THE
HANDY
LITERATURE
ANSWER
BOOK

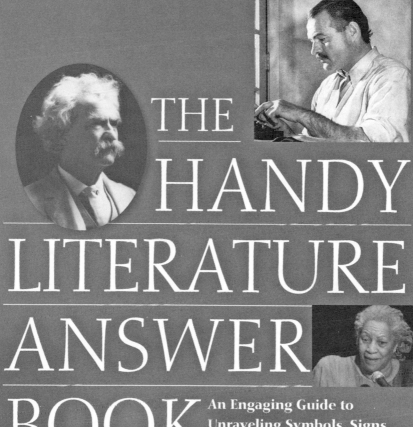

THE HANDY LITERATURE ANSWER BOOK

An Engaging Guide to
Unraveling Symbols, Signs,
and Meanings in Great Works

DANIEL S. BURT, PH.D., AND DEBORAH G. FELDER

VISIBLE INK PRESS

Detroit

About the Authors

 **Daniel S. Burt** received his Ph.D. in English and American literature from New York University. He has taught undergraduate and graduate courses in writing and literature at NYU, Wesleyan University, Trinity College, Northeastern, Wentworth Institute, and Cape Cod Community College for more than thirty years. He served for almost a decade as a dean at Wesleyan University. Since 2003, he has been organizing literary and historical tours of Ireland as the co-owner and founder of Unique Irish Tours. A former director of the NYU in London program, Daniel has led study groups to Russia, Spain, Britain, and Ireland. Daniel lives on Cape Cod.

Daniel is the author of *Understanding Literature*, Next Thinking, 2012; *The Novel 100: A Ranking of the Greatest Novels of All Time*, Facts On File, revised ed. 2010; *The Literary 100: A Ranking of the Most Influential Novelists, Playwrights, and Poets of All Time*, Facts on File, revised ed. 2009; *The Drama 100: A Ranking of the Greatest Plays of All Time*. Facts on File, 2008; *The Chronology of American Literature*, Houghton Mifflin, 2004; *The Biography Book: A Reader's Guide to Nonfiction, Fictional, and Film Biographies of More Than 500 of the Most Fascinating Individuals of All Time*, Oryx, 2001; and *What Do I Read Next?: A Reader's Guide to Current Genre Fiction*, Gale Research, 2000.

 **Deborah G. Felder** is a graduate of Bard College, where she studied drama and literature. She worked as an editor at Scholastic, Inc., and has been a freelance writer and editor for over thirty years. The author of twenty books, including fiction and nonfiction, she has written books and articles for middle grade, young adult, and adult readers. She has also written book reviews for *The New York Times Book Review*, *Kirkus Reviews*, and *Publishers Weekly*. Deborah is the co-owner and founder of Unique Irish Tours with her husband, Daniel Burt.

Deborah's published works include *100 American Women Who Shaped American History*, Bluewood Books, 2005; *A Bookshelf of Our Own: Works That Changed Women's Lives*, Citadel Press, 2005; *Fifty Jewish Women Who Changed the World*, Citadel Press, 2004; *The 100 Most Influential Women of All Time: A Ranking Past and Present*, Citadel Press, revised ed. 2001; *A Century of Women: The Most Influential Events in Twentieth-Century Women's History*, Birch Lane Press, 1999; and *The Kids' World Almanac of History*, Pharos Books, 1991.

Also from Visible Ink Press

The Handy Law Answer Book
by David L. Hudson, Jr., J.D.
ISBN: 978-1-57859-217-3

The Handy Literature Answer Book
By Daniel S. Burt and Deborah G. Felder
ISBN: 978-1-57859-635-5

The Handy Math Answer Book, 2nd edition
by Patricia Barnes-Svarney and Thomas E.
    Svarney
ISBN: 978-1-57859-373-6

The Handy Military History Answer Book
by Samuel Willard Crompton
ISBN: 978-1-57859-509-9

The Handy Mythology Answer Book
by David A. Leeming, Ph.D.
ISBN: 978-1-57859-475-7

The Handy New York City Answer Book
by Chris Barsanti
ISBN: 978-1-57859-586-0

The Handy Nutrition Answer Book
by Patricia Barnes-Svarney and Thomas E.
    Svarney
ISBN: 978-1-57859-484-9

The Handy Ocean Answer Book
by Patricia Barnes-Svarney and Thomas E.
    Svarney
ISBN: 978-1-57859-063-6

The Handy Pennsylvania Answer Book
by Lawrence W. Baker
ISBN: 978-1-57859-610-2

The Handy Personal Finance Answer Book
by Paul A. Tucci
ISBN: 978-1-57859-322-4

The Handy Philosophy Answer Book
by Naomi Zack, Ph.D.
ISBN: 978-1-57859-226-5

The Handy Physics Answer Book,
    2nd edition
By Paul W. Zitzewitz, Ph.D.
ISBN: 978-1-57859-305-7

The Handy Presidents Answer Book,
    2nd edition
by David L. Hudson
ISB N: 978-1-57859-317-0

The Handy Psychology Answer Book,
    2nd edition
by Lisa J. Cohen, Ph.D.
ISBN: 978-1-57859-508-2

The Handy Religion Answer Book,
    2nd edition
by John Renard, Ph.D.
ISBN: 978-1-57859-379-8

The Handy Science Answer Book,
    4th edition
by The Carnegie Library of Pittsburgh
ISBN: 978-1-57859-321-7

*The Handy State-by-State Answer Book:
    Faces, Places, and Famous Dates for All
    Fifty States*
by Samuel Willard Crompton
ISBN: 978-1-57859-565-5

The Handy Supreme Court Answer Book
by David L Hudson, Jr.
ISBN: 978-1-57859-196-1

The Handy Technology Answer Book
by Naomi E. Balaban and James Bobick
ISBN: 978-1-57859-563-1

The Handy Texas Answer Book
by James L. Haley
ISBN: 978-1-57859-634-8

The Handy Weather Answer Book,
    2nd edition
by Kevin S. Hile
ISBN: 978-1-57859-221-0

PLEASE VISIT THE "HANDY ANSWERS" SERIES
WEBSITE AT WWW.HANDYANSWERS.COM.

THE HANDY LITERATURE ANSWER BOOK

Visible Ink Press®
43311 Joy Rd., #414
Canton, MI 48187–2075

Visible Ink Press is a registered trademark of Visible Ink Press LLC.

Most Visible Ink Press books are available at special quantity discounts when purchased in bulk by corporations, organizations, or groups. Customized printings, special imprints, messages, and excerpts can be produced to meet your needs. For more information, contact Special Markets Director, Visible Ink Press, www.visibleinkpress.com, or 734–667–3211.

Managing Editor: Kevin S. Hile
Art Director: Mary Claire Krzewinski
Typesetting: Marco DiVita
Proofreaders: Shoshana Hurwitz and Stephanie Scarlet
Indexer: Larry Baker
Cover images: Toni Morrison (Angela Radulescu), all other images public domain.

Cataloging-in-Publication Data is available from the Library of Congress.

10 9 8 7 6 5 4 3 2 1

Printed in the United States of America.

Table of Contents

HOW TO READ DRAMA … 243

HOW TO READ LITERARY NONFICTION … 339

CRITICAL APPROACHES TO LITERATURE … 373

Photo Sources

Acknowledgments

The origin and orientation of this book can be traced to several sources: our parents, for having instilled in us a love for literature; the English teachers and literature professors who taught us how to love literature even more by teaching us how to read it; and the many students for whom it has been a privilege to teach the art of reading literature. We are grateful to all for the many contributions (intended or otherwise) to this book. Samuel Johnson famously declared, "When a man knows he is to be hanged in a fortnight, it concentrates his mind wonderfully." Add to hanging: teaching a course and writing a book. We are grateful for the privilege afforded us in asking and answering questions about how to read literature and hope that the result of all that concentration proves to be a benefit to our readers.

Our thanks to Kevin Hile for his editorial insights during the course of this project; Roger Jänecke for his much-valued advice and many courtesies; and our agent, Roger Williams, for introducing us to Visible Ink Press.

Introduction

Few would contest the truism that what we deem literature is one of the greatest achievements of human civilization. A culture is defined and judged by the buildings and monuments it constructs, by the laws it makes, but especially by the literature it produces. Prehistoric cave paintings, the first and oldest surviving reflections of the world created some 40,000 years ago, include hand stencils, a prototype of literature itself, powerfully communicating the essence of literary expression: "This is me." "I was here." "I matter." "Remember me." Long-dead voices and vanished cultures retain their ability to speak to us in the present only through literature. Literature alone confirms William Faulkner's famous assertion: "The past is never dead. It's not even past." To hear what an age thought and felt most directly and intimately, we must read the literature that it has left for us. But our interest in literature is not just antiquarian. More than precious cultural artifacts, literature provides the most fundamental service ever devised. It teaches us how to be human. At a basic level, we learn to function as human beings by intuition and by imitation, by the earliest examples and instructions of those closest to us—our parents, relatives, friends, and teachers. At the deepest level, however, to learn what human nature is and the multiple dimensions of human experience in all times and places, literature becomes our principal and most valuable guide and instructor.

If civilization and culture recognize literature as a singular human achievement, as our window into the past, the world, and ourselves, literature's hold on the individual is no less esteemed or revered. Can you imagine a home without some books? Why are they not as disposable as most of the consumables that enter and exit our dwellings? Why do we throw out yesterday's newspaper but hold on to that novel read in college long after we know whodunit and why? Test your devotion to literature by imagining purging your bookcase. Do you send the unwanted or battered copies to the landfill? Most likely not. You recycle by donating to your local library or some other exchange to provide the book with a new home and a new owner. Why? Because you know at some visceral, intuitive level that those books continue to be relevant and to have persistent value, not on the commercial exchange perhaps but on the human one. That's the essence of what literature is, and that's why we value it so highly. So much of what we possess is time stamped with an inherent obsolescence: clothes wear out, appliances break down, electronics must be replaced by newer models. Not literature.

However, recognizing the cultural and personal benefits of literature does not necessarily mean that our encounters with literature are either continual or do not meet with some resistance. We may acknowledge literature's importance, but the challenge of reading what Matthew Arnold called "the best that has been thought and said" can often mar our experience with literature. *Ars longa, vita brevis* (Art is long, life is short), as the saying goes. We know that literature is good for us, but how much relish do we have for most things in our lives that are good for us: sensible diet, exercise, self-assessment? Like fine art and cultural treasures consigned to the museum to be visited and admired on occasion, volumes of great literature await activation on our bookshelves, but the call doesn't come. We know it's there; we know its value, but the remote is easier and the social media feed is irresistible. Moreover, somehow we have convinced ourselves that a now-dimly recalled encounter with a literary classic sometime in high school or college means that we have definitively extracted its treasures and transferred all the meaning it possesses to memory. Nothing could be further from the truth.

Great works of literature change over our lifetime because we change over our lifetime. Twain's *Adventures of Huckleberry Finn* experienced at twelve is qualitatively different when experiencing it at twenty, thirty, forty, and so on. Imagine the notion of once seen, forever mastered applied to a great painting: "I saw Van Gogh's *Sunflowers* in my art history class decades ago, and I'm done with that." It's equally absurd to relegate a great work of literature to a long-ago, vaguely recalled meeting. You may have checked it off your bucket list, but don't think that the literary work is done with you. Instead, a new version of each great classic is waiting for each version of yourself that emerges with age.

Why do we, therefore, resist literature? This is the opening question that animated this book: that is, why, even though we may acknowledge literature's crucial appeal and importance, is reading literature such a challenge that results in our resistance and deferral of the pleasure that literature provides? The short answer to this is because reading literature can be hard. It can delight, certainly, but great works of literature place demands on us that other forms of entertainment do not. We can follow a television program while sending a text message and carrying on a conversation, but try doing that while reading a great work of literature that insists on our undivided attention.

We try to address the demands literature makes by offering both general and specific advice to guide your reading. We start with an attempt in chapter one to define literature: when and where did it originate and what is its fundamental nature? What makes literature a unique form of human communication and self-expression? Central to our definition of literature is the recognition that the reading skills we employ to extract information from everyday writing (a newspaper, instructional manual, a textbook, for example) are not the same reading skills that literature demands. One important reason why reading literature presents such a challenge is that we tend to misread it based on our reliance upon everyday reading skills that focus on information extraction. Literature demands a different kind of reading competence, one more directed by the *how* than by the *what*, one more attuned to the questions literature presents rather than the explicit answers it provides. Everyday reading caters to our often-distracted, impatient, multitasking reading habits; literature requires our full engagement with the implicit rather than with the explicit. By confusing these two kinds of reading experiences—everyday versus literary—we imperil our ability to rise to the challenges of literature. We also can become frustrated when a reliable everyday reading method fails to deliver the same results when reading literature. Frustration leads to abandoning literature for more accessible and immediately gratifying pastimes.

In chapter two we look at the various ways in which literature should NOT be read: not expecting as we do in everyday reading a kernel of truth delivered with a headline or a helpful first paragraph summary. Literature generates meaning by multiple means, implicitly rather than explicitly, by suggestion rather than by directive, in a style that is expressive rather than transparent as in a journalistic account. Neither is literature a coded message to be deciphered by the initiated but as a kind of force field of multiple and various meanings and significance, readily available to all. On a walk in the woods we don't ask, "What do the woods mean?" Instead we bask in the various pleasures that the woods afford us. Reading literature is no different.

What does a work of literature mean is one of the last questions to ask, after first looking for the various ways the work generates that meaning. To assist in attending to these questions, we offer five key questions that you can ask of any work of literature to begin the process of appreciating the method and significance of a literary work: 1) What is the significance of the title? (Often this is the only hint the author provides on the focus of a work); 2) Why does it begin when it does? (What is the catalyst that generates the drama?); 3) What is the conflict (What are the forces in opposition?); 4) How is the conflict resolved? (What changes as a result of the conflict?); 5) Why does it end when it does? (What is resolved? How has the situation introduced at the beginning changed?) With these five questions in mind, an engaged reader of literature should be able to rise to the challenge of most literary works in ways that will enhance both the appreciation of a work's methods and its various meanings.

What follows are chapters devoted to the shared and unique resources and possibilities of each of five dominant literary forms: poetry, short story, novel, drama, and literary nonfiction. We attempt to define the form in comparison with the others. Literature is about choices the author makes: why this and not that? What results from the choices made? In each chapter, we summarize the various choices each literary form establishes. By understanding these choices—for example, what can't you do in a short story that a novel can provide and how does that affect the reading experience—you can enhance both your appreciation of the challenges a writer faces and how they have been surmounted.

You cannot really appreciate a sporting event beyond the most superficial (and often misleading) level without knowing the rules that apply. The same is true for reading the various types of literature. You don't have to become a pedant; you don't necessarily have to know the difference between a dactyl and an anapest to appreciate a poem's method, but you do need to understand the capacity of words to serve meaning, association, sound, and rhythm. By doing so, you begin to understand how a poem works to achieve its effects. In each chapter, we apply key concepts of method to readings of specific works to underscore the ways in which meaning and technique are related.

A core principle that we attempt to illustrate throughout these chapters is that a great literary work sets the rules by which it needs to be read, understood, and appreciated. In this regard, a single reader response most definitely does not fit all. This is particularly true when reading modern literature in which the operating principles that governed the literature of the past seem to be irrevocably altered, demanding a new set of critical responses. A fundamental problem in approaching literature is the assumption that the same reading response used for one literary work will by necessity work for another. Imagine a trip to a museum of fine art in which you start with the Middle Ages and all the many Madonna and Child paintings. You move to the Renaissance and see that two dimensions have become three, and the subject of art has shifted from divine to secular sources. Continue in time to see the world depicted in intimate, eye-deceiving realism to the disruption of Impressionism, Post-Impressionism, and Abstract Expressionism. A set of rules during each artistic era determining what deserves artistic treatment and how are asserted and demand to be acknowledged in assessing achievement. One set of rules becomes inadequate to judge another. Jackson Pollack's drip paintings are not failed Rembrandts. You cannot use the same criteria for judging a Vermeer, a Matisse, or a Rothko.

The same is certainly true of literature. One era's set of assumptions and methods do not prescribe other practices, and judging one work by an inadequate or inappropriate critical criteria misinterprets that work. It is simply not a valid critical response to complain that one is not the other as it would be to complain that you dislike a tragedy because it is not a comedy. Eliot's *The Waste Land* cannot be assessed using the standards derived from Milton's *Paradise Lost*. The rules are different and need to be judged accordingly.

Consider these three openings from novels from different eras that treat a similar subject: the growth and development of a central protagonist:

> An author ought to consider himself, not as a gentleman who gives a private or eleemosynary treat, but rather as one who keeps a public ordinary, at which all persons are welcome for their money. In the former case, it is well known that the entertainer provides what fare he pleases; and though this should be very indifferent, and utterly disagreeable to the taste of his company, they must not find any fault; nay, on the contrary, good breeding forces them outwardly to approve and to commend whatever is set before them. Now the contrary of this

happens to the master of an ordinary. Men who pay for what they eat will insist on gratifying their palates, however nice and whimsical these may prove; and if everything is not agreeable to their taste, will challenge a right to censure, to abuse, and to d—n their dinner without control.

Henry Fielding, Tom Jones

Whether I shall turn out to be the hero of my own life, or whether that station will be held by anybody else, these pages must show. To begin my life with the beginning of my life, I record that I was born (as I have been informed and believe) on a Friday, at twelve o'clock at night. It was remarked that the clock began to strike, and I began to cry, simultaneously.

Charles Dickens, David Copperfield

Once upon a time and a very good time it was there was a moocow coming down along the road and this moocow that was coming down along the road met a nicens little boy named baby tuckoo....

His father told him that story: his father looked at him through a glass: he had a hairy face.

He was baby tuckoo. The moocow came down the road where Betty Byrne lived: she sold lemon platt.

O, the wild rose blossoms

On the little green place.

He sang that song. That was his song.

O, the green wothe botheth.

When you wet the bed, first it is warm then it gets cold. His mother put on the oilsheet. That had the queer smell.

His mother had a nicer smell than his father. She played on the piano the sailor's hornpipe for him to dance. He danced:

Tralala lala,

Tralala tralaladdy,

Tralala lala,

Tralala lala.

James Joyce, A Portrait of the Artist as a Young Man

What should be evident from the above examples is that each represents three very different assumptions about the rules of engagement in the novel, and that the rules for one do not apply to another. With Fielding, we have a confident narrative voice of the cultured impresario commencing a guided tour and establishing good companionship and witty observations for the journey. Any heavy lifting of interpretation he will handle, so Fielding makes it clear that the reader can sit back and enjoy the show. With Dickens, the point of view shifts from Fielding's confident, detached, and decisive narrator to the more limited first person, and the reader is alerted that this will be more of a journey of discovery in which even the claim that he "shall turn out to be the hero of my own life" is very much to be determined. By shifting the perspective from Fielding's omniscience to a limited first person, Dickens introduces the notion of unreliability here, putting the reader on notice that appearance and reality may diverge, that others, not the narrator, may be the focus, even that "hero" might not be a characteristic that the story will reveal. Dickens, therefore, problematizes the narrative, forcing the reader into a much more active and skeptical engagement with his story than what Fielding establishes. With Joyce, authorial distance collapses totally into the sequence and association of child's consciousness itself. There is no retrospective here, no authorial guidance. It is up to the reader to make sense of what is unmitigated linguistic stimuli. Who exactly is speaking here? What are we to make of the rapid shifts of ideas and images? We are far from Fielding's confident and cultured showman and Dickens's earnest striver after the meaning of his life. Joyce offers the data of experience that requires the reader to reveal the pattern of coherence.

Fielding, Dickens, and Joyce each establish the ground rules for how his novel should be read, and the rules governing one do not necessarily apply to the other. Are you allowed to prefer one set of assumptions and methods to another? By all means, but what does not work critically is judging one from the standards of the other. Joyce is not a failed Fielding or Dickens; he intends something very different and expects the reader to judge his performance by the rules he sets himself.

In each chapter on the literary forms we try to account for changes to literary subjects, values, and methods that you will face, suggesting that, although literary works all share some common characteristics, your reading skills need to adapt to the rules each work establishes.

In the final, eighth chapter, we examine critical theory and critical approaches to literature as the various lenses that can be used to guide interpretations of a literary work. We provide a brief overview of how literary criticism developed and the key assumptions various critical theories and approaches make about the author, text, and reader. The fundamental lesson that literature should offer to its reader is literature's multiplicity and depth. Criticism of literature should enhance these notions, not reduce literary works to a single truth or a single approach. We try to emphasize in our discussion the ways in which the general reader can profit from these critical perspectives. As in the previous chapters, we guide you to an awareness of techniques and approaches that will enhance your appreciation of literature.

Our hope is that this guide will help you to better understand what makes literature

and each literary genre so distinctive, and that you will not only know *how* to read literary works but will also have a greater appreciation of what you are reading. Then, any resistance to the challenge of reading literature will shift to active engagement and understanding of literature's great gift in the discovery of our humanity and our mutuality. The good news is that literature is patient, awaiting your activation of a dialogue between "the best that has been thought and said" and you. We hope that we have anticipated the questions that you would have asked and provided the answers to make that dialogue both lively and meaningful.

WHAT IS LITERATURE AND WHY DO WE READ IT?

What do we mean by the word "literature"?

Like the old chestnut, "I may not know much about art, but I know what I like," literature seems to depend on the eyes of the beholder. We know it when we see it. In this sense, literature is essentially writing of value but value beyond the merely practical. Rarely does a recipe, a textbook, a text message, or even a newspaper account qualify as literature. They are dependable carriers of useful information, vital for human communication, but not literature as most understand it—not cherished, preserved, or reread for pleasure. So, how is the writing we consider literature different? The value literature provides is far more elusive and abstract: dealing less with answers than essential questions. We live in the often chaotic rush of experience; literature functions like an indispensable freeze-frame or snapshot, stopping time for a close examination of the world and ourselves. We need literature, therefore, to make sense of experience and to discover what matters most in our lives and others' lives over space and time.

What makes literature "literature"?

Nonliterary, everyday writing, which we will explore in more detail in Chapter Two, is valued for one crucial imperative: an ability to transfer information from text to reader as clearly and concisely as possible. This kind of writing is a vital but readily discarded form of writing. Who saves yesterday's newspapers to reread? Once the information is delivered, the message has served its purpose and can be dispensed with, only now valuable to remind the reader of any key information. Literature is something else entirely: less informational and more expressive, less about providing practical answers but posing the greatest questions about the world and our relationship with it, in which *how* is as important as *what*.

What is deemed literature also is a collective agreement rather than a matter of personal taste. Tradition and custom, that is, the collective wisdom of others both past and

As an English word, "literature" emerged in the fourteenth century and was derived from the Latin *lit(t)era* for "letters" and *lit(t)eratura* for "learning, writing, and grammar." Originally, "literature" designated not a text but a reader: one who was acquainted with the written word; that is, a literate person. In the eighteenth century, the meaning of literature shifted to describe printed texts rather than those who read them. The earliest definition of literature as literary production can be found in lexicographer Samuel Johnson's *Lives of the English Poets* (1779), although Johnson failed to define literature in this sense in his famous and influential *A Dictionary of the English Language* (1775). The definition of literature as a compendium of writing was originally broadly conceived to include all written texts. Literature in this sense meant the "art of the written word."

present, help to mold a contentious and shifting canon of literary worth, rising and falling like a literary stock market, reflecting long- and short-term value and current supply and demand. We may think we know literature when we see it, but that's largely because we have been instructed in what to look for and what to value. Literature as a concept simply is not possible without a critical tradition that has privileged some literary expressions over others. Literature, therefore, is a collective, cultural enterprise determining literary value. Literary history is replete with examples of overpraise and overlooked genius: Who valued Melville's *Moby-Dick* when it first appeared? Fitzgerald's *The Great Gatsby* failed to find an initial audience and was not even mentioned in most obituaries of the novelist when he died in 1940. Today, both are ranked among the greatest American novels. Imagine the reaction of their contemporaries to today's accepted critical valuation that the two greatest American poets of the nineteenth century are Walt Whitman and Emily Dickinson. Who?

The vagaries of literary reputation and an all-too-often shortsighted contemporary critical estimation may suggest that questions of what constitutes literature are missing an algorithm or critical calculus to reach certainty. Yet, such a quantitative approach to literature obscures literature's more qualitative essence. The Victorian poet and critic Matthew Arnold (1822–1888) defined culture in *Culture and Anarchy* as the study of perfection "to make the best that has been thought and known in the world current everywhere." Substitute literature for culture in Arnold's formulation, and you have at least a working definition of literature: "the best that has been thought and known in the world." How to find it and what to look for is the core subject of this book.

How was literature defined in the nineteenth century?

During the nineteenth century, the scope of what was meant by literature gradually narrowed to refer primarily to imaginative and creative writing: poetry over prose, fiction rather than nonfiction, expressive rather than merely informational writing (such as instructional texts and journalism). Literature thereby took on a *qualitative*, rather than merely a *quantitative* (all things written), distinction. Literature, in this sense of the term, designated the best possible examples of writing, those most valued by tradition and consensus to be included in a literary canon of authors and types of literature, principally poetry, drama, and fiction.

How has literature been defined in the twentieth and twenty-first centuries?

Throughout the twentieth century and into the twenty-first, the distinctions that once characterized literature and what kind of works a literary canon should include have become increasingly challenged and debated. Space has been made for writing formerly excluded from canon inclusion. For example, few would have accepted comic books in the 1940s and 1950s as works of literature. However, graphic novels are now a widely accepted literary form and, therefore, deemed literature. Nonfiction writing, formerly the reserve of the utilitarian, has contributed a vital new literary subgenre: creative nonfiction. Writers of literary genres such as mysteries, romances, horror, and science fiction have long been considered as purveyors of popular literary entertainment but not literature. However, works in these genres have entered the literary canon in the twentieth and twenty-first centuries. In many ways, the concept of what literature is has expanded back to its broader, eighteenth-century definition as the "art of the written word."

What is the best definition of literature?

The challenge faced in determining a viable definition of literature is whether to work from too broad a definition (all written work) or too narrow, excluding works whose appeal and importance in the cultural moment are unavoidable. At the beginning of the nineteenth century, for example, few literary critics accepted the novel as worthy to be considered literature. The novel's popularity and evolution as an art form as the century progressed allowed it to achieve its accepted important literary status.

Although the boundaries of what constitutes literature are unstable and often contentious, certain elements are central to any workable definition of literature. First and foremost is that literature refers to written works, texts that can be read. It is a pleasure to see a performance of *Hamlet*,

Actor Scott Shepherd portrays Hamlet in a modern Berlin production of Shakespeare's play. A play such as Hamlet is regarded as great literature not just because of what it says but how it says it, as well as critical consensus.

3

but its inclusion as a work of literature derives from our ability to appreciate the poetry of Shakespeare's words while reading the play.

What characteristics define a work of literature?

We often ignore the distinction that allows some written work to be considered literature and other kinds of writing that is commonly called "literature." We might, for example, consult "literature" on how to apply for a passport, open a bank account, or play a musical instrument. We expect this kind of literature to provide us with practical information and instruction that we can use. We don't expect the writing to be necessarily entertaining or interesting: We don't read it for the fun of it or for a source of pleasure. We read it for the information it provides, and we require that it be written clearly and succinctly to deliver the information we need. Its language is usually clear and concise; it does not call attention to itself or obscure its message. Once we have discovered what we need to know, this kind of literature has served its purpose as a carrier or deliverer of information. We would only reread it if we needed a reminder about the information we were seeking or the steps of the instructions we should follow. The kind of writing that provides information is the opposite of what we characteristically mean by literature. In this definition, literature may have no practical benefit at all.

How have others defined literature?

One of the best ways to define literature is to be instructed by past practitioners of the art. The Roman poet Horace described poetry (and by extension all literature) as containing the power to instruct *and* delight. Those who offer the kind of writing we normally designate as literature provide us with both. They delight us with discovery, with the shock of recognition, with the thrill of encountering something both strange and familiar. At the same time, writers of literature increase our understanding of how humans think and feel by allowing us inside human consciousness and enabling us to experience human thought and feeling through their characters and the events that shape their characters' progress within a story. Writers, moreover, can overcome the limitations of space and time for us. The entire world is miraculous and accessible always and everywhere in works of literature, and the past can speak to us: it is the way in which we can claim kinship, closeness, and affinity with individuals who have been dead for centuries or for millennia. Writers of literature have created the only working time machine in which the past (as well as the future) becomes our present. Let's allow some of those literary voices to define literature further:

"The purpose of literature is to turn blood into ink."

T. S. Eliot

"Literature, real literature, must not be gulped down like some potion which may be good for the heart or good for the brain—the brain, that stomach of the soul. Literature must be taken and broken to bits, pulled apart, squashed—then its lovely reek will be smelt in the hollow of the palm, it will be munched and rolled upon the tongue with relish; then, and only then, its rare flavor will be appreciated at its true worth and the broken and crushed parts will again come together in your mind and disclose the beauty of a unity to which you have contributed something of your own blood."

—Vladimir Nabokov

"I think we ought to read only the kind of books that wound or stab us. If the book we're reading doesn't wake us up with a blow to the head, what are we reading for? So that it will make us happy, as you write? Good Lord, we would be happy precisely if we had no books, and the kind of books that make us happy are the kind we could write ourselves if we had to. But we need books that affect us like a disaster, that grieve us deeply, like the death of someone we loved more than ourselves, like being banished into forests far from everyone, like a suicide. A book must be the axe for the frozen sea within us. That is my belief."

—Franz Kafka

"Literature duplicates the experience of living in a way that nothing else can, drawing you so fully into another life that you temporarily forget you have one of your own. That is why you read it, and might even sit up in bed till early dawn, throwing your whole tomorrow out of whack, simply to find out what happens to some people who, you know perfectly well, are made up."

—Barbara Kingsolver

"To subvert is not the aim of literature, its value lies in discovering and revealing what is rarely known, little known, thought to be known but in fact not very well known of the truth of the human world. It would seem that truth is the unassailable and most basic quality of literature."

—Gao Xingjian

"[Literature is] a process of producing grand, beautiful, well-ordered lies that tell more truth than any assemblage of facts."

—Julian Barnes

"Great literature is simply language charged with meaning to the utmost degree."

—Ezra Pound

"Literature is where I go to explore the highest and lowest places in human society and in the human spirit, where I hope to find not absolute truth but the truth of the tale, of the imagination and of the heart."

—Salman Rushdie

5

"Literature adds to reality, it does not simply describe it. It enriches the necessary competencies that daily life requires and provides; and in this respect, it irrigates the deserts that our lives have already become."

—C. S. Lewis

What characteristics do these descriptions of literature share?

What is common to all of the above descriptions of literature is its power and privilege: literature takes its reader beyond the surface of things, though that surface is the crucial starting point to essence—blood (Eliot), smell (Nabokov), imagination and heart (Rushdie). Literature powerfully duplicates our world (Kingsolver); its lies tell more than factual truth (Barnes), and works like an "axe for the frozen sea within us" (Kafka), irrigating "the deserts that our lives have already become" (Lewis).

Literature serves to disorient and reorient the reader to truths, not necessarily from its faithful representation of experience but its creative repossession of experience in ways in which meaning and relevance radiate.

How do you know you are dealing with literature? Nabokov would argue that a reader should read "the book of genius" (that is, literature) "not with his heart, not so much with his brain, but with his spine. It is there that occurs the telltale tingle...."

How did literature originate?

The development of literature depended on the greatest accomplishment in human history. Human beings first had to develop language: the ability to communicate meaning through vocal sounds that began to be associated with particular things. Think of an infant's slow language development from producing idiosyncratic (and incomprehensible) sounds to learning to associate certain sounds with objects and concepts (food and hunger, for example). It's an extraordinary achievement that only humans have developed so extensively. The mastery of language skills allowed us to communicate not just basic observations and responses (food here, pleasure/pain) but also the most complex and abstract concepts (freedom, alienation), as well as the syntactical rules to combine words into larger constructs like sentences.

The essential building block for the construction of literature is, therefore, language. The association of verbal sounds with particular things led to the ability of humans to communicate with one another as they evolved. As literary and linguistic scholar Michael D. C. Drout put it, "As soon as someone figured out that you could influence another person by creating a poem or telling a story, we had literature." With language, individuals could begin to express ideas and begin the process of performing in language to delight and instruct through stories and song (or poetry). Oral literary compositions that have survived include the *Iliad* and the *Odyssey* by Homer in an anonymous transcription of performances of his great epics and in written versions of Greek poetry and drama. Oral literary composition still survives in tribal, nomadic cul-

This ancient Greek sarcophagus includes scenes from Homer's epic *Iliad*. Works by Homer and others of the time began as oral compositions that were later—fortunately for us—transcribed for posterity.

tures today in Africa and Asia in which the transmission of important history, myth, story, and legend are oral rather than written.

What must the earliest literature have been like?

We can image the first literature, although it was lost to time because it was unrecorded. In the proverbial cave by firelight, a speaker recounts the events of a recent hunt, and, by comparison, another describes a similar or different hunt. With either, storytelling emerges, with details selected to achieve an effect on the audience (illustrating fear or the challenge of the combat). As soon as one of the speakers imitates one of the participants instead of merely narrating events, whether hunter or quarry, the first drama debuts. In response to the performance, perhaps an audience member joins in to honor the occasion with a response of pleasure, and poetry arises: expressions of ideas and feelings taking the form of a song or a speech.

It is not a stretch to extend this scene of storytelling, drama, and poetry to other topics essential for a community's well-being: stories that embody their values, dramas and poems that explain origins and natural phenomena, like the seasons or what happens after death. Literature, thereby, takes the form of the history of a community in the events and individuals who matter most and in a community's myths and legends that give shape and meaning to their world.

Stories that impose a pattern on the chaos of experience, dramas that show those patterns, and poetry that can express—like a handprint drawn on cave wall—identity

7

and shared experience are the essential ingredients and expressions of literature. The need to express—We were here. This is how we lived, felt, and survived—seems so basic that it is hard to imagine human beings without a literature to accompany us on that evolutionary journey.

Vladimir Nabokov offers an alternative origin story for literature that clarifies a key component. "Literature was born," he argues, "not the day when a boy crying wolf, wolf came running out of the Neanderthal valley with a big gray wolf at his heels: literature was born on the day when a boy crying wolf, wolf and there was no wolf behind him. That the poor little fellow because he lied too often was finally eaten up by a real beast is quite incidental. But here is what is important. Between the wolf in the tall grass and the wolf in the tall story there is a shimmering go-between. That go-between, that prism, is the art of literature." Nabokov's origin fable asserts that the lie of the boy crying wolf and the lie of literature are the same. Why cry wolf in the wolf's absence in the first place? The difference between the real and invented wolf are the essential questions we face in examining literature.

Beyond language, what was essential for the development of literature?

Literature as an artifact, as opposed to oral literary expression, would ultimately depend on the next great cultural breakthrough: the representation of language in writing. In the West, writing first developed in the southern Mesopotamia region of Sumer (c. 3400 B.C.E.) in the form of markings on clay tablets in a script known as cuneiform. These early texts served economic and administrative purposes in records of possessions and trading transactions. The earliest form of writing used two-dimensional symbols for objects, but the true breakthrough occurred with the use of arbitrary symbols representing sounds. Combining them could represent a word, graphically representing language, which eventually evolved into the first alphabet.

By the third millennium B.C.E., Mesopotamian scribes using this new alphabet system were copying down instructions, hymns, poetry, and myths, including favorite stories and performances from the oral tradition. The first author of literature known by name was the high priestess of Ur, Enheduanna (2285–2250 B.C.E.), whose hymns in praise of the Sumerian goddess Inanna survive. Literature's oldest surviving written fictional story is the *Epic of Gilgamesh*, the questing adventures of a Sumerian king amongst monsters and gods, originally based on a series of Sumerian poems and tales dating from around 2100 B.C.E. Writing, spread by the Phoenicians, would reach Egypt, Greece, Rome and the vast Roman Empire, and beyond.

What are the key components of literature?

Literature depends on the interactions of three key components:
- Author
- Text
- Reader

Each is dependent on the other, and each plays a crucial role in defining the reading experience of literature. Literary criticism, particularly beginning in the mid-twentieth century, has challenged previous understandings of each component, but it is still possible to get a sense of how the author, text, and reader work together in literature.

What is the role of the author in literature?

A work of literature begins with an author-creator tasked with converting vision into language, producing a text that can be read. Although authors face countless choices on how to proceed, they are bound by a few key limitations. Converting vision (abstract ideas and feelings) into a voice that can be understood by a reader, the author has only three fundamental choices: word choice (or diction), in which the author selects particular words to reflect meaning; the placement of those words into grammatical units called sentences (or syntax); and the arrangement of those syntactical units into larger constructs (paragraphs, stanzas, chapters, scenes, etc.). The author, moreover, has a template to work from in the traditional literary forms available—poetry, drama, fiction, and nonfiction—each with its own rules of composition that can be imitated or modified. At the core of the literary endeavor is the author's desire to communicate with a reader, sharing or shaping meaning by the text produced.

The extent to which an author is truly a free agent or bound by the rules of language and form determined by culture and historical forces is one of the contentious issues surrounding our evolving critical understanding of literary works. Modern literary criticism has radically challenged the primacy of the author in the creation of literature. Previous approaches to literature have endowed authors with a godlike power over their creations, asking readers to master an author's biographical and cultural authority to explain a work or to decipher the buried truths that he or she has concealed within the text. Literary criticism, such as New Criticism and the Reader Response theory, have instead shifted the primary locus of literature to the text and the reader.

What is the role of the text in literature?

An author's vision—the abstract ideas and feelings—to be expressed and communicated to the reader must be given voice in the words selected and in the arrangement of those words into sentences and in the combination of those sentences into larger organizational groupings, such as paragraphs, stanzas, scenes, etc. These choices form the text that the reader must translate back into vision, reversing the process of vision to voice by the author. Depending on the author's ability to choose correctly, what the author intended to communicate is transferred to the understanding (or vision) of the reader. An author's vision leads to a choice of voice; that voice is translated back to the reader's vision, and the two should match up. However, misreading can happen because language, whether spoken or written, can fail to communicate intended meaning: an author might have chosen incorrectly, or the reader may have misinterpreted the choices offered. A simple example of this is an author who wants to communicate danger and chooses a text that says: "There is a fire!" But the reader might perceive fire as beneficial and misread the author's meaning, so danger is not communicated. Because the building blocks of text is language with multiple meanings and shifting connotations, the text is always problematic if the goal is to understand with certainty exactly what the author intended to say.

Texts, therefore, must be interpreted, that is, analyzed for both explicit and implicit meanings. Since it is impossible to know with any certainty what an author intends, one alternative is to discount the intentions of the author and concentrate on whatever meaning the text generates. As D. H. Lawrence famously declared, "Never trust the teller, trust the tale." New Criticism in the twentieth century would reject the notion that deciphering an author's intention is a central goal of literature. Literature, they argued, is not a secret message planted by the author to be decoded but a dynamic field of multiple meanings, generated because of, despite of, and indeed regardless of the author. In this model, literature is a textual world that the author has set in motion but does not control; the reader controls the text through interpretation.

However, a text should not be confused with the reality that it represents in the same way that we should not confuse language with what it signifies. A text is a map rather than the territory it represents, and, like any good map, a text must transform reality: Route 1 is not blue as your map has it, and not every turning and elevation can be included. This leads to an important understanding about reading literature: it is life simplified, framed, and translated in the interest of larger truths. To remind ourselves about the artifice of the text may undermine the illusion that we are reading life, not an artful version of it, but such a recognition stimulates a greater understanding and appreciation of the ways and means that literary artists construct a world and generate meaning.

Literature does not stand alone nor is it subject only to the author's intentions. The reader is also a factor. The interpretation of literature depends, at least in part, on the reader's knowledge, cultural background, age, and other factors.

What is the role of the reader in literature?

The communication circuit of literature is incomplete without a reader. Authors need a projected reader in mind to help shape the choices in translating vision to voice. That reader may be a version of the author, trying to understand what in fact the author is trying to say, or a fictionalized audience whose needs for understanding and pleasure are accommodated, modified, or sometimes challenged. In a famous essay by literary theorist Walter Ong, "The Writer's Audience Is Always a Fiction," he provocatively declared, "The text constructs its ideal reader." In Ong's view, a successful author fictionalizes an imagined reader, and the actual reader becomes the ideal reader imagined.

Actual readers likewise construct notions of who authors are and what they intend, but such an assumption of an all-knowing and ever-guiding authorial presence in a text is a delusion. This, at least, is the radical assertion of Roland Barthes in his influential essay "The Death of the Author" (1968). Barthes argued that since it is impossible to know with any certainty the intentions of authors, living or dead, readers should concentrate instead on the text itself in a search for meaning unfettered by questions of authorial intent.

Readers are still left with the daunting challenge of interpretation: assessing the text for meaning and significance in works of literature that by definition are multiple and complex. Lacking a direct, secure route to meaning from either the author or the text, the reader is left with the challenge of interpretation: the analysis and evaluation of possible meanings suggested by the text.

How do the three components of literature—author, text, and reader—come together in interpretation?

Although a case can be (and has been) made for the primacy of each of the three components of literature—author, text, and reader—interpretation that both elucidates and illuminates depends upon a knowledge of the demands, limits, and possibilities of all three.

If an author's intentions remain essentially unknowable or untrustworthy, the reader can still profit from some understanding of the times and culture out of which the author produced the text. Knowing, for example, what a particular word meant in Shakespeare's time or what a certain allusion referred to can at least avoid the interpretative fallacy of judging by inappropriate or anachronistic standards. An apple need not apologize for not being an orange, and an interpretation not balanced by at least some insights about the author can mislead rather than illuminate. Similarly, thorough knowledge of a text leads to better interpretations. Just as one cannot expect to communicate unless one knows the language used, knowledge of the conventions of the literary forms—the elements writers use to produce meaning in literature—are essential.

The most valuable interpretations of literature open up works rather than reducing them to simplistic analysis. Great works of literature are by definition complex and challenging but repay the effort readers make coming to terms with a literary work thoughtfully, deliberately, and skeptically.

Why do we read literature?

Before engaging with the challenges of reading literature, it is worthwhile to address some questions that are assumed but rarely examined, namely, why do we read literature at all, and is it in fact good for us?

For as long as any of us can remember, we have accepted that reading is necessary and beneficial and that reading literature is even better. But what makes this so? In school, our teachers, particularly our literature teachers, assume the importance of their subject: it's self-evident to them but often not to their students. Few disagree with the notion that literature is valuable, useful, and esteemed, but why exactly? What about literature justifies the time and effort it takes to read and understand it? Hippocrates observed, "Art is long, life is short," so why should we bother?

Does literature make us better?

In 2013, philosophy professor Gregory Currie touched off a war of words with a *New York Times* essay, "Does Great Literature Make Us Better?" (June 1). Currie takes on the notion that "exposure to challenging works of literary fiction is good for us." It's a belief, he points out, that is widely accepted and rarely if ever challenged: "That's one reason we deplore the dumbing-down of the school curriculum and the rise of the Internet and its hyperlink culture. Perhaps we don't all read very much that we would count as great literature, but we're apt to feel guilty about not doing so, seeing it as one of the ways we fall short of excellence. Wouldn't reading about Anna Karenina, the good folk of Middlemarch and Marcel and his friends expand our imaginations and refine our moral and social sensibilities?" Currie's answer to this question is unfortunately no, or rather that there is no evidence to support the assumption that we become a better person from our exposure to great literature. Currie argues that there is no causal link between reading great literature and moral excellence. "Can you be confident," Currie asks, "that your intelligent, socially attuned and generous friend who reads Proust got that way partly because of the reading? Might it not be the other way around: that bright, socially competent and empathic people are more likely than others to find pleasure in the complex representations of human interactions we find in literature." Currie's basic complaint is that we have accepted the core idea of literature's moral benefit on faith, not based on evidence, and that "we need to go beyond the appeal to common experience and into the territory of psychological research" for proof of the proposition that literature is good for us. Currie is confident "we can look forward to better evidence." However, he is "less optimistic about what the evidence will show."

Gregory Currie, a philosophy professor at the University of York, has argued that, despite impressions to the contrary, there is no evidence that reading great works of literature makes one a better person somehow.

How was Currie's thesis that there is no evidence that literature makes people better rebutted?

As one would expect, Currie's undermining a cherished belief in literature's moral value prompted impassioned refutations. One of the best was by science writer Annie Murphy Paul in *Time* (June 3, 2013), "Reading Literature Makes Us Smarter and Nicer." Paul counters that the research Currie calls for is in fact available in studies that demonstrate "that individuals who often read fiction appear to be better able to understand other people, empathize with them and view the world from their perspective." Paul goes on to argue that these benefits are at risk in a contemporary reading culture that privileges information processing over the reading skill literature demands. According to Paul, "'Deep reading'—as opposed to the often superficial reading we do on the Web—is an endangered practice, one we ought to take steps to preserve as we would a historic building or a significant work of art." By failing to do so, Paul asserts, we "imperil the intellectual and emotional development of generations growing up online, as well as the perpetuation of a critical part of our culture: the novels, poems and other kinds of literature that can be appreciated only by readers whose brains, quite literally, have been trained to apprehend them."

Paul contends, "Use it or lose it." Literature, as opposed to other kinds of reading, trains readers to slow down the reading process to provide "deep readers time to enrich their reading with reflection, analysis, and their own memories and opinions. It gives

13

them time to establish an intimate relationship with the author, the two of them engaged in an extended and ardent conversation like people falling in love." To illustrate the difference between shallow and the deep reading literature demands, Paul recalls literary critic Frank Kermode's distinction between "carnal reading" (hurried, utilitarian information processing) and "spiritual reading" (for pleasure, reflection, analysis, and improvement), insisting that the former cheats young people "of an enjoyable, even ecstatic experience they would not otherwise encounter" and that the latter provides "an elevating and enlightening experience that will enlarge them as people," showing them "someplace they've never been, a place only deep reading can take them."

How can the benefits of reading literature be measured?

Paul's refutation of Currie's argument, however, falls short of tackling directly his central question: Does reading literature make us better morally? The research suggests that reading literature (deep or spiritual reading) makes us better (or at least different) readers compared to our informational processing skills, but doesn't refute Currie's challenge about moral betterment. Currie, on the other hand, rests his argument on the lack of empirical evidence to support the betterment proposition. Yet, his argument leaves unconsidered other crucially unproven notions, namely, language acquisition. There is no scientific consensus on why and how humans developed language. That absence, however, surely doesn't invalidate language's importance. We take our understanding of language acquisition on faith. Why not also have faith in literature's benefit?

Currie and Paul lead us to consider a much more fundamental question: not does literature make us better humans, but how and why does literature make us human in the first place? Reading literature may or may not contribute to moral excellence, and it may or may not be responsible for developing reading skills of vastly more importance than information processing. But the core benefit of reading literature rests on an even more fundamental assertion: literature instructs us in our humanity. Currie and Paul are looking for quantitative answers for a qualitative experience, and what matters most about literature in our lives is potentially lost in a search for data to quantify it.

How does literature make us human?

How does a person become human? How does one acquire a human nature? Well, instinct certainly supplies key components. We are hardwired to express core human traits for physical survival, for example. Parents and other teachers are responsible for many of the moral components of our nature, offering us instruction (as well as reward and punishment) in how we should behave and how we act in relation to others. But how do parents and teachers learn the lessons of human behavior that they transmit? Experience, says John Locke, but such a system of experiential learning does not tell the whole story. How does someone, for example, born and bred in the tropics acquire an understanding of snow and ice? Experience may be limited and inadequate. This is how reading comes into play and how literature functions in expanding our experience to encompass a wider view of our human nature and experience.

What about the questions beyond behavior, such as "Who am I?" How do humans derive a sense of identity, individuality, and personality? Again, experience determines much: we become the result of our past experiences, but since our experience is naturally limited, we turn to literature to enhance and expand our understanding of human nature and the world. We come to know who we are in relation to those around us because literature both expands our acquaintances and deepens (and complicates) our understanding. Literature, therefore, plays a pivotal role in our becoming fully human.

Literary critic Harold Bloom, in his survey of Shakespeare's canon, *Shakespeare: The Invention of the Human,* argues not just that Shakespeare is the paramount representor of our humanity but also the inventor of it! The notion that human identity is dynamic and ever-changing is, according to Bloom, Shakespeare's innovation and legacy to mankind: "Personality, in our sense, is a Shakespearean invention, and is not only Shakespeare's greatest originality but also the authentic cause of his perpetual pervasiveness." We may challenge Bloom's rhetorical question, "Can we conceive of ourselves without Shakespeare?" but not the role literature plays in that construction. As Bloom explains, "[Shakespeare's] few peers—Homer, the Yahwist, Dante, Chaucer, Cervantes, Tolstoy, perhaps Dickens—reminds us that the representation of human character and personality remains always the supreme literary value, whether in drama, lyric, or narrative." *Who am I?* is perhaps the single most intriguing and perplexing question we can ask and is answered invariably in response to literary representations that are simultaneously lenses—bringing the world and its inhabitants into focus—as well as a mirror in which we can introduce ourselves to ourselves.

How does literature expand our experience?

Human beings are functionally prisoners of space and time. We cannot physically be in two or more places at once or inhabit more than the present. Other than in memory, the past is lost to us, and the future only takes shape in the present. The limitations of space and time are immutable conditions of human life, or are they? This is precisely what literature allows us to do: evade the tyranny of space and time. In works of literature, we are not bound to a single physical space but can simultaneously be here and there, widening our geographical reach to extend our knowledge and experience. In works of literature, we can begin to see the world and ourselves from multiple vantage points that our physical restraints otherwise pre-

Books open up our world and provide us with experiences we are unable to have firsthand. They allow us to travel in time and space beyond the limitations of real life.

vent. But literature enhances our view not just from multiple vantage points in space but also from multiple perspectives. You can only see the world through another's eyes in literature. Film may suggest a perspective, but literature delivers one clearly. The result is our ability to reconstruct our sense of the world in various dimensions. Our physical eyes only look one way. We don't even have the capability of seeing the back of our heads except in reflection. With literature, no such physically restricted sight applies. We can see the world from as many perspectives as there are witnesses who have set their vantage point and perspectives down on paper.

Literature additionally allows us to travel not just in space but in time as well. The only effective time machine ever devised comes to us in the books we read. In literature death does not silence, and the only practical way to evade our mortality is to write something of value that keeps our thoughts and feelings alive. Immortality is only possible in literature. In Shakespeare's famous Sonnet 18 ("Shall I compare thee to a summer's day?"), the speaker boldly asserts the lover's superiority over everything in nature, claiming in conclusion, "So long as men can breathe, or eyes can see, / So long lives this, and this gives life to thee." The "this" here is the poem Shakespeare has written, and he is right: centuries after the subject of the poem has passed away, she still lives on in the poem we read today. It may have taken a Shakespeare to deliver on that claim, but literature, that is, writing read and passed on for its value, stops time. Shakespeare has been dead for four centuries except in the plays and poems that are as vital and pulsing with life (including his life experiences) as ever. In literature, the dead still talk to us beyond any grave. Literature allows us to agree with William Faulkner, who declared, "The past is never dead. It's not even past."

So, how is literature good for us?

The best answer to the question "Why read literature?" is less about making us better people or better readers and more about making us ourselves, or rather testing our evolving notions of who we are and the world we live in against the greatest responses to those key questions—what is human nature and human experience—ever expressed, is this: If we neglect literature, we risk living in a restricted, narrow world, bound by the limitations of time and space. To see more and experience more than what a single life can provide, we depend on literature. Whether we are morally better or smarter or nicer from our exposure to literature is somewhat beyond this crucial point: without literature our humanity is jeopardized, an unwise self-centeredness is unopposed, and the opportunity for human growth and understanding is lost.

We often resist and evade what is good for us—a sensible diet, regular exercise, and constructive criticism. It's far easier to eat whatever we like, to limit a commitment to hit the gym for the week following our New Year's resolution, and to put off any serious performance reviews whether on the job or off. Human nature may depend on literature, but human nature is also more prone to procrastinate and defer the challenge literature clearly provides. The sugarcoating of literature's pill is that it is (or can be) pleasurable medicine that entertains as well as instructs.

In emphasizing the ways in which literature is good for us, it is also important to say how literature need not be good for us at all, or rather its benefits exceed the practical. Does a walk in a forest make us better human beings? Why do we listen to music, dance, sing? Sure, all of these have practical benefits—good exercise, self-expression, and social encounters—but are these really the core motives for doing these activities? So much of what we do in life we do because we enjoy it, regardless of utility and benefit. Literature may offer benefits, but those benefits may not be realized unless literature rewards the reader with pleasure and entertainment.

What's the connection between literature and entertainment?

Literature's basic and ultimately sustaining appeal is that it pleases. We read literature for the sheer pleasure it gives us. Whatever instruction we derive from works of drama, poetry, fiction, and creative nonfiction is directly connected to the entertainment they provide. Horace in his *Ars Poetica* observed that poets (and by extension any writer of literature) "deliver at once both the pleasure and the necessaries of life." Literature should both "instruct and delight," according to Horace, but without the delight, instruction rarely follows. There's no question that literature teaches us about human nature and human experience, but at its core is something more visceral and self-indulgent. Practical benefit is well down the list of literature's core appeal. Think about why you might like to dance. Do you do it just because it is good cardiovascular exercise, that is, for its health benefit, or because of the sheer pleasure of movement to music? Perhaps a more apt analogy to literature, since reading is a more passive activity in appreciating another's performance in words, is attending a sporting event. There, you aren't playing yourself but are watching others. Why? For the sheer pleasure of attending an athletic contest whose outcome is unknown and whose performers can be admired for their exceptional skills. Reading literature is similar. Literature may be read because we feel it might be good for us, but that's not the primary reason for experiencing it. We read it to appreciate a view of the world, a view of life that we never had before, for the sheer thrill of discovery, for insights, experiences, and feelings that have never been better expressed, and for the sheer beauty of a work's language and expression.

Moreover, literature in this sense is inexhaustible, not to be dispensed with once the transfer of information takes place. The greatest works of literature—*King Lear, Anna Karenina, The Waste Land*—deliver few if any answers but instead pose the best possible questions that continually puzzle and delight. A work of literature has depth and complexity, which invite continual rereading. One way to know if you are reading literature, instead of informational writing, is that the work demands to be reread, repeatedly releasing its treasure of truth and pleasure. As Ezra Pound, the American poet and critic, succinctly put it, "Literature is news that stays news": universal in its meanings, perennial in its relevance, and absorbing across generations and cultures.

We also read literature for the beauty and intricacy of its language. Unlike informational writing, which strives to make its message clear and concise, the language of literature is often more or less the message. Literary works can generate a complexity of response simply by the power and intensity of its language.

What role does escape play in literature's appeal?

Unquestionably, a significant element of literature's core delight is vicarious escape. "Escapism" is frequently a pejorative, implying avoidance, seeking distraction and relief from unpleasant realities, and literature certainly can achieve these ends. What we read can be a diversion and pleasant respite from our complicated and too often unsatisfying actuality. This is not surprising since literature can offer a pleasing alternative reality in which experience comes with a clear beginning, middle, and ending, decisive actions (unlike our daily life that can seem random, chaotic, and inconclusive), and characters that more neatly fit into clearer moral categories like heroes and villains, unlike those we encounter in real life. Consider your life on a typical day. Note how little it resembles some kinds of literature: little that will shape your future happens decisively on a typical day. Beginning, middle, and ending? Not really. One day succeeds another in an unbroken string with important events only occasionally disturbing an undramatic routine. Often the most important events in one's life are initially overlooked and only obvious years later when the complicated consequences of an event become obvious. Are you the hero or villain of your own story? The question seems odd even to ask. We would hope to be characterized by the moral certainty of heroism, but too often, if we are honest, we are mixed, grey characters, far more complex than the simplified moral portraits some literature provides.

While "escapism" sometimes has a negative connotation of avoiding life, literature can both offer escapism and a heightened sense of reality that helps round out our humanity.

Literature, therefore, can offer a pleasing escape from the world as it is into a world as it might be or should be. Instead of doubt, literature can provide assurances; instead of frustrating complexity, literature can offer pleasing resolutions; instead of contradictions and inconsistencies, literature can provide certainties and agreeable simplifications. That is, some literature, but not all. Great literature offers escape into a heightened reality that equips us, in Horace's phrase, with the "necessaries of life" to complete our humanity.

What kinds of pleasure does reading literature provide?

Beyond the utility of literature—learning from the best that has ever been written by others—it serves as sheer delight, pleasing us in several different and important ways.

- The pleasure of the imagination: In the escape that reading literature provides through vicarious identification and comparison with other lives, places, and times, we activate our imagination, that uniquely human ability to explore an alternative set of ideas and experiences that are outside our present environment and that may not even be real. As opposed to perception that receives and processes information from the outside world—light, sound, shape—and finds meaning in it—a sunset, a symphony, a house—in imagination, the process is reversed. Translating the words we read into what they signify, we populate an inner world in which imagery is created from the memory. For example, we read "house" and conjure a representation of a house from memory. It is our imagination, the complex interweaving of perception and memory that literature activates, releasing a latent creativity that pleases. The writer may provide the blueprint, but the reader builds literature's many rooms, and like any satisfying occupation, literature gratifies our imaginative and creative abilities.

- The pleasure of analysis: Literature activates a different kind of pleasure in its problem-solving. Why does doing a crossword puzzle give pleasure? Why are we attracted to what W. B. Yeats called "the fascination of what's difficult"? Given human nature's tendency to procrastinate and avoid so many labors, why do we relish the special challenges that literature sets for us? Some literature, so-called "page-turners," seem effortless: sit back and enjoy the ride; others that can be labeled "page-stoppers" impede our progress, forcing us to use more than imagination to conjure scene and situation. We need to bring to our reading the closest analytical skill we possess to uncover sometimes complicated, implied motivations and relationships, significance and meaning. Think of the investigation skills mystery writers set for their readers. No doubt the answers will be finally provided, but the questions still baffle and demand active analysis to crack the case. We may not be blessed by Sherlock's uncanny insights, but the fun of a mystery is to test our skills against those of the featured investigator. Great literature may not be constructed around problem-solving as explicitly as a mystery, but it calls for our active involvement in the translation of clues into patterns of significance and meaning. The "a-ha!" moment of clarity, like the completed crossword, is the pleasure of being tested and passing the challenge.

- The pleasure of aesthetic appreciation: One of literature's greatest pleasures is the appreciation of the skill and performance of the literary artist. Literature's medium is language as color is the medium of the artist and sound is the medium of the musician, and the craft on display by the greatest writers is a thing of beauty. As John Keats asserts, "A thing of beauty is a joy forever," and literature summons up that joy in appreciating a well-turned phrase, a perfectly crafted scene or image, experience designed and patterned to release a shock of recognition. We enjoy performance by the best, whether dancers, guitarists, or athletes. They show us something special that we cannot do as well or at all, but we can still appreciate their exceptional skills and accomplishments. Literature is no different. We can all write, but likely not a sonnet as sublime as Shakespeare's or a novel as profound as Tolstoy's *War and Peace*. Neither therefore discourages but inspires and pleasingly stimulates. Just as our appreciation of the greatness of Jimi Hendrix is enhanced by our own fumbling attempts to master the rudiments of the guitar, so, too, is the aesthetic pleasure of literature enriched when the reader understands the basic rules of literary construction, which we will cover in this book.

Why is literature resistible?

Why then, with literature's evident benefits and apparent pleasures, do readers reject literature for other less demanding forms of enrichment and entertainment? No doubt one answer to that question is that reading great literature is a challenge, and like any complicated task (cooking, playing an instrument, etc.), expertise and the pleasure of accomplishment do not come easily or at least without some instruction and practice. You cannot simply pick up a guitar and make it behave like a master; you cannot expect a literary masterpiece to unlock its many treasures without some training and practice. In our instant-gratification culture, the challenge of literature seems more like gratification deferred. We know that literature is good for us, and, somewhat guiltily, postpone the challenge to another day. This is particularly the case with modern literature that seems at times written only for the specialist. We have all read that James Joyce's *Ulysses* is the greatest novel of the twentieth century, but how many have been baffled by the first section and never gone further? Modern poetry and drama are no less intimidating because they break so many rules and ask us to understand them in ways far different

Think of the literary world as being like an art museum displaying the works of many masters. Each master has a unique style, yet there are certain principles of painting that they have in common. Understanding these central principles will help you to appreciate any art form.

than what we have mastered. You may, for example, have learned to "read" and appreciate the expressive realism of a Vermeer or a Rembrandt, but how do you then use those same skills to appreciate Picasso, Pollack, and Rothko? Readers of literature must contend with different intentions and methods in which a single standard of evaluation and appreciation does not apply. An apple need not apologize for not being an orange, and Pollock is not a failed Rembrandt. To understand his art, we need to understand what he is trying to do and the rules he has set himself. Likewise, literature operates under multiple sets of intentions and methods, and to rely on only one can lead to frustration and ultimately abandoning certain works of literature as incomprehensible and unsatisfying. To read literature properly, you need first to learn how to read it at all.

This is why we will begin our consideration of literature with how NOT to read it before proceeding to the basic skills that should allow you to enjoy and understand various forms and types of literature.

HOW NOT TO READ LITERATURE

Where do you start?

The starting point for learning how best to read any work of literature is an understanding that literature requires a different set of reading skills and approaches than those we have mastered for nonliterary, everyday reading. Confusion between the two kinds of reading can lead to frustration and miscommunication, as well as explaining the seemingly insurmountable challenges reading some literature produces. Reader resistance to literature can be exacerbated by previously taught approaches that simply do not help. Let's then consider how NOT to read literature along with some suggestions of how best to read it.

DON'T READ LITERATURE LIKE YOU DO ORDINARY WRITING

How is reading literature different from other kinds of reading?

The way we need to read literature is fundamentally different from the way we read regularly. Regular reading is the kind of reading we do daily: reading emails, text messages, newspapers, and magazines, even books such as this one. The emphasis in this kind of everyday reading is on extracting necessary information (for example, what time and where to meet, who won the game and by what score, the formula needed to master the problem in a textbook). Once the extraction of the desired information happens, the message is no longer needed. Unless we need to be reminded of specific details, we never need to revisit this kind of everyday reading. It's disposable, valuable only as a carrier of the information that we need. Once we get that message, there's no need for the messenger any longer. How often do we reread yesterday's newspaper? Why do so many college students rent rather than buy their assigned textbooks? The idea of reading them again after processing their information is unfathomable!

What are the characteristics of everyday reading?

Everyday reading is written to reflect the practical purpose it serves. It is all about delivering information as clearly and directly as possible, with an emphasis on clarity, conciseness, and coherence. Anything that obscures the message is a drawback in everyday reading, which aspires to a high level of transparency to display the message as clearly as possible. Whatever muddles key information, particularly through a writing style that calls attention to itself rather than its message, is to be avoided. In everyday reading, meaning is explicit, on its surface. If it calls attention to itself as writing, the reader may be distracted from its primary purpose: to receive useful information.

Consider this text message: "Meet me 9 P.M. Friday to see a movie at the mall." This is clear and to the point: the crucial information is when, where, and why. But what if the message was this: "Dare I suppose that you would grace me with your presence to traverse the evening streets to unite for a showing of flickering images as the sun declines on the last evening of the work week...." The message is obscured by the display of florid and overelaborate language, unsuited for its purpose: to arrange a date and time to meet. In everyday reading, meaning is primary, and anything that delays or disguises that meaning is a detriment.

Therefore, newspaper articles try never to "bury the lead," that is, they try to begin with the information that is most important and avoid forcing the reader to search for it: how many died in the fire, what was the final score of the game, what did the president actually say. The core information of most importance to the reader is clarified at the outset (announced by a helpful headline summary) with details that answer the key questions: what, when, where, why, and how made clear. Leaving out any of these, the writer fails in a primary mission to inform the reader as clearly and concisely as possible. Imagine your disappointment if an account of a game left out the final score or if an account of a fire did not offer some details about possible causes.

In ordinary, daily writing, such as composing a text on a phone, the language should be direct, straightforward. One would not use an overly artistic style with florid prose to set up a business meeting.

How is reading literature different from everyday reading?

Literature—how it is designed, what its purpose is, and how it needs to be read—is different from and often contrary to the methods of everyday writing and reading. For one thing, most works of literature rarely have a single, easily extracted meaning, a core piece of information to be transmitted. What exactly is the core takeaway from Shakespeare's *Hamlet*, for example? Simplified responses like "Believe in ghosts," "Never trust an uncle who becomes your stepfather," or "The play's the thing" are reductively absurd in contending with Shakespeare's great drama because literature rarely has an explicit, easily extracted "message." As Hollywood mogul Samuel Goldwyn has been credited with saying, "Just write me the comedy. Messages are for Western Union." Goldwyn demonstrates here the core difference between literature and other forms of writing in which information processing, that is, extractible messages, is paramount. Meaning in literature, instead of being on the surface and at the outset as it is in everyday reading, is more often implicit, suffused throughout the work in its various elements: in its plot, characterization, setting, etc. In poetry, meaning can turn on a single word or image. Rather than striving for an unobstructed transparency, literature can be as much about *how* as *what* in which style can serve as important lenses to focus meaning and significance. Literature calls attention to itself as written because how it expresses itself can often be the point.

Literature is also not a disposable carrier of nuggets of information. Literature (as opposed to everyday reading) invites us back again and again to re-experience what it offers and to reassess its meanings. Literature continues to communicate meaning and significance over time, and, most remarkably, to shift its meaning based on our perspective. We have all had the experience of taking up a classic work of literature after several years and finding in it details and significance we missed the first (or fifth) time through. What has changed is not the work of literature exactly but our experiences that are now reflected in the text. One's perception of Shakespeare's grand drama on aging under existential threat, *King Lear*, is a different experience read in one's twenties than it is in one's seventies. This is true because reading literature, as opposed to everyday reading, requires full reader participation, activating not just our informational processing skills but our analysis, imagination, and emotions. These change over time in every person, and those changes explain how works of literature are more dynamic than everyday reading.

Readers should keep this in mind if they are tempted to say, "I read *Huckleberry Finn* in high school: Been there, done that." All of the greatest works of literature need to be read every five or ten years during a reader's life not because they have changed but because you have.

DON'T JUST READ LITERATURE, REREAD IT

Why does literature need to be reread?

Literature's dynamism and ever-shifting meanings and significance underscore another key reading principle that sets it apart from everyday reading. As Vladimir Nabokov declared, "One cannot *read* a book: one can only reread it." By book, Nabokov means liter-

25

Russian-American novelist Vladimir Nabokov believed that rereading a book was essential to fully grasp its artistry.

ature, and as he explains, "A good reader, a major reader, an active and creative reader is a rereader.... When we read a book for the first time the very process of laboriously moving our eyes from left to right, line after line, page after page, this complicated physical work upon the book, the very process of learning in terms of space and time what the book is about, this stands between us and artistic appreciation." Nabokov goes on to explain that the barrier in reading between process and perception is noticeably absent when we view a painting, for example: "We do not have to move our eyes in a special way even if, as in a book, the picture contains elements of depth and development. We have no physical organ (as we have the eye in regard to a painting) that takes in the whole picture and can enjoy its details. But at a second, or third, or fourth reading we do, in a sense, behave toward a book as we do towards a painting."

It's not just the physical act of reading that distracts on a first reading from the "depth and development" of literature. Every exposure to something new is enhanced with familiarity, versions of rereading. For example, how much of the view is evident on the first time on a steep mountain hike? Most of us are mainly concerned with making it to the top, conserving energy for the unknown challenges, and spending most of our time watching our footing. But what happens the second time up the same trail? You have a better sense of the distance and the energy needed. Strain gives way to a more relaxed approach based on familiarity, and now the view comes more into focus.

Perhaps an even better example is the experience we have all had watching a film for a second time. For a complex mystery or thriller, so much of our first viewing is concentrated on just the basics: what exactly is going on? Which character is that again? On a second re-view, so much that had been missed before—details and clues—become apparent and obvious. This is no less true for reading literature. No great literary work reveals all it has to say on a first reading. The depth and nuance with which literature is written demands rereading.

Are rereadings better readings?

Rereading is essential in opening up literature's treasures, but are rereadings the best readings? As literary scholar Patricia Meyer Spacks argues in *On Rereading,* her account of a year spent rereading classic literary works, "Reading a book, or rereading it, we enter into relation not only with the text but with an imagined author. Rereading it, we relate also to one or more versions of our past selves. Examining the textures of those relationships, we learn both about ourselves and about complicated connections informing the mysterious process of reading." On her rereading journey, she was reacquainted not just with previous literary friends and foes but also to herself at various stages of her reading life. What she discovered was not all positive. She did find value in books she previously dismissed as uninteresting, but she also was disappointed by other works she had greatly admired in the past. "We read to recapture the thrill of a book first encountered twenty years earlier," she writes, "and the thrill has mysteriously vanished. We remember a wonderful story, and the story has turned into a cliché. The change may attest to our maturity, but it feels like a loss." Spacks reaches an ambivalent conclusion: "Rereading has turned out to be rich in paradox. A conservative activity that holds on to the past, it is also potentially revolutionary, overturning judgments and repudiating assumptions. What once you failed to notice jumps up to alarm or delight you. Rereading gives the self permission and space to think, to play, and to meditate. It can feel like self-enlargement. In some ways it proves more personal even than initial acts of reading, given its engagement with earlier versions of the self."

What about the value of a first reading?

A case can be made that rereading is too detached, too analytical, with the emotional power of literature, once unanticipatedly released on a first reading, now diminished with familiarity. There's something to be said about the first time for anything we do.

Are rereadings in fact possible?

As Spacks discovers, rereading can be as unsettling as it is essential for deepening an encounter with literature. Perhaps the reason for this is best captured by critic Verlyn Klinkenborg in an essay "Thoughts on the Pleasures of Being a Re-Reader." "The real secret of rereading," Klinkenborg declares, "is simply this: it is impossible. The characters remain the same, and the words never change, but the reader always does. Pip [in Dickens's *Great Expectations*] is always there to be revisited, but you, the reader, are a little like the convict who surprises him in the graveyard—always a stranger." Klingenborg argues here that every encounter with a work of literature is essentially a first reading since the reader's experience and perception always changes.

If Klingenborg is correct that each reading of a literary work is a first reading by a different self, it is still the case that multiple readings result in enhanced understanding (whether of the text or your previous self). The surface appeal of a work, its forward momentum of plot and incident, falls away, allowing other pleasures to take hold in reflection and appreciation of the craft displayed.

It's special because of its novelty, freshness, and surprise. Literary scholar J. Donald Adams has written that "reading *War and Peace* for the first time is one of the greatest literary experiences; reading it again and again is to realize the immeasurable gulf that is fixed between a merely good book and a great one." The difference that Adams registers here is between the enviable literary experience of the first-timer and the more seasoned evaluative appreciation of the veteran rereader. Which is better?

French literary theorist Roland Barthes in "The Pleasure of the Text" draws a distinction between books that provoke pleasure and those that stimulate what he calls *jouissance* (bliss). For Barthes, rereading may cause pleasure, "but not my bliss: bliss may come only with the *absolutely* new."

It is certainly possible to envy a first encounter with a great work of literature because once read, it can only be reread, with the magic of its initial spell replaced by other attractions, sometimes taking us behind the curtain to notice how the trick was accomplished. Does the magic still work if you know how it was done? While one can envy a first-time reader for the initial pleasures that rereaders can no longer experience, it also needs to be said that the first time doing most things, as thrilling and surprising as they can be, are rarely well done or are fully satisfying. What about the first time you drove a car? Exhilarating, certainly, but you were likely so concerned with the process (hands positioned at ten and two, looking straight ahead and in the rearview mirror, footwork untried and tested) that the pleasure of expertise is lacking. Once the process is mastered, full enjoyment follows. There's something like this regarding reading literature. A first encounter with any work of literature is so strange and unfamiliar that it can be hard to get your bearings. It can shock and surprise, certainly, but with familiarity, understanding increases and pleasure deepens. Ideally, reading literature should aspire to retaining the thrills of the first time allied with the appreciation that comes with deeper understanding. In other words, readers should retain their memory of their first time with a work of literature (as we do with other firsts in our lives) while cultivating the reading expertise that comes from repeated readings.

One way around the first-time versus rereading dilemma is that the more we read literature, the better our first readings become.

DON'T READ LITERATURE PASSIVELY

Why does literature require active reading?

Whether reading for the first time or rereading, literature demands more than passive absorption of information. So much of what we read every day is made easy for us. In today's print and online world, sources vie for our easily distracted and limited attention spans by catering to readers and viewers with sound bites, memes, and easily digested encapsulations. Our focus of attention is deemed so easily diverted that most cable news programs include crawls of headlines and breaking stories to distract us if the main story proves unengaging. Concentration required to process complex subjects has been replaced by instant absorption. We become more passive consumers of data and not attentive, thoughtful readers. Such an approach to reading undermines the active reading skills literature requires.

There are some kinds of literature, thrillers for example, that feature a break-neck plot that sweeps up the characters and the reader in the ride. We have all experienced what are often called "good reads," books that can be consumed in a single sitting, "page-turners," with a relentless forward momentum that propels the reader effortlessly to the final page.

A passive reading of a book does not lend itself well to absorbing the material it contains.

Other "good reads" are facilitated not by an irresistible plot but by a guiding narrator, directing and focusing the reader's attention. Novels, particularly the great Victorian novels of Charles Dickens, William Makepeace Thackeray, George Eliot, Anthony Trollope, and others, come equipped with a helpful narrative presence who can be depended upon to alert readers to issues of importance (it has been said of George Eliot: "Take seriously anything she repeats three times!"). The all-knowing, supportive narrator in these books is responsible for the book's heavy reflective lifting, and the reader can sit back in a comfy chair with a companionable assistant for the reading labors.

Much to the chagrin and often frustration of readers, modern literature eliminates such assistance, whether in a breathless plot or narrative guide, and readers are forced into an active, cocreative role in the reading process. Modern literature—whether poems, short stories, novels, or drama—at times resembles television crime shows in which the investigative team confronts a baffling, chaotic crime scene, and through laborious attention to the various clues—broken ashtray, blood splatter, tread marks— they clear up by the end of the episode what happened, by whom, and why, as initial chaos is reassembled into order and significance. Reading literature is similar. The reader needs to be the lead criminal investigator, actively sorting the data provided for meaning and significance. It's natural enough to prefer a good read to a hard read, but as literary scholar Malcolm Bradbury has argued, "A conventional good read is usually a bad read, a relaxing bath in what we know already. A true good read is surely an act of innovative creation in which we, the readers, become conspirators." Literature requires a reader as inventive co-creator and conspirator in an active, dialectical reading process.

What is an active dialectical reading process?

Active dialectical reading is a process by which the reader engages in a silent dialogue with a literary work through active questioning of the writer's choices. Why this word, scene, event, or outcome and not some other? What and how does each signify? The dialectic may seem somewhat one-sided. Neither the text nor its author answer the reader's questions directly, and the reader's interrogation of the text leads not to definitive answers but insights, which emerge in the reader's engagement with the text. According to Reader Response literary criticism, meaning does not exist in a text but *in* the interaction between the reader *and* the text. Therefore, the reader, not the text or the author, generates whatever meaning a literary work possesses, which is only generated in the reader's active engagement. Waiting for a text to signal meaning, as in a news article with a banner headline or useful encapsulation and summary, is futile. This is the reason that many readers resist the challenges of literature: because we are forced out of a passive reading process and required to bring the full weight of analysis, reflection, and emotional empathy to bear in reading literature. Sit back, relax, and let the text entertain and enlighten is NOT the way literature works, or at least not the way that the greatest literary works behave.

What does active reading require?

Engaged dialectical reading requires effort, concentration, attention to detail, and, through practice, a growing expertise to know the best questions to ask and where to look for the answers. Analysis and reflection (thinking through the implications of what is read) is crucial to active reading. As Edmund Burke famously observed, "To read without reflecting is like eating without digesting." Instead of being a passive passenger in the vehicle of a literary text, awaiting a destination and justification for the time spent, active readers are closer to copilots with the writer, sharing in the duties and responsibilities of the trip. The motto "It's not the destination that matters; it's the journey" aptly applies to the active reading process literature requires.

The eighteenth-century Irish philosopher, author, orator, and political theorist Edmund Burke advocated reflecting on the material one reads after reading it.

What are the five key questions to ask when reading a work of literature?

In thinking about what questions to ask any literary text, you cannot do better than these five. Answering them, based on the evidence that the work provides—whether in a poem, short story, novel, or drama—will take you far in establishing an active dialectical reading process and arriving at answers about meaning and significance.

Question 1: What is the title?

The title in a literary work is sometimes the only explicit suggestion by the author what the work is about and what should focus the reader's attention. Ask yourself: why this title and not some other? What does the title suggest in terms of what the focus and meaning of the work is? If the work is a novel, how do the chapter titles (if any) suggest what to expect next?

Question 2: Why does it start here?

Like the viewfinder in a camera that frames a picture, the beginning of a literary work reveals a great deal about the focus and purpose of the work. Ask yourself: why does the work start here and not some other place? What is important about the initial information that is given? About the initial situation? It has been said that there are only two plots in literature: setting off on a journey or the arrival of a stranger. In other words, literature often shows a status quo disrupted. Does this concept apply? Is there some routine, habit, condition that is challenged? How and why?

Question 3: What is the conflict?

Drama is conflict: the opposition of desires, goals, ambitions. This is no less true in poetry and fiction as it is in drama. Find the conflict, and find the significance of that conflict. What are the oppositions? Conflict can come between individuals and circumstances (nature, time, etc.), individuals with each other, and individuals with themselves. Isolate the explicit or implied conflict in the work to locate its dramatic center.

Question 4: How is the conflict resolved?

If conflict is the dramatic center of literary works, framing the tensions and movement in a work, how the conflict is resolved is crucial in determining significance.

Why is active reading so hard?

Students who struggle in literature classes often complain, "Why does reading literature have to be so hard? Can't it just be enjoyed?" Perhaps. There are some popular literary works that please without effort, but great works of literature rarely come without a cost in a reader's involvement and effort. Great literature's subjects, ideas, and methods challenge, and their enjoyment deepens with the effort put in to read thoughtfully. Most works of literature deserve—and demand—to be read attentively, seriously, and actively, with time and effort, as does any other complex and challenging activities. Do any activities in life yield their pleasures without experience and practice? How enjoyable or satisfying was your first time picking up a guitar? Skiing downhill? Learning to drive? None of these activities are immediately doable (or even initially enjoyable). They require effort and practice. The same is true for reading literature actively. Inexperienced readers can enjoy literature, but active readers will see more, hear more, learn more, and enjoy more because they will know what to look for, and the various sources of enjoyment will deepen and expand as expertise in reading develops.

What happens in the confrontation? What change in the initial situation is evident? Does the central character (or speaker) come to a new or different insight, conclusion, or action? What does the resolution tell us about a revealed aspect of human nature or the human experience?

Question 5: Why does it end here?

Think of the conclusion of a work of literature as completing the frame of the viewfinder: what is revealed? Why end here and not some other place? What is resolved or left unresolved? Why? Compare how the work ends with how it began. What's different? What's the same? What has changed?

DON'T SPEED-READ LITERATURE

Why isn't speed the thing in reading literature?

A useful corollary to the need to be an active reader is that literature requires you to slow your reading down. In elementary school being labeled a "slow reader" was grounds for concern and intervention. Speed—processing reading material quickly with retention—was the goal, and it was important training for the challenge ahead in informational processing that escalated in secondary school, college, graduate school, and beyond.

But speed-reading works of literature simply does not work. Speed-readers often miss the point completely. Literature demands that you slow your reading speed down. Speeding through a great work of literature may allow you to tick off that particular box on your reading to-do list, but what you will remember of the experience is directly connected with your putting a brake on your usual reading speed. The mantra of the slow-cooking movement is "low and slow": reduced heat and extended cooking time will bring out flavor. The mantra for reading literature ought to be "slow and slower": reduce your reading pace so you begin to absorb fully the details, nuances, and flavors. What you notice in the world around you is directly connected to the speed you travel. At high speed, the world is a blur, with only your destination as the primary goal. The same is true for reading literature: slowing your reading down does not just enhance the view. It also allows details to move from short-term to long-term memory, improving retention while interrupting the rush to the end with reflection and the dialectical questioning that literature requires.

The Irish novelist Jamie O'Neill, author of *At Swim, Two Boys* (2001), once confessed to a creative writing class that instead of a "page-turner," he aspired to write a "page-stopper," that is, a novel so loaded with significance and beauty that a reader would only reluctantly give in to the next page. This may seem an impossible or impractical standard, but O'Neill's central point is that he wanted his readers to linger, not to rush to the end, not to miss what was meticulously included both to delay the reading and reward the stopover.

How can you become a slower, active reader?

You can reduce your reading speed in several ways:

- Read with a purpose. Go beyond the surface appeal of being entertained to a more active and reflective interrogation: why is this (or isn't this) entertaining? What do I like about what I read and why? Posing these questions as you read, not just afterward, will positively slow your reading speed and encourage engagement.

- Read critically. Concentrate not just on the *what* but also the *how* of a literary text. Pause to consider why you like what you do: word choice, turn of phrase, characterization. Ask how the

Although there are techniques you can learn to speed-read a book—and this might be useful for, say, a business manual from which you just want facts—absorbing good literature requires a deliberate, slow, and careful approach.

drama comes about. What provides the suspense, the surprises? What's the crisis and the resolution? Again, thinking through these issues as you go puts a break on your rush to the end in a positive way.

- Read with a pen/pencil in hand. Nothing slows reading down better than some system of annotation, reading with pen or pencil in hand. Obviously, this only works for the books you own, but you can photocopy poems, short stories, and even passages of longer works to write down your reactions as you go. Underline words you do not understand and look them up, if not immediately, then after completing a stanza, paragraph, scene, or chapter. Ask the text questions: why X and not Y? Why this detail and not some other? Why this turn of events? And note tentative answers in the margins of the text. Annotation encourages the dialectic reading process, the dialogue with the text, that reading literature requires. The act of writing out comments, even underlining key passages, will slow your reading down as well. However, dispense with the highlighter. Painting large swaths of text does little more than add color. Highlighting is passive annotation. Force yourself into active annotation by interrogating the passage in your marginal comments: why did I pause at this passage? Why do I think this passage is significant?

- Pause as directed. As you read, follow the directions in the text to pause or even stop your reading. In a poem, notice the sentence and stanza breaks. Pause to assess. In a drama, let scenes and acts signal moments to stop for reflections and assessment. Pause to ask questions: Why this scene? Why start and stop here? What has been achieved in this unit of the play? Jot down your thoughts. For a novel, obey the end of the chapter signs to halt. Again, pause to reflect on this particular unit of the text:

how does it logically follow what came before and what follows? How and why is this chapter here in the first place?

- Summarize often. It is always helpful to keep a reading notebook that forces you to make sense of what you have read by summarizing key points and reactions divided by units in the work, such as a poem's stanza, a drama's scene or act, a novel's chapter. The act of doing so ensures time for reflection and attention to details that might have been missed in a rush to finish. Afterward, you have a helpful document to assist your memory in recalling important elements of structure and details.

- Reread by units. To slow your reading down, reread as you go through a text, not just after you finish one. A second reading of a stanza, scene, chapter, even a paragraph, before you proceed to the next dramatically slows your progress while enhancing engagement and understanding. Some readers may find this approach disruptive to the narrative flow of a work. In a short lyric or short story, you can complete the entire work before closer inspection. In longer works, pause at the main breaks: scenes or acts in drama, chapters in novels.

Some or all of these methods will slow your reading down dramatically to the thoughtful, reflective, and active level reading literature requires.

DON'T READ LITERATURE ONLY TO IDENTIFY

Why is reading for identification with characters and situation limiting?

One of literature's greatest pleasures is the vicarious identification with its situation, story, and characters, but that should not be the only goal of your imaginative engagement. We have all heard and made reviews of literary works: "It is so lifelike"; or "The same thing happened to me"; or "The central character is just like me." These comments reflect one of literature's chief assets: to function like a mirror, offering our world and ourselves for closer inspection. Self-reflection is one of the core values that literature provides, but it should not come at the expense of another crucial function: to act as a lens, bringing into focus the unfamiliar and taking us beyond our experience for a chance to identify with other people, places, and events. It is meant not to reassure but to unsettle. "Reading is the sole means," writer Joyce Carol Oates insists, "by which we slip voluntarily, often helplessly into another's skin, another's voice, another's soul." Often, this experience can be disconcerting and disorienting, setting up resistance. Literature can show us what is uncomfortable, distorted and troubling reflections that still hit their target of resemblance, relevance, and truth. For literature to work as a lens, readers need to go beyond a narrow capacity for imaginative identification. That is, readers should resist a critical standard to overrate works of literature that show them what they think they know about themselves and the world as praiseworthy, while undervaluing works that fail to flatter or that take us beyond our comfort zone of familiarity.

Vladimir Nabokov, in his opening lecture on how to read literature to his college classes, identifies two types of imagination at play. "First, there is the comparatively lowly kind, which turns for support to the simple emotions and is of a definitely personal nature," he argues. "A situation in a book is intensely felt because it reminds us of something that happened to us or to someone we know or knew. Or, again, a reader treasures a book mainly because it evokes a country, a landscape, a mode of living which he nostalgically recalls as part of his own past. Or, and this is the worst thing a reader can do, he identifies himself with a character in the book. This lowly variety is not the kind of imagination I would like readers to use." Nabokov instead asks from his students a more "authentic instrument" of the imag-

Award-winning author and Princeton University creative writing professor Joyce Carol Oates once said that reading is the only way we can really penetrate another person's voice and soul.

ination, which he calls "impersonal imagination and artistic delight." It operates, Nabokov explains, in "an artistic harmonious balance between the reader's mind and the author's mind" in which "we ought to remain a little aloof and take pleasure in this aloofness while at the same time we keenly enjoy—passionately enjoy, enjoy with tears and shivers—the inner weave of a given masterpiece." What Nabokov seems to be saying here is that we need to limit our identification to see and understand literature in full: "The reader must know when and where to curb his imagination and this he does by trying to get clear the specific world the author places at his disposal. We must see things and hear things, we must visualize the rooms, the clothes, the manners of an author's people." In other words, we must go beyond what we know of the world to see with clarity what the literary artist knows of the world.

As literary critic Jeffery Perl contends, "It is no trick to like what you like. It is no trick to understand what you understand." Literature demands that we go beyond the familiar, to learn to like what we did not formerly like, to understand what we formerly did not understand. A simple identification to like only what you have liked, to see only what you have seen, is not what literature offers. "Literary works quite often 'know' things that the reader does not know," argues literary theorist Terry Eagleton, "or does not know yet, or perhaps will never know."

Identification, with literature's story, setting, or characters, is an initial response to the power of literature, but it should not be the last or necessarily the best. Few readers of Poe's short story "The Tell-Tale Heart" can or would "identify" with the homicidal maniac narrator, but that doesn't diminish or dismiss the power and insights of the

35

story. No reader has ever gone through what Gregor Samsa experiences in Franz Kafka's "The Metamorphosis," being transformed overnight into an insect. A critical response, based on simple identification, "That couldn't happen," or worse, "That never happened to me," misses the point of Kafka's story and is a barrier to understanding what Kafka is exploring. It may never have happened in life, but it has in the confines of Kafka's story that invites readers to enter new and startling imaginative territory.

Most of what happens in literature features circumstances that we simply would not want to experience in life—murdering your father and marrying your mother in Sophocles' *Oedipus* or damning an entire crew in pursuit of a monstrous white whale in Melville's *Moby-Dick,* for example—but literature permits us to do so imaginatively at a safe distance to allow for reflection, analysis, and empathy. Resist the temptation to limit your imaginative engagement in literature to what you already have experienced. Allow literature to extend your identification beyond what you know to learn and experience what you do not.

DON'T READ LITERATURE FOR MEANING (FIRST)

Why is a search for meaning in literature potentially misdirected?

A recommendation to defer the search for meaning in literature may seem counterintuitive: isn't finding meaning the goal and the point of reading it? Why else do it? It is certainly true that meaning and significance is a paramount reward in literary works. Life is chaotic and far too often random and inconsequential, but literature is not. It is patterned and ordered in ways designed to release consequence, purpose, impact, and understanding. Meaning in literature can justify the efforts made to contend with often complex and challenging texts. But readers should be careful about how to search for meaning and to resist the temptation to treat literature like everyday reading whose central point is readily expressed. Meaning and significance do not necessarily come as easily or obviously elsewhere. Think of other activities you do: what precisely is the "meaning" of a hike in the woods? What is the meaning of that particular rock or tree? What is the meaning of a dance performance or a musical concert? The questions seem irrelevant and beside the point. Certainly, all have significance and, therefore, meaning in our lives, but what they are can be elusive and difficult to articulate. Literature resembles these activities in that its significance and meanings are multiple and very possibly ineffable. What exactly is the meaning in *Hamlet*? Where do you start? Where do you stop?

Meaning in literature comes in the plural and can defy encapsulation. Therefore, interviewers who ask authors what is the meaning of their work usually are met with a blank stare. Few great works of literature begin with meaning that is carefully embedded in verse, scene, or story. Instead, multiple meanings are released from incident, character, and details. Meaning in literature is not detachable from the myriad insights literature stimulates, which must be gathered by close, active reading, not dug up like buried treasure.

Far too often a reader in pursuit of meaning distorts or overlooks literature's processes for generating meaning. Literature is not a coded message needing to be deciphered. Literature is also rarely an argument or a thesis by indirect means. Too often, particularly in literature classes, that's the impression teachers seem to suggest, often unintentionally. On display in the lesson is the result of a more experienced reader demonstrating the meanings that can be found, but the message to the students is that the "game" of literature is only to anticipate what the teacher has found, rather than to derive its significance themselves from the process of close reading and reflection. Too often the "how" of literature gives way to an exclusive consideration of what does the text

How does reading literature resemble a cocktail party and a foreign city?

In thinking about the pursuit of literary meaning, consider two analogies: a cocktail party and an unfamiliar, foreign city and its culture. How do you make "sense" of either of these? In the cocktail party, guests usually don't come with name tags and certainly not with helpful cards to indicate personality and beliefs, so how do you size up your fellows? By close observation: by surface details of dress and behavior, in inspection of tone and temperament that comes from what they say and how they say it. First impressions can be misleading, we know, and truly to get to know someone, additional effort beyond a casual encounter will be needed.

Consider another analogy: traveling to a foreign city and enjoying its culture. How do you make sense of where you are and what exactly is going on? The answer is by familiarity. You may be armed with a guidebook and map to help direct your exploration, but the best approach is immersion, plunging into the life of the city while always observing, alert for details and patterns that lead to understanding. Hypotheses based on evidence, such as this street leads to that street, this behavior suggests these values, need to be tested in comparison to corroborating or contradictory evidence. With sufficient time and effort, you find your way around and gain understanding.

In neither case—cocktail party or foreign city—is understanding immediate or simple. It's not a matter of finding a secret key to unlock important truths but requires active engagement and questioning. In both cases, meaning and significance are outcomes that follow rather than direct our encounters. Literature is similar. Readers need to immerse themselves into a work of literature, shift evidence, form hypotheses, and test them against more evidence and examples, letting meaning and significance become the outcome of this process.

mean, neglecting precisely the ways meaning in literature is generated: organically out of the details of its construction. Students of literature, thereby, become more concerned with "cracking the code" than attending carefully to processes by which various meaning is generated in a work of literature.

The narrator in Joseph Conrad's great novella *Heart of Darkness* draws a distinction between the storytelling style of other seamen and that of his mariner Marlow: "The yarns of seamen have a direct simplicity, the whole meaning of which lies within the shell of a cracked nut. But Marlow was not typical … and to him the meaning of an episode was not inside like a kernel but outside, enveloping the tale which brought it out only as a glow brings out a haze, in the likeness of one of these misty halos that sometimes are made visible by the spectral illumination of moonshine."

Conrad here signals how the reader should pursue meaning in his work (and all great literature): not with an eye for the kernel of truth but in a projection emanating from the literary work. Meaning is not a core truth but an enveloping and irreducible illumination extending outward. Readers in pursuit of meaning and significance need to look up and about in as many directions as the literary work shows. Meaning is not the kernel but the shell. As literary theorist Terry Eagleton has argued, "The most common mistake students of literature make is to go straight for what the poem or novel says, setting aside the way that it says it. To read like this is to set aside the 'literariness' of the work—the fact that it is a poem or play or novel, rather than an account of the incidence of soil erosion in Nebraska."

What should you look for before you tackle the question of meaning in literature?

Instead of immediately trying to answer the question "What does it mean?", readers are better served by deferring this one until several others are addressed. Ask first:

- Where and when are we? Who is speaking?
- Where are we going, and what's going on here?
- What conflicts are evident?
- How are the conflicts evident, and how are they resolved?
- What attracts my attention here?
- What do I find familiar about the work? Disturbing, challenging, or strange?

Questions like these take the reader more deeply into the literary work, where meanings come into focus.

Why do details matter in reading literature?

It is commonly said that God (or the devil) is in the details. In literature, meaning and significance are to be found there, too. All literature is a collection of choices made, from the words selected to the sentences constructed and arranged in larger units of paragraphs, stanzas, scenes, and chapters. Asking why this and not that forces the reader into a direct dialogue with the way literature generates its meanings: in the details. It's best to assume that everything in a work of literature is there for a reason—every character, scene, detail of setting, image, metaphor, matter—at least as tentative sources of significance. That is not to say that every detail must be read as a symbol, as a potential stand-in for something more abstract and figurative. Sometimes, as Freud allegedly declared, "A cigar is just a cigar." But details could be read as symbols and merit the reader's close attention. By slowing reading to notice the details of a literary work, readers establish a knowledge base that leads to deeper understanding of the author's purpose. It will also root the work in your imagination first, the foundation upon which analysis and reflection should be built. Everything considered together—details, imagination, analysis, and reflection—leads to meaning.

How should you read literature?

Here is a simple checklist of how to approach reading literature:

- Slow down your reading: The goal should be not to finish a work of literature as soon as possible but to slow down your reading so that you attend to what is being said.

- Reread: Rereading a literary work or passages a second time tends to open up the work and more fully display what it is about. A first reading of any literary work will provide an overview; subsequent readings allow you to examine it closely and see more about how it works and what it means.

- Read critically: that is, thoughtfully and actively. Reading literature is not, as we have said, a passive activity in which you expect to have the key information delivered to you as directly as possible (as in everyday reading). Literature's meanings are multiple, and the questions they raise require your active pursuit of meaning. You need to function almost like a cocreator in a work of literature, actively attending to all the evidence you are presented with and formulating interpretations based on that evidence (more on this later).

- Engage in a dialogue with the work: ask it questions. The very best way to read literature is to ask questions continually of the text: Why did the author provide this detail? Why did a character react this way? What would have resulted had this happened and not that? Asking questions like these forces you to engage with the work of literature at a deep level in which its significance becomes clearer.

- Annotate: The best way to engage in the kind of dialogue suggested above is to read with a pen in your hand. By

One way to read literature actively is to go right ahead and write notes of your observations, questions, and reactions right on the page, or simply underline key passages.

underlining and writing in the margins, you will slow your reading and pose the kinds of questions that will help you to understand a work of literature. You will also have identified key passages and issues to raise in discussions and to consider when writing about the work.

- Summarize: Write a brief summary of each poem or story, the acts of a play, chapters of a novel. This serves as a useful way of keeping the work fresh in your mind and helps to convert your memory from short-term to long-term. Summaries are often the basis for any analysis or writing about literature, so get in the habit of writing summaries to aid your understanding of exactly what happened in a story, poem, novel, or play.

- Ask critical questions: Beyond summarizing what happens in the literary work you are reading, consider other essential questions, such as: How does the literary form (poem, play, story, or novel) help determine what the work is and its methods? What about knowledge of the author? Does that help you to understand what is intended? How about the cultural context? Do you need to know something about the time in which the work was written, the historical era, the cultural values that are expressed here? Posing these kinds of questions can help in important ways with your understanding about a writer's intentions and the effect the work of literature is intended to have.

HOW TO READ POETRY

What is poetry?

Poetry, of all the literary genres, is the most elusive to define because of its capaciousness and contradictions. It is written in different forms—verse, prose, and drama—which means that boundaries limiting what poetry is and is not are impossible to draw. Here is a typical dictionary definition of a poem: "A composition designed to convey a vivid and imaginative sense of experience, characterized by using condensed language, chosen for its sound and suggestive power as well as its meaning, and by such literary techniques as structured meter, natural cadences, rhyme, or metaphor." This definition doesn't exactly narrow things down. Is every composition "designed to convey a vivid and imaginative sense of experience" a poem? Hardly. Don't other forms of writing—an essay or a short story—similarly use "condensed language" with words chosen for their suggestive power as well as for meaning? And what about these elements of literary technique, such as meter, rhyme, natural cadences, or metaphor? Poems can't be exclusively defined as writing that has meter because a lot of poetry is nonmetrical. Neither is poetry confined to writing that rhymes because many poems don't use rhyme. Much poetry uses figurative language such as metaphor and is intense and emotional—but the same is true for powerful prose. Natural cadence—rhythm or inflection—is found in the short story, novel, and drama, particularly in the way characters speak. In fact, whatever characteristics you try to apply to poetry are never typical of all poetry or exclusive to poetry alone.

What is this thing we call "poetry," though?

Etymology is of limited usefulness. The word *poetry* is derived from the Greek *poien*, meaning "to make" or "to create." But all forms of literary expression are similarly made or crafted. *Prose*, as opposed to poetry, comes from the Latin *prosa* and *proversus*, meaning "turned to face forward" or "straightforward." Is poetry, therefore, in comparison

41

"roundabout" or "indirect"? This distinction might help to clarify why poetry has a reputation for difficulty but doesn't much help to explain what exactly poetry is.

What is the best way to define poetry?

A definition of poetry may better be approached less as a distinct genre of literature and more as a method or manner of expression: the poetic. We can refer to prose poems and poetic novels, while certain verses ("Thirty days hath September, April, June, and November …") resist categorization as poetry at all. The poetic comes closer to what makes poetry so distinctive: expression through a careful choice and arrangement of words, achieving its impact through the resources of language—the nuances and subtlety of diction, syntax, and language's musicality—that may be found in other literary forms but none so directly or powerfully as in poetry.

What makes a work of literature poetic and not just prosaic? Distinguishing the two can be problematic, since prose can certainly have poetic qualities, and poetry (such as in some free verse) can seem rather prosaic.

How have other poets defined poetry?

It would be natural to expect that poets, at least, should be able to tell us exactly what they are trying to create. They do tell us a great deal about the nature of poetry and the poetic but in a poetic rather than "straightforward" prose way. Poet Robert Frost (1874–1963) once famously ruled the question of what exactly poetry is to be out of order when he declared, "Poetry is the kind of thing that poets write." However, Frost did offer a more thorough definition of poetry: "Poetry is when an emotion has found its thought and the thought has found words." Here is a sampling of what other poets have said about their craft:

> As imagination bodies forth
> The forms of things unknown, the poet's pen
> Turns them in shapes and gives to airy nothing
> A local habitation and a name.
> Such tricks hath strong imagination,
> That, if it would but apprehend some joy,
> It comprehends some bringer of that joy.
>
> —William Shakespeare, *A Midsummer Night's Dream*

> Poetry … is … a speaking picture, with this end: to teach and delight.
>
> —Sir Philip Sydney

Poetry is thoughts that breathe, and words that burn.

—Thomas Gray

I would define the poetry of words as the rhythmical creation of beauty. Its sole arbiter is taste. With the intellect or with the conscience it has only collateral relations. Unless incidentally, it has no concern whatever either with duty or with truth.

—Edgar Allan Poe

I read a book and it makes my whole body so cold no fire can ever warm me, I know that is poetry. If I feel physically as if the top of my head were taken off, I know that is poetry.

—Emily Dickinson

[Poetry is the] best words in the best order.

—Samuel Taylor Coleridge

The proper and immediate object of Science is the acquirement or communication of truth; the proper and immediate object of Poetry is the communication of pleasure.

—Samuel Taylor Coleridge

I have said that poetry is the spontaneous overflow of powerful feelings: it takes its origin from emotion recollected in tranquillity: the emotion is contemplated till, by a species of reaction, the tranquillity gradually disappears, and an emotion, kindred to that which was before the subject of contemplation, is gradually produced, and does itself actually exist in the mind.

—William Wordsworth

Poetry is indeed something divine. It is at once the centre and circumference of knowledge; it is that which comprehends all science, and that to which all science must be referred. It is at the same time the root and blossom of all other systems of thought; it is that from which all spring, and that which adorns all; and that which, if blighted, denies the fruit and the seed, and withholds from the barren world the nourishment and the succession of the scions of the tree of life. It is the perfect and consummate surface and bloom of all things; it is as the odor and the color of the rose to the texture of the elements which compose it, as the form and splendor of unfaded beauty to the secrets of anatomy and corruption.

—Percy Bysshe Shelley

Poetry is at bottom a criticism of life; that the greatness of a poet lies in his powerful and beautiful application of ideas to life—to the question: How to live.

—Matthew Arnold

[Poetry is] speech framed ... to be heard for its own sake and interest even over and above its interest of meaning.

—Gerard Manley Hopkins

Poetry is emotion put into measure. The emotion must come by nature, but the measure can be acquired by art.

—Thomas Hardy

Out of the quarrels with others we make rhetoric; out of the quarrel with our-selves we make poetry.

—William Butler Yeats

[Poetry is] the rhythmic, inevitably narrative, movement from an overclothed blindness to a naked vision.

—Dylan Thomas

Poetry is what in a poem makes you laugh, cry, prickle, be silent, makes your toe nails twinkle, makes you want to do this or that or nothing, makes you know that you are alone in the unknown world, that your bliss and suffering is for-ever shared and forever all your own.

—Dylan Thomas

Poetry is not a turning loose of emotion, but an escape from emotion; it is not the expression of personality, but an escape from personality. But, of course, only those who have personality and emotions know what it means to want to escape from these things.

—T. S. Eliot

Poetry is a search for syllables to shoot at the barriers of the unknown.

—Carl Sandburg

Poetry is life distilled.

—Gwendolyn Brooks

Poetry is language at its most distilled and most powerful.

—Rita Dove

Poetry is the art of creating imaginary gardens with real toads.

—Marianne Moore

Poetry is above all a concentration of the power of language, which is the power of our ultimate relationship to everything in the universe.

—Adrienne Rich

A poem is an interruption of silence, an occupation of silence, whereas public language is a continuation of noise.

—Billy Collins

Poetry is language in orbit.

—Seamus Heaney

What are the common characteristics of these definitions of poetry?

These statements of what poetry is, how it operates, and its effects share some key elements: poetry is clearly different from "public language," "Science," and language that is not "distilled and most powerful," "in orbit," capable of taking the top of your head off and causing your toenails to twinkle. Poetry gives to "airy nothing" a "local habitation and a name." It produces "imaginary gardens" out of "real toads." It is "naked vision," penetrating and exposing "the form and splendor of unfaded beauty." The poets quoted above show us that poetry is clearly a privileged and powerful lens and mirror, one that evokes a magical and sacred essence. But how did the art of poetry come to evoke such lyrical description? What are the attributes that define the essence of a poem? The answers may best be found by looking at poetry's origin, its special qualities, and the choices poets make to unleash its latent power.

What do poems do?

Poetry seems to come from some deep impulse humans have that needs expression; it arises when no other form of expression seems capable of conveying what the poet is thinking or feeling. Many of us have had the experience of feeling great joy or emotional pain: coming home for the holidays and feeling an overwhelming sense of well-being and happiness or feeling great sorrow and grief at a loss, such as a death of a loved one. Attempting to verbalize those feelings is what poetry is about. Poems may tell a story but they need not. A poem can be only about a thought or a feeling, something both inconclusive and fleeting, in which the poem itself is an attempt to understand or come to terms with what prompted the emotion or thought. Poetry is first and foremost an exploration into things unknown, giving it form, naming

Rita Dove, poet laureate of the U.S. Library of Congress from 1993 to 1995, defined poetry as "language at its most distilled and most powerful."

45

and visualizing a previous, in Shakespeare's phrase, "airy nothing" and converting the abstract to the specific.

At its most basic level, poetry allows us to give voice to what we are thinking and feeling, converting abstract emotions or ideas into a concrete setting or situation, expressed in powerful language that can communicate to another what we feel and think.

Why should you read poetry?

If poetry gives its creator a voice, a means of self-expression, what exactly does the reader gain in listening to the words of a poet? Poetry, like all other forms of literary expression—drama, stories, and novels—is primarily a form of communication. All human beings are unique and different as well as similar, experiencing such core emotions as love, hate, fear, and joy, but we are prompted by the particulars of our individual lives and times. Poetry helps to remind us how much we share with others when a poem turns what is unique or particular into collective relevance. Poetry, because it can voice a fleeting emotion or idea, can have a greater sense of intimacy and directness than other literary expressions. The reader gains a privileged view of a life. Therefore, one of the fundamental reasons to read poetry is to compare our experiences with another's. The reader of a poem can experience both the shock of the unfamiliar, extending our understanding and compassion to ideas and emotions we have never experienced as well as the thrill of recognition, seeing our own thoughts and emotions visualized and verbalized by another person in an artful and captivating way.

What is the origin of poetry?

Poetry predates literacy and, like storytelling, is one of humankind's earliest and greatest accomplishments. Language to communicate evolved into language to recreate what was memorable for a group or a culture—births, deaths, brave actions, disasters, battles, etc.—and to please and entertain—language appreciated as much for its form and facility as for its content. In oral cultures, the earliest poems were recited or sung, set to a rhythmic pattern with repetition of sounds as an aid to memory and retelling before writing was available. The metrical line (so many beats per line unit) and formulaic phrases (regularly recurring words filling out a metrical pattern, such as "wine-dark sea" and "rosy-fingered dawn") allowed Homer to create his massive epics the *Iliad* and the *Odyssey* afresh with each performance.

What is the earliest surviving poetry?

Some of the earliest surviving writing is poetry, preserved on monoliths, runestones, tablets, and papyrus. Poetic fragments survive that document everything from genealogical records, historical accounts, practical instructions, love songs, and fictional stories. The oldest surviving work of fiction is the Egyptian poem "The Tale of the Shipwrecked Sailor" in Heriatic from around 2500 B.C.E. The first surviving long, narrative poem is the *Epic of Gilgamesh*, preserved in cuneiform from around 2000 B.C.E. Besides the Homeric epics (c. eighth to seventh century B.C.E.), epic heroic poems were produced in India—the *Ramayana* and the *Mahabharata*. The first poetry collection is the Chinese *Book of Songs,* all from the first millennium B.C.E. Poems are collected in the Old Testament, and the first named written poet is believed to be Hesiod, writing in Greek between 750 and 650 B.C.E. Hesiod's *Theogony* is an essential source for our knowledge of Greek mythology, and his *Works and Days* offers an early form of self-help advice in verse.

Who was the first to apply literary criticism to poetry?

Nearly as ageless as the earliest poetry are the attempts to define, categorize, and assess poetry. The earliest surviving work of literary criticism, Aristotle's *Poetics* (c. 335

The tablets containing the ancient Assyrian poem *Epic of Gilgamesh,* currently housed at the British Museum, date back some four thousand years.

B.C.E.), includes a chapter on the origin and development of poetry. In it, Aristotle asserts that poetry sprang from two conditions, each of which is deep-seated in human nature: the instinct for imitation in which we delight in representing the world and our experiences, and the instinct for harmony and rhythm. "Persons, therefore," Aristotle argues, "starting with this natural gift developed by degrees their special aptitude, till their rude improvisations gave birth to Poetry." He identifies two main directions of poetry: toward the imitation of noble actions, which produced hymns to the gods, epic poetry, and tragedy, and toward the imitation of the "actions of meaner persons," which produced satire and comedy.

How did literary critics after Aristotle categorize poetry?

Later critical followers of Aristotle in the Middle Ages and Renaissance would identify three major genres of poetry: epic (or narrative), dramatic, and lyric. The latter, designating an intense expression of the speaker's emotions or feelings, is named for the lyre, the small, stringed, harplike instrument used to accompany a performance. First practiced in Greece around the seventh century B.C.E., lyrical performances sung by large choruses honored the Greek god Dionysius. Lyric poetry would eventually lead to the invention of drama as a performer stepped out of the chorus to imitate a character instead of singing about him.

Poetry, therefore, is fundamental to the creation and methods of literary expression. If the Aristotelian "imitation of an action," that is, storytelling and self-expression, form the primary core of literature, then poetry can be defined as the shaping of those stories and expression in ways that are memorable and pleasing.

How does poetry work?

Poetry works in a contrary manner. As in the distinction made earlier between everyday reading and reading literature, poetry aspires not to transparency (the direct, unambiguous transfer of meaning) but to a multivalent expressiveness in which not a single meaning but several are revealed, produced by multiple means. This is not to say that poets resemble Hamlet's errant players, whose artifice obscures and distorts, but that poetry's impact and meaning are created because of, not despite, linguistic forms and resources. Said another way, poetry aspires not to a literal but a figurative transfer of meaning. Poetry proceeds indirectly as Emily Dickinson (1830–1886) observed:

> Tell all the truth but tell it slant—
> Success in Circuit lies
> Too bright for our infirm Delight
> The Truth's superb surprise
> As Lightning to the Children eased
> With explanation kind
> The Truth must dazzle gradually
> Or every man be blind—

Poems "dazzle gradually," finding their way to truth circuitously not from direct statement but through fully empowering language to delight and instruct. In this way, poetry is language patterned and arranged in such a way that significance emerges.

What makes poetry so "difficult"?

We are surrounded by poetry every day in the song lyrics we listen to, in advertising jingles, in memorable turns of phrases that delight and surprise us. Poetry is often our go-to form of literary expression that attracts amateurs and professionals alike. It is rare to find anyone who has not tried his or her hand at composing a poem. Plays, novels, and even short stories seem more for the initiated and the specialist. Poetry is for everyone. Why then should this most persistent, ubiquitous, and accessible expression have such a reputation for difficulty?

Poets can come from unexpected places. Are song lyrics poetry? Absolutely, and when Bob Dylan won the Pulitzer Prize in 2008 and the Nobel Prize in Literature in 2016 for refining the boundaries of literature, he proved that point definitively.

How should we understand poetry?

Part of the answer is how we have been instructed to understand poetry: less as a form of vital and compelling human expression to be savored and more as a cryptically coded message to be deciphered (and endured). Literature teachers too often fixate on the methods of poetry without first explaining why these methods deserve our attention. It is like being taught how to read music before learning how to appreciate it.

How does a poem mean?

Years ago, the poet and critic John Ciardi (1916–1986) wrote a handbook titled *How Does a Poem Mean?* His title challenged the expected question—*What Does a Poem Mean?*—and the wrong impression that, like everyday writing, poetry's meaning can be extracted and the delivery system disposed of. This makes as much sense as asking what is the meaning of a dance, a musical performance, or a baseball game. We seek these out for the pleasure they give us, not to extract a reductive meaning. They all have significance, but that significance is multiple: in the pleasure they afford, in the appreciation for a skillful performance, even in the communal experience they supply or the sense of accomplishment they offer the participant. Ciardi's approach to poetry reminds us that meaning in poetry, like these activities, is various and that poetry is best approached, after enjoyment, by understanding the ways poets generate significance. Robert Frost's description of poetry as a "performance in words" suggests an emphasis on the *how* of poetry and offers a sensible way for readers to approach their encounter with poetry: as a performance, first to be savored, and, with increasing familiarity, to be appreciated for the skills demonstrated.

Why is it necessary to think about poetry as more than simply "performance in words"?

Approaching poetry as performance helps but does not eliminate poetry's perceived difficulty. Poetry's contrary approach to delivering meaning compared to everyday reading,

49

its compressed and intensified use of language with an emphasis on the nuances of its diction, the patterning of its form, and the musicality of its sounds test readers' patience and attentiveness. Few of us share to such a degree poet William Butler Yeats's "fascination of what's difficult." We mainly prefer the simple to the complex, the explicit to the implicit, the transparent to the opaque, the direct to the indirect, at least in everyday communication. Poetry's alternate methods can strain understanding and require both effort and expertise. Imagine, for example, attending an unfamiliar sporting event—cricket, curling, sumo wrestling. How much of the sport can you appreciate until you know its rules and standards of excellence? Similarly, reading and understanding poetry require extending your appreciation of the choices poets make and the impact of those choices on our enjoyment and understanding.

How should you read a poem?

Poetry, more than any other form of literature, requires active and attentive reading. Like all forms of literature, poetry invites, even demands, rereading. Imagine you are visiting a new city for the first time. What do you see? How is your experience different, enhanced, and deepened by a second or third visit? The same is true of your encounter with poetry. Each poem you read and reread takes you someplace you have not visited before. Apply some of the same principles you would use in navigating a new city. Try to understand the landscape, while at the same time realizing that familiarity leads to awareness.

Poetry is often best appreciated when it is read aloud, which is why poetry reading events, such as this one in Berlin, Germany, draw appreciative audiences.

How else can you read a poem?

Another helpful way of encountering a poem is to approach it like a drama. Who is the speaker? What is the situation or crisis that prompts the poem? What is the conflict that establishes the tension or provides the suspense? How is the conflict resolved? What has changed over the course of the poem in the speaker's situation or awareness? Answering these questions can take you far in your understanding of a poem.

What are some other suggestions for experiencing a poem?

- Read straight through. In an initial reading, get a feel for the entire poem without worrying about what you don't know or understand. Don't get hung up on a word that you don't understand or a syntax that needs to be untangled. These can wait for rereading.

- Slow down. You can't speed-read a poem any more than you can speed-listen to your favorite music, so slow down and listen.

- Read aloud. Most poems are meant to be heard. By vocalizing a poem, you can better feel its rhythm and hear its music. Reading, as opposed to hearing a poem, can resemble reading a musical score rather than listening to it. Hearing a poem enhances understanding.

- Write down a summary of the poem. After reading and rereading a poem, enhance your understanding by writing a summary of it. Identify the speaker and situation, the conflict and resolution. Try to answer the five key questions to ask any work of literature:

  What is the significance of the title?

  Why does the poem start when it does?

  What is the conflict in the poem?

  How is the conflict resolved?

  Why does the poem end when it does?

- Focus on what surprises you. Particularly in a second or third reading, focus on what strikes you as unique or different about the poem. It may be something unfamiliar or something that you recognize as true to your experience. Are there words that stand out, call attention to themselves, or defy normal usage? Do the ideas expressed take some unexpected turn? Does the poem gratify your expectations or challenge them?

- Ask why this and not that. Literature is all about choices, and one of the best methods to arrive at an understanding of a poem is to interrogate it regarding the choices it makes: Why this word and not some other? Why this arrangement of lines? Why this break into stanzas and not some other pattern? By answering these questions, readers can begin to understand what is distinctive about the poem and how it produces its meaning and significance.

51

How should poetry be read for its words?

A poet only has words to communicate an idea or an emotion. While this is also true for a playwright and a fiction writer, words are even more central to poets because so much of the meaning and significance of poems comes exclusively from the words themselves. A play's words become dialogue heard and enacted onstage; fiction's words become a story, which a poem may tell but does not have to, displaying only a feeling or an impression. To communicate, a poet depends on the power of the words alone to carry the burden of significance. One way to define poetry is to say that the poet, more so than the fiction writer or playwright, makes more extreme or unusual use of words, taking fuller advantage of both words' meaning and sound to produce significance.

Why is it important to pay particular attention to the words in a poem?

Accordingly, to understand any poem, you must attend to its words. This may seem obvious: how can you read at all without understanding the words used? But attending to the words of a poem is more demanding and complicated than what we are used to in everyday reading. When you read a newspaper, for example, words that call attention to themselves are distracting, taking the reader away from the principal advantage of the words: to gain information as clearly and concisely as possible. In poems, words play a much more complex and important role in producing meaning and significance, and you need to pay attention to the multiple components of words. Words possess three distinct components: their denotation, connotation, and sound.

What is a word's "denotation," and why is it important?

The most basic component is a word's denotation, or dictionary definition. Knowing what a word means is, of course, fundamental to reading itself. But a word's meaning can be tricky since word meanings over the centuries change. You might encounter, particularly in poems written centuries ago, unfamiliar words or familiar ones that seem to be used in strange ways. Here are some examples of words whose meanings have completely changed over time:

Artificial—originally meant "full of artistic or technical skill." It now means "contrived or false."

Nice—derives from the Latin for "not to know" and referred to a person who was ignorant or unaware. Now it means "pleasant or agreeable."

Awful—meant "full of awe," that is, something wonderful or amazing. It now refers to the opposite: something bad, unpleasant, or horrific.

Counterfeit—this once meant a perfect copy, a word of praise. Now it refers to a fake or a sham.

Make sure, therefore, to consult a dictionary carefully to make sure you understand precisely what a particular word meant at the time it was selected by the poet. A good dictionary will list multiple meanings with indication of when a particular definition applied. This will help you determine exactly the right denotation for the words in a poem.

What is a word's "connotation"?

A second crucial component of a word is its connotation: its associations, positive or negative, that a word carries and accumulates over time and through social custom and usage. Words may mean the same things but have markedly different connotations. To describe someone who is stubborn, you might say he is strong-willed (a positive connotation) or pigheaded (an extremely negative connotation). It used to be that you bought a "used car," but dealers now refer to "previously owned cars" because that has a far better connotation. In the 1920s, if you said, "He's a square," you would have given a compliment. The connotation for square was solid, down-to-earth, and unshakable. From the 1950s on, a square meant dull or old-fashioned. A good dictionary will also indicate the positive and negative connotation of a word, and because poets are careful in selecting words with the exact denotation and connotation they desire, this information can be crucial in fully understanding a poem's words.

What's so special about the words that are chosen for poems?

The one characteristic that most poets share is a fascination with words. For the poet, words are far more than just a means to an end but vital elements to appreciate and enjoy just for themselves. Emily Dickinson, for example, used to read a dictionary for pleasure, just to savor words and their definitions. Dickinson, like most poets, loved the look, the sound, the associations words have, the meanings they evoke, and their power to instill ideas and images in the mind. Like all poets, Dickinson struggled sometimes to find exactly the right words to express the most complex feelings and ideas, and, like a great musician, to orchestrate those words into verbal music.

Why are the "sounds" of words important?

A third major component for words is their sounds. Words are ultimately collections of sounds that have been translated into language, like notes in music. When we hear language, we hear those sounds. When we read, we see the representation of those sounds. Poets, unlike writers who use language primarily to convey information, often choose words for their sound as well as for their meaning. Edgar Allan Poe (1809–1849) famously defined poetry as "music … combined with a pleasurable idea," a definition underscoring the primacy of sound words provide. In a song, the lyrics are accompanied by the music. In a poem, the lyrics or words of the poem *are* the music. Poets, therefore, select words to enhance musical effects. They rely on repetition of sounds, such as alliteration (the repetition of identical consonant sounds, for example, "tongue twisters"), assonance (the repetition of identical vowel sounds, for example, "moon in June"), and rhyme (the repetition of the final vowel sound and all the subsequent sounds after this vowel sound, for example, "breath and death"). By using such sound effects, poets can create a pleasing "music," while calling attention to the words and underscoring significance and meaning.

How does a poem's rhythm contribute to the quality of its sound?

One other central sound quality in a poem is its rhythm. In a song, a drum can mark the beat in the movement of the music. In a poem, rhythm is created by the arrangement of words and is affected by controlling elements like line length (short lines create a faster rhythm; longer lines a slower one), the combination of short and longer words in phrases that affect reading speed, and how lines end or run on to the next line. The former halts the reader, and the latter moves the reader faster from line to line. All of these effects enhance the poem's musicality and contribute to meaning as well as enjoyment of a poem.

AN ANALYSIS OF EMILY DICKINSON'S "I LIKE TO SEE IT LAP THE MILES"

How should you read a particular poem for its words?

With these aspects of words and their uses in mind, let's look closely at how a poet, in this case Emily Dickinson, exploits the capacity of words to affect meaning. Read it straight through just to get a sense of the poem's overall subject. For your second reading, linger on individual words. Make sure you understand all of them. Look up any others you don't understand in a dictionary. Try your hand at writing a brief, prose summary of the poem. Translate it in your own words. Try to identify anything that strikes you as unusual or peculiar in the poem: this might be an odd comparison or a strange choice of words. Try to identify a rationale for the comparison or the word choice. Do they help explain the subject of the poem and the attitude or feelings of the poem's speaker?

"I Like to See It Lap the Miles"

I like to see it lap the miles,
And lick the valleys up,
And stop to feed itself at tanks;
And then, prodigious, step

Around a pile of mountains,
And, supercilious, peer
In shanties by the sides of roads;
And then a quarry pare

To fit its sides, and crawl between,
Complaining all the while
In horrid, hooting stanza;
Then chase itself down hill

And neigh like Boanerges;
Then, punctual as a star,
Stop—docile and omnipotent—
At its own stable door.

What should you notice first about the poem?

What should have been initially striking in your reading is that Dickinson never explicitly names her subject, referring only to "it." By doing so, the poem takes on the character of a riddle, forcing the reader to answer, "What laps the miles ... licks the valleys up ... feeds itself at tanks," etc. In a first reading, several words point to the obvious answer: a horse, which neighs and stops at a stable door. However, other details suggest that, if a horse, it is some kind of superhorse that can step around a "pile of mountains" and pare a rock quarry, like a piece of fruit. No ordinary horse could do this. Looking closer at the language and details, the answer becomes clearer. The solution to the riddle, of course, is a train en-

gine, which is described in the context of a well-known synonym for a railroad engine in Dickinson's day, an "iron horse."

How does Dickinson use personification in her poem?

What's arresting about Dickinson's description and her word choices here is that she personifies the inanimate engine with attributes associated with an animal or a superhuman creature. In other words, she takes the figurative (iron horse) and applies it literally. Look at the verbs in the

\American poet Emily Dickinson.

55

first stanza—*lap, lick, stop, feed, step*. Only one, *step*, is an action we normally associate with the action of a train. The others apply more to a person or animal. So, the poem opens with a riddle—What is it that the speaker likes?—and clues that only figuratively, not literally, apply. In a literal sense, a train doesn't lap, lick, feed, or step, but that's exactly what the poet tells us this train appears to do, and the reader is forced to try to work out how in fact these words apply to a powerful and fleet-moving train engine. Diction—word choice—here is crucial in visualizing what exactly the speaker likes about what is seen and how she feels about it. For Dickinson's speaker here, what she likes is the immense power of the engine.

How do Dickinson's other word choices enhance the poem's meaning?

Look even closer at the word choices. In line one, "lap" could mean what an animal, like a cat, dog, or a horse might do to eat or drink by taking in food or liquid by its tongue ("The cat lapped its milk," for example). To "lap the miles," in this context, suggests consuming them, devouring them with a steady, easy motion. This sense of lap is echoed in the second line with a similar word, "lick." There is another sense of lap as well, that is, overtaking a competitor in a race to become one or more laps ahead. Both senses of the word fit the context here: the engine easily consumes distance and leaves anyone or anything far behind. Remember that when this poem was written in the nineteenth century, a railroad engine was the fastest thing on earth, making obsolete the former standard for speed on the ground—the horse. It is an interesting holdover to the previous era that we still measure motion in "horsepower."

Why do Dickinson's word choices matter?

So, attending to Dickinson's word choice in the first stanza, we begin to comprehend what the speaker likes: the sense of power in the train's ability to "lap the miles," "lick the valleys up," "feed itself at tanks" (that is, refuels the water for its steam engine), and "step around mountains." Consider how Dickinson's word choices capture a sense of the engine as a giant of enormous power. Try substituting other words for lap, lick, feed, and step, and note how the image of the train changes. "Step," for example, seems exactly the right word to choose, rather than "move" or "run," if you wanted to conjure a sense of graceful power: a train can simply step around a mountain. By describing the mountains as a "pile" diminishes their stature, while increasing the train's importance. From the perspective of the powerful train, the majesty and size of a mountain is reduced to just a "pile," something easily disposed of by a simple sidestep.

How does Dickinson continue to personify the engine in her poem?

Dickinson continues to select words that personify, that is, bestow human (or animal) characteristics on an inanimate object. The engine can "peer" in at shanties, "pare" (that is, cut like a piece of fruit) a quarry (a large, deep pit from which stone is extracted), "crawl between" the cut, "complaining all the while," and then "chase itself down hill," "neigh" and "stop … At its own stable door." The speaker has, therefore, painted a portrait of a train's journey, lapping the miles, licking the valleys up, being refueled, passing shanties along the route, crawling through an opening in a rock quarry, while "complaining all the while / In horrid, hooting stanzas," before rushing downhill with a shriek and arriving, "punctual as a star," "docile and omnipotent" (easiness and power combined) at its resting place ("its own stable door").

What does Dickinson admire about the train?

By attending to Dickinson's word choice, we begin to understand what exactly the speaker admires: the effortless, graceful power of the train, its combination of mas-

One must carefully read Dickinson's poem "I Like to See It Lap the Miles" to understand that what she is describing in her verse is a locomotive.

sive force and explosive energy that overpowers all it encounters. The train the speaker here conjures up is more like a giant of superhuman or superanimal dominance who conquers all nature: valleys, mountains, quarries, uphill and down, and can still arrive at its destination, "punctual as a star," an ever-fixed and dependable point in the night sky.

What may not be so admirable, according to Dickinson's word choices?

So, this is something that the speaker likes or admires, right? Well, yes and no. The speaker in line one explicitly says she likes all that follows, but an implicit ambiguity enters the poem again based on the words chosen and their connotations that begin to sound some negative notes added to the sense of admiration and desirability explicitly stated. Look again at the word choices. The adjective "prodigious" to characterize the step around a "pile" of mountains conjures up the image of a giant who can tower over mountains, diminishing the natural grandeur of a mountain into a mere pile, a heap. But what about the use of the word "supercilious" to describe the way the engine peers in at the "shanties by the sides of roads"? Supercilious means behaving in a superior, proud, and arrogant manner and has a decidedly negative connotation: here, the giant seems to be looking down on those humans living humbly beside the tracks. Combined with the animalistic connotations of "lap," "lick," and "feed," there is a sense here of a devouring giant, scornful of the human agents who, after all, created it in the first place. The undertone here, based on the word choices and their connotations, is that a powerful force has been unleashed to challenge the primacy of both nature and humanity. This man-made object is more powerful than either nature or man, which it devours, scorns, and masters. Here, Dickinson seems to be suggesting not only how exciting this new technology is but also how potentially dangerous and problematic it might be as well.

What is it about the engine's noise and size that personally affects Dickinson as a poet?

To make this point even closer to home and more personal, note Dickinson's word choice to describe the way in which the engine complains going through the quarry's rock opening: "In horrid, hooting stanza." "Horrid" is a sinister word to describe the sound a laboring engine makes, but also, why use the word "stanza" to characterize that sound? "Stanza" is a word associated with the poet's own method and technique: poems are arranged into stanzas. Dickinson's poem has four of them, which forms its units. Is Dickinson suggesting that the sound made by the engine has invaded not just the outside landscape but also her own territory as a poet? The speaker's voice, which would normally be shaped into stanzas, is dominated or diminished here by the louder voice of the engine. Is this the new poetry that we will be forced to listen to? Are these the new sounds of our inanimate creations that rival any human voice as the engine challenges for mastery any human or animal force? Dickinson suggests this in later characterizing the engine's neigh "like Boanerges," the name given to Jesus's disciples James and John, meaning "son of thunder." The word is associated with the power of a preacher to command attention and transfix a congregation. That seems exactly what this engine is doing here: commanding all our attention to try to understand its meaning.

What are "explicit" and "implicit" meanings in the poem?

Again, these associations emerge only when the reader looks closely at the words Dickinson uses and their implications. Every poem contains explicit meaning—what actually is said and happens—but also meaning that is implicit in how something is said. Notice how far we have come from a fairly straightforward description of the movements of a train. Positives connect with negatives, and a complex attitude, far more ambiguous than the rather bland "like" at the opening of the poem, begins to emerge by paying attention to the particulars of the words Dickinson chooses and what they imply. By attending to these implications, the poem's meaning becomes richer and deeper.

How does Dickinson's use of structure and pattern enhance the poem's meaning?

A final aspect of Dickinson's strategy of word choice and arrangement is its structure and patterning of sounds to enhance meaning. Organized into four stanzas, the entire poem is a single sentence. This gives the poem a kind of suspended animation, a breathless quality as we race from line to line to get to the end of the sentence to draw our breath, echoing the movement of the engine. Note that the end of the sentence comes exactly at the end of the train's journey as it arrives at the station. It comes to rest as the reader comes to rest at the end of the poem.

To underscore a sense of exhilarating movement, Dickinson further relies on run-on lines, pausing briefly at line three of each stanza with a dash, while adding details with no fewer than five "Ands" and two "Thens." Eight-syllable lines alternate with six-syllable lines to further echo speed. These words and their arrangements into lines and stanzas mimic the furious pace of the engine, a rhythm that enhances the meaning of the poem. The words are further patterned by alliteration: *l*ike, *l*ap, *l*ick; *s*upercilious, *s*hanties, *s*ides; *h*orrid, *h*ooting; *s*tanza, *s*tar, *s*top, *s*table; *d*ocile, *d*oor. These are keywords, whose importance is underscored by Dickinson using alliteration to call attention to them.

By looking at the words closely, by paying attention to what they mean and how they sound, you see how much you can make of a poem's meaning and how you can begin to appreciate the artistry of a master poet.

How should a poem be read for its comparisons—metaphors and similes?

If words are the fundamental building blocks of poetry, then the poet's skill in using words to embody ideas and emotions is what constitutes poetic ability and achievement. The Greek philosopher and critic, Aristotle, asserted that, of all the poet's facilities with language, the use of metaphor—relating one thing with another—was supreme. "The greatest thing by far," Aristotle declared, "is to be a master of metaphor. It is the one thing that cannot be learned from others; it is also a sign of genius, since a good metaphor implies an eye for resemblance." Identifying resemblances, that is, translating a concept or an emotion into specifics that can be seen, felt, and understood, is a central mission for any poet. As we saw in Emily Dickinson's poem, she employs direct comparisons such as "like Boanerges," as well as extended comparisons. The "it" of line one, what the speaker likes, is defined by comparisons (human and animal) that convert the abstract and general to the specific, drawing on the associations supplied by those comparisons.

Aren't metaphors and similes what all poetry is about, though?

It could be argued that finding and naming resemblances is basically what all poetry (and literature for that matter) is about. The Scottish poet Robert Burns (1759–1796) famously wrote, "Oh, my love is like a red, red rose." He turns through metaphor the abstract quality of love into something tangible and concrete: a red rose. Burns here uses a specific kind of comparison, a simile, comparing two distinct things by using a connective word such as *like* or *as*. A more direct identification using a metaphor would have been: "My love is a red, red rose." The speaker is not saying literally that his love *is* a rose but is speaking figuratively, using language to associate or compare distinct things. We don't know what Burns' love is like. However, by connecting what he feels with what we know or associate with a red rose, his love is embodied, and the abstract becomes tangible. We can then apply the

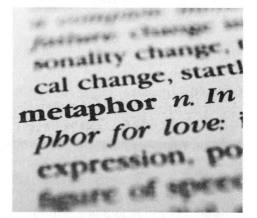

Metaphors are used in prose and poetry as a way of describing one thing in terms of another. The best poets employ metaphor in original and creative ways.

associations of a rose—beautiful, delicate, valued, fleeting—to help us understand more precisely what Burns is feeling and saying about his love.

What is the difference between our everyday use of figurative language and a poet's use of metaphor and simile?

The main difference between our everyday use of metaphor and simile and a great poet's is that figurative language in an effective poem is usually more striking because of its originality and freshness. Metaphor and simile tend to wear out with use, and their effectiveness in creating in our mind a vivid picture can fade. An odd, unusual, or creative comparison that once sounded fresh can eventually diminish into stale cliché with overuse. Whoever first coined such similes as "cool as a cucumber" or "happy as a clam" was a genius in finding resemblances that had never been used before, and the comparisons were so effective and inspired (who ever thought clams were happy!) that as they entered our language, we ceased to even think about the resemblance suggested by the comparison. A good example is the expression "It's as cold as hell." *As hell* once was an effective simile—as in "hot as hell" or "mad as hell"—but what sense does it make linked to cold? Charles Dickens begins *A Christmas Carol* making fun of overworked and meaningless comparisons when he writes:

> Old Marley was as dead as a door-nail.

> Mind! I don't mean to say that I know, of my own knowledge, what there is particularly dead about a door-nail. I might have been inclined myself to regard a coffin-nail as the deadest piece of ironmongery in the trade. But the wisdom of our ancestors is in the simile; and my unhallowed hands shall not disturb it, or the Country's done.

> Dickens here points out how ineffective some comparisons can become. What a writer—whether poet, novelist, or playwright—strives to do is to show us things and ourselves from a fresh perspective. Dickens does that himself a few pages later by describing Marley's glowing face looking "like a bad lobster in a dark cellar."

Why is the poet's individual viewpoint significant?

A poet's principal job is to get us to see things from a new or unfamiliar viewpoint. It's how poets extend our knowledge of the world and of human experience. Robert Frost declared, "An idea is a feat of association, and the height of it is a good metaphor." Frost reminds us here that the process of thought means recognizing resemblances. The only way we recognize anything—a chair, a table, or a wall, for example—is because we associate the one we see with others in our experience and recognize the resemblance. More abstract, complex concepts are similarly defined by what they are like or what they resemble.

How should you read a poem for its comparisons?

Let's examine how a great poet—William Shakespeare (1564–1616)—generates meaning and significance through artful comparisons. Shakespeare's famous Sonnet 18 is a love

> ## How do we use metaphor and simile in everyday communication?
>
> The use of figurative language, such as through the use of similes and metaphors, is by no means exclusive to poets and poetry. We all use metaphors and similes every day to communicate more effectively. We might refer to "cabin fever," a "broken heart," "the setting sun," "a loose cannon," "a melting pot," "like a bull in china shop," "white as a ghost." We don't mean that literally we have a fever, that a heart is actually broken, etc. Instead, we use metaphor and simile to describe more vividly and concretely a feeling or idea.

poem and an attempt by the speaker in the poem to describe his love, always a tricky business! It is a response to the unstated question "How would you describe me?" or "How do you love me?" There are probably no more dangerous questions in a love relationship than these. Say too much and you risk being charged with insincere flattery. Say the conventional and forfeit originality. Say too little and … well, you can just imagine.

So, how does Shakespeare solve this problem?

Read the poem at least twice and then consider Shakespeare's use of metaphor and simile.

> Shall I compare thee to a summer's day?
> Thou art more lovely and more temperate:
> Rough winds do shake the darling buds of May,
> And summer's lease hath all too short a date:
> Sometime too hot the eye of heaven shines,
> And often is his gold complexion dimm'd;
> And every fair from fair sometime declines,
> By chance, or nature's changing course, untrimm'd;
> But thy eternal summer shall not fade,
> Nor lose possession of that fair thou owest;
> Nor shall Death brag thou wander'st in his shade,
> When in eternal lines to time thou growest;
> So long as men can breathe, or eyes can see,
> So long lives this, and this gives life to thee.

As previously suggested, after reading any poem several times, look up any words you don't understand and try to summarize what is said. Most summaries can be prose translations of the poetry, but here is a line-by-line translation of Shakespeare's Elizabethan language into a more modern version:

Shall I compare you to a summer's day?
You are lovelier and milder:
Rough winds shake the beloved buds of May,

And summer is far too short:
Sometimes summer's sun is too hot,
And often it goes behind clouds,
And everything that is beautiful sometime will lose its beauty,
By chance or nature's alteration that cannot be controlled;
But your youth shall not fade,
Nor lose the beauty that you possess;
Nor will death claim you for his own,
Because in these eternal lines you will live forever;
As long as there are people who breath and see,
So long will this poem live on and make you immortal.

Why does Shakespeare compare the lover in his sonnet to "a summer's day"?

Shakespeare begins his sonnet with a direct question to his lover: "Shall I compare thee to a summer's day?" The speaker is asking what is the connection or resemblance between the lover and a summer's day. Responding to the unstated question of the lover, "What am I like?" or "What do you feel for me?", the speaker offers an analogy: an association between the lover and the characteristics of a summer's day to determine how the two compare. Most would agree that of all the days in a year, a summer's day is the finest, the most desirable and preferred, so how does the lover stack up against such a thing? Compared to a summer's day, that is, to the implied simile "You are like a summer's day," the speaker concludes forcefully in line two: the lover is lovelier and more temperate (that is, showing more moderation, less prone to extremes) than a summer's day, then proceeds to explain why. In line three, the speaker explains that sometimes "Rough winds do shake the darling buds of May." In other words, summertime can be disrupted by storms ("rough winds"). The implied comparison calling the lover more temperate suggests that the lover is more consistent, more constant than summer, whose "lease" (that is, whose possession of nature) is all too short. "Lease" is a perfect word (a metaphor) to describe summer: it is temporary, not permanent, which would be implied by ownership as opposed to leasing a property. Moreover, the speaker further explains, sometimes a summer's day, instead of being too stormy, can be too hot or too mild or too overcast ("his gold complexion dimm'd," another metaphor). Note that the comparison here has shifted from a metaphor associating

William Shakespeare compares the beauty of a woman favorably to that of a summer's day in his Sonnet 18. The extended metaphor elevates the subject at hand as superior to even the blessings of Nature.

the lover with summer in the first four lines to what summer is most associated with: the sun. The lover is now described as superior to both. Compared to a summer's day, the lover is lovelier because she (or he) is more consistent and less given to extremes of mood. Unlike the sun, the lover is neither too hot nor obscured by clouds.

What is the significance of the sun's "gold complexion"?

The comparison that the sun's "gold complexion" can be diminished or reduced by clouds leads the speaker to a new comparison and the core of the sonnet's analogy associating the lover to a summer's day. If even the sun's "gold complexion" can be dimmed, so, too, as the speaker admits, everything that is beautiful must eventually lose its beauty. Here, however, is a tricky turn to the argument. If that is true, if everything must fade, if even the constant sun is "dimm'd" and loses its force and power, isn't the lover's beauty included here? The poem's comparison has led the speaker into a potential trap, forcing an acknowledgment that the lover is not superior to all that is beautiful in nature because the lover's beauty as well must decline and fade as summer gives way to fall and winter. Summer (and, by implication, youth and beauty) won't last, and the seasons ("nature's changing course") must unalterably shift from summer to fall and winter, from bloom to fruit to harvest and to death. The implied comparison here associates these seasonal changes with an individual's "seasons" of youth, giving way to age and decay.

What is the dilemma the speaker faces in the poem concerning his lover and summer?

Reminding the lover that you too are fated to age and decline risks shifting the poem from praise to censure or insult. The genius of the poem is how the speaker gets around this dilemma. It happens in line nine, signaled by the forceful words. "But thy eternal summer shall not fade." The "but" here dramatically marks the contradiction with what was previously asserted: that all beauty must fade. The lover is unlike everything else in nature because compared to a summer's day, the lover possesses "eternal summer," not the summer of nature, which is temporary and changeable, but one that is unalterable, that is, beyond the reach of time. The speaker further argues that the lover's beauty will never diminish, and, in fact, the lover will not die.

How is the poem's lover eternal?

The speaker's ingenious solution to this riddle of how the lover is not like a typical summer's day but is instead an eternal summer's day, immune to "nature's changing course," is contained in the nature of the poem itself. The lover is eternal, forever beautiful and alive, because of these lines, which can circumvent and defeat the natural course of decay and death. The poem is eternal now, and the lover in it will remain forever young and immortal. The speaker asserts that the lover will not decline or lose the beauty the lover possesses or owes to nature "When in eternal lines to time thou growest," that is, as you are converted into these lines of verse. As a poetic subject here, the lover will not decline or die but will be enhanced ("growest") by the power of this poem to celebrate the lover. Because these lines will live forever, the speaker immodestly proclaims, so, too, will the lover live forever, like eternal summer. Time, the vicissitudes of nature, and age all have been surmounted here by the poem's final analogy. The lover as the subject of the poem is superior to everything else in nature: a summer's day and whatever blossoms and comes to fruition in the summertime. As long as anyone can still read these lines, the speaker concludes, then all will know of the lover's beauty and superiority, ensuring the lover's immortality and undiminishing permanence.

What else does Shakespeare suggest is eternal and immortal?

Through this declaration, Shakespeare's speaker makes a bold assertion: only in literature are we able to defeat death and our natural mortality. In literature, our voice is never stilled, and we, in effect, never die. It may have taken a poet as masterful and as memorable as Shakespeare to deliver on this promise to the lover, but indeed, it is true. The lover of Shakespeare's poem has long ago died and his or her beauty has faded, but in reading this poem, the lover lives again, undiminished and cherished in "eternal summer."

What might be the real subject of Sonnet 18?

One could argue that Shakespeare's sonnet is less a poem celebrating the lover than a poem about the power and superiority of the poet! What is finally on display here is not a description of the lover. We don't ever learn what the lover actually looks like to justify the poem's praise. Instead, the ultimate comparison is not the lover to a summer's day but with the power of the poet to transform and redeem the world.

William Shakespeare, perhaps more so than any other writer, is the master of metaphor, of associating ideas and emotions with contexts that bring them to life. When reading poetry, be alert to all comparisons—to similes and metaphors—because that is how a poet sees the world and manages to convert the chaos of experience into order and understanding.

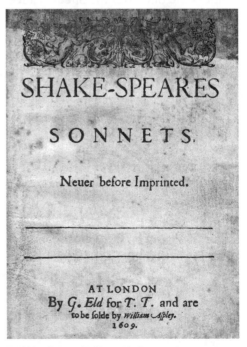

A 1609 edition of William Shakespeare's sonnets. The Bard was as adept at poetry as he was at writing stage plays.

What are other examples of original and striking uses of comparisons in poetry?

> When the evening is spread out against the sky / Like a patient etherized upon a table
>
> —T. S. Eliot, "The Love Song of J. Alfred Prufrock"

Life's but a walking shadow, a poor player
That struts and frets his hour upon the stage
And then is heard no more: it is a tale
Told by an idiot, full of sound and fury,
Signifying nothing.

—William Shakespeare, *Macbeth*

She is all states, and all princes, I.

—John Donne, "The Sun Rising"

What happens to a dream deferred?
Does it dry up
like a raisin in the sun?
Or fester like a sore—
And then run?
Does it stink like rotten meat?
Or crust and sugar over—
like syrupy sweet?
Maybe it just sags
like a heavy load,
Or does it explode?

—Langston Hughes, "Harlem"

My heart aches, and a drowsy numbness pains
My sense, as though of hemlock I had drunk.

—John Keats, "Ode to a Nightingale"

The land's sharp features seem to be
The country's corpse outleant.

—Thomas Hardy, "The Darkling Thrush"

The City now doth, like a garment, wear
The beauty of the morning; ....

—William Wordsworth, "Upon Westminster Bridge"

I'm a riddle in nine syllables,
An elephant, a ponderous house,
A melon strolling on two tendrils.
O red fruit, ivory, fine timbers!
This loaf's big with its yeasty rising.
Money's new-minted in this fat purse.
I'm a means, a stage, a cow in calf.
I've eaten a bag of green apples,
Boarded the train there's no getting off.

—Sylvia Plath, "Metaphors"

But I've no spade to follow men like them.
Between my finger a squat pen rests.
I'll dig with it.

—Seamus Heaney, "Digging"

I was of three minds,
Like a tree
In which there are three blackbirds.

—Wallace Stevens, "Thirteen Ways of Looking at a Blackbird"

How does it feel, how does it feel?
To be without a home
Like a complete unknown, like a rolling stone.

—Bob Dylan, "Like a Rolling Stone"

I do not love you as if you were salt-rose, or topaz,
or the arrow of carnations the fire shoots off.
I love you as certain dark things are to be loved.
in secret, between the shadow and the soul.

—Pablo Neruda, Sonnet 17

How should a poem be read for imagery and symbols?

If words are the essential building blocks of poetry, and comparisons—uses of metaphor and simile—are an essential method of relating ideas and emotions, of making the abstract understood, an equally fundamental resource of the poet is the use of imagery and symbolism. Poetry appeals to our sense of sound in the musicality of word choice and rhythm employed by the poet, but it also appeals to our other senses in the mental images or pictures it describes. An image is a word or a group of words that evokes a mental representation of an object or an action perceived by our senses. An image communicates an impression of a sight, sound, touch, taste, or smell that helps the reader visualize and experience what is going on in poems. Therefore, both to enjoy and understand poetry, pay attention to the images poems create.

How does imagery in poetry work?

Poetic images operate not just to add vivid sensory details but also by conjuring details that connect with the reader's memory and imagination, producing an emotional as well as sensory reaction. Ezra Pound (1885–1972) famously defined an image as "that which presents intellectual and emotional complex in an instant of time." For Pound, the image became the basis for an early twentieth-century poetic movement called Imagism, devoted to "clarity of expression through the use of precise visual images." Imagism was a reaction to the perceived abstraction, clichés, and "emotional slither," in Pound's phrase, of Romantic poets, which needed to be revitalized by exactness of observed detail, fresh metaphors, and economy of language. The importance of the poetic image is also asserted in T. S. Eliot's conception of the objective correlative. "The only way of expressing emotion in the form of art," Eliot writes, "is by finding an 'objective correlative'; in other words, a set of objects, a situation, a chain of events which shall be the formula of that particular emotion; such that when the external facts, which must terminate in sensory experience, are given, the emotion is immediately evoked." Said more succinctly by poet William Carlos Williams (1883–1963): "No ideas but in things."

Imagery, these poets asserted, could show rather than tell, providing the reader with a direct, objective alternative to the most abstract and subjective ideas and emotions. Rather than telling the reader what to think or feel, images could serve as the language of thought and feeling.

Poet and critic Ezra Pound was a leading proponent of Imagism in poetry, which stressed precision, clarity, and economy of language.

What are some examples of poetic uses of imagery?

That time of year thou mayst in me behold
When yellow leaves, or none, or few, do hang
Upon those boughs which shake against the cold,
Bare ruin'd choirs, where late the sweet birds sang.
In me thou see'st the twilight of such day
As after sunset fadeth in the west,
Which by and by black night doth take away,
Death's second self, that seals up all in rest.
In me thou see'st the glowing of such fire
That on the ashes of his youth doth lie,
As the death-bed whereon it must expire
Consumed with that which it was nourish'd by.
This thou perceivest, which makes thy love more strong,
To love that well which thou must leave ere long.

—William Shakespeare, Sonnet 73

The winter evening settles down
With smell of steaks in passageways.

67

Six o'clock.
The burnt-out ends of smoky days.
And now a gusty shower wraps
The grimy scraps
Of withered leaves about your feet
And newspapers from vacant lots;
The showers beat
On broken blinds and chimney-pots,
And at the corner of the street
A lonely cab-horse steams and stamps.

—T. S. Eliot, "Preludes"

The apparition of these faces in the crowd;
Petals on a wet, black bough.

—Ezra Pound, "In a Station of the Metro"

What thoughts I have of you tonight Walt Whitman, for I walked down the side-
streets under the trees with a headache self-conscious looking at the full moon.

In my hungry fatigue, and shopping for images, I went into the neon fruit supermarket, dreaming of your enumerations!

What peaches and what penumbras! Whole families shopping at night! Aisles
full of husbands! Wives in the avocados, babies in the tomatoes!—and you, Gar-
cia Lorca, what were you doing down by the watermelons?

—Allen Ginsberg, "A Supermarket in California"

Whirl up, sea—
Whirl your pointed pines,
splash your great pines
on our rocks,
hurl your green over us,
Cover us with your pools of fir.

—Hilda Doolittle, "Oread"

And the ghostly, creamy coloured little tree of leaves
white, ivory white among the rambling greens
how evanescent, variegated elder, she hesitates on the green grass
as if, in another moment, she would disappear
with all her grace of foam!

—D. H. Lawrence, "Trees in the Garden"

You stand at the blackboard, daddy,
In the picture I have of you,
A cleft in your chin instead of your foot
68   But no less a devil for that, no not

Any less the black man who
Bit my pretty red heart in two.
I was ten when they buried you.
At twenty I tried to die
And get back, back, back to you.
I thought even the bones would do.

—Sylvia Plath, "Daddy"

You do not have to be good.
You do not have to walk on your knees
for a hundred miles through the desert repenting.
You only have to let the soft animal of your body
love what it loves.
Tell me about despair, yours, and I will tell you mine.
Meanwhile the world goes on.
Meanwhile the sun and the clear pebbles of the rain
are moving across the landscapes,
over the prairies and the deep trees,
the mountains and the rivers.
Meanwhile the wild geese, high in the clean blue air,
are heading home again.
Whoever you are, no matter how lonely,
the world offers itself to your imagination,
calls to you like the wild geese, harsh and exciting—
over and over announcing your place
in the family of things.

—Mary Oliver, "Wild Geese"

When does an image become a symbol?

As Ezra Pound (1885–1972), T. S. Eliot (1888–1965), and Williams show, an image can function beyond its literal meaning, carrying more significance than sensory details. Evoking a more complex idea or emotion beyond its literal meaning, an image may become a symbol. An image allows the poet to compress a mood, idea, and emotion into sensory details; a symbol offers an expansion of meaning and significance. Put simply, a symbol represents something else. Words themselves are symbols, sounds and letters that stand for objects, actions, ideas, and qualities. We negotiate the symbolic continually: an octagonal red sign symbolizes stopping; the skull and crossbones signifies danger. Arms raised designates surrender. Each communicates a meaning beyond itself. Carl Jung (1875–1971) defined a symbol as "a term, a name, or even a picture that may be familiar in daily life, yet that possesses specific connotations in addition to its conventional and obvious meaning." Coleridge characterized the symbol brilliantly as "a translucence of the special … in the individual."

69

What are some conventional and cultural examples of symbols?

Symbols can be conventionally and culturally determined: scales stand for justice; a dove represents peace; a lion, strength; a lily, purity; a rose, beauty. A nation's flag stands for a homeland, patriotism, and a nation's history. A cross, a Star of David, and a star and crescent represent three world religions. Other symbols are called literary or contextual symbols because they can function contrary to conventional meaning, explained by the context of a literary work. For example, white conventionally signifies purity and innocence (at least in Western culture), but Herman Melville (1819–1891) has the white whale in his novel *Moby-Dick* mean something very different. A poet like William Butler Yeats was notorious for his private symbolism—the winding stairs, the gyre, the swan, and arcane images derived from the occult, his experiments with automatic writing, and Irish mythology that depend on the context of his poems to unravel.

Swiss psychiatrist and founder of analytical psychology Carl Jung was fascinated by symbols and archetypes, a pursuit that influenced his field, but poets already well understood the power of symbols.

How do you know when an image becomes a symbol?

Poetry, in its methods of verbal compression and argument through imagery, is particularly susceptible to evoking the symbolic, the meanings of which can be powerfully suggestive, nuanced, and multiple.

How should you handle the symbolic in poetry?

The best strategy in dealing with symbols in poetry is to delay the impulse to rush to a symbolic interpretation. Let the details and images in a poem be their literal selves first. Sometimes, a surface detail, even when evoked by a powerful image, is still just a surface detail, important nevertheless, but not a symbol. Symbols handled by great poets are not imposed on a poem as an artificial stimulant of meaning but grow organically from the poem itself, by its tone and emphasis, by an image's prominence, placement, and repetition. A tree in a poem need not symbolize a cross, night need not be sinister, and not every room symbolizes confinement. Let the poem work out the relevance of an image's symbolism. Does the poem call attention to a particular image? Does it appear in a prominent place in the poem: in the title, for example, the first or last detail mentioned? Are references to the particular object, action, or gesture repeated? Do they connect logically and emotionally with the poem as a whole?

In Herman Melville's *Moby-Dick* the white sperm whale of the title served as a symbol for Captain Ahab's obsession with revenge, as well as the nature of evil, fate, and the mysteries of existence.

What is the logic within images and symbols?

In an allegory, X = Y; in a symbol, X may = Y, Z, or Q, or all three simultaneously. Images are promoted to the symbolic when they expand, not reduce, meaning and significance. For instance, what exactly does the white whale represent in Melville's *Moby-Dick*? We can count the possibilities. Because effective symbols carry multiple associations, it is best to handle a symbolic interpretation tentatively. For example, rather than saying that Melville uses the white whale to explicitly mean something, we would say that Melville seems to suggest or Melville may be suggesting what the white whale may represent. Interpretations that discover only one possible meaning in a symbol either point to an inferior poem or a reductive reader.

In reading poetry, therefore, pay attention, not only to the images used but also to the possibility that those images might carry important additional meanings and significance. To see how images and symbols work to produce meaning and significance in a poem, let's look at an example.

What is a good example of reading a poem for its imagery and symbols?

Here is William Wordsworth's most famous and perhaps most beloved poem, "I Wandered Lonely as a Cloud," primarily due to its vivid imagery. In it, the speaker attempts to convey the beauty of nature and the feelings evoked by that beauty.

71

I wandered lonely as a cloud
That floats on high o'er vales and hills,
When all at once I saw a crowd,
A host, of golden daffodils;
Beside the lake, beneath the trees,
Fluttering and dancing in the breeze.

Continuous as the stars that shine
And twinkle on the milky way,
They stretched in never-ending line
Along the margin of a bay:
Ten thousand saw I at a glance,
Tossing their heads in sprightly dance.

The waves beside them danced; but they
Out-did the sparkling waves in glee:
A poet could not but be gay,
In such a jocund company:
I gazed—and gazed—but little thought
What wealth the show to me had brought:

For oft, when on my couch I lie
In vacant or in pensive mood,
They flash upon that inward eye
Which is the bliss of solitude;
And then my heart with pleasure fills,
And dances with the daffodils.

What is the origin of "I Wandered Lonely as a Cloud"?

The poem recalls an incident in April 1802, when Wordsworth and his sister, Dorothy, were walking near a lake at Grasmere, in England's Cumbria. They came upon a shore lined with daffodils. Dorothy Wordsworth described the scene in her diary:

When we were in the woods beyond Gowbarrow park we saw a few daffodils close to the water side, we fancied that the lake had floated the seeds ashore & that the little colony had so sprung up—but as we went along there were more & yet more & at last under the boughs of the trees, we saw that there was a long belt of them along the shore, about the breadth of a country turnpike road.... Some rested their heads on stones as on a pillow for weariness & the rest tossed & reeled & danced & seemed as if they verily laughed with the wind that blew upon them over the Lake, they looked so gay ever glancing, ever changing. This wind blew directly over the lake to them. There was here & there a little knot & a few stragglers a few yards higher up but they were so few as not to disturb the simplicity & unity & life of that one busy highway ...—Rain came on, we were wet.

Why is "I Wandered Lonely as a Cloud' such an effective poem?

The effectiveness of Wordsworth's poem stems not just from its simplicity and directness but also from the poet's ability to convey the beauty of the scene and the feelings it evoked in language that the reader understands first with the senses and then with the intellect and emotions.

How does Wordsworth begin his transformation of the scene to a poem?

Wordsworth's sister vividly describes the scene in prose, and Wordsworth attempts to render it in poetry. Note what Wordsworth changes, however. Gone is any reference to the "we" in Dorothy's account (or the rain and wet). Wordsworth instead emphasizes the isolated, solitary speaker: "*I* wandered lonely as a cloud." Before setting the scene, therefore, Wordsworth chooses to begin with the speaker's condition, characterized by the simile "lonely as a cloud." It's the poem's first powerful image: the speaker imagines himself untethered and isolated as a cloud above the ground. The comparison asks the reader to consider: how is a cloud lonely? How does the comparison capture the speaker's feelings at the outset of the poem? A cloud moves without will or purpose. It is acted upon by the prevailing wind that determines its course. So, we get the sense in Wordsworth's comparison of the speaker aimlessly walking, without a plan or destination, "high o'er vales and hills," detached and above the scene on the ground. In other words, nothing is holding him or fixing his attention.

How does Wordsworth describe what captures his attention?

However, all that changes suddenly: "When all at once I saw a crowd / A host, of golden daffodils." Both metaphors Wordsworth chooses here—"crowd" and "host"—to describe the daffodils personifies them in human terms. We normally wouldn't describe many daffodils as a "crowd" or a "host," meaning a mass of people, such as an army. Wordsworth employs personification, figurative language that bestows human characteristics upon the nonhuman, after using a form of reverse personification, conferring nonhuman characteristics upon a human by associating the speaker with a cloud. Above them, the speaker sees this crowd or host of golden daffodils, "fluttering" and "dancing in the breeze." Note how the movement of a cloud, conditioned by the prevailing wind, is echoed here in the imagery of fluttering and dancing, the latter metaphor another instance of personification. Here, however, the movement of the daffodils contrasts with the lonely movements of the speaker as a cloud. The daffodils are moving with purpose; they are dancing. Daffodils can't dance literally but figuratively: that's what they seem to be doing from the speaker's perspective. Stanza one, therefore, sets the scene, paints a vivid picture of the daffodils, moving in the breeze, beside the lake. It's the imagery—the golden daffodils beside a lakeshore—that the reader "sees" based on the details on which Wordsworth chooses to focus.

73

What does the second stanza tell us about Wordsworth's experience?

The second stanza further visualizes through imagery and metaphor what the daffodils look like, or, more precisely, what they remind the speaker of, that is, what they resemble. There are so many daffodils that they are "Continuous as the stars that shine" in the Milky Way, a "never-ending line" along the shore. The imagery of countless stars making up the Milky Way creates a sense of a vast number that seems infinite. However, having taken us out to the farthest reaches of space to convey the multitude of the daffodils, the speaker comes back to earth in the final two lines of the stanza. He gives the previous suggestion of the infinite ("never-ending line") a number ("Ten thousand") and returns to the human personification of flowers dancing. They are "Tossing their heads," something that we normally associate with humans and not flowers, engaging in a "sprightly dance," again, what humans, not flowers, do. We need to remember the initial statement of the speaker—his loneliness—is now contrasted with the gaiety and community of the flowers, whose attractions seem irresistible to the speaker.

How does the third stanza convey Wordsworth's delight?

The third stanza contrasts the dancing waves of the lake with the dancing daffodils, which "Out-did the sparkling waves in glee." "Glee" is a human quality, an expression of joy in which the speaker projects onto the inanimate daffodils. The daffodils have become more than literal flowers, a representation of human values and emotions. Their delight is contagious, and the speaker declares: "A poet could not but be gay, / In such a jocund company." Wordsworth makes an important distinction here. He doesn't say anyone "could not but be gay," only a poet, and the rest of the poem will increasingly concern the poet's mission and skill in recalling and celebrating such a natural scene. Stanza three concludes with the statement that the speaker did not realize at the time "What wealth the show to me had brought." Gaiety, the initial contagious response at seeing the daffodils, here shifts to "wealth" or value upon recollection.

How does the final stanza explain the meaning of what Wordsworth has experienced?

The final stanza explains what he means. Often since, the speaker declares, "In vacant or in pensive mood," he has seen with "that inward eye," his imagination, the dancing daffodils, filling his heart with pleasure. A final distinction is made, however, in his imaginative recollection of the scene. He is no longer the lonely wandering cloud, isolated and alone, but his heart has joined with the daffodils in their dance. The speaker's ability to recall this particularly vivid scene, "In a vacant, or pensive mood," that is when again lonely, mentally wandering like the cloud in the opening line, brings contentment and connection that joins the isolated individual to the wider, joyful world of nature.

AN ANALYSIS OF WILLIAM BUTLER YEATS'S "THE LAKE ISLE OF INNISFREE"

What is an example of a poem that expresses longing for a well-loved place?

Let's follow Wordsworth's most famous poem with the most celebrated poem of the great Irish poet William Butler Yeats (1865–1939). As in Wordsworth's poem, we know from the poet's own words what prompted his poem. Born in Ireland, Yeats spent most of his childhood living in London, where his artist father trained and worked. The family struggled to make ends meet, and Yeats spent his happiest time with his mother's well-to-do family on the northwest coast of Ireland in Sligo, the landscape of which forever haunted Yeats's imagination and which he called "the land of heart's desire." Yeats was a poet of the Irish Celtic Revival: a late nineteenth- and early twentieth-century culturally based literary movement that attempted to create poetry that was uniquely Irish rather than British in origin and standards.

What inspired Yeats to create a poem based on Innisfree?

In a radio broadcast in 1932, Yeats preceded his reading of "The Lake Isle of Innisfree" by saying:

> When I was a young lad in the town of Sligo, I read Thoreau's essays, and wanted to live in a hut on an island in Lough Gill called Innisfree, which means "heather island." I wrote the poem in London when I was about twenty-three. One day in the Strand, I heard a little tinkle of water and saw in a shop window a little jet of water balancing a ball on the top. It was an advertisement, I think, for cooling drinks, but it set me thinking of Sligo and lake water.

> Like Wordsworth's poem, therefore, the speaker in Yeats's poem is imagining a natural scene.

How should you read the poem?

As you read the poem, concentrate on the images that bring the scene to life to your senses—its sights and sounds.

"The Lake Isle of Innisfree"

I will arise and go now, and go to Innisfree,
And a small cabin build there, of clay and wattles made:
Nine bean-rows will I have there, a hive for the honey-bee,
And live alone in the bee-loud glade.

And I shall have some peace there, for peace comes dropping slow,
Dropping from the veils of the morning to where the cricket sings;
There midnight's all a glimmer, and noon a purple glow,
And evening full of the linnet's wings.

I will arise and go now, for always
night and day
I hear lake water lapping with low
sounds by the shore;

While I stand on the roadway, or on
the pavements grey,

I hear it in the deep heart's core.

What can you learn from the title and the speaker?

The island of Innisfree on Lough Gill in Ireland remains a natural and uninhabited place, at least in
the imagination, for escaping the bustle of life.

The title of Yeats's poem, "The Lake Isle of
Innisfree," focuses our attention on that
place, which we learn in stanza one is the
desired destination of the poem's speaker, who declares his attention to "arise and go now
… to Innisfree." The situation prompting the poem, therefore, is that the speaker, is someplace else and feels compelled to leave it, to escape to Innisfree. The implied question the
poem raises is why? Why go to Innisfree? We get some answers in the language and imagery used to describe what the speaker intends to do when Innisfree is reached. The
speaker intends to build a "small cabin," simply constructed from clay and wattles (a
framework of interlaced branches and twigs). Beyond a simple shelter, the speaker intends
to grow his own food ("Nine bean-rows will I have") and a hive to collect honey. The images (the bean-rows and beehive) here create a picture in the reader's mind of an idyllic,
simple, rustic retreat that allows the speaker "to live alone in the bee-loud glade." This final
image adds sound to the visual imagery of life on the island desired by the speaker.

How is the poem's initial situation developed?

Stanza two addresses the issue of why the speaker wants to go to Innisfree in the first
place. What is compelling the speaker to declare an intention to "go" (repeated twice to
stress an urgency in line one) to Innisfree. The speaker declares that "I shall have some
peace there." So, the speaker implies a lack of peace in his present situation and possibly the source of the conflict in the poem, between a desire for escape and peace suggested by life on Innisfree and the speaker's current situation. On Innisfree, "peace
comes dropping slow," and the speaker visualizes this abstraction in the following examples: "Dropping from the veils of the morning" (suggesting the shadowy scene of
first light), "to where the cricket sings" (another image combining the visual and auditory), to the look at the landscape at midnight ("all a glimmer," that is, shining faintly
with a wavering light), and at noontime, which has a "purple glow" (Yeats explained
that he was referring to the reflection of purple heather on the water around the island). The speaker concludes his examples of the nature of peace on the island with a
description of "evening full of the linnet's wings." The sound of the linnet, a small bird,
flapping its wings will be, in the speaker's imagination, the dominating sound. The place,

How did Henry David Thoreau inspire "The Lake Isle of Innisfree"?

The American writer Henry David Thoreau (1817–1862), whose essays Yeats claimed as inspiration for the poem, is the author of *Walden,* a chronicle of the author's time spent in a small cabin beside Walden Pond in Massachusetts. It is a famous treatise on independence and self-reliance in which Thoreau explains:

> I went to the woods because I wished to live deliberately, to front only the essential facts of life, and see if I could not learn what it had to teach, and not, when I came to die, discover that I had not lived.... I wanted to live deep and suck out all the marrow of life, to live so sturdily and Spartan-like as to put to rout all that was not life, to cut a broad swath and shave close, to drive life into a corner, and reduce it to its lowest terms.

The speaker in Yeats's poem is following a similar intention: to seek seclusion and authenticity in another version of *Walden* on the island of Innisfree. The images in stanza one conjure up a life of plainness and austerity in a small cabin, of order ("Nine bean-rows will I have"), self-sustained by food grown and cultivated by the speaker.

in other words, will be so quiet and tranquil that a bird flapping its wings can be heard. All the visual images here—the veil of morning light, the glimmering light at midnight, the purple glow of noon—help the reader to see Innisfree through the imagination of the speaker, while auditory images—the cricket singing and the sounds of linnets' wings—add to the visual peaceful sounds. All support the notion of peaceful isolation, undisturbed by anything other than the natural: the routine of the day, from morning to midnight, and the sounds of crickets and birds (to accompany the "bee-loud glade" of stanza one). So, we now realize that the speaker here is seeking peace and implying that his current circumstances are the opposite of the world conjured up in Innisfree.

How is the conflict resolved?

Stanza three returns to the initial situation that prompted the poem, using the exact same words, "I will arise and go now," of the first line. Here, the speaker reminds himself (and the reader) of his determination to depart for Innisfree. The wording is significant. "Arise" is a word normally associated with waking up from sleep: we arise from our beds. Another sense of the word is something that has come into being, emerging, or becoming apparent: "New difficulties have arisen." *Arise*, therefore, suggests both urgency and a previous state of inaction, lethargy, even sleepiness replaced by a call to action. Adding the word "now" to *go* underscores this determination and the resolve of the speaker. Whatever he is feeling or experiencing, he is determined to put an end to it by departing immediately for Innisfree. Stanza three clarifies the necessity that the speaker is feeling to depart and seek peace on Innisfree. He says he actually "hears lake water lapping with low sounds on the shore" even as he stands "in the roadway, or on the pavements grey." Finally, the speaker makes clear his present situation in key images. In contrast to the peaceful, natural isolation of Innisfree, he is clearly in a man-made place, a city or town. In contrast to the sound of water lapping on a shore, he is on a roadway or "pavements grey," experiencing what they imply: the sound of traffic, of vehicles and pedestrians, not the comforting sounds of "lake water lapping." The image of grey concrete pavement contrasts with the previous colorful imagery of "noon a purple glow." The poem's images contrast a black-and-white urban scene with the Technicolor-imagined lake island. The reader now understands what is driving the speaker: a discontent with life in the grey city. This is is portrayed in two images: roadways and pavements and a passion for an alternative, an escape into a peaceful, natural world of color with only the sounds of bees, crickets, and linnets.

What else is resolved in the poem?

The poem establishes the conflict between the here and the there, between the speaker's current situation and his desired alternative—life on Innisfree. The final line of the poem offers a surprising resolution to this conflict. The speaker explains that he hears the sounds of the lapping water of the lake "in the deep heart's core." This is significant because of what it implies, particularly at the close of the poem, which underscores its importance. By explaining that the sounds he hears come from his "deep heart's core," the speaker implies that that actually is where Innisfree is. The imagined island is not so much an actual, physical destination but a place conjured by the imagination, created by memory and the visualization of the speaker. The last line, therefore, implies that the speaker need not "arise and go now" to Innisfree. Instead, the speaker at the conclusion realizes he is already in Innisfree in his imagination, that the journey has already been accomplished.

What is missing in the poem?

Missing in the conclusion of the poem is any repetition of his determination to "arise and go now." The final realization of the poem is that the consolation of the speaker need not be the actual but the imagined. The real Innisfree is certainly much more complicated and much less ideal than the one conjured by the speaker. Do you think life in isolation on such an island would be as problem-free as it seems in the speaker's imagination? All the unpleasantness of living in a clay and wattled cabin, sustained by "nine bean-rows" and a hive for honeybees, is left out, replaced by perfect days of peace and quiet, interrupted only by the sounds of crickets and linnets. We know that actually living on the island in this way probably cannot sustain this description, but that's the point: in the imagination, perfection is possible. In the imagination, we need not actually go to Innisfree or live there at all, but we can achieve the results of doing so, refined and perfected into a desired feeling of peace and tranquility.

What makes Yeats's poem so successful?

Yeats's haunting poem is about the power of the imagination, of the capacity of language and poetry itself, to provide an alternative to reality, replacing the hard, grey facts of life with images and feelings that challenge them, that console and compensate. Yeats's success in this poem is his ability to conjure up an alternative place that is sharply seen and heard, while at the same time shifting its location from actuality to where all our desires reside: in our "deep heart's core."

How should a poem be read for its drama?

If the core resources of poetry are diction, metaphor, and imagery, poetry's power— its suspense and dynamic energy—mainly comes from its drama, its ability to engage the reader in circumstances and situations that test our understanding of human nature and human experience. Robert Frost, always a reliably quotable source on poetic methods, stated: "Everything written is as good as it is dramatic.… [A poem is] heard

Irish poet and Nobel Prize winner William Butler Yeats remains one of the giants of twentieth-century literature.

as sung or spoken by a person in a scene—in character, in a setting. By whom, where, and when is the question." Even though poems can express a single feeling or fragmentary thought or feeling, they are usually presented dramatically, that is, in a situation or setting prompting the feeling or thought, with an imagined speaker (not always the poet) and conflict that is the essence of drama. Each of the poems we have already examined can be profitably studied from the perspective of the dramatic questions Frost poses here ("By whom, where, and when is the question"). In some poems, much of the drama—its circumstances and conflicts—may be implied or are beneath the surface as in Emily Dickinson's "I Like to See it Lap the Miles," in which the speaker only eventually contradicts the first line about liking the train described. In other poems, however, the drama is unmistakable and in the forefront of the poem, forcing the reader to confront the poem in many of the same ways as we read and understand a drama.

What is an example of a "dramatic" poem?

With his poem "Ulysses," Alfred, Lord Tennyson (1809–1892), gives us a dramatic monologue—that is, a poem that takes the form of a speaker addressing a silent listener who is revealed within the context of a dramatic situation. By the end of the poem, the reader learns not only about the speaker's personality, desires, and needs but also about the time, setting, key events, and other characters involved in the dramatic situation. Read "Ulysses," but first answer these questions:

1. Who is speaking?

2. To whom?

3. What are the circumstances?

4. What is the speaker's goal?

5. What do we learn about the speaker from what he says and how he says it?

Here is the full text of Tennyson's "Ulysses":

AN ANALYSIS OF TENNYSON'S "ULYSSES"

ULYSSES

    It little profits that an idle king,
By this still hearth, among these barren crags,
Matched with an agèd wife, I mete and dole, measure out and distribute
Unequal laws unto a savage race,
That hoard, and sleep, and feed, and know not me.

I cannot rest from travel: I will drink
Life to the lees: all times I have enjoyed
Greatly, have suffered greatly, both with those
That loved me, and alone; on shore, and when
Through scudding drifts the rainy Hyades
Vexed the dim sea: I am become a name;
For always roaming with a hungry heart
Much have I seen and known; cities of men
And manners, climates, councils, governments,
Myself not least, but honoured of them all;
And drunk delight of battle with my peers,
Far on the ringing plains of windy Troy.
I am a part of all that I have met;
Yet all experience is an arch wherethrough
Gleams that untravelled world, whose margin fades
For ever and for ever when I move.
How dull it is to pause, to make an end,
To rust unburnished, not to shine in use!
As though to breathe were life. Life piled on life
Were all too little, and of one to me
Little remains: but every hour is saved
From that eternal silence, something more,
A bringer of new things; and vile it were
For some three suns to store and hoard myself,

80

And this grey spirit yearning in desire
To follow knowledge like a sinking star,
Beyond the utmost bound of human thought.

    This my son, mine own Telemachus,
To whom I leave the sceptre and the isle—
Well-loved of me, discerning to fulfil
This labour, by slow prudence to make mild
A rugged people, and through soft degrees
Subdue them to the useful and the good.
Most blameless is he, centred in the sphere
Of common duties, decent not to fail
In offices of tenderness, and pay
Meet adoration to my household gods,
When I am gone. He works his work, I mine.

    There lies the port; the vessel puffs her sail:
There gloom the dark broad seas. My mariners,
Souls that have toiled, and wrought, and thought with me—
That ever with a frolic welcome took
The thunder and the sunshine, and opposed
Free hearts, free foreheads—you and I are old;
Old age hath yet his honour and his toil;
Death closes all: but something ere the end,
Some work of noble note, may yet be done,
Not unbecoming men that strove with Gods.
The lights begin to twinkle from the rocks:
The long day wanes: the slow moon climbs: the deep
Moans round with many voices. Come, my friends,
'Tis not too late to seek a newer world.
Push off, and sitting well in order smite
The sounding furrows; for my purpose holds
To sail beyond the sunset, and the baths
Of all the western stars, until I die.
It may be that the gulfs will wash us down:
It may be we shall touch the Happy Isles,
And see the great Achilles, whom we knew
Though much is taken, much abides; and though
We are not now that strength which in old days
Moved earth and heaven; that which we are, we are;
One equal temper of heroic hearts,
Made weak by time and fate, but strong in will
To strive, to seek, to find, and not to yield.

Who is the Ulysses of the poem?

The poem's title identifies the speaker and helps us understand the dramatic context. To understand the poem, we must know something about Ulysses, its speaker. Ulysses (the Roman name for the Greek warrior Odysseus) is the famous Greek hero who devised the stratagem that ended the ten-year siege of the ancient city of Troy and the Trojan War. Ulysses, who came up with the idea for the Trojan horse that allowed the Greeks to enter the walled city, and was largely responsible for the Greeks' ultimate victory over the Trojans, took ten more years trying to return home to his island kingdom of Ithaca, where he reigned

Alfred, Lord Tennyson published the poem "Ulysses" in his 1842 collection, *Poems,* which would be his third collection but his first major success.

as king. His exploits during his long trip home are chronicled in Homer's great epic poem *The Odyssey.* After many adventures, Ulysses finally reaches his home in Ithaca, where he is reunited with his devoted wife Penelope and his son Telemachus. Homer's poem ends with Ulysses resuming his reign as Ithaca's king and restoring the order and harmony of his kingdom that had been disrupted during his twenty-year absence.

How does Tennyson update Ulysses' story?

Tennyson's poem provides an update on Ulysses' story, picking up a detail from Homer's *Odyssey* in which the prophet and seer Tiresias predicts Ulysses' eventual successful return to Ithaca but further foresees that Ulysses will undertake a new voyage that will eventually lead to his death "from the sea." Tennyson imagines Ulysses handing over his authority as king of Ithaca to his son Telemachus, justifying his decision, and setting off on this final voyage. Years have passed since he returned home from his wandering after the Trojan War. Penelope is described now as "an agèd wife," and clearly, Ulysses is bored and discontent with his responsibilities as king in which "I mete and dole / Unequal laws unto a savage race." Ulysses, the great Greek war hero and legendary wanderer and adventurer, is frustrated and unfulfilled with the dull routine of governing his kingdom that is made up of a "savage race" who seems only to "hoard and sleep and feed" and "know not me." The first of the three sections of the poem ends with making clear Ulysses' current dilemma or crisis: his conflict between his responsibilities as a king over his uninspiring subjects and his own conception of himself as an indomitable adventurer.

Do we know to whom Ulysses is speaking?

It is unclear in this opening section to whom Ulysses is speaking. It could be that these are his internal, unvoiced thoughts because it is unlikely that he would be addressing his subjects in such derogatory terms. What is clear from the form of the poem—written in blank verse, that is, unrhymed iambic pentameter (five pairs of unaccented syllables followed by accented ones in each line)—is that we get the fluid, natural quality of actual speech. To understand the poem, the reader needs to listen carefully to what Ulysses says (and doesn't say), and the way he says it as he both intentionally and unintentionally reveals himself to us.

How do the words in the first section of the poem reveal Ulysses to the reader?

Look again at the words Ulysses uses in the first section of the poem. In the first line, he identifies himself as an "idle king," beside a "still hearth," and among "barren crags" in his island kingdom. Ulysses says that he finds little pleasure ("profit") in such a life of inaction. He is now idle, and his former fiery, intense life in war and wandering has declined to a "still hearth" amidst unproductive "barren crags." He describes his life "Matched with an agèd wife" fulfilling his royal responsibilities with the words "mete and dole," suggesting measuring out in small, trivial quantities "Unequal laws to a savage race." Clearly, neither Ulysses' domestic life with Penelope nor his royal activities bring him satisfaction, living among and reigning over a people whose existence is limited to basic functions and instincts, who "hoard, and sleep, and feed." Theirs is a life of stagnant routine, and Ulysses rejects this definition for himself (they "know not me").

What does Ulysses mean by "me"?

The "me" to which Ulysses refers is the subject of the next, much longer section of the poem in which he clarifies who he thinks he is and contrasts his past with his present, his passions and desires with the dull, inactive world in which he finds himself. Ulysses devotes only five lines to commenting on his present situation but offers the next twenty-seven lines to reveal his sense of himself. In contrast to the idle king he has become, Ulysses declares, "I cannot rest from travel." He aspires to live life to the fullest, to drink life even down to the "lees." The "lees" here suggest that although Ulysses acknowledges his life is nearing its end, that, like his wife, he, too, is "agèd," he will challenge his current reality with another, closer to his most cherished aspirations. Compared to the "still hearth" and "barren crags" of Ulysses' present, stagnant existence, he conjures up a life of action, movement, and productiveness in his recollections of his past. There are "scuddy drifts" of wandering clouds, like the formerly ever-wandering Ulysses. There are the "rainy Hyades" that "vexed the dim sea," whose rain contrasts with the "barren crags" of Ithaca. In this landscape of motion and continual change, Ulysses sees his own valued identity as one who is "always roaming with a hungry heart." Ulysses' true self, as he confesses, is a man in motion, a man of action, whose heart is hungry for new experiences and new challenges. Having traveled widely and experienced a multiplicity of "manners, climates, councils, governments," Ulysses concludes, "I am a part of all that I have met," that is, his existence and identity is intertwined with his past experiences, not his present, dull, royal routine. For Ulysses, experience is an "arch" revealing the "untraveled world" beyond. To illustrate his current dilemma, he supplies a metaphor: a sword that begins to rust when unused. Instead, Ulysses will resist doing nothing until the "eternal silence"

83

of death arrives. He will not "store and hoard" himself in idleness but will "follow knowledge like a sinking star, / Beyond the utmost bound of human thought."

How does the poem shift from private musings to public declarations?

Having revealed his essence as a man of action who craves new experiences that test his emotional and intellectual mettle, Ulysses now addresses both his son Telemachus and presumably an audience of his subjects. If the first two sections represent more a soliloquy than a monologue, that is, words said to himself rather than to an audience, the next two sections of the poem are clearly public utterances. "This my son, mine own Telemachus" suggests that Ulysses here is presenting his son to an unstated audience in some kind of ritual transference of power, introducing Telemachus as his heir and successor. Ulysses is stepping down from the reign of Ithaca, leaving his "scepter and the isle" to his son to fulfill the father's former royal responsibilities. Although called "well-loved of me," Ulysses praises Telemachus mainly for being good at all that is small. Justifying his choice of his son to follow him as ruler, Ulysses praises Telemachus's good judgment ("discerning to fulfill this labour"), his "slow prudence" to "make mild / A rugged people," and his steady persistence ("through soft degrees") to "Subdue them to the useful and the good." Rather than offer any superlatives about his son, Ulysses instead defines him negatively, calling him "Most blameless," that is, least objectionable, which is hardly a ringing endorsement! Telemachus is "centred in the sphere / Of common duties," implying Ulysses' different sphere of the uncommon, heroic duties that he is now to pursue, which Ulysses judges superior. Telemachus is praised for his prudence, his dedication, his decency, and his devotion to honoring the gods. He is, in other words, the perfect candidate to take on the onerous task of ruling a community that Ulysses is happily abandoning. His final dismissal of kinship with his son is unmistakable: "He works his work, I mine."

How does Ulysses justify his status as a ruler?

Having dismissed his devoted Penelope and the love he should have for her in only two words ("agèd wife"), Ulysses devotes eleven lines to his son, largely to say that his unexceptional qualities, at least in comparison to those that Ulysses has attributed to himself in the previous stanza, make him the proper ruler of a savage and rugged people who are best governed by someone who is "slow," "soft," "blameless," and "decent." Ulysses seems to suggest that the Ithacans are now well matched: a dull, plodding, uninspired people now have a ruler in their own image.

What has been further revealed about Ulysses at this stage of the poem?

That Ulysses is so condescending and patronizing in describing his own son points up the egotism of the speaker here. In stanza one we can sympathize with the boredom of rule that is tedious and uninspiring. However, readily relegating his own son to such service seems to suggest that Ulysses cares little either for the fate of Ithaca or his offspring. He is directed elsewhere in pursuit of his heroism. As much as we can admire Ulysses' determination, his aspirations, there is also something disturbing and off-putting in his diminishing of important responsibilities over "common duties" in favor of his preferred existence of adventure and wandering. Tennyson seems to be offering two sides to the heroic Ulysses and the hero in general. Heroes are great because they are exceptional, but that same exceptionality makes them ill-suited for the world of normalcy. Having complained about the narrow selfishness of his people, Ulysses shows himself here equally self-centered and irresponsible. His desires for heroic action and notoriety cause him to oppose the values we associate with unity, order, and harmony, namely love, family, and community. Tennyson here dramatizes the contradictions of the hero: a person of great confidence and self-reliance who is not willing or even able to do the often tedious but essential tasks of everyday normal life.

A 1909 illustration by E. M. Synge from the "Story of the World" series depicts the return of Ulysses. In Homer's version, he returns alone, but in Tennyson's version some of his mates survived the voyage.

How does Tennyson resolve the contradictions in Ulysses' character?

If Ulysses loses some of our sympathy in the third section of the poem by his condescending and patronizing words about his son, he reclaims our admiration in the poem's fourth and final section. Having dispensed with his domestic and royal responsibilities, Ulysses now is prepared to depart and urges his former comrades to join him. Here, Tennyson departs from Homer's *Odyssey* because in Homer's telling, all those who traveled home to Ithaca with Ulysses from Troy were eventually killed. Ulysses returns home to Ithaca alone. In Tennyson's version, some of Ulysses' former shipmates ("My mariners") have survived, and Ulysses tries to recruit them for one last adventure together. He concedes now what he has only implied before: "you and I are old" but that "old age hath yet his honour and his toil." Death may be coming, Ulysses declares, but "something ere the end, / Some work of noble note, may yet be done." In a beautiful series of images, Ulysses says:

> The lights begin to twinkle from the rocks:
> The long day wanes: the slow moon climbs: the deep
> Moans round with many voices. Come, my friends,
> 'Tis not too late to seek a newer world.

Acknowledging the possibility that they may never return and that their voyage may be perilous ("that the gulfs will wash us down"), Ulysses offers them the consolation that their ultimate destination might be the Happy Isles, the final resting place of the heroes, including the greatest of them all, Achilles. Ulysses here is summoning up his and their sense of themselves as heroes worthy of a place in the Happy Isles, even though "We are not now that strength which in old days / Moved earth and heaven; that which we are, we are." We few, Ulysses declares, share "one equal temper of heroic hearts," and, though time and circumstances have weakened us physically, our will, he declares, remains strong "To strive, to seek, to find, and not to yield."

What is the significance of the poem's last line?

This last line of the poem, which was chosen as the motto of the 2012 Summer Olympic Games in London, offers Ulysses' final testament in pursuing aspirations over any other consideration. This is, of course, an inspiring and noble sentiment, claiming greatness as our ultimate goal in life. Tennyson wrote the poem after the death of a close friend and said that the poem expressed his own "need of going forward and braving the struggle of life" after that loss. As inspiring as Ulysses' final words are, the drama revealed in the poem—its conflict and characterization—is far more complex than just the idea of living life to the fullest. What Ulysses says and doesn't say and how he says it reveals a fully human portrait of multiple dimensions. All heroes are by their nature egotistical and self-centered, who thrive in the realm of the exceptional, not the mundane. Tennyson asks us to think about what makes a great hero and what we should admire or criticize about heroic greatness. What's more important, the poem asks us to consider: the "common duties" of a Telemachus or the ever-questing, never-resting Ulysses? Is home a place of nurture and completion or only a destination for departure? These are intriguing questions raised by Tennyson's drama here.

To recap, what are the key considerations in understanding poetry?

1. Poets and poetry must rely on words both to communicate their ideas and convey feelings and emotions. Accordingly, to understand a poem, you need to look closely and understand the diction of a poem—its word choice—and consider the three components of words: their denotation (dictionary definition), their connotation (the positive or negative association), and their sound. All three contribute to the overall effects of a poem and its significance. Make sure you know what each word means, and, using a good dictionary, understand a word's connotation. One great way to start any encounter with a new poem: pay attention to any unexpected word, any word that is unfamiliar, or any familiar word used in an unfamiliar or unexpected way.

2. One of the most important of a poet's resources with words are metaphors, the relating of one idea or emotion with something else to make the abstract more concrete. Metaphors are the art of resemblances. When reading a poem, pay close attention to comparisons.

3. To make the abstract and general specific and concrete, poets help their readers see through imagery, communicating an impression of a sight, sound, touch, taste, or

smell that helps the reader visualize and experience what is going on in poems. To understand a poem, concentrate on the mental pictures the poem displays.

4. Poetry is fundamentally dramatic. To get to the core of what a poem means, identify the speaker and situation that prompts the poem and the conflict which is revealed. Read a poem like you would a drama: who are the characters, what obstacles are apparent, and what resolution is reached? By answering these questions, you will be well underway toward understanding poetry.

What are the key elements to consider when responding to poems?

First Response

- What stands out on a first reading? What's familiar and unfamiliar? What about the situation is unusual? Does the poem meet your expectations or challenge them?

Speaker & Tone

- Who is the speaker? What details reveal the speaker's situation or personality? Tone or attitude?
- Are there any contradictions between what the speaker says and does or implies?
- Is the speaker reflecting on an earlier experience or attitude?

Audience

- To whom is the speaker speaking?

Structure & Form

- Does the poem proceed in a straightforward way or at some point or points does the speaker reverse course, altering his or her tone or perception?
- Is the poem organized into sections? What may account for them?
- What is the effect on you of the form—say quatrains (stanzas of four lines) or blank verse (unrhymed lines of ten syllables of iambic pentameter)?

Center of Interest

- What is the poem about?
- Is the theme stated explicitly or implicitly?

Diction

- How would you characterize the language?
- Is there anything unusual about the language in word choice and connation?
- What is the role of figurative language—metaphor, simile, personification?
- Does any image in the poem take on a symbolic significance? How and why?

Sound

- What is the role of sound effects, including repetition of sounds (for instance, alliteration and rhyme)?
- If there are unexpected stresses or pauses, what do they communicate about the speaker's experience?

87

HOW TO READ SHORT STORIES

What are the earliest short stories?

Storytelling—accounts of real or fictional people and events intended to entertain or instruct an audience—is a basic attribute of human beings and the way by which we make sense of our experiences. We continually use our storytelling skills to attempt to communicate significant actions or insights selected from our past and present experiences. When asked "How was your day?", we respond with stories selected from the day's events, often embellishing our accounts with our feelings about the people involved or past experiences that relate to our experience of the events. Jokes are basically stories intended to amuse and astonish us by a revelation of the unexpected, the incongruous, or the disconcerting.

We can imagine the earliest humans doing just this: telling an audience about a past event, such as a hunt, and arranging the event into a sequence of narrated actions with a beginning, middle, and end to inform and entertain their listeners.

Written versions of stories have existed in one form or another throughout recorded history. Written stories were sometimes referred to as "tales," which suggest the form's oral origin: performed to hold an audience of listeners, not readers. Short narrative tales date as far back as Ancient Egypt; short stories of biblical people and events are a feature of the Old Testament (Jonah and the whale, the story of Ruth) and appear as accounts of Jesus's life and preaching in the New Testament. In fact, Jesus is one of the earliest published short story tellers. He preached, as recorded in the New Testament, in parables: short stories with characters in specific situations to illustrate a moral lesson. Collections of short stories appeared during the Middle Ages and the Renaissance, such as *The Arabian Nights* and Boccaccio's *Decameron*. Geoffrey Chaucer, English literature's first great figure, based his greatest imaginative work, *The Canterbury Tales*, on a collection of verse short stories. The famous fables attributed to the ancient Greek slave and storyteller Aesop were originally part of the oral storytelling tradition and were not collected and transcribed until three centuries after his death (believed to be 584 B.C.E.). In 1484, merchant, writer, and printer William Caxton became the first to translate and print a collection of *Aesop's Fables* in English. The fables, with their closing moral lessons, were initially meant for adults and later served as ethical guides, especially for children.

Where and when did the short story as a literary genre originate?

Even though short stories have been told and written for as long as literature has existed, the emergence of the short story as a distinct literary genre is relatively recent. Only in the nineteenth century did writers begin to treat a short narrative tale, which eventually began to be referred to as a short story, as a distinct and specialized form of narrative art with its own unique rules and methods.

Where should we look for the best evidence for the emergence and development of the modern short story?

The best starting place is probably in America. The short story has been called America's unique contribution to narrative art, like jazz to music and baseball to sports.

Why did Americans pioneer the development of the short story?

Why the short story should develop significantly in America is a complicated story connected to the uniqueness of American literary history and development. The earliest full-length novels in America did not appear until the 1790s, well behind the development of the novel in Europe. Novelists in America had to share the expenses of publication with publishers, and there were no international copyright laws to prevent American publishers from reprinting popular European novels for free. Accordingly, there was little incentive to pay homegrown authors for their novels. Magazines, however, offered a more secure means for publishing American writers' works. By the 1820s, America had more than a hundred magazines. To fill them, short stories began to appear—sketches, sentimental/moral lessons, Indian stories—which were used to add spice and variety to a magazine's fare. Almost all were published anonymously. Washington Irving, the author of such classic short tales as "Rip Van Winkle" and "The Legend of Sleepy Hollow," published his stories in a series of sketchbooks under a pseudonym. Titled *The Sketch Book of Geoffrey Crayon, Gent.*, Irving's stories, which came to be known simply as *The Sketch Book* or *Washington Irving's Sketch Book*, were published from 1819–1820 in seven installments.

The original impulse for published stories was didactic and moralistic. Fiction, particularly from the Puritan perspective, had an unsavory reputation. Considered a form of lying, the short story could justify its existence by its moral teaching. Stories had titles such as "The Exemplary Daughter," "Miseries of Idleness and Affluence," "The Pangs of Repentance," "The Progress of Vice," and "The Imprudent Parents." These early American short stories resembled the parable or a prose sermon, yet they also began to display what was unique in the American landscape: character and the formation of an

American identity. By the 1830s and 1840s, the short story had become a kind of laboratory for redefining narrative effects.

What was the earliest critical definition of the short story?

American nineteenth-century author Edgar Allan Poe is the short story's first great critical theorist who claimed artistic integrity for such a casual and hybrid literary form—part joke, part sketch, part sermon—insisting that the tale (or short story) deserved consideration as second only to lyric poetry as the supreme literary expression. In 1842, Poe favorably reviewed Nathaniel Hawthorne's collection of short stories, *Twice-Told Tales*. Praising the artistry of Hawthorne's stories (many of which examine the heart and soul of the Puritan experience), Poe delivered what is still considered the fundamental critique of the artistic intentions and methods of the short story.

How did Poe define the short story?

Opposing contemporary and conventional wisdom that valued the epic poem or tragedy as the supreme literary expressions, Poe contended, "The tale proper, in my opinion, affords unquestionably the fairest field for the exercise of the loftiest talent." For Poe, "unity of effect or impression is a point of the greatest importance," and such unity is simply not possible in anything that "cannot be completed at one sitting." Reading a long poem, a five-act tragedy, or a novel with frequent interruptions over many reading sessions causes the reader, in Poe's estimation, to lose focus, and the full impact of a work is diminished or diluted. Imagine someone sitting in front of you at a movie theater who interrupts the movie you are watching by frequent trips to the snack bar. How much of the impact of the film would therefore be lost? Poe mounted a similar claim for stories short enough to be read in a single sitting, without distracting interruptions. Poe argued that longer works of literature lack "the immense force derivable from totality" and insisted, "During the hour of perusal the soul of the reader is at the writer's control. There are no external or extrinsic influences—resulting from weariness or interruption."

What, according to Poe, should be the method of the short story writer?

Having made his case for the superiority of the short story, Poe goes on in his re-

Edgar Allan Poe was an American master of the short story, especially the macabre tale. Early American authors penned short stories for sale in periodicals to earn their income.

91

view to describe the methods the short story writer should follow to achieve the totality of unity and force of impression: "A skillful literary artist," according to Poe, "has not fashioned his thoughts to accommodate his incidents; but having conceived, with deliberate care, a certain unique or single effect to be wrought out, he then invents such incidents—he then combines such events as may best aid him in establishing this preconceived effect." Poe maintained that with deliberate care and craft, the short story writer should attempt to produce a certain unique or single effect. First deciding on the effect, the writer then invents and arranges incidents, characters, and details to produce a story. Everything must contribute to a pre-established design.

What are the key assumptions about the short story that emerge from Poe's analysis?

There are two:

1. Short stories operate under a principle of exclusion (Poe: "In the whole composition there should be no word written, of which the tendency, direct or indirect, is not to the one pre-established design"). Compression and intensity are produced by this exclusion by limiting the number of characters, setting, and incidents and selecting only what will contribute to the desired effect. The short story, therefore, willingly sacrifices certain elements that longer narratives, like novels, provide: fully established background of characters and incident as well as full narrative action of beginning-middle-end.

2. The short story writer must know what it is he or she is after and work toward it. Short stories must be preplanned and consciously crafted. Poe suggests that the short story writer must set out to achieve a "unity of effect or impression" and that all must contribute toward achieving this.

How does the short story compare with poetry?

Like lyric poetry, the short story restricts its attention to life in miniature: to a single situation, to something elusive or fragmentary. Unlike a novel, the short story usually does not tell a life story with multiple characters and events. Instead, a short story, like a poem, can consider a single incident. A short story usually locates its interest in a more fully developed setting and situation, but many of the same techniques used by poets, including the reliance on words and images to carry significance, equally apply in a short story. Short stories share with poetry the intensity of compression in which

How can the short story best be defined?

Poe's analysis offers some important distinctions that define the nature and the method of the short story. To clarify these distinctions, it is helpful to compare the short story to other literary genres—poetry, drama, and the novel.

every element—plot, setting, characterization, theme, imagery, symbol, voice, and tone—combines to create the unified effect of the story. As much as you should read a short story as a drama, you should also rely on skills developed in reading poetry to locate significance in a story.

How does the short story compare with drama?

The major difference between a short story and drama is that plays mostly dispense with a narrator and instead confine the focus on characters in dialogue with one another. In a short story (as in a novel), a narrator, whether a first person "I" narrator or a third person serving as an objective or omniscient narrator, directs the reader's attention, providing background to a story and commentary on the action that can include description and analysis of what a character is thinking and feeling. Drama can dispense with description because the scenes and characters are immediately visible to the audience. The analysis of characters in a play is confined to what characters say about themselves and other characters and through what is revealed about both in what they say and how they say it. Stories, like drama, are also dependent on conflict, and the crisis in a story may be between a character or characters and external forces, other characters, or within characters themselves. The same operation of conflict, climax, and resolution that drives a drama applies to most short stories as well. The key to reading and understanding short stories is to find the conflict and follow it to its climax and resolution. At the same time, you should be focused on where the significance in a story is to be found.

To understand the difference in material and method between a short story and drama, think of the difference between a five-act and a one-act play. One act has to have a unity of effect, fewer characters, and economy of action and incident. In a five-act play, a playwright can feature a host of characters, multiple settings, and several plotlines converging together.

How does the short story compare with the novel?

One way of looking at the short story is to see it as a novel in miniature. But such a view can miss what is unique and original about the short story. Unlike a novel, a short story strives to reveal character through a single action and under stress. The purpose of the story is accomplished when the reader comes to know what the true nature of a character or situation is. The novel tends to show character developing as a result of a series of actions (stressful or otherwise), gradually emerging. The pace of a novel is far more leisurely. Expansion is the prime advantage of the novel, which has many scenes, characters, incidents, and settings. Compression and intensity are the prime ingredients and advantages of the short story. The novel, as we will see in the chapter "How to Read the Novel," was created to extend artistic interest over the ordinary as well as extraordinary experience. Short stories give the writer a means of capturing fleeting experience and aspects of character and incident in depth instead of breadth. The novel (at least in the eighteenth and nineteenth centuries) is defined by its amplitude and panoramic nature—its centrifugal pressure—expanding outward in increasing detail to capture many characters and scenes over a wide expanse of narrative time. The short story reverses the process to the centripedal—featuring a contracted time period, with fewer characters and scenes.

To understand the contrast between the short story and the novel, consider the difference between painting in oil and painting in watercolor. Oil painting allows for a larger canvas in which more careful delineation is possible. Watercolors are quick drying, emphasizing immediacy of technique and less precision of depth.

What can be learned by applying Poe's principles to one of his own stories?

Let's test Poe's theories about the short story against his own practices in one of his most famous short stories, "The Tell-Tale Heart."

First, let's summarize the tale. The narrator recounts how he murdered an old man because of his pale blue, film-covered eye. On seven successive nights, he crept stealthily into the old man's room, making sure that he could not be seen. Then he would open his lantern just enough so that a single, narrow beam of light would shine on the "vulture eye" he so hated. Since the eye was never opened, however, the narrator was unable to complete his crime because his enemy was not the old man—whom he even claims to have loved—but his hideous eye. On the eighth night, however, the old man awakens and realizes that someone was in the room. The narrator remains perfectly still and silent, and for nearly an hour, he senses the old man's mounting terror. Exulting in his power, the narrator trains his light on the dreaded eye and becomes aware of a dull, thudding repetitious sound he assumes is the beating of the old man's heart. Maddened, he springs from his hiding place with a scream, pulls the old man to the floor, and throws the bed on top of him. His victim soon dies, and the narrator dismembers the corpse, which he hides beneath the floor of the old man's room. Soon after finishing his gruesome work, three policemen arrive at the door, explaining that a neighbor heard a suspicious scream during the night. The narrator tells the officers that his own bad dream caused him to scream and that the old man was away from home. He invites them to search the house, then asks them to sit down with him for a chat. He places his chair directly over the spot where the old man's remains are concealed. Initially, he is confident that the police suspect

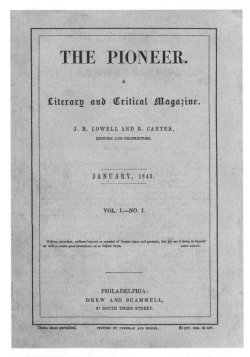

Poe's "The Tell-Tale Heart" first appeared in the January 1843 issue of *The Pioneer*.

nothing but, after they show no intention of leaving, he becomes increasingly nervous. Then the sound he had heard before, which he believed was the old man's heartbeat, begins again. In extreme agitation, the narrator begins pacing the room. His agitated talk turns to ranting and, convinced that the policemen know of his crime, he finally bursts out a confession, begging them to tear up the floorboards and discover the dismembered corpse and the "hideous heart" that torments him.

In encountering any short story for the first time, read it at least twice: the first time just to get your bearings, to identify the essential information of characters and situation; the second time paying more attention to individual details like the word choice, tone, and imagery. As a final test of your reading comprehension, write out a summary of the story, noting what happens and why and who the characters are. Try your hand at summarizing "The Tell-Tale Heart" and then compare with the following summary.

How might we analyze "The Tell-Tale Heart"?

Poe specializes in tales of psychological horror, and "The Tell-Tale Heart" is one of his most famous and most masterful short stories. Let's consider how it adheres to the principles of the short story Poe outlined in his review. First, consider Poe's "Principle of Exclusion." We can see clearly that Poe eliminates details that we might expect would be there to explain the situation and characters. Apply the famous formula for an effective newspaper article: Who, What, When, Where, and Why.

Who?

None of the characters are named here, neither the narrator, the old man, or the three policemen. Instead, we only get the most basic identifiers: the victim is an old man, and the policemen are identified only by their roles. We have nothing with which to identify the narrator, such as his age, status, or relationship with the old man.

When/Where?

Neither do we know when the events take place or where. Did the murder take place long ago or recently? The setting seems to suggest a city scene in which neighbors are close enough to hear screams, but we don't know what city. "Policemen" suggests a modern setting (police as a designator of law enforcement is a nineteenth-century invention) or at least contemporary with the story's publication date, but no details are offered to supply any more specifics of time and place.

What?

The recounting of the murder of the old man and the narrator's confession are the only activities in the story. We don't know what the relationship is between the old man and the narrator, and we don't know what happens after the narrator confesses his crime: is he now speaking from prison? Before his trial? Who exactly is he speaking to? The police interrogators? The readers? We simply do not know because Poe has eliminated any background or summary information to answer these questions.

Why?

This is clearly the most intriguing question that the story prompts: why *does* the narrator kill the old man in the first place, and why does he confess his crime to the police? The only thing we know for sure is that the narrator initially rejects the notion that he is mad and all the conventional reasons usually offered for such a crime: hatred of the old man and greed. In fact, his account of the murder and its aftermath is intended to disprove the narrator's madness and to demonstrate his sanity. Unanswered, at least explicitly, is any evidence that helps clarify motive here. There is no objective narrator to evaluate what the murderer, who may or may not be mad, is saying and why or to help our assessment as to whether the narrator has succeeded in convincing his audience that he is not mad.

Why does Poe withhold information in "The Tell-Tale Heart"?

By any standard of journalistic thoroughness, therefore, "The Tell-Tale Heart" violates all the accepted rules of specificity. Information we expect has been excluded here. Consider why. One effect of this exclusion is to force the reader to become a more active participant in deciphering the story. By omitting information, Poe enhances the suspense of the story. We don't quite know what to expect because we have so little evidence to help us anticipate the action and understand the characters. Moreover, by excluding everything but the essentials, the crime and its aftermath, Poe increases the intensity of the story. There is nothing provided that isn't essential for our understanding, nothing distracts us from the key situation of the crime and the confession. If Poe had filled in the blanks in the story with details, would the story have been better or worse? Probably worse since those details are really unnecessary in the context of the essentials provided. With so little information supplied, every detail assumes added significance. Test this statement by going back to the story and try to eliminate parts of the story. Can any be taken away without changing the story significantly or weakening its impact? How would the story have been different without the first paragraph? Without any of the subsequent paragraphs or sentences? What you begin to see is that each part of the story is there for a reason, sustaining the overall impression and unity of the story.

Having excluded all but the necessary details, does Poe achieve the "unity of effect and impression" that he insists is the goal of the short story writer?

To answer this question, consider your reaction to the story. What is unusual or striking here, and what are you left with at the end of the story?

Dominating the story from first to last is the narrator's voice. Poe made a conscious decision here to have the story told from the perspective of the murderer. What if he had chosen a different perspective, say, an omniscient narrator who could have penetrated the minds and feelings of all the characters here: the murderer, the old man, the police? Such a narration would have given us answers: what were these characters thinking

> ## How would one characterize the narrator of Poe's story?
>
> **W**e are confined to the perspective of the narrator, who speaks in nervous bursts of broken sentences, initially assuring his audience/reader that he is not insane. The story's famous first line, "True—nervous—very, very dreadfully nervous I have been and am; but why *will* you say that I am mad?", immediately and dramatically involves us in the story. It poses the central question that we must answer: is the narrator mad or isn't he? The words here support the narrator's mental instability that the narrator continues to deny throughout the remainder of the story. Instead, he insists that his careful, premeditated plan and the stealthy manner in which he carried out the murder of the old man and the dismembering and concealing of the corpse was far too clever an accomplishment for an insane man. However, every detail offered to prove his sanity instead leads the reader to the inescapable conclusion that he is completely insane.

and feeling and possibly the motive for the murder, but would the story have been better? Probably not. Poe realized here that what you leave out in a short story can be as important (even more important) than what you include. What unifies the story is Poe's skillful, unnerving depiction of the narrator's psychological state.

What does the narrator reveal?

The second paragraph of the story immediately addresses the issue of motive. The narrator states, "Object there was none. Passion there was none. I loved the old man. He had never wronged me. He had never given me insult. For his gold I had no desire." Instead of these conventional reasons for murder—vengeance, enmity, greed—the narrator offers an odd reason for the crime: "I think it was his eye! yes, it was this! He had the eye of a vulture—a pale blue eye, with a film over it. Whenever it fell upon me, my blood ran cold; and so by degrees—very gradually—I made up my mind to take the life of the old man, and thus rid myself of the eye forever." What does the narrator's obsession with the old man's eye tell us about him? For one thing, that he is fixated on a particular detail that only a madman would cite as a reason for murder. Also, the narrator reveals his premeditation ("so by degrees—very gradually"). His is not a rash act, a moment's emotional response, but a long-calculated decision brought on by a growing repulsion and horror over the old man's eye. We learn that it is really the eye that the narrator wants to kill, and each night he enters the old man's room, "just at midnight," only to find the eye closed: "But I found the eye always closed; and so it was impossible to do the work; for it was not the old man who vexed me, but his Evil Eye." The eye here becomes a symbol: it is described as both a "vulture eye" and an "Evil Eye." Both tell us something about the narrator and his psychological state. A vulture is a bird of prey that chiefly feeds on decaying flesh and reputedly appears in anticipation of the death of a sick or injured animal or person. Seeing the eye as that of a vulture suggests the narrator's paranoia as well as his sense of being a victim, perhaps unconsciously acknowledging his mental sickness. Someone with an "Evil Eye" is believed to be able to cause injury or bad luck with a look. The narrator has, therefore, attributed to the old man's eye animalistic and supernatural malevolence. That the narrator projects so much in the physical detail of the old man's eye as well as the elaborate absurdity of the nightly ritual and daily concealment of his intent underscores the narrator's mental instability and madness, despite his assertions to the contrary.

What do we learn about the murder in Poe's story?

On the fateful eighth night, the routine changes. This time, the old man is awake, and his eye can be seen:

> It was open—wide, wide open—and I grew furious as I gazed upon it. I saw it with perfect distinctness—all a dull blue, with a hideous veil over it that chilled the very marrow in my bones; but I could see nothing else of the old man's face or person: for I had directed the ray as if by instinct, precisely upon the damned spot.

Focusing his lantern light on the offending eye, the narrator, with his self-proclaimed "over-acuteness of the sense," begins to hear the beating of what he perceives to be the old man's heart. A more plausible explanation would be that the narrator is hearing his own heartbeat, accelerating as he pursues his violent intent. The story's title directs our attention to the importance of this heartbeat, and its prominence in the story begins here. Fear that the sound might be heard by neighbors causes the narrator to strike:

> But the beating grew louder, louder! I thought the heart must burst. And now a new anxiety seized me—the sound would be heard by a neighbour! The old man's hour had come! With a loud yell, I threw open the lantern and leaped into the room. He shrieked once— once only. In an instant I dragged him to the floor, and pulled the heavy bed over him. I then smiled gaily, to find the deed so far done. But, for many minutes, the heart beat on with a muffled sound. This, however, did not vex me; it would not be heard through the wall. At length it ceased. The old man was dead.

First making sure that the old man is indeed dead and the heart has stopped beating entirely, the narrator next grue-

A 1919 illustration by Harry Clarke of Poe's depicting the murder in "The Tell-Tale Heart."

somely disposes of the body, concealing the dismembered corpse under the room's floorboards.

What happens when the police arrive?

Having chronicled the crime, the narrator next reports on the consequences as the policemen arrive. Noise, presumably the old man's shrieks rather than his heartbeats, has awoken the neighbors, and the police investigate. The narrator explains how successfully he was able to deal with the police, offering plausible explanations for the noise (his own nightmare) and the absence of the old man (absent in the country). His relaxed confidence in the interview allays any suspicion from the police, and it appears that the narrator has pulled off the perfect crime: an undetected murder. However, the narrator's hearing again the beating heart causes him to confess all:

> It grew louder—louder—louder! And still the men chatted pleasantly, and smiled. Was it possible they heard not? Almighty God!—no, no! They heard!—they suspected!—they knew!—they were making a mockery of my horror!—this I thought, and this I think. But anything was better than this agony! Anything was more tolerable than this derision! I could bear those hypocritical smiles no longer! I felt that I must scream or die! and now—again!—hark! louder! louder! louder! louder!

> "Villains!" I shrieked, "dissemble no more! I admit the deed!—tear up the planks! here, here!—It is the beating of his hideous heart!"

It is the auditory hallucination of the still-beating heart of a dismembered corpse that leads to the confession of the crime, the climax of the story, and unmistakable evidence of the madness of the narrator. The supernatural here serves a psychological purpose revealing the underlying dementia of the narrator. He hears the old man's still-beating heart. A more realistic explanation is that it is the narrator's own heartbeat, accelerating from his guilt. Poe has used the story to take us inside the mind of a murderous madman with all the psychological acuity of his paranoia, projections, self-confidence, and helplessness.

The unity of effect or impression here is the psychological awareness that the reader achieves over the course of the story. One single event—the murder of the old man—serves to uncover the madness that the narrator denies but which every detail in the story asserts.

What principles about the short story does Poe's story underscore?

In reading and understanding "The Tell-Tale Heart," a couple of key principles in approaching short stories are evident:

- In a short story, assume everything is there for a purpose. Every detail, no matter how seemingly insignificant, may contribute to the significance of the story. As an attentive reader, your job is to relate each of these items to the "big picture" of what the story concerns.

- In a short story, try to determine what all of the elements in a story—setting, situation, description, conflict, resolution, imagery, symbols—are helping us to understand something unique, unusual, or provocative about human nature or the human experience.

How have authors understood the short story?

The short story is the art of the glimpse; it deals in echoes and reverberations; craftily it withholds information. Novels tell all. Short stories tell as little as they dare.

—William Trevor

A short story is a love affair; a novel is a marriage. A short story is a photograph; a novel is a film.

—Lorrie Moore

A short story is like a kiss in the dark from a stranger.

—Stephen King

I believe that the short story is as different a form from the novel as poetry is, and the best stories seem to me to be perhaps closer in spirit to poetry than to novels.

—Tobias Wolff

I'm a failed poet. Maybe every novelist wants to write poetry first, finds he can't and then tries the short story, which is the most demanding form after poetry. And failing that, only then does he take up novel writing.

—William Faulkner

In a rough way the short story writer is to the novelist as a cabinetmaker is to a house carpenter.

—Annie Proulx

Find the key emotion; this may be all you need to find your short story.

—F. Scott Fitzgerald

A short story is confined to one mood, to which everything in the story pertains. Characters, setting, time, events, are all subject to the mood. And you can try more ephemeral, more fleeting things in a story—you can work more by suggestion—than in a novel. Less is resolved, more is suggested, perhaps.

—Eudora Welty

You see I'm trying in all my stories to get the feeling of the actual life across—not to just depict life—or criticize it—but to actually make it alive. So that when you have read something by me, you actually experience the thing.

—Ernest Hemingway

What is the best way to read a short story initially?

In encountering any short story for the first time, read it at least twice: the first time just to get your bearings, to identify the essential information of characters and situation; the second time paying more attention to individual details like the word choice, tone, and imagery. As a final test of your reading comprehension, write out a summary of the story, noting what happens and why and who the characters are. Finally, answer the five key questions:

1. What is the significance of the title?
2. Why does the story begin when it does?
3. What is the story's conflict?
4. How is the conflict resolved?
5. Why does the story end when it does?

A National Medal of Arts and PEN/Faulkner Award winner, author Tobias Wolff believes that the best short stories were more like poetry than short novels.

Where should you look to understand a short story and to reveal its significance?

All writing, especially writing literature, is about making choices: what words to choose, how to organize them into sentences, how to arrange sentences into larger units (paragraphs, stanzas, chapters, etc.). A fundamental question to ask any literary text is "Why this and not that": why this work, this detail, this organization, and not some other.

Writers of literature make choices to produce both understanding and significance. In the short story, which works from Poe's principle of exclusion—excluding everything that does not contribute to the intended outcome—readers need to assume that every element in a story is potentially meaningful. Short stories require the same kind of focus on language as a poem does to reveal significance. Short story writers, like poets, depend on word choice as a fundamental resource in generating meaning and significance, and the same ways of analyzing the expressive power of language when reading poetry applies in attempting to read and understand short stories. Like poetry, short stories depend on the power of compression, creating the most from the least.

Beyond close attention to a short story's language, readers should consider the choices writers make in controlling the key elements in any story: character, plot, point of view, setting, imagery, and symbolism.

What is the appeal of plot and character in short stories?

Whenever you hear or read a story, the first things you usually pay attention to and are most interested in is what is happening in the story and to whom. Plot and character are the foundations of fiction: it is why we are attracted to reading stories in the first place. Human nature and human experience are the two grand subjects of literature. We are naturally curious about those we care about (our family and friends) and what happens to them. However, one of the basic attractions of literature is extending our view into the lives and adventures of characters who may resemble us or who cause us to re-evaluate assumptions about who we are and the world around us. Plot helps us to understand how the world works, while character helps us to test our sense of self against others.

How does plot operate in a short story?

If Poe is correct that the chief advantage of the short story is that it can be read in one sitting, it is usually the plot that guarantees we finish a story in a single sitting. The plot pushes us forward to turn the pages and find out what happens next. But what exactly is a plot?

A plot usually centers on human beings engaging in actions or being acted upon by external forces, or both. Besides physical events, stories may involve psychological developments, with the action internal within a character. Think of plot in the sense of a scheme: for example, bank robbers plotting their crime. In this sense a plot is an artful arrangement of events to help explain why characters behave in the ways they do.

What's the difference between a story and a plot?

There's a difference between a story and a plot. They may seem to be the same thing (a narrative account of some action with a beginning, middle, and end), but they aren't. A story, as opposed to a plot, is the straightforward account of everything that happens in the order that it happens. A plot is the way events are selected and arranged with an emphasis not only on what happened but on why it happened. In other words, plots involve cause and effect, not just one event following another. The English novelist E. M. Forster illustrated the difference between story and plot by this example. Here's a story: *The king died and then the queen died.* This is a succession of events, simply organized temporally: this happened and then this happened. Here's a

In Shakespeare's *Hamlet,* Claudius, the king of Denmark, and his queen, Gertrude, die in Act V (Nikolai Osipovich Massalitinov and Olga Knipper shown here in a 1911 Russian production). The difference between story and plot is that story says what happened to them, but plot explains why it happened. Without plot, the play would not be very compelling.

plot: *The king died and then the queen died of grief.* Events are now connected by cause and effect: the death of the king led to the death of the queen from grief. For Forster, a story asks "And then?" (X happens and then Y happens). A plot asks "Why?"

How do you recognize the difference between story and plot in a short story?

In many short stories, you may notice a clear discrepancy between straightforward chronological events and the revealed causal sequence of those events. In other words, plots don't have to be chronological. There may be flashbacks to earlier events, or information about past events may be withheld and then revealed. One useful exercise in understanding a short story: convert it back to its original story (the chronological sequence of events). In examining the difference between the story and the actual plot, you can learn a great deal about the author's intentions and construction of the plot. For example, why does the writer begin the story when it does? Is the chronology upended, that is, do details from the past follow present action? Does foreshadowing point toward future events? These elements reveal how straightforward stories are transformed by the choices a writer makes into meaningful plots.

Turning "The Tell-Tale Heart" back into a story, for example, would eliminate the opening paragraph of the narrator's justification of his actions, shifting it to the end of the story. The story would proceed day by day until the narrator actually murders the old man, and the reader would not know that a murder was to happen until the fateful eighth night. Instead, in Poe's plot, the confession comes first, then the murder, with the crime used to "prove" the murderer's sanity. Story as chronology is replaced with an emphasis on the why of the action, its causes and effects.

What's the importance of plot in reading a short story?

The greatest of all theorists concerning plot is the ancient Greek philosopher and critic Aristotle, whose *Poetics* is the earliest work of literary criticism. Aristotle's focus in *Poetics* is on tragic drama, but his analysis also applies to fiction. For Aristotle, plot is the primary end, or soul, of tragedy. According to Aristotle, plot is the artful "arrangement of incidents" into a beginning, middle, and end. Each should lead directly (by "causal necessity") to the next. Each part of an effective plot, each episode, is unalterable and essential, in Aristotle's view, to an impression of the whole. If an episode can be eliminated or repositioned, the plot is defective.

What can you learn about the beginning of a short story?

In reading a short story, you should always ask, why start here? Why not in some other place or at some other time? Since a short story usually deals with a single incident or a single conflict or crisis, ask, what has initiated the action? Consider the analogy of a catalyst in a chemical experiment. A catalyst is something that accelerates the rate of a chemical reaction. In a short story, a catalyst is the circumstance/event/occurrence that changes the norm. Usually, beginnings in stories establish the story's routine that will

103

be disrupted. The disruptive agent or catalyst (a stranger arrives, a challenge is identi-fied, a task is undertaken) breaks the routine and initiates the plot ("the king dies").

Try to identify (a) the norm and (b) the disruptive agent or catalyst that sets the action of the plot moving. Is the agent another character? Within a character? Is the character the victim of circumstance? Also, consider what background information is given and why. Why are the initial details of the story relevant to your understanding of the norm or what is at risk in its disruption?

What can you learn from the middle of a short story?

It is in the middle of a short story where conflicts and complications usually develop from the disrupting agent or catalyst. The conflict is the result of the circumstances identified in the beginning of the story. It might be a crucial moment in a character's life; the result of a decision made by a character that leads to a break from the status quo; a new and deeper sense of self-knowledge or self-awareness; some kind of crisis of belief that causes a person to re-examine previously held assumptions; or a value crisis in which a character is forced by circumstances to decide how to make a moral or ethical decision. Central to the middle of many short stories is suspense; that is, uncertainty over how things will turn out, who did what, what the effects on the characters or events will be, and when and how the climax will occur.

What else should you look for in the middle of a short story?

Short stories signal significance in various ways. One thing to watch for in the middle of a story is foreshadowing—an anticipation or a glimpse of things that will happen later. Foreshadowing contributes both to suspense by raising expectations and stakes and to the reader's focus on how certain details, circumstances, or characters' choices might have unintended consequences.

Another important signal of meaning that may occur in both the beginning and middle of a story is repetition—repeated elements that call attention to especially im-

What does a short story reveal, and what does it conceal?

Almost everything included in a short story is meaningful—every scene, every detail, perhaps every word. But a short story can't, nor should it, feature every-thing that happens during the series of events it is relating. Whatever is not sig-nificant to the action or a story's meaning is typically left out. Therefore, a key question to ask is what things are omitted? Great writers are careful and deliber-ate in selecting what to include. So, pay attention to the gaps (what is withheld). This will help focus your attention on the importance of what is included. Ask your-self, why feature this scene, this description, this detail? How do these elements contribute to my understanding of what this story is about and what it means?

portant aspects of the story. By these means, a short story writer underscores significance and goes beyond the literal to suggest images that become symbols—important resources for generating meaning in a story. Note any repetition of details. They could suggest a pattern in or an element of the story that carries important significance.

What can you learn about the ending of a short story?

A climax or resolution is expected in any effective ending to a short story. The climax is the peak moment of drama in which the conflict, introduced in the beginning of the story and developed in the middle, is resolved. It is the decisive turn of events when characters carry out one or more (or all) of the following significant acts: they experience a meaningful change, make a significant discovery, or learn a significant lesson.

The key question to ask is how is the conflict of the middle of the story resolved? Does the climax or resolution follow logically from the previous episodes, or is it a surprise? Does it develop naturally and plausibly from the previous events, or does it seem imposed on the characters? Does the climax seem logical or artificial? We all have experience watching a movie in which the complications are resolved plausibly, based on what we know of the characters and their circumstances. We have also probably seen films that solve their complications by arbitrary turns of fortune (a character gains an inheritance) or a coincidence (a remarkable concurrence of events without apparent causal connection). In the best films and stories, characters cause their climaxes, and the ending satisfies the reader because it seems a natural development from what has gone before. Readers should look closely at the story's climax to determine what is resolved, as well as what the climax tells you about the overall meaning of the story.

What happens after the climax of a short story?

Essential to the ending of a short story is the denouement (literally the "unknotting") of the story's complications: how the complications developed in the middle are resolved. Sometimes, a story will end abruptly with no apparent resolution. Sometimes, the denouement is left up to the reader to determine. The key question to ask is how does the story end? What has happened to the character and his/her condition that were established before the disrupting event occurred? Has the norm returned, or has some fundamental alteration ensued? How has the central character changed due to the events in the story? What lessons, if any, are offered in assessing any changes? Are those changes explicit in what is said and done or implicit, by what is not said or done, or implied by details? Are the loose ends of the story tied up satisfactorily? Simply put, are you satisfied that the ending is appropriate, given what has come before and the characters involved?

Always ask yourself: why does the story end the way it does? What does the ending reveal about a character's fate? The difference between a short story stopping abruptly and an effective ending is that the latter gives a sense of completeness and leaves you satisfied that you have gained some significant knowledge of human nature and the human experience. You may want to know more about these characters and their progress (or lack of progress), but the journey you have taken with them still seems to you worth your time and energy.

Questions to Ask for Understanding Plot

1. What initially defines the norm in the story, that is, the situation that will be disrupted?
2. What is the disruptive agent or the catalyst for the action in the story, such as the arrival of a new character, an event/situation that requires a response, a journey, a choice?
3. How does this disruption illuminate the conflict in the story? What is the conflict?
4. How is the conflict resolved? What event or action brings about the resolution of the conflict?

How do characters compare to plot in importance for understanding a short story?

If our most important interest in hearing or reading a story is "What happened," our next most important question is likely "To whom?" Aristotle ranked character in the secondary position after plot in his listing of the most important elements in tragedy, contending that you could still have an effective tragedy even if the characters were not as interesting or as artfully developed as the plot. But most of us want both an interesting story and characters we can identify with or are intrigued by. In fact, it is somewhat simplistic even trying to separate plot from character, to separate the story's actions and the people involved in carrying them out.

Characters, the created persons who appear or are referred to in all stories, can be literature's greatest attraction. Literature offers us the opportunity to learn about and imaginatively enter the lives of people we would otherwise never encounter, to understand their lives and situations, and to sympathize, even empathize, with them. We have all heard criticism of stories in which the critic praised, more than anything else, identification with the characters. This means that the skillful writer managed to create in a character's portrait a mirror in which readers could see something of themselves.

How does a writer create characters?

Characterization refers to the methods and techniques a writer uses to represent people and to enable us to know and relate to them. Here are some of the most important means of characterization to pay attention to:

While Aristotle felt that plot was more important than character for a story, most authors since then would agree that characters that are not two dimensional are essential to make a tale come to life.

106

Telling—The most direct method of characterization is when we are simply told by the story's narrator what the characters are like as they are first introduced or gradually as they reappear in the story.

Showing—What a character is like can come out through the character's actions, which may be presented without interpretive comment from a narrator, leaving the reader to conclude what a character is like from what she or he does. To only tell what a character is like is often less effective than showing a character in action.

Saying—What a character is like can be brought out by having other characters say things about him or her. Be careful, however. What a character says depends on how those characters relate to one another. It's a subjective view and may be biased and even unreliable. A great deal can also be learned about a character by what she or he says. Dialogue (conversation between characters) is a crucial characterization technique. Pay attention to what characters say to one another, how they say things, as well as what they don't say.

Entering a Character's Mind—What a character is like can be revealed through his or her thoughts or feelings. A writer sometimes takes us directly into a character's mind, directly reporting what a character thinks or feels, or through first-person narration in which a character can tell us what she or he was thinking or feeling. Choosing how to narrate a story is one of the most important decisions a writer can make, and the reader always needs to consider who is telling the story and how.

Motivation—Besides knowing what characters are like, we want to know why they make the decisions and choices they do. This important aspect of characterization is motivation: the reasons, explanations, or justifications behind a character's behavior. Motivation usually grows out of a sense of what characters deeply want or desire and how that leads them to act in specific situations.

Consistency—A great deal is revealed about characters by the way in which they handle situations, especially difficult, problematic, or tragic situations or relationships. For characters to be plausible, they must be consistent in the way they deal with circumstances. If they respond to a situation one way at one time and differently at another, there must be clear reasons for the difference, that is, their inconsistency must be understandable and believable.

What types of characters are featured in short stories?

Short stories make use of characters in varying degrees of complexity and importance. Here are some useful distinctions in considering characters:

Round/Flat—The English novelist E. M. Forster originated the terms *round* and *flat* to distinguish the differences in complexity among characters. Round characters are multidimensional, multisided, complex, and, therefore, often challenging to understand. They may act inconsistently, at times contradictorily, forcing the reader to reconcile their seemingly incompatible ideas or behaviors. Round characters are also dynamic in that they are shown changing and growing because of what happens to

107

them. A round character may appear differently at the end of the story than at the beginning as a result of actions taken or insights achieved. Flat characters are generally less fully developed than round characters. Compared to the more organic round characters, flat characters are more functional and mainly serve to facilitate the plot. They are usually more static, not shown as changing, and are represented through only one or two main personality features or traits. Unlike round characters, they rarely surprise us: what you see is usually what you get. Flat characters are not necessarily liabilities in a story. A character with only one or two traits can still be interesting and add to the meaning of a story, while not claiming as much interest or importance as the round character.

Major/Minor—Major characters in a story are usually round or dynamic, while minor characters are usually flat. Minor characters are sometimes stock characters, stereotypes easily recognized from popular convention and frequent use (for example, the absent-minded professor, the femme fatale, the loyal sidekick). In a short story, there is rarely the time to develop more than one character in a rounded way. Look for the role minor characters play in acting upon or bringing out the major character. They can be obstacles to the main character's desires or foils to contrast with the major character.

Hero/Villain—The conventional distinction between hero and villain, good guy and bad guy, is less effective in describing characters in modern short stories than in older melodramatic works that depend on characters that easily fit into unmistakable moral categories of good and evil. Characters, particularly in modern short stories, tend to contain elements of both hero and villain battling internally for preeminence. While it is certainly possible to describe characters as heroic and villainous, characters in short stories, more often than not, defy simple moral categories.

Protagonist/Antagonist—These terms (derived from the Greek "first combatant" and "opponent or competitor") describe important relationships between characters. The protagonist referred to the first actor in a Greek tragedy and, therefore, its central character. The antagonist is the character (or force) opposed to the protagonist that leads to

Even though a character such as Darth Vader from the "Star Wars" films is seen as pure evil, a back story is given to the character to make him more than a two dimensional film. Modern fiction tends to stay away from melodramatic stereotypes.

the central conflict of the story. In examining any story, it is useful to identify the protagonist and antagonist and to localize the central conflict and its resolution that determines their fates.

What questions should one ask to best understand characters in short stories?

1. What key traits are supplied in the story to help understand the characters? (These could be something said about the character by the narrator or another character or something the character says/thinks/does.)

2. Is the character defined by only one or two traits or by several? Are they contradictory? Is there a contradiction between what a character says or thinks and what he or she does?

3. Does the character change over the course of the story? From what to what, and what causes any change?

4. Are there any insights gained by the character over the course of the story? What are they?

5. What are the roles or functions of other characters in the story? Do they serve as obstacles or foils to the central character? Do they help to focus on the story's central conflict?

"THE GIFT OF THE MAGI"

How do I read O. Henry's "The Gift of the Magi" for plot and character?

To see how plot and character is handled by a master storyteller, read O. Henry's famous 1906 story "The Gift of the Magi." Read the story at least twice, and at the end of your second reading, write out a summary and compare it to the summary that follows.

What is the plot of "The Gift of the Magi"?

On Christmas Eve in a shabby city apartment, Della Young is crying because she has only $1.87 to buy a Christmas present for her beloved husband, Jim. The impoverished couple's only treasures are Della's beautiful chestnut hair and the gold watch that once belonged to Jim's father and grandfather. Della suddenly comes to a decision and leaves the flat. She enters a dry goods shop and sells her hair for twenty dollars. After searching for several hours, Della finally locates a present she considers worthy of her husband: a simple but elegant platinum chain for his watch. Returning home, Della curls her shorn hair, hoping that Jim will love her just as well with her new hairstyle. When Jim arrives, he looks at his wife in stunned silence. Della explains that she has sold her hair so that she could buy him a Christmas present. Jim embraces her and finally explains that he too has a present for her: the expensive tortoiseshell combs she has long admired, which would be perfect for her long hair. Della is nevertheless delighted with her gift and reminds Jim that her hair grows quickly. Then she presents the watch chain to Jim, only to learn that to buy the combs, Jim has sold his gold watch.

How does O. Henry's story share Poe's "exclusion principle"?

Like Poe, O. Henry, which was the pen name of William Sydney Porter (1862–1910), was a master of compression and exclusion, including only the key details to create the story's atmosphere and central situation. "The Gift of the Magi" begins, symbolically, on Christmas Eve, with Della fretting over her lack of money to buy her husband a Christmas present. As Della sobs, the narrator takes the reader on a brief tour of the Youngs' $8-per-week flat, emphasizing their impoverishment. The "shabby couch," the useless letterbox, and the broken electric doorbell are all vivid details of the couple's financial decline, particularly contrasting with the rather aristocratic name: Mr. James Dillingham Young. We learn that the "'Dillingham' had been flung to the breeze during a former period of prosperity when its possessor was being paid $30 per week." That salary has contracted to $20 a week, leaving but $12 per week after the rent is paid. Without wasting too many words, O. Henry conveys clearly to the reader what kind of life the Youngs are living and the challenges they face. Without these details, we will not understand the issues involved in the action of the story.

Rising up from her sobbing over her lack of funds to buy Jim a present, Della looks into the pier-glass mirror, and the narrator focuses on her long, cherished, chestnut hair, along with Jim's gold watch, the only two treasures that the couple possess. Making a decision, Della hurries out, and the first movement, or the beginning of the story, is concluded.

What do we learn from the beginning of the story?

The norm is set with an accounting that defines the Youngs' present, impoverished circumstances: once more prosperous, they now reside in a shabby apartment flat on an income that has only managed a surplus of $1.87 after scrimping and saving. What's the disrupting agent or catalyst for the action in the story? It's the Christmas holiday with its tradition of exchanging presents. If the story did not take place during Christmas, there would be no urgency for her to gain more money for a gift. Della would like to give Jim a Christmas present, but she hasn't enough money to do so. What will she do?

The beginning of the story, therefore, establishes the norm of the couple's poverty and the disruptive situation (Christmas) that require some response, some action to be taken. An obstacle has been introduced that needs to be overcome. Della first responds with tears over her seemingly hopeless situation but then clearly makes a decision that causes her to leave the flat. Her deadlock over her lack of funds is replaced with movement outside the apartment. We don't know yet what she has decided or where she is going, just that some plan is underway, some decisive action whose consequence is yet to be discovered. Note that we have a plot here, not just a sequence of chronological events. Della leaves the flat, caused by her predicament. Cause (Della's lack of funds for a gift) leads to effect (she takes some action to remedy her situation), and the story's plot begins. It's not "This happens and then this happens" but "This happens because this happens."

What about the middle and the end of the story?

The middle movement of the story is what Della does in response to her predicament and its results. We learn that her solution to her crisis of a lack of funds is to sell her treasured hair to Madame Sofronie for $20, enough to buy Jim a platinum chain for his gold watch. Della's solution establishes a conflict and suspense: how will Jim react to her new hairstyle, to the loss of one of their two treasured possessions? Della sits waiting for Jim's return, and, after he arrives, O. Henry delays giving us Jim's full reaction to aid the suspense. By the end of the story, we know clearly why Jim is so shocked at his wife's new appearance. The combs he has purchased after selling his watch are now useless. Seeing things mainly from Della's point of view, we, like her, suspect only that Jim is disappointed by how his wife now looks. Eventually, the suspense over Jim's reaction is ended by him saying:

> "Don't make any mistake, Dell," he said, "about me. I don't think there's anything in the way of a haircut or a shave or a shampoo that could make me like my girl any less. But if you'll unwrap that package you may see why you had me going a while at first."

Unwrapping the package, Della discovers the combs and the explanation of Jim's stunned reaction. All is not yet lost because, as Della says, "My hair grows so fast, Jim!" It is only when Della gives Jim his present that the story's climax occurs. To buy the combs, Jim has sold his watch (not something that will grow back), making the gift of the platinum chain useless.

How does O. Henry arrange the climax?

O. Henry has saved the information about Jim's similar conflict over a lack of funds to buy a present for Della until the very end of the story as the couple in the story's climax is forced to face the consequence of their similar decisions: they have both sacrificed their treasures to buy a gift for the other that is no longer needed. The combs cannot be displayed in Della's short hair, and the watch chain has no watch to display. However, O. Henry saves his final surprise for the end of the story. The consequence of the conflict over the Youngs' lack of money for Christmas gifts seems frustratingly ironic and heartbreaking. Both characters have solved the obstacle they face by selling their personal treasures for gifts for each

O. Henry was one of the most talented short story writers America has ever produced as evidenced by his famous tale "The Gift of the Magi," a masterpiece of literary craftsmanship.

111

other, gifts that make no sense without those treasures. This could, therefore, be a story of despair, of how the best of intentions are undone, but it isn't. Della and Jim's true treasures are not the watch or the hair but the love each has expressed by their generosity on behalf of the other. The story ends reminding the reader why gifts are given at Christmas in the first place and comparing those first gift-givers, the Magi, to Della and Jim:

> The Magi, as you know, were wise men—wonderfully wise men—who brought gifts to the baby Jesus in the manger. They invented the art of giving Christmas presents. Being wise, their gifts were no doubt wise ones, possibly bearing the privilege of exchange in case of duplication. And here I have lamely related to you the uneventful chronicle of two foolish children in a flat who most unwisely sacrificed for each other the greatest treasures of their house. But in a last word to the wise of these days, let it be said that of all who give gifts, these two were the wisest. Of all who give and receive gifts, such as they are wisest.

> Everywhere they are wisest. They are the Magi.

How does the story end?

The story ends by asking the reader to consider how "the uneventful chronicle of two foolish children in a flat who most unwisely sacrificed for each other the greatest treasures of their house" are in fact "the wisest" and "are the Magi." O. Henry doesn't explain exactly why this is the case, leaving it up to the reader to agree or disagree. The Magi gave precious gifts to a humble baby born in a stable whom they perceived to be the son of God, an embodiment of ultimate spiritual values. The Magi were called "The Wise Men" because they recognized great significance and worth despite the humble setting of the stable where the baby rested. In this story, Jim and Della similarly recognize the significance and value of the other despite their own humble setting. Their gifts, like those of the Magi, are the sacrifice of what is most precious to each for the other, an act of love and generosity that O. Henry suggests is their greatest present and greatest treasure. The realization of what really matters, their love, not their possession, is the source of their wisdom.

O. Henry's conclusion here only works if the plot connects with characterization. Della and Jim need to be selflessly devoted to each other for the story to have its happy ending. If they were more selfish, they would not have sold their most prized possessions in the first place; neither would they have reacted the way they did on learning that they had each sacrificed the object of each of their gifts. There are no recriminations or expressions of regret or self-pity. Jim dismisses the potential tragedy of the situation in a few reassuring words:

> "Dell," said he, "let's put our Christmas presents away and keep 'em a while. They're too nice to use just at present. I sold the watch to get the money to buy your combs. And now suppose you put the chops on."

Jim here signals what is more important than the gifts: their domestic life together, in other words, their love and devotion to one another that is far more important than any gift or any lost physical treasure. Throughout the story, O. Henry carefully provides details that foreshadow Jim's generosity here and the couple's love for one another that supports O. Henry's final assertion of their wisdom. At the very beginning of the story, Della is upset at having so little money to buy Jim a gift, not for anything for herself. Seeing the worth of her long hair, her most prized possession, Della willingly sacrifices it out of generosity. We learn that Jim was never late coming home from work, suggesting his eagerness for Della's company and his consistency. He assures Della that no alteration of her appearance "could make me like my girl any less," and he quickly dismisses the selling of his watch, perhaps to spare the feelings of his wife. All these details establish the couple's loving and generous relationship that helps to explain O. Henry's final assertion about Jim and Della's wisdom.

What about the characterization in the story?

It should be said, however, that neither Della nor Jim are complex characters. They don't change over the course of the story. Instead, they are consistent in their behavior based on the two major traits that define them: love and generosity. For a story to be effective, fully rounded characters with mixed character traits of strengths and weaknesses are not always essential. Instead, believability is needed. Do Della and Jim seem too good to be true? If so, O. Henry's story runs the risk of being more a sentimental fairy tale rather than a plausible dramatization of human nature and the human experience. The more believable a story is, the more the events seem possible and the characters credible, the more likely the reader will respond to the events with interest and empathize with the characters.

How is meaning affected by point of view in a short story?

Next to the arrangement of story into a plot and characterization, the way in which a story is narrated—its point of view—is crucial for our understanding of it. Point of view is a key choice a writer makes, one with serious consequences in how we make sense of the story and arrive at its significance. Think of point of view like the camera's position in a film for recording the action. What kind of camera angle works best? And why? Is the camera far above the action to capture the entire scene or close up to focus on a particular detail or character's reactions? Does the camera angle shift from one perspective to another or stay focused in one place or through the perspective of a single character? These questions, applied to a short story's point of view, will help to guide your understanding of the story and help you gain valuable insights on the overall focus of the story and its meaning.

What are the key distinctions to consider when evaluating the point of view in a short story?

- Who is the narrator? Determining a story's point of view starts with who is telling the story. Does the story use a first-person or "I" narrator or a third-person or "he or she" narrator? Is the narrator named or unnamed? Does the narrator participate in the action as a major or minor character, or does the narrator observe and record the action, looking on only from the outside? Does an unidentified voice relate what happens from outside the events, or is it someone able to tell us what one or more characters is thinking and feeling?

- Where is the narrator? Equally important to identifying the narrator in a story is the narrative vantage point. Again, think of this in terms of a camera angle. Is the camera positioned to show everything? Or is it limited to selected details or perspectives, showing only what a single character could see? Does the perspective enter the mind or feelings of a character? Does the perspective shift? In a story, you might be told everything that is going on inside and outside a character so that you know all that happens and the reasons why. Or you can see everything from the outside but nothing from the inside, so you must deduce the characters' motivations, thoughts, and feelings for yourself. Or your perspective can be restricted to what only one character sees and believes. Finally, you can be told things from different perspectives as the story progresses, sometimes switching back and forth. Each of these options has its own benefits and consequences and affects the reader's understanding of the story.

- When is the story? Stories allow perspective in time as well as space. Unlike film, which usually shows events as they are occurring, stories necessarily relate events after they have happened. As you read, you need to ask to what degree is the narrator looking back on past events. Are they recent or from the distant past? Can you tell how long ago? Does it matter how much time has passed? Does the narrator tell things differently now from the way he or she saw it earlier? Does the narrator's knowledge of all that happened inform how he or she narrates the story? In other words, does the narrator foreshadow the outcome of the story? Or are key pieces of information withheld? For what purpose?

The questions of Who, Where, and When in a story's narration are key decisions that the writer makes that greatly affect how you read a story and how you understand its significance.

Ask of a story: why this perspective and not another? How is the story changed if another point of view is employed, from a different character, angle, time, or place? By asking these questions, you should be able to gain a better understanding of the outcome the writer was attempting to gain by choosing the narrative method selected.

Point of view—through whose eyes the reader views a story—has a significant effect on how a story can be interpreted.

What are the advantages and disadvantages of first-person narration?

A first-person point of view is identified by the narrator's use of "I" or "we" in telling the story. First-person narration takes us back to the origin of storytelling as oral performance. We have all experienced someone telling us a story, whether a friend or family member. The advantages of this type of narration are credibility, sympathy, and intimacy. Hearing a story told directly by someone generally enhances its believability. We may know the person well and may believe him or her to be trustworthy and therefore credible. A first-person narrator can enhance credibility by appearing to be genuine and honest. The first-person narrator can also confess important thoughts and feelings, giving us an intimate view of the speaker's motivation and desires. In a story, this first-person technique enhances the possibility of identification and sympathy with the narrator, who seems to be talking directly to us and sharing his or her most intimate secrets. First-person narration also increases intensity, moving the vantage point closer to the action and the participants. A first-person narrator is usually directly involved in what is being narrated, while a third-person narrator is further removed, like the difference between an eyewitness testimony and a summary of that testimony.

First-person narration, however, is necessarily limited. It can only tell about what the narrator experiences or observes. It cannot penetrate other characters' minds or feelings, and it may not fully know the implications of what is experienced. A first-person narrator might be too limited by naiveté, bias, age, inexperience, prejudice, or knowledge to understand or appreciate the implications of what she or he is talking about. With these limitations, the reader, who may understand more than the narrator, needs to be alert not to miss the implications that the narrator cannot grasp. An active reader of a story narrated in the first person must always be attentive to the discrepancy between what the narrator says and what is happening because the gap between the two can be revealing.

Since a first-person narrator is limited and subjective, there is always an issue of trustworthiness at play in this kind of narration. If the narrator tells the story accurately and honestly (as far as we can tell), the narrator appears reliable. We can believe or trust what is said. However, in some cases, we may suspect that a narrator is not telling the whole truth or is distorting some things, perhaps deliberately to make them look better or to justify behavior or unintentionally because of the limitations of the narrator's understanding or sympathies. The reader, therefore, needs to try to determine what can be trusted and when to raise questions and make allowances or corrections in what we are being told. Again, ask yourself why this particular narrator? How would the story be different with another choice?

What are the advantages and disadvantages of third-person narration?

One way of moving beyond the subjective, limited, and possibly unreliable vantage point of first-person narration is to employ a third-person narrator, a story's objective guide who is not confined to a limited consciousness or perspective and is presumably not biased toward or against a character or outcome. A third-person narrator is not involved in the story as a participant, is therefore without an apparent vested interest in any outcome, and appears more objective and trustworthy than a first-person narrator. Third-person narrators can appear like scientists observing an experiment, carefully recording exactly what is happening and why. This kind of narration may sacrifice intimacy since the scientist must be detached and above the action to record it all.

There are various types of third-person narration, each with its advantages and disadvantages:

- *Third-Person Omniscient Narration.* When a story is told by an external narrator who seems to know everything about the events (both present and past) and is capable of seeing into the minds and hearts of more than one character, the point of view is referred to as third-person omniscient (that is, "having unlimited knowledge"). The advantage of third-person narration, beyond its reliability, is flexibility. Imagine a film shot only from the perspective of a single character versus multiple cameras capturing the action from multiple points of view, both inside and outside several characters. At times, such a narrator can describe what happens or what characters are like from the outside, either objectively or by conveying opinions about them. At other points, the narrator may relate things from within the perspective of one character or tell what that character or other characters are thinking, feeling, or experiencing.

Keep in mind, however, that omniscient point of view doesn't mean the narrator must tell the reader everything about the events or all of the characters. No story can tell everything that happened nor record everyone's full reactions. Just because the narrator can see into every character doesn't mean the narrator will do so. An omniscient narrator will usually reveal the thoughts or feelings of only a few characters but not all of them. The omniscient narrator might also withhold crucial information, offering it later or not at all. This means that the omniscient narrator voluntarily limits what she or he relates. The third-person narrator could and does go inside characters to reveal their thoughts and feelings but does not always have to do so.

- *Third-Person Limited and Objective.* An omniscient third-person narrator has the flexibility to tell a story from multiple perspectives but does not have to. Limited omniscience in a third-person narration is called third-person objective point of view or third-person limited point of view. In third-person objective narration, the narrator does not penetrate the minds of any of the characters or explain why any of the characters do what they do. The narrator describes events only from the outside, leaving it to the reader to draw conclusions from the details and dialogue provided. In third-person limited point of view, the narration is purposely limited to a single perspective.

- *Free Indirect Discourse.* This is a type of third-person narration in which an omniscient narrator renders the thoughts of another character without the intervening "he said" or "she thought," embedding a character's speech or thoughts directly into an otherwise third-person narrative. Such a narrative allows the writer to slip in and out of a character's consciousness while eliminating the boundaries between third- and first-person narration and taking advantage of the principal asset of first-person narration—intimate access—and the greatest asset of third-person narration—reliability. The writer can, in this way, render a character from the inside without being permanently tied to that perspective. Pioneered by writers like Johann Goethe, Jane Austen, and Gustave Flaubert, free indirect discourse is frequently employed in the modern short story by writers as diverse as James Joyce and Elmore Leonard.

How should the reader assess third-person narration?

When you are considering the kind of third-person narration a writer chooses, ask yourself why a writer might prefer omniscient, objective, or limited narration. What is gained? What is lost? A writer may prefer third-person omniscience to make sense of a complex story, making sure the reader is fully informed about several characters' motives and behavior. A third-person objective narration might be preferred to increase the reader's engagement in a story. If readers are not told what a character is thinking or feeling, we must answer those questions for ourselves, based on the evidence supplied. We, therefore, are forced to become more active readers, rather than passive recipients of information. By withholding key information, by choosing third-person limited narration, surprises are possible. The writer who uses third-person limited narration might also want to focus exclusively on the developing perspective of a single, central character rather than the complete perspective of several characters or with the meaning and significance of every action clearly known and presented. By employing free indirect discourse, a writer might want to achieve the intimacy and authenticity of first-person narration, while retaining the ability to go beyond its limitations.

Checklist for Reading for Point of View

- ☑ Notice who is telling the story (the narrator) and the point of view (the perspective or vantage point) from which the story is told.
- ☑ If first person, access the degree of naïveté and reliability.
- ☑ If first person, are there any gaps or discrepancies between what the narrator says and what the evidence of the story reveals?
- ☑ If third person, is it omniscient (all-knowing, often anonymous reporter), third-person objective (a reporter of words and actions but not thoughts or motives), third-person limited (a partially knowing observer or participant), or a combination of third- and first-person narration (free indirect discourse).
- ☑ Consider the impact of the choice of point of view, narration, and perspective. What is achieved by the narrative method selected? What is sacrificed? How does the method of narration help frame the point or significance of the story?

What are the other elements in a short story that communicate significance and meaning?

If plot, characterization, and point of view constitute the essential building blocks of any story, meaning and significance are signaled in several other ways, which need to be considered by an active reader looking to understand a story fully. All creative writers convert abstract ideas into specific details. The challenge for the reader is to convert those specifics back into meaning so that the details of the story are transformed into universal relevance. This means that the story of a specific character in a unique series of actions must express significance beyond itself to be interesting or engaging. Think about a story you might tell to someone about something that happened to you. This story is, of course, interesting to you because it happened to you. But how can you make it interesting to someone else? How can you convert the specifics of your story to relevance for someone else? How do you go from the particular to the universal? This is the central challenge in all literature.

A third-person, omniscient narrator is rather like a god overseeing not only the actions in the story but also the thoughts and feelings of all the characters. Through the narrator, the reader, too, sees all that is happening.

One way to do this is to load every aspect of the story with significance so that a reader better sees beyond the specifics to important meaning. To reach meaning in a story, writers make full use of all the details available to them. Recalling Poe's prescription for a successful short story, a masterful storywriter wastes nothing and excludes everything that does not contribute to the story's effect and meaning. Readers should assume that *everything* in a story has a purpose. Let's consider key details in the specifics of a story and how they generate meaning and significance.

What can be learned from a short story's setting?

Stories are usually orientated in a specific place and time. Characters are generally seen in a particular setting. In some stories, the setting is barely noticeable; in others, setting can become a force in the plot and can even create the conflict. A story can, for example, test a character in nature as in Jack London's "To Build a Fire" or Stephen Crane's "The Open Boat." In such cases, the setting becomes the antagonist, producing the conflict that the human character must overcome and affecting the development of those characters. The way in which characters cope with their settings can often become a major component of the story. Do they accommodate themselves to their environments or struggle against their environments?

In evaluating any story, examine where the action of the story takes place. Is it an exterior or an interior setting? Urban or rural? Peaceful or threatening? Look closely for the details that signal the specifics of a story's setting. What evidence is supplied to allow you to understand and visualize the setting? What impact does the setting have on the characters and the conflict? Ask yourself how the story might be different in a different setting? Contrasting settings are also important: Does the setting shift significantly from one place to another? What is the impact of the shift of setting and its implication on the story and the characters?

As important as *where* a story takes place is *when* a story occurs. The specific or approximate time for the action of a story can be indicated explicitly or implicitly (by reference to a historical event, for example, or by descriptions of the way people talk, act, or dress). When a story takes place is often based solely on when the story was written or published as much as by telling details or obvious dating. This historical basis provides insights into characters' attitudes and circumstance and prevents anachronistic interpretations: attributing contemporary values to past periods when issues of gender, race, and class markedly differed from today's values.

Look closely at the setting in a story and consider the implications of when and where the action happens. Does the setting tell us anything important about the characters? Does it help clarify what the characters are like and the circumstances they are facing?

Setting can also be crucial in evoking atmosphere, that is, the mood or emotional tone that surrounds and permeates the story. A setting on a deserted country road on a stormy night contributes to apprehension in characters and readers alike. The same setting on a fresh, spring day establishes different associations that the story may gratify or challenge. The atmosphere of a story helps to establish a story's tone—the way writers convey attitudes toward the story. Is the story's tone hopeful or anxious? Should you expect a positive or a negative outcome? Writers can raise these questions by calling attention to the details of the setting. An active reader needs to be attentive to the implications of these details.

As you consider setting in any story, watch for connections to other aspects of the story, such as characters, conflicts, or actions. Master storytellers, following Poe's exclusion advice, rarely describe anything just for the sake of description. Rather, you should assume that details like setting matter greatly in generating significance in a story and try to arrive at how the setting contributes to a story's meaning.

What can be learned from the images stories use?

Just as in poetry, one of the most important resources a writer has is the power of visualization through imagery—the details that help the reader see, hear, smell, touch, and even taste the particulars in a story. Through its imagery, the abstract and the general in a story become concrete and specific. It is how a story begins to live in our minds as a felt experience rather than just recounted facts. The great fiction writer Joseph Conrad (1857–1924) famously declared, "My task which I am trying to achieve is, by the power of the written word, to make you hear, to make you feel—it is, above all, to make you see.

That—and no more, and it is everything." To make the reader see, writers like Conrad supply sensory details, or images, to aid our visualization. The active reader of a short story needs to be alert for these details and how they serve both to bring a story to life and contribute to its meaning.

If Poe is correct in asserting that in a masterful story every detail supports the desired effect of the story, then you should pay attention to each detail, no matter how trivial it may seem, for its impact. In this way, everything in a story is potentially both itself and something beyond itself, that is, both surface detail and symbol.

How do symbols operate in a short story?

A story's symbol represents both itself and suggests more significance than its literal meaning alone. A symbol in a story may be an object, a character, or an action. We are surrounded by symbols every day: a red traffic light immediately communicates stop. A wedding ring is more than just a piece of jewelry because of what it signifies about a couple's devotion and commitment. A hundred-dollar bill, which is literally a piece of often soiled paper, stands for so much more.

Polish-British author Joseph Conrad used imagery in his fiction to try to make his readers feel as if they were in the story. For Conrad, to make his readers "see ... is everything."

Conventional symbols—the Christian cross, the Muslim star and crescent, the Jewish Star of David, or a nation's flag—communicate symbolic meanings widely. Conventional symbols might also include things that have gained traditional meanings: winter, the setting sun, and, at least in Western culture, the color black all can suggest or symbolize death or loss, while spring, the rising sun, and green evoke associations of life, youth, and new beginnings. Writers often use conventional symbols such as these to reinforce meaning in their stories. They also employ what are called literary symbols, or unique, specific details that the larger context of the story elevates to the prominence of meaning beyond the literal.

Symbols, whether conventional or literary, usually convey multiple possible meanings. Careful readers should not reduce them to a single, definite meaning. Instead, in discussing symbols, it's best to avoid saying "X = Y." Instead, say "X may *represent* Y" since we can never be certain what exactly a writer intended in the use of a symbol or exactly what one meaning a symbol communicates since a symbol, by its nature, has multiple meanings.

How can you recognize a symbol?

Even though almost anything can take on symbolic significance, not every object, character, or action in a story needs to be symbolic. Details can still be important and essential in a story without becoming symbols, serving functional rather than symbolic importance. Sometimes, a surface detail is just that: a surface detail and no more. It is not necessary to force every detail in the story to do double service as both detail and symbol. Readers should always consider: What does this detail add to the story? Why is it included? Is it there functionally, to help the reader visualize the setting or the action, or does it suggest even more significance?

A key test for symbolic status of any detail in a story is its prominence. Objects that are mentioned repeatedly, described in detail, or appear in noticeable or strategic positions (at the beginning or end, in the title, or at a crucial moment) may point toward a meaning beyond themselves and therefore become symbols.

In assessing the symbolic in a story, it is wise to consider what Ernest Hemingway said about symbols in his stories:

> No good book has ever been written that has in it symbols arrived at beforehand and stuck in. That kind of symbol sticks out like raisins in raisin bread. Raisin bread is all right, but plain bread is better. I tried to make a real old man, a real boy, a real sea and a real fish and real sharks. But if I made them good and true enough they would mean many things. The hardest thing is to make something really true and sometimes truer than true.

Hemingway suggests that readers should assume the literal first and let the story dictate additional associations. If you suspect that a detail might serve as a symbol in a story, ask yourself whether that interpretation is plausible within the context of the story. Can you find other evidence, other details to support your interpretation? Does the potential symbol meet the test of prominence (in placement or repetition)? Short stories are not coded messages that need to be deciphered. Skillful writers usually let the meaning of a story and details that become symbolic grow out of the story's circumstances organically rather than be added onto a story. If you cannot find other details in the story that help to clarify the association you think may be suggested, then you may be misinterpreting a surface detail for a symbol. Ultimately, a symbol needs to make sense based on the evidence in the story.

Checklist for Reading for Setting and Symbol

☑ Be attentive to setting in a literary work:
- Setting in terms of place both in its broad sense and in its sense of narrower, individual places
- Setting in time
- Setting as historical, social, and cultural context

☑ Be aware of the different effects setting can have in a work, whether it reveals character, conveys atmosphere, reinforces meaning, or serves as a symbol or occasionally almost as a character.

☑ Be able to explain the difference between an image or action or character that is only itself and one used as a symbol (an image or action or character that also embodies an idea).

☑ Know the formal devices commonly used for indicating that an image, action, or character may be a symbol: repetition, description, prominent placement (title, beginning, ending, climactic scene), or a sense of weightiness or significance beyond the literal function in the work. Be able to use those signals to perceive when a work is using symbols.

"THE STORY OF AN HOUR"

How do you use plot, character, point of view, setting, imagery, and symbolism to interpret a short story?

Let's bring together all the key elements of short stories we have discussed and which writers employ to generate meaning in their stories—plot, character, point of view, setting, imagery, and symbolism—in an analysis of Kate Chopin's "The Story of an Hour."

First read the story at least twice, then write out a summary indicating the major characters and situation in the story. Compare your summary with that below.

What is the plot of "The Story of an Hour" by Kate Chopin?

Chopin (1850–1904) writes of the surprising end of Mrs. Mallard, a young, married woman with a heart condition. Her sister, Josephine, informs her delicately that her husband, Brently, has been killed in a railroad disaster. After weeping in her sister's arms, Mrs. Mallard retreats to her upstairs room to be alone. There, she notices the signs of spring outside, and her shock and grief turn to feelings of new possibilities that her life now offers her. She begins to say to herself over and over, "Free, free, free!" Eventually, she leaves her room, descending the stairs, where her sister and her husband's friend Richards are waiting at the bottom. Suddenly, the front door opens to reveal Brently Mallard, who had never been on the doomed train. The doctors decide that Louise Mallard died because of heart failure, "of the joy that kills," brought on by the happy news of her husband's return.

How do you read this story for plot?

Start your analysis with where the writer begins, with the story's title and the initial situation that establishes the crisis or conflict that arises. The title, "The Story of an Hour," focuses the reader's attention on the very brief period in which several crucial things happen: Mrs. Mallard learns of the death of her husband, Brently, reassesses her life as a wife and now as a widow, and dies from shock at the surprise return of her husband. Notice that the story opens not with details about the Mallards' married life or specifics about the setting but the single detail that Mrs. Mallard was "afflicted with a heart trouble." This necessitates the care her sister Josephine takes in breaking the news of the railroad disaster and Brently being on a list of the killed, "in broken sentences; veiled hints that revealed in half concealing." The disruptive agent or catalyst for the story is the information of Brently's death that needs to be delivered to Mrs. Mallard. Her heart condition, affecting the way in which everyone needs to behave toward her so that her heart is not further weakened by the shock of her husband's death, is crucial information both for the plot (foreshadowing the story's climax) and for the characterization of Mrs. Mallard. This detail immediately establishes dramatic tension and suspense because we do not know how Mrs. Mallard will handle the news of her husband's death.

The conflict in the story emerges directly from the disruptive news of Brently Mallard's presumed death in the railroad accident. How will Mrs. Mallard deal with this news? Initially, she responds to the news conventionally: weeping "with sudden, wild abandonment in her sister's arms." She seeks solitude in her room, and there, the complications occur. As she struggles with her grief, she also must accommodate herself to a new realization that she is now free and glad to be so. Although still stunned by grief, Mrs. Mallard begins to feel a change coming over her owing to her growing awareness of the world outside her room: "There was something coming to her and she was waiting for it, fearfully. What was it? She did not know; it was too subtle and elusive to name. But she felt it, creeping out of the sky, reaching toward her through the sounds, the scents, the color that filled the air." She eventually understands that what she is feeling is liberation and revitalization brought on by her newly independent status. No longer married to Brently, she is thrilled by the prospects that now open for her as a single woman.

Suspense is generated as Mrs. Mallard re-emerges from her room: how will she express her realization, how will she reconcile the feeling of grief expected of her and the liberation that she is actually feeling? Before this can be answered, the surprise arrival of Brently Mallard produces the story's climax. The heart condition afflicting Mrs. Mallard, mentioned at the opening, finally takes its toll: Mrs. Mallard dies, presumably from shock at the surprise appearance of her husband. In the denouement to the story, the doctors diagnose their assumed cause of her death as "the joy that kills," in other words, Mrs. Mallard's great happiness at her husband's safe return. The reader, however, privileged to have accompanied Mrs. Mallard inside her room where her most private thoughts and feelings are revealed, realizes that this diagnosis is incorrect, or, rather, both right and wrong. Based on what we have learned about Mrs. Mallard, we realize that it is not joy that kills her at being reunited with her husband but more likely losing the joyful liberation she experienced after his "death," or it could be that Brently's return provokes an overwhelming guilt in Mrs. Mallard about her joyful feelings of freedom at her husband's expense. It may be guilt, not regret, that produces the shock that kills her. It could be a combination of both. We don't know this for sure: the doctors think differently, and Chopin does not offer an opinion or inform us what exactly Mrs. Mallard is feeling when she sees her returned husband. To reach this conclusion, we must integrate what happens in the story with what we begin to learn about Mrs. Mallard's character.

How do you read it for character?

On a first reading of the story, readers may find Mrs. Mallard an unsympathetic character, someone who appears callous, selfish, and unnatural in her reaction to the death of her husband. Instead of expressing expected grief, she ecstatically revels in a newly discovered sense of freedom so soon after learning of her husband's presumed death. Chopin complicates our reaction to Mrs. Mallard's transformation by giving us virtually no details about the couple's relationship that might justify the character's feelings of relief at the news. Looking more closely at Mrs. Mallard through the details and information Chopin does supply, however, we can reach a more balanced view of her not as a heartless monster but as a more sympathetic victim of a repressive, male-dominated society that severely restricts a woman's sense of self and opportunities.

First, consider her name: it is "Mrs. Mallard" up to paragraph seventeen of the twenty-three-paragraph story. Names in stories can be very significant, and here, Mrs. Mallard's identity is totally connected with her marital status. Her name is her husband's last name and the designation "Mrs." to signal that she is his wife. Only when her sister, Josephine, tries to coax her out of her room do we learn Mrs. Mallard's given name: Louise. Symbolically, this occurs after Mrs. Mallard has accepted a new identity brought on by the sense of freedom and possibility her husband's presumed death has provoked. It is inside her room in private, which Chopin allows us to enter with her, that the complexity of Louise Mallard's character and situation are revealed.

Initially, does Mrs. Mallard's behavior upon receiving the news of her husband's accident strike you as odd or different from what you would expect? Chopin writes, "She did not hear the story as many women have heard the same, with a paralyzed inability to accept its significance." Instead, Mrs. Mallard immediately passes over an expected grieving stage of denial to full acceptance in which "She wept at once, with sudden, wild abandonment, in her sister's arms." Does this indicate her rapid accommodation to the news of Brently's death? Does it foreshadow her rapid transformation from grief to joy? Possibly. What is clear is that when her initial paroxysm of tears passes, "she went away to her room alone. She would have no one follow her." Mrs. Mallard's initial reaction is followed by a desire to be alone. Why? She may want to be alone with her

Kate Chopin's "Story of an Hour" was first published in 1894 in *Vogue* magazine. It was highly controversial at the time for its portrayal of a woman being relieved by the news of her husband's death.

private grief, a normal reaction, but her decision to take her own counsel alone is also a sign of her growing independence and self-sufficiency.

Inside her room, Mrs. Mallard continues to grieve, sobbing periodically, "as a child who has cried itself to sleep continues to sob in its dreams." However, she also is described looking out the opened window:

> She could see in the open square before her house the tops of trees that were all aquiver with the new spring life. The delicious breath of rain was in the air. In the street below a peddler was crying his wares. The notes of a distant song which some one was singing reached her faintly, and countless sparrows were twittering in the eaves.

> There were patches of blue sky showing here and there through the clouds that had met and piled one above the other in the west facing her window.

All of these details—the signs of "new spring life," the "breadth of rain in the air," the sounds of a peddler "crying his wares," and the "notes of a distant song"—all contrast with her mourning. It is as if she has gone into the room to be alone with her grief and instead hears and sees invitations to widen her perspective and expand her prospects. Almost against her will, "The vacant stare and the look of terror that had followed it went from her eyes. They stayed keen and bright. Her pulses beat fast, and the coursing blood warmed and relaxed every inch of her body." Instead of grief, Mrs. Mallard is overcome with a sense of relief. Chopin writes:

> She did not stop to ask if it were or were not a monstrous joy that held her. A clear and exalted perception enabled her to dismiss the suggestion as trivial. She knew that she would weep again when she saw the kind, tender hands folded in death; the face that had never looked save with love upon her, fixed and gray and dead. But she saw beyond that bitter moment a long procession of years to come that would belong to her absolutely. And she opened and spread her arms out to them in welcome.

Welcoming the new possibility of her life now freed from her marriage responsibilities, Mrs. Mallard clarifies exactly what she will not miss of her former life:

> There would be no one to live for during those coming years; she would live for herself. There would be no powerful will bending hers in that blind persistence with which men and women believe they have a right to impose a private will upon a fellow-creature.

In just a few words, Chopin characterizes married life as the imposition of a "powerful will bending hers in that blind persistence with which men and women believe they have a right to impose a private will upon a fellow-creature." Marriage, therefore, is not depicted as mutually supportive but rather as a contest of wills for dominance, not as equality but as capitulation to the stronger will of the other. Mrs. Mallard concludes that "she had loved him—sometimes. Often she had not." But she decides that love is irrelevant "in the face of this possession of self-assertion which she suddenly recognized as the strongest impulse of her being!" What matters most to her now is not the past but the present and the sense of "self-assertion" she now feels: "'Free! Body and soul free!' she kept whispering."

What does this tell us about Mrs. Mallard? As Brently Mallard's wife, she has felt dominated by his strong will to the exclusion of her own, that she has both loved and not loved in her relationship with him but that all questions of love, "the unsolved mystery," are less important than what she is now feeling as a newly liberated and independent person. Implied is Chopin's suggestion that marriage, particularly under the restrictions of a time in history that severely limited what women could do and become, forces women to subsume personal identity and selfhood. In the era of Chopin's story, wives were dominated by and subservient to their husbands. It was assumed that the domestic world inside the home was a woman's only province, and anything beyond— work, politics, or society—belonged to the husband. Mrs. Mallard's reaction to her sudden release from her marital role is described like a captive who has been imprisoned and is now being freed. Several details make this clear. Like a starved woman, Mrs. Mallard is described as "drinking in a very elixir of life through that open window." She signals her transformation: "Her fancy was running riot along those days ahead of her. Spring days, and summer days, and all sorts of days that would be her own. She breathed a quick prayer that life might be long. It was only yesterday she had thought with a shudder that life might be long." As a married woman, she felt that her life could not be endured. Now free, she prays that "life might be long." With a "feverish triumph in her eyes," she exits the room like "a goddess of Victory."

It is the nature and the intensity of Mrs. Mallard's feelings here that help the reader understand that she clearly did not die overjoyed by Brently's return home safely. Instead, we realize that the joy she experienced inside her room at the prospect of her independence is abruptly ended with his return. We don't know precisely what kills Mrs. Mallard: it could be disappointment or guilt, but we have been given the evidence to see Mrs. Mallard as a complex character who experiences contradictory emotions. She is a perfect model for Forster's concept of a "rounded character," one with multiple sides who surprises us, not a flat character who is what she is and remains that way. We watch Mrs. Mallard change from shock and tears to joy to shock again and, in the process, have learned important information about what she has felt and is feeling.

What is the point of view in Chopin's story?

How we gain access to Mrs. Mallard is greatly impacted by Chopin's arrangement of narrative point of view. In a story so focused on a single character's reactions—Mrs. Mallard's—it might seem an obvious choice to narrate the story in her own words. First-person narration would have provided intimacy and a clear understanding of the conflicting emotions and thoughts that Mrs. Mallard experiences after the news of Brently's death. But how could she have narrated her own death? By having Mrs. Mallard tell her own story, the full consequence of Brently's return home would have been lost. Now dead, Mrs. Mallard could not provide the doctors' diagnosis of what killed her, nor would there have been the same sense of irony in their misdiagnosis. So, instead of first-person narration, Chopin chooses third-person, but shifts among omniscient, limited, and objective third-person narrative. However, note that even though Chopin's narration allows her to tell all and from multiple viewpoints, she does not. Instead, she strategically restricts the viewpoint to focus on her central character. Chopin also withholds crucial information—the fact that Brently is not dead but alive—to set up the story's major surprise that produces the climax. A story's narration is rarely one kind only. Most stories show their authors strategically cutting between multiple narrative points of view and techniques. By noticing when these shifts happen and what they accomplish, the reader gains insight into the focus and potential meaning in a story.

"The Story of an Hour" opens from the vantage point of omniscience. The narrator summarizes what two characters—Josephine and Richards—are concerned about in breaking the news to Mrs. Mallard, whose heart condition is named. By the third paragraph, the narration is limited to Mrs. Mallard's perspective: what she is doing and feeling. This is intensified as the narration moves inside Mrs. Mallard's room with her. We don't know what is going on outside the room among those inside the house until Josephine calls her sister to come out. Chopin has purposely restricted her focus to Mrs. Mallard's point of view as the narrator describes what she is seeing and hearing from her vantage point in the room. As we begin to learn what Mrs. Mallard is going through and feeling, the all-knowing, third-person narrator merges with Mrs. Mallard's consciousness to such an extent that it is as if she is narrating. The confusing emotions and conflicting thoughts are delivered directly with very little analysis on the part of the narrator. The third-person narration is so limited here that it almost becomes a first-person narrative. Read again the several paragraphs describing Mrs. Mallard's thoughts inside the room and notice how they appear to be coming from her and not from an all-knowing narrator. By doing so, Chopin increases suspense as Mrs. Mallard is shown trying to sort out her thoughts and conflicting emotions. A different narrative strategy of full omniscience would have quickly summarized exactly Mrs. Mallard's situation, motives, and prospects.

After a single paragraph from Josephine's perspective outside the room, the viewpoint shifts back to Mrs. Mallard as she re-emerges. Chopin includes both how Mrs. Mallard looks from the outside ("like a goddess of Victory") and what Mrs. Mallard is thinking (that life might be now long). The final shift of perspective moves from Mrs. Mallard to Brently:

> Some one was opening the front door with a latchkey. It was Brently Mallard who entered, a little travel-stained, composedly carrying his grip-sack and umbrella. He had been far from the scene of the accident, and did not even know there had been one. He stood amazed at Josephine's piercing cry; at Richards' quick motion to screen him from the view of his wife.

The narrator then only tells us that Richards failed in shielding Mrs. Mallard from seeing her husband's sudden arrival. The narrator does not describe what happens when she sees him and its fatal consequence. There is then a clear gap in the story as it moves ahead to the doctors' perspective on the cause of Mrs. Mallard's death. The actual death must be surmised from this information. Why withhold this important revelation? Why does Chopin decide not to give us the explicit details of what happens after Mrs. Mallard sees her husband? The obvious answer is for the shock effect, for the surprise. The reader, like Mrs. Mallard, experiences a shock here in learning of Mrs. Mallard's death in the last sentence of the story. Another reason is to focus attention on the doctor's misdiagnosis of the "joy that kills." By doing so, Chopin underscores the significance of her story: how for a woman like Mrs. Mallard, newly liberated from a repressive and self-denying marriage, learning of her husband's survival kills the joy that she has discovered and finally kills her. Our understanding of this is established by Chopin's artful arrangement of narrative point of view and perspective.

Kate Chopin wrote stories ahead of their time with their themes of women struggling to find worth and identity in the male-dominated world of the nineteenth century.

What is the setting in the story?

The single setting of the story is the Mallards' home. Chopin, like Poe in "The Tell-Tale Heart," offers very few particulars: no city or town is named nor when the story takes place. The single detail of a railroad accident helps to establish the time of the story as contemporaneous with when the story was published—in the 1890s, when railroad passenger travel was the norm. At least one other detail—the peddler crying his wares—similarly suggests a nineteenth-century setting, when the designation "peddler" for a street seller was common.

Why the lack of specifics here? The best way to answer that is to further ask: What would additional details have added to the story? We have already mentioned how withholding Mrs. Mallard's first name serves the story's theme, and the single key detail offered about her is her heart condition, a crucial factor in the story. Chopin is clearly employing Poe's exclusion principle of eliminating all unnecessary information to focus attention on what is critical. The critical focus in this story is the news of Brently's death and how Mrs. Mallard responds. All information beyond this is irrelevant and unneeded. Only what contributes to the story's theme and outcome needs to be included.

The vital setting for the story is Mrs. Mallard's room within her house, where she retreats to be alone. Symbolically, this setting, cut off from prying eyes or the need to behave in a certain way that might be expected of her, allows Mrs. Mallard the opportunity to be herself, to express honestly her reactions to her husband's presumed death. The sights and sounds outside the window serve as an invitation to Mrs. Mallard to break out of her confinement, reflecting her growing awareness of future possibilities now that she is freed from her restrictive marriage. The setting of a closed room symbolically reflects the confinement Mrs. Mallard feels in her marriage. Her liberation is associated with the outside world "creeping out of the sky, reaching toward her through the sounds, the scents, the color that filled the air" and is demonstrated by her leaving the room "with a feverish triumph in her eyes" like "a goddess of Victory." Chopin uses her setting to reflect what Mrs. Mallard is feeling, allowing external details to stand in for her internal state of mind.

One other aspect of setting is crucial for our understanding of the story: gender assumptions that apply in the time frame of the story. Written today, "The Story of an Hour" would make little sense. Most contemporary women do not feel the same sense of restriction in their roles as wives. Women have won equality of opportunity outside the home that would have been unimaginable in Chopin's day. Neither is the expectation of deferring to the superior judgment of the male in a marriage relationship the same today. Chopin was shockingly ahead of her time in forecasting the issues of women's liberation to come, but knowing how women were expected to behave and the roles they were expected to play in the 1890s is crucial for an understanding of the issues Mrs. Mallard faces and how and why she reacts to her husband's presumed death the way she does.

What imagery and symbolism can be found in "The Story of an Hour"?

Finally, Chopin underscores key themes and significance by calling attention to specific details in the story, some of which take on the impact of symbols. Undoubtedly, the greatest of these is the detail that Mrs. Mallard is suffering from "a heart trouble." It becomes obvious as the story develops that Mrs. Mallard's heart trouble is not just physical but emotional. "Heart" in this case refers not just to the organ in her body but also to her affections and the source of her emotional life. As a sufferer of heart disease, physically, she must be cared for, not exposed to shocks of any kind. As a sufferer of emotional heart disease, she has been cut off from a vital engagement with the world. That connection begins again as she takes in the world outside her room, drinking in the "very elixir of life through that open window." The heart disease that finally kills her is associated both literally with her physical ailment and symbolically with the return of Brently and, with it, her former repressive condition.

The test for whether an image or story detail is symbolic is placement and prominence. Chopin focuses the reader's attention on Mrs. Mallard's heart condition at the outset of the story and at the conclusion, in a sense framing the story with this detail. The importance of the heart, therefore, is unmistakable in the context of the story as a whole. In terms of what Mrs. Mallard is feeling and undergoing, the heart serves a clear symbolic purpose.

There is another key detail of the story: Brently's presumed death in a railroad accident. Are we expected to see more to this event than just a surface detail of the story? Is the railroad accident also a symbol? While readers may disagree, there is insufficient evidence in the story to suggest that Chopin is using this event to say something about modern travel or the perils of industrialism. The steam-driven railroad train could, of course, be used symbolically as we have seen in Emily Dickinson's poem "I Like to See It Lap the Miles." Chopin calls little attention to the railroad accident, offering no details that force the nature of the accident into any kind of prominence that might support a symbolic interpretation. There is no suggestion that the train serves as anything more than its literal role as the source for an accident that supposedly killed Brently. Chopin could have substituted another source for the accident as easily with little impact on the story. The train, therefore, is unlikely to serve as a symbol in the story.

What is striking about "The Story of an Hour" is the absence or withholding of images and details until Mrs. Mallard retreats into her room and then looks out the window. It is almost as if a black-and-white factual description of the circumstances suddenly bursts into color and sound in a succession of sensory images—of sight and sound—that breaks the previous mood of grief and serves to initiate Mrs. Mallard's self-assessment. The details can be taken both literally—what is happening outside the window—and symbolically. Chopin uses the conventional symbols of spring: the trees "all aquiver with the new spring life," nourishing rain, a bird's song, and blue sky to suggest new life starting again, all of which serve to reflect what is going on inside Mrs. Mallard. The imagery Chopin chooses helps Mrs. Mallard to understand the contrast between her former existence as Brently's wife as a way of life that had to be endured and what she is now joyfully feeling. Readers are helped to this understanding because we have all felt the appeal and attraction of a fine, spring day that signals the end of winter, which forces us indoors, bundled up against the elements. Similarly, Mrs. Mallard feels the sense of renewal and revitalization that nature shows in the spring. By emphasizing these details, Chopin helps the reader not just to understand what Mrs. Mallard is going through but also to feel it themselves.

In analyzing "The Story of an Hour," we have looked at each of the major elements of a short story—plot, characterization, point of view, imagery, and symbolism—to show how each contribute to meaning and significance in a story. By concentrating on these elements, both how they operate and interact, an active reader should be able to identify not just what a story is about but also what a story means.

NINETEENTH-CENTURY SHORT STORIES

How did the short story develop during the nineteenth century?

Poe's groundbreaking critical theorizing about how the short story functions was prompted by his recognizing the achievement of Nathaniel Hawthorne in the form, but Hawthorne did not originate the development of the American short story. That distinction, according to most literary historians, belongs to Washington Irving, America's first professional man of letters. Influenced by the blending of folk, fantasy, and realistic elements in the short tales of German Romantic writers such as E. T. A. Hoffmann and Heinrich von Kleist, Irving produced *The Sketch Book*, a miscellany of essays and stories, published to great acclaim serially from 1819 to 1820. It includes his most enduring short stories, "Rip Van Winkle" and "The Legend of Sleepy Hollow." Marking a distinctive new kind of narrative form, the development of the American short story begins with *The Sketch Book*. Writing to a friend in 1824, Irving initially dismisses the story form "merely as a frame on which to stretch my material." He adopted "the mode of sketches and short tales rather than long works, because I choose to take a line of writing peculiar to myself." Irving, however, warms to his choice for "a constant activity of thought and a nicety of mind" in the shorter form, compared to the longer narrative, in which "the author may often be dull for half a volume at a time." "In these shorter writings," Irving observes, "every page must have its merit. The author must be continually piquant; woe to him if he makes an awkward sentence or writes a stupid page."

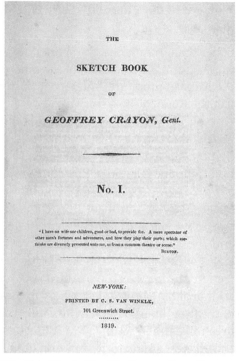

The Sketch Book of Geoffrey Crayon, Gent., first published in 1819, was created by Washington Irving as a way of selling his stories.

What were Washington Irving's principal contributions to the development of the short story?

In pioneering the development of the sketch and prose tale that would become the short story, Irving achieved commercial success and acclaim in a literary form that previously had been regarded as ephemeral and of little value, more journalistic filler than literature. But Irving's success spawned imitators. Irving's friend, Walter Scott, would subsequently publish what is recognized as the first modern short story in England, "The Two Drovers" (1827), and Irving primed the market for American short stories that would foster the literary career of Hawthorne, Poe, and others. In addition, Irving helped to define a flexible narrative form that could include whimsy, the uncanny, and pointed observations about contemporary life along with a reliance on American scenes and customs that would significantly contribute to the creation of an indigenous American literature. If his American successors—Hawthorne, Poe, and Melville—are credited with enhancing the dramatic effectiveness and compression of the evolving short story, of pushing its exploration of moral and psychological concerns, it is still Washington Irving who set the paradigm and possibility for the short story to function as a work of literature.

Where else does the short story emerge in important ways in the nineteenth century?

Other than in America, the short story would emerge as an important literary form in Russia during the first half of the nineteenth century. The cofounding figures of modern Russian literature—Alexander Pushkin and Nikolai Gogol—would also help establish the Russian short story tradition. According to Pushkin's biographer Henri Troyat, "Inexplicably, the whole of Russian literature preceded from [Pushkin's] genius. Poetry, novels, short stories, history, theater, criticism—he had opened up the whole gamut of literary endeavor to his countrymen." Synthesizing European models and Russian folk traditions and fairy tales, Pushkin published the five short stories comprising *The Tales of the Late I. P. Belkin* (1831) and his best-known work outside Russia, "The Queen of Spades" (1834), a brilliant story combining a realistic setting of contemporary life with suggestive folk and fairy-tale elements, creating a haunting atmosphere of manipulation and corruption. Gogol would achieve his initial literary success absorbing the influences of German romanticism in the comic folktales of his native Ukraine in the collection *Evenings on a Farm Near Dikanka* (1831). He would turn his attention to the cosmopolitan life of St. Petersburg in the collection *Arabesques* (1835), depicting for one of the first times in Russian literature the lives of the petty strivers in a depersonalized, dreamlike urban setting. Two subsequent "St. Petersburg Tales" followed, both among the greatest short stories in world literature: "The Nose" (1836), which dramatizes the mysterious disappearance and eventual return of a vain, ambitious bureaucrat's nose, and "The Overcoat" (1942), which concerns the efforts of an impoverished clerk to claim self-esteem by purchasing a new overcoat. When it is stolen, his appeal for assistance goes unheeded, and he subsequently dies, returning as a ghost to haunt the Important Personage who rejected the clerk's appeals in life. Both stories imbue the mundane with fantasy, joining psychological projections with social criticism that anticipates so much subsequent Russian literature, a debt acknowledged famously by Dostoevsky, who declared, "We all came out from under Gogol's 'Overcoat.'"

What about developments of the short story in France?

In France, the importance of the short story initially comes less from the actual stories produced but more from the short story method that Gustave Flaubert (1821–1880) incorporated in all his narratives—his tales and novels—thereby redesigning the core principles of narrative art that would become a major feature of modern fiction. In several crucial ways, modern fiction begins with *Madame Bovary*. Prior to Flaubert, fiction was chiefly regarded as a popular entertainment, lacking in intellectual seriousness or aesthetic accomplishment. He would help to turn the novel and short fiction into an art form so patterned that every detail contributed to the intended effect and as capable of rendering beauty and truth as poetry, drama, or the epic. Flaubert's fifty-six-month, nightly seven-hour struggle to complete his masterpiece—the descent of his title character deluded by romantic illusion into tawdry affairs and finally destroyed by the conjunction of her nature and an inhospitable provincial environment—represents the birthing pains of a new kind of fictional narrative. In his search for the *mot juste* and a unity of effect, Flaubert was essentially attempting to incorporate into the novel the methods of the short story, of Poe's principle of exclusion, in which every narrative element contributed to the ultimate effect and significance of the work as a whole. "The goal I have set for myself will be achieved by others," he wrote in a remarkable series of letters that chart his progress during the composition of *Madame Bovary,* "thanks to me, someone more talented, more instinctive, will be set on the right path. It is perhaps absurd to want to give prose the rhythm of verse (keeping it distinctly prose, however), and to write of ordinary life as one writes history or epic (but without falsifying the subject). I often wonder about this. But on the other hand it is perhaps a great experiment, and very original."

Best known for *Madame Bovary,* Gustave Flaubert was a champion of literary realism.

What was Flaubert's principal contribution to narrative art and the history of the short story?

Flaubert accomplished a revolution in fiction's subject matter and style. By presenting such an unrelentingly objective depiction of ordinary life, by making the trivial and the mediocre the source for the deepest moral and poetic exploration, he replaced fictional idealization and falsification of character and scene with a meticulous portrait of the unexceptional and the ignoble. No previous novel had been so carefully designed with each part fitted into an elaborate whole. To decipher the novel's significance, the reader needed to employ the same skills usually reserved for poetry, discerning the layered implications of diction, image, repetition, contrast, and comparison. According to Flaubert, "The artist in his work must be like God in his creation—invisible and all-powerful: he must be everywhere felt, but never seen." He denied the reader direct, subjective narrative guidance and in doing so established an important modernist principle of composition, raising the bar in the art of fiction by insisting that the reader play an active role in uncovering the patterns beneath the surface of things, subverting the expected fictional delights, and substituting a coherent fictional universe held together by the force and clarity of the novel's vision.

Flaubert demonstrated for the first time that the narrative principles of the short story, first identified by Poe, could serve as the dominant methods of both the longer novel and short fiction.

133

How were Flaubert's innovations expressed in the nineteenth-century French short story?

Flaubert applied his narrative method to the short story only at the end of his career. Three years before his death, in 1877, Flaubert published *Three Tales,* a collection of three stories, "A Simple Heart," "The Legend of St. Julian the Hospitalier," and "Herodias." Particularly in "A Simple Heart," the story of an unremarkable and seemingly pointless life and death of a servant woman, Flaubert treats an unheroic, unexceptional subject, one of the "little men" (or in this case "little women"), which Irish writer Frank O'Connor called the true subject of the short story, and replicated the method of narrative compression and unified effects pioneered in *Madame Bovary,* which would become his principal legacy to the modern short story.

Both subject matter and method would be perfected in the short story by Flaubert's protégé, Guy de Maupassant (1850-1893), who stands alongside Anton Chekhov as the great innovators of the modern short story. Both would not only pioneer dominant methods of the short story but also would establish short fiction as a legitimate form for serious literary consideration.

What were Maupassant's contributions to the development of the short story?

Flaubert served as a literary guardian for Maupassant, introducing him to Zola, Turgenev, and other proponents of Flaubertian realism and naturalism. Drawing on his experiences during the Franco-Prussian War, Maupassant published his first as most enduring short story, "Boule de Suif," in 1880. It became both a popular success and literary achievement that Flaubert proclaimed "a masterpiece that will endure." Maupassant followed it over the next decade with a steady stream of some three hundred short stories, including the collection *La Maison Tellier* in 1881, and such highly regarded stories as "A Parisian Affair," "Femme Fatale," "Deux Amis," "Mother Savage," and "Mademoiselle Fifi." His stories are characterized by an unflinching realism, depicting life which he regarded as "brutal, incoherent, disjointed, full of inexplicable, illogical, and contradictory disasters." Maupassant opened new fictional territory in his uncensored, gritty subject matter, in his descriptive details and quirks of behavior for psychological insights, and in his tightly organized dramatic construction that usually builds to a decisive climax. Maupassant would influence and be imitated by later short story writers as diverse as Henry James (whose "Paste" reworks Maupassant's "The Jewels"), O. Henry (whose surprise endings and ironic coincidences owe much to Maupassant, in "The Necklace," for example), to Hemingway (whose "Big Two-Hearted River" echoes Maupassant's "Love"), and to Raymond Carver (who adapted Maupassant's "Guillemot Rock" in "So Much Water So Close to Home"). Maupassant's dramatic method, emphasizing suspense and surprise, would provide one direction for the modern short story. The other would come from Anton Chekhov.

ANTON CHEKHOV

How did Chekhov contribute to the development of the modern short story?

Anton Chekhov (1860–1904) has the distinction of revolutionizing two different literary forms: the short story and drama. Although he would not complete his first important play until 1895, he wrote stories continually beginning in 1879, when he began his medical training at Moscow University, noting in 1899 that "I have written and published more than 10,000 pages of stories and tales in twenty years of literary activity." Publishing his work in weekly newspapers, sometimes with a one-hundred-word limit, Chekhov initiated technical innovations in the short story that have become standard practice ever since. Like Maupassant, Chekhov's focus was on ordinary life, stripped of the propriety and idealization of previous fiction, for a closer approximation of the unflattering, evanescent, contradictory, and inconclusive nature of experience itself, infused with a rigorous objectivity. "To a chemist there is nothing impure on earth," Chekov declared. "The writer should be just as objective as the chemist; he should liberate himself from everyday subjectivity and acknowledge that manure piles play a highly respectable role in the landscape and that evil passions are every bit as much a part of life as good ones." For Chekhov, the writer's central duty is neither to resolve complexities nor pass judgments but to provide "the correct formulation of a problem." Chekhov insists that "it is not the writer's job to solve such problems as God, pessimism, etc.; his job is merely to record who, under what conditions, said or thought what about God or pessimism. The artist is not meant to be a judge of his characters and what they say; his only job is to be an impartial witness…. Drawing conclusions is up to the jury, that is, the readers. My only job is to be talented, that is, to know how to distinguish important testimony from unimportant, to place my characters in the proper light and speak their language."

How did Chekhov arrange his questions?

For Chekhov, "the correct formulation of a problem" required a radical application of Poe's exclusion principle in which "Everything that has no direct relation to the story must be ruthlessly thrown out. If you write in the first chapter that a rifle hangs on the wall it must without fail fire in the

Russian author Anton Chekhov was an innovator of both drama and short story forms.

second or third chapter. And if it isn't going to fire, it musn't hang, either." He advised fledging writers to eliminate the first half of their stories: "One ought to write so that the reader understands what is going on without the author's explanations, from the progress of the story, from the characters' conversations, from their actions. Try to rip out the first half of your story; you'll only have to change the beginning of the second half a little bit and the story will be totally comprehensible. And in general there ought to be nothing unnecessary."

Chekhov's stories thrust the reader into the action without much exposition, letting the action and details speak for themselves. He advised writers to "cross out as many adjectives and adverbs as you can." Chekhov would pioneer a minimalist approach in service of an unmitigated perception of scene and character, yet, compared to Maupassant's realistic exactitude, Chekhov focuses on the aura or atmosphere surrounding his stories, more like an impressionist painter, so that objective reality resonates with symbolic significance.

What were Chekhov's radical innovations in the short story?

In a remarkable canon of stories, including "The Bet," "The Grasshopper," "Misery," "The Death of a Government Clerk," "The Black Monk," "A Doctor's Visit," "The Princess," "A Living Chronology," "The Huntsman," and "The Lady and the Dog," which Vladimir Nabokov called "one of the greatest stories ever written," Chekhov changed the operative principles of the short story by replacing what English writer William Gerhardie called the "event plot" that dominated the structure of all short stories before Chekhov, in which plot is all important and shaped with a clear beginning, middle, and decisive resolution. As writer William Boyd explains, "The revolution that Chekhov set in train—and which reverberates still today—was not to abandon plot, but to make the

How did Chekhov redefine the plot in the short story?

If Chekhov shares Maupassant's focus on the unexceptional and undisguised truth of experience as well as the Frenchman's intensity of compression and unity of effects, he strongly departs from Maupassant's reliance on plot contrivance of decisive action producing suspense, surprises, and clear resolutions. In many Chekhov stories, an incident may occur, but often, a static situation is merely exposed and remains unresolved, much like one's life. Chekhov's stories are often open-ended, with their effects trailing off without culminating or decisive outcomes, resolved when the situations that define the characters are captured. The question Chekhov's stories pose is not "What happens next" or even "What just happened," but "What could happen," given these characters and their situation. Chekhov, therefore, by de-emphasizing plot in his stories, forces the reader to attend to the stories' details, atmosphere, and the externals that point toward concealed significance.

plot of his stories like the plot of our lives: random, mysterious, run-of-the-mill, abrupt, chaotic, fiercely cruel, meaningless." As Boyd further elaborates, "For the first time in literature the fluidity and randomness of life was made the form of the fiction."

What was Chekhov's influence on the modern short story?

Chekhov's drama of the undramatic would become his principal legacy for literary modernism in the twentieth century, reflected in the stories of writers like James Joyce, Ernest Hemingway, Virginia Woolf, Katherine Mansfield, Elizabeth Bowen, Raymond Carver, John Cheever, Alice Munro, and many more. For Woolf, Chekhov's example demanded a completely different set of assumptions and reader response: "[Chekhov's] stories are inconclusive ... and proceed to frame a criticism based upon the assumption that stories ought to conclude in a way we recognize. In so doing we raise the question of our own fitness as readers." She explains, "Where the tune is familiar and the end emphatic—lovers unite, villains discomfited, intrigues exposed—as it is in most Victorian fiction, we can scarcely go wrong, but where the tune is unfamiliar and the end a note of interrogation or merely information that they went on talking, as it is in Tchekov [sp.], we need a very daring and alert sense of literature to make us hear the tune, and in particular those last notes which complete the harmony." It would be the short story writers in the twentieth century who would help familiarize readers with the modern short story's unique performance.

What are the characteristics and who are the chief innovators of the modernist short story?

Both Maupassant and Chekhov stand behind short story innovations by the modernist writers in the first part of the twentieth century with their unexceptional, nonheroic subjects, artful economy and unity of effects, and Maupassant's dramatic and Chekhov's nondramatic structures. In fact, it can be argued that the aesthetic of the short story— its severe economy of ends and means—first displayed in the novel by Flaubert, applied by Maupassant and Chekhov, and further refined by Henry James, Joseph Conrad, D. H. Lawrence, Virginia Woolf, Katherine Mansfield, and others became the norm of modernist fiction. What makes modernist novels so challenging in large part is that the intensity and compression of the short story has been transferred to a longer narrative in which the modernist novel functions much like a short story. In Joyce's *Ulysses,* for example, a passing detail (Bloom's potato talisman), first mentioned in chapter four ("potato I have"), does not come into play until chapter fifteen, hundreds of pages later, and Joyce expects the reader to hold this detail, and his entire encyclopedic narrative, in mind to make sense of it. Modernist novelists demand the close concentration formerly reserved for poetry and shorter fictions that was to be read in a single sitting.

Two writers, James Joyce and Ernest Hemingway, especially encapsulate the methods of the modernist short story, refining and renaming the methods of Maupassant and Chekhov, while establishing the dominant mode of the modern short story.

JAMES JOYCE

What were Joyce's contributions to the modern short story?

In both theory and practice, James Joyce revolutionized the short story in its internal operation and the larger narrative purposes that a series of linked stories could serve. The fifteen short stories Joyce produced were written between 1903 and 1905 and collected in *Dubliners* in 1914 after a decade-long publication struggle involving eighteen separate submissions to fifteen publishers.

From the outset, Joyce intended each story to serve a wider purpose. "My intention was to write a chapter of the moral history of my country," Joyce declared, "and I chose Dublin for the scene because that city seemed to me the centre of paralysis. I have tried to present it to the indifferent public under four of its aspects: childhood, adolescence, maturity, and public life. The stories are arranged in this order." Story cycles or linked narratives are as old as *One Thousand and One Nights,* Malory's *Le Morte d'Arthur,* Boccaccio's *Decameron,* and Chaucer's *The Canterbury Tales.* In the nineteenth century, short story collections unified by theme, subject, characters, and geography, such as Irving's *The Sketch Book* (1819–1829), Turgenev's *A Sportsman's Sketch* (1852), Melville's *The Piazza Tales* (1856), and Sarah Orne Jewett's *The Country of the Pointed Firs* (1896), preceded *Dubliners,* but none were with the highly developed, overarching theme and the groundbreaking unified patterning of realism and symbolism that Joyce provided. *Dubliners* would set the example for the modern short story sequence that would be followed by such linked story collections such as Sherwood Anderson's *Winesburg, Ohio* (1919), Hemingway's *In Our Time* (1925), Richard Wright's *Uncle Tom's Children* (1938), Faulkner's *Go Down, Moses* (1942), J. D. Salinger's *Nine Stories* (1953), John Updike's *Olinger Stories* (1964), Alice Munro's *Lives of Girls and Women* (1971), Raymond Carver's *What We Talk About When We Talk About Love* (1981), Gloria Naylor's *The Women of Brewster Place* (1982), and Tim O'Brien's *The Things They Carried* (1990).

How does Joyce's *Dubliners* change the realistic standard of the short story?

Dubliners not only demonstrated the patterning of individual short stories into an extended narrative whole, linked by theme, characters, and details, but it also set a new realistic standard for modern fiction. Joyce shared with Maupassant and Chekhov a focus on the unexceptional and unheroic, documenting the lives of ordinary Dublin-

Irish author James Joyce is best remembered for works such as *Ulysses* and the short story collection *Dubliners.*

ers in all their tawdry insignificance. But Joyce extends verisimilitude to the extreme realism of naturalist writers like Zola and others who aspired to a near-photographic exactitude. Joyce reflects this in *Dubliners* in his meticulous reconstruction of the Dublin cityscape, preserving the names of shops and pubs and orchestrating his characters' movements with the precision of a map and a stopwatch. (What is remarkable is that most of the stories in *Dubliners* were written from abroad, during Joyce's self-exile from Dublin in Trieste, with Joyce armed only with his astounding memory, *Thom's Dublin Directory,* and family at home willing to verify topographical details on research forays.) *Dubliners* offers the first example of the even more massive documentation in *Ulysses* that prompted Joyce's declaration that "I want to give a picture of Dublin so complete that if the city suddenly disappeared it could be reconstructed out of my book."

Fear of lawsuits from named businesses or individuals readily identified from their fictional counterparts was one of the reasons publishers were scared away from *Dubliners.* No less forbidding was Joyce's uncensored subject matter and sexual frankness. "It is not my fault that the odour of ashpits and old weeds and offal hangs round my stories," Joyce insisted. "I seriously believe that you will retard the course of civilization in Ireland by preventing the Irish people from having one good look at themselves in my nicely polished looking-glass." Joyce intended an unflinching group portrait of the citizens of Dublin in which the environment enveloping his characters is explored with painstaking accuracy down to the type of trees outside a Dublin church and the exact route and the time it would take for his characters to circumnavigate the city.

From the conflict between the individual and the environment came *Dubliners'* overarching, unifying themes of paralysis, decay, and death that infect nearly all of the stories' characters and define each story's situation. As Joyce explains, "I have written it for the most part in a style of scrupulous meanness and with the conviction that he is a very bold man who dares to alter in the presentment, still more to deform, whatever he has seen and heard." Nothing is mitigated or falsified, all is stripped down to essentials, Joyce declares, establishing an unprecedented level of fictional truth telling.

How does Joyce extend the short story's realism in *Dubliners?*

The challenge Joyce faced as an extreme realist who insisted on clinical objectivity without subjective, authorial intervention is how to achieve significance and relevance, how to convert the specific into the universal. In other words, how to tell individualized stories that communicated a collective truth about the nature of Dublin and modern urban life. "If I can get to the heart of Dublin," Joyce insisted, "I can get to the heart of all the cities of the world. In the particular is contained the universal." But how to unlock these core truths? His answer is contained in his concept of the "epiphany."

What did Joyce mean by an "epiphany"?

Joyce began his fictional career collecting the rare data for his eventual stories in what he called "silhouettes," fragments of encounters, overheard conversations, and observations from ordinary Dublin life. From these, Joyce developed the literary technique he called the "epiphany," the transformation of the ordinary into transcendent meaning. Joyce secularized the term from the Christian liturgy that describes the manifestation of divinity to the Magi in a Bethlehem stable to encompass a sudden revelation of meaning, what he described as the unexpected "revelation of the whatness of a thing" in which the "soul of the commonest object … seems to be radiant." An epiphany was meant to be a "sudden spiritual manifestation either in the vulgarity of speech or of gesture or in a memorable phase of the mind itself." Transformation of the actual into the abstract is the key function of the epiphany. What Joyce was after is recorded by his brother Stanislaus during a ride on a streetcar: "Do you see that man who has just skipped out of the way of the tram? Consider if he had been run over, how significant every act of his would at once become. I don't mean for the police inspector. I mean for anybody that could know them. It is my idea of the significance of trivial things that I want to give two or three unfortunate wretches who may eventually read me." Joyce points to the challenge of his epiphanic method: how to let the man skip out of the way of the tram and yet still give the reader the "significance of trivial things" as if he had been run over, in which every detail contributes to the meaning of the incident. How to balance the mundane and the significant? Surface and symbol?

How does the epiphany function in Joyce's stories?

Joyce's epiphanies work like a spotlight, momentarily illuminating a scene and freezing it in an instant to reveal its meaning. It also functions like a magnifying glass, intensifying and underscoring what is shown to force the reader to consider every detail. In Joyce's stories, every element, no matter how seemingly trivial, is included for a purpose, and it is the reader's job to decipher that purpose. Ironically, as Poe demonstrated, by omitting authorial commentary and conventional dramatic action, the reader is forced to listen for the single word that explains the story, to notice the simple gesture that reveals a complex set of relationships, an instant in which the actual reveals a deeper significance. *Dubliners* establishes the operating principles by which the stories need to be read:

1. The writer presents and never explains; the reader must interpret. As Joyce's surrogate Stephen Dedalus explains in *A Portrait of the Artist as a Young Man,* echoing Flaubert: "The artist, like God of the creation, remains within, or behind or above his handiwork, invisible, refined out of existence, indifferent, paring his fingernails."
2. The writer strives for a presentation so focused that authorial commentary is unnecessary and redundant.
3. Every detail functions like a potential symbol, expressing both its objective reality and deeper meaning. In this way, Joyce irradiates the trivial with significance.
4. It is the reader's job to put the discrete pieces together, like the pattern of imagery in a poem, by association, comparison, and contrast, to find meaning.

How do the stories in *Dubliners* operate?

Dubliners shows Joyce applying his notion of the epiphany as well as expressing his dual interest in realism and symbolism. We are presented with fifteen slices of Dublin life, ob-

How does Joyce's epiphanic method reflect the techniques of literary modernism?

Joyce's technique of the epiphany shows him working out the central problem of the artist in the twentieth century, expressed in the choice between realism and symbolism. On the one hand, fiction was opening new territory of reality rarely examined before: sexuality, psychology, and the pressure of class, gender, and environment in the formation of modern identity and behavior. On the other hand, writers were seeking a way of penetrating actuality, to go beyond surface experience, to arrive at essential, universal truths. Reality therefore was processed for its symbolic significance. Joyce is at the center of these tendencies. *Dubliners* is a collection of realistic slices of life, portrayed it in all its grimness, vulgarity, and triviality. There are no heroes or villains and, like most of our lives, very little of importance ever happens in a Joyce story. Joyce attempts to mine this unexceptional material for its hidden significance, and the stories become much more than just photographical realism. Details are arranged to uncover essential truths and symbolic association, bringing together both modes: realism and symbolism in a rich construct that neither invalidates the concrete nor ignores the "whatness of a thing."

jective rendering of average or ordinary experiences. For the most part, the stories avoid the conventionally dramatic. Although Joyce manages a Maupassant-like, "twist-in-the-tale" story ("Two Gallants"), most of the stories resist either a surprise ending or decisive climax. Perhaps the best example of Joyce's Chekovian nondramatic drama is "Ivy Day in the Committee Room" in which Joyce anticipates his protégé Samuel Beckett's *Waiting for Godot* by dramatizing waiting as a group of cynical electioneerers await their pay from their candidate, settling for a case of porter and the recitation of a patriotic poem that mocks their fall from devotion and principles. Joyce works here and in his other stories by indirection, implying much but asserting little. His method is presentative, lacking the guidance of the author to explain significance. Each story captures scenes, setting, and character with unflattering honesty, offering a moment of comprehension, of insight or lack of it, in the life of his principal characters. Each story, therefore, is built to release that epiphany, whether in the characters or the reader alone.

Moreover, each story sheds light and clarity on the others as expressed in the title of one of the stories, "Counterparts." Joyce here instructs us to see each story as representative, as a metaphor for a larger, universal theme: the state of modern life. Each story must be considered in its sequence, like individual chapters in a novel, connected by recurrent image and situation. Think of collage or montage as an organizing principle. The full meaning of each story is only revealed in relationship to the whole. The effect is a cumulative significance as each story is set next to what precedes and follows it, picking up meaning and insight from one story to the next. Joyce's style of "scrupu-   **141** lous meanness" suggests a clinical detachment, an objective viewpoint that will render each scene with brutal clarity. But the writer is not just the cameraman recording Dublin life as he found it. All is strategically arranged to reveal important aspects of itself. Joyce's method is Poe's principle of exclusion taken to its ultimate extreme, in which everything must help to render the effect intended. Nothing is random or incidental. Like a modern poetic sequence, such as T. S. Eliot's *The Waste Land,* Joyce works by association, establishing a rich and nuanced verbal texture of surface and symbol.

ANALYSIS OF JOYCE'S "ARABY"

What does "Araby" suggest on an initial reading?

Here is a summary of one of Joyce's most famous stories in *Dubliners*, "Araby": A nameless narrator, after describing his drab Dublin neighborhood and his youthful activities with his friends, describes his infatuation with his friend Mangan's sister, whom he watches for through a lowered blind in the front parlor of his home and walks behind on their way to school. One evening, she addresses him and asks if he is planning on going to the Araby bazaar. When he learns that she cannot attend, he volunteers to bring her a present from the bazaar. On the night of the bazaar, the boy waits for his uncle to return home with the money needed to travel to and attend the fair. By the time he sets off to Araby, it is late. The train he takes is deserted, and, when he enters the hall, the exhibition area is nearly empty, the attendants uninterested, and the wares on display unacceptable for the mission he has undertaken. The story ends with a brief but bitter insight: "Gazing up into the darkness I saw myself as a creature driven and derided by vanity; and my eyes burned with anguish and anger."

A typical reaction to a first reading of "Araby" is "What just happened?" Joyce omits key elements a reader might expect in a story. A first-person account as the narrator reflects on a past event, it's the story of an adolescence's romantic longing, but note that neither the narrator is named nor is the object of his affection, who is only identified as "Mangan's sister." She is visualized only by the details that enthrall the narrator: "Her dress swung as she moved her body and the soft rope of her hair tossed from side to side." And "The light from the lamp opposite our door caught the white curve of her neck, lit up her hair that rested there and, falling, lit up the hand upon the railing. It fell over one side of her dress and caught the white border of a petticoat, just visible as she stood at ease just visible as she stood at ease." We don't know what she actually looks like, other than her impression on the narrator. She is given only one line of direct address: "It's well for you." Clearly, this is a one-sided love story about the romantic infatuation of the narrator and his determination to bring her something back from the bazaar as a token of his devotion.

What is even more striking is Joyce's main emphasis on the journey to Araby, including the narrator's frustrating wait for his uncle's return home and the late arrival. We can anticipate the narrator's frustration at what he finds there, but the story's final line: "Gazing up into the darkness I saw myself as a creature driven and derided by vanity; and my eyes burned with anguish and anger," forces the reader back into the story to make sense of the narrator's realization, the anguish and anger of his tears, and his assessment as a "creature driven and derided by vanity." The story seems conventionally unfinished, dependent on all the preceding details and elements to explain its resolution.

Consider the five key questions here.

What is the significance of the title?

"Araby" literally refers to the narrator's destination, where he hopes to find something to bring "Mangan's sister," embodying his feelings for her. Like so much in *Dubliners*, it is based on an actual detail of Dublin life, on an historical charity bazaar that occurred in 1894, when Joyce was twelve.

This surface detail of Dublin life takes on a figurative meaning in the story, reflecting the exotic escape that the narrator's love represents in his romance with Mangan's sister. As the destination of the narrator's quest, it also localizes the contrast between dreamy desire and the reality that the boy must reconcile. The title "Araby," therefore, offers the reader an important clue about the story's focus in the contrast between escape and confinement, the exotic and the mundane, desire and disappointment, and appearance and reality. Note then that the title announces the combination of surface and symbol, the literal and the figurative that the entire story will develop.

Why start here?

The opening paragraph is crucial to establish the key themes of the story: "North Richmond Street, being blind, was a quiet street except at the hour when the Christian Brothers' School set the boys free. An uninhabited house of two storeys stood at the blind end, detached from its neighbours in a square ground. The other houses of the street, conscious of decent lives within them, gazed at one another with brown imperturbable faces."

North Richmond Street is an actual location on Dublin's north side, where Joyce lived during his school years. It is still exactly as Joyce described it in "Araby." It is a dead-end street (blind) with a Christian Brothers' School at the top end. Again, Joyce's surface details are authentic, but note how his word choice and details push toward the symbolic. The street being blind establishes the personification that Joyce uses to create an environment of drab unenlightenment, as "The other houses of the

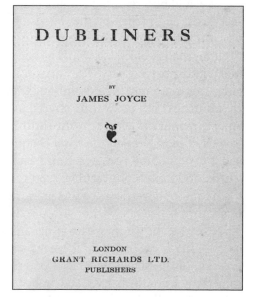

Title page from the 1914 edition of Dubliners, which includes Joyce's story "Araby."

143

street, conscious of decent lives within them, gazed at one another with brown imperturbable faces." The street's blind complacency is only disturbed "when the Christian Brothers' School set the boys free," suggesting that the students are imprisoned. Class and religion are revealed as dual agents of repression. The story's second paragraph, describing the narrator's house, extends the theme of decay: Its former residence was a priest who died "in the back drawing-room," and "Air, musty from having been long enclosed, hung in all the rooms." Its "waste room" is "littered with old useless papers," with a few damp and yellowing books, and a "wild garden behind the house" with "a central apple-tree and a few straggling bushes under one of which I found the late tenant's rusty bicycle-pump." Critics have made much of the significance of the titles of the books, including *The Abbot* and *The Devout Communicant*, the back garden's Edenic apple-tree and the rusty pump. Religious echoes and imagery of disuse and decay establish a setting inhospitable for either spiritual enlightenment or romance.

What is the conflict in "Araby"?

With just a few surface details that point to symbolic meaning, Joyce prepares the story for the catalyst that will produce the story's central conflict. Recalling playing outside in the winter dusk as evening darkness descends, illuminated by "feeble lanterns," the narrator is part of a collective "we" and "our" until Mangan's sister appears "to call her brother in to his tea," and "we left our shadow and walked up to Mangan's steps resignedly." Her figure, "defined by the light from the half-opened door," produces the shift from "we" to "I" for the first time: "I stood by the railing and looked at her." She is defined by light, and the narrator is drawn from the shadowy darkness by her image.

It would be a repeated glimpse of her image that the narrator begins obsessively to seek, each day, hidden by the "blind" of his front parlor, waiting for her departure for school and his following her from afar, never speaking, "yet her name was like a summons to all my foolish blood." It would be her image that "accompanied me even in places the most hostile to romance." The narrator here makes explicit the story's conflict: the challenge to sustain romance, desire, and transcendence in the drab and antithetical Dublin environment with its "flaring streets, jostled by drunken men and bargaining women, amid the curses of labourers, the shrill litanies of shop-boys who stood on guard by the barrels of pigs' cheeks, the nasal chanting of street-singers, who sang a come-all-you about O'Donovan Rossa, or a ballad about the troubles in our native land." The sights, smells, and sounds of street life, captured here in a handful of precise images, represent the narrator's adversaries to sustaining his romantic illusion, in which "I imagined that I bore my chalice safely through a throng of foes." The boy's hopeless adoration is given purpose when he finally speaks to her and learns that she cannot attend the Araby bazaar because her convent school is having a retreat (a repetition of the note of religious repression of the boy's Christian Brothers' School). The narrator promises to bring her something from the bazaar, and Araby takes on the figurative destination of a romantic quest: "The syllables of the word Araby were called to me through the silence in which

my soul luxuriated and cast an Eastern enchantment over me."

How is the conflict resolved?

Having established the story's key opposition in the conflict between love, desire, and transcendent meaning and the environmental forces hostile to all three, Joyce counters the narrator's elevated longing with a series of down-to-earth obstacles that betrays his quest. His uncle's drunkenness and self-centered forgetfulness delay the departure until "people are in bed and after their first sleep," according to the uncle, who makes a mockery of the speaker's exotic and solemn Araby by seizing the focus with a beside-the-point recitation of the sentimental poem "The Arab's Farewell to His Steed." The evening streets are "thronged with buyers," anticipating the commodification of romance that will follow. The car in the special train to the bazaar is deserted and bare as will be the bazaar when the boy arrives: "I found myself in a big hall girdled at half its height by a gallery. Nearly all the stalls were closed, and the greater part of the hall was in darkness. I recognized a silence like that which pervades a church after a service." The boy's version of Chapel Perilous of the questing knight resembles a deserted church too late for the transcendence intended. Approaching the center of the hall "timidly," the boy sees only two men "counting money on a salver," as if toting up the offerings of the departed worshippers, an echo of the moneylenders in the temple. Araby, like Dublin, is only for buyers and sellers, the boy realizes as he recalls his mission and seeks out an object to purchase as a proper token of his devotion and love. At a stall, he overhears the young woman attendant flirting with two men with English accents (suggesting Ireland's usurpation even of romance). The language of love here is translated into an inane back-and-forth over what the young woman did or did not say. Finding nothing to serve his purpose, the boy realizes his "stay was useless," and he returns to the middle of the bazaar to the sound of the money jingling in his pocket, a culminating end note for his failed quest and its vanity in which love and desire is commercialized and commodified.

Why does "Araby" end when it does?

The story ends with a climactic fade-to-black: "I heard a voice call from one end of the gallery that the light was out. The upper part of the hall was now completely dark." The darkness here resonates with the opening in "blind" North Richmond Street and the winter shadows, illuminated by Mangan's sister in the doorway. She is the light calling the speaker out of the dark and glimpsed from behind the blinds of his front room, yet with the collapse of his quest and defeat of a meaningful expression of the love he feels, the boy reverts to the condition before romance lifted him momentarily out of the dreary, unilluminated status quo. The fade-to-black is followed by a final elucidation, the story's epiphany: "Gazing up into the darkness I saw myself as a creature driven and derided by vanity; and my eyes burned with anguish and anger." By Joyce's definition, an epiphany is the "revelation of the whatness of a thing" in which the "soul of the commonest object ... seems to be radiant." What is revealed here? Clearly, the boy is shaken by his experience into a realization that he is "a creature driven and derided by vanity." The whatness of Dublin as a "centre of paralysis," destructive of romance and self-destructive for anyone who seeks to gratify longing and desire, has been realized. Such an ennobling impulse can only be in vain, and the boy's final epiphany is a recognition of his own self-deluding vanity that recasts him as a questing knight. He now realizes how absurd such illusions are. Reality clearly has won against any dream of escape (to the exotic realm of Araby) and for fulfillment. However, in a story in which blindness suffuses the details, the final words imply vision: "My eyes burned with anguish and anger." Joyce ends emphasizing not just what the boy feels but also what he sees. Anguish suggests severe mental and physical torment that may lead to self-pity and resignation, but anger suggests an alternative toward change, if directed at himself, or attack, if focused outward toward all "that is most hostile to romance." The story serves both cases: it has presented an inner portrait of adolescent love with all its foolish striving and self-magnification, while also exposing the pettiness, stagnation, and crassness in the Dublin environment that is life- and love-destroying and that must be resisted.

How does Joyce's arrangement of his stories in *Dubliners* enhance meaning?

The narrator's anger here is clarified when "Araby" is considered in its *Dubliners* sequence, in relation to the stories that precede and follow it. "Araby" is the third story and the last of a trilogy of first-person stories of boyhood. The first, "The Sisters," concludes with the boy's stunned silence learning the truth about the old priest and his mentor who has died from the priest's sisters. In the second, "An Encounter," a day's absence from school for an adventure leads to an encounter with a pervert and the boy's realization of his own desperate reliance on his companion, who "I had always despised … a little." In the first story, the boy displays no explicit self-awareness from the lesson he learns; in the second, the vanity of the boy's self-confidence is revealed. In "Araby" more vanity is exposed, but now anger is added, suggesting a developmental process from helpless childhood to struggling adolescence. Joyce will continue his developmental sequence of frustrated striving in the following stories of young adulthood ("Eveline," "After the Race," "Two Gallants," and "The Boarding House") to maturity ("A Little Cloud," "Counterparts," "Clay," and "A Painful Case") and public life ("Ivy Day in the Committee Room," "A Mother," and "Grace") before the summation of "The Dead."

Each story picks up meaning from the previous stories and passes on meaning to the next as in a modern poetic sequence, like "The Waste Land," or an album like *Sgt. Pepper's Lonely Hearts Club Band*. Each story can stand alone, but a full understanding only emerges when each is considered in relation to others. The individual short story collectively forms a greater, novel-like whole. Joyce's *Dubliners* would pioneer the modern short story sequence that harnesses the compression and intensity of the short story to a more expansive pattern of meaning.

Besides Joyce, who else created the model for the modernist short story?

In addition to Chekhov and Joyce, the writer who would help define the modern short story for a world audience is Ernest Hemingway. Few other writers have entered the modern consciousness and dominated literary sensibility as Hemingway has done. In his time as America's most famous writer, Hemingway was also America's greatest literary export; his influences can be felt in every culture where his books are read as his works help to define modern themes, attitudes, and a new fictional technique. Not since Poe's theory of short fiction has an American's technique technique for the short story so dominated the form as has Hemingway's method of suggestive indirection and minimalism.

AMERICAN SHORT STORY INNOVATIONS IN THE TWENTIETH CENTURY

What are the characteristics of the famous Hemingway style?

Hemingway's notorious, stripped-down, "just the facts" style, much imitated but rarely so well duplicated, developed from his journalistic training. The style sheet of the *Kansas City Star,* where Hemingway began as a cub reporter in 1917, provides a good prescription for the literary style that he would make famous:

- Use short sentences
- Use short first paragraphs
- Use vigorous English
- Be positive, not negative
- Avoid using adjectives
- Tell an interesting story

Hemingway would adapt these rules in his first important collection of short stories, *In Our Time* (1924). The stories of *In Our Time,* which should be read as a narrative sequence, like Joyce's *Dubliners,* trace for the first time the archetypal Hemingway hero who would recur in his work. Nick Adams is shown at various stages of his development attempting to cope with different traumas as the threat of death and destruction engulf him. Spare and specific, the characteristic Hemingway style emerges in force. "If a writer of prose knows enough about what he is writing about," Hemingway declared, "he may omit things he knows and the reader, if the writer is writing truly enough, will have a feeling of those things as strongly as

American author Ernest Hemingway had a distinct style combining a deceptively simple sentence structure with compelling stories.

147

though the writer had stated them. The dignity of movement of an iceberg is due to only one-eighth of it being above water."

Hemingway's variation on Poe's principle of exclusion and Joyce's epiphanic method is his so-called iceberg principle of excluding all but the essential details, presenting what's on the surface that allows the reader to penetrate to their depths by his artful selection and arrangement. In the masterpiece that closes *In Our Time,* "Big Two-Hearted River," a precisely rendered account of a fishing trip, evokes Hemingway's version of T. S. Eliot's *The Waste Land,* while in one of his most famous stories, "Hills Like White Elephants," a young couple's apparently inconsequential conversation while waiting for a train conceals a fraught struggle over an abortion and the evidence that forecasts the destruction of their relationship that is revealed to the reader by paying close attention to both what is said and what isn't.

Like Chekhov and Joyce before him, Hemingway crafted some of the most influential short stories in the modern canon that set the rules by which short fiction would continue to operate and be read: actively, noting every detail, attuning to what isn't said or shown as much as what is, and gaining the most from the least.

What about the short story in the postmodernist period?

What is striking about the short story during the modernist period of the first half of the twentieth century is not only the heightened status writers like Hemingway gave it but also the way its methods began to dictate the construction of longer narratives. It can be argued that modernist novels challenge readers so much in part because they share with short fiction the sense that every detail matters and must be activated in the reader's memory even in an extended narrative of hundreds of pages. In other words, modernist novelists, like Joyce and Faulkner, apply the same techniques to their long narratives as to their short ones, with the corresponding challenge to the reader's stamina and endurance. It is one thing to master the details of a seven-page short story; it is another thing entirely to be expected to do the same for *Ulysses* and *Absalom, Absalom!*

If the modernists raised the status and expanded the possibilities of the short story by extending its compression and intensity to longer narratives, other writers have continued to push the form in interesting and challenging ways since the end of the modernist period. Critic Susan Lohafer in her study, *Coming to Terms with the Short Story*, provides a useful summation of the direction of the American short story in the second half of the twentieth century and beyond: "It branched out southern and suburban and ethnic and far."

"Southern" refers to the works of writers such as William Faulkner, Flannery O'Connor, Katherine Anne Porter, Eudora Welty, and others whose stories universalize a regional approach that has sustained the short story since the nineteenth century. "Suburban" describes the writers beginning in the 1950s, such as J. D. Salinger, John Cheever, Shirley Jackson, John Updike, Joyce Carol Oates, Raymond Carver, Tillie Olsen, Grace Paley, Ann Beattie, and others, who have chronicled the post-urban American landscape and the angst of its consumer-dominated, and for many, its dislocated, society. "Ethnic" reflects the opening for alternative voices other than those of the white Christian majority, such as Bernard Malamud, Philip Roth, Cynthia Ozick, Grace Paley, Richard Wright, Zora Neale Hurston, James Baldwin, Alice Walker, Jamaica Kincaid, Gish Jen, Amy Tan, Jhumpa Lahiri, Bharati Mukherjee, Louise Erdrich, Leslie Marmon Silko, N. Scott Momaday, Junot Díaz, Sherman Alexie, Sandra Cisneros, and so many others who have made the short story into a distinctly pluralistic, multicultural tool of communication. By "far," Lohafer has in mind anti-realists and fabulists, such as John Barth, John Barthelme, Robert Coover, Lorrie Moore, Lydia Davis, George Saunders, and others, authors of self-reflective metafictions and language and formal experimentation that extends the boundaries and bounty of short fiction.

What about developments in the short story beyond the United States?

Lohafer's categories provide a useful sense of the diversity and energy of the contemporary American short story, but any suggestion of American hegemony in the achievement of the contemporary short story is misleading and misses a central point about the form today in its global reach and appeal. Although Americans certainly have excelled in the short story form, its international reach is unmistakable. We have already considered the influence of great Russian and French innovators behind the development of the modern short story. Great short fiction masters are represented and influential in other national literatures as well: Franz Kafka is a giant of both German-speaking literature and modernism, whose short fiction stands behind the anti-realistic fiction alternative of the contemporary fabulists. Italian short story master Italo Calvino is similarly important as a legacy figure. The creative explosion of Latin and South America in the second half of the twentieth century includes remarkable imaginative achievements in short fiction by Jorge Luis Borges, Gabriel García Márquez, Julio Cortázar, and others. Ireland has long excelled in the short story, producing such major practitioners as Seán Ó Faoláin, Frank O'Connor, Mary Lavin, John McGahern, Brian Friel, Edna O'Brien, Elizabeth Bowen, Anne Enright, and more. Canada is well represented by such short story masters as Alice Munro, Mavis Gallant, Carol Shields, and Margaret Atwood. Japan has produced Haruki Murakami, Yusunari Kawabata, and Kenzaburo Oe, and in China, Lu Xun, Mo Yan, and Rao Xueman. African authors include Chinua Achebe and Nadine Gordimer.

As interpreted by these writers and many more, the short story has proven both durable and elastic enough to serve multiple cultures, diverse senses of reality, and literary techniques. There is no indication that either the vitality or the reach of the short story will not continue undiminished.

What makes a novel different from a short story?

Both the short story and the novel are narrative forms in which the same elements already discussed—plot, characterization, point of view, imagery, setting, and symbolism—apply. However, the novel's expansive form brings additional challenges and strategies for reading and understanding. The obvious difference between the short story and the novel is length. Most textbooks and dictionaries tell us that a novel is a work of fiction almost always written in prose, at least 150 to 200 pages long. The textbook definition usually also distinguishes novels (as works written in prose) from classical epics, like the *Iliad, Odyssey,* and *Aeneid,* which are all very long poems. As we have previously mentioned, the short story is a fictional work short enough to be read in a single sitting. As Poe explained, the short story works by exclusion: eliminating everything that does not directly contribute to the overall significance and meaning of the story. For the short story, compression and intensity are paramount, with a story usually limited to one or a very few characters and a single incident that provokes or dramatizes the story's central interest.

How does reading a novel compare to reading a short story?

A novel replaces compression with expansion. Instead of a principle of *exclusion*, novels operate from a principle of *inclusion*. Too long to be read in a single sitting, a novel takes its time, featuring multiple characters and several incidents over a time scheme that can encapsulate weeks, months, years, even a lifetime. If short stories reveal themselves in glimpses, in brief snapshots, novels work by meticulously and comprehensively directing attention both outwardly, revealing entire communities and social organizations, and inwardly, exploring the innermost recesses of human nature: how we think and how we feel.

Why is the length of a novel important?

A novel's length allows it to extend its focus over years and its characters through multiple major events. Because the reading time of a novel may be far longer than for a short story or for most plays or films, the novel encourages a close, intimate relationship between the characters in a novel and the reader. We can get to know characters in a novel far better than we know anyone else other than ourselves. However, the length of a novel imposes important demands on its author and its reader: if the reading experience must be broken up into readable portions, how can those parts cohere as a satisfying, unified, and complete whole? If a reader must, by necessity, put the novel aside for a while and pick it up again, how is the reader to be reminded about the characters and situations and appreciate the significance of the work? These are unique issues for the novel and need to be taken into consideration as we examine how novels work and achieve their effect.

What longer prose narrative forms existed before the novel?

Length, however, is only one important consideration in characterizing the novel. Another is where the novel came from and what innovation in narrative fiction it delivered. The term "novel" comes from the Italian word *nouvelle,* meaning new. What exactly was new about this form of storytelling that began to emerge in eighteenth-century Europe?

"Novel" was a designation to distinguish it from earlier prose narrative forms, including biography, history, and especially, the romance. The romance, as a storytelling form, dates to antiquity, though the most familiar examples are probably the medieval stories of King Arthur and his knights. Romances vary widely, but they do have some common features:

1. The setting of a romance is usually remote and, perhaps, exotic, like that of a fairy tale. Its setting is usually generic: the forest, for example, not Sherwood forest. Any forest will do.

2. The characters in a romance are also sketched broadly—handsome prince, beautiful princess—and may include larger-than-life figures, such as dragons and wizards. In the romance, characters are mainly types: embodiments of abstract moral values, such as nobility, chivalry, courtesy, or villainy. Those who are not completely virtuous are likely to be embodiments of vice and evil. There is little distinction between Galahad, Lancelot, or the Red Cross Knight: all are noble heroes. That's all you need to know.

3. The action of a romance is equally typical: a quest or a confrontation between hero and villain. There's often some sort of magic in a romance. The romance is a form that has no trouble depicting the supernatural and the allegorical.

For modern versions of the romance, think of the Harry Potter novels, the *Lord of the Rings* trilogy, or the *Star Wars,* movies. In fact, the opening of *Star Wars*: "A long time ago, in a galaxy far, far away," serves as a perfect descriptor of the romance, locating its action not in the here and now but in the long ago and the faraway.

How did the novel originate, and how did it compare to the romance?

The subjects and methods of the romance were challenged in the eighteenth century by a new kind of narrative entertainment that came to be known as the novel. What was new or "novel" about this new kind of storytelling was a commitment to realism. Realism can be defined as the accurate representation of the way things are with an emphasis on *individual*, *average*, and *ordinary* experience. The new prose fictions of the eighteenth century, evolving in England and France, replaced the earlier romantic narrative interest in general and universal experience with a truthful reflection of individual experience. As one critic of the new form observed:

An illustration by Arthur Rackham of a 1917 edition of *The Romance of King Arthur*. The romance is a lengthy narrative form that preceded the novel.

> The Romance is a heroic fable, which treats of fabulous persons and things. The novel is a picture of real life and manners, and of the times in which it is written. The Romance, in lofty and elevated language, describes what never happened nor is likely to happen. The novel gives a familiar relation of such things as they pass every day before our eyes, such as may happen to our friends, or to ourselves, and the perfection of it is to represent every scene, in so easy and natural a manner and to make them appear so probable as to deceive us into persuasion (at least while we are reading) that all is real, until we are affected by the joys and distresses of persons in the story, as if they were our own.

This description illustrates the radical change in literary temperament that produced the novel. The notion that ordinary experience, without fantasy and idealization, merits literary and artistic attention, that the stories of ordinary folks, not flawless knights and noble ladies, could entertain readers or even deserved to be chronicled at all, represented a shift from abstraction in Western art to representation. The novel turned away from the romance's extravagant situations, virtuous characters, remote and exotic settings, and its heroic, implausible actions to represent the actual experiences of individuals within contemporary settings. The long ago and faraway of the earlier romance was replaced by the here and now. Novelists attempted to chronicle the actual world accurately as governed by the laws of probability.

Novel vs. Romance

Novel	Romance
Reality conveyed in detail.	Refuses to do so.
Relies on probability to convince; story and characters are believable.	Strives for the marvelous; believability not as important as beauty and moral.
Characters take center stage.	Action more important.
Characters are particularized individuals, not necessarily noble or paragons.	Characters are general types, usually aristocratic paragons of virtue or villainy.
Empirical method: representation of ordinary life.	Symbolic method: generic, universal settings and situations.
Appeal is recognition: seeing ourselves.	Appeal is surprise: startle with the unusual.
Life presented as it is.	Life presented as it ought to be.

What are the defining characteristics of the novel?

To develop a more exact and useful definition of the novel, we need to go beyond the issue of length to draw a distinction with another long prose narrative like the romance and to emphasize the new novel's interest in specificity, in individualized and recognizable experience. The novel (again distinguished from the earlier romance) has two major dimensions: one sociological, the other psychological.

A novel can describe an entire society. It's no wonder that novels are frequently described as the forerunners of modern sociology. Novels in their length and complexity can expose the often hidden connections among entire classes of people. The sociological dimension of the novel is crucially important because novels are almost always concerned with social distinctions, social hierarchies, and social values. Dealing with the actual experience around them, novelists noticed these things long before sociologists codified them. Novels, therefore, function like a telescope, bringing the unseen, external world closer for inspection.

What else makes the novel a unique literary art form?

At the same time, novels offer us a vivid sense of how particular individuals think and feel. Whereas plays and films are forced to concentrate on externals—how a character moves or speaks—novels are free to probe the inner recesses of both mind and heart. To do so, the telescope becomes a microscope, revealing often hidden reality beneath the surface of behavior. By the end of a novel, we may have developed a deep sympathy and, perhaps, a close identification with the characters. We learn not just what they do (as in a drama) but also why and how they think and feel. In addition to examining human communities, then, the novel explores the contours of consciousness itself. Some of the most important scenes in a novel may involve no interactions between characters or no

dialogue at all. In such scenes, characters may be sitting quietly, reflecting on their thoughts or feelings. Because the novel can go slowly and deeply, such scenes may allow us to trace very subtle shifts in feeling or mood. Therefore, in the greatest novels, we come to know certain characters—Emma Bovary, Pierre Bezukhov, Leopold Bloom, the Invisible Man—far better than any other actual person we know, except perhaps ourselves.

What is the scope of a novel?

The novel, then, has both an outward dimension, helping readers to explore society and its workings, as well as an inward dimension, taking readers inside a character's head and heart. The sociological and psychological aspects of the novel form are closely related. Indeed, the novel's close attention to the relationship between society and the self or the individual is one of its

American author Lorrie Moore compared the difference between a short story and a novel to the difference between a photograph and a movie.

defining features. It is the novel's flexibility in shifting from telescope to microscope, from the sociological to the psychological, that helps to explain its popularity and persistence.

How have others described the novel?

It is only a novel … or, in short, only some work in which the greatest powers of the mind are displayed, in which the most thorough knowledge of human nature, the happiest delineation of its varieties, the liveliest effusions of wit and humour, are conveyed to the world in the best-chosen language.

—Jane Austen

No one says a novel has to be one thing. It can be anything it wants to be, a vaudeville show, the six o'clock news, the mumblings of wild men saddled by demons.

—Ishmael Reed

A short story is a love affair, a novel is a marriage. A short story is a photograph; a novel is a film.

—Lorrie Moore

If you only write when inspired, you may be a fairly decent poet, but you'll never be a novelist.

—Neil Gaiman

155

Writing a novel is a terrible experience, during which the hair often falls out and the teeth decay. I'm always irritated by people who imply that writing fiction is an escape from reality. It is a plunge into reality and it's very shocking to the system.

—Flannery O'Connor

People wonder why the novel is the most popular form of literature; people wonder why it is read more than books of science or books of metaphysics. The reason is very simple; it is merely that the novel is more true than they are.

—G. K. Chesterton

You don't read Gatsby ... to learn whether adultery is good or bad but to learn about how complicated issues such as adultery and fidelity and marriage are. A great novel heightens your senses and sensitivity to the complexities of life and of the individuals, and prevents you from the self-righteousness that sees morality in formulas about good and evil.

—Azar Nafisi

The novelist teaches the reader to comprehend the world as a question.... In a world built on sacrosanct certainties the novel is dead. The totalitarian world ... is a world of answers rather than questions. There, the novel has no place.

—Milan Kundera

[To a question whether it is easier to write a novel than a short story] Yes, sir, you can be more careless. You can put more trash in it and be excused for it than a short story—that's next to the poem. Almost every word has got to be almost exactly right. In the novel you can be careless, but in the short story you can't.

—William Faulkner

The novel is the one bright book of life. Books are not life. They are only tremulations on the ether. But the novel as a tremulation can make the whole man alive tremble.

—D. H. Lawrence

I think the reason novels are regarded to have so much more "information" than films is that they outsource the scenic design and cinematography to the reader.... This, for me, is a powerful argument for the value and potency of literature specifically. Movies don't demand as much from the player. Most people know this; at the end of the day you can be too beat to read but not yet too beat to watch television or listen to music.

—Brian Christian

There are three secrets to writing a novel. Unfortunately, nobody knows what they are.

—W. Somerset Maugham

Ah, Sir, a novel is a mirror carried along a high road. At one moment it reflects to your vision the azure skies, at another the mire of the puddles at your feet. And the man who carries this mirror in his pack will be accused by you of being immoral! His mirror shews the mire, and you blame the mirror! Rather blame that high road upon which the puddle lies, still more the inspector of roads who allows the water to gather and the puddle to form.

—Stendhal

A novel is never anything but a philosophy expressed in images. And in a good novel the philosophy has disappeared into the images.

—Albert Camus

There is a great deal to be said in favour of reading a novel backwards. The last page is as a rule the most interesting, and when one begins with the catastrophe or the dénouement one feels on pleasant terms of equality with the author. It is like going behind the scenes of a theatre. One is no longer taken in, and the hair-breadth escapes of the hero and the wild agonies of the heroine leave one absolutely unmoved. One knows the jealously guarded secret, and one can afford to smile at the quite unnecessary anxiety that the puppets of fiction always consider it their duty to display.

—Oscar Wilde

If you read the novel in more than two weeks, you don't read the novel really.

—Philip Roth

We read novels because we want to see the world through other experiences, other beings, other eyes, other cultures.

—Orhan Pamuk

What changed to make the novel possible as a popular literary form?

What explains the narrative shift from the romance to the novel? What historical/social conditions helped make the novel possible and help to explain both its preoccupations and appeal? To answer these questions, we need to go back a century or so before the emergence of the English novel in the early years of the eighteenth century, to the Elizabethan era of Shakespeare at the close of the sixteenth century and one of history's greatest flowerings of literary expression: in London's playhouses. Plays had been performed throughout the medieval period, but there had been nothing quite like Elizabethan drama in its interest in secular life and human psychology. The medieval morality and mystery plays took as their subjects biblical stories and the central concern of salvation: How should we understand God's will and achieve everlasting happiness with Him in heaven? The plays being staged during the Elizabethan period by Shakespeare and others took up secular subjects: how individuals act in society, in love, in marriage; how historical events

157

happened, and the conflicts individuals contend with in competing earthly desires. This shift of emphasis is attributable to many factors, such as the advances of science and the explorations that began to map the world. In thought, a new scientific rationalism that depended on the empirical method, that is, the direct observation of physical phenomenon, was beginning to be applied not only to the physical sciences but also to the realm of human behavior. Throughout the seventeenth century there were numerous attempts to classify people according to types, to determine inductively from observations the principles that governed behavior. Writers also were applying the empirical method to history and politics. Such attempts show a shift away from dependence on divine law and religious dogma in explaining experience to empirical methods of observations. Shakespeare and his fellow Elizabethan playwrights began the process of exploring

Pulitzer-winning American author Philip Roth believed that novels should be consumed intensely for no more than a couple weeks.

human psychology and social relations in ways never previously attempted. During this period, drama was preeminent as the popular literary form. Poetry and romances were literary media for the educated elite; drama was inclusive, accommodating even the illiterate. The great questions of the age would be aired in the playhouses.

Even though the Puritans, who came to power in England in the 17th century, had a devastating effect on English drama by closing the theaters for eighteen years, from 1642 to 1660 would have an indirect, positive impact on the creation of the novel. Opposed to drama and literature of any kind as forms of lying and occasions for idleness, the Puritans, whose religious beliefs stressed personal faith as revealed in direct contact with the word of God contained in biblical scripture, stimulated an increase in literacy that created a sufficient popular audience for the novel. If the way to salvation rested on your ability to read the Bible, as the Puritans believed, you had the motivation to read as never before. This led to the first of two cultural changes that would make the novel possible: an increase literacy rate.

How did a growing middle class contribute to the popularity of the novel?

The second cultural change was an increase in leisure time that would make novel readers possible. To view an Elizabethan play, you needed just a penny and roughly two hours. To read a novel, you needed considerably more discretionary income, as well as more leisure time. The Puritans' rise to power coincided with a steady growth of a new middle class, with sufficient means to afford the luxury of novel reading. Books were still a luxury item, but enhanced printing technology lowered costs and made possible other print forms, like the broadside and the newspaper, which brought writing to an emerging mass audience. A growing market economy for literature shifted support for writers from patrons to the public, who demanded artistic treatment of their world reflected in artistic forms. The old feudal order of the nobility supported by a peasantry was radically changing. An upper class remained as did a vast laboring class, but a new middle class of professionals, tradesmen, and shopkeepers was evolving. This new class was far less interested in the adventures of noblemen in far-off, magical forests—the leading ingredient of prose romances that preceded the novel—and wanted to read about their own experiences and characters like themselves. Under the patronage system, literature largely gratified the tastes and values of the noble patrons in chivalric tales of the nobility. With the rise of a market economy for literature, authors were quick to gratify the taste of a mass audience for the here and the now, not the long ago and faraway. A new class of readers called for a new literary art form, and the novel was born.

What were the crucial social changes that this new literary form began to reflect?

The novel, pioneered in England, took shape during a period of convulsive social change. In this period, England developed the world's first capitalist economy. England also was beginning to grapple with issues of urbanization, industrialization, and globalization. To understand such changes—and assess their impact on the novel—we need to review the emergence of new economic structures and social values.

England prior to the eighteenth century was still essentially an agrarian society, with a feudal structure of powerful nobles supported by a laboring peasant class. Steadily, in the seventeenth century and into the eighteenth, the rural economy was becoming more centralized. Common lands were being enclosed or appropriated by the wealthiest families. As a result, subsistence farming and self-sufficient living were less of an option for rural people. These details are important be-

The Industrial Revolution not only brought about changes in technology, the economy, and society as a whole, it also had an impact on literature. Novels were often explorations of the convulsive social changes of the eighteenth, nineteenth, and twentieth centuries.

159

cause one characteristic of a capitalist economy, according to economic historians, is that it offers most people little choice but to work for wages.

How did a rising population, the economy, and trade become important factors?

In the city, partly because of the developments mentioned above, the population began to rise dramatically. London in 1700 had a population of 350,000. By 1750, the population had doubled to 750,000—making it the largest city in the Western world, twice as large as Paris or any other European city. By the 1790s, as textile producers opened larger factories, the population of industrial cities, such as Manchester and Birmingham, began to explode as well. The new phenomena of urbanization and industrialization had arrived. Through all of this, England also experienced an early form of what we now call globalization. The growth of England's first modern industry, textiles, depended on international trade. Cotton had to be imported from the West Indies and other parts of the world and then shipped back out again in the form of cloth and other goods.

These three developments—urbanization, industrialization, and globalization—would have an enormous impact on the national imagination—England's sense of itself and its values. The older social order that was being displaced was one dominated by fixed communal values, sustained by a stable, ordered hierarchy in which everyone knew his or her place on the social ladder that was determined at birth: you were what your father was. As limited as this could be, at least you knew who you were and what your responsibilities were in your community. Especially important to this image was a sense of communal solidarity and mutual obligation. English society was hierarchical, with clear divisions between rich and poor, but those at the very top were able and willing to accept responsibility for the welfare of those at or near the bottom.

How did the novel respond to the social and economic changes of the eighteenth and nineteenth centuries?

With the emergence of a new social order, this traditional image would prove difficult to maintain. Rural landlords were often accused of placing their own interests ahead of those of their tenants, not least because of the highly controversial enclosure of common lands. The situation in London and other cities was even more chaotic. In search of wages, newcomers entered the city with no idea where they would be living or working. There is no social welfare net to catch those who fail. These sweeping changes raised questions of personal identity: who am I if I can no longer answer "I am what my father was"? Or "I'm from this village, where I was known by everyone"? It also raised questions of social responsibility and moral values. In a society where economic self-interest is an increasingly important motivation, what kind of behavior is considered worthy and admirable? At a time of increasing class conflict, what happens to traditional ideas of social cohesion and shared responsibility? Moreover, the capitalist system was in the process of transforming the traditional feudal society of noble and peasant, rich and poor, and creating a new class system. How do these new urban, industrial workers fit into the society? What are they if they are neither one nor the other,

> ### What are characteristics of the
> ### first great novels in the eighteenth century?
>
> Examining the first important novels, we can see clearly the break from the earlier romance narrative tradition and the consideration of these social and psychological issues of the new world of urbanization, industrialization, and globalization.

neither noble nor peasant? What assumptions about their station, their lot in life, now applied? How does the individual fit into this increasingly fluid social system in which money is beginning to trump birth and background? As traditional moral authorities appear less reliable, how can one develop a sense of right and wrong? Which values should be upheld, and why?

All of these questions the new novel would begin to address. The novel initiated a long evolution in answering the age's decisive questions: who am I, and how do I fit into this new society?

Who was Daniel Defoe, and why was he important to the development of the novel?

Daniel Defoe (1660–1731) is credited as the originator of the English novel with *Robinson Crusoe* (1719). Defoe, a trader, manufacturer, journalist, and sometime undercover political operative, is the quintessential new man of the eighteenth century, whose middle-class background and experiences would help to shape a new art form, the novel. A fictionalized version of an actual shipwreck account, *Robinson Crusoe* has the familiar romantic situation: an adventure in a remote, exotic setting. We would expect then, if we were reading a romance, Crusoe's story to be an episodic account of all his amazing adventures. What we read instead is the opposite. Until the character Friday appears three-quarters of the way into the novel, nothing very extraordinary occurs. Instead, we watch Crusoe gradually and methodically domesticate his exotic setting. Crusoe is no warrior knight but a middle-class house-husband who creates in the wilds a respectable domicile. There are no dragons, no monsters, and very few cannibals, but there is much discussion about how to make a tea set and raise Crusoe's living standard.

MOLL FLANDERS

Why is Daniel Defoe's *Moll Flanders* important?

In *Moll Flanders* (1722), Defoe further extends the boundaries of the novel. Having domesticated the exotic and replaced romance with realism in *Robinson Crusoe,* Defoe's follow-up is a confession of a woman cut adrift from conventional class, gender, and

161

moral imperatives, who is forced to subsist in the contemporary urban jungle. The full title warns the reader that Moll's story is as remarkable, exciting, and ultimately edifying as that of any questing knight or modern male adventurer: *The Fortunes and Misfortunes of the Famous Moll Flanders, &c. Who was Born in Newgate, and during a Life of continu'd Variety for Threescore Years, besides her Childhood, was Twelve Year a* Whore, *five times a* Wife *(whereof once to her own Brother) Twelve Year a* Thief, *Eight Year a Transported* Felon *in Virginia, at last grew* Rich, *liv'd* Honest, *and died a* Penitent, *Written from her own Memorandums.*

British author Daniel Defoe is most remembered for penning *Robinson Crusoe,* which is the second-most translated book of all time after the Bible.

It is safe to say that Moll Flanders—Whore, Wife, Thief, Felon, Rich, Honest, and Penitent—is the most complex heroine who had ever taken center stage in a novel before. Not since Chaucer's Wife of Bath had a woman with a comparable earthy vitality and authenticity been celebrated in literature. Challenging the gender convention of the passive and virtuous disembodied female, Moll would initiate a new conception of the empowered heroine—willful, ambitious, contradictory, and resourceful—the literary progenitor for later female protagonists like William Makepeace Thackeray's Becky Sharp in *Vanity Fair*, the title characters in Charlotte Brontë's *Jane Eyre* and Zola's *Nana*, Carrie Meeber in Dreiser's *Sister Carrie*, Lilly Briscoe in Wharton's *The House of Mirth*, and Scarlett O'Hara in Mitchell's *Gone with the Wind*. Moreover, with her frankly rendered consciousness in which her narrative reads like an extended interior monologue, Moll Flanders claims kinship with her namesake: Joyce's Molly Bloom. In what E. M. Forster called a "masterpiece of characterization," Defoe initiated in *Moll Flanders* what would become a dominant tradition of the English novel: a narrative of growth and development in which the historical moment, social conditions, and gender assumptions all contribute to the making of an individual. Moll is the first great heroine of the English novel with a mythic dimension, composed in equal measure of particularity and universality. In discussing *Robinson Crusoe*, Coleridge famously attributed to Defoe the power to make "me forget my specific class, character, and circumstances" and to raise "me into universal man. Now that is Defoe's excellence. You become a man while you read." In the case of *Moll Flanders*, you become a woman.

What were the origins of Defoe's *Moll Flanders*?

After a long and turbulent career as a struggling businessman and journalist, Daniel Defoe, at the age of sixty, followed up the enormous success of his first novel, *Robinson Crusoe*

(1719), with his first fully developed fictional account of a criminal, *The Life, Adventures, and Pyracies, of the Famous Captain Singleton* (1720). Defoe's fascination with London's criminal underworld was stimulated when, also in 1720, he began writing for *Applebee's Weekly Journal* whose specialty was the biographies of criminals and their gallows confessions. Throughout 1721, Defoe was a regular visitor to Newgate prison. There, he likely met the notorious convict, Moll King, and from her heard accounts of the adventures of her friend, thief and whore "Callico Sarah" (Sarah's nickname, after a kind of cloth targeted by thieves, may have suggested to Defoe another, Flanders, or Flemish lace, to serve as Moll's surname). As scholar Gerald Howson suggests, "It seems likely that Defoe sought [Moll King] out when she was under sentence of death, as a suitable subject for a criminal pamphlet.... After her reprieve, the pamphlet grew into the novel, the first of its kind in English." If *Robinson Crusoe* was based on Defoe's reading of Alexander Selkirk's memoir, *Moll Flanders* originated from Defoe's firsthand research and direct knowledge of the ways and means of contemporary urban life and its demimonde. Beyond its contemporaneousness and authenticity, the uniqueness of *Moll Flanders* rests in Defoe's ingenious and original amalgam of previously incompatible narrative forms.

How did interest in crime and criminality shape *Moll Flanders?*

Ballads, broadsides, and chapbook biographies and confessions of notorious criminals constituted a major part of the popular literature of the time. Fictional accounts of crimes and criminals go back to the picaresque narratives that first appeared in sixteenth-century Spain, a series of loosely connected episodes in the life of a *picaro*, a rogue, outlaw, or transgressor of established social and moral values. As critic Martin Halliwell has argued, "Written within and set against the backdrop of a society in transition from fixed feudal relationships to a more flexible social structure in which the middle classes began to have significant economic and moral influence, the picaresque foreshadows the novel, charting the rise of bourgeois individualism in its exploration of the tensions between oppressive societies and disaffected individuals." Defoe would incorporate the methods and subjects of the picaresque in the emerging English novel that would be subsequently employed by his successors, most notably Henry Fielding and Tobias Smollett. Defoe's contribution to the picaresque tradition would be to feature a female picaro. Moll's gender and the inclusion of her adventures of love as well as crime links Defoe's narrative further to another proto-novel form, the so-called amatory tale, as practiced by Defoe's contemporary Eliza Haywood in one of the period's bestsellers, *Love in Excess* (1719–1720). Derived from the earlier prose romances, the amatory tale selects love and sexual passion as a principal narrative focus while retaining the romance's idealized, stock characters and generalized settings and situations. Defoe's version of the amatory tale in *Moll Flanders* adds the specificity and concreteness that would define the transition from romance to novel. Love in Defoe's novel is firmly rooted in the particularity of place and personality. Never before in fiction had the amatory been shown in its full practical and commercial contexts as experienced by a new kind of lover who is alternatively victim and transgressor, passionate and calculating.

How does *Moll Flanders* proceed?

Moll's account of her life begins with what little she knows about her birth and infancy. Her mother was a petty thief who escaped hanging by "pleading her belly," giving birth to Moll in Newgate, before being transported to America when her daughter was six months old. Somehow having fell in with a tribe of gypsies (Moll's recollections are plausibly vague), she was abandoned or escaped to Colchester at the age of three and is put into the care of a poor woman paid for maintaining parish orphans. At the age of eight when she is intended to go into service, Moll resists, asserting instead that she desires to become

A nineteenth-century illustration from *Moll Flanders*. Interestingly, the novel was not attributed to Defoe until 1770, nearly forty years after the author's death.

a gentlewoman, which she defines as being able "to work for myself, and get enough to keep me without that terrible bugbear going into service." Moll here announces her life's mission: to gain independence and autonomy. Hers is a radical redefinition of gentility as not a matter of birth or breeding but as self-sufficiency within the reach of even someone with no fixed social position and limited financial possibilities but with drive, natural resources, and determination. At the outset of Moll's story, Defoe establishes an intriguing social, class, and gender conundrum: how is survival and self-actualization possible for a person like Moll? What are her options contending with the seemingly insurmountable limitations of class, economics, and gender without the boost of birth, background, and means? Defoe's response comes in the series of subsequent survival challenges Moll faces that collectively demonstrate a complex nexus of sexual, economic, and moral necessity in the formation of an individual's character and destiny.

After her guardian dies when Moll is fourteen, she is taken in as the companion of two daughters of a local gentry family. Learning by "imitation and enquiry," Moll proves to be naturally superior in intelligence than these privileged girls, but it is her physical assets which most directly affect her future as she is seduced by and becomes the mistress of the family's eldest son. When he gratifies Moll with both sex and money, the essential pattern of Moll's career is established in her association of sexuality with profit and social advancement. When her lover accedes to his younger brother's proposal of marriage to Moll, his betrayal steels her to control her emotional attachments and to use her physical attractions as the means to gain the independence and sustenance it requires. Married for five years to the brother of her seducer, Moll frankly confesses, "I never was in bed with my husband, but I wished my self in the arms of his brother ... I committed adultery and incest with him every day in my desires...." After her husband's death, Moll conducts the first in a series of accountings that follow all her subsequent marriages and affairs in which she calculates profit and loss, like a periodic quarterly report. Consigning her two children to her in-laws, Moll sets out with her accrued savings for London determined to remarry profitably. "I had been tricked once by that cheat called love," she insists, "but the game was over; I was resolved now to be married or nothing, and to be well married or not at all." Entering the London marriage market, Moll learns the value of disguise, role-playing, and adapting one's identity to attract suitors. Her next husband is a tradesman who squanders both his and Moll's savings, goes bankrupt, and abandons her. Moll's third husband is a sea captain, whom she accompanies to America. There, to her horror, Moll discovers that her mother-in-law is her mother and that she has married her own half brother. Concealing this anguishing secret for several years, Moll finally returns to England, where she becomes the mistress of a married gentleman who maintains her and the son she bears him until, repenting his immorality, he ends their relationship. Next, agreeing to marry a banker after he has divorced his wife, Moll, portraying a gentlewoman of means on a visit into Lancashire, becomes infatuated with a man she believes is a rich Irish peer. They marry, each convinced that the other is rich. Jemmy turns out to be a penniless fortune-hunter like Moll. When the truth is discovered, they agree to separate, reluctantly on Moll's part, as her passion for Jemmy overpowers practical necessity for the first time. Back in London, Moll disposes with the child Jemmy fathered and bigamously marries the now-divorced banker with whom she lives happily until his investments fail and he dies from despair.

Why does Moll turn to crime, and what are the consequences?

Now at the age of forty-eight, destitute and "past the flourishing time ... when I might expect to be courted," Moll begins to steal to survive, justifying her actions by asserting that "a time of distress is a time of dreadful temptation, and all the strength to resist is taken away; poverty presses, the soul is made desperate by distress, and what can be done?" Despite an initial reluctance and pangs of guilt, Moll, resourceful as ever, soon masters and ascends to the top of her new profession, whose ways and means Defoe elaborately documents. Eventually, she is caught and taken back to where she began, Newgate. Defoe's vivid description of prison life is one of the high points in the novel; another is Moll's dramatized process of self-assessment and repentance brought on by her incarceration. Having over a lifetime successfully evaded the limiting circumstance of her lot with inventiveness and ingenuity, Moll must now contend with the intractable reality of prison, which causes her to "degenerate into stone; I turned first stupid and senseless, and then brutish and thoughtless, and at last raving mad...." Moll's self-recovery and renewal begins with her discovery that Jemmy is a prisoner as well, awaiting execution as a highwayman. Moll blames herself for Jemmy's descent into crime, and her compassion and sympathy for the afflictions of another are transformative: "I bewailed his misfortunes and the ruin he was now come to, at such a rate, that I relished nothing now, as I did before, and the first reflections I made upon the horrid detestable life I had lived, began to return upon me, and as these things returned my abhorrence of the place I was in, and of the way of living in it, returned also; in a word, I was perfectly changed, and became another body." Condemned to death, Moll achieves a spiritual conversion, aided by a visiting minister who leads her to repentance, not out of fear of punishment but for her offense to God and others. The minister secures a commutation of her sentence and transportation to America, and Moll manages to convince Jemmy to seek the same fate and to accompany her. There, with the aid of an inheritance from Moll's mother, the pair becomes successful planters in Carolina, returning eventually to England, "where we resolve to spend the remainder of our years in sincere penitence for the wicked lives we have lived."

How does *Moll Flanders* conclude?

By the end of her story, Moll completes the accepted pattern of the spiritual biography—from innocence to sin, repentance, and redemption (morally and financially). It has been argued that her reclamation, in the words of critic G. A. Storr, the "gradual, fairly systematic development of the heroine's spiritual condition," unifies the novel's episodic structure. Such a view is contested by another that asserts that the power of the novel derives not from its morality but from its sins, not from Moll's repentance but from her transgressions. In such a view, Moll's is the story of an irrepressible, clear-eyed individualist who manages to circumvent a hostile environment and expand her possibilities by her adaptability and continual self-invention. The critical debate over how to interpret Moll and her career centers on Defoe's handling of his volatile and often contradictory protagonist, whose moralism is often at odds with her actions and attitudes. Is the pride Moll expresses in her criminal accomplishments and the obvious relish she takes in narrating some of her sinful ways, which contrasts with the insights of her conversion, meant to be ironic or evidence of Defoe's mishandling, of forgetting his spiritual theme in the face of a more compelling actuality? Ultimately, it is not the novel's consistency but its contradictions that have fascinated readers for nearly three centuries. The power and persistence of Moll Flanders as one of the greatest characters of the English novel derive from her rich mixture of virtue and villainy. A mixture of cupidity and conscience, Moll offers novel readers access to a unique heroine, one who evades and expands simple moral and psychological distinctions. *Moll Flanders* points out the ways in which the emerging novel, with all its complexity of characterization and context, exceeds the possibilities of either the romance or the spiritual fable.

THE HISTORY OF TOM JONES, A FOUNDLING

Why is Henry Fielding's *The History of Tom Jones, a Foundling* important?

The History of Tom Jones, a Foundling (1749) by Henry Fielding (1707–1754) has been called not just the first great masterwork of the English novel but "the greatest literary work of the eighteenth century." In it Fielding clearly announces his assault on conventional decency and decorum by putting at the center of his novel a young man of dubious birth and questionable morality. To tell the story, Fielding employs the romance's episodic quest structure, but Tom is not a noble Galahad or Gawain but a bastard forced to make his own way in contemporary England, not in the forest primeval. His adventures are those anyone might expect to face on the road as he journeys to London. Along the way, Fielding provides a social panorama of contemporary life that justifies his calling his novel "a comic epic in prose."

What was the reception to *Tom Jones,* and how did it compare to other novels of the time?

Tom Jones was an immediate, notoriously popular success, selling out its entire first edition of two thousand copies before the official publication date, February 10, 1749; by the end of the year, three additional edi-

Best known for his satire *Tom Jones,* British novelist and playwright Henry Fielding commented on the failings of society.

tions had appeared. Fielding's first readers were both entranced and appalled by the novel's rough-and-tumble exuberance, wide social canvas, and frank urbanity, dubbing it both "the most lively book ever published" as well as "low" and "vicious." The novel's precise title, *The History of Tom Jones, a Foundling,* clearly announced its assault on conventional decency and artistic propriety by putting at the center of the fiction a young man who, like Moll Flanders, had no social standing and only his wits and good nature to sustain him. One contemporary even suspected that the earthquakes that shook London in 1750 were divine retribution for the book's popular success.

The book's seismic jolts have been felt ever since. Among critics and literary historians, Fielding and *Tom Jones* have commonly been paired with Samuel Richardson (1689–1761) and his contrary, nearly contemporaneous masterwork, *Clarissa* (1747-1748), marking out the two different paths the English novel would take: inward, in Richardson's treatment, to explore the wellsprings of human personality and consciousness, or in Fielding's outward movement toward the rich panorama of English society, customs, and human affairs. In Dr. Samuel Johnson's famous denigration of Fielding's achievement, Richardson's "characters of nature" were judged superior to Fielding's "characters of manners" with as great a difference between the two novelists "as between a man who knew how a watch was made, and a man who could tell the hour by looking on the dial-plate." Coleridge counters, asserting that *Tom Jones,* along with Sophocles' *Oedipus* and Ben Jonson's *The Alchemist,* were "the three most perfect plots ever planned" and that reading Fielding after Richardson "is like emerging from a sick-room heated by stoves into an open lawn on a breezy day in May." Fated to be continually linked in the literary mind, like Tolstoy and Doestovsky, Keats and Shelley, Hemingway and Fitzgerald, Fielding and Richardson have long served as the rivals they were in life, representing central opposed tendencies in the novel between plot and character, comedy and tragedy, manners and consciousness, the telescope versus the microscope."

What in Fielding's background explains the nature of *Tom Jones*?

Fielding's background, compared to Defoe's and Richardson's, was not middle class but distinguished, and his classical education, legal training, and wide-ranging exposure to high and low life as well as his experience as a dramatist who came to the novel late provided the ideal conjunction of personal qualities and the cultural moment to establish the novel in England as a rival form to poetry and drama. The novel's eventual emergence as a dominant artistic medium owes much to Fielding's genius in blending his comic and dramatic vision to the flexible and expansive narrative form of the novel that he helped devise. Fielding's career as a dramatist ended in 1737 with the passing of legislation restricting the number of authorized theaters, prompted by Fielding's attack of the Walpole government in his plays. The same year, Fielding entered the Middle Temple to study law, and the legal career that took him throughout the country increased his wide knowledge of English life. After 1748 Fielding became one of the most famous of the Bow Street magistrates, closely associated with human suffering and the moral issues that absorbed him and are reflected in his writing.

Fielding took up fiction prompted in part by the publication in 1740 of Samuel Richardson's first novel, *Pamela, or Virtue Rewarded*, which was arguably, after *Don Quixote,* the second-bestselling novel internationally. It is the story of a virtuous maid-servant heroine who rebuffs the unwanted attentions of the rakish Mr. B. before winning his genuine affection and marriage. Fielding set out to puncture Richardson's genteel sentiment and what he perceived to be his false idealization, first in the pastiche, *Shamela* (1741), in which a heroine's virtue is only a pretense to inflame her lover and to manipulate an advantageous marriage. A similar attack on Richardson's sentimentality provides at least the initial ironic focus of Fielding's other masterwork, *Joseph Andrews* (1742). In Fielding's comic parody, Richardson's Pamela is now married to Squire Booby, and her brother, Joseph Andrews, has his virtue assaulted by Booby's sister in a delightful reversal of Richardson's plot. However, what began as a satire on the perceived narrow and hypocritical sentimental virtue in *Pamela* grows into one of the English novel's first great social satires, in which Fielding's good humor and sympathy embrace a wider comic conception of human nature as a blend of frailty and goodness, corruption and virtue. *Joseph Andrews* is also significant for announcing and previewing Fielding's radical narrative departure "hitherto unattempted in our language." Fielding's version of the novel—his "comic romance" or "comic epic poem in prose"—draws on the conventions of the earlier prose romance, epic, and drama but differs from them by its action being more extended and comprehensive, containing a much larger circle of incidents, and introducing a greater variety of characters. It differs from the serious romance in its fable and action in that in the one, these are grave and solemn, so in the other, they are light and ridiculous; it differs in its characters by introducing persons of inferior rank, and consequently of inferior manners, whereas the grave romance sets the highest before us lastly, in its sentiments and diction, by preserving the ludicrous instead of the sublime.

Fielding offers a new definition for the fledgling novel as a hybrid form incorporating the epic's wide vision of central cultural values, comedy's admission for attention of ordinary characters and scenes, and drama's artful arrangement of incident into a skillful plot.

How does *Tom Jones* proceed?

Fielding's claim of creating a comic epic is most masterfully fulfilled in *Tom Jones.* In his story of the adventures of the low-born protagonist, whose generic name suggests an ordinary English Everyman, Fielding introduces a character whose disreputable birth and blend of virtues and flaws extends the novel's realism. By rejecting previous idealization of perfect character types, Fielding paves the way for a frank consideration of the actual ways of the world and a clear-headed conception of human nature. Tom is no paragon; he has all the excesses of youth, perfectly suitable for his entry into a wider world of dupes and knaves, whose outstanding characteristics are their imperfections. The novel begins in the Somersetshire of Fielding's youth, where Tom, whose indiscretions include loving his neighbor's daughter, Sophia Western, cause him to lose the support of Squire Allworthy. He is cast out of the rustic, yet Edenic, Paradise Hall to embark upon a revealing journey through English society. Fielding's account of Tom's education in the ways of the world combines the episodic looseness of the picaresque road narrative—in which the novelist presents an ever-widening cast of characters, scenes, and incidents—with the tight control of the mystery and suspense novel, putting at the center of Tom's story the sensational secret of his birth. Supporting Fielding's social panorama is a formal structure of breathtaking symmetry.

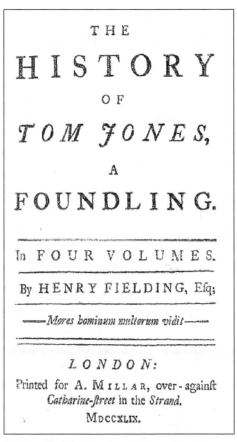

THE

HISTORY

OF

TOM JONES,

A

FOUNDLING.

In FOUR VOLUMES.

By HENRY FIELDING, Efq;

——*Mores hominum multorum vidit*——

LONDON:

Printed for A. MILLAR, over-againſt *Catharine-ſtreet* in the *Strand.*
MDCCXLIX.

Published in 1749, the picaresque, coming-of-age story *Tom Jones* is one of the earliest English works to be classified as a novel.

The novel is divided into eighteen books and subdivided into three equal portions corresponding to the story's principal settings—Somerset, the road to London, and London itself. Each setting features a female—Molly Seagrim, Mrs. Waters, and Lady Bellaston—to tempt Tom and complicate his true love for Sophia. At the inn at Upton, the novel's exact midpoint, Fielding reverses the novel's narrative pressure from Sophia's pursuit of Tom to his pursuit of her, which will only be resolved when the questions of Tom's identity are revealed and his own recognition of his moral failings is accepted at the novel's breathless and triumphant conclusion. All is controlled by the shaping presence of the book's narrator, whose ironic, though compassionate, sympathy insists on a moral standard that embraces man's weaknesses as well as his vitality and accepts the world as it is, even as it is shown very much in need of the good sense the narrator supplies.

There had simply never been anything quite like Fielding's performance in English fiction before. The author of the play *Don Quixote in England* succeeded in a Cervantine equivalent in the English novel, sharing with *Don Quixote* an epic-like depiction of his age's customs and values and offering the amplitude that had previously been achieved in English narrative by Chaucer alone.

What has been the impact and importance of *Tom Jones?*

Like England's first great literary artist, Chaucer, Fielding numbered the classes of men while providing both delight and instruction in human nature and action. If breadth dominates over depth in Fielding's bravura performance, if a convincing inwardness of character is missing in the often emblematic Hogarth-like quality of Fielding's portraiture in pursuit of the universals of human nature, *Tom Jones* compensates in unparalleled enjoyment as well as in the crucial innovations the author brings to the novel form: the harnessing of wide learning and classical tradition to fashion an imaginative structure that rivals poetry and drama as a medium for truth-telling and a massive criticism of life. In the wake of *Tom Jones,* the commonplace realism of Jane Austen, the picaresque and suspenseful marvels of Dickens, Sterne's self-reflective novel as artifice, and the prose epic of Joyce become conceivable.

What about the novel's inward, psychological interest during its earliest evolution?

All three novels—*Robinson Crusoe, Moll Flanders*, and *Tom Jones*—show an interest in the experience of ordinary characters who are neither flawless heroes nor unmitigated villains. Note that all three novels' titles are their central characters' names. This makes clear the novel's interest in particularized characters in particularized settings, in the case of the last two contemporary urban English life.

If the novel pioneered realism over romance and focused on the actual over the fanciful, we can also see evidence of an interest in the interior world of consciousness itself. One of the earliest examples is the French novel *The Princess of Clèves* (1678) by Madame de La Fayette (1634–1693). It shifted the novel's focus from action and adventure to the characters' thoughts and feelings, thereby claiming the distinction of being the first truly psychological novel.

WOMEN CHARACTERS IN EARLY NOVELS

How did *The Princess of Clèves* compare with other forms of French fiction?

In seventeenth-century France, the *roman* designated a fictional narrative of considerable length, set in a remote historical period, dramatizing, usually with numerous subplots connected through coincidence, the extraordinary adventures of heroic characters, who after many challenges to prove their worthiness finally are rewarded with a happy ending in marriage. By the 1660s, the *roman* had become synonymous with the untruthful, and different narrative forms began to emerge to gratify the reader's demand for the *vraisemblable,* for lifelikeness and plausibility. One was the so-called *nouvelle historique* that blurred the distinction between history and fiction by connecting invented characters and situations with historical settings and actual figures. Another was the quasi-historical narrative known as the memoir that purported to offer the private rather than the public side of historical events. Both of these more realistic alternatives to the *roman* that anchored invention in verisimilitude would be employed in *The Princess of Clèves.* It begins by locating its action not in the remote past of the romance but in the more immediate past during the previous century and the reign of Henri II. With its initial emphasis on glamorous court life, the reader is led to expect either the elaborate extravagances of the romance or the private scandals of the powerful. Instead, emphasis shifts to the arrival at court of Mademoiselle de Chartres and her mother to arrange an advantageous marriage. The preliminary description of the intrigues at Henri's court provides the backdrop to the rather mundane process of wooing that commences. The conflict between appearance and reality, the disjunction between how people act and what they truly feel, generates the novel's drama. Mademoiselle de Chartres eventually accedes to her mother's wishes and agrees to a loveless marriage to the Prince de Clèves.

How did Madame de La Fayette elevate character to the center of her novel?

Having altered the direction of the romance from marriage to its consequences, Madame de La Fayette further violates romantic conventions by shifting emphasis from a sequence of adventures imposed on her characters to plausible circumstances caused by the characters themselves. The core of the drama becomes the internal conflict over the Princess de Clèves' duty to her husband, whom she does not love,

Marie-Madeleine Pioche de La Vergne, comtesse de La Fayette was the first author in France to publish a novel, 1678's *The Princess of Clèves,* which is also considered to be the first psychological novel.

171

and a man whom she does. Her conscience prevents infidelity, and, although she attempts to hide her true feelings behind a decorous public mask, the split that ensues between her outward behavior and her deepest feelings forces her to try to resolve her conflict by confessing to her husband with disastrous consequences. It is clear in the enigmatic questions raised by *The Princess of Clèves*—Is deception better than truth? What is the cost of passion and truth to self?—that we are no longer in the nether, fantasy domain of the romance but in the ambiguous and challenging new interior world of the novel.

How is Samuel Richardson important to the further evolution of the novel?

In the English novel, if Defoe is widely credited with first tapping into the novel's primary resource of actual life, and Fielding is mainly responsible for establishing the affinity between the novel and the epic and drama, then Samuel Richardson (1689–1769) played two equally crucial roles in establishing the novel: he made it respectable as a vehicle for serious moral and social exploration, and he began the process of turning the novel inward to delineate the private realm of consciousness, showing how an individual perceives the world and the complex issues underlying motivation.

Richardson was a self-educated businessman who had risen from apprentice to journeyman to respected tradesman and official printer for the House of Commons. His skill as a letter writer resulted in a publisher's offer for him to write a book of sample letters, models of style and behavior for an increasingly literate but unpolished public. Richardson's efforts in imagining various individuals' responses to different experiences led him in 1740, at the age of fifty-one, to interrupt his work on *Familiar Letters* and expand a story he was told of a beautiful, young serving girl who resisted her master's seduction attempts until, won over by her virtue, he married her. "Little did I think," Richardson remarked concerning the origin of *Pamela* (1740), "of making one, much less two volumes of it. But when I began to recollect what had, so many years before, been told me by my friend, I thought the story, if written in an easy and natural manner, suitably to

the simplicity of it, might possibly introduce a new species of writing." Nothing quite like the immediacy and intensity of Pamela's letters to her parents concerning Mr. B.'s assault on her virtue had been written in a novel before, and Richardson's work became an international sensation.

Why is Richardson's *Clarissa* important?

Richardson followed *Pamela* with the momentous *Clarissa* (1747–1748). At nearly a million words, it is one of the longest novels ever written. Compared to the Cinderella-like wish fulfillment of *Pamela,* in which the heroine's virtue rehabilitates her

British author and printer Samuel Richardson was known for his epistolary novels.

rakish pursuer, *Clarissa* offers a far more realistic challenge to the concept of "Virtue Rewarded" that must accommodate Clarissa's elopement with a libertine, her rape, and eventual demise unalloyed by poetic justice beyond a spiritual consolation that virtue is its own reward. Compared to *Pamela,* Richardson's social observation is more acute and his psychological exploration far more complex. His heroine, like Pamela, is still a moral paragon, but Clarissa's self-awareness is brought to the forefront of the drama as she is pressed to hold on to her idealistic principles in a complex practical world of mixed and disguised motives. As in *Pamela,* Richardson's epistolary method achieves a closeness of view and immediacy through his strategy of writing "to the moment," with the correspondent dealing directly with experiences as they occur. However, *Pamela* is close to a monologue in which almost all the letters are written by the heroine herself, with Pamela's naiveté crucial for the unfolding action. In *Clarissa* Richardson widens his approach and drama by including multiple correspondents. The reader, therefore, gains access to both Clarissa's and her seducer, Lovelace's, thoughts as well as a multidimensional perspective on their circumstances by contrasting viewpoints. By strategically cutting from one correspondent to another, Richardson aids verisimilitude by advancing the story more plausibly from several angles of view. The overall effect is an enhancement of both breadth and depth over Richardson's achievement in *Pamela*, while involving the reader actively in the complex issues of right behavior and self-awareness that the novel raises. By locating narrative interest in the workings of human consciousness itself, Richardson discovered one of the novel's great and continual subjects.

Why does it matter that women are the central characters in these novels?

It is worth noting that the central characters in both de La Fayette's and Richardson's novels are women. This is significant for two reasons. The first is that the novel with its emphasis on the actual and the ordinary would bring domestic life and women's perspectives within the range of literary focus for the first time. The second is, as Madame de La Fayette shows, the novel would diminish the barriers for woman writers. Women dramatists and poets were extremely rare due to a lack of opportunity and education that largely put those literary forms out of reach.

Women represented three-quarters of the novel-reading public during the eighteenth century. They liked to read what other women had written, and it is estimated that about half of the two thousand novels published in England during the eighteenth century were by women. Women's strengths were held to be the home and the heart. The outside, non-domestic world of politics and business was a masculine preserve to which women had no ready access or expertise. Women, however, could write with knowledge on domestic subjects and the drama of courtship and marriage. No need for higher education, to which women were denied. Women novelists, such as Aphra Behn, Eliza Haywood, Delarivier Manley, Maria Edgeworth, Mary Wollstonecraft, Ann Radcliffe, and Fanny Burney, published significant English novels during the seventeenth and eighteenth centuries, establishing a market for literary works by women. They were the forerunners of the novel's first master practitioner, Jane Austen (1775–1817).

JANE AUSTEN

Why does Jane Austen matter?

If the novel's earliest practitioners mapped out its dual sociological and psychological boundaries, it is Jane Austen who united both for the first time at the outset of the nineteenth century. Austen turned the novel into an undisputed truth-telling instrument and made it a serious rival to poetry and drama in its artistry. By learning from one of the novel's greatest practitioners, the reader can enhance an appreciation and understanding of the art of the novel.

How did Jane Austen view herself as a novelist, and how have others viewed her?

Designating Jane Austen as a paragon of the triumph of the novel would have shocked (and even embarrassed) the author, who, with characteristic modesty, described herself as "the most unlearned and uninformed female who ever dared to be an authoress" and who disparaged her artistry as "the little bit (two inches wide) of ivory on which I work with so fine a brush, as produces little effect after much labor."

Such an exalted designation would have mystified her contemporaries, most of whom did not know the name behind her anonymous works and would have stupefied the next generation of English novelists during the Victorian period. There is no evidence, for example, that Charles Dickens ever read or even heard of novels written by Jane Austen. Charlotte Brontë reacted so violently against a critic who called Jane Austen a "prose Shakespeare" that she fumed that Austen "ruffles her readers by nothing vehement, disturbs him by nothing profound." Ralph Waldo Emerson characterized her novels as "vulgar in tone, sterile in artistic invention, imprisoned in the wretched conventions of English society." More than one critic, echoing Austen's own self-deprecation, has labeled her a skilled miniaturist rather than a weighty artist with a grand vision. What she leaves out of her novels seemed to many so crucial to our understanding of human nature and what we have come to expect to belong in the novel. They contain few views on man's mortality in philosophical or existential terms; almost nothing about our earthly destiny in grand social or metaphysical

Jane Austen's half dozen novels were critiques of landed gentry society in England.

terms; little on our deepest personal compulsions. Even Henry James, who of all novelists might appreciate Austen's great subtlety and achievement, complained, "With all her light felicity, Jane Austen leaves us hardly more curious of her process, or the experience in her that fed it, than the brown thrush who tells his story from the garden bough." Virginia Woolf echoes James by stating that "of all great writers she is the most difficult to catch in the act of greatness." Allow Mark Twain the final negative comments: "A library without a volume of Jane Austen must be a good library even if it contains no other books."

Why is Jane Austen so popular today?

Modern readers of Jane Austen's works (and viewers of so many acclaimed film and television adaptations) must be perplexed by these complaints. For her contemporary fans, Austen is an unfailing refuge compared to the chaos and clashing modern values governing class and gender. Austen's readers are struck by her rigid social rules but also by her novels' clear moral distinctions and well-behaved (and charmingly dressed) characters. In our social world of apparently no rules, Austen's carefully calibrated social manners and certainties of class and customs point out what we have lost, yet Austen offers her readers far more than nostalgia.

What is left out of Jane Austen's novels, and what is included?

Austen excludes from her novels the artificial accelerants of plots involving hairbreadth escapes, murders, kidnappings, mystery, and suspense and saturates her stories in the ordinary, unexceptional details of everyday life, avoiding extremes of situation or characters. Accordingly, her readers must radically adjust their expectations in reading her

What can you learn about reading the novel from Jane Austen?

Critics and enthusiasts alike risk missing Austen's true genius. Far from being a complacent conservative, Austen needs to be viewed as a true literary revolutionary who broke new fictional ground, making the novel for the first time an important truth-telling medium. One literary historian has argued that Jane Austen is the earliest English novelist "to be read with the feeling that she depicts *our* life, and not a life placed back somewhere in history, or off somewhere in imagined space." Modern fiction, beginning with Austen, demanded that the reader accept neither a nobleman nor a saint as the subject of the novelist's most intense moral and psychological exploration. Instead, Austen insisted that the undramatic crises of everyday life provide the best focus of insight not only into human nature but also into deeper moral significance. Her range is purposely limited to what she knew best. "Three or four families in a country village," she once remarked, was her ideal subject for a novel.

novels. She does not pretend to offer what most novelists before and since have often relied on to engage reader interest. Long before the hit situation comedy *Seinfeld*, Jane
Austen decided to write novels "about nothing," excluding from consideration character of unmitigated virtue or villainy usually encountered in fiction and the exciting series of exceptional situations designed to keep a reader turning the pages. Instead,
Austen, like *Seinfeld*, tries to create her drama out of the unremarkable, featuring mixed
characters in situations we can readily recognize. The great literary critic Lionel Trilling
once said, "The novel is a perpetual quest for reality," and Jane Austen took us further
in that quest than any other novelist before her (and few since). Austen provides not
the distortions and exaggerations of other novels designed to cater to a reader's craving
for escape from the complexities of life but a bracing glimpse of yourself in the mirror,
with all your imperfections. The musician and writer John Lennon once said, "Life is
what happens when you are busy making other plans." That's precisely Austen's point:
our lives are a succession of small, undramatic moments between the next great anticipated event. That's where we live, and to overlook this is to miss the real drama of any
human life. Her version of "nothing happens" is where, ironically, most of the crucial
drama of our lives takes place. James Joyce once said that if his novel *Ulysses* is not
worth reading, then life is not worth living. That same challenge is true for Austen's
novels. Neglect her subjects at your own peril; if you find nothing in her novels to engage your interest or sympathy, what does that say about your interest and involvement
in your own life that is chiefly remarkable for the absence of the extraordinary?

What lessons on how to read a novel can be learned from Jane Austen?

Austen takes to their logical conclusion the interest in realism, sociology, and psychology of the originators of the novel in the seventeenth and eighteenth centuries. What
lessons does she teach in how to read and understand the novel?

1. Let each novel generate its own drama out of the collisions and conflicts between
   self and society. All of Austen's novels are built on the courtship struggles of her
   heroine protagonists, showing how a choice of a mate is not just a question of
   heart but of head, moral compass, and pocketbook. Austen demonstrates how so
   much more is at stake than what we usually consider by romantic comedy. Austen,
   and other great novelists, extends our definition of what is truly dramatic.

2. Be careful to judge novels by what they attempt to do (not by what they don't).
   Dismissing Jane Austen's novels because they lack the plot stimulants like violence, coincidence, and a contrived sequence of breathless action is like resisting
   a comedy because it isn't a tragedy and vice versa. Better to ask: What does the
   novel achieve by omitting elements that we are used to finding in novels? In their
   absence, what keeps our attention and propels us forward?

3. Pay attention to the little things. They matter most. Watch how external forces of
   class and gender assumptions affect character. Austen shows us that, like the climate, humans exist in a social environment. Self, severed from Society, can be

dangerous as Marianne Dashwood in *Sense and Sensibility,* Elizabeth Bennet in *Pride and Prejudice,* and Emma Woodhouse in *Emma* learn only too well. Similarly capitulating to social demands can be self-destructive, as Anne Elliott learns in *Persuasion.* Finding the proper balance between self and society can become one of the great dramas, too often overlooked in the interests of page-turning.

4. Look beneath the surface for the interior drama of character. What characters say and do is undoubtedly significant, but what they don't say or do can be equally crucial. Some of the greatest scenes in Austen's novels are the quietest, those moments of reflection and insight when thoughts and feelings take center stage.

5. Consider how a definition of human nature and human experience is being delineated. The ultimate test of any novel is what it adds to our understanding of ourselves and our society. All of a novel's mighty arsenal of effects—its cast of characters, particularized settings, gradual development—have these simple aims: surprise us by something we don't know or provide the shock of recognition of what we always knew but never before saw or felt so clearly.

What challenges did novelists like Jane Austen face?

As accomplished and important as Jane Austen's novels are, she never became a bestselling author. Her most popular novel, *Pride and Prejudice,* sold just 1,750 copies during Austen's lifetime. In 1814 when Austen published her masterpiece, *Emma,* it took six months to sell out its first edition of 1,250 copies. By contrast, Walter Scott's first novel, *Waverley,* sold 6,000 copies in its first six months, and Maria Edgeworth's novel *Patronage* sold 8,000 copies on its first day of publication. While great success was possible for a novelist, the risk was considerable as well. Production costs kept editions small (500–1,000 copies for an unproven author), and it was cheaper to reprint popular works than risk the cost of unsold new editions. Novelists could sell their copyright upfront, minimizing risk but foregoing any royalties if a book was successful. Jane Austen sold her copyright to *Northanger Abbey* for £10 and *Pride and Prejudice* for £110. Novels were also published "on commission," like

Elizabeth Bennet, the protagonist of *Pride and Prejudice,* must struggle to navigate the ins and outs of English society as do Austen's other heroines.

today's vanity presses in which the author is responsible for all printing and advertising costs. Requiring considerable upfront cost and risk, this method at least ensured the novelist would reap the rewards of a novel's success. Jane Austen published several of her novels on commission: *Sense and Sensibility* (for a profit of £117), *Mansfield Park* (for a profit of around £310) and *Emma* (for a profit of £221). During her lifetime, Jane Austen earned less than £1,000 from her novels.

Why did Jane Austen publish her novels anonymously?

Publishing a novel meant entering the marketplace and earning from your labors, which was not considered a respectable activity for the daughter of a gentleman, like Jane Austen. Therefore, she published her novels anonymously and kept the full knowledge of her authorship to family and friends, although she was "outed" by the Prince Regent, who admired her works and demanded to meet the author.

The novel itself contributed to concealing one's identity as an author. William Makepeace Thackeray would write that in his childhood in the 1810s when Austen published her novels, "To the largest part of the reading public … the novel, like the pole-cat was known only by name and a reputation for bad odour." Queen Victoria was allowed no novels in her youth except devotional ones. Parents were likely to restrict their children's reading of novels to certain wholesome authors and not on Sundays. The low reputation of the novel was certainly the reason that the distinguished poet of the age, Walter Scott, kept his identity a secret when he turned to the novel for money. He became "The Great Unknown," producing in his series of historical novels, beginning with *Waverley* in 1814, the bestselling novels of the first three decades of the nineteenth century.

What changes affected the novel following Jane Austen?

During the nineteenth century in England, the novel would become the dominant literary form, the form of expression most suited to the age. The transformation of social life by urbanization, industrialization, and globalization accelerated in unprecedented ways, and the novel became its chronicles.

Between the beginning of the Victorian era (1837) and its end (1901), Britain was transformed into the world's first industrial and urban society. Before the nineteenth century, most of the British populace still lived in the countryside; during the Victorian era, there would be a dramatic shift to the cities, with London becoming the greatest city of them all. The population of London in 1801 was just under one million (not quite double its size in 1700). It would become the largest city on earth, the first city ever to reach a million inhabitants. By the end of the century, London's population had swelled to around 6.5 million, one-fifth of the population of Britain and Wales (compared to one-twentieth in 1800), equal to the combined populations of Europe's four other great cities: Paris, Berlin, Vienna, and St. Petersburg. By 1900, the London that Defoe in the eighteenth century could have traversed in four miles had expanded to eighteen, covering seventy square miles.

EMMA

How is *Emma* Jane Austen's masterpiece?

If *Pride and Prejudice* remains Jane Austen's most popular and endearing novel, the exuberant achievement of her youth, *Emma,* is her mature masterwork, the apex of Austen's skills as a social satirist, psychologist, and dramatist—the ultimate justification of her assertion that "3 or 4 Families in a Country Village is the very thing to work on." *Emma* combines both the comic social drama of Henry Fielding and the inner exploration of character derived from Samuel Richardson in such a masterful, culminating synthesis that a case can be made that it is the first great display in English of the novel's fullest potential and mastery. Such a high claim certainly was not immediate. The novel's first 1816 edition of 1,250 copies sold in six months, but a second edition did not appear until well after Austen's death, in 1833. Jane Austen herself had misgivings about her novel, fearing that "to those readers who have preferred 'Pride and Prejudice' it will appear inferior in wit, and to those who have preferred 'Mansfield Park' very inferior in good sense." Even more troublesome was her fear that she had created a heroine "whom no one but myself will much like." *Emma* is the longest of Austen's novels and the most psychologically rich with the closest focus on her heroine's inner development, signaled by its being the only one of her novels named for its protagonist. It also most fully exploits Austen's reliance on the commonplace details of ordinary life with which to construct her social dramas. *Emma* depicts a year in the life of the Surrey village of Highbury, in which nothing out of the usual happens beyond the natural cycle of births, deaths, and marriages and the various unexceptional comings and goings in a self-enclosed, provincial community.

How does *Emma* proceed?

Like all of Austen's novels, *Emma* explores the progress of its heroine to the altar, a romantic drama that is fundamentally a process of growth and education into the ways of the world and human nature. Unlike her other novels, *Emma*'s protagonist is hampered neither by a lack of fortune nor status, having only the disadvantage of her own immaturity to complicate her destiny: "Emma Woodhouse, handsome,

The title page from the 1909 edition of *Emma,* Jane Austen's masterwork of her mature years as an author.

clever, and rich, with a comfortable home and happy disposition seemed to unite some of the blessings of existence; and had lived nearly twenty-one years in the world with very little to distress or vex her." With her mother dead, her older sister married and living in London, and her father a hypocondriacal "valetudinarian," Emma is the uncontested mistress of Hartfield, the most prominent household in Highbury, which she dominates. With only her brother-in-law's older brother, Mr. Knightley, willing to criticize her, Emma is afflicted with the "power of having rather too much her own way, and a disposition to think a little too well of herself."

The novel opens significantly with the departure from Hartfield of Emma's former governess and companion, Miss Taylor, who has married the Woodhouses' neighbor, Mr. Weston, leaving Emma on her own for the first time. Emma flatters herself that she has succeeded in arranging the match, and she looks about for another opportunity for matchmaking. She befriends Harriet Smith, "the natural daughter of somebody," and recklessly decides that Harriet is the perfect match for the local vicar, Mr. Elton. To clear the way, Emma must convince Harriet that her attachment to the local farmer Robert Martin is beneath her and intimidates Harriet into rejecting his proposal when it comes. Indulging in a romantic fantasy, Emma is guilty of a series of social errors that underscore her blindness, vanity, and snobbery. Her encouragement of Mr. Elton on behalf of Harriet is ultimately misperceived by the clergyman as evidence of Emma's own interest in him, and she is comically blindsided by his proposal following a Christmas party at the Westons that concludes the novel's first volume. Mr. Elton's drunken impertinence exposes Emma's errors of judgment. Her exaggerated sense of her own importance and infallibility and her snobbish prejudices all prevent her from seeing correctly the social reality or the natures of those around her. She ends this first stage of her development by swearing off future matchmaking (while violating her prohibition almost instantaneously). Emma has played with love and romance by proxy through Harriet; however, the stakes will subsequently increase as she allows her own affections to be engaged, and she also finds herself the victim of another's scheming and manipulation.

What are the conflicts in *Emma*?

Part of Emma's problem is that life in Highbury has grown too stale and complacent, and her superiority has been assumed rather than earned. Three newcomers will help Highbury to awaken from its moribund routine, revive its social obligations, and reaffirm its principles. They will also help Emma complete her education. One is the estimable Jane Fairfax, the talented young niece of Miss Bates, a garrulous Highbury spinster. Brought up and educated by Colonel and Mrs. Campbell as a companion to their daughter, Jane has returned to Highbury to visit her aunt and grandmother after her friend's marriage to Mr. Dixon. Jane is Emma's equal (or superior) in everything but fortune and consequently is not one of Emma's favorites. Another visitor is Mr. Weston's son by his first marriage, Frank Churchill, who lives with his aunt and uncle and has finally come to Highbury to pay his respects to his father's new bride. The agreeably sociable Frank flirts with Emma, and the pair enjoys a secret joke at Jane's expense alleging that she has had an unhappy love affair with her friend's husband, Mr. Dixon, who seems to be the only possible source for the gift of a piano that Jane receives. The third newcomer is the former Augusta Hawkins, now married to Mr. Elton. An ill-bred parvenu, Mrs. Elton challenges Emma for social dominance in Highbury and offers her a pointed comparison to her own tendency toward vanity and snobbery: "Mrs. Elton was a vain woman, extremely well satisfied with herself, and thinking much of own importance.... She meant to shine and be very superior, but with manners which had been formed in a bad school, pert and familiar." The bad breeding of both husband and wife is in evidence at the long-awaited ball at the Crown Inn. Their snub of Harriet is answered by Mr. Knightley, who, foregoing his previous reluctance to dance, saves the embarrassed Harriet by becoming her partner. It is a fateful act that causes Emma to acknowledge his superiority and to see Knightley as a potential partner as well. The following day, Harriet is beset by a band of gypsies (the novel's one extraordinary circumstance) and is rescued by Frank Churchill. Harriet's later confession to Emma that she is now over Mr. Elton and prefers someone more superior leads Emma to think that she must mean Frank. She willingly accedes to her friend's preference, matchmaking yet again.

What is the novel's climax?

As summer arrives, the complicated tangle of relationships reaches a crisis point. Jane prepares to accept a governess position arranged through Mrs. Elton; Frank is inexplicably out of humor at the news; and Mr. Knightley has finally reasserted his social responsibilities as one of the principal landowners by reviving the social life of his estate of Donwell Abbey. The excursion to his home stimulates a more ambitious journey to Box Hill, where Frank caters to the worst of Emma's imperious tendencies with a game in which each of the party are commanded to entertain Miss Woodhouse by saying one clever thing, "or two things moderately clever—or three things very dull indeed." Miss Bates chooses the latter, prompting Emma's unpardonably rude remark: "Ah! ma'am, but there may be a difficulty. Pardon me—but you will be limited as to number—only three at once." The entire novel will turn on this witty remark at Miss Bates's expense that crystallizes all of Emma's shortcomings. These are made painfully (and tearfully) clear to

"*Say 'No' if it is to be said.*"   *She could really say nothing*

An illustration by Chris Hammond for the 1898 edition of *Emma* depicts Mr. Knightley and Emma.

181

Emma in Mr. Knightley's later rebuke. She is mortified for the hurt she has caused an old family friend who deserves her respect and compassion and for eliciting Mr. Knightley's poor opinion of her behavior. Repentant, Emma visits Miss Bates the next day, an act of reformation and an acknowledgement of her error that pave the way for the comic conclusion of the novel that depends on Emma's maturation.

How does *Emma* conclude?

In rapid succession, complications give way to three weddings. Frank's aunt dies suddenly, and it is revealed that Frank has been secretly engaged to Jane all along. His duplicity and manipulation are the final telling comparison with Emma's own behavior, which also has been at times far from open and honest. Emma's first thought, however, is for "poor Harriet," who she assumes to be in despair over the news. Instead, in the great comic revelation in the novel, Harriet admits that she has set her sight not on Frank but on Mr. Knightley. It was Knightley's chivalric treatment of her at the ball, not Frank's rescue from the gypsies, that has earned Harriet's affections after Emma encouraged her to aim higher than her station might otherwise have allowed. Emma is shocked into a recognition of her blindness and folly: "With insufferable vanity had she believed herself in the secret of everybody's feelings; with unpardonable arrogance proposed everybody's destiny. She was proved to have been universally mistaken. She had brought evil on Harriet, on herself, and she too much feared, on Mr. Knightley." Equally powerful is her realization "that darted through her with the speed of an arrow that Mr. Knightley must not marry anyone but herself."

After two previous proposals—Mr. Elton's and Frank's confession that is misperceived as a proposal by Emma—the way is now clear for the culminating and appropriate third. Misunderstanding the other's feelings—Knightley that Emma is in despair over Frank's engagement and Emma over the presumed affection between Knightley and Harriet—the couple comes to a satisfactory agreement in the end. As for the exact words of Knightley's proposal and Emma's acceptance, the author retreats to a discreet, generalizing distance: "What did she say?—Just what she ought, course. A lady always does.—She said enough to show there need not be despair—and to invite him to say more himself." To add to the happy conclusion of reconciliation and unity, Harriet is granted a second proposal from Robert Martin, the original object of her affection, to make up the third match. Emma has learned crucial lessons about her own nature and her responsibilities in an adult world. The final view is provided by Mrs. Elton, who laments the absence of white satin and lace that makes Emma's wedding a "most pitiful business." However, Emma's maturation in her nature and her social responsibility makes it one of the most satisfying comic culminations in which someone who, in her own words seems "to have been doomed to blindness," finally sees clearly. It is the essential step, in Austen's mind, for a heroine to assume her proper station as an adult and a wife.

As in all her novels, marriage is not a simple, sentimental climax but the result of a complex moral and social negotiation that reveals much about human nature and experience. To reach the altar triumphantly, Emma must first learn painful lessons about self-deception and the ego's often dangerous drive for mastery and control. Emma, like the reader, is schooled in the complicated matter of living, in which common sense and clarity replace self-deception and delusion.

THE ENGLISH NOVEL AFTER JANE AUSTEN

What made London so exceptional in the development of the novel?

There simply had never been this concentration of people in one place before. As one writer observed, "London is more than a city: it is a whole kingdom in itself." London at the end of the nineteenth century had more inhabitants than Ireland, Switzerland, and Australia; it had twice the population of Norway or Greece. There were more Irish in London than in Dublin; more Scots than in Aberdeen; more Roman Catholics than in Rome. It had become the capital of capitals, with a greater concentration of personal wealth than anywhere else on earth, alongside the world's most miserable slums. It was accurately described as "the city of dreadful contrasts."

What were some of London's "dreadful contrasts"?

London was both thrilling in its enormity and diversity, exhilarating in its energy, and terrifying in its density, confinement, and dislocations. As Henry James observed, "immensity was the great fact" of London and that "it is the biggest aggregation of human life—the most complete compendium of the world." London contained all the trappings of the world's undisputed superpower, the inner sanctums and playgrounds of the monarchy, parliament, and the wealthiest citizens in the world, alongside overflowing cesspits, disease-ridden streets, rampant prostitution, and criminality. It was estimated that a third of London's population (about a million people) in mid-century lived in filthy, ill-constructed courts and alleys, in decrepit houses and single rooms. Unlike Paris and New York, London had no coherent development dictated by an urban designer or by a rational grid pattern. London, instead, like a Darwinian species, evolved spontaneously. Dislocation and relocation were constant. Nothing ever stood still in London; nothing was constant except continual change and movement. London, therefore, became a particularly new and modern phenomenon: the megalopolis that was spawning a new form of human life and human possibility.

CHARLES DICKENS

How is Dickens's rise as a novelist reflected in the urban scene?

Charles Dickens (1812–1870) would become the first great novelist of city life at a time when the city itself became the embodiment of modern civilization. It can also be argued that the novel as an art form is essentially a city art form that originated in response to the needs and interests of a new urban audience in the eighteenth century. An art form that required popular support rather than a patron's subsidy needed an urban concentration of readers. The phenomenon of the urbanization of society is the crucial social fact of modern life that writers were quick to respond to. Balzac in France attempted to guide readers through the various substrata of Parisian life; Dostoevsky would do the same in the second half of the nineteenth century in Russia—but no writer before him (and few after him) would explore the implications of the modern city more thoroughly than Dickens.

How did Dickens use the city as a backdrop to explore urban life?

Dickens's art coincided with an enormous change in human history, and he was the first major writer to realize the aesthetic possibility of London's new urban world that was generating a new kind of human energy, as well as a new challenge to traditional conceptions of human nature and the human experience. Dickens would begin his writing career conducting his readers into the labyrinthine complexity of London, providing a coherent report of the bewildering phenomenon of a newly emerging urban society of street folk, outcasts, criminals, costermongers, and clerks. Dickens would explore the positive and negative sides of London's impact, joyfully celebrating its life-affirming energy and probing its darker, sinister secrets and threats.

What do Dickens and his novels tell us about modern city life?

It has been said that Dickens may have been the last person to know London in full and as a whole. His expertise in London street life became his initial contribution to English fiction and the source of his first notoriety as a writer. Here was someone whose imagination not only could take readers to places that they had never visited before but also could make sense of the chaos of London life and reveal its organizing principles, its classes, and values. His early fiction is suffused with London's power, its exuberant diversity, its messy multiplicity. Dickens fed off London's energy and needed it to stimulate him. For him, London was his "magic lantern." He declared, "A day in London sets me up again and starts me." He was no less haunted by its threats and horrors. Being lost and victimized in a heartless city is, in a sense, Dickens's great theme in

Possibly the most popular novelist of nineteenth-century England (and still popular today, of course), Charles Dickens expressed concern in his books for his country's lower classes.

all his books. He was the first novelist to explore fully the ways in which a great modern, industrialized city like London could thwart human desires and cripple both physically and psychologically. He was one of the first to recognize that traditional human relationships were undergoing profound changes in the crucible of the modern industrialized city. Dickens revealed London's most sinister paradox: it was a busy, noisy multitude where one could easily feel alone or get lost in the crowd. London's multiplicity and grandness ironically pointed up the insignificance of the individual, and Dickens was the first to probe the psychological implication of modern alienation, paranoia, even madness and psychosis. Dickens would create some of the first recognizably modern characters: individuals who become their jobs, whose lives are completely ruled as mechanical parts in a vast, urban system that they do not control. Moreover, the threat of crime and disease forces individuals to seek safety and refuge in more confinement and greater class division that further isolates individuals. His great social theme would become the connection among classes and individuals that Londoners—and all of us—ignore at our peril.

ANALYSIS OF CHARLES DICKENS'S
THE PICKWICK PAPERS

What was the backstory to *The Pickwick Papers*?

What is initially striking about Dickens's remarkable achievement in his first novel is the sense of the collision of the accidental with the incendiary genius of a twenty-four-year-old, relatively obscure journalist and parliamentary reporter. *The Posthumous Papers of the Pickwick Club* (later more familiarly known as *The Pickwick Papers*) launched Dickens's career as a novelist to unrivaled heights, helped to establish the novel as the dominant literary form of the Victorian period, and set the model for the ways fiction would be published for a significant portion of nineteenth century. All because Dickens, who was not the first choice of publishers Chapman and Hall, was hired to supply the text for a series of cockney sporting sketches for a picture book to be published in monthly installments by the popular illustrator Robert Seymour (1798–1836). Most established writers would have rejected both the scheme of relegating their words as a mere accompaniment to the book's illustrations and the installment form of publication, a method previously reserved for cheap reprints of standard works, religious tracts, and vulgar comedies. Dickens, however, who had begun to get noticed for his series of views of London street life, *Sketches by Boz*, jumped at the chance to earn £14 for each monthly installment. He could be married to his intended, Catherine Hogarth, and begin in earnest his career as a full-time writer.

What happened next is one of the great publishing stories of all time. Dickens convinced Chapman and Hall to modify Seymour's original concept of views of the sporting misadventures of a group of townsmen to give the writer "freer range of English scenes and people." Dickens was no sportsman, but he was reporting on provincial elections in stories filled with details about contemporary customs and characters that he wanted to exploit through the travels of Samuel Pickwick and his fellow club members—Nathaniel Winkle, the amateur sportsman; Augustus Snodgrass, the aspiring poet; and Tracy Tupman, the romantic bachelor. As Dickens's control over the project increased, Robert Seymour watched his own part in what was originally his concept shift to a secondary position by the sheer force of the young writer's imagination and ambition. The illustrator dutifully completed the revision of his drawings for the series' second number and then committed suicide.

An illustration by Robert Seymour for Dickens' *Pickwick Papers*.

How did Dickens alter the original conception and transform the novel?

Seymour's death in 1836 caused Chapman and Hall to consider abandoning the project, but Dickens offered a plan to alter it. Dickens proposed increasing the monthly text from twenty-four to thirty-two pages and reducing the number of illustrations from four to two per installment. *Pickwick Papers* was thereby transformed into a novel, giving Dickens more space to develop his characters and situations. With his introduction of Sam Weller, Mr. Pickwick's cockney servant in Number 4, sales of the series exploded. The initial printing of 1,000 copies of Number 1 was cut in half for Number 2, but with Number 4, sales increased to over 20,000 per month. By the conclusion of the novel's installment run, monthly sales had risen to 40,000 copies, and the novel had become a phenomenon. Pickwick merchandise flooded the market: hats, canes, cigars, jest books, and china figurines. There also were Pickwick songs, dances, stage productions, and unauthorized sequels. Judges read the issues during breaks in trials, while the poor pooled their pennies to buy each installment, with the illiterate having each read to them. The book's initial audiences were drawn to Dickens' inventiveness and were transfixed by the young author's ability to craft a fresh, comic masterpiece out of stock characters and situations. As a result of the success of *Pickwick,* the installment form of publication became popular—all of Dickens's following thirteen novels would appear in monthly or weekly installments, either separately or as part of a periodical offering. This trend increased the novel's appeal by putting book ownership into the hands of individuals who previously could not afford one. *Pickwick* allowed readers to extend payments for novels over a nineteen-month period, made it possible for publishers to recoup their costs during the same period, and established an unprecedented relationship between novelist and audience as monthly sales figures gave the writer a clear reaction to a work in progress.

How is *Pickwick* structured?

It is not surprising, given the inherited conception and improvised nature of publication, with Dickens inventing his story as he went along, that the *Pickwick Papers*, or, more precisely, *The Posthumous Papers of the Pickwick Club Containing a Faithful Record of the Perambulations, Perils, Travels, Adventures and Sporting Transactions of the Corresponding Members,* begins as a series of picaresque episodes and interpolated tales. Pickwick and his companions set out from London to Rochester, where they fall in with the rascally Alfred Jingle, who gets Winkle involved in a duel. They move on to Dingley Dell and the home of the Wardles, where Jingle reappears and elopes with Mr. Wardle's sister. Jingle is pursued, and Mr. Pickwick, ever in need of a practical guide, engages the irrepressible, street-smart Sam Weller as his servant, providing a cockney Sancho Panza for the idealistic and naive Quixote-like Pickwick. Together they visit Eatanswill during a parliamentary election and Bury St. Edmunds, where Jingle and his own servant Job Trotter resurface. Both are again pursued to Ipswich, where at an inn Mr. Pickwick accidentally enters the bedroom of a middle-aged lady during the night, provoking a conflict with her admirer. The novel proceeds, therefore, to new locations, situations, and characters with little unity beyond the episode nor with much depth of characterization beyond comic types. However, the novel's episodic structure finally develops into an actual plot when Mrs. Bardle, Pickwick's London landlady, confused over his intentions, falls into the hands of sharp-practicing lawyers and brings a suit against him for breach of promise. The trial, one of the novel's and literature's comic triumphs, results in a judgment for the plaintiff, and Mr. Pickwick, who refused to pay the damages, is imprisoned for a time. Pickwick by this time has been transformed in Dickens' handling from something of a comic cliché to a moral force and archetype of innocence and benevolence. The novel concludes with a satisfying comic resolution of most of the novel's difficulties, including the regeneration of Jingle, the long-delayed marriage of the perennial bachelor Winkle, and Pickwick's retirement from his travels into a small community of fellowship and good intentions.

What is Dickens's achievement in *Pickwick*?

Pickwick is a triumph of Dickens's ability to animate characters and scenes, creating a rich, exuberant catalogue of unforgettable situations and dialogue. It is also the beginning of the novelist's ever-expanding pantheon of remarkable fictional portraits, including the coachman Tony Weller, medical students Bob Sawyer and Benjamin Allen, the Fat Boy, the rapacious lawyers Dodson, Fogg, and Mr. Serjeant Buzfuz, and a host of others. The novel allowed Dickens to develop his imaginative muscle while learning to control his powers under the pressure of installment publication. At this early stage of his career, Dickens could apologetically observe in the preface written after the novel's installment run that "no artfully interwoven or ingeniously complicated plot can with reason be expected." He would go on to write the most artfully interwoven and complicated plots imaginable in this "detached and desultory form of publication," producing mystery novels, such as *Bleak House, Little Dorrit, Great Expectations,* and *Our Mutual Friend,* which are also massive social and moral fables. *Pickwick Papers* announced the arrival of a writer whom Edmund Wilson called the "greatest dramatic writer the English had had since Shakespeare," who, like Chaucer, magnificently "numbered the classes of men." If *Pickwick* lacks the artistry, daring social themes, and accomplishment of Dickens's later works, it is still one of the comic treasures of English and world literature, marking the beginning of the novelist's incredible ability to reshape the world imaginatively in ways that continue to be described as "Dickensian."

SERIAL NOVELS

How did novels in serial form become popular?

Readers who did not subscribe to a circulating library could still get new novels after Dickens pioneered the practice of serial publication with *The Pickwick Papers* in 1837. Dickens's first novel transformed the way novels were published, making it a mass-market entertainment.

What was the advantage of serial novel publication?

With the serial installment method of novel publication that Dickens pioneered, which would be imitated by others, readers could buy in paper wrappers a novel in monthly parts. Each installment was thirty pages, usually with two illustrations. The cost was a shilling a part in nineteen monthly installments, the last a double issue with author's forward, table of contents, and a *frontis* illustration. At the end of the run, readers could take the part issues back to the bookseller (or stationers) to be bound. Novel readers could, therefore, have novels for a pound (two-thirds the cost of a normal three-volume novel) and spread out the cost over a year and a

Periodicals such as the popular *The Strand* published novels in serial form, including the Sherlock Holmes stories of Sir Arthur Conan Doyle. This form of publication helped give rise to the "cliffhanger" to encourage customers to buy the next issue.

half in manageable monthly payments. This method was responsible for expanding the novel-reading public into a mass market of book owners. Publishers liked the form for its high circulation with income monthly, revenue from advertising, and their ability to spread out their costs to the author and printing costs over the run. Authors liked it for its financial rewards, which reached them while the book was coming out.

How did the serial form create the art of the "cliffhanger"?

Publishing a novel in serial form, despite the almost impossible challenges, benefited both author and reader. Serial publication enhanced suspense since readers had to wait a month to see what happened next. There would be no looking ahead to the last chapter. The serial form also created a bond between author and reader that is unknown today. There was a sense of the novel coming fresh from the author's pen, reinforced by the fact that often novelists had not finished a book before it started its run in parts. Dickens, early in his career, wrote two serials at once. He juggled the monthly installments of *Pickwick,* started a weekly serial (*Oliver Twist*), and before that concluded, launched another monthly novel (*Nicholas Nickleby*). He only reported having one moment of panic under the pressure of serial publication: he was in a stationery shop when he overheard a lady inquiring for the latest number of *David Copperfield*. She was told it would be out at the end of the month, and Dickens knew he hadn't written a word of

---

How did the serial form enhance the relationship between novelist and reader?

If a novelist could "turn in the space," the relationship achieved in serial publication restored novel writing to something like the original storytelling context of performance. It would be the closest novelists would get to live performance. Like an actor onstage, the novelist could gauge audience reaction during the performance: monthly or weekly sales immediately communicated a response and prompted adjustments. In *Martin Chuzzlewit*, for example, disappointing initial sales caused Dickens to send his protagonist off to America and a new change of setting. In *David Copperfield*, the original for Mrs. Mowcher, the novel's dwarf hairdresser, wrote to Dickens to complain about her characterization, and Dickens altered his plan, shifting Mrs. Mowcher from a villain to a hero. Dickens would receive advice as he went along about what should happen in his novels, whether Nell, for example, should die in *The Old Curiosity Shop*. The relationship between installment author and reader has been described as "something continual, confidential, something like personal affection." Novel writing this way was a challenge and test of ability which Dickens drew strength from; others, like Eliot, rejected it. Such catering to audience demand helped keep the novel an all-purpose, inclusive entertainment.

it: "Once, and but once only in my life, I was frightened." The strain was enormous and was not for the faint of heart. Charlotte Brontë refused a publisher's suggestion that she write a serial, and George Eliot rejected an offer from Dickens himself to supply one of his magazines with a novel in part. Dickens reported that she had said she "couldn't turn in the space."

What were some disadvantages of the serial form?

Disadvantages, however, were also sizable, beyond the stamina and discipline required. Each part needed to be nearly self-sufficient; each needed to advance the action and involve the major characters. With weekly or monthly breaks between installments, novelists needed to remind readers about who the characters were and what the situation was. Often, the design of the whole needed to be subordinated to the demands of the monthly or weekly unit. Each needed to end at a moment of crisis or suspense to ensure interest in the next installment.

The serial form encourages a loose, flexible design, prone to improvisation and padding. The easiest kind of narrative to attempt in a serial was the journey, sending your characters off on a series of episodic adventures; each could introduce new characters and circumstances. This is precisely what Dickens relied upon in his first novel and serial, *The Pickwick Papers*. At its conclusion, Dickens rather apologetically confesses that in this "detached and desultory form of publication, no artfully interwoven or ingeniously complicated plot can with reason be expected." For Dickens, through *Oliver Twist, Nicholas Nickleby, Barnaby Rudge, The Old Curiosity Shop, Martin Chuzzlewit, Dombey and Son*, and *David Copperfield*, starting a new serial was quite literally a journey into the unknown. With Dickens later novels such as *Bleak House, Great Expectations*, and *Our Mutual Friend,* he managed to cut his material to the demanding mystery and suspense pattern that required careful planning.

How did magazines affect the development of the novel?

In the end, another form of cheap novel publishing devoured all the others. If Dickens pioneered the monthly serial novel, he also engineered its nemesis: the successful magazine serial. Magazines would prove to be the death knell for the separate monthly part serial. With a magazine, for a few pennies, a reader could get his installment of a novel and much else besides. Dickens himself launched a monthly magazine for his work as well as a popular weekly publication that began to supply serial fiction to the masses. *A Tale of Two Cities* and *Great Expectations* both came out in weekly installments, which were smaller than monthly ones and usually only a chapter or two, with even less "room to turn" and even more a problem of controlling action and climaxes. The mass market meant subservience to editorial control and censorship that Dickens circumvented by being his own editor and owner. Other novelists, such as Thomas Hardy, would not be so lucky, and one of the chief reasons Hardy abandoned the novel was because of the cuts insisted on to bring his novels out in a family-oriented periodical.

Learning the manner of novel production enhances the reading experience of Victorian fiction and helps promote understanding: what challenges novelists faced and how they were able to surmount them.

What did Charles Dickens and the other great Victorian novelists contribute to the art of the novel?

Dickens and his fellow Victorian novelists would, like Jane Austen before them, take the sociological and psychological focus of the novel to its logical conclusion. Dickens, with a seemingly inexhaustible interest in and retention of the world around him, would produce some of the most memorable characters in literature. For Dickens, dramatic collisions of character

Like Dickens, William Makepeace Thackeray influenced the novel form by writing about ordinary, flawed people in such works as *Vanity Fair*.

and incident produced the illumination he required. Other Victorians would more strictly follow the route laid out by Jane Austen toward the real, eschewing the extraordinary. William Makepeace Thackeray (1811–1863) chose for his masterpiece *Vanity Fair* (1847–1848) the subtitle "A Novel without a Hero," as revolutionary a statement as any later modernist experiment. By doing so, Thackeray suggests an enhanced realistic standard in which not paragons but unexceptional, flawed individuals and their far-from-idealized daily routines should take center stage, initiating the psychological realism and the drama of ordinary life that would be adapted and modified by many subsequent novelists during the period. As Thackeray's biographer Gordon Ray summarizes, "Thackeray's novel achieves for the first time in English the effects of massive realism: among the novelists of the world, indeed, only Stendhal and Balzac had earlier shown how to establish character in society by deluging the reader with information concerning the daily routine, the employments, the pleasures, and the manners of their figures." Thackeray in crucial ways clears the ground of melodramatic excesses and idealization of character that would make the construction of the modern novel possible.

VICTORIAN NOVELS

What other novelists provide insights on the emerging culture of the nineteenth century?

Other English novelists, such as William Thackerary, George Eliot, Anthony Trollope, and Thomas Hardy, would follow Dickens into the labyrinth of the modern urban, industrial environment and the breakdown of traditional rural life. Honoré de Balzac, in his massive series of novels, *The Human Comedy,* and Emile Zola would similarly document the impact and consequences of modern life. In Russia, Fyodor Dostoevsky would become one of the great novelists of alienation and spiritual loss in the modern urban setting. These novelists, in advance of modern sociology and psychology, were the principal guides to their age, fulfilling the promise of the novel as a truth-telling instrument.

How were novels published during the Victorian period?

The most obvious difference between today's novels and those published during the Victorian period is the lack of distinction among novel readers then. Today, a clear distinction is made between serious and important works of fiction, designated "literary" or "high-brow," and novels that dominate the bestseller list, regarded as "popular" or "low-brow." During the Victorian period, almost every serious and important novel was also a bestseller. This is an extraordinary accomplishment. Serious or literary novels (though the literary designation did not yet exist) were addressed not only to an intellectual elite and the highly educated but also to the common reader. Like Elizabethan drama, the Victorian novel was inclusive and vital because of, not despite, its attempt to appeal to the widest possible audience.

How did novels reach a large, popular audience?

Novel readers needed to become novel buyers. The story of the achievement of the Victorian novel and how to understand it is directly related to changes in the novel's production and availability.

There were several ways of getting novels into the hands of Victorian readers. The commonest form was in three small volumes, like bound paperbacks but with wide margins and more space between lines. The cost (for most of the century) of such books was 31 shillings (about $300). This is more than 1 percent of an acceptable middle-class income of £100 per year. Consequently, most Victorians were book borrowers rather than owners. Circulating libraries stepped in to deliver books for an annual subscription: usually less than the cost of a single, three-volume novel. Separate volumes made for convenience of sharing as an entire family could share a rented novel one volume at a time. Three-volume novels, however, meant many pages for authors to fill, producing what Henry James described as the "loose, baggy monster": the characteristic panoramic, multiple-character, Victorian novel of complex plots.

One- or two-volume novels were rare. They were unpopular with publishers due to the tyranny of the circulating libraries (who wanted to keep costs high). One-volume novels were usually reserved for cheap reprints two or three years after original publication.

How did the Victorian novel pioneer the genre of "social realism"?

Chronicling a rapidly changing culture produced by urbanization and industrialization, the Victorian novelists would become their era's primary historians and social scientists. Dickens, Thackeray, and others, in their capacious, three-volume form, would pioneer a radically new fiction: the novel of the social group, of multiple characters juxtaposed and contrasted to become colossal critiques of life. Perhaps the greatest example of that, and the Victorian novel's truth-telling achievement, is George Eliot's *Middlemarch* (1871–1872). With its subtitle "A Study of Provincial Life," *Middlemarch* attempts nothing less than a portrait of an entire community during the crucial historical period of 1829–1831, which saw Catholic Emanci-

The Western world was undergoing tremendous technological, political, and social changes during the reign of Britain's Queen Victoria, events that are reflected in the literature of the day.

pation, the death of George IV, and the election of 1831 that would produce the first Reform Bill extending voting rights. During that time, traditional English customs, authority, and values were tested, and Eliot's contemporary world emerged. To make that happen, she needed a fourth volume to contain her sprawling tale of four connected plot centers and multiple characters, which collectively formed a nuanced, interdependent social web that was tied to a particular historical moment. As Eliot's attempt to achieve a comprehensive vision, *Middlemarch* is a supreme example of the novel's art both as a culmination of the Victorian push to assert a realistic standard for fiction and in registering essential truths about who we are and how we act.

How should you read the Victorian novel?

Here are some suggestions for reading and understanding the Victorian novel:

1. *Don't be daunted by the Victorian novel's length.* No question that at thirty-two pages for twenty monthly installments (640 pages in total), the Victorian triple-decker is one of the longest novels you are likely to encounter. The canvas is wide, often panoramic, connecting a large cast of characters, multiple settings, and a variety of situations. Unity may come from a life story (*David Copperfield*) or central themes (the law in *Bleak House;* the prison in *Little Dorrit*). There usually is a steady accretion of detail until an entire society and its pressures are invoked. Length contributes to our understanding, so settle in for a long but hopefully memorable journey.

2. *Read like a Victorian.* The best way to take that journey to try to and replicate the reading experience of the Victorian novels' first readers. You may not want to take nineteen months go through one of Dickens' or Thackeray's monthly serials, but knowing how they were divided and pausing at the installment breaks to consider the impact of each part and its connection to the whole should greatly assist your understanding and pleasure. Unfortunately, not all editions come equipped with the part breaks, so seek those that do. In a pinch, the many helpful Victorian novel

websites or reference works devoted to the individual authors can provide them. One site, mouseholdwords.com, will send you part installments of several Victorian novels to a schedule you designate. Whenever possible, try to read an edition that includes all the original illustrations. Dickens worked closely with his illustrators; Thackeray did his own illustrations for several of his novels, and "reading" the illustrations provides invaluable insights.

3. *Watch the novel.* Over the years there have been many outstanding film and television productions of classic Victorian novels. With some exceptions, film versions tend to be such abridgements that they fail to provide both the depth *and* breadth that is the Victorian novel specialty. More successful are the multipart serials that better approximate the reading experience.

4. *Become a Victorian.* All Victorian novels provide a rich surface realism that depends on knowledge of customs, geography, and contemporary events that elude most modern readers. Annotations, so much a part of reading Shakespeare, have not yet appeared in most editions of Victorian novels. Instead, readers can consult the many available guides to Victorian life that help answer questions about daily life during the period that the novels reflect.

HOW ARE NOVELS CONSTRUCTED?

What models of construction did novelists imitate?

At the emergence of the novel in the eighteenth century, novelists had multiple structural models to imitate or adapt. Long prose romances preceded the novel, and most employed an episodic arrangement of sequential events organized around a quest or a journey. The sections of the episodic narrative can be independent and detachable from what comes before or follows, like individual beads on a string, which are infinitely expandable. In the medieval romance, the narrative concludes when the quest is completed with each episode testing the questing hero and providing obstacles to the goal; in the picaresque romance, the story ends when the road does. Defoe, in *Moll Flanders*, and Fielding, in *Tom Jones,* would build their novels atop an episodic, journeying substructure, with each section a way-station on their protagonist's journey. In *Moll Flanders*, it is a life story and redemptive journey from sin to salvation; in *Tom Jones,* it is the hero cast out of his home and separated from his beloved, enduring all the setbacks and consequences before being reunited with both.

The other structural model available for the trailblazing novelists in the eighteenth century to consider employing is drama. Plays organize their episodes into scenes but then group these into larger units of acts that are patterned as simple as beginning-middle-end or conflict, rising-action, climax, falling-action, denouement. Dramatic structure converts the seemingly random, consecutive nature of the episodic story into the cause-and-effect arrangement we call plot. "And then … and then" is replaced by "this happens because that happens." It is this dramatic method that Jane Austen would pioneer in the novel, replacing a string of unrelated characters and incidents into a carefully crafted drama. In the episodic novel, characters seem little more than willing passengers under the forward pressure of the vehicle of incident. In the dramatic structure of Austen and others, characters cause the incidents and suffer the consequences for their actions.

A third literary structure available to early novelists is the epic. Synonymous for its length and breadth, the epic showed how a long narrative could be controlled. In the case of Homer's *Iliad*, action is shaped dramatically, following the consequence of Achilles' fateful withdrawal from combat at Troy, or, as in Homer's *Odyssey,* it is shaped episodically, chronicling the many homecoming adventures of the wandering Odysseus. Other great epics like Virgil's *Aeneid*, Dante's *The Divine Comedy,* and Milton's *Paradise Lost* employ both Homer's dramatic and episodic structure. The essence of the epic's length and breadth is its aspirations to reflect an entire culture's history and values. Compared to the poetic lyric's interior focus on thought and feeling, the epic extends its focus outward from the individual to a collective, social awareness: the values that define the Greek Heroic Age or that account for the founding of Rome and its values in the central medieval and Protestant Christian myths of belief. The epic, whether heroic or religious, aspires to be a summation, encyclopedic in what it offers, expansive rather than selective. There is something of this aspiration in Fielding calling his novel, *Tom Jones,* a "comic epic in prose." Fielding establishes the role of the novel to serve a sociological function in describing how we act and the rules of behavior that we follow. Once again, Jane Austen would refine this tendency, demonstrating not just how episodic structure can be turned into drama but how the sociological impulse of the epic can be combined with the lyrical focus on psychology and feeling.

How are the three organizing principles of the novel—episode, drama, and epic—demonstrated in the Victorian novel?

These three organizing principles are central to the construction of the classic Victorian novels. Again, Dickens is the exemplar as his career shows him moving from the episodic to the dramatic and epic modes, even as he had to contend with the demands of serial publication.

For more than a hundred years, publishing concerns dictated the novel's length. (The contemporary novel unfolds organically as determined by the internal forces of the narrative.) Most novels had to fill three volumes, and the initial question of structure that Dickens and others faced was how to do that. Dickens's initial answer to that question, and the easiest to manage, was an episodic structure, making possible a series of incidents and characters originating from his apparently inexhaustible imagination. Since Dickens launched his novels before he had worked out with any certainty where they would end up, the episodic construction was ideal. Dickens knew he needed to fill thirty pages monthly (or about twenty pages weekly), delivered in two to three chapters that could develop a single incident or make progress in multiple storylines. Initially, Dickens's method was mostly improvisational, more concerned with each part as a self-contained unit than the overall sum of the parts. Only occasionally would a collection of incidents, such as Mr. Pickwick's breach of promise case and its consequences, adhere to a central dramatic unity. Dickens's facility of extending episode into drama would grow as he developed as a novelist. If episode drove the vehicle, dramatic unity became the ultimate destination. We can see this clearly in Dickens's development through his first seven novels. All are episodic but gradually, in novels such as *Dombey and Sons*, *Martin Chuzzlewit*, and *David Copperfield*, Dickens began to master the art of plot emanating from, rather than inflicted upon, his characters. Episode gives way to a developing dramatic method. By the second half of his career, the dramatic method is so pronounced that his great mature masterpieces, such as *Bleak House, Little Dorrit, Great Expectations,* and *Our Mutual Friend* are all cut to the most demanding narrative structure of all, the mystery, which demands careful preplanning and expert control.

Dickens would also make a benefit of his multivolume form by taking on the epic formulation of the widest possible social focus. His great mature works, besides being mysteries, can be described as novels of the social group, in which a large cast of characters and several subplots are unified thematically. In *Bleak House*, for example, a long-disputed case over wills and legacy draws together the highest classes with the lowest in a massive indictment of social injustice and a dramatization of social interdependence. Themes, particularly social themes, would become another organizing principle along with episode and drama for the massive Victorian novels. In this way, Dickens would pioneer what became the characteristic Victorian novel: a string of stirring episodes, harnessed by an evolving dramatic and thematic unity.

How do chapters work in the novel?

For Dickens and other novelists, the novel's key building block is the chapter, and it is worth looking more closely at the nature of chapters in novel construction.

Chapters serve an essential function in the novel, so much so that it is hard to imagine the existence of the novel without them. Imagine a narrative of even modest length, say two hundred pages, appearing with no chapter divisions. Where would you pause in your reading, and, more importantly, how would you find your way back? Like an essay with a single paragraph with multiple topic sentences, a novel without chapter breaks invites confusion. But chapters serve as more than a reading aid.

As scholar Nicholas Dumes points out in an essay, "The Chapter: A History," "The first authors who wrote in chapters were not storytellers. They were compilers of knowledge, either utilitarian or speculative, who used chapters as a way of organizing large miscellanies…. These chapters, unlike the 'books' of epic poetry, were what we would now call finding aids: devices for quickly locating specific material in long texts that were not meant to be read straight through." The most famous chapter divisions are those in the Bible, with a uniform division into chapter and verse established in the thirteenth century. William Caxton, who introduced the printing press into England in 1476, famously divided the text of Thomas Malory's *Morte d'Arthur* into chapters in his 1485 edition, helping to establish the chapter as the unit of division in prose narratives. As the novel developed in the eighteenth century, chapter divisions were a standard feature and no doubt served as a helpful accommodation to the many novice readers attracted to the new literary form. Fielding's *Tom Jones* is divided into eighteen "books," befitting the author's attempt to write a "comic epic in prose," and then into titled chapters, such as "The Introduction to the Work, or Bill of Fare" and "Containing such grave Matter, that the Reader cannot laugh once through the whole Chapter, unless peradventure he should laugh at the Author." Witty and self-denigrating to match and introduce the far-from-serious spirit of his comedy, Fielding's chapters were also strategic. As the writer explains, "those little Spaces between our Chapters" serve as "an Inn or Resting-Place, where [the reader] may stop and take a Glass, or any other Refreshment,

With Charles Dickens developments in a story were the result of actions taken by the characters, rather than characters having events inflicted upon them (scene from Dickens' *David Copperfield* showing David falling in love with Dora).

as it pleases him," with the chapter titles serving as signposts for the next stage of the journey, ready when the reader is.

Fielding's notion of the breaks afforded by chapter divisions as a "Resting-Place" is a crucial one because it encourages a pause to consider what the chapter has offered and prepare for what is to come. Chapter divisions become, therefore, narrative way-stations to slow down our reading for reflection and analysis and to allow our setting out fresh into the next chapter. Laurence Stern, in his masterpiece *The Life and Opinions of Tristram Shandy, Gentleman* (1760–1767), provides his readers with a "chapter upon chapters," in which he argues that "chapters relieve the mind—and they assist—or impose upon the imagination—and that in a work of this dramatic case they are as necessary as the shifting of scenes." For Sterne, as Dumes summarizes, a chapter encourages "our immersion by letting us know that we will soon be allowed to exit and return to other tasks and demand. Coming and going—an attention paid out rhythmically—would become part of how novelists imagined their books would be read."

How do authors build novels by chapters?

Thus far, we have mainly considered chapters from the reader's perspective—to break up the narrative journey for rest and reflection and to find our way back—but what about chapters as structural units for the novelist's benefit? In chapters, between the breaks, novelists had a self-contained narrative unit to develop dramatically as a kind of minidrama with a beginning-middle-ending of an incident, as well as to shift to a new setting or scene or to advance the narrative time by hours, days, months, or years. Such shifts add narrative variety, can expand a focus by comparison or contrast, and can function like individual scenes in a drama as segments of action that form a dramatic whole. Chapters may pave the way for a major event or turning point, as well as show the consequences leading to the next decisive action. Novelists, therefore, can control their narrative, enhance suspense and surprise, and fuse individual episodes into a sustained drama by a deft handling of chapters.

For several of Dickens's novels, his "number plans" survive, his chapter-by-chapter monitoring of the progress of his novels. What they show clearly is Dickens keeping an eye on the organization of each installment, deciding what should go into each of the two to three chapters of each number. An additional column suggests his attention to where his story is headed and how his parts will eventually adhere to a dramatic whole. Asking in a note about a character appearance or plot turn, Dickens tells himself "not yet," clearly suggesting his concern for the general, if not the exact, narrative direction

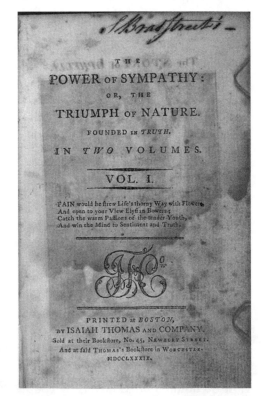

he was developing. A master of suspense, Dickens would also use his chapters to advance action on several fronts, cutting back and forth from various narrative centers or subplots, while not above using these cuts at key moments of suspended interest to enhance a reader's desire to continue. In a letter written during the composition of *David Copperfield,* Dickens mentions his method of "moves": "I feel, thank God," he writes, "quite confident in the story. I have a move in it ready for this month; another for next; and another for the next." By moves, Dickens meant exciting turns of events that propelled the story forward. His chapters were key in leading up to these moves and developing them dramatically, while interweaving in and out of several stories and constantly stopping one plot and starting another.

Dickens shows how important and strategic chapters are in novel construction. The strength and stress of the storytelling wall is distributed among multiple narrative bricks, and the readers, like the

The Power of Sympathy by William Hill Brown is considered the first published American novel. An epistolary novel set in Boston, it was printed in 1789.

author, need to keep the focus on both the parts and the developing whole of the novel, asking such key questions:

- Why is this chapter here? Why this chapter and not some other?
- How does the chapter connect with what preceded and followed it?
- What would the result be if the chapter was removed?
- What does the chapter contribute to an understanding of the novel as a whole?

Questions such as these should lead to a deeper understanding of the novel's methods and overall purpose and meaning.

What about the "Great American Novel"?

In tracing the development of the novel in the eighteenth and nineteenth centuries, we have largely concentrated on British fiction. It was mainly English writers who established the core directions that the novel would follow in replacing the make-belief of the romance with the actuality of the novel. Similar trends, however, can be found in France, Germany, and Russia as the novel evolved as an important literary form. But what about America? Why no mention of the developing novel there? The reason is that external factors delayed the development of the novel in America. Although the novel in England began with Daniel Defoe's *Robinson Crusoe* in 1719, the consensus choice for the first American novel, William Hill Brown's *The Power of Sympathy,* was not published until 1789. A moralistic, epistolary novel set in Boston and drawing on distinctly local affairs, Brown's novel marks the beginning of American fiction, well after development of the European novel. Why was this?

How did the American novel evolve?

The condition that would make the novel a popular literary form—a literate middle class with sufficient leisure time to generate a market for reading—was late developing in the frontier society of colonial America. Also, drama, secular poetry, and fiction languished due to Puritan disapproval so that an indigenous American literary tradition was late developing compared to Europe.

As late as 1820, the British critic Sydney Smith asked, "In the four quarters of the globe, who reads an American book? Or goes to an American play?" The few American novels that did appear were derived from British models. The first bestselling American novel was Susanna Rowson's *Charlotte Temple* (1794), modeled on the English novel of domestic sentiment; H. H. Brackenridge's *Modern Chivalry* (1792, 1815) adapted the English picaresque, satirical novel derived from Henry Fielding, and the best of the earliest American novelists, Charles Brocken Brown, transferred the English Gothic romance to an American setting. Brown's impressive string of novels before his early death—*Wieland* (1798), *Arthur Merwyn* (1799), *Ormond* (1799), and *Arthur Huntley* (1799)—employed supernatural elements to serve psychological and social purposes. Brown helped to define the romance tradition of the American novel and was to be a significant influence on subsequent writers such as Edgar Allan Poe and Nathaniel Hawthorne. Even the groundbreaking American subjects of James Fenimore Cooper's

One crucial factor in the novel's late development was the economic reality of American book publishing, which contributed significantly to the struggles of writers, particularly novelists, to emerge from the long shadow cast by the British. Although a national copyright law was enacted in 1790, international copyright protection was not established until 1891, leaving American printers free to pirate the latest works by popular British novelists such as Walter Scott and Charles Dickens. Because American readers could acquire the best of British writers in cheap reprints, there was little economic incentive for publishers to support American writers who expected to be paid. Most American writers consequently found it difficult to survive by their writing; only those who produced works of exceptional distinction and popularity were rewarded. The one market that was open to American writers was the many periodicals that could accommodate short fiction. This is largely why the American short story, as practiced by Poe, Hawthorne, and others, preceded publication of America's first great novels.

The Spy (1821), through his five Leatherstocking Tales (1823–1841), were Cooper's attempt to replicate Walter Scott's historical novel in an American setting.

Why were nineteenth-century American novels considered "romances"?

The romance would also persist in the American imagination far longer than in Europe, where it was replaced by the social realism of the emerging novel. Hawthorne's *The Scarlet Letter* (1850), the American novel's first undisputed masterpiece, is built on a solid romance foundation of the symbolic and allegorical from America's Puritan past. Melville's *Moby-Dick* (1851) is encyclopedic in its documentation of whaling but is animated by the romance's quest after a monster of the deep, lit by Shakespearean tragic thunder. Called by its first reviewers a "rhapsody run mad," *Moby-Dick* baffled readers and was dismissed as "an intellectual chowder of romance, philosophy, natural history, fine writing, good feeling, [and] bad sayings." Realism would not challenge the romance in the American imagination until the post-Civil War period, when a proto-realistic movement of writers, dubbed local colorists, would tap into the rich resources of regional scenes, speech, and customs to revitalize writing enervated by the war while paving the way for an increasingly realistic aesthetic that became the dominant mode of American literary expression during the period.

How did realism evolve in the American novel?

The greatest of the regionalists was Mark Twain (1835–1910). In his masterpiece, *Adventures of Huckleberry Finn* (1884), Twain transformed a boy's adventure tale into what

Lionel Trilling called "one of the world's great books and one of the central documents of American culture." With Huck and Jim's trip downriver into the heart of racial conflict, Twain released the poetic resources of the American vernacular and the dramatic and thematic possibilities of the landscape, earning his friend William Dean Howells's praise as "the Lincoln of our literature." Although an overstatement, Ernest Hemingway's oft-quoted claim that "all modern American literature comes from one book by Mark Twain called *Huckleberry Finn*" is not far off the mark.

Hawthorne, Melville, and Twain are the foundation figures of the American novel tradition. They began the quest for its perfect embodiment that would become known as "The Great American Novel," an ideal that subsequent writers would try to capture.

Mark Twain combined realism and humor to create one of the greatest novels of the nineteenth century, *Huckleberry Finn*.

How did the novel evolve from a popular literary entertainment to the modern novel?

The golden age of the Victorian novel represented a never-duplicated conjunction between the highest aspirations of the writer's art and mass popular appeal. Never again would the best novels—the most ambitious, challenging, and controversial—have a consistent home on the bestseller list. At some point during the nineteenth century, the divide between "highbrow" and "lowbrow" novels began, producing the modern book culture with the so-called literary works battling for attention with the much more popular (and less ambitious) genre fiction—romances, westerns, mysteries, and fantasy.

What influenced the creation of a new kind of novel and led to a break with the Victorian novel's ability to reach the widest possible audience?

One unmistakable turning point in the shift between popular and literary is the publication of George Eliot's *Middlemarch* (1871–1872), which represented a radical break in the way Victorian novels were written and published. Virginia Woolf would declare that *Middlemarch* is "one of the few English novels written for grown-up people."

GEORGE ELIOT'S *MIDDLEMARCH*

How do Eliot's background and experience as a novelist impact *Middlemarch*?

Coming to fiction late, at the age of thirty-eight, following a career as a reviewer and critic, George Eliot (the pseudonym for Mary Anne Evans) (1819–1880) set out to widen the intellectual range of the novel by making fiction a medium for serious social, psychological, and moral inquiry. She also was determined to alter the basic Victorian fictional formula by replacing the appeal of idealization and the melodramatic with a careful analysis of commonplace experience and mixed characters. Her first book of stories, *Scenes from Clerical Life* (1858), set the pattern for her subsequent novels with its insistence that ordinary life is the proper realm for fiction, that flawed characters should be viewed with tolerance and sympathy, and that dramatizations of human behavior should be accomplished through what she called "aesthetic teaching." As she declared, "Art must be either real and concrete or ideal and eclectic. Both are good and true in their way, but my stories are of the former kind. I undertake to exhibit nothing as it should be; I only try to exhibit some things as they have been or are." The three novels that followed—*Adam Bede* (1859), *The Mill on the Floss* (1860), and *Silas Marner* (1861)—owe much of their power and appeal to the author's childhood memories of provincial Warwickshire. When these sources began to run dry, Eliot attempted a departure in *Romola* (1863), a historical novel of fifteenth-century Florence. Eliot traveled to Italy and researched the customs and values of a different time and culture with the eye of the social scientist. With *Romola* Eliot learned to go beyond her own memories to see an entire society as a complex, interconnected whole. This deepened and widened her scope as a novelist when she returned to more familiar English scenes for her last three novels—*Felix Holt* (1866), *Middlemarch* (1871–1872), and *Daniel Deronda* (1874–1876). All three are massive novels of the social group in which Eliot attempted to display what she called the "invariability of sequence": the laws of social order and principles of moral conduct, including both the complex forces underlying characters' actions and the social, historical, and political climate in which her characters move.

How did George Eliot conceive and write *Middlemarch*?

Middlemarch began to form in the writer's mind as early as 1869 in a journal entry listing "Novel called Middlemarch" as one

Mary Ann Evans (a.k.a. George Eliot) is perhaps most remembered for her novel *Middlemarch*. Her fiction is noted for its realism, provincial settings, and psychological insights.

of her proposed tasks for the year. Originally, her scheme concerned the single figure Tertius Lydgate, the doctor whose altruistic and scientific aspirations would be tested against the limitation of English provincial life. Eliot set her story during the period of 1829–1831—the crucial years of Catholic Emancipation, the death of George IV, the general election of 1831, and the passage of the first Reform Bill of 1832, in which traditional authority and values were tested. It is estimated that between 1868 and 1871, Eliot read over 290 works of history, philosophy, and science to help her reconstruct the past and gain a critical perspective on it, yet the story languished, and Eliot turned in 1870 to the story of another idealist, Dorothea Brooke, whose aspirations for a wider life would, like Lydgate's, be similarly hampered by actual life. At some point in 1871, Eliot decided to join her manuscript of "Miss Brooke" with the early "Middlemarch" material. The challenge the novelist then faced was the "fear that I have too much matter, too many 'momenti.'" Eliot would need to solve the dramatic problems of joining an expanded novel reconstructing an entire social scene with four major plot centers: the story of Dorothea Brooke's marriage to the pedant Casaubon and her subsequent attraction to his nephew, the artistic Will Ladislaw; Lydgate's marriage to the conventionally materialistic Rosamond Vincy and his professional life in Middlemarch; a third individual in search of a vocation, Fred Vincy, and his relationship with the sensible, practical Mary Garth; and the circumstances surrounding the self-righteous businessman Bulstrode, whose secret and fall from grace in the Middlemarch community would be used to join the novel's many parts.

To complete her ambitious plan, Eliot realized that she required four volumes, not the standard three. Her common-law husband, George Henry Lewes, proposed to her publisher a scheme borrowed from Victor Hugo's plan for *Les Misérables,* which was to bring the book out in half-volume, bimonthly parts at a total cost of double the usual £1 for an installment novel, like those of Dickens and Thackeray. The arrangement was a significant departure from Victorian publishing practices. Eliot's novel would be carefully crafted and composed before it began to appear in parts and published at a cost that restricted a wide popular readership. *Middlemarch* was thereby aimed at a highbrow audience reflecting the heightened intellectual ambitions and assumptions of its author. For good or ill, the English novel after *Middlemarch* would begin to challenge the old three-decker format that had dominated the form since Walter Scott's Waverley novels, while unraveling the synthesis between popular and serious literature that Victorian novelists such as Dickens and Thackeray had fashioned since the 1830s. With *Middlemarch*, the battle to secure the novel's respectability as more than popular entertainment, to claim equal footing with poetry and drama as an instrument of truth and moral seriousness, was finally won.

How does *Middlemarch* proceed?

Middlemarch, with its subtitle, "Study of Provincial Life," shares with Balzac's intention in his *Human Comedy* to relate individual lives to the wider historical scene as well as Thackeray's interest in observing society in depth. Challenging a novel reader's conventional expectations, Eliot insisted that ordinary life and unexceptional, often flawed characters are the novel's proper subject matter. Dorothea Brooke is a "latter-born" St. Theresa, "helped by no coherent social faith and order which could perform the function of knowledge for the ardently willing soul." She is an ardent idealist in search of a great cause and an opportunity for self-expression, who will be shown in conflict with her own nature and the narrow conditions of her circumstances. Rejecting the standard notion that marriage should be the novel's climax, Eliot substitutes a detailed study of the aftermath of Dorothea's choice as she accepts a man whom she perceives to be a kindred spirit, the scholarly Casaubon, who fails to provide her with the expansion into the noble life of mind and spirit she seeks. Lydgate's desire to advance medical science and to remain independent to do good works is similarly compromised, both by the petty and practical world of Middlemarch and what Eliot calls his "spots of commonness," his conceit and ambitions for social advancement that cause him to succumb to the superficial charms of the materialistic Rosamond. Dorothea and Lydgate, as well as a wide cast of characters, are all examined against a fully elaborated social hierarchy from Middlemarch's gentry and farm families through the professional and laboring classes. All are related to a particular historical moment in which traditional values face the pressure of change in the reforming spirit of the age.

The major action in the novel is brought on mainly by such natural circumstances as marriage and death. Resisting exceptional dramatic situations, the novel's integrative narrative perspective concentrates on what Eliot calls "the suppressed transitions which unite all contrasts," the buried threads of personality and circumstance that explain and cause the novel's relationships, conflicts, and resolutions. *Middlemarch* presents an elaborate social web needing mainly ordinary pressure to set the whole in motion. The novel's major plot stimulant is Bulstrode's secret that leads to the novel's major crisis, which brings about Lydgate's diminished prospects and produces Dorothea's final self-assertion in her accepting her affection for Will Ladislaw in defiance of propriety. In the end, idealism is tested in an arena of conventionality with mixed outcomes. Fred Vincy finds his way through practical, earned labor; Lydgate manages a respectable, successful career but regards his life as ultimately a failure; and Dorothea's triumph of spirit and ultimate satisfaction are muted and misunderstood by the world. As Eliot concludes, "Certainly those determining acts of her life were not ideally beautiful. They were the mixed result of young and noble impulse struggling amidst the conditions of an imperfect social state, in which great feelings will often take the aspect of error, and great faith the aspect of illusion." To see the world and individuals correctly, Eliot asserts, readers must extend their sympathy and widen their understanding of the causes and effects of human behavior from a comprehensive vantage point that the novel provides.

What defines the importance of *Middlemarch*?

The greatness of *Middlemarch* derives ultimately from Eliot's taking the novel simultaneously to the inwardmost recesses of private consciousness and outwardly to the weblike complexity of social life, in which each individual is a separate junction point in an interrelated whole. Few other novels have managed such a remarkable presentation of private and public life. In the subtlety and reach of Eliot's fiction to achieve a comprehensive vision of who we are and how we act, *Middlemarch* is one of the supreme achievements in the art of the novel both as a culmination of the Victorians' push to assert a realistic standard for fiction and to point the way for the novel as an instrument to measure essential truths. It has been called "the summa of Victorian realism" (George Levine); "one of the supreme classics of European fiction" (David Daiches); and "the only truly representative, truly great Victorian novel—all other candidates, including the rest of George Eliot's fiction, being either too idiosyncratic or too flawed" (David Lodge). Straining the limits of the novel's expandability, pushing the form's capacity to accommodate multiple

An illustration of Dorothea and Will from the 1910 edition of *Middlemarch*. The strength of the novel lies in Eliot's penetration of her characters' inner worlds.

plotlines and an extensive cast of characters into a massive, panoramic whole, George Eliot certainly produced one of the most ambitious English novels. "No other Victorian novel approaches *Middlemarch*," V. S. Pritchett has argued, "in its width of reference, its intellectual power, or the imperturbable spaciousness of its narrative."

In its research, its intellectual aspirations to capture human life in as full a context of cultural, sociological, and political awareness as had ever been attempted in the novel before, *Middlemarch* is both a departure from and a farewell to the improvisational and episodic Victorian novel. George Eliot willingly separated her novel from the reach of the widest-possible popular audience in both the cost to acquire it and the intellectual patience and background required to appreciate it. The English novel, after *Middlemarch*, would have two principal directions: as popular entertainment and as a serious instrument to explore moral and psychological truths. These two directions would only occasionally converge in the novel's future course.

What corollary event predicted a radically new kind of fiction?

A new kind of fiction that would define the modern novel appeared in France nearly twenty years before *Middlemarch* with Gustave Flaubert's heroic struggle to publish *Madame Bovary* (1857). Flaubert's fifty-six-month, nightly seven-hour struggle to complete his masterpiece—the descent of his title character, deluded by romantic illusion, into tawdry affairs and finally destroyed by the conjunction of her nature and an inhospitable provincial environment—represents the birthing pains of a new kind of fictional narrative. Gustave Flaubert (1821–1880) devoted weeks to individual scenes and days to a single page in search of the *mot juste,* producing an art form so patterned that every detail contributed to a unity of effects as capable of rendering beauty and truth as poetry, drama, or the epic. To decipher the novel's significance, the reader needs to employ the same skills usually reserved for poetry, discerning the implication of diction, image, repetition, contrast, and comparison. Flaubert denied the reader direct, subjective narrative guidance, declaring, "The artist in his work must be like God in his creation—invisible and all-powerful: he must be everywhere felt, but never seen." Flaubert here articulates a key principle of the evolving modern novel, insisting that the reader play an active role in uncovering the patterns beneath the surface of things, while subverting expected fictional delights and substituting a coherent fictional universe held together by the force and clarity of the novel's vision.

Why was *Madame Bovary* considered a scandalous novel?

The reception of *Madame Bovary* is equally predictive of things to come for the modern novel. Replacing fictional idealization and falsification of character and scene with an unflinching portrait of the mundane and the ignoble, Flaubert stirred a hornet's nest of condemnation. *Madame Bovary* was initially published serially with Flaubert fighting demanded cuts, protesting, "You are objecting to details, whereas actually you should object to the whole. The brutal element is basic, not superficial." He was charged with "outrage of public morals religion" and brought to trial in which he bitterly predicted a guilty verdict, but ironically he found in the legal affair, "sweet recognition for my labors, noble encouragement to literature." Instead, he was acquitted, and the novel became a notorious *succès de scandale.*

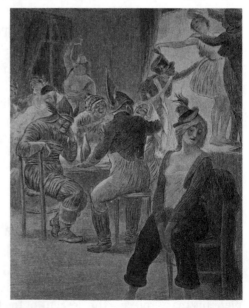

In both *Madame Bovary* and *Middlemarch,* the lineaments of a new kind of modern novel were materializing: an organic form, not fitted to a predetermined, three-volume structure and a meticulously preplanned, unified whole that was dramatic, not episodic or improvised. Flaubert and Eliot would pioneer novel construction closer to the principle of exclusion of the short story, in which every element contributes of an intended effect. They also would show a willingness not only to forego a wide popular audience but also a disposition to provoke them, testing the limits of acceptable subjects and their treatment in literature. These would become the core precepts of a new, modern novel.

Emma Bovary is dressed as a transvestite attending a ball in this illustration from Flaubert's scandalous novel.

THE MODERN NOVEL

What is meant by the term "modern"?

Every age sees itself as "modern," so what gives the so-called modernist period its distinctive claim to modernity? The term "modernist" was coined to designate a discontinuity from the values of predecessors in the nineteenth century. There is nothing unusual about succeeding generations breaking with a previous era in a search for new forms of expression or new ways to understand a changed world. It can be argued, however, that in no period in Western history has change been so profound and therefore demanded a more radical alteration to capture that change than in the modernist period, roughly the period between 1870 and 1950. Virginia Woolf famously declared, "In or about December 1910, human character changed," and D. H. Lawrence would assert, "It was in 1915 that the old world ended." Both writers sound the essential credo of the modernist that the modern world has unalterably been changed, requiring a radical response, such as in Ezra Pound's modernist rallying cry, "Make It New."

What were these changes?

The major assaults to the sense of certainty, order, and belief that produced this sense of an altered world include the following:

- New technologies in work, transportation, and communication changed the culture and produced new pressures on human interactions, sense of self, and connectedness to place and traditions.

- Darwin's theory of evolution displaced man from the center of the universe, replacing the notion of divine purpose with natural forces that found more cogency not in man's will and reason but in sheer brute survival.

- Marx showed the ways in which economic forces and class struggle shape consciousness, producing a dominant psychological characteristic of alienation as the individual is shown cut off from the means of finding satisfaction in work or economic security in the dehumanizing operation of competition.

- Freud destabilized inherited notions of the self with his idea that we are driven by forces we do not understand or even acknowledge to exist: the unconscious, our sexual drives, the role played by the trivial details of everyday life. Freud offered a more complex notion of human consciousness more shaped by the irrational than by reason.

- Einstein's special theory of relativity (1905) showed that time and motion are not absolute but relative to the observer, thus fundamentally challenging the Newtonian worldview.

What are the chief characteristics of the modern novel?

In one sense the modern novel is a culmination of its initial pursuit of the real, opening aspects of actual life in sexuality, gender relations, even biological functions that

In another sense, instead of being merely an outgrowth or extension of its past, the modern novel represented a radical break. Like all modern literature, it would emerge in response to a fundamental shift in cultural values brought about by the assault on certainty in the ideas of writers such as Darwin, Marx, Nietzsche, Freud, and Einstein. As early as 1853, poet and essayist Matthew Arnold declared, "The calm, the cheerfulness, the disinterested objectivity have disappeared: the dialogue of the mind with itself has commenced." Under attack, Arnold suggests, are the philosophical, religious, and cultural absolutes that had been the operating principles for understanding and behavior, for one's sense of place in the universe and in society. A new, modern world, very different from the past, seemed to be underway.

had never been reflected in literature before and had been discreetly avoided even in the massive realism of the Victorian novel. Thackeray complained privately that he could never depict a "complete man" in his novels; Hardy had to go to such absurd lengths not to offend (for example, finding Angel Clare a wheelbarrow instead of carrying two maids across a flooded road in *Tess of the d'Urbervilles*) that he abandoned the novel to be left alone with his poetry. Testing the limits of the acceptable inevitably led to collisions with accepted standards of taste that eventually altered the core relationship between novelist and readers. Dickens, Thackeray, and the other Victorian novelists were not the opposition to their audience, even in some of their harshest criticism of social wrongs and moral weaknesses. However, modern novelists saw themselves disaffected from and antagonists to their society, willing to sacrifice sales and unwilling to accommodate a large popular audience, insisting instead that their audience must accept their increasingly challenging and demanding works.

JAMES JOYCE'S *A PORTRAIT OF THE ARTIST AS A YOUNG MAN*

What is the background for Joyce's novel?

"At the age of twenty-one," Joyce's biographer Richard Ellmann astutely observed about the origins and impact of *A Portrait of the Artist as a Young Man*, "Joyce had found he could become an artist by writing about the process of becoming an artist." The shape and texture of the modern novel and the literary revolution that Joyce would help to initiate are clearly glimpsed in his interpretation of a traditional subject—the story of a youth's education and development. Literary critic Harry Levin argued, "The history of the realistic novel shows that fiction tends toward autobiography," that "the increasing demands for social and psychological detail that are made upon the novelist can only be satisfied out of his own experience." Joyce responded by transforming the *Bildungsroman* (or more precisely the *Künstlerroman*, the story of the formation of an artist), previously attempted by such novelists as Goethe in *Wilhelm Meister,* Dickens in *David Copperfield,* Flaubert in *The Sentimental Education,* and Samuel Butler in *The Way of All Flesh,* with an experimentally daring, concentrated and symbolic density that make other versions seem shallow and stale by comparison. In its focus on the formation of consciousness and identity, in its fusion of the realistic and the symbolic, and in its grafting of the subjective expressiveness of the lyric and the selective economy of the short story onto the longer narrative form, *Portrait* is in many ways the prototypical modern novel, setting a dominating theme and influential method for modern fiction.

What challenges did Joyce face writing and publishing *A Portrait of the Artist as a Young Man*?

Joyce's decade-long labor on a fictional version of the development of an Irish renegade artist in *Portrait* reflected the critical stages of his evolution as a novelist. The first version of his self-portrait, written on a single day in January 1904, was the narrative essay "A Portrait of the Artist," which anticipated both Joyce's eventual intention—to capture the stages of an artist's development from infancy—and his method of recreating the past as a "fluid succession of presents." Joyce incorporated several of the epiphanies or fragmentary revelatory incidents he had collected to dramatize his version of the artist's evolving sensibility from religious zeal, through sexual awareness, to secular celebration as well as the necessary liberation from the constraints of homeland, church, and family. The essay was rejected by the Dublin magazine editor who had first commissioned it with the justification that "I can't print what I can't understand." Responding to this rejection, Joyce on his birthday (February 2, 1904), in the words of his brother, Stanislaus, "decided to turn his paper into a novel.... It is to be almost autobiographical, and naturally as it comes from Jim, satirical. He is putting a large number of his acquain-

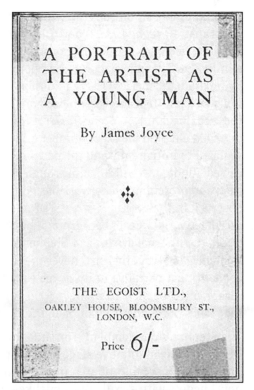

A PORTRAIT OF
THE ARTIST AS
A YOUNG MAN

By James Joyce

THE EGOIST LTD.,
OAKLEY HOUSE, BLOOMSBURY ST.,
LONDON, W.C.

Price 6/-

James Joyce's *A Portrait of the Artist as a Young Man* imaginatively explores the awakening of the main character's intellectual and spiritual beliefs.

209

tances into it, and those Jesuits he has known." Joyce set out to record in naturalistic detail his life up to his accepting his artistic vocation and exile from Ireland. Portions shared with the Irish writer and editor George Russell led to an invitation to write a short story for the *Irish Homestead*. This would result in Joyce beginning the groundbreaking sequence of stories that became *Dubliners* and the refinement of Joyce's epiphanic and symbolic methods, the essential components of his future novels. Called *Stephen Hero*, by 1906 the manuscript had grown to 914 pages, about half its proposed length. The 383 pages that survive, rescued by Joyce's sister Eileen after the author had thrown the manuscript into a fire, are longer than the final published version and cover what would be eventually reduced to the final eighty pages of *Portrait*. The cuts and the radical foreshortening of his autobiographical material are a result of Joyce's decision in 1907, after finishing "The Dead," the final story of *Dubliners,* to rewrite *Stephen Hero* completely "in five chapters—long chapters." Serialized in *The Egoist* from 1914 to 1915, *Portrait* was finally published in America in 1916 and in England in 1917, after it had first been rejected by every London publisher to whom it was submitted and printers refused to take the job when *The Egoist* attempted to publish it in book form.

How does the final version of *A Portrait* proceed?

With an emphasis on selection, compression, and intensity, Joyce pared the episodic, naturalistic *Stephen Hero* down to the essential, intimate stages of his surrogate, Stephen Dedalus's developing consciousness. Transitions and authorial comment were eliminated. The fully elaborated supporting characters recede from the stage, and clarifying dramatic incidents were minimized to serve only as a shadowy backdrop or sounding board for Stephen's internalized drama. Compared to the characterized members of the Dedalus family in *Stephen Hero*, for example, in the reshaped *Portrait,* Stephen is not even clear on the exact number of his siblings, and his love, Emma Clery, has been reduced to initials only and the occasion for a poem and a later resentment over a perceived slight. Joyce filters all through Stephen's consciousness that processes events, past, and present into a network of significance through association. As Harry Levin has observed in the revised *Portrait,* "Drama has retired before soliloquy." Although Joyce sacrificed a richness of background, he gained a closeness of focus that directly reproduces the internal dynamic of Stephen's identity and the pressures that shape his consciousness in ways that had never previously been attempted in a novel. In place of a conventional narrative unity, Joyce establishes a poetic, cinematic logic in which the reader must be alert to the recurrent image, parallels, and juxtaposition to elucidate the stages of Stephen's emotional, intellectual, and artistic evolution.

Stephen's development from infancy through childhood, adolescence, and maturity is organized into five stages made up of a series of episodes, each an epiphany illuminating a significant step in Stephen's education and gestation as an artist. The novel begins with a brilliant, fuguelike overture recording Stephen's earliest recollections and infant capacities. Differentiating reality only very broadly through his senses, Stephen can distinguish between his mother and father by touch and smell. As an incipient artist, he responds to his father's stories, to the power of language, and expresses his first creativity in song and dance. However, when he declares that he will become a father himself by marrying the girl next door, Stephen is ordered to apologize under threat of eagles who will pull out his eyes. The scene closes with Stephen's first poem and a symbolic summary of much of the novel in miniature: Stephen in defensive hiding against vengeful authority, representative of the various father figures—his own father, the Jesuit fathers, and his fatherland—that he must eventually overcome.

Stephen Dedulus's last name is a reference to the Hellenic myth about Daedulus, the man who built wax wings to fly and whose son, Icarus, died using those wings.

How is *A Portrait* structured?

Each of the subsequent stages of Stephen's education is characterized by a different school. In the first, Stephen is a boarder at the prestigious Clongowes Wood in which the sensitive boy endures bullying and the school routine while mentally and emotionally attempting to make sense of the baffling larger world. The novel's first great dramatic scene of the Christmas dinner dispute that splits his family over whether the Church was right or wrong in deserting the Irish nationalist leader Parnell becomes a crucial lesson for Stephen in his own testing of authority that culminates in his first rebellion in which he stands up to the undeserved "pandying" by Father Dolan.

In chapter two, Stephen's short-lived triumph of self-assertion is undercut by his family's financial decline that takes the Dedaluses from the respectable suburbs to grim Dublin and Stephen's next school at Belvedere. Stephen struggles to maintain his independence and achieve his dream of beauty and fulfillment against his increasingly squalid family conditions and pressures to submit to the conventional beliefs of his schoolmates and the Jesuit fathers, culminating in his second major rebellion: his carnal sin with a prostitute that ends the chapter. Chapter three represents the final assault by the forces of authority to coerce his submission that takes the form of a tour de force reconstruction of a hellfire-and-brimstone sermon that produces in Stephen a temporary repentance and mortification of the senses. Chapter four leads to the novel's climax of Stephen's epiphany on Dollymount Strand in which he accepts his vocation as an artist: "He would create proudly out of the freedom and power of his soul, as the great artificer whose name he bore, a living thing, new and soaring and beautiful, impalpable, imperishable." Stephen embraces not the cold certainty of religious faith or conformity before an intractable Irish reality but the call to create permanent beauty out of the sensual world that surrounds him: "To live, to err, to fall, to triumph, to recreate life out of life!"

211

Chapter five, Stephen's undergraduate education, the longest section of the book, shows his preparation for his artistic life and exile in the aesthetic theories that will sustain him and the nets of family, friends, church, and homeland that continue to exert their pull on his independence. It is this section of the book that the reader's sympathy toward Stephen is most severely tested. Unwilling to make any concessions that might humanize him, priggish and pedantic, Stephen gathers strength for his flight into exile, but the novel offers little confirmation of Stephen's gifts beyond his assertions of artistic integrity and a collection of aesthetic declarations. To assess Stephen's final progress, it is essential to remember Joyce's qualifying phrase in his title, "as a Young Man," which suggests that Stephen has still a long way to go to become the mature artist. The degree to which Joyce meant Stephen to be viewed ironically is one of the central critical debates over the novel. Clearly, the reader is meant to sympathize with Stephen's facing down the obstacles that stand in his way, but throughout the book his triumphs are quickly deflated with Stephen's rhapsodic assertions the only result of his artistry. Joyce himself confessed to being "extremely hard on that young man.... I haven't let this young man off very lightly, have I? Many writers have written about themselves. I wonder if any of them has been as candid as I have." As the novel concludes in Stephen's diary fragments on the verge of his departure from Ireland, he is given a final, famous, lyrical exultation: "Welcome, O life! I go to encounter for the millionth time the reality of experience and to forge in the smithy of my soul the uncreated conscience of my race." However, Joyce was not yet done with his young artist. Stephen is next seen back in Ireland from his short-lived Parisian exile to refight his previous struggles and to encounter a new father: the cuckolded Irish Jew Leopold Bloom in *Ulysses*. Joyce had shifted, as Stephen's aesthetic theory forecasted, from the lyrical mode of *Portrait* to the epical and dramatic mode of *Ulysses* and the ultimate confirmation of the artistic process.

THE NOVEL AND MODERNISM

What was the influence of World War I on modernist thought?

Darwin, Marx, Freud, Einstein, Nietzsche, and others all eroded a faith in religion, moral certainty, progress, and reason. The catalyst for the full acceptance of the implications of these ideas was World War I, which slaughtered an entire generation, bringing home the realization that previous conceptions of progress and human values were now inoperative. How could God exist to allow such carnage? The technological promise of industrialization led to the invention of more efficient means of self-destruction. Humanity's right to a certain dignity by virtue of its special place in creation was cancelled by the ignominy of trench warfare.

How did Ernest Hemingway describe a new kind of postwar literature?

The supremacy of reason in human affairs was debunked by the madness of the war. Hemingway memorably has his protagonist Frederic Henry, in his 1929 novel, *A*

Farewell to Arms, say:

I was always embarrassed by the words sacred, glorious, and sacrifice and the expression in vain. We had heard them, sometimes standing in the rain almost out of earshot, so that only the shouted words came through, and had read them, on proclamations, now for a long time, and I had seen nothing sacred, and the things that were glorious had no glory and the sacrifices were like the stockyards at Chicago if nothing was done with the meat except to bury it. There were many words that you could not stand to hear and finally only the names of places had dignity. Certain numbers were the same way and certain dates and these with the names of the places were all you could say and have them mean anything. Abstract words such as glory, honor, courage, or hallow were obscene beside the concrete names of villages, the numbers of roads, the names of rivers, the numbers of regiments and the dates.

The modernist agenda very much begins with the dilemma Frederic Henry identifies: language, literature, and all belief had to be reassessed under the pressure of this new understanding. Heaven for the first time in Western civilization seemed empty. Much of modernist literature is born from this spiritual confrontation with emptiness. With the cosmos and society either without order or so disordered to defy understanding, writers sought new principles for order: what can you believe in the absence of the possibility of belief?

What themes did modernist novelists explore?

Modernist novelists would turn to the isolated, alienated, vulnerable individual, establishing the central preoccupation of modernist art with human consciousness and the process of perception itself. There are clear parallels in the visual arts: in the movement from realism to impressionism, that is, capturing the viewer's coloring of the external world in the act of perception. In Post-Impressionism, there is a further movement toward abstraction, in reaching truth via distortion. Cézanne famously declared: "Exactitude is not truth." Picasso and the Cubists would shatter the features of the human face and reassemble body parts in grotesque methods of caricature. Modernist novelists would perform a similar shattering.

What else made the modern novel different from earlier works?

The modern novel would reject established notion of plot as inauthentic and falsifying. Time in the modernist novel would be broken into nonchronological, nonlinear fragments glimpsed from limited perspectives. Removed is the comforting God's-eye view of the omniscient narrator, replaced by a limited, often unreliable point of view. Character and identity are not held together by an overarching theory of human types or psychology. Individuals and experience itself are shown as multiple, contradictory, and illusive, forever eluding our grasp and our understanding.

Given this fragmentation, there is a search for a new form of organization. Plots with clear beginnings, middles, and ends, indeed even causes and effects, are ruled re-

213

ductive and simplistic. Instead, the novel began to rely on juxtaposition as in a collage in which the connection between scene, incident, and significance must be supplied by the reader. Consciousness itself would be rendered directly in the associational, often illogical, moment-to-moment sequence of ideas, feelings, and memories. All of these elements would result in a modern novel strikingly different from earlier versions.

Differences between the Nineteenth-Century Novel and the Modern Novel

	Nineteenth Century	Modern
Subject	Broad, crowded, and comprehensive	Narrow and deep
Plot	Paramount and theatrical	Neglected, avoids arrangement of events into dramatic climaxes
Character	Central, viewed primarily from the outside through manners and dialogue	Sensibility over personality/what one thinks rather than what one does/viewed from inside and unconscious as well as conscious life
Society	Non-alienated, fixed, accepted	Disaffected, fluid
Scope	Normal life, wide angle, panoramic	Exceptional, still life
Technique	Recognition of familiar and representative	Shock of the unfamiliar
Structure	Episodic, loose, emphasis on message	Patterned by image and situation like mosaic/montage; emphasis on medium
Point of view	Omniscient and authoritative	Limited and unreliable

What are examples of the modern novel and its assault on established novel conventions?

- *Les Rougon-Macquart* (1877–1893) by Emile Zola—Zola embarks on writing a twenty-novel cycle to systematically study an historical period (1851–1871) and an entire social hierarchy in depth, particularly the working class, which Balzac's *Human Comedy* neglected. Using recurring characters, Zola traced the influence of heredity and environment through several generations in such powerful works as *L'Assommoir, La Terre*, and *La Debacle*. Zola applied the methods of the social scientist to the novel and turned it into a powerful moral and political truth-telling instrument.

- *The Brothers Karamazov* (1880) by Fyodor Dostoevsky—Freud regarded Dostoevsky's final book as "the most magnificent novel ever written," in which its central themes—its concern with human alienation, the inadequacy of reason, its depiction of a fragmented, unstable world, and its attempts to rediscover a core of permanent values—have contributed more to the content and shape of modern fiction than any other single novel. In depicting the disintegration and redemption of a family, it is one of the towering narratives for its sheer daring in coming to terms with the knottiest problems of the human heart, mind, and soul.

Modern artists such as Picasso recognized that exacting realism did not necessarily equate to truth, and modern novelists came to the same conclusion in an effort to shatter old truths and force new meaning upon experiences.

- *The Portrait of a Lady* (1881) by Henry James—The culminating work of James's early period, the "first of Henry James's book to sound with the ring of greatness," according to one critic. *Portrait* is the first American novel to absorb and expand upon the lessons of social and psychological realism by such European writers as Stendhal, Balzac, Turgenev, and George Eliot. Replacing American novelists' previous reliance on romantic adventure for the internal drama of consciousness in a solidly rendered social setting, James pointed the way the novel would increasingly follow in the modern period.

- *Germinal* (1885) by Émile Zola—Arguably, the angriest novel ever written in its relentless depiction of individuals and a community locked in an epic struggle with natural, social, and economic forces beyond their control. Few novels deal as extensively or as intimately with the world of work, and despite Zola's reputation as an objective, naturalistic clinician who simply recorded what he saw, *Germinal* is documentation processed by a mythic imagination.

- *The Mayor of Casterbridge* (1886), *Tess of the d'Urbervilles* (1891), *Jude the Obscure* (1896) by Thomas Hardy—Hardy's masterworks show how the specifics of local customs and regional elements can be suffused with the universal for some of the starkest views of human existence outside of the plays of Shakespeare and Attic tragedy. His artistic vision tested the limits of censorship and the commercial restrictions of the novel form while offering an imaginative expansion to the dicta of

215

fictional realism by reintroducing an oral storytelling tradition and ballad structure with its emphasis on unusual and exceptional action. "Art is disproportioning," Hardy asserted, "(i.e., distorting, throwing out of proportion) of realities, which if merely copied or reported inventorily, might possibly be overlooked. Hence realism is not Art."

- *The Red Badge of Courage* (1895) by Stephen Crane—Achieved a radical refinement of the novel's methods, conjoining external details and internal states, pioneering a literary version of impressionism that caused novelist Robert Stone to declare that with this novel, "American literature entered the modernist age."

- *Sister Carrie* (1900) by Theodore Dreiser—One of the seminal texts of American realism, Dreiser's novel, in the words of novelist John Dos Passos, "opened the way through the genteel reticences of American nineteenth-century fiction for what seemed to me to be a truthful description of people's lives. Without Dreiser's treading out a path for naturalism none of us would have had a chance to publish even." Dreiser fundamentally liberated American literature to pursue the widest and most ignored truths and to capture the modern experience in all its complexity and contradictions.

- *The Wings of the Dove* (1902), *The Ambassadors* (1903), *The Golden Bowl* (1904) by Henry James—James's mature masterworks defined the ways and means of the modern poetic novel of consciousness. Densely layered and nuanced, James's novels limit and restrict the reader's view, turning perception itself into an experiential process of shifting angles and moral complexity. James located the novel's power to penetrate the recesses of consciousness itself while investing simple circumstances with an unprecedented depth and subtlety.

- *Nostromo* (1904) by Joseph Conrad—His most ambitious and profound novel is a moral and political fable of an entire imagined country. No other of Conrad's novels achieves so vast and so comprehensive an assessment of human motives and relationships, refracted by multiple perspectives and a narrative that scrambles cause and effect into a nonlinear sequence that the reader must labor to decipher.

- *In Search of Lost Time* (1913–1927) by Marcel Proust—Proust redefined the novel's operating principles of both causality and chronology, in which conventional plot and stable characterization are bypassed for a complex and intimate unlocking of the essential, buried, multivariable texture of experience itself. At more than 4,000 pages, it is one of the most ambitious novels ever attempted, in which the years between about 1840 and the opening decades of the twentieth century, with a cast of some 200 characters, are depicted with an incomparable poetic intimacy and subtlety that the novel had never previously managed.

- *Sons and Lovers* (1913) by D. H. Lawrence—One of the earliest and best examples of the British proletarian novel, detailing life in a small mining community with an insider's familiarity, it has also been called the "first Freudian novel in English," one of the earliest applications of Freud's emphasis on subconscious and the irrational in human experience.

- *The Good Soldier* (1915) by Ford Madox Ford—Represents an end and a beginning: the culmination of the nuanced moral comedy of manners of Henry James and in its endlessly refracting indirectness and suggestiveness and its subtle display of consciousness and narrative unreliability, a forecast of how the novel would increasingly be written in the postwar era.

- *Petersburg* (1916/1922) by Andrey Bely—Credit for making the modern city the central character is usually given to James Joyce for *Ulysses,* but that distinction is more accurately attributed to *Petersburg,* the greatest example of Russian modernist fiction, which Vladimir Nabokov declared "one of the four great masterpieces of twentieth-century prose" along with *Ulysses, The Metamorphosis,* and *In Search of Lost Time.*

- *Women in Love* (1920) by D. H. Lawrence—Nothing like its treatment of sexual relationships and personal identity had previously been attempted, and few other novels have ever provided such an ambitious interweaving of its psychological-moral-cultural-historical themes. For critic F. R. Leavis, the novel is "one of the most striking works of creative originality that fiction has to show."

- *Ulysses* (1922) by James Joyce—Despite its reputation for its difficulty, it is one of the most human stories ever written. No single day in human history has been as fully or as brilliantly captured than June 16, 1904, nor has any novelist created a greater protagonist than Leopold Bloom, who has been called "the most *complete* figure in modern fiction, if not indeed in all Western fiction." Joyce ventured further than anyone previously into the complex labyrinth of modern experience while as one of the novel's supreme symbolists, Joyce set out to irradiate the myriad mundane data of existence with universal significance.

- *The Magic Mountain* (1924) by Thomas Mann—The great philosophical novel of the twentieth century in which Hans Castorp's stay in a mountaintop tuberculosis sanatorium becomes an intellectual and emotional drama of education and development that explores Western culture in crisis and the ongoing mysteries of existence.

- *The Great Gatsby* (1925) by F. Scott Fitzgerald—Fitzgerald's take on *The Waste Land* is the defining novel of the receding American dream that is alternatingly an acid satire and a lyrical evocation of loss and desire.

- *Mrs. Dalloway* (1925) by Virginia Woolf—Shows the full emergence of Woolf's distinctive voice and the experimental method she would employ in her subsequent fiction. Like Joyce's *Ulysses* in its exploration of a city on a single day, Woolf's novel is more lyrical than epic, more personal and centripetal, less encyclopedic in attempting to render human experience, though no less profound in its representation of the mysteries and wonderment of existence.

- *The Trial* (1925) by Franz Kafka—The archetypal modern novel: fragmentary, bewildering, disturbing, and inexhaustibly challenging in its symbolic and interpretative possibilities. It is certainly the classic fable of the modern bureaucratic victim, of contemporary alienation, and the ultimate persecution complex. Defines "Kafkaesque."

- *The Counterfeiters* (1926) by André Gide—One of the prototypical metafictions that problematizes how we see and express the world. It is one of the modernist wonders that rewrites the rules of the novel and liberates them for more complex and challenging exploration of experience and consciousness: simultaneously a novel of ideas, a meditation on the psychology of literary creation, and a comprehensive portrait of manners and morals in the period before and after World War I.

- *To the Lighthouse* (1927) by Virginia Woolf—Her masterpiece is one of the seminal works of modernist fiction and the ultimate justification of her experimental method in her ability to give form to the flux of human experience and consciousness.

- *A Farewell to Arms* (1929) by Ernest Hemingway—There are few better depictions of the values that defined the post-World War I generation. It is a novel that unequivocally announces Hemingway's essential theme of war and survival that he would return to again, whether on the battlefield or in symbolic or ritualized versions in bullfighting, fishing, or big game hunting.

- *The Sound and the Fury* (1929) by William Faulkner—America's first great modernist novel, reflecting both the native tradition of Poe, Hawthorne, Melville, and James and the European innovations of Conrad, Joyce, and others. Faulkner's family saga fractures chronology and objectivity to reassemble a narrative mosaic of a personal, family, regional, and ultimately universal tragedy, of sexual corruption, suicide, madness, and jealousy—ideas that Faulkner would return to again in works that established him as America's greatest modernist novelist.

- *The Man without Qualities* (1930–1943) by Robert Musil—Unfinished at nearly 1,800 pages, it has been called "the supreme example in Western literature of the novel of ideas" and "a compendium of contemporary uncertainty." Like the best modernist works, the novel tests the limits of fiction to contain the widest possible perception of experience and the moral, philosophical, and psychological currents underlying human actions. There are few novels better at diagnosing the breakdown of beliefs and values of the modern world and one of the most intriguing in their search for a way out of the morass of doubt and despair.

- *The Sleepwalkers* (1932) by Hermann Broch—One of the most intellectually ambitious and innovative novels of the twentieth century, it is, in the words of one critic, "the first attempt at an 'epistemological' novel" in which *Sleepwalkers* attempts nothing less than a comprehensive account of the intellectual and moral forces in Germany that culminated in World War Two, as well as a diagnosis of the metaphysical patterns underlying the modern age.

- *Malloy, Malone Dies, The Unnameable* (1951-1953) by Samuel Beckett—For all its dislocations and frustrations, Beckett's trilogy is one of the most exhilarating of modern novels, treating the dilemma of experience in a radically new manner that

How is reading the modern novel different from earlier fiction?

It is worth noting that we have largely made our peace with modern architecture; we flock to see the latest Picasso, Cubist, or abstract expression shows. We have Paul Klee and Kandinsky, even Dali prints, above our sofas; we accept the dissonance and atonality of much modern music and appreciate the imagistic overload of film and television, but the modern novel is often resisted as too demanding and too difficult, a form to be endured (and therefore avoided) rather than enjoyed. The reason for this may be that, although we have come to terms with the conventions and methods of other modern arts, we still may be using a set of criteria, a set of assumptions and expectations appropriate for earlier novels that simply no longer apply. The way we read Jane Austen and Charles Dickens simply does not work for Conrad, Joyce, Woolf, and others. Try applying a standard derived from Rembrandt, Vermeer, and David to Monet, Cezanne, Manet, Van Gogh, Picasso, Pollack, and Rothko, for example. To allow these paintings appropriate expression, we need to meet them on their own terms, to try to understand what they are trying to do, not to critique them for what they never intended. In encountering such works as *Heart of Darkness, A Portrait of the Artist as a Young Man, Sons and Lovers, Ulysses, Mrs. Dalloway, To the Lighthouse,* and *The Sound and the Fury,* and other modern novels you will quickly discover that established assumptions of what a narrative should be—a story with a clear beginning, middle, and end with a definite resolution and characters who are easily categorized in moral, social, and psychological terms—have been fundamentally altered. The rules about how a novel should look and proceed have radically changed.

forces the reader to re-evaluate virtually every assumption about life, language, thought, and expression.

- *Invisible Man* (1952) by Ralph Ellison—Called "the veritable *Moby-Dick* of the racial crisis," the novel for the first time in literature illuminated the African American experience with the sophistication, density, and daring of the greatest modernist masters, such as Eliot, Faulkner, and Joyce. While suffusing his narrative with the American vernacular, Ellison also created something uniquely his own, offering the prose equivalent of two of America's greatest cultural contributions: the blues and jazz.

What are some suggestions on how you should read the modern novel?

1. *Read it like a short story.* The modern novel generally rejects the loose episodic pattern of eighteenth-century or Victorian novels for the more compressed, preplanned, and tightly patterned method closer to the principle of exclusion in the short story in which every element—diction, imagery, and details—matter. In

many ways, this is why the modern novel is so demanding: the unity of effects derived from short fiction that can be achieved in a single sitting has been extended to the longer novel. Like the short story, the modern novel generates significance by image and symbols as much as by action. Apply the same skills previously discussed in our section on the short story to the modern novel: assume every detail counts and try to relate each part of the narrative to an emerging whole.

2. *Read it like a poem.* It is interesting to note that many of the great modernist novelists were also poets: D. H. Lawrence, James Joyce, William Faulkner, even Ernest Hemingway, and a poetic sensibility pervades the modern novel. Like a poem, the modern novel depends on the power of its language—in the words it chooses and in its image patterns—as much as by the traditional structural elements of drama. Use the skills discussed in our section on poetry in reading the modern novel.

3. *Put the pieces of the puzzles together.* So much of the modern novel is fragmented: time and space are dislocated; linear development and causality are replaced by simultaneity, spatial form, and recurrence rather than progression. Just as it is helpful in a short story to turn the plot back into a story (a chronological sequence), do the same to the modern novel. By reassembling the parts into a coherent sequence, you gain insights into what the dislocations achieve in the novel's strategy.

4. *You are the novel's investigating detective.* Few modern novels make use of the helpful, if at times garrulous and intrusive, omniscient narrative guide of the eighteenth-century or Victorian novel. In those novels, you can sit back and be shown what to pay attention to and be told why it is important. Modern novels largely concede that responsibility to the reader. You are on your own. Modern novels, therefore, increase the demand to be an active reader, ever alert to significance, constantly sifting evidence to reach conclusions about meaning. Instead of third-person omniscient, modern novels mainly rely on first person or third-person limited. In a modern novel, narrators rarely are completely reliable. Their subjective, limited viewpoint needs to be questioned and cross-examined: how is bias and subjectivity getting in the way of revealed truth? Imagine your role in the modern novel as skeptical investigator attempting to reach the truth about what has occurred and its significance. Don't expect the novelist to assist directly, but look closely at the evidence presented: the title, the context for the action, the conflict, the resolution, and where you wind up.

5. *Ask yourself: Why?* Ultimately, in dealing with all the challenges of the modern novel, an important question needs to be answered: what is gained from all this effort? If there is no compensation, no reward, what is the point of the exercise? Many readers intimidated or baffled by the challenges of the modern novel rush into the comforting arms of genre fiction (like the historical novel, the romance, or mystery), in which the rules are clearer and the effort to wrestle the form into meaning is diminished. Ultimately, however, the effort required by a modern novel is built on the recognition that the simplification and idealization of other novels missed the won-

der and complexity of our lives. Modern novels, the argument goes, must be complicated because the life it is pursuing is complicated. Let Virginia Woolf, from her essay "Modern Fiction," more eloquently explain:

Examine for moment an ordinary mind on an ordinary day. The mind receives myriad impressions—trivial, fantastic, evanescent, or engraved with the sharpness of steel. From all sides they come, an incessant shower of innumerable atoms, and as they fall, as they shape themselves into the life of Monday or Tuesday, the accent falls differently from of old; the moment of importance came not here but there; so that if a writer were a free man and not a slave, if he could write what he chose, not what he must, if he could base his work upon his own feeling and not upon convention, there would be no plot, no comedy, no tragedy, no love interest or catastrophe in the accepted style.… Life is not a series of gig lamps symmetrically arranged; but a luminous halo, a semi-transparent envelope surrounding us from the beginning of consciousness to the end. Is it not the task of the novelist to convey this varying, this unknown and uncircumscribed spirit, whatever aberration or complexity it may display, with as little mixture of the alien and external as possible? … Let us record the atoms as they fall upon the mind in the order in which they fall, let us trace the pattern, however disconnected and incoherent in appearance, which each sight or incident scores upon the consciousness. Let us not take it for granted that life exists more fully in what is commonly thought big than in what is commonly thought small.

How has the novel evolved in the modern and postmodern eras … and beyond?

The energy and the spirit of modernism would gradually be succeeded by a new set of cultural responses that has been labeled postmodernism. This highly contested term is used to characterize philosophical ideas and artistic reactions in the second half of the twentieth century that acknowledge even further destabilization of core certainties at the most basic level of mind and language itself. In postmodernism, all truth, even artistic truths, and the very notion of reality itself are problematic, even illusory, undermined by language itself that fails in its mission to reflect reality. For the postmodernist novelist, any artful arrangement, whether in plots or stable characters, especially in the most elaborate modernist constructions, are consoling delusions. Randomness and fragmentation are not to be resisted in the causality and orderliness of art but accepted as postmodernism's steady state.

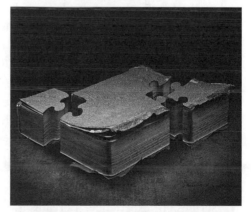

Modern fiction can pose a greater challenge to readers than novels of earlier centuries; they are more like puzzles that the reader, as detective, has to piece together in order to give the work's meaning clarity.

221

RALPH ELLISON'S *INVISIBLE MAN*

What is the significance of *Invisible Man*?

Only a few novels written in the second half of the twentieth century are certain to last as essential texts for their own and future times, and *Invisible Man* by Ralph Ellison (1914–1994) is unquestionably one of these. Literary critic Frederick Karl has called it an achievement that "needs no second act" and "a touchstone of the 1950s," while a *Book Week* poll of prominent authors, critics, and editors conducted in 1965 ranked *Invisible Man* "the most distinguished single work" published in the previous two decades. Judged by F. W. Dupee to be "the veritable *Moby-Dick* of the racial crisis," *Invisible Man* has entered the canon of American and world literature, as Saul Bellow observed in 1995, as a book that "holds its own among the best novels of the century." Critics continue to debate the degree to which *Invisible Man* is a universal or racial expression and the implications of the novel's lessons in democracy, identity, and history. What is unquestionable is that for the first time in literature, Ellison illuminated the African American experience with the sophistication, density, and daring of the modernist masters, such as T. S. Eliot, William Faulkner, and James Joyce, whom he admired. By suffusing his narrative with the American vernacular, Ellison also created something uniquely his own, refracting African American experience into a groundbreaking and influential prose equivalent in his themes and structure to America's greatest cultural contributions: the blues and jazz. As his friend novelist Albert Murray explained, *Invisible Man* represents "par excellence the literary extension of the blues. It was as if Ellison had taken an everyday twelve bar blues tune (by a man from down South sitting in a manhole up North in New York signifying about how he got there) and scored it for full orchestra." In this sense Ellison should be compared with the American musical geniuses Louis Armstrong and Duke Ellington, whose works and methods echo throughout his novel as a similar artistic originator, synthesizer, and liberator. *Invisible Man* is equally one of the most profound meditations on what it means to be an American and one of the great artistic battles to contain identity, consciousness, and the complexity of the American experience in a radical new form consistent with the novelist's mission that Ellison embraced. As the novelist remarked in a 1955 interview:

> I feel that with my decision to devote myself to the novel I took on one of the responsibilities inherited by those who practice the craft in the United States: that of describing for all that fragment of the huge diverse American experience which I know best, and which offers me the possibility of contributing not only to the growth of literature but to the shaping of the culture as I should like it to be. The American novel is in this sense a conquest of the frontier; as it describes our experience, it creates it.

How did *Invisible Man* originate?

According to Ellison, the conception for his novel came to him in the summer of 1945 while on sick leave from the merchant marine, recovering from a kidney infection at a friend's Vermont farm, "reading *The Hero* by Lord Raglan and speculating on the nature of Negro leadership in the United States." Ellison recalled that "creatures from Afro-American fables—Jack-the-Rabbit and Jack-the-Bear—blended in my mind with figures of myth and history" and "images of incest and murder, dissolution and rebirth whirled in my head" when he suddenly typed "I am an invisible man," the novel's opening line, "and I gasped at the range of implication." The novel would take him the next five years to complete and was finally published in 1952. As Ellison summarized his challenge and intention in his introduction to the novel's thirtieth anniversary edition, "I knew that I was composing a work of fiction, a work of literary art and one that would allow me to take advantage of the novel's capacity for telling the truth while actually telling a 'lie,' which is the Afro-American folk term for an improvised story.... I knew that I could draw upon the rich culture of the folk tale as well as that of the novel, and that being uncertain of my skill I would have to improvise upon my material in the manner of a jazz musician putting a musical theme through a wild star-burst of metamorphosis. By the time I realized that the words of the Prologue contained the germ of the ending as well as that of the beginning, I was free to enjoy the surprises of incident and character as they popped into view."

How does *Invisible Man* proceed?

Framed by its prologue and epilogue of Ellison's nameless protagonist, who has retreated to his basement room illuminated by 1,369 light bulbs, *Invisible Man* traces the theme of selfhood and invisibility through his central character's recollections from boyhood through college, exile to New York City and infatuation and ultimately betrayal by the manipulative Brotherhood to eventual insights into the meaning of his racial, national, and personal identity. The stages of Invisible Man's development proceed through a series of reversals dramatized by surrealistic dislocations and symbolically haunting imagery. There is simply no greater dramatic scene in modern fiction than the "Battle Royal" that initiates the protagonist's career. He is asked to deliver his high school valedictory address on racial deference at a smoker attended by white community leaders but must first participate with nine other young, blindfolded blacks in combat with one another. They are rewarded in a scramble for coins on an electrified rug. This chilling, expressionistic scene that forecasts much of the novel's incidents crystallizes black experience into a set of rich symbolism while initiating Invisible Man's discovery of his invisibility.

Armed with a college scholarship in his presentation briefcase that will bear the totems of his encounters with the wider world that refuses to see him beyond its own projections and manipulative needs, Invisible Man will be tested into self-knowledge and awareness. "It's a novel about innocence and human error," Ellison remarked about the patterning of the novel's action, "a struggle through illusion to reality." Invisible Man is initially disturbed and puzzled by his grandfather's deathbed advice, so different from the humility and deference his grandson initially accepts as the means for success: "Live with your head in the lion's mouth. I want you to overcome 'em with yeses, undermine 'em with grins, agree 'em to death and destruction, let 'em swoller you till they vomit or bust wide open." This riddle—how yes can become no and vice versa—will not be finally solved until the novel's conclusion in which the novel's protagonist has learned the lesson of his invisibility and its consequences and responsibilities.

At a college modeled on Ellison's own alma mater, Tuskeegee Institute, the naively earnest Invisible Man is initially anxious to succeed by endorsing the school's mission based on racial accommodation. However, he is expelled by accidentally exposing a white trustee, Mr. Norton, to a lowly sharecropper, Trueblood, who captivates the white man with the heart-rending story of his incestual relations with his daughter and by taking

The winner of the National Book Award for his *Invisible Man,* Ralph Ellison tackled the problem of identity and democracy in America.

Norton to recover to the Golden Day, a saloon-brothel frequented by black veterans on an outing from their asylum. Allowing an unflattering view of black experience, Invisible Man has committed an unpardonable error, according to the school's manipulative president, Dr. Bledsoe, who declares that "the only way to please a white man is to tell him a lie!" Black power and success are reached, according to Bledsoe's dictum, by subterfuge and illusion: by wearing a mask and letting whites see only what they think they want to see. Dispatched to New York to expiate his crime, Invisible Man is given a stack of introductory letters to help him find work that eventually are discovered to be the equivalent of his grandfather's interpretation of the testimonial he carries in his briefcase: "To Whom It May Concern … Keep This Nigger-Boy Running."

Invisible Man's experiences in New York include work for the Liberty Paint factory, mixing in black drops to make its white paint whiter ("If It's Optic White, It's the Right White"), confinement at the factory's hospital, and identity reprogramming until finally discharged back to Harlem. Through his oracular skills, Invisible Man comes to the attention of the white-controlled Brotherhood, who provide him with a new identity and occupation as "chief spokesman of the Harlem District" for their radical cause. Eventually, Invisible Man learns that despite the rhetoric of equality and social justice espoused by the Brotherhood, the group is no less manipulative or as willing to grant the autonomy of blacks as the community leaders at the smoker. Neither radical politics, black nationalism as represented by the rabble-rouser Ras the Exhorter, nor the shapeshifting, hipster Rinehart and his "vast seething, hot world of fluidity" provide Invisible Man with a workable solution for his dilemma to define himself and his responsibilities, though all help to expose his challenge. Others he encounters—Trueblood, Wheatstraw, Mary Rambo, Brother Tarp, and Tod Clifton—offer alternatives in transcendence and survival that echo the insight of the veteran he meets on the bus north: "Play the game, but don't believe in it.… Learn how it operates, learn how *you* operate.… The world is possibility if only you'll discover it." As Harlem explodes into riot in one of the novel's most impressive expressionistic scenes, Invisible Man has been betrayed yet again, forcing him underground, where the act of recalling his experiences leads to the novel's final illumination.

How does *Invisible Man* conclude?

Ultimately, by accepting his invisibility, the Invisible Man asserts control of his destiny. Invisibility offers possibilities, a nullity upon which identity can be creatively and liberatingly fashioned. As the Invisible Man gradually understands, "When I discover who I am, I'll be free." Through confronting the challenge of his invisibility, he also penetrates to the core of the American experience in which the delineation of identity is the central cultural imperative. He also approaches the full implication of his grandfather's deathbed advice "to overcome 'em by yeses": by taking America at its word, by affirming the principles of American democracy, that despite all the evidence to the contrary, the individual can validate and vindicate his humanity and begin to give shape and purpose to his identity.

Few novels have penetrated so deeply into the core American problem of identity and democracy as *Invisible Man*. Richard Wright asserted that the Negro is "America's metaphor," and Ellison, his former protégé, has applied it masterfully. As Ellison conceived it, his novel framed the essential questions: "Who am I, what am I, how did I come to be? What should I make of the life around me?… What does American society mean when regarded out of my *own* eyes, when informed by my *own* sense of the past and viewed by my *own* complex sense of the present?" Ellison's answers in *Invisible Man* reach far beyond protest, victimage, and sociology through its aspirations and achievement to the universals implied in the novel's concluding sentence: "Who knows but that, on the lower frequencies, I speak for you?"

How does randomness and fragmentation influence postmodern novels?

The impact of these notions on the postmodernist novel is reflected in a further retreat from synthesis and conclusions about human nature and human experience. If the modernists asked the question "What can we believe in the absence of the possibility of belief?" then the postmodernists ask, "What can we know in the absence of the possibility of knowing anything?" Postmodernist novelists mainly invoke the great stories and myths ironically as parodies. Hence, Thomas Pynchon in the postmodern classic *The Crying of Lot 49* (1966) send his protagonist, Oedipa Maas, on a detective quest to uncover the existence of a counterculture, a vast network of alternative modes of communication, only to end the novel at the climactic moment when Oedipa presumably will learn either the truth or confirm her own madness. John Barth in *The Sot-weed Factor* (1960) repurposes the eighteenth-century novel as an absurdist mash-up. E. L. Doctorow in *Ragtime* (1970) violates the rules of plausibility of the historical novel, answering the charge that

225

historical figures like Henry Ford, Freud, Jung, and others never did what he has them do: "I'd never read that J.P. Morgan and Henry Ford met. But for me their meeting was unavoidable.... So have they met? They have now" and "What's real and what isn't? I used to know, but I've forgotten. Let's just say that *Ragtime* is a mingling of fact and invention—a novelist's revenge on an age that celebrates nonfiction."

As exhilarating and creative as the postmodern novel can be, there is a clear sense in its reach and confidence that the era of the novel as epic summary of an age is over. The novel, like our mass media, has fractured into multiple markets, narrow-casting rather than broadcasting. Excellent novels persist, but they seem narrower and deeper rather than wide and expansive, more lyrical in evoking private ideas and emotions rather than epic in encapsulating an entire time and place.

TONI MORRISON'S *BELOVED*

What is the signicance of *Beloved*?

There is perhaps no better justification for the challenging modernist and postmodern methods of chronological dislocation, fragmentation, and blending of fantasy and realism than the remarkable attempt to come to imaginative terms with the enormity of slavery and the American past in *Beloved* (1987) by Toni Morrison (1931–). How better to emphasize a repressed, traumatizing past than to bury it and allow it only gradually to emerge in disjointed, lethal images? How appropriate in a present haunted by the past that a spirit from the host of the anonymous dead should magically appear and compel an exorcism? *Beloved* is thus far Morrison's most ambitious and most fully realized novel, a masterpiece of almost unbearable power and seemingly inexhaustible cultural, psychological, and humane relevance. In a work of shattering emotional intensity and historical synthesis, Morrison has crafted one of the essential fictional works of the second half of the twentieth century.

What is the background behind and origin of *Beloved*?

Having come to novel writing late in a career occupied by teaching and editorial work, Morrison published her first novel, *The Bluest Eye,* in 1970 when she was thirty-nine. This lyrical exploration of racial and gender identity was followed by *Sula* in 1974. Both books were critically praised for their poetic prose, emotional intensity, and unique interpretation of African American experience from the largely neglected woman's perspective. Neither book was a popular success, and both novels were out of print when Morrison published her breakthrough novel, *Song of Solomon,* in 1977, the novel that established her reputation as a dominating voice in contemporary fiction world-

Author and educator Toni Morrison earned both the American Book Award and a Pulitzer Prize for her critically acclaimed novel *Beloved.*

wide. *Song of Solomon* shows Morrison extending her range, employing a male protagonist for the first time, Milkman Dead, whom critic Margaret Wade-Lewis has called "undoubtedly one of the most effective renderings of a male character by a woman writer in American literature." His quest to find a family legacy and to decipher his racial identity is a complex and resonant interweaving of myth and history that draws on black folklore, oral tradition, and classical archetypes. This expansiveness is continued in her next novel, *Tar Baby* (1981), in which Morrison continues an imaginative search for identity in the confrontation between blacks and whites, along with her characteristic fusion of fantasy derived from the black American folktale and realism but here placed in a global setting that encompasses the entire African Diaspora.

Tar Baby was a bestseller and prompted *Newsweek* to do a cover story on the writer. Ironically, Morrison felt at the time that her writing days were over. "I would not write another novel to either make a living or because I was able to," she later recalled. "If it was not an overwhelming compulsion or I didn't feel absolutely driven by the ideas I wanted to explore, I wouldn't do it. And I was content not to ever be driven that way again." The compulsion came reluctantly as Morrison began to confront the legacy of slavery, a subject obscured, in Morrison's words, by a "national amnesia." *Beloved* would become an effort of re-memory, the deliberate act of reconstructing what has been forgotten, which the author defined as "a journey to a site to see what remains have been left behind and to reconstruct the world that these remains imply." In an act of bearing witness, of giving voice to the unspeakable, Morrison set out "to fill in the blanks that the slave narrative left," to "part the veil that was frequently drawn" in which the full

227

ramifications of the slave experience could be probed, and its costs embodied in psychological, emotional, social, and cultural terms.

The inspiration for her story came from Morrison's editorial work on Middleton Harris's documentary collection of black life in America, *The Black Book*. Morrison became fascinated by a historical incident from a newspaper clipping contained in Harris's collection entitled "A Visit to the Slave Mother Who Killed Her Child." It concerns a journalist's report on a runaway slave from Kentucky, Margaret Garner, who in 1855 tried to kill her children rather than to allow them to be returned to slavery. Successful in killing one, Margaret Garner would provide the historical access point for *Beloved* as Morrison explored imaginatively the conditions that could have led to such a horrific act and its consequences on the survivors.

How does *Beloved* proceed?

Narrated in a series of flashbacks assembled gradually from the limited perspective of its characters, *Beloved* opens in 1873, eighteen years after the defining trauma in the life of Sethe, a former slave on a Kentucky farm called Sweet Home. Sethe lives in an isolated house outside Cincinnati with her eighteen-year-old daughter Denver and the ghost of Sethe's dead baby girl, named by the inscription on her tombstone, Beloved. The novel's setting during the Reconstruction Period is symbolically appropriate for Sethe's search for wholeness, the effort to rebuild an identity, a family, and a community shattered by the enormous toll and dehumanization of slavery. A clear chronology of events in Sethe's life emerges only eventually as numerous characters—her mother-in-law Baby Suggs, the black river man Stamp Paid, and Sethe's fellow slave: the last of the Sweet Home Men, Paul D, and others—allow their experiences to emerge painfully through a protective repression.

In 1848 the teenage Sethe is sold to Mr. Garner at Sweet Home as the replacement for Baby Suggs, whose freedom has been purchased by her son Halle, whom Sethe marries. When Mr. Garner dies in 1853, the farm is placed in the hands of an overseer called "Schoolteacher," who transforms Mr. Garner's more benign regime with a brutal and calculated indifference to the humanity of the Sweet Home slaves. When one is sold, the rest plot their escape in 1855. On the eve of departure, the pregnant Sethe is attacked by Schoolteacher's two nephews. As one holds her down, the other submits her to "mammary rape," sucking the milk from her breasts. Unknown to Sethe, this violation is witnessed by Halle, who is incapable of assisting his wife. The event leads to his derangement and disappearance. Sethe sends her three children to join the emancipated Baby Suggs in Ohio and eventually reaches freedom there herself after giving birth to her daughter, Denver. The four other Sweet Home Men are either brutally killed or imprisoned. Sethe enjoys only twenty-eight days of freedom before Schoolteacher arrives to take her back. Rather than allowing her children to be returned to slavery, Sethe tries to kill them. Three survive, but Beloved's throat is cut. Arrested and sentenced to hang, Sethe is pardoned due to the intervention of abolitionists and allowed to return to Baby Suggs's home at 124 Bluestone Road, where she is shunned by the black community. The vengeful spirit of her murdered child also takes up residence, drives away Sethe's two sons, contributes to Baby Suggs's death, and holds Sethe and Denver in her spell until the arrival in 1873 of Paul D.

How does *Beloved* conclude?

Paul D is able to expel the ghost, temporarily breaking the hold of grief, seclusion, and despair that has locked Sethe and Denver in a continual, debilitating past. Paul D offers the possibility of family and future, but neither Paul D nor Sethe are

Morrison explores the negative effects of blacks trying to disassociate themselves from the slavery they experienced in their past in *Beloved* (*Slaves Waiting for Sale* [1861] by Eyre Crowe).

truly ready to put their past behind them. As if to insist that both must confront that past, the ghost returns in bodily form as a young woman (appearing the age Beloved would have been had she survived) and claims sanctuary. A sinister presence, Beloved's voracious obsession with food and Sethe's love split the incipient family apart. The revelation that Sethe has killed her daughter drives Paul D away, and Beloved claims complete dominance over Sethe as the physical embodiment of her crippling conscience. Increasingly obsessed with righting the wrong to Beloved that cannot be corrected, Sethe loses her job and all contact with the outside world. Neglected and starving, Denver is forced to reach out to the larger community for assistance, an act that finally will break the hold Beloved has over Sethe. As the black women of the community who had previously ostracized Sethe for her murder now come to her assistance, a version of Schoolteacher's arrival at the house is reenacted as the elderly Mr. Bodwin, who had gained Sethe's pardon in 1855, and is mistaken by the deranged Sethe as a slave catcher. She is prevented from stabbing him with an ice pick, but her climactic gesture of striking out—not at the victims of slavery in her former assault on her children but at its presumed agent—forces Beloved to vanish and prepares the way for the novel's concluding reconciliations and affirmations. Sethe at first despairs at losing her child yet again, but her complete breakdown and retreat from life, following the previous example of Baby Suggs, is halted by the return of Paul D, whose acceptance of Sethe and the past asserts his willingness and her ability to face the future. Contrary to Sethe's belief that her children were her "best things," that her all-encompassing love was the essential justification for her to kill them rather than allow them to be returned to slavery, Paul D insists, "You your best thing, Sethe. You are." The revelation he offers Sethe suggests that the past need not tyrannize but must be fully confronted with wholeness the result of self-respect *and* selflessness, of individual autonomy and participation in a sustaining wider human community.

Morrison has supplied a unique lesson in the ramifications of the legacy of slavery from a perspective that has previously been ignored: as an institution with devastating consequences on the family, sexuality, and psychological and emotional wholeness. In her handling, racial, personal, and national history come together in an essential myth that probes a collective scar and suggests where healing can be found.

SUBGENRES OF THE NOVEL

What are the main subgenres of the novel?

If modern novels can be divided between popular entertainment and serious literary works, they also can be further grouped by several subgenres. A frequent retreat for the novelist in these postmodern times, as well as the refuge for readers craving a less demanding, more familiar story has been genre fiction—the historical novel, mystery, fantasy, and science fiction—in which the rules of engagement are more definitively fixed. Much of genre fiction is formulaic, aimed not at challenging or disrupting the reading experience but at providing sheer entertainment. However, you can also find genre novels that attempt to do much more than just gratify a taste for the familiar. To close our consideration of the novel, let's look at three of the most popular novel genres.

THE HISTORICAL NOVEL

What are the chief characteristics of the historical novel?

Of all the novel's genres, the historical novel has proven to be the most popular (in terms of presence on the bestseller lists) and the most persistent, attracting first-time novelists, veterans of the form, and literary novelists to its challenges. Historical fiction endures even though it remains one of the most demanding and contested of fictional genres. By invading the domain of the historian with an intention to elucidate the past as well as to entertain, the historical novelist must serve two opposed standards, satisfying the often contradictory goals of historical and imaginative truth. Not bound by the same restrictions as the historian to report only what is known and verifiable, the historical novelist is free to look beneath the facts for insights, to fill in gaps in the record with speculation and surmise. Historical novelists must balance the demands of representing the historical record accurately and telling a good story and often imaginatively compensating for gaps and deficiencies in that record. Taking too much latitude with the facts of history distorts the truth and shatters the illusion of authenticity; taking too little, and the sheer data of history never come to life.

How do you define the "historical" in historical fiction?

Most novels—with the exception of science fiction that is set in the future or fantasy novels usually set in an imagined, alternative world outside historical time—deal with the past. Yet not all novels are truly historical. Central to any workable definition of historical fiction is the degree to which the writer attempts not to recall the past but to recreate it. In some cases, the period, setting, and customs of a novel's era are merely incidental to its action and characterization. In other cases, period details function as little more than a colorful backdrop for characters and situations that could as easily be played out in a different era with little alteration. So-called historical "costume dramas" could, to a greater or lesser degree, work as well with a change of clothing in a different place and time. The novels that we can identify as truly historical, however, attempt much more than incidental period surface details or interchangeable historical eras. What justifies a novel's designation as "historical" is the writer's efforts at providing an accurate and believable representation of a specific era. The writer of historical fiction shares with the historian a verifiable depiction of past events, lives, and customs. In historical fiction, the past itself becomes as much a subject for the novelist as the characters and action.

How can you identify and evaluate a historical novel?

The litmus test for identifying and evaluating the historical novel is whether the author uses his or her imagination—and often quite a bit of research—to evoke an earlier time. Sir Walter Scott (1771–1832), who is credited with "inventing" the historical novel in English during the early nineteenth century, provides a useful criterion in the subtitle of *Waverley*, his story of Scottish life at the time of the Jacobite Rebellion of 1745: "'Tis Sixty Years Since." This supplies a possible formula for separating the created past from the remembered past. What is unique and distinctive about the so-called historical novel is its attempt to imagine a distant period before the novelist's lifetime. Scott's sixty-year span between a novel's composition and its imagined era offers an arbitrary but useful gauge to distinguish between the personal and the historical past. The distance of two generations or nearly a lifetime provides a necessary span for the past to emerge as history and forces the writer to rely on more than recollection to uncover the patterns and textures of the past.

How should you read the historical novel?

Realizing the dual directions of the historical novel between the historian's emphasis on the verifiable and the novelist's imaginative invention, the best approach to reading a historical novel is to do the following:

1. Read it like history. Assess as best as you can the historical reliability of the novel. Responsible historical fiction writers will alert readers in a preface or afterword what liberties from the historical record were taken. Other-

Celebrated poet, playwright, and novelist Sir Walter Scott has been credited with developing the historical novel as a genre.

231

wise, you must rely on your own sense of the historical past, its customs and speech patterns, to judge how convincing the novel is as a historical record.

2. Read it like a novel. Clearly, historical novelists will be trying to do more than just offer a reliable historical account. They will use the methods of fiction, whether in the arrangement of narrative events into a convincing plot or in focusing on a historical or invented character to illuminate the historical past. It's worth noting that all historians select and shape their material into compelling versions of the past. Great historians are also great storytellers who master some of the same skills as their imaginative novelist counterparts: the vivid use of details, nuances of characterization, suspense in narrating events that still surprise even if outcomes are known. In assessing a historical novel, look for the same elements of well-crafted storytelling. Departures from the verifiable, such as imagined conversations or thoughts, can be acceptable provided they seem plausible and consistent with the historical record that is known or established by the novel. Radical departures into the realms of surmise and the hypothetical demand some justification or the illusion of historical truth will be eroded or violated.

THE MYSTERY NOVEL

How does the mystery novel differ from the literary novel?

While there are often mystery elements in the literary novel, as well as novels in which a mystery is central to the plot—such as *Northanger Abbey, Jane Eyre, The Woman in White, Great Expectations*, and *Rebecca*—mystery as a genre denotes a work of fiction that *primarily* focuses on the solving of a problem or puzzle. It is usually, but not always, connected with one or more crimes, such as homicide, theft, fraud, or espionage. Mys-

---

What is the origin of the word "detective"?

The word "detective" was coined in the mid-nineteenth century as shorthand for "detective policeman" but was not yet in use when Edgar Allan Poe created C. Auguste Dupin, a character considered to be the first fictional investigator. Dupin is featured in three of Poe's short stories: "The Murders in the Rue Morgue" (1841), "The Mystery of Marie Roget" (1842), and "The Purloined Letter" (1844). The scion of a once wealthy family and now living in Paris under humble circumstances, Dupin is the precursor of what was later known as the "gentleman detective," a subset of freelance investigators either from the aristocracy or educated to be a "gentleman." Dupin investigates with the help of the stories' anonymous narrator, and he is connected with "G," a prefect of police who seeks his help with cases. Possessed of a formidable intellect, Dupin relies on a combination of deductive reasoning and creative imagination to solve crimes.

tery novels are often subcategorized as "detective fiction," "crime novels," "spy fiction," or "thrillers."

Who are the main characters in the mystery novel?

The main protagonist in mystery fiction, and especially in a mystery series, is usually one or more detectives connected either officially or unofficially (a spouse, for example) with police departments (most notably in police procedural mysteries) or government agencies. However, the protagonist in a mystery can also be a private, or "consulting," detective (Sherlock Holmes, Sam Spade, Easy Rawlins, Hercule Poirot, Precious Ramotswe) who may or may not work with the police during an investigation. In the case of historical (but also in some modern) mysteries, the detective-protagonist can be anyone who is either directly or tangentially connected with the problem to be investigated and solved either by profession or by coincidence or both (for example, Robert Langdon in *The Da Vinci Code*).

Who was the first police detective in a novel?

The first police detective in a novel is Inspector Bucket in Charles Dickens's *Bleak House* (1853). Although not a main character, Bucket carries out several investigations that are

An illustration from the Edgar Allan Poe mystery "The Purloined Letter," featuring detective C. Auguste Dupin, who is often considered the first crime investigator to appear in a work of fiction.

integral to the novel's plot. Dickens is thought to have based his detective on Charles Frederick Field, an inspector at Scotland Yard's newly formed Detective Branch, whom Dickens sometimes accompanied in his investigations.

What are some other characteristics of fictional detectives?

Like C. Auguste Dupin and Inspector Bucket, detectives in mysteries generally possess very clear character traits, which are easily recognizable to readers and which are expected features of each novel in which they appear: Sherlock Holmes, the most famous of all, is an eccentric genius; Agatha Christie's Hercule Poirot is sartorially fastidious and relies on his "little gray cells" to solve crimes; Christie's Miss Marple is an elderly English spinster whose fluttery manner hides a deep understanding of human nature and great powers of deduction; Dashiell Hammett's Sam Spade and Raymond Chandler's Philip Marlowe are world-weary, urban tough guys; Dorothy Sayers' gentleman detective, Lord Peter Wimsey, affects the attitude of an effete aristocrat to confound possible suspects.

Mystery novels often feature detective-protagonists who offer us more depth to their characters than the formula requires. One example is Scotland Yard Commander Adam Dalgliesh, P. D. James's melancholy police detective and poet. Dalgliesh is a complicated man, whose conflicted feelings about his personal past and his relationships with women inform and occasionally compromise his cases. But because mysteries present problems that must be solved, Dalgliesh ultimately satisfies the reader's need for investigations that ultimately lead to a solution.

What is the importance of secondary characters in mysteries?

Mystery fiction relies on the conflict of protagonist vs. antagonist. Antagonists in mysteries are generally one or more persons pursued and apprehended, but each suspect or potential suspect, as well as characters who in some way hamper an investigation (for example, a person in authority who disputes the methods used by the detective-protagonist), can be considered antagonists. Secondary characters can also include friends and family members, who may either serve the plot by suggesting another path of investigation, pointing out a clue, or act as a distraction for the detective-protagonist. The most famous example is Sherlock Holmes's friend Doctor Watson, who serves as a foil to display Holmes's virtuosity but also as a stand-in for the reader, tasked with asking our questions—who, what, why, when, and how—that Holmes can then brilliantly answer.

Why are plot, setting, and culture particularly important in a successful mystery novel?

More than any other literary genre, mystery fiction relies at its core on the simple plot formula of problem, investigation, solution, and identification and apprehension of a culprit. However, although a detective-protagonist and even secondary characters may have recognizable and expected character traits, there can be depths to a character's personality and experience that can elevate this simple formula, and, depending on the deftness of the author, bring it closer to literary fiction in offering more than just entertainment.

One example is Steig Larsson's gifted but deeply troubled Lisbeth Salander, a researcher and skilled computer hacker with an eidetic memory, a traumatic past, and a gift for concealing her identity. Salander is introduced in *The Girl with the Dragon Tattoo* (2005), where her research into a disgraced journalist leads her to a series of past murders.

Setting and culture can similarly influence the ways in which a problem occurs, and an investigation progresses: Alexander McCall Smith's *The Number 1 Ladies Detective Agency* mystery series takes place in Botswana; Tony Hillerman's detective series featuring Lieutenant Joe Leaphorn and Sergeant Jim Chee of the Navajo Tribal Police explore themes relating to the experience of American Indians in the Southwest. When reading a mystery novel, ask yourself how characterization, setting, and culture affect the various elements of the plot and how these elements are related.

Why does point of view matter in mysteries?

In a mystery novel, points of view may shift back and forth between the detective-protagonist and secondary characters. Mysteries ask readers to solve the problem along with the investigator, and shifting points of view can provide an advantage for the reader: to learn something about a suspect that the detective-protagonist doesn't know yet. If the point of view shifts, ask yourself why. What is achieved by such shifts? The artful arrangement of perspective can be as crucial as camera angles in a film.

What about suspense versus surprise?

Suspense and surprise are core ingredients of any well-told story. For the difference between the two, consider the words of the master of film suspense, Alfred Hitchcock:

> There is a distinct difference between "suspense" and "surprise," and yet many pictures continually confuse the two. I'll explain what I mean.

> We are now having a very innocent little chat. Let's suppose that there is a bomb underneath this table between us. Nothing happens, and then all of a sudden, "Boom!" There is an explosion. The public is surprised, but prior to this sur-

---

Why is the presence of a "red herring" a crucial plot device in mystery fiction?

A staple of mystery fiction, the red herring is a literary plot device that is designed to lead the detective-protagonist and by extension, the reader, toward a false conclusion. Red herrings can include suspects, objects, or additional crimes that serve as false clues during an investigation. The red herring is crucial in helping to distract or delay the usual arrangement of a mystery plot to a climactic revelation. If the solution is too easy, the mystery fails, and red herrings serve to complicate the plot.

prise, it has seen an absolutely ordinary scene of no special consequence. Now, let us take a suspense situation. The bomb is underneath the table and the public knows it, probably because they have seen the anarchist place it there. The public is aware the bomb is going to explode at one o'clock and there is a clock in the decor. The public can see that it is a quarter to one. In these conditions, the same innocuous conversation becomes fascinating because the public is participating in the scene. The audience is longing to warn the characters on the screen: "You shouldn't be talking about such trivial matters. There is a bomb beneath you and it is about to explode!"

In the first case we have given the public fifteen seconds of surprise at the moment of the explosion. In the second we have provided them with fifteen minutes of suspense. The conclusion is that whenever possible the public must be informed. Except when the surprise is a twist, that is, when the unexpected ending is, in itself, the highlight of the story.

The successful mystery novel depends on both: there needs to be suspense to keep the pages turning as well as the surprising final revelation, Hitchcock's "Boom!"

Ultimately, the test of whether a mystery succeeds or fails is whether it can deliver both effectively: engagement in the problem/puzzle as well as the satisfying surprise that the mystery writer has carefully prepared for so that the reader's response, after initial astonishment, is "How did I not see that coming? It all makes sense now."

How can mysteries be elevated to literary status?

It is incorrect and misleading to suggest that reliance on a mystery formula only results in entertainment, that a mystery cannot become something more ambitious. After all, the first mystery in Western literature is Sophocles's great tragedy *Oedipus the King*. Oedipus sets out to end the plague that afflicts Thebes by following the instructions of the Delphic oracle and solving the mystery of who killed his predecessor, Laius. Sophocles has the play's initial mystery serve much more profound ends by replacing the initial mystery of who killed Laius with the more existential question that Oedipus must solve: Who am I? Sophocles's murder mystery takes in issues of free will and fate, the role of the gods in human affairs, even whether knowledge itself is desirable. Sophocles also constructs the first great metamystery in which Oedipus the detective becomes Oedipus the culprit: searching for Laius's killer, Oedipus learns he is the one he is looking for. Sophocles's mystery pushes

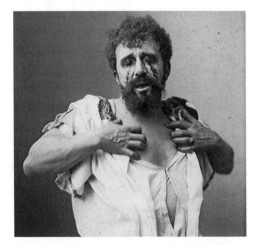

Oedipus the King by Sophocles may be regarded as not just a tragedy but also a mystery.

his characters to unsuspected disclosures, more than justifying the form of withheld truth and its gradual revelations.

What other literary works use mystery as more than a vehicle for puzzle solving?

One famous example is William Shakespeare's *Hamlet*, which is, of course, many things, but its engine to reach them is a murder mystery: who killed the title character's father? Shakespeare spoils the surprise by having the king's ghost identify the killer in Act 1, but the detective Hamlet still must try to prove the truth of the ghost's accusations and bring the guilty to justice. Another example is Henry Fielding's *Tom Jones*, which puts a central mystery—the parentage of Tom Jones—at the center of his great comic epic, the revelation of which is saved for his finale.

How did Charles Dickens begin to incorporate the mystery genre into his novels?

Perhaps no writer better shows the larger purpose mystery can offer than Charles Dickens, who began his novel career with episodic improvisation: without the preplanning that mysteries require to plant and reap a central mystery. In *Oliver Twist*, his second novel, Dickens mastered the great lesson that would hereafter drive his narratives: "Make 'em laugh. Make 'em cry. But most of all make 'em wait." *Oliver Twist* employs the central mystery of Oliver's parentage and expertly withholds outcomes of events to enhance suspense. Readers of the original monthly serial had to wait three months to learn that the installment's final line, "a cold deadly feeling crept over the boy's heart; and he saw or heard no more," is a bit premature!

How did Dickens focus on mystery in *Bleak House*?

Mystery and suspense, however, would grow in importance to become the main event. *Bleak House,* at the midpoint of Dickens's career, would set the mystery pattern for virtually all his next six novels. The mysteries in *Bleak House* are numerous: Why does Lady Dedlock react so violently when she sees a lowly copyist's handwriting? Who is Esther Summerson? To answer these questions and unveil other secrets, the characters (and reader) are forced to become detectives, and their investigations slowly but inevitably tie together the novel's entire massive social panorama. Dickens asks, "What connexion can there be between the place in Lincolnshire, the house in town, the Mercury in powder, and the whereabouts of Jo the outlaw with the broom.... What connexion can there have been between many people in innumerable histories of this world, who, from opposite sides of great gulfs, have, nevertheless, been curiously brought together." In *Bleak House*, mystery and detection make a social and psychological point, becoming both the central subject and method of the novel. Here, mystery is put to the service of great literature.

What makes a modern mystery novel more than just a puzzle to be solved?

Some mysteries, like a completed crossword puzzle, are disposable when the puzzle is solved—determining the person or persons responsible for the crime is enough. But other mysteries use the elements of detection and withheld information, together with compelling and often complicated characters and the cultures in which readers encounter them, to propel the reader forward, even reaching epistemological and existential truths along the way. George Bernard Shaw observed that melodrama, that debased entertainment concoction, was of "first-rate literary importance because it only needs elaboration to become a masterpiece." The same is certainly true of mystery and indeed of any of the novel's subgenres. The challenge is in the elaboration and the intention to offer more to a reader than a simple "whodunit."

SCIENCE FICTION AND FANTASY

How do science fiction and fantasy novels differ from other kinds of novels?

Science fiction and fantasy are both forms of "speculative fiction," a term that refers to any work that contains futuristic or supernatural elements. Each genre can contain both elements and are based on imaginary realities, settings, and situations, but there are clear differences between the two.

How is science fiction defined?

It can be difficult to define science fiction because the genre has come to be considered by authors and critics to comprise two types—"hard" and "soft"—as well as a wide range of subgenres and themes. In general, science fiction can be defined as fiction that draws on imaginative concepts outside the realm of everyday experience, usually with components that include scientific theory and innovation, and often explores the potential consequences of scientific applications. According to Robert A. Heinlein, the author of the classic science fiction novel *Stranger in a Strange Land* (1961): "A handy short definition of almost all science fiction might read: realistic speculation about possible future events, based solidly on adequate knowledge of the real world, past and present. And on a thorough understanding of the nature and significance of the scientific method."

What is the difference between "hard" and "soft" science fiction?

Hard science fiction is generally based upon the natural sciences, especially physics, astrophysics, chemistry, or advanced technology, in an attempt to create future worlds. Authors known for this type of science fiction include Isaac Asimov (*I, Robot*, *The Bicentennial Man*) and Arthur C. Clarke (*Childhood's End*, *2010: Odyssey Two*). In contrast, "soft" science fiction draws from the social sciences, such as psychology, sociology, economics, and political science, focuses on character and emotion, and can be set in a technologically advanced future. Authors of "soft" science fiction include Ursula LeGuin ("The Hainish Cycle"), Philip K. Dick (*Do Androids Dream of Electric Sheep?*, "We Can Remember It for You Wholesale"), and Ray Bradbury (*The Martian Chronicles*, *Fahrenheit 451*).

Where did science fiction originate?

In one of literature's most remarkable creation stories, science fiction was invented by an eighteen-year-old on her summer holidays! She is Mary Shelley (1797–1851), and her creation, *Frankenstein,* is every bit as astonishing as the monster Victor Frankenstein builds. Mary Shelley, the daughter of radical thinkers William Godwin and Mary Wollstonecraft, who died giving Mary Shelley birth, in 1814 fell in love with the already married poet Percy Bysshe Shelley. In 1816, the couple traveled to Geneva to stay at the chateau of fellow Romantic poet Lord Byron. The weather that summer was cold and rainy, forcing the party inside. For entertainment, they challenged themselves to concoct the best ghost story. Mary, recalling conversations between her soon-to-be hus-

Mary Shelley could be said to have written the first science-fiction novel, *Frankenstein.*

band (after his wife's suicide) and Byron about electricity and its effect making a severed frog's leg twitch and a corpse move, had a kind of waking dream in which she "saw the pale student of unhallowed arts kneeling beside the thing he had put together. I saw the hideous phantasm of a man stretched out, and then, on the working of some powerful engine, show signs of life, and stir with an uneasy, half vital motion. Frightful must it be; for supremely frightful would be the effect of any human endeavor to mock the stupendous mechanism of the Creator of the world." Mary Shelley's contribution to the contest clearly succeeded, and, encouraged by Percy Shelley to develop her story, she produced the novel *Franken-stein; or, The Modern Prometheus,* published in 1818.

What are the elements in *Frankenstein* that make the novel science fiction?

In a single, accidental stroke, Mary Shelley had conceived one of horror's most enduring franchises, but what about science fiction? Mary Shelley's innovation as she developed her novel was to reverse the standard procedure of previous Gothic horror fiction, which usually dispelled the apparently uncanny incidents of the supernatural at the end by offering a naturalistic and plausible explanation: the statue moved because it was the villain all along intent on terrifying the heroine, etc. What Mary Shelley did differently is put the plausible explanations for the wonders in her novel at the beginning, providing, if not a scientific prescription, a believable, rational explanation of Victor Frankenstein's mastery of his "unhallowed arts." We are shown his studies, including a list of sources, and his perfecting the technological skills that lead to his creating life. The extraordinary is not merely explained away as a misconception but grows out of a speculative science. By doing so, Mary Shelley set the procedures for all subsequent science fiction that attempts to base its wonderment in the stuff of science and technology. With such a powerful myth as *Frankenstein* at its inception, it is not surprising that countless authors have followed Mary Shelley's lead.

What are the classic subgenres of science fiction?

- *Time travel.* A staple of science fiction and a subgenre that sometimes blurs the distinction between science fiction and fantasy, time-travel fiction features one or more characters that travel in time by various means. In Mark Twain's *A Connecticut Yankee in King Arthur's Court* (1889), the first major novel about time travel, the protagonist travels back to the titular location after a blow on the head. The most famous early example of the subgenre is H. G. Wells' *The Time Machine* (1895), in which the main character, an inventor, uses a time machine to travel many millennia in the future. In Robert Heinlein's 1941 novella, *By His Bootstraps*, a graduate student in metaphysics uses a Time Gate as his conduit to the past and future and is forced to confront the temporal paradoxes caused by his actions. A contemporary example is *The Time Traveler's Wife* series by Audrey Niffenegger. The novels feature Henry, born with a genetic defect that leads to frequent time jumps and temporal anomalies, as well as his wife, Claire, and their daughter, Alba, who is also capable of time travel. Another example is the popular *Outlander* series by Diana Gabaldon in which a twentieth-century nurse time travels to eighteenth-century Scotland.

- *Alternate history.* This subgenre is based on the premise that a different past would alter the historical timeline, either through time travel or simply an imaginary construct. Examples include Philip K. Dick's *The Man in the High Castle* (1962), which presents an America dominated by the winning Axis powers in the aftermath of World War II, and the novels of Harry Turtledove, which include the author's *Worldwar* and *Colonization* series.

- *Apocalyptic and post-apocalyptic fiction.* Fiction in this subgenre is concerned with the destruction of the world through cataclysmic events that include war, ecological or natural disaster, an astronomic event, or the aftermath of such events. Examples include the 1933 novel *When Worlds Collide* by Philip Wylie and Edwin Balmer, in which Earth's existence is threatened when two exoplanets enter the solar system, and Nevil Shute's *On the Beach* (1957), which takes place during the aftermath of a nuclear war that has destroyed most of life on earth and will eventually kill the humans who remain.

- *Dystopian fiction.* Related to post-apocalyptic fiction, dystopian novels focus on future societies characterized by oppressive and monolithic governments often aided by technology, a breakdown of ethical values, and personal as well as organized revolts against the system. The most famous examples include Aldous Huxley's *Brave New World* (1931), George Orwell's *Nineteen Eighty-four* (1949), and Anthony Burgess's *A Clockwork Orange* (1962). More contemporary examples are Margaret Atwood's *A Handmaid's Tale* (1985) and P. D. James's *Children of Men* (2006).

- *Space opera.* Science fiction adventure novels are set mainly in space with an emphasis on interplanetary battles featuring futuristic weapons and advanced technology. Space operas rely on the simple formula of good vs. evil and hero vs. villain. Notable authors who have contributed to this subgenre include Isaac Asimov (the *Foundation* series) and Orson Scott Card (the *Ender's Game* series).
- *Other science fiction subgenres.* These include cyberpunk, steampunk, biopunk, military science fiction, superhuman science fiction, the space western, social science fiction, mundane science fiction, feminist science fiction, and numerous others. These distinct subgenres use many elements that characterize science fiction but often veer into the realm of fantasy.

How does fantasy differ from science fiction?

Although science fiction and fantasy are both examples of speculative fiction with clear overlap between the two, which can be called "science fantasy," there are fundamental differences. Authors of fantasy fiction create worlds that might draw upon historical eras but which never could have existed. Playwright, screenwriter, and producer Rod Serling, the creator of the classic TV show *The Twilight Zone,* offered this definition of the basic difference between fantasy and science fiction: "Fantasy is the impossible made probable. Science

fiction is the improbable made possible." According to George R. R. Martin, the author of the *Game of Thrones* series: "The best fantasy is written in the language of dreams. It is alive as dreams are alive, more real than real ... for a moment at least ... that long magic moment before we wake."

What are the elements that characterize fantasy fiction?

Elements that characterize fantasy fiction—magic or the supernatural, the appearance of fantastic creatures, and themes culled from folklore or mythology—can be traced back to such works as Shakespeare's *A Midsummer Night's Dream* and *Sir Gawain and the Green Knight*, a late fourteenth-century Middle English chivalric romance written by an unknown author that is set during the time of King Arthur. The first modern fantasy novel is considered to be George MacDonald's *The Princess and the Goblin* (1872), a novel for children. During the nineteenth century, authors of

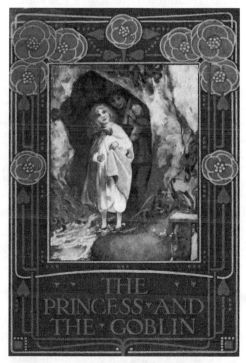

The Princess and the Goblin by George MacDonald is an early work of fantasy fiction that was released in 1872. It is said that J. R. R. Tolkien was influenced by the book.

241

fantasy fiction for adults as well as children included Lewis Carroll (*Alice in Wonderland, Through the Looking-Glass*), H. Rider Haggard (*She, The People of the Mist*), and Jules Verne (*Journey to the Center of the Earth, Twenty-Thousand Leagues under the Sea*). Because they contain elements of science fiction, Verne's novels can also be categorized as "science fantasy." Twentieth-century examples, in addition to Martin's *Game of Thrones* series, include J. R. R. Tolkien's *The Hobbit* and the *Lord of the Rings* trilogy, Philip Pullman's *His Dark Materials* trilogy, and Neil Gaiman's *Stardust*.

What should you look for when reading either science fiction or fantasy?

As with any work of fiction, when reading science fiction or fantasy, you should pay close attention to plot, character, themes, and points of view as well as the presence of such literary devices as backstory, cliffhangers, *deux ex machina,* flashbacks or flash-forwards, foreshadowing, the framing of the story, whether the story begins in the middle of a sequence of events, and plot twists. Ask yourself whether these literary constructs come together in a satisfying story and whether they enhance or detract from the quality of what you are reading.

What should you look for when reading science fiction?

When reading science fiction, you should determine whether one or more of the following elements conform to the genre: a story that is set in the future and includes advanced technology and weaponry; settings in outer space or below the earth's surface; characters that are aliens, as well as technologically advanced characters like robots, androids, and holograms; scientific principles that contradict accepted and applied physical laws, including faster-than-light travel, teleportation, time travel, wormholes, other dimensions, and parallel universes; settings or scenes that feature alternative timelines or history; and stories set at a time that features a different social system. Consider whether the author has succeeded in presenting a speculative world that seems plausible to you.

What should you look for when reading fantasy fiction?

Fantasy fiction can seem as plausible as science fiction, even though its speculative qualities are different. Elements to look for that set fantasy fiction apart from science fiction include a story set on Earth or on an earthlike world and with social systems that might reflect Earth's medieval period, Earth's ancient history, or at a time before recorded history; plots, themes, and characters suggested by folklore, world mythology, and even fairy tales and which sometimes involve a mission or a quest; fantastic creatures such as dragons, fairies, goblins, and giants; and the use of magic or sorcery. When reading fantasy fiction, ask yourself if the author has successfully created a world, as well as characters and situations, which, although imaginary and implausible, is entirely believable.

Ultimately, the test for reading and evaluating any work of science fiction or fantasy is the same as for mystery, historical fiction, or, indeed, any literary novel or work of literature: how and why does it please? The best will do even more. They will reveal something new, unexpected, or provocative about human nature and the human experience.

HOW TO READ DRAMA

Why does drama matter in understanding literature?

Charles Dickens once declared, "Every writer of fiction writes in effect for the stage." His assertion can be expanded to say that all writers of literature of any kind—playwrights, fiction writers, and poets—write if not for the stage, then with drama in mind. Robert Frost famously defined poetry as "a performance in words" and added "Everything written is as good as it is dramatic." Both Dickens and Frost suggest that drama is fundamental to all literature and that to understand any literary work, you need to find the drama. To do so, always look for a literary work's conflict in a specific situation involving a speaker or characters in an imagined setting and situation. Great writers usually don't start with an idea and then invent a story to illustrate it but with a circumstance, a character, and a crisis, in which meaning and significance grow out of the exploration of all three. This is no less true for a poem, a story, or a novel as it is for a play. Therefore, understanding how drama works is valuable not just for an appreciation of the plays you see and read but also in all your encounters with literature.

What is drama?

Drama is one of the oldest forms of verbal art, as old as storytelling itself. It is easy to imagine the earliest storyteller, who instead of just describing an action or event pretended to be the person or thing portrayed, giving birth to drama. The word *drama* derives from a Greek word meaning "to do, act, or perform," so drama differs from fiction and poetry in its performance aspect. Instead of merely telling a story, a drama enacts its story with individuals pretending to be other characters in a re-created situation.

What is the difference between drama and theater?

Theater describes drama in performance. It is the place where drama is presented, and the term has come to mean drama that is presented live before an audience. Dramas can be read   243 for pleasure and so-called "closet dramas" are written to be read rather than performed, but most dramas are best imagined and appreciated as scripts for performance in a theater (or on film). Reading a play resembles examining the score of a musical work: it gives instructions on how a drama should look and sound when performed before an audience.

Drama, as written by the playwright, is comparable to other literary forms, relying on the same kinds of resources: language, plot, characterization. Theater, however, transforms the literary text of the playwright into a collaborative performance involving actors, a director, set lighting, and costume designers. In addition, an essential component of theater is the audience, whose reactions and responses are essential for the success and impact of a performance.

What are the advantages and disadvantages of reading a drama?

Reading drama, you only have the playwright's words for the dialogue among the characters as well as any stage directions for the action or details regarding how a character looks or the settings the playwright imagines. While watching a play performed, however, the playwright's instructions or descriptions are unnecessary because you see and hear the characters in action and in a materialized location in front of you. You do not need descriptions of what characters are wearing because you see their costumes; you don't have to imagine the setting because it's there onstage. Performed dialogue also takes full

There is quite a difference between reading a play and watching it performed onstage. Attending a play in person saves one the trouble of reading stage directions and character and setting descriptions.

advantage of tone, emphasis, and gesture (absent on the page), as well as the reactions of the listener that must be imagined by a reader. Moreover, seeing drama performed in real time can produce an immediacy and intensity that the reading experience, subject to distractions and interruptions, cannot match without considerable effort.

Because so many elements of a live dramatic performance are missing when reading drama, you need to supplement the text with the details that are omitted on the page. Playwrights, knowing that actors will interpret the dialogue, may leave instructions on reactions and movement to the stage director or individual interpretation, and you, as a reader, therefore, need to stage the drama in your imagination: trying to hear the dialogue spoken and reacted to by individualized characters who are not statically waiting for their next lines but are dynamically involved in the scene. By doing so, the reading of drama, meant to be seen and heard, can at least achieve some of the vitality and impact of a live performance.

While there are major advantages to watching drama performed, there are also benefits derived from reading it. In performance, there are no pause or rewind buttons to aid in understanding what is said or done. Reading allows you to linger on lines and scenes, looking up words you don't understand or construing meaning and implications of actions by careful review. None of this is possible in a live drama performance. Much can be missed live that can be better appreciated and understood by your own reading pace. Reading also allows you to reread, to revisit scenes to understand them better, or to juxtapose scenes out of their sequence, underscoring parallels or repetitions that you could easily miss in performance.

The ideal way of appreciating and understanding drama is to read and to view a performance, gaining insights from what each can supply.

How is drama similar and different from poetry and fiction?

Dramatic literature both shares and departs from elements used by other literary forms like poetry and fiction. Like the poet, the dramatist, who builds the play out of words spoken, must rely principally on the resources of language to communicate meaning, drawing on the same assets of diction, sound, and rhythm for dialogue to exemplify the speakers and communicate the action. Dramatists, however, have the additional means of *showing* language through dynamic action onstage. Characters deliver their lines with emphasis and gestures that a poem on the page cannot so easily supply. Poetry can be written as a dialogue among two or more speakers, but most poetry, especially lyric poetry, concerns introspective, subjective feelings and emotions. These are a challenge for the dramatist because the inner life of characters must be externalized onstage. Characters in a play can, of course, tell what they are feeling or thinking, but showing us this onstage directly is difficult. Shakespeare addressed this restriction by pioneering the soliloquy, a character's direct address to the audience of thoughts and feelings, as a form of interior monologue. Mainly, however, dramatists must rely on showing the inner life of a speaker, not directly, as in poetry, but indirectly through what a speaker says (and doesn't say), does, and what other speakers say about that character.

Poetry also may or may not tell a story. It can be about an idea or a feeling, not a sequence of events with a clear beginning, middle, or ending. Drama, however, except for the most experimental kind, is characteristically a narrative art form like the short story and the novel. Aristotle defined tragedy (and by implication all drama) as "an imitation of an action," in which story, or the sequence of events forming a plot, is preeminent. A common definition of drama is that it is storytelling in dialogue, although this is somewhat misleading. You can have dramas as monologues with single speakers onstage. You can also have dramas in which there are no spoken words at all. If "dialogue" in a definition of drama is debatable, "storytelling" is much more certain. Common to virtually all definitions of drama is the notion of an exciting, emotional, or unexpected series of events or set of circumstances. This is a characteristic shared by the short story or novel but with the difference that fiction narrates its story and drama enacts it, embodying its storytelling in actual characters in action that an audience (or readers in their imagination) watches unfold. Because characters and setting are shown onstage, drama can dispense with a central fictional resource: an external narrative perspective supplying details of how a character looks or acts and where the action takes place. All of these elements are shown in a drama. Dramas can be framed by the limited point of view of a character, but the omniscient perspective of fiction is not possible. As in the introspection of poetry, narrators in fiction can penetrate the inner thoughts and feelings of characters that drama must externalize in dialogue and action. Plays can employ a narrator onstage with a privileged view of the actors and the action, or, as in the case of the chorus in ancient Greek drama, provide commentary and analysis, but those conventions tend to be the exception to the rule: drama must show its stories unfolding in real time, relying on its imagined characters and series of events to do so.

Most dramas resemble the compressed methods of the short story more than the expansive manner of the novel. Novels can, of course, cover the events of a lifetime, chronicling both the exceptional and the commonplace, incorporating a multiplicity of characters, each with his or her own narrative arc and interest. Drama more readily conforms to the principle of exclusion of the short story: restricting interest to fewer characters in a more contracted sequence of time and cohesive action focused on one or a few key characters in a single or a few settings. Aristotle described the ideal of tragic action in a drama as conforming to the unities of place, action, and time: in a single setting, a single action (without subplots), in real time, without chronological interruptions, such as flashbacks or flash-forwards. In drawing a distinction between the expansive, novel-like Epic and Tragedy, Aristotle observed, "Tragedy endeavors, as far as possible, to confine itself to a single revolution of the sun, or but slightly to exceed this limit, whereas the Epic action has no limits." Playwrights over the century have both practiced and violated Aristotle's conception of the dramatic unities, but what the unities were meant to achieve, intensity through compression, remains a consistent dramatic characteristic, which it shares with the short story.

Like a short story, dramas depend on an economy of elements. Poe insisted that the power of a short story is made possible by its being designed to be read without interruption over the course of about an hour. Drama must likewise contend with the limited attention spans and endurance of its audience. Shakespeare famously referred in the Prologue to *Romeo and Juliet* to "the two hours' traffic of our stage," in effect describing the temporal limit to the dramatist's art. Certainly, dramatists before and since have expanded (and contracted) those two hours. An uncut modern production of the 4024 lines of *Hamlet* easily stretches beyond the four-hour mark. The Royal Shakespeare Company's dramatic adaptation of Dickens's *Nicholas Nickleby* in the 1980s lasted eight and half hours, presented in two parts that could be seen on successive nights or in a single go with a dinner break. Other play sequences like Shakespeare's history cycles or all of Synge's plays have been presented in marathon productions, yet two hours more closely resembles the rule, particularly for films, of a theatrical production.

Given this limitation, drama, like the short story, is built around conflict and crisis: the collision of characters within themselves or with others at key turning points in the characters' lives. While the novel can record more than the exceptional, the short story and drama rarely do. As Alfred Hitchcock observed, "What is drama but life with the dull bits cut out." Dramatic exclusion is seconded by the dual master short storyteller and dramatist, Anton Chekhov, who famously declared, "If in the first act you have hung a pistol on the wall, then in the following one it should be fired. Otherwise don't put it there." In trying to understand drama, therefore, you should apply the observations already made about the short story, keeping in mind what makes drama different and distinctive.

The famous Globe Theater in London is a faithful reproduction of the one that was torn down in 1645. At the original theater, audiences from all ends of the social spectrum were brought together to attend Shakespeare's plays, making the dramas great equalizers of the poor and illiterate with the rich and educated.

What are the unique elements of drama?

Although drama shares certain features of other literary forms, it is instructive to underscore the characteristics that also make it unique. The core of drama's power comes from it being watched instead of listened to or read. With its characters and actors visualized, drama possesses immediate and unforgettable qualities that other forms of literature cannot so easily duplicate. Infants learn by watching before their listening or reading skills develop, and this remains true as we grow. Being shown how to do something is frequently more instructive and lasting than reading a set of instructions; seeing some event, such as a fire or sporting event, is much more memorable and affecting than just reading or hearing an account of it. Drama, therefore, achieves an extraordinary hold on its audience by its power of visualization, and this resource is so central that the term for theater itself, which comes from the Greek, means "the seeing place."

Another distinctive characteristic of drama is its accessibility. Drama does not require its audience to be literate. This is one reason that drama dominated as popular entertainment and instruction in eras when literacy rates were low and the cost of printing kept written literature out of the hands of most consumers. Drama lowers barriers of education, class, or cost (at least until more recently for live theater) that are central consideration in poetry and fiction. Shakespeare's audiences at the Globe—rich and poor, commoners and nobles, educated and illiterate—could attend performances for a penny. In our own day, drama has long been a feature of free television, even as the cost of attending the theater has become more prohibitive. Drama can be enjoyed and understood without the mastery and means often required of literary texts.

A final important quality of drama as a literary form, beyond its immediacy and accessibility, is what it adds to a literary experience. Drama can enhance its visualization with stagecraft to enrich and contribute to a play's meaning and impact. The audience sees and hears the characters in action, but performances can also benefit from stage effects like lighting, music, choreography, and scenery that can complement language in ways that a text cannot. This is why a play's text gives only a partial impression of what a drama in performance can become and why seeing drama enhances simply reading it.

How others have described drama, plays, playwrighting, and the theater?

Drama assumes an order. If only so that it might have—by disrupting that order—a way of surprising.

—Vaclav Havel

When the drama attains a characterization which makes the play a revelation of human conduct and a dialogue which characterizes yet pleases for itself, we reach dramatic literature.

—George Pierce Baker

Drama is based on the Mistake … all good drama has two movements, first the making of the mistake, then the discovery that it was a mistake.

—W. H. Auden

The basis of drama is … the struggle of the hero towards a specific goal at the end of which he realizes that what kept him from it was, in the lesser drama, civilization, and, in the greater drama, the discovery of something that he did not set out to discover, but which can be seen retrospectively as inevitable.

—David Mamet

Everything written is as good as it is dramatic. It need not declare itself in form, but it is drama or nothing.

—Robert Frost

A play is fiction—and fiction is fact distilled into truth.

—Edward Albee

A play should give you something to think about. When I see a play and understand it the first time, then I know it can't be much good.

—T. S. Eliot

A playwright must be his own audience. A novelist may lose his readers for a few pages; a playwright never dares lose his audience for a minute.

—Terence Rattigan

A dramatist is one who believes that the pure event, an action involving human beings, is more arresting than any comment that can be made upon it.

—Thornton Wilder

On the stage it is always *now*; the personages are standing on that razor edge, between the past and the future, which is the essential character of conscious being; the words are rising to their lips in immediate spontaneity…. The theater is supremely fitted to say: "Behold!"

—Thornton Wilder

The drama may be called that part of theatrical art which lends itself most readily to intellectual discussion; what is left is theater.

—Robertson Davies

Inevitably, a dramatist writes one play, his director interprets another, the actors perform a third and the public sees a fourth and altogether different one.

—John Harvey

[Drama is the] just and lively image of human nature, representing its passions and humours, and the change of fortune to which it is subject, for the delight and instruction of mankind.

—John Dryden   249

I regard the theatre as the greatest of all art forms, the most immediate way in which a human being can share with another the sense of what it is to be a human being.

—Oscar Wilde

Only in a problem play is there any real drama, because drama is no mere setting up the camera to nature; it is the presentation in parable of the conflict between Man's will and his environment; in a word, of problem.

—George Bernard Shaw

Great drama is great questions or it is nothing but technique. I could not imagine a theater worth my time that did not want to change the world.

—Arthur Miller

The structure of a play is always the story of how the birds come home to roost.

—Arthur Miller

Drama is akin to the other inventions of man in that it ought to help us to know more, and not merely to spend our feelings.

—Arthur Miller

For me, playwriting is and has always been like making a chair. Your concerns are balance, form, timing, lights, space, music. If you don't have these essentials, you might as well be writing a theoretical essay, not a play.

—Sam Shepard

GREEK AND ROMAN DRAMA

What are the origins of drama?

Drama's beginnings are obscure, but a connection can be traced between the earliest drama and oral poetry, such as chants and hymns, in religious rituals. Greek drama, the earliest known recorded drama in the West, derived from the religious festivals that paid tribute to Dionysus, the god of fertility, wine, and revelry, who was celebrated and worshipped in choral song and dance. Aristotle in the *Poetics* (c. 335–323 B.C.E.), the earliest extant account of how drama originated, asserts that it began with the speeches of "those who led the dithyramb," the choral lyrics honoring Dionysus, and that comedy came from a group of singers and dancers representing satyrs—half men, half goats— who were the attendants of Dionysus. At some point during the sixth century B.C.E., a choral leader began to impersonate an imaginary character and to imitate, rather than to narrate, the story of a deity or a mythical hero. Later, second and third actors were added, combining choral performance, dance, recitations, and dialogue.

A fourth-century B.C.E. stone relief shows the god Dionysus with an escort and theatrical masks. The worship of Dionysus through song and dance is said to be the origin of theater.

Tradition credits the Greek actor and playwright Thespis (none of whose plays survived) with first combining the choral songs and dances with the speeches of a mask actor in an enacted story. As the first known actor, Thespis is memorialized in the term *thespian,* a synonym for an actor. It is believed that Thespis first performed his plays at festivals throughout Greece. In 534 B.C.E., Athens reorganized its annual spring festival, the Great or City Dionysia, as a theatrical contest in which choruses competed for prizes in a festival that lasted for several days. During the City Dionysia, performed in an open-air theater that held audiences of fifteen thousand or more, business was suspended, and prisoners were released on bail for the duration of the festival so that all Athenian citizens could attend. The first day was devoted to traditional choral hymns followed by the competition in which three dramatists each presented three tragedies and a comic satyr play. Only the full-length works of four ancient Greek playwrights survive: the tragedies of Aeschylus, Sophocles, and Euripides (thirty-two plays in total) and the comedies of Aristophanes (eleven plays).

How were ancient Greek dramas performed?

Since so many theatrical terms and methods derive from the Greeks, an awareness of these conventions should enhance understanding of the ancient Greek dramatic tradition and subsequent refinements up to modern theater.

The first Greek dramatic performances, growing out of the rituals and sacrifices of the Dionysian festivals, were centered around a sacrificial altar, or thymele, on the sa-

251

cred ground near the temple of Dionysus. The circular space around the altar was called the *orchestra,* or "dancing place," for the singing and dancing celebrants. The orchestra would be relocated to an area at the base of sloping hills to accommodate more spectators. Eventually, wooden and stone benches were built on the slope surrounding the orchestra, called the *theatron,* or "seeing place," from which we get the term "theater." In Athens, the erected theater for dramatic performances could accommodate more than 15,000 spectators, the city's largest place of assembly. The backdrop for the semicircular performance space was known as the *skene* (meaning "hut" or "tent," from which we derive the term *scenery*), a structure for entrances and exits and a changing room for the actors that could also represent a play's setting, such as the exterior of a palace. Eventually, the skene became a permanent building, the roof of which could be used in a performance. A raised area in front of the skene, the *proskenion* (from which we get the term *proscenium),* could provide a space for displaying scenery and for stage machinery. One of the three main mechanical devices in the ancient Greek theater was the *eccyclema*, a small, wooden wheeled platform that could be used to change the setting or to display a tableau, such as a slain victim and the murderer and his bloody weapon. Violence in Greek drama almost always took place offstage, but the eccyclema could be used to show what had happened. Another device was the *mechane*, or "machine," a sort of crane operated by a pulley system that could be used to show a character appearing or disappearing by supernatural means. This is how the term *deus ex machina* ("god from the machine") originated, referring to divine intervention. The third device was the *theologeion,* a narrow, movable platform atop the skene where the gods in heaven were represented overlooking the earthly action below. Passages on either side between the auditorium and the skene, called the *parados,* provided access for the audience and could be used for entrances and exits of the actors and the chorus.

The audience at the Great or City Dionysia, Athens' annual five-day festival in late March, usually entered the theater at daybreak, prepared to stay until sundown. Usually, four or five plays were produced each day: three linked or separate tragedies, followed by one or two comedies or so-called satyr plays, boisterous and bawdy satires. Comic dramatists, who presented one play each, also competed. Tickets were small, leaden coins with a theatrical emblem. It is uncertain whether performances were exclusively for men or if women, children, and slaves could also attend.

Ancient Greek playwrights served as writers, composers, choreographers, designers, directors, and sometimes actors. Since dramatic performances were part of the state-sponsored religious worship, they were overseen by an *archon,* or magistrate, who selected the competing dramatists and approved their submissions. The archon would also name the *choregus,* a wealthy citizen who, on a rotating basis, shared with the state the expenses for each dramatist; hired the actors, musicians, and chorus; and was responsible for rehearsal expenses and the cost of costumes and set decoration. Service as a choregus was a public responsibility, compelled by law. Competition among dramatists, actors, and choragi was intense, and each choregus tried to outdo the others in magnificence of the scenery, stage effects, and costumes. Consequently, the cost of mount-

The ancient theater at Epidauros can still be visited by tourists today in Greece, where the art form originated around the sixth century B.C.E.

ing productions was exorbitant: they could only produce four plays for one performance only. Only one of the three dramatists (and choregi) would win the prize: an ivy wreath.

What about actors in ancient Greek dramas?

In the earliest Greek drama, a single actor interacted with the chorus. Eventually, second and third actors were added. The actors were all male, as were the members of the chorus, though the chorus might have included boys. The actors were hired professionals who usually performed more than one role (with never more than three actors in any Greek drama).

Greek dramatic costume had three outstanding features: the mask, the *cothurnus*, a high-soled boot, and the tunic and mantle. The masks were usually made of linen covered with plaster, but other materials, such as cork and wood, could also be used. On the mask, the main traits of the character were depicted in exaggerated outline. Because the effect of the mask would be lost on the audience in side view, actors mainly faced the audience to declaim their lines with sufficient volume and expression to be heard clearly in the enormous, open-air theater. The *cothurnus*, or tragic boot, served to increase the height of the actors, with the thickness of the sole varied according to the dignity and rank of the character. The *cothurnus* was not worn by comic actors. The costumes were like ordinary Greek attire, differing mainly in color, style, and magnificence: a brilliantly colored and patterned tunic undergarment and an overgarment, or mantle, which was also brightly colored, with some colors associated with a character's rank, such as purple for royalty. Comic actors could be outfitted with a phallus and could be grotesquely padded into ludicrous shapes.

The chorus was also masked but their tunics and mantles were closer to normal dress, suggesting their function to represent the ordinary public. The chorus, who were usually amateurs from the general body of citizens, served multiple functions in Greek drama: to set the mood and comment on the central themes of the drama, to give background information, and to interpret the characters' actions. The chorus would interact directly with the actors, questioning and advising characters, serving as a kind of collective fourth actor in the drama. In Sophocles's *Oedipus,* for example, the chorus

253

represents the concerned Theban citizens petitioning, questioning, and advising Oedipus as well as reflecting on the impact and consequences of the action. The chorus could recite or sing their lines, and most of the choral songs were accompanied by dances. In tragedy, such dances were called the *emmeleia,* which were graceful and majestic in their motions. The comic dances were called the *kordax,* which was much coarser and lascivious, echoing the raucous satyr rituals out of which comedy developed. As Greek drama developed, the size of the chorus changed. Aeschylus purportedly reduced the chorus from fifty to twelve; Sophocles increased its size to fifteen. The reduction of size and importance of the chorus reflects the shift of importance from the choral songs to the dialogue of the actors, from a chiefly lyrical to a primarily dramatic form of art.

What, according to Aristotle, are the key elements of drama?

Aristotle's *Poetics* supplies far more than drama's origin story. His analysis is undoubtedly the single most important guide to drama and core concepts of the dramatist's art that have dominated understanding ever since. In the *Poetics*, Aristotle defines all art as an "imitation of nature" and distinguishes drama from poetry as an "imitation of an action." He provides the accepted division of dramatic form into comedy and tragedy based on the imitation of inferior and superior action. "Comedy is ...," Aristotle explains, "an imitation of characters of a lower type," which "aims at representing men as worse, Tragedy as better than in actual life."

Although Aristotle's promised full analysis of comedy was either never completed or has been lost, further distinctions between comedy and tragedy, and the key elements of dramatic art, are found in the *Poetics'* predominant consideration of tragedy. Aristotle defined tragedy as "an imitation of an action that is serious, complete, and of a certain magnitude" with six key components, which he ranked in order of importance:

Plot—For Aristotle, the most important resource of the tragic dramatist is "the arrangement of the incidents," not simply as a succession of events but also as the way they are presented to the audience. In Aristotle's view, tragedies in which the outcome depends on a tightly constructed cause-and-effect chain of actions are superior. The plot must be "complete," having a "unity of action," by which Aristotle means that the plot must be structurally self-contained, with each action leading inevitably to the next and each necessary for the completion of the whole. The worst kinds of plots, according to Aristotle, are "episodic," in which incidents succeed one another "without probable or necessary sequence," not caused by the characters but imposed upon them or including action extraneous to a unified plot. Aristotle suggests that a dramatic plot may be simple, having only a "change of fortune" (*catastrophe*) or complex (preferred), with both a "reversal of intention" (*peripeteia*) and a "recognition" (*anagnorisis*) derived from the catastrophe. Aristotle explains that a *peripeteia* occurs when a character produces an effect opposite to that which was intended, while *anagnorisis* "is a change from ignorance to knowledge, producing love or hate between the persons destined for good or bad fortune." In the best tragic drama, Aristotle contends, the *peripeteia* leads directly to the *anagnorisis*, which in turn creates the *catastrophe*, producing the final "scene of suffering."

Character—In a successful tragedy, Aristotle believes, character should support plot. The *Poetics* seems to suggest that it is possible to have an effective tragedy without notable characters but not without a closely designed plot. Characters' motivations in an effective tragedy should be an intricately connected part of the cause-and-effect chain of actions. According to the *Poetics,* the protagonist should be renowned and prosperous, so a change of fortune in the tragic protagonist's fall is conspicuous. This change "should come about as the result, not of vice, but of some great error or frailty in a character." Such a plot is most likely to generate pity and fear in the audience for "pity is aroused by unmerited misfortune, fear by the misfortune of a man like ourselves." In the ideal tragedy, claims Aristotle, the protagonist will mistakenly bring about his own downfall due to *harmartia*, a greatly debated term that has been commonly translated as "tragic flaw" but might be better termed "tragic capacity": not just because of the protagonist's shortcomings but also because of the protagonist's unique nature. Aristotle explains that the tragic dramatist should produce four key character traits: 1) characters should be "good" regardless of status in life, that is, the best representatives of gender and station in life; 2) characters should be appropriate and suitable for the occasion; 3) characters should be true to life; and 4) characters should be consistent. As in the structure of the plot, Aristotle insists that "in the portraiture of character, the poet should always aim either at the necessary or the probable. Thus, a person of a given character should speak or act in a given way, by the rule either of necessity or of probability; just as this event should follow that by necessary or probable sequence."

Thought—Aristotle defined the third most important component of tragic drama as "the faculty of saying what is possible and pertinent in given circumstances." Thought in Aristotle's usage is more commonly treated as "theme," the central idea or core truths presented in a work of literature, which, according to him, are "found where something is proved to be, or not to be, or a general maxim is enunciated." The major difference between thought or theme in other works of literature and in drama is that it is derived indirectly from what drama must show rather than what a poem or fiction might tell directly. In drama, Aristotle insists, "the incidents should speak for themselves without verbal exposition."

Diction—For Aristotle, diction, "the expression of the meaning in words," is no different in drama than in verse or prose, the core resource that writers use to express their meaning. In drama, word choice is principally reflected in dialogue, serving both to characterize each speaker and reflect on the action as it transpires onstage. Aristotle argues that the tragic dramatist should avoid artificial grandiloquence for clarity and appropriateness: "The perfection of style is to be clear without being mean."

Song and melody—Aristotle regarded song as the chief "embellishment" the tragic dramatist employs to enhance and underscore the emotional impact of drama's action. Ancient Greek dramas were written in verse and chanted or sung onstage. Such an embellishment is unique to drama in performance. Poetry may aspire to the condition of music, as Poe alleges, but drama can incorporate song and music directly in its appeals. In later drama, song and melody remain potent in musical theater and especially in opera, in which song carries much of the meaning of a play.

Spectacle—Aristotle means by spectacle what we see onstage, which presumably includes a play's scenery, costumes (including the masks of the actors), choreography, and any stage machinery that could produce such effects as the tragic heroine being carried into the heavens at the end of Euripides's *Medea*. Lighting effects did not apply to ancient Greek outdoor, daytime performances, but Aristotle would likely have regarded

The Greek philosopher Aristotle said that tragedy must elicit a response of pity and fear from the audience.

lighting as one more part of a play's spectacle, important in its "emotional attraction" but dependent "more on the art of the stage machinist than on that of the poet." Fear and pity, the central emotions tragedy evokes and purges in the audience, says Aristotle, "may be aroused by spectacular means, but they may also result from the inner structure of the piece, which is the better way, and indicates a superior poet." If the plot is skillfully constructed, Aristotle insists, "he who makes the tale told will thrill with horror and melt with pity at what takes place…. Those who employ spectacular means to create a sense not of the terrible but only of the monstrous, are strangers to the purpose of Tragedy."

What, according to Aristotle, is the purpose of tragedy?

Having characterized the six key elements of the dramatist's art, Aristotle relates them to tragedy, which he defines as "an imitation of an action that is serious, complete, and of a certain magnitude … in the form of action, not of narrative; through pity and fear effecting the proper purgation of these emotions." The purpose of tragedy, therefore, according to Aristotle, is to show a sequence of action that elicits a response of pity and fear in the audience that results in the "purgation of these emotions." This is the much-debated Aristotelian concept of *catharsis* in which the tragic dramatist, having aroused these powerful emotions in the spectator, achieves a therapeutic release of them. The audience of a tragedy witnesses and experiences vicariously disturbing events—the consequences of patricide and incest, in the case of Sophocles's *Oedipus*—in which the destruction of the tragic protagonist elicits the spectator's fears about these experiences and pity for the protagonist's suffering. The tragic hero serves as a kind of scapegoat to represent the community. The term "scapegoat" derives from the ancient Hebrew practice of letting a goat loose into the wilderness after symbolically laying the sins of the people upon it. Ironically, there is an echo of this in the meaning of the word tragedy itself: from the Greek "goat song," referring either to the ritual slaying of goats during the Dionysian rituals or the performance of the goatlike satyr figures in the processions in Dionysius's honor.

Aristotle's notion of catharsis, the therapeutic expelling of otherwise repressed emotions, goes to the core of drama's power and importance. In watching, as opposed to listening or reading, an audience powerfully confronts moral and existential issues, such as, in the case of Greek drama, the role of the gods in human affairs, free will versus fate, questions of justice and equality, gender assumptions, and many more. By watching the consequence of characters' actions, the spectator can test beliefs and experience extremes avoided in normal life. Drama can, therefore, provide a powerfully realized lesson in how to act and offer the psychological benefit of confronting our fears and anxieties to allow us to control them. For the ancient Greeks, drama, as in a religious ritual, allowed the audience to experience ultimate questions not in the abstract but viscerally in the embodied action onstage.

How does Sophocles's *Oedipus* reflect Aristotle's conception of the ideal tragedy?

Throughout the *Poetics*, Aristotle draws his examples of the tragic dramatist's methods from Sophocles's *Oedipus*, and a closer look at this play serves to clarify Aristotle's concepts as well as to illustrate the nature of ancient Greek drama and its achievement.

No other drama has exerted a longer or a stronger hold on the imagination than Sophocles's *Oedipus*. Tragic drama that is centered on the dilemma of a single, central character largely begins with Sophocles and is exemplified by his *Oedipus*, arguably the most influential play ever written. The most famous of all Greek dramas, Sophocles's play, supported by Aristotle in the *Poetics*, set the standard by which tragedy has been measured for nearly two and a half millennia. For Aristotle, Sophocles's play featured the ideal tragic hero in Oedipus, a man of "great repute and good fortune" whose fall, coming from his horrifying discovery that he has killed his father and married his mother, is masterfully arranged to elicit tragedy's proper cathartic mixture of pity and fear. The play's relentless exploration of human nature, destiny, and suffering turns an ancient tale of a man's shocking history into one of the core human myths.

Sophocles began his career as a playwright in 468 B.C.E. with a first-prize victory over Aeschylus in the Great or City Dionysia, the annual Athenian drama competition. Over the next sixty years, he produced more than 120 plays (only seven have survived intact), winning first prize at the Dionysia twenty-four times and never earning less than second place, making him unquestionably the most successful and popular playwright of his time. It is Sophocles who, according to Aristotle, introduced the third speaking actor to drama, creating the more complex dramatic situations, and deepened psychological penetration through interpersonal relationships and dialogue. Favoring dramatic action over narration, Sophocles brought off-stage action onto the stage, emphasized dialogue rather than lengthy, undramatic monologues, and purportedly introduced painted scenery. Notably as well, Sophocles replaced the connected trilogies of Aeschylus with self-contained plays on different subjects at the same contest, establishing the norm that has continued in Western drama with its emphasis on the intensity and unity of dramatic action. At their core, Sophocles's tragedies are essentially moral and religious dramas pitting the tragic hero against unalterable fate as defined by universal laws, particular circumstances, and individual temperament. By testing his characters so severely, Sophocles orchestrated adversity into revelations that continue to evoke an audience's capacity for wonder and compassion.

Sophocles took the already familiar story of Oedipus and transformed it from heroic tale into a dramatic tragedy by focusing on the consequences of the discovery of his identity.

Like most ancient Greek dramas, the story of Oedipus was a well-known myth familiar to Sophocles's audience. Sophocles chose to tell Oedipus's story at its end, focusing not on how he came to power but on the consequences of the revelations about his identity. Sophocles's great innovation was to turn Oedipus's horrifying circumstances into a drama of self-discovery that probes the mystery of self-hood and human destiny.

The play opens with Oedipus secure and respected as the capable ruler of Thebes, having solved the riddle of the Sphinx and gained the throne, as well as Thebes' widowed queen, Jocasta, as his reward. Oedipus, therefore, meets Aristotle's ideal as a man "who is hightly reknowned and prosperous" at the play's outset. Plague now besets the city, and Oedipus comes to Thebes's rescue once again after learning from an oracle that the plague is a punishment for the murder of his predecessor, Laius. Oedipus swears to discover and bring the murderer to justice. The play, therefore, begins as a detective story, the first in Western literature, with the initial mystery, "Who killed Laius?" Oedipus initiates the first in a seemingly inexhaustible series of dramatic ironies as the detective turns out to be his own quarry. Oedipus's judgment of banishment of Laius's murderer seals his own fate. Pledged to restore Thebes to health, Oedipus is in fact the source of its affliction. Oedipus's success in discovering Laius's murderer will be his own undoing, and the seemingly perceptive, riddle-solving Oedipus will only truly see the truth about himself when he is blind. To underscore this point, the blind seer Teiresias is summoned. He is reluctant to tell what he knows, but Oedipus is adamant: "No man, no place, nothing will escape my gaze. / I will not stop until I know it all." Finally goaded by Oedipus to reveal that Oedipus himself is "the killer you're searching for" and the plague that afflicts Thebes, Teiresias introduces the play's second, even more striking mystery: "Who is Oedipus?"

Oedipus rejects Teiresias's horrifying answer to this question, that Oedipus has killed his own father and has married his mother as part of a conspiracy with Jocasta's brother Creon against his rule. In his treatment of Teiresias and his subsequent condemning of Creon to death, Oedipus exposes his excessive pride, wrath, and rush to judgment, character flaws (*harmatia*) that are connected to his considerable strengths of relentless determination to learn the truth and fortitude in bearing the consequences. Oedipus, therefore, shows not just weaknesses but strengths, not just tragic flaws but a tragic capacity that defines him and causes his destruction. Jocasta comes to her brother's defense, while arguing that not all oracles can be believed. By relating the circumstances of Laius's death, Jocasta attempts to demonstrate that Oedipus could not be the murderer, while ironically providing Oedipus with the details that help to prove his culpability. In what is a marvel of ironic plot construction, each step forward in answering the questions surrounding the murder and Oedipus's parentage takes Oedipus a step back in time toward full disclosure and self-discovery.

As Oedipus is made to shift from self-righteous authority to doubt, a messenger from Corinth arrives with news that Oedipus's supposed father Polybus is dead. This intelligence seems again to disprove the oracle that Oedipus is fated to kill his father. Oedipus, however, still is reluctant to return home for fear that he could still marry his mother. To relieve Oedipus's anxiety, the messenger reveals that he himself brought Oedipus as an infant to Polybus and his wife Merobe. Like Jocasta whose evidence in support of Oedipus's innocence turns into confirmation of his guilt, the messenger provides intelligence that will connect Oedipus to both Laius and Jocasta as their son and as his father's killer. The messenger's intelligence produces the crucial recognition for Jocasta, who urges Oedipus to cease any further inquiry. Oedipus, however, persists, summoning the herdsman who gave the infant to the messenger and was coincidentally the sole survivor of the attack on Laius. The herdsman's eventual confirmation of both the facts of Oedipus's birth and Laius's murder produces the play's staggering climax.

Aristotle would cite Sophocles's simultaneous conjunction of Oedipus's recognition (*anagnorisis*) of his identity and guilt with his reversal of intention (*peripeteia*)—condemned by his own words to exile as Laius's murderer—as the ideal artful arrangement of a drama's plot to produce the desired cathartic pity and fear.

The play concludes with an emphasis on what Oedipus will now do after he knows the truth. No tragic hero has fallen further or faster than in the real time of Sophocles's drama in which the time elapsed in the play's action coincides with the performance time. Increased intensity derives from the compression of the action in the single setting outside Thebes's palace. Oedipus is stripped of every illusion of his authority, control, righteousness, and past wisdom and is forced to contend with a shame that is impossible to expiate—patricide and incestual relations with his mother—in a world lacking either justice or alleviation from suffering. Oedipus's heroic grandeur, however, grows in his diminishment. Arguably, a victim of circumstances, innocent of intentional sin whose fate was preordained before his birth, Oedipus refuses the consolation of blamelessness that victimization confers, accepting in full his guilt and self-imposed sentence as an outcast, criminal, and sinner. He blinds himself to confirm the moral shame that his actions, unwittingly or not, have provoked. It is Oedipus's capacity to endure the revelation of his sin, his nature, and his fate that dominates the play's conclusion. Oedipus's greatest strengths, his determination to know the truth and to accept what he learns, exemplifies one of the most pitiable *and* admired of tragic heroes. The now blind Oedipus has been forced to see and experience the impermanence of good fortune, the reality of unimaginable moral shame, and a cosmic order that is either perverse in its cruelty or chaotically random in its designs, in either case defeating any human demand for justice and mercy.

The chorus summarizes the harsh lesson of heroic defeat that the play so majestically dramatizes:

Look and learn all citizens of Thebes. This is Oedipus.
He, who read the famous riddle, and we hailed chief of men,
All envied his power, glory, and good fortune.
Now upon his head the sea of disaster crashes down.
Mortality is man's burden. Keep your eyes fixed on your last day.
Call no man happy until he reaches it, and finds rest from suffering.

Few plays have dealt so unflinchingly with existential truths or have as bravely defined human heroism in the capacity to see, suffer, and endure in expressing the power and possibilities of drama to affect an audience.

What happened to drama after the ancient Greeks?

Athenian drama of the fifth century B.C.E. is the first great flowering of Western dramatic art. With Athens' ultimate defeat in its devastating war with Sparta (404 B.C.E.), the death of Alexander the Great (323 B.C.E.), and the collapse of the Macedonian empire he created, by the second century B.C.E., Greece became a province of the next great Mediterranean empire: Rome. A great assimilating culture, the Romans would absorb from the Greeks their pantheon of the gods (renamed), key concepts of government, jurisprudence, and science, as well as the Greek theatrical tradition but with significant alterations.

Tradition dates the beginning of Roman drama to 240 B.C.E. when a Greek named Livius Andronicus from Tarentum, a settlement in southern Italy, first presented Latin translations of Greek plays at the *Ludi Romani*, the annual festival in Rome of games and entertainments. Horace traced the origin of Roman theater further back to the Etruscan Fescennine songs—improvised satrical and bawdy choral performances of masked singers at harvest and wedding celebrations—associated with the Etruscan city of Fes-

As with many other things that were originally Greek (philosophy, religion, art, architecture), the Romans adopted Greek theater as their own as evidenced by these amphitheater ruins in what is now Turkey but was once part of the Roman Empire.

cennium. Livy pointed to another Etruscan source in the 364 B.C.E. arrival to Rome of Etruscan musical and dancing performers. Improvised dialogue was subsequently added to these performances, first by amateurs and later by professionals, and, according to according to Livy, the Romans derived the Romans derived their term for actors (*histriones*) from the Etruscan word *ister,* affirming an Etruscan basis for Roman drama. Livy called these early theatrical entertainments *satura,* or medleys of song, dance, and dialogue. Another native source for Roman drama is the so-called *Fabula Atellana.* Named for the town in Campania where they are thought to originate, these were short farces performed by masked actors employing, as in the *commedia dell'arte,* stock characters such as the clown, the glutton, the braggart, the gullible old man, and the trickster. Roman drama, therefore, was an amalgam of Greek models and indigenous farcical, satirical, musical, dance, and bawdy elements.

Roman plays were performed during festivals several times a year, but, unlike the Athenian drama competitions, were not the centerpiece of the celebration. Roman stage plays instead had to compete with other popular forms of entertainment, including athletic competitions, gladiatorial fights, chariot races, and animal baiting for audience share. Roman playgoers lacked the sophisticated appreciation of dramatic tradition acquired by the Greeks and demanded diversion and amusement over edification or challenge by provocative and disturbing themes. For the ancient Greeks, drama was a combination of religious ceremony, civic duty, and shared communal opportunity to encounter profound existential issues. The Romans preferred comedies to tragedy and belly laughs to catharsis.

There were no permanent theaters in Rome before 55 B.C.E., so plays were performed on temporary wooden stages made to resemble a city street. Most actors were slaves owned by a theatrical company's manager or freedmen of notoriously low esteem who could be beaten for a bad performance. Eliminated in the Roman theater was the chorus, which also abandoned the Attic drama's episodic division between dialogue and song.

What did the Romans contribute to the history of drama?

Virtually all surviving Roman dramas were adaptations of ancient Greek plays. The only surviving Roman tragic dramatist is Seneca (4 or 5 B.C.E.–65 C.E.), five of whose nine extant tragedies are adaptations from Euripides. The two Roman comic dramatists whose works have come down to us are Plautus (c. 254–184 B.C.E.) and Terence (c. 195–159 B.C.E.), who provide us with our only complete examples of Greek New Comedy.

The only works of tragedy that survive the Roman Empire are those by Seneca the Younger, and many of these works were actually adaptations from the Greek Euripides.

Compared to the raucous, profane, and intellectually daring Old Comedies of Aristophanes—along with Greek tragedy, the singular achievements of Attic drama—New Comedy, popularized by the Greek dramatist Menander (none of whose plays have survived in complete form), is much more staid, earthbound, and less daring. Aristophanes's cutting satire and wild leaps into fantasy are replaced by a much less controversial comedy of family and domestic life. New Comedies are the first "situation comedies," drawing on more realistic situations, like the complications of thwarted lovers, and employing stock characters, such as the wily merchant, the cunning slave, the boastful soldier, and the cruel father. Although far from the domestic realism of later dramas, the version of New Comedy practiced by the Roman playwrights took drama from the palace to recognizable settings and characters, reflecting contemporary values and the more familiar world of the audience. If drama during the time of the Romans falls short of the profound exploration of a culture's deepest fears and anxieties—a standard set by the ancient Greeks—it did pioneer a new set of theatrical conventions and realistic expectations that would become an important legacy.

How and why was drama rediscovered after the fall of the Roman Empire?

With the collapse and dissolution of the Roman Empire in the fifth century, drama virtually disappeared in the West. The bulk of Greek and Roman plays were lost, and the purpose of the grand outdoor amphitheaters, built by both the Greeks and Romans, were largely forgotten.

What is most striking about the re-emergence of drama in the Middle Ages is the role played by the Christian Church both in stopping the classical dramatic tradition and in fostering the conditions for drama's revival. The number of theaters and performances of Roman drama reached a high point in the fourth century before significantly waning. Drama's decline to near extinction was precipitated both by the breakup of the Roman Empire and the burgeoning Christian Church's opposition to an art form with distinctively pagan roots. Theologians regarded drama as an illusionist art allied to idolatry, magic, and devilry. Church authorities actively dissuaded Christians from attending performances, threatening excommunication of anyone who went to the theater rather than to church on holy days. Actors were forbidden the sacraments unless they foreswore their profession. The last recorded dramatic performance in the classical tradition occurred in Rome in 549 B.C.E., and for almost a half millennia organized theatrical performances ceased in Western Europe with the remnants of an acting tradition fitfully maintained by occasional and slapdash performances by traveling entertainers.

Ironically, the Church, which had played such a decisive role in closing the theaters and halting a literary dramatic tradition, revised the art form in ways similar to its originating conditions that preceded the emergence of formal drama in Greece in the sixth century B.C.E. As classical comedy and tragedy originated from religious celebrations and rituals, Western drama would be restored in the Middle Ages from a comparable

After the fall of Rome, theater did not revive itself until the Middle Ages, when the Christian Church began supporting performances of a religious nature, such as mystery plays, depictions of stories from the Bible. This illustration depicts a performance of the mystery play of Saint Clement.

spiritual foundation to serve a parallel religious need. Antiphonal songs, sung responses or dialogues, like the dithyramb in Greek proto-drama, were eventually incorporated into celebrations from the liturgical calendar, such as Christmas, Epiphany, and Easter. Short, illustrative scenes evolved to vivify worship for a congregation that did not understand Latin, the liturgical language. First performed in the monasteries and churches around the tenth century with clergymen or choirboys as actors, liturgical dramas would by the thirteenth century grow far too elaborate—with multiple scenes, actors, and stage effects—for proper staging indoors. Performances moved outdoors with nonclerical actors and secular organizations like trade guilds producing vernacular Mystery plays, scriptural dramas representing scenes from the Old and New Testament; Miracle plays, dramatizing incidents from the lives of the saints; and Morality plays, enacting the allegorical spiritual struggle of an average individual.

Like Attic Greek plays, medieval drama, therefore, evolved out of religious ritual and was supported by wealthy citizens (like the Athenian *choregi*) or organizations to serve both a civic and religious function. As the Greek choral performances in honor of Dionysus were expanded to enact the stories of multiple gods and heroes, medieval drama gradually became more secularized by incorporating aspects of familiar life and recognizable situations and characters in its performances. Enacted episodes from the liturgical calendar were joined to form complete cycles of biblical plays in increasingly more complicated productions involving realistic stage effects. Religious dramas became all-purpose moral entertainments combining serious devotional and didactic purposes with low comic, often bawdy, farce. By the fifteenth century, religious drama had re-established a strong, robust theatrical tradition in Western Europe that would be combined with the rediscovery of the classical dramatic tradition in the Renaissance to create the second great explosion of dramatic achievement in Elizabethan England.

ELIZABETHAN DRAMA
AND SHAKESPEARE

What explains the second great flowering of Western drama during the Elizabethan period?

There is a risk of oversimplification in attempting to relate one era to another and equating the set of cultural conditions that produced significant literary achievement, but it is interesting and instructive to compare the first great flowering of drama in fifth-century B.C.E. Athens with the second great flowering in late sixteenth- and early seventeenth-century London. Both the Age of Pericles and the Elizabethan period were eras of energized possibilities, of challenge to previous conceptions of the world and human capabilities. The Athenian state would create the world's first democracy, made possible by the radical notion that the individual could both understand the world and could claim self-determination over it. Attic drama would come to reflect the challenges and consequences of these ideas, in the conflicts between fate and free will, in the complicated contradictions of freedom and justice, personal and civic responsibility. Drama seems to thrive when the age's great questions need to be tested and experienced. In fifth-century B.C.E. Athens, the conjunction of the cultural moment, with its attendant great questions and challenges, the means of a popular dramatic tradition, and great literary genius united to create a great home for theater.

The Elizabethan period shares something of that same conjunction of forces. The Renaissance's rediscovery of classical learning and its faith in a secular humanism originated in Italy during the fourteenth century and initiated a period of cultural achievement that spread throughout Europe and stands behind the energy and accomplishments of Elizabethan England in the sixteenth century. In virtually every aspect of human life—in architecture, the visual arts, music, poetry, science, and technology—innovation and new possibilities, symbolized by the voyages of discovery that would circle the globe, formed the cultural *zeitgeist*. New literary forms and expression derived from the shift from Latin to the vernacular, and the development of the printing press aiding the distribution of new learning and literary expression, were also crucial factors in the Elizabethan cultural moment.

No less important was the history of Europe and England in the sixteenth century to form the key conditions for Elizabethan achievement. The Protestant Reformation, incited by Martin Luther in 1517, would challenge Catholic hegemony in Europe, undermining the Roman Church's authority, and emphasizing the individual's direct experience of God, unmediated by priestly authorities. In England, Henry VIII dramatically brought an end to the state-sponsored Catholic Church for a leap into religious self-determination. Under Elizabeth I, England was victorious over Catholic Spain, vanquishing the invading Armada in 1588. Into this mix of nationalistic and secular triumph, a means of expressing the era's key values and issues emerged in the rise of theaters throughout London that would attract the age's greatest literary talent, William Shakespeare. The conjunction of moment, means, and genius is complete.

How did Elizabethan drama compare to that of the ancient Greeks?

The Elizabethan period shared more than a similar cultural moment with the ancient Greeks. The Elizabethans also duplicated some of the key elements of the earlier theater and its methods (with several important differences). Both theaters were mainly open-air in semicircular auditoriums. Instead of the theater in Athens that could hold 15,000 or more, Elizabethan theaters were considerably smaller, accommodating about 3,000, though with several theaters offering productions, about 10,000 to 20,000 per week attended performances in London. As in ancient Greek drama, Elizabethan plays used male actors exclusively. On the ancient Greek stage, only three masked actors performed multiple parts. The unmasked Elizabethan performances could include twenty to thirty actors. The Elizabethans, like the Romans before them, eliminated the chorus, but performances could feature songs and dancing. Elizabethan drama is, like Attic drama, mainly a verse drama. The Elizabethans pioneered blank verse (with regular meter but unrhymed lines, usually iambic pentameter). It was first used in the 1561 play *Gorbo-duc* by Thomas Norton and Thomas Sackville and perfected by Christopher Marlowe, whose "mighty line" in such plays as *Tamburlaine* (1587) and *Dr. Faustus* (1592) would become a major inspiration for Shakespeare.

The Elizabethan theater, like that in ancient Greece, closed the semicircular, partially galleried viewing area on three levels with a skenelike structure for entrances and exits on the first-level raised platform stage. The second level could be used as an additional performance space, representing a parapet of a castle or a balcony as in *Romeo and Juliet.* The third level housed the musicians and the various sound effects, such as a dropped cannonball to mimic thunder. "Groundlings" stood in the area reserved for performance in the Greek orchestra ("the dancing place"). Otherwise, bench seating on three levels surrounded the stage as in the ancient Greek theater, or "seeing place." Unlike the Greek theater, the roof galleries provided cover during inclement weather. Elizabethan scenery as in the ancient Greek theater was minimal, usually restricted to props, such as a throne. The onstage columns supporting the upper levels of the skene could be used to suggest a tree or screen for an actor to see the action onstage and not be seen. The smaller, more intimate Elizabethan theater led to a more naturalistic acting style since actors did not have to be heard in a 15,000-seat auditorium. The absence of masks likewise contributed to a more realistic and lifelike performance with actors making full use of facial expressions and reactions.

The essential difference between Attic drama and the Elizabethan, however, is that the latter is mainly a commercial enterprise, neither state-sponsored nor funded (though patrons like the Athenian *choregi* were still important to sustain and protect an acting company) nor confined to annual festival competitions. Elizabethan plays were performed in repertory based on the plays' ability to attract an audience. Unlike the single performance of a Greek play at an annual festival, Elizabethan plays would remain in the repertory if they remained popular. In this sense, Elizabethan drama is closer to Roman theater, in which plays competed with other forms of popular entertainment, like bear-baiting. However, if comedy was paramount among Roman audiences, the Elizabethan playwrights were closer to ancient Greeks in presenting tragedies as well as pioneering new dramatic forms, such as histories, romances, and masques, to attract their audience. Women, non-Athenian citizens, or slaves may or may not have attended ancient Greek dramas. No exclusions existed in the Elizabethan theater. All comers, for the price of a penny, would be admitted (additional charge for gallery seating). The dramas the Elizabethans devised needed to appeal to a diverse audience, rich and poor, high-born and low-born. This is clearly reflected in the rich variety of Elizabethan drama.

How and why does Shakespeare reign supreme as history's greatest dramatist?

Discussion of Elizabethan drama begins and ends with William Shakespeare. There are other important Elizabethan dramatists, such as Christopher Marlowe and Ben Jonson, but Shakespeare reigns supreme as the greatest of all dramatists, whose plays are more produced, read, and studied than any other playwright. Why is this the case?

What we know for sure of his biography comes from a few scanty records that fix Shakespeare's birth, marriage, the baptism of his three children, and his later theatrical successes as an actor and playwright. Shakespeare was born in Stratford-on-Avon in the geographical center of England, a rural community of fewer than two thousand. His father was a prosperous and prominent tradesman, bailiff, and alderman, who suffered a decline in fortune and prestige. It is likely that Shakespeare was educated at the local grammar school, where he was exposed to the Latin classics. At the age of eighteen, he married a farmer's daughter, Anne Hathaway, who bore him three children, Susanna in 1583

A statue of William Shakespeare in Leicester Square, London, depicts a thoughtful Bard, the undisputed king of drama.

and twins Hamnet and Judith in 1585. What Shakespeare did or experienced in the next seven years, before records locate him in London as a successful playwright and actor, remains a mystery. By 1594 records show that he was a shareholder in London's most celebrated stage company under the patronage of the Lord Chamberlain. His early plays include the comedies *Comedy of Errors* (1592), *Two Gentlemen of Verona* (1594), *Love's Labour's Lost* (1594), and *A Midsummer Night's Dream* (1595); historical chronicles *Henry VI* (1590), *Richard III* (1592), and *Richard II* (1595); and the tragedies *Titus Andronicus* (1593) and *Romeo and Juliet* (1594). Shakespeare also achieved literary distinction as a poet with *Venus and Adonis* (1593) and *The Rape of Lucrece* (1594). He would continue his nondramatic writing with his masterful sonnet cycle that circulated among his friends and was published in 1609. The achievement evident in the sonnets alone would have secured Shakespeare a prominent place in English literary history.

By the late 1590s, Shakespeare's prominence and success allowed him to purchase a large home in Stratford, New Place, and to secure the rank of a gentleman. Around 1610 Shakespeare retired to Stratford, although he continued to write a series of romances or tragicomedies that include *Cymbeline* (1609), *The Winter's Tale* (1610), and *The Tempest* (1611) before his death in 1616 at the age of fifty-two.

It is impossible to write briefly of Shakespeare's achievement in a literary canon that includes over thirty plays, the vast majority of which are crucial for an understanding of literary history and the dramatic tradition, and resist reduction even to the conventional categories of comedies, tragedies, and histories. It is only possible here to point to some of the central qualities that define Shakespeare's genius. One place to start is with the dramatic tradition that Shakespeare inherited and revolutionized. As with all of literature's greatest figures, Shakespeare's work is derived from a complex blend of time, place, and particular genius.

Shakespeare is fundamentally a great assimilator of the popular dramatic tradition joined with the humanist energies released by the Renaissance and the expansive freedom of expression and form that the Elizabethan stage allowed. Prior to the Elizabethan dramatists, the English theater offered mainly religious and allegorical themes. Shakespeare, preeminently, returned drama to the exploration of secular human experience and a reflection of the actual life of English and world history, shaped by a remarkable grasp of the commonplace and the subtlety of behavior and psychology. He established the link with the great ancient Greek playwrights in reviving drama as a medium for the most profound exploration of human existence. Extending the rules of classical drama, he created an expressive dramatic form that would serve as a model for a romantic alternative to the classical norm of order and balance and helped establish the tension between classicism and romanticism that defines modernism.

Shakespeare divided his efforts fairly equally among the four major categories available to him in drama—tragedies, comedies, histories, and romances—and turned the potential limitations of the Elizabethan theater, with its bare, open stage, into a great strength as his expressive language compensated for limited stage effects. With characters ranging from king to clown, Shakespeare captures believably the high heroism of a character like Hotspur in *Henry IV* and his opposite in Falstaff; the tortured melancholy of youth in *Hamlet* and the anguish of age in *King Lear*, and the delightful follies of love in his comedies as well as love's corruption in *Othello* and *Macbeth*. Expressed in his remarkable expressive language, as Thomas Carlyle observed, "woven all of sheet-lightening and sunbeams," Shakespeare exploited the widest vocabulary of any English creative writer and fashioned an unsurpassed pattern of dazzling and functional imagery, yet Shakespeare's greatness essentially rests not principally on either his daunting range or virtuosity but rather in his power to communicate, to reveal ourselves in the mirror of his art.

What is the best way to understand and appreciate Shakespearean drama?

With all that said, understanding Shakespeare's plays present certain challenges. The obvious initial barriers are Elizabethan English and culture. Language and customs change, and Shakespeare's plays demonstrate that clearly. There are countless words in Shakespeare's plays readily understood by his contemporary audience that we no longer use or whose meanings have changed. This is reflected in the long blocks of annotations on each page of a modern text of a Shakespeare play that

Actors at the restored Globe Theatre in London are shown performing Shakespeare's *The Tempest*. To gain a full appreciation of the Bard's work, it is helpful if modern readers combine a reading of his plays with a viewing of live performances.

translate his usage into modern equivalences. This can be distracting, turning your experience with Shakespeare into an exercise in decoding, not drama, of ever-shifting gaze between the lines and the meaning. Equally daunting are Shakespeare's references to historical, geographical, and cultural details that would have been evident to his contemporaries but are lost on a modern reader or viewer. Shakespeare could also assume intimate audience familiarity with material like the Bible, ancient myths, and folklore for which a modern reader needs assistance, and the annotations grow.

The good news is that a reader's disorientation on entering Shakespeare's dramatic world diminishes considerably in performance. Seeing or hearing a Shakespeare play shifts the focus from the words to the action that usually eliminates the need for extensive footnotes. The ideal method for enhancing an understanding of Shakespeare's plays is to combine the reading with a listening or viewing experience. Here are some suggestions on how to do this:

1. Start with a plot summary to provide an overview of what the play is about. There are numerous synopses of Shakespeare's plays available online and elsewhere. Look for scene-by-scene summaries, like those available in *The Shakespeare Encylopedia* or *Shakespeare A–Z*. Even better: consult a scene-by-scene summary that incorporates quotations from the play, highlighting important passages.

2. Read from a good, annotated, scholarly edition that will provide useful background material on the plays and Elizabethan customs along with line-by-line notes clarifying words and references. Several collected editions are available, such as *The Norton Shakespeare, The Riverside Shakespeare,* the *Bevington Shakespeare,* the *RSC Shakespeare,* and *The Complete Pelican Shakespeare*. Before investing in one of these collections, do some comparison on how each organizes material and annotates. Go with the edition that seems most accessible for you. The gold standard for single-play editions has long been the Arden, but other excellent individual play editions are available from Norton, Yale, Oxford, and Cambridge. Electronic book editions (collections and single plays) are also available with hypertext links to annotations and helpful search features. Increasingly as well, apps have been appearing focused on individual plays with audio clips and commentary from leading Shakespearean actors and directors.

3. Read and reread scene by scene. On a first reading, ignore the annotation and just concentrate on the action. This is where a scene-by-scene summary is handy before or after your first reading. On a second reading, concentrate on a line-by-line examination that either shifts your gaze from lines to notes or considers the notes after finishing a passage or scene.

4. There is no better enhancement to your reading experience than by hearing or seeing the play in performance. Seek out an unabridged audio or film version of the play from your local library. The BBC Shakespeare project undertaken in the 1970s and 1980 that filmed versions of all of Shakespeare's plays is available on disc, and the Royal Shakespeare Company has issued many versions of their acclaimed pro-

ductions. Hearing the play is not as good as also seeing it, but you are more likely to secure an unabridged audio recording than film versions that are often heavily edited. In a pinch, supplement your second reading of each scene by reading aloud. This helps to slow your reading so you concentrate on each word. In giving voice to the words on the page, you can gain important insights on how lines can be delivered, hearing the emphasis and the rhythm of the verse.

5. After your close reading of each scene and supplemental listening or viewing, go through the play again from start to finish, concentrating on larger issues suggested by the language and the action, such as:

    a. What are the key events that establish, ignite, and resolve the play's central conflicts?

    b. How is each character defined? Consider what the characters say (and do not say), do, and what others say about them or do to them.

    c. Which characters emerge as the center of the action, or who undergoes the most significant changes or realizations? Consider how key characters begin the play and end it. What is the play saying about human nature in what is revealed about the characters?

    d. What does the play's setting contribute to the action? Why does the setting shift, and how do the shifts help define the conflict and its resolution?

    e. What's the overall outcome of the play? What have you learned over the course of the play about the human experience?

Force yourself to write your responses to these and other questions raised by the play. Try to be as specific as possible, going back to the play to record significant lines that help you explain your answer. Writing your responses often clarifies your thoughts; writing down key quotations will help you recall the play's specifics.

Let's apply some of these questions to a reading of Shakespeare's *A Midsummer Night's Dream*.

HOW TO READ A SHAKESPEAREAN PLAY: ANALYZING *A MIDSUMMER NIGHT'S DREAM*

What is some background information about *A Midsummer Night's Dream*?

A Midsummer Night's Dream is Shakespeare's first comic masterpiece and remains one of his most beloved and performed plays. It is easy, however, to overlook what a radically original and experimental play this is. *A Midsummer Night's Dream* is the triumph of Shakespeare's early playwriting career, a drama of such marked inventiveness and vision that its first audiences must have only marveled at what could possibly come next from this extraordinary playwright. In it, Shakespeare changed the methods of stage comedy that he inherited from the ancient Greeks and Romans by dizzyingly multiplying his plotlines and by bringing the irrational and absurd delusions of romantic love center stage. He established human passion and gender relations as comedy's prime subject, transforming such fundamental concepts as love, courtship, and marriage that have persisted in our culture ever since. If that isn't enough, *A Midsummer Night's Dream* makes use of its romantic intrigue, supernatural setting, and rustic foolery to explore essential questions about the relationship between art and life, appearance and reality, truth and illusion, and dreams and the waking world, which anticipate some of the most experimental modern writers. *A Midsummer Night's Dream* represents a kind of declaration of liberation for the stage, in which, after its example, nothing seems either off limits or impossible.

The plot focuses on three parallel stories: the trials and experiences of two sets of lovers who have ventured into the forest world of the Fairy King and Queen and their minions and a group of rough craftsmen attempting to stage a production of "Pyramus and Thisbe" for the wedding of the Duke of Athens. Complications abound due to the mischief and mistakes of the Fairy King's chief retainer, Puck.

What five key questions should you ask about the play?

Let's begin with recalling the five key questions that can be asked of any work of literature:

1. What is the significance of the play's title? How does the title announce what we should expect in the play? What themes might be explored in the play?

2. Why does the play begin when and how it does? How does the opening of the play establish possible themes and set in motion the conflicts to come?

3. What are the play's conflicts? Conflict is the essence of drama. Conflicts can be those between a character and his/her circumstance, between characters, and most interestingly within characters. What are the conflicts in the play, and how do they help us to understand what the play is about and its significance?

4. How are the conflicts resolved? The resolution of a play's conflicts is called the climax. When and how does the climax occur, and how is the resolution of the conflict revealing about the significance and meaning of the play?

5. Why does the play end when it does? Both the beginning and ending of a play frame the action, directing the reader/audience's attention in a particular way. What does the play's conclusion tell us about the meaning of the play?

What about its title?

Consider the first essential question—why the title? Remember that a title, whether from a play, poem, story, or novel, is the author's initial, and in some cases only, direct suggestion about significance in a work of literature. The title focuses our attention on key themes or the central subject of the work. So, what about *A Midsummer Night's Dream?* Shakespeare's title immediately signals the difference between what happens when we are awake and when we sleep and dream. In a dream, anything might happen; anything is possible. Shakespeare seems to be alerting us here that we can expect the unexpected in this play, that the rules that govern the ordinary world do not apply, and instead of the predictable and familiar, we should expect the unforeseen and extraordinary. It is also helpful to understand what Shakespeare (and his original audience) understood about midsummer night. In English folklore, the night of midsummer was when a maid could dream and see the identity of the man she would wed. So, Shakespeare's audience would have immediately expected that a play with this title likely concerns love and courtship.

What conflict opens the play?

That's exactly the subject indicated at the beginning of the play as Theseus, the Duke of Athens, expresses his impatience awaiting his marriage to Hippolyta, the queen of the Amazons, who, based on Greek legend,

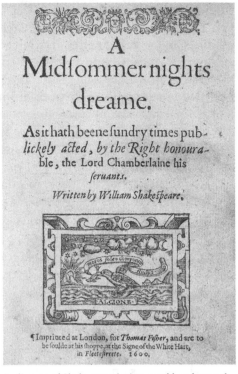

Audiences of Shakespeare's time would understand full well the meaning behind the title "A Midsummer Night's Dream" as a reference to a young woman's dreams of marriage.

was first defeated in battle by Theseus and then fell in love with him. Former enemies are now lovers looking forward to their wedding. Romance and its fulfillment, however, are undercut by the arrival of Egeus, who has come to complain about his daughter's own romance. Instead of accepting Demetrius, the suitor Egeus has selected for her, Hermia has been, according to her father, "bewitched" by Lysander and wants to marry him instead. Egeus demands that the Athenian law that establishes a parent's absolute authority over a child be invoked and that if Hermia refuses to wed Demetrius, she must either die or become a nun, "chanting faint hymns to the cold, fruitless moon." So, the anticipated happy outcome of Theseus' relationship with Hippolyta contrasts with the unhappy circumstance that Hermia's choice—Lysander—is not approved by her father, and his choice—Demetrius—is frustrated by Hermia's rejection of him as a suitor. Love and romance are shown moving in two opposite directions: toward fulfillment in marriage and love's destruction in the alternatives—death or celibacy—that Hermia is forced to choose.

How does Shakespeare extend the play's opening conflict?

Note how at the outset of the play, a conflict emerges in which Hermia and Lysander's desire for each other collides with an obligation to a marriage that is not a choice but a social arrangement determined by a parent, whose authority is sanctioned by the state. The romance of Lysander's courtship of Hermia is contrasted with Egeus's understanding of love as enchantment and irrelevant to the more important business of marriage, which seems more like an advantageous business merger than the fulfillment of passionate desires.

Theseus, despite his own romantic feelings for Hippolyta, reluctantly supports Egeus's demand and offers the lovers a deadline—his own nuptial day—to comply or to suffer the consequences. Left alone, Hermia and Lysander decide to resolve the conflict by eloping, where, free from Athenian law, they may marry. Helena, another unhappy lover, now enters. She is in love with Demetrius, whom Egeus has encouraged to pursue Hermia. To comfort her, Lysander and Hermia tell her their plan to meet the next night in the woods by moonlight and elope. After they leave, Helena decides that she will alert Demetrius to the elopement and follow him into the woods. At the end of the scene, all four lovers are headed into the woods for the complications that will follow.

Drama *is* conflict, and Shakespeare immediately establishes in the play situations that produce opposition and opponents: Egeus versus Hermia and Lysander, Demetrius versus Hermia and Lysander, and Helena versus Demetrius. So, the second essential question—why does the play begin when it does?—can be answered by showing how the opening of the play establishes the central concern of love and romance and how the initial conflicts motivate the subsequent actions of the central characters.

How are the conflicts resolved?

The answers must await the dizzying complications that follow when the lovers enter the midsummer night's moonlit wood, which is also the destination of Bottom and his acting troupe. Like the opening of Scene 1, we are again in the company of royalty, Oberon and Titania, the king and queen of the fairies. Like Theseus and Hippolyta, they have been at "war," but over the possession of a lovely boy, a changeling, stolen from an Indian king. So, even in the fairy world, we see how "the course of true love never did run smooth." Oberon and Titania's love complications—his jealousy over the boy and her aggravation over his demands—join those of the four Athenian lovers as problems that need to be solved over the course of the night. Shakespeare's strategy is to take a theme of the compli-

Shakespeare's play includes a tangled web of personal relationships that counterbalance obligation and romance, alliances and rivalries. (*Hermia and Lysander* [1870] by artist John Simmons.)

273

cation of romantic love and then show variations on it, establishing comparison and contrast as he proceeds.

What complications develop in the play?

Drama—particularly comic drama—depends on complications. In shifting the scene from the daylight world of Athens, ruled by law and Theseus, to the nighttime world of the forest, ruled by the Fairy King and Queen, Shakespeare embodies an alternative reality in which all sorts of transformation and disordering can be accomplished. The main agent for this is Puck, the mischief maker, who is dispatched by Oberon for the love juice that will be used in his plot to gain the changeling from Titania. Cupid's arrow has missed its mark, hitting a flower instead, which is yet another example of love gone astray. Placing the love juice into Titania's eyes while she sleeps will cause her to fall in love with the first thing she sees upon waking. Here, Shakespeare clearly suggests how fickle love can be, how when in love, we see what we want to see, not necessarily reality. Just as Cupid's arrow goes astray, so, too, will Oberon's plot go astray as he witnesses Demetrius's rejection of Helena and orders Puck to put some of the love juice in his eyes to make Demetrius fall back in love with her. Puck instead puts the potion in Lysander's eye, adding to the complications.

As Titania goes to sleep, Hermia and Lysander finally appear, attempting their elopement, but in the dark woods, Lysander has lost his way to his aunt's house, necessitating their sleeping in the woods. While they sleep, Puck enters, and administers the love potion to Lysander instead of Demetrius as Oberon intended. So, multiple complications have occurred: Lysander and Hermia have lost their way through the woods, and Puck has mistaken his intended target. After Puck leaves, Demetrius enters pursued by Helena. Intent on finding Hermia, Demetrius leaves Helena. She wakes up the sleeping Lysander, who instantly forgets his former devotion to Hermia by declaring his undying love for the startled Helena. By the end of the scene, the complications have greatly increased. Now neither Lysander nor Demetrius love the woman who loves him: Hermia loves Lysander, who loves Helena, who loves Demetrius, who loves Hermia. Like a dance in which the partners are scrambled, the entry into the woods by the Athenian lovers has produced complications, confusion, and suspense over how all will be resolved. On the theme of love and romance, Shakespeare also underscores here how fickle affections can be, how certain lovers often are, yet how quickly their feelings change. Is love, therefore, to be trusted?

How does coincidence and accident complicate the action?

In the world of a dream, coincidences can predominate along with the extraordinary, like the fairies and their supernatural powers. To the coincidence of Demetrius and Helena crossing the path of Hermia and Lysander is now added the proximity of Bottom and his men and the sleeping Titania to allow her to see Bottom upon waking and to fall hopelessly in love with him due to the love-potion. Although it would certainly be funny to have the Queen of the Fairies dote on a rough-hewn weaver like Bottom, giving him the head of a donkey by Puck's mischievousness is far funnier! By having the regal Titania lavish praise and flattery on the ridiculous Bottom—half man, half ass—further makes a point about love: it is subjective; it is in the eye of the beholder. Someone in love sees what he or she wants to see rather than what is. Bottom's transformation, first with his donkey's head and later as the love object of the Fairy Queen, echoes a persistent theme of the play. Love is transforming, but so, too, is the world: what seems so clear in the daylight world of Athens is transformed in the moonlight realm of the forest and in dreams. What is real and what is illusion? What's the difference between appearance and reality? These questions are key themes in the play.

By correcting Puck's error, Oberon makes things even more complicated and confused! Note how in the topsy-turvy world of the dream, the initial situation has now become completely reversed. At the beginning of the play, Hermia was loved by both Lysander and Demetrius, and Helena was loved by no one. Now Helena is loved by both men and Hermia by neither. However, the seeds for the happy resolution of the complication are partially planted since now at least Demetrius' affections have returned to Helena. It will take yet another dose of the love juice and the proper alignment of the lovers—Lysander beside Hermia and Demetrius beside Helena—to correct all the complications and confusion.

How are the complications resolved?

Before resolving the lovers' dilemma (and the play's multiple conflicts), the stress and strain between the two couples explode into verbal and intended violence. Lysander and Demetrius vie to outdo the other in denying their former vows of love for Hermia and their unswerving devotion to Helena. Hermia enters, knowing only that Lysander had disappeared from her side while she was asleep. The confusion now reaches its hilarious crescendo with Hermia's arrival to discover that now Helena is the object of both suitors' passion, not her. Each of the women believes the other is conspiring against her in "foul derision." Hermia believes that the other three have joined together to make fun of her and that Helena has won Lysander because she is taller than Hermia. Helena contradicts her previous friendship as a schoolgirl with Hermia, calling her a vixen and confessing how she betrayed their trust by revealing the elopement to Demetrius. The accusations escalate into a foolish frenzy brought on by the confusion that causes Hermia to call their very identities into question by asking, "Am I not Hermia? Are you not Lysander?"

As the foursome exit with recriminations and threats of violence, Oberon steps in to make things right, taking advantage of another flower's juice that acts as an antidote to the first. This Puck will apply to Lysander, and Oberon himself will do the same to Titania after he has claimed the changeling. Puck, imitating the voices of Lysander and Demetrius, leads them on a fruitless pursuit of each other until, exhausted by their chase, they fall asleep alongside their appropriate partner: Lysander beside Hermia and Demetrius beside Helena.

How does Act 5 resolve the conflict?

Generally, in a Shakespearean five-act play, Act 1 establishes the conflict; Act 2 provides the complications; Act 3 is the turning point or escalation of the conflict that leads to Act 4's climax; and the final resolution is in Act 5. Shakespeare manages to accomplish the turning-point action that will at least resolve the fate of his young lovers in Act 3. However, Titania's situation needs the initial scene of Act 4 to accomplish resolution.

As the scene opens, Titania is lavishing affection and attention on Bottom, who, as the only mortal character in the play actually to see the fairies, finds himself completely at home in Titania's and her fairies' care. As Titania and Bottom sleep, Puck and Oberon enter, and the charm is removed from Titania's eyes and the ass's head is removed from Bottom. Oberon declares that Bottom will think his experience was no more than "the fierce vexation of a dream." Before restoring Bottom, Titania is shown whom she doted on. The king and queen, now restored to harmony, declare their intention of dancing the next night to bless Theseus's wedding as the morning lark signals the return of day.

A scene from *A Midsummer Night's Dream,* depicting the characters Bottom, Titania, and Puck in Act 3, by artist Charles Buchel.

The green world of the forest, night, and the fairies give way to the normal world as Theseus arrives, accompanied by Hippolyta and Egeus on a morning hunt. The hunting party finds the four lovers asleep. Lysander and Demetrius attempt to explain why they are in the forest and that Demetrius no longer loves Hermia and his former passion for Helena has been restored. Theseus tells Egeus that he overrides a father's wishes with respect to his daughter and declares that the two couples shall be married when he and Hippolyta are, and all return to Athens. In keeping with the spirit of the green world, in which individual desires predominate over law and reason, Theseus reverses his previous position as the custodian of law in favor of supremacy of hearts and desires.

How are the issues of love and romance resolved in the play?

Demetrius' declaration of undying, unshakable love for Helena is ironic since we know that he is still under the effect of the love potion, and the audience understands that his certainty about his love is enchantment. Shakespeare has shown throughout the play that love is irrational, volatile, subjective, and fickle and that the reality of love is often at odds with what lovers say it is.

After the lovers leave, Bottom wakes up and confesses, "I've had a dream, past the wit of man to say what dream it was. Man is but an ass if he go about to expound this dream." Throughout the play, Shakespeare has blurred the distinction between the waking world and our dreams. Bottom's questions about his experiences—what can be believed and what is the truth?—are the core questions of the play.

Most romantic comedies end in reconciliation, harmony, and especially marriage, the traditional personal and social fulfillment of love. Disorder, misunderstanding, and conflict are all resolved positively (as opposed to tragedy that ends in death, disorder, and destruction). Here, Shakespeare arranges three marriages and a reunited and reconciled Oberon and Titania. As in a dance, all have found their rightful partners, and the complications that opened the play are happily resolved in favor of the transformative power of love, which is stronger than parental authority, the laws of the state, or even the fickleness and confusion of the lovers.

Why does the play end like it does?

Although order and normalcy are restored in the final act, it opens with a consideration of the strange experiences the lovers have recounted to Hippolyta and Theseus. He says the lovers' story is "more strange than true." According to Theseus, lovers and madmen have "seething brains," whose senses cannot be trusted. Theseus then delivers his famous speech comparing the imaginations of the lunatic, the lover, and the poet:

> The lunatic, the lover, and the poet
> Are of imagination all compact.
> One sees more devils than vast hell can hold;
> That is the madman. The lover, all as frantic,
> Sees Helen's beauty in a brow of Egypt.
> The poet's eye, in a fine frenzy rolling,
> Doth glance from heaven to earth, from earth to heaven.

In his analysis, all three see whatever their imagination conjures and, therefore, none is trustworthy. Theseus's speech is central to the main theme of the play, in which Shakespeare has shown the way the world is transformed by the imagination and our subjective viewpoint. Ironically, the play has displayed all three kinds of imaginative distortions from characters who have acted like lunatics, lovers, and poets!

What is the purpose of the play-within-the-play?

If Theseus' speech provides a key commentary on the play, so, too, does the play-within-the-play, performed by Bottom and his troupe. Although performed with hilarious incompetence, the tragic story of Pyramus and Thisbe, frustrated lovers who die because of their love, is remarkably close to the other story unfolding in the previous acts. If the tragedy of Pyramus and Thisbe is subverted by the workmen's comic performance, so, too. has the other potential tragedy been circumvented by the absurd antics of Lysander, Hermia, Demetrius, and Helena. As Lysander and Demetrius joke at the expense of the inept performers, the reader/audience should remember how absurdly the men themselves behaved in the woods. We also know that Demetrius, who does most of the disruptive jesting, still has the love juice in his eyes that causes him to love Helena, so who is more foolish: the inept amateur performers or the earnest lover convinced of his sincerity who really has been tricked into loving another?

The main instigator of the comic complications in the play, Puck, is given the final words of the play. After all the humans have departed, Puck enters with a broom, "To sweep the dust behind the door," in other words, to restore cleansing order to all who are resting inside "this hallowed house." Oberon and Titania, with all their attendants, enter to bless the brides and grooms. Puck then turns to address the audience directly, asking forgiveness for any offenses the play might have caused. He suggests, "If we shadows have offended, / Think but this, and all is mended: / That you have but slumbered here." The play has been like a dream, full of distortions and dislocations, and ultimately innocent: we cannot control visions in sleep. In a play about the transformative power of love, the fancy of imagination, and the delusions they can conjure, the suggestion that the audience has been sleeping and witnessing but a dream is the perfect ending!

So, recall the final two of our essential five questions to ask about any work of literature: how is the conflict resolved, and how and why does the play end? Act 5 shows how all the previous misunderstandings and conflicts are subsumed in the harmony and unity of marriage. By ending the play so happily, Shakespeare affirms his comic intentions. This is a play about the ultimate triumph and power of love surviving all obstacles—parental and personal—that block its fulfillment. The forces unleashed in the forest—the supernatural and the imaginative—are aligned to the power of love itself to transform actuality with desire. Once the lovers have returned to daylight and the normal world, all the oppositions to their desires are magically dispelled. But Shakespeare does not stop with just the happy ending of a marriage celebration. By staging a play-within-a-play, Shakespeare cleverly organizes a kind of funhouse mirror in which actors watch characters perform as actors, while we watch all perform for us. Illusion multiplies, and it becomes difficult to sort out what is real and what is pretend. And that's precisely Shakespeare's point about love: is it real or just imagined? Can it be trusted? Does the lover really see the loved one or only what he or she wishes to see through the haze of desire and longing? We are all a bit like Theseus's lunatic, lover, and poet. We all see what we want to see, while insisting that we see the truth.

What is Shakespeare saying about the nature of drama in the play?

Finally, Shakespeare poses some interesting questions about drama and literature as well. Is it real? Or is it just a dream? Nothing we just read or saw be performed actually happened. It's either made up exclusively of language or by actors pretending to be someone they are not in a situation that only takes place onstage, not in the real world. At the end of the play, Shakespeare, through Puck, gets us to ask: what did I just read or see? Is it real or a dream? Where is truth to be found: when we are awake or when we dream?

What happened to drama after the Elizabethan period?

The vibrant Elizabethan theater in which Shakespeare and others thrived from 1572 to 1642 supported eighteen acting companies, seventeen London playhouses, and a long list of playwrights, including John Webster, John Marston, Thomas Heywood, Thomas Middleton, John Fletcher, Francis Beaumont, William Rowley, Philip Massenger, and John Ford, who were collectively responsible for over six hundred published plays.

Ben Jonson was one of the most prolific and influential of the playwrights of Elizabethan England. Also a poet, actor, and critic, he was particularly noted for his satirical works.

The most significant playwright of the period, besides Christopher Marlowe and Shakespeare, was undoubtedly Ben Jonson (1572–1637). In the history of English drama, he is exceeded only by Shakespeare and George Bernard Shaw in contributing more plays to the permanent national repertory. Jonson was the master of the urban satirical comedy of manners, in plays such as *Every Man in His Humour, Volpone*, and *The Alchemist,* that brought authentic and unflattering contemporary subjects within dramatic range and harnessed disparate, rowdy Elizabethan life to the classically derived rules of dramatic construction that would define theatrical ideals for the next two centuries. It was Jonson who insisted that drama was more than entertainment but a high literary art rivaling the epic or poetry. It was Jonson, more than any other English dramatist, who helped to establish plays as literature, capable of the most serious inquiry into human nature and social life. Shakespeare is inimitable; however, it can be argued, more subsequent playwrights claim their descent as a "son of Ben."

This great second flowering of drama abruptly ended in 1642, when Parliament, now in the hands of the Puritans who regarded plays and performances as sinful, closed the theaters. Acting companies, playwrights, and actors who received patronage from the monarch and nobility were conspicuous targets for the anti-Royalists who came to power during the English Civil War and period of the Commonwealth. Although intended as a temporary ban "while these sad causes and set Times of humiliations do continue," the law prohibiting performances of plays continued for the next eighteen years until the Restoration of the monarchy under Charles II in 1660.

One of Charles's first acts was to reopen the theaters, and the king granted patents to Thomas Killigrew and Sir William Davenant to form companies to mount productions. Killigrew formed the King's Company; Davenant the Duke's Company. Both added actresses to their casts and constructed new indoor theaters in Drury Lane and Covent

Garden to cater to an audience mainly of the upper echelon of London society. Initially, the theaters depended on the earlier works of Shakespeare, Jonson, Beaumont, Fletcher, and others, but gradually, new dramatic forms emerged to gratify the aristocratic tastes of Restoration audiences—heroic, verse drama, and comedies of manners. The new English stage, very different from the rough-and-tumble, socially inclusive Elizabethan and Jacobean theater, gratified a more elite audience keenly sensitive to social distinction, who valued wit above all things in their stage entertainments. Their taste was reflected in the so-called Restoration comedies, produced between 1669 and 1710, written by George Wycherley (*The Country Wife* [1675] and *The Plain Dealer* [1676]), George Etherege (*The Man of Mode* [1676]), John Vanbrugh (*The Provoked Wife* [1697]), William Congreve (*Love for Love* [1695] and *The Way of the World* [1700]), and George Farquhar (*The Recruiting Officer* [1706] and *The Beaux' Stratagem* [1707]). Restoration comedies, reflecting the period's social values, are usually set in fashionable parts of London in the gardens, houses, and drawing rooms of the leisured classes, reflecting their audience's concern with manners in highly topical, often cynical and licentious, complicated plots, occasions for the display of witty dialogue.

As England lost and recovered its national theater in the seventeenth century, other European nations were forging their own, particularly in Spain and France.

EARLY EUROPEAN DRAMA

What were the characteristics and achievements of the Spanish Golden Age of drama?

In Spain, classical drama, introduced by the Greeks and the Romans to the Iberian Peninsula, gave way to the liturgical dramas of the Middle Ages with secular theater barely kept alive by traveling entertainers and performers in short farces. Spaniards traveling to Italy brought back the *comedias humanísticas* of the Renaissance, and performances of classically inspired dramas were supplemented by Italian theatrical troupes who came to Spain in the mid-sixteenth century. Plays were performed at the royal court, in aristocratic households, and in open courtyards (*corrales*), with the first permanent open-air theater established in Madrid in 1579. Performances were given by daylight with a stage ordinarily representing the two-story facade of a house with balconies on a Madrid street. As in the Elizabethan theater, a pit served as a place for the groundlings, and the upper windows of the surrounding houses served as boxes. Women spectators were segregated in an area known as *la cazuela* (the stewpan), but onstage, women's parts were played by actresses.

It was the great Spanish playwright Lope de Vega (1562–1635) who formulated a new dramatic form, the *comedia nueva*, the full-length Spanish secular play that initiated a century-long flowering of Spanish Golden Age drama from the 1580s to the 1680s. His plays broke with the Aristotelian dramatic tradition as interpreted during the Renaissance, which dictated a strict separation of comedy and tragedy within a five-act structure and a restricted number of dramatic characters and situations. Vega instead pioneered a flexible and varied dramatic form aimed at appealing to his audience. In his dramatic treatise *Arte nuevo de hacer comedias en este tiempo* (1609; *The New Art of Writing Plays*), he declared his artistic independence from the established rules of dramatic decorum and expounded a liberated dramaturgical method. Vega insisted that his plays were based on an assimilation and refinement of classical rules and the Spanish popular tradition. He believed the action of the *comedia* should be confined to three acts encompassing exposition, complication, and denouement with a premium on sensation and suspense. He

Second in prominence perhaps only to Miguel de Cervantes, Lope de Vega was a prolific playwright who helped usher in the Spanish Golden Age of drama.

eschewed a highly stylized and allusive poetic style and narrow, proscribed subjects, preferring an expressive method aimed at capturing the richness of everyday life. "When I set out to write a play," he observed, "I lock up all the rules under ten keys, and banish Plautus and Terence from my study.... For I write in the style of those who seek the applause of the public, whom it is but just to humor in their folly, since it is they who pay for it." If art imitates nature, Vega asserted, the variety of nature is infinite and so should be the subjects represented onstage. To supply the variety his audience demanded, he mixed the comic and the tragic, allowed noble characters to interact with the humble, and violated the unities of time and place, asserting that a Spanish theatergoer grows impatient if he is not shown in two hours "all human history from Genesis to the Last Judgment." Unapologetic in his catering to his audience's often unsophisticated taste, Vega viewed his plays, dashed off for money, as inferior to his other writings. All show signs of haste and repetition, and if few of them rise to the level of Shakespearean depth and profundity in the complexity of their characterization or ideas, they still serve an important liberating function in the history of Western drama. To reach his audience, Vega turned drama into a stirring vehicle for embodying an age's values in a form flexible enough to incorporate stories from ancient mythology, the Bible, the lives of the saints, legends, ancient and Spanish history, and the social life of contemporary Spain. On his stage, kings mix with commoners, and both are entitled to comic or tragic treatment. He transformed the often crude Spanish dramatic folk tradition with a new artistry, while he expanded the rigidly proscribed neoclassical drama by his genius and the breadth of his vision into an all-purpose entertainment that could both give pleasure and mount an effective criticism of life.

281

Vega propagated multiple new genres and refinements of older forms, producing religious plays, pastoral dramas, mythological plays, historical dramas derived from past and contemporary events, and plays of intrigue and adventure turning on jealousy and revenge. Several of his plays have entered the canon of world dramatic literature, including *El acerode Madrid* (*Steel in Madrid*), *El caballero de Olmedo* (*The Knight of Olmedo*), *El castigo sin venganza* (*Punishment without Revenge*), *El perro del hortelano* (*The Dog in the Manger*), and *El major alcalde, el rey* (*The Best Magistrate, the King*). Lope de Vega is the foundation figure of Spanish drama, about whom it has been said, he "gave Spain its theatre, and Spain in turn gave her theater to Europe."

What were the characteristics and achievements of French drama during the seventeenth century?

France also built a national theater that developed neoclassical tragedy and comedy during the seventeenth century.

In their adaptations of Spanish and classical source material, as in Pierre Corneille's *Le Cid* (1637) and Jean Racine's *Phèdre* (1677), French playwrights returned drama to the tightly controlled construction of the classical theater. As its name implies, neoclassical, or "new-classical," ideals derived from the recovery and dissemination of classical texts during the Renaissance, particularly in drama, of Aristotle's *Poetics* that specified methods and standards for tragedy that proponents of neoclassicism would adapt and modify into a set of rules governing dramatic practice that returned to the values and conventions of classical Greek drama. The two key concepts of neoclassical drama are verisimilitude and decorum. The conception of *verisimilitude* (*vraisemblance*), being true to life, derived from Aristotle's dramatic theory of mimesis in which drama imitated nature. Neoclassical drama, therefore, needed to be believable, depicting characters and situations derived from nature and supported by the so-called Aristotelian unities: plays should have a single action (without subplots), be confined to a single place, and occur over a period of no more than twenty-four hours. Decorum prescribed that characters must speak and behave suitably for their age, gender, and social class, and the mixing of high and low characters, comedy and tragic scenes, must be avoided. Neoclassical drama can appear, particularly to a modern audience, cripplingly formalized and limited. It would take a great dramatist such as Racine to demonstrate what could be achieved by adhering to (and violating) the rules of neoclassical tragedy that would dominate European theater conventions until the emergence of modern drama at the end of the nineteenth century.

French comedy as practiced by the great Molière (the stage name of Jean-Baptiste Poquelin, 1622–1673) would become a similarly important legacy for world drama. Along with Aristophanes, Molière is the great innovator of comic drama. Together, the pair marks out the boundaries for comedy, and it is to Molière that one can point to its revival as a serious reflection of human nature and experience, as well as the perfection of theatrical conventions that have maintained their powers in the hands of such different artists as Samuel Beckett, Eugène Ionesco, and Charlie Chaplin. It is also to Molière that one must look principally for the legitimatization of comic theater in the

West, establishing a classical repertory and, largely in his honor, a national theater, the Comédie-Française. After more than three hundred years, Molière, like Shakespeare, continues to dominate the theater that he helped to create.

French comedy of Molière's day was largely based on the Italian *commedia dell'arte*, to which Molière was extensively exposed on his troupe's tour of the southern provinces. Based on set comic routines, the *commedia* depended on stock roles familiar to the audience and witty improvisations by the actors, which included topical references. Molière mastered the farcical base upon which he began to build a new kind of comedy while elevating the comic form to the serious aspirations of tragedy. If comedy before Molière was exclusively rough-and-tumble entertainment and low humor, he

French playwright Jean-Baptiste Poquelin (Molière) was another master of satire in Europe, but his plays got him in hot water with the Catholic Church, especially for *Tartuffe*.

would help transform it into a critique of life, expanding the range of the knockabout farce and stock characters to encompass social satire and the reflection of the reality and experience of his audience. His *The School for Wives* (1662) began a remarkable series of literary masterpieces that included *Tartuffe* (1664), *Don Juan* (1665), *The Misanthrope* (1666), and *The Miser* (1668). All show Molière's skill in adapting traditional comic conventions to the new uses of character comedy in which he exposes the vice and folly embodied in the excesses of his characters. In his widening of theatrical forms to incorporate a comedy of ideas, Molière is one of the major innovators of Western drama. Only a few subsequent dramatic inventions, whether the spectacle of romantic drama or the symbolic antirealistic techniques of modern drama, cannot be traced to Molière for precedence. The comic vision of Molière that expresses the discrepancy between how we would like to be seen and who we truly are sets the tone for much modern literature, from the antiheroic to the absurd, in which the sanity of Molière's exposed truths is the essential consolation.

READING NEOCLASSICAL DRAMA—MOLIÈRE'S *TARTUFFE*

What makes *Tartuffe* so controversial and influential?

Tartuffe is one of the most contentious plays ever produced and the subject of the seventeenth century's greatest censorship battle. Molière's shockingly delightful drama about religious belief radically redefined the targets and ends of comedy. That Molière would comically treat such a subject in a religiously sensitive age that still dealt with heresy at the stake was daring in the extreme, if not foolhardy. That his critics misperceived the play's exposure of false piety and religious hypocrisy as an attack on religion itself suggests that *Tartuffe* hit a sensitive nerve. It is easy to condemn the bias and blindness of Molière's clerical contemporaries at the time of his death, still smarting from the stings of *Tartuffe*. However, the play retains its ability to shock and touch audiences in sore spots, and the need to be able to distinguish true piety amidst sham is no less urgent today than it was in seventeenth-century France.

How does Molière's biography and career help to inform *Tartuffe*?

Controversy, such as that surrounding *Tartuffe* and Molière's passing, was a constant in the playwright's career, beginning with his return to Paris in 1658 after a twelve-year provincial tour as actor, manager, and playwright with a struggling theatrical troupe. During this apprenticeship period, Molière perfected his craft as a comic *farceur* and playwright, converting elements from traditional French farce and the Italian *commedia dell'arte* into a radically new comic drama that challenged tragedy as a vehicle for delivering the most serious and profound truths. If seventeenth-century French tragedy had formulated a clear set of rules and conventions, French comedy was another matter when Molière took it up. The crude slapstick of French farce with its stock characters and exaggerated situations was enjoyed by the populace, while the sophisticated preferred the dignity, verisimilitude, and profundity of tragedy. Literary or high comedy needed to be similarly serious and refined. Molière, who developed his skills on the popular stage, would revolutionize French comedy by fusing the farcical with proscribed elements of neoclassical drama and the aspirations of serious drama. He showed that comedy as well as tragedy could reach psychological depths and essential human themes and that the caricatured distortions of farce aided rather than prevented the exploration of human nature and social experience. His was an innovative character comedy based on the life-like portrayal of contemporary manners but with the theatrical inventiveness that provoked hearty laughter at human foibles and pretensions. Many were not amused.

In 1662, Molière presented *L'École des Femmes* (*The School for Wives*), a play about a middle-aged man's scheme to prevent becoming a cuckold by raising his bride from girlhood isolated from the corruptions of society. Despite great commercial success, his satirical comedy that exposed the excesses and unflattering inclinations of the *beau monde* prompted charges of the playwright's immorality and defiance of dramatic decorum. The play touched off the so-called *La guerre comique*, which became, after the controversy over Corneille's *Le Cid,* seventeenth-century France's second great debate over the ends and means of drama. To the charge that he had violated good taste by exposing the vices of the respectable and overturned the rules of dramatic decorum by provoking ridicule with his comic exaggeration of serious matters, Molière insisted that he had observed drama's fundamental rule by pleasing his audience. Preferring to treat

How was Molière's burial influenced by his writing?

On February 17, 1773, Molière coughed up blood while performing the title role in his final comedy, *Le malade imaginaire* (*The Imaginary Invalid*). That the already desperately ill Molière should end his theatrical career pretending to be a hypochondriac is one of the theater's great dramatic ironies. He died a few hours after the performance at his home of a lung embolism. The priests at the parish of Saint Eustace, where he had been baptized, refused him last rites and the opportunity for the conventional deathbed renunciation of his profession that would have allowed the excommunicated actor to be buried in holy ground. France's greatest dramatist was finally buried, in the words of critic Nicholas Boileau, in a "piece of land obtained by supplication" through the intervention of Louis XIV on behalf of his friend. The king managed to persuade the archbishop of Paris to grant Molière a Christian burial but only in the dead of night without a public ceremony of mourning. The clergy refused to forgive Molière for his presumed impious and blasphemous attack on religion in *Tartuffe*, which had been first performed almost a decade before in 1664, and only reluctantly bowed to royal persuasion.

Molière's tomb.

men as they are rather than as they ought to be, the playwright insisted that comedy must represent "all the defects of men, and especially the men of our own time." Throughout the debate, Molière insisted on a new realistic standard for drama that would extend the range of comedy with the goal of correcting men's vices by exposing them, by instructing reason and moderation (the neoclassical ideals), and by wittily showing their violations.

How did *Tartuffe* develop?

The ultimate test for Molière's conception of comedy would come with *Tartuffe*. An initial three-act version of the play was first performed for the king at Versailles during a lavish spring fête. It provoked shocked condemnation from the queen mother, from church officials, and from lay members of the Company of the Holy Sacrament, the era's spiritual thought police engaged in the protection of morality and orthodoxy. In the grip of the Counter-Reformation, the Catholic Church in France was divided into two dominant rival factions of the Jesuits and the puritanical Jansenists. Both sides saw themselves the target of Molière's satire, and less than a week after its first performance, religious and moral pressure groups forced a royal ban. Molière was condemned as "a demon dressed in flesh and clothed as a man, and the most outrageously impious libertine who has ever appeared in centuries" by one cleric who called for the playwright to be burned at the stake. The ban led to Molière's five-year struggle to justify his play and his method and to get *Tartuffe* performed and published. He insisted that his tar-

285

get was neither religion nor the truly pious but those who merely pretended to be and who used religion to conceal and justify their vices. Molière insisted that instead of belittling moral values, his play was the most effective way to support morality by attacking "the vices of these times through ludicrous depictions." In 1667, a second five-act version of the play with a new title, *L'Imposteur,* and a renamed title character (Panulphe) premiered in Paris. It likewise was immediately banned. Molière's theater was closed, and the archbishop of Paris decreed that anyone performing in, attending, or reading the play would be excommunicated. Molière appealed to the king, who was away from Paris with his army at the time, arguing that the play was dangerous neither to religion nor the genuinely pious and threatened to stop writing comedy altogether if these "tartuffes" were unchallenged. Louis let the ban stand but agreed to reexamine the case upon his return to Paris. On February 5, 1669, the ultimate version of the play, now entitled *Le Tartuffe, ou l'Imposteur*, finally opened to great acclaim and commercial success as well as lingering clerical resentment.

What is Molière's main innovation in the play?

The most striking structural innovation in the play is keeping Tartuffe offstage until the second scene of the third act, the climax of most five-act dramas. His absence underscores Molière's focus not on Tartuffe but on his guilt and the consequence of his deception. The opening scenes, recording the family's breakdown through the patriarch Orgon's falling for the lures of a religious hypocrite, was called by Goethe "the greatest and best thing of the kind that exists." The household has been ruptured by Tartuffe's arrival into two warring factions: Orgon and his mother, Madame Pernelle, who have

What are Molière's achievements in *Tartuffe*?

Tartuffe has gone on to become Molière's most widely read and performed play. Its title character is among drama's greatest comic characters, and the story of his rise and fall as a devious usurper in the respectable bourgeois household of Orgon and his family is a masterpiece of characterization, social satire, and theatricality in its multiple discovery scenes and reversals. The basic elements of the comedy are inherited. The parasite, the tyrannical father, young, put-upon lovers, and scheming servants recall the cast in Roman comedies. Tartuffe, the unctuous *faux dévot*, resembles the seductive Vice in the medieval morality plays. The uncovering of a fraud in which a cozener preys on the weaknesses of sinners and the gullible has its basis in the medieval and farce traditions, as well as such previous comedies as Ben Jonson's *Volpone* and *The Alchemist*. Molière's originality rests in the psychological and social uses he makes of these elements, working out believable motivations for his characters while embodying in their often ludicrous behavior serious social themes.

been taken in by Tartuffe's cant and pose of fervent religiousness, and the rest of the household, including Elmire, Orgon's wife; Cléante, his brother-in-law; Orgon's daughter and son, Mariane and Damis; and Mariane's maid, Dorine. Orgon's household, a microcosm of society, has been perverted and inverted by Tartuffe, who has made himself "master in the house." Orgon (originally played by Molière) is blinded by Tartuffe's promises of spiritual salvation and neglects and violates the temporal demands of love and responsibility he rightfully owes to his wife and children and is unable to see what is so evident to the others, that Tartuffe is a hypocrite and selfish manipulator. The family's patriarch prefers the illusions Tartuffe supplies to reality, and the opening scenes make clear the consequences of Orgon's self-delusion. Dorine summarizes the perverse overthrow of proper relations that afflicts Orgon: "He dotes on him, embraces him, and could not have, I believe, more tenderness for a woman he loves." Cléante, Molière's voice of reason and moderation, tries to get his brother-in-law to see clearly:

> There's a vast difference, so it seems to me,
> Between true piety and hypocrisy:
> How do you fail to see it, may I ask?
> Is not a face quite different from a mask?
> Cannot sincerity and cunning art,
> Reality and semblance, be told apart?
> Are scarecrows just like men, and do you hold
> That a false coin is just as good as gold?
> Ah, Brother, man's a strangely fashioned creature
> Who seldom is content to follow Nature,
> But recklessly pursues his inclination
> Beyond the narrow bounds of moderation,
> And often, by transgressing Reason's laws,
> Perverts a lofty aim or noble cause.

Orgon has transgressed "Reason's laws" and perverted religious faith by succumbing to its shows rather than its substance, while immoderately overthrowing judgment in his selfish pursuit of personal salvation. He thereby becomes a petty tyrant in his home, willing to sacrifice all he is responsible for—wife, son, daughter, and property—to his desires, while casting out all who dissent as damned heretics. Orgon's violation of his parental responsibility is made clear when in Act 2 he breaks Mariane's engagement to Valére and orders her to marry Tartuffe, whom Mariane despises.

How is the play's conflict developed with the onstage arrival of Tartuffe?

Having established a dysfunctional family, the result of Tartuffe's deceptive manipulation, Molière finally brings the culprit onstage in Act 3 with one of the stage's greatest entrance lines. "Hang up my hair-shirt," Tartuffe instructs his manservant, "put my scourge in place." His orders are clearly to impress Dorine, whom he likewise orders to "cover that bosom, girl. The flesh is weak." The weaknesses of the flesh will become Tartuffe's undoing as he takes the stage at the height of his powers over Orgon and initiates his own downfall. Molière addressed the late arrival of Tartuffe by stating that "I have employed … two entire acts to prepare for the entrance of my scoundrel. He does not fool the audience for a single moment; one knows from the first the marks I have given him; and from one end to the other he says not a word and performs not an action which does not paint for the spectator the character of an evil man." The preparation establishes the play's delightful dramatic irony as the audience is in no doubt, despite Orgon's blindness, of what lies behind Tartuffe's every word, gesture, and action. Tartuffe's downfall will come, as it does in most of Molière's plays, from immoderation and succumbing to the illusions of power and control. So confident is Tartuffe in his power over Orgon that he risks exposure by attempting to seduce Elmire. His initial lustful attack, overheard by Damis, is reported to Orgon, and, when confronted, Tartuffe blatantly confesses the truth: "Yes, brother, I am an

The name Tartuffe—the fraud who tries to control the fortunes of a wealthy family—has entered the French lexicon as a synonym for a hypocrite who pretends to be virtuous.

evil, guilty, wretched sinner filled with iniquity, the greatest rascal ever." Tartuffe's confidence that he will not be believed is confirmed when Orgon instead disinherits his son and hands over his patrimony to his now-adopted son, Tartuffe. Elmire realizes that Orgon, impervious to argument, must see Tartuffe unmasked, and she stage-manages the play's comic triumph. With Orgon concealed under a table, Tartuffe renews his pursuit of Elmire, while revealing both his lusts and contempt for the morality he has espoused by urging her to ignore both "Heaven's wrath" and her scruples:

> No one shall know our joys, save us alone,
> And there's no evil till the act is known;
> It's scandal, Madam, which makes it an offense,
> And it's no sin to sin in confidence.

Tartuffe, however, finds himself in Orgon's, not Elmire's, arms, and his unmasking is finally complete.

How does Molière manage the play's climax?

Molière follows Orgon's discovery of Tartuffe's hypocrisy and the realization of his own gullibility, however, with a reversal. Orgon's breakthrough is too late. Tartuffe is now legally the master of all that Orgon owns and controls Orgon's destiny because he has been given a chest containing treasonable evidence against his patron. Villainy appears triumphant, and, although Orgon is reunited with his family and chastened into the correct obligations toward them, the disorder and inversion that the hypocrite Tartuffe has unleashed appear complete with the family's eviction. Again, it is Tartuffe's greed and overconfidence in his ability to control all and complete his *coup d'état*, which leads him to denounce Orgon as a traitor and thereby become known to the authorities as a wanted criminal. The king serves as the play's *deus ex machina,* able to see through Tartuffe's schemes, and orders his arrest. It is the king, the wise and sensible patriarch of the French nation, who restores order in Orgon's household (as he does in his kingdom) and allows Orgon to benefit by the sobering lesson of his errors and delusions. A marriage between the reunited lovers, Mariane and Valére, closes the comedy.

How best to assess the play's conclusion?

Although *Tartuffe* invites the complaint that its ending is overly contrived—that events so thoroughly motivated by the characters themselves are now imposed on them to produce the desired poetic justice (as well as flattery of a royal patron)—in a thematic sense, the play's ending is thoroughly satisfying. Orgon and the audience have been instructed in the difference between artifice and authenticity, appearance and reality, falsehood and truth. The hypocritical religious zealot has been unmasked both by his own excesses and a monarch who possesses the reasonableness and moderation so needed by his subjects to ensure that hypocrisy can be exposed. The king also has the good sense to allow Molière's comedy a hearing.

READING NEOCLASSICAL DRAMA–RACINE'S *PHÈDRE*

Why is *Phèdre* significant?

If Molière is master of French neoclassical comedy, Jean Racine (1639–1699) is France's preeminent neoclassical tragedian, and *Phèdre* is his essential masterpiece. It is both the culminating achievement of French neoclassical tragedy and the artistic justification for a set of stage conventions that often strikes modern audiences as overly narrow, severe, and artificial.

What are the basic conventions of neoclassical tragedy?

The rules and methods of neoclassical drama that Racine adhered to are the strict observance of the unities of time, place, and action. Incidents needed to be confined to twelve to twenty-four hours in a single location. Subplots and inessential characters and scenes are eliminated, and stage action must grow out of a central, believable dramatic situation. To reach the desired seriousness of purpose and elevation required for

289

tragedy, characters needed to be of noble rank, and their language reflected their breeding and status. Characters were denied physical contact, and any violence took place offstage. As highly stylized as the Japanese Noh play, neoclassical drama seems impossibly formal and restrictive, particularly from the perspective of Shakespeare's freedom of expression and expansiveness or compared to the graphic naturalism of modern dramatists, which spares its audience little. Racine in *Phèdre*, however, clearly shows how to make a virtue out of limitations, achieving an almost unbearable intensity and psychological penetration within the prescribed neoclassical rules that sacrificed breadth for depth and stirring action for inner conflict.

Jean Racine was the master of seventeenth-century French tragedy.

How did Racine handle the constrictions of neoclassicism?

Despite abiding by the neoclassical stage conventions, Racine's dramas are marked by a radical assault on other standards of his day, particularly its melioristic humanism, and a rejection of a popular preference for tragicomedy with its happy ending and assumed providential will in which the good are rewarded and the evil are punished. Racine returned drama to the bleak and severe tragic vision of Euripides and an examination of the often crippling paradoxes of human nature, unsupported by sustaining illusions of a benign divine order or faith in an unconquerable human will. His plays explored the darkly sinister workings of human passions and compulsions that are as irresistible as they are destructive. As a theatrical craftsman, Racine was the master of dramatic intensity achieved through an economy of means. With stirring action restricted offstage, Racine concentrated interest within the characters themselves, providing an unprecedented interior view of motive and temperament. By doing so, Racine pointed theater toward the modern conception of drama as inner conflict. If Molière radically altered the history of dramatic comedy, Racine accomplished the same transformation of tragedy, joining the classical and the modern into a powerful dramatic synthesis.

How does Racine's biography inform his works?

Racine was born in 1639 into a lower-middle-class family in a small, provincial town northeast of Paris. Orphaned at age four, he was raised by his grandmother and sent in 1649 to be educated in the religious community of Port-Royal, the center of Jansenism, the austere Catholic sect akin to Calvinism that emphasized predestination and man's essentially corrupt nature. Theater was an anathema to the Jansenists, and the conflict between their spiritual teachings and more temporal, secular attractions would dominate Racine's temperament throughout his life. Racine remained at Port-Royal until he was seventeen, acquiring a solid education, particularly in classical literature, which equipped him well to pursue a literary career. As a university student, he achieved some notoriety for his poetry, and, after two years of training for the priesthood, Racine began his drama career in Paris. He was befriended by Molière, whose company performed Racine's first play, *La Thebaide* (*The Theban Brothers*), in 1664. It failed with audiences, but Molière persisted on behalf of the younger playwright, producing a lavish and successful production of Racine's second play, *Alexandre le Grande,* in 1665. During the play's initial run, Racine offended his mentor by unethically offering it to a rival company. A final break with Molière followed when Racine persuaded his mistress, one of Molière's leading actresses, to join a rival company. The two playwrights never spoke again. Despite his theatrical rivalries, quarrels with the Jansenists, and serial affairs with actresses, Racine subsequently produced the seven plays that established his reputation as the master of French classical tragedy: *Andromache* (1667), *Brittanicus* (1668), *Berenice* (1670), *Bajazet* (1672), *Mithridates* (1673), *Iphigenia* (1674), and *Phèdre* (1677). With stories borrowed from classical and biblical sources, Racine's plays take for their themes the potentially damning effect of human passion in which love often resembles hatred in its intensity and tendency toward self-destruction. After the production of *Phèdre*, Racine experienced a religious conversion that led him to abandon the theater and to reconcile with the Jansenists. In a famous quip, it was said that after his conversion, "Racine loved God as he loved his mistresses." He obtained the position of royal historiographer and spent his last twenty-two years chronicling the activities of the king and his court. He wrote two religious plays, *Esther* (1689) and *Athalie* (1691), before falling from the king's favor in 1698, a year before he died.

What is the origin and significance of *Phèdre*?

Phèdre is, therefore, Racine's final secular drama, and, in his own estimation, "probably the clearest and most closely-knit play I have written." Based on Euripides' *Hippolytus* (428 B.C.E.), *Phèdre* follows, in Racine's words, "a slightly different route from that author as regards the plot." Euripides dramatized the revenge of Aphrodite, goddess of love, on Hippolytus, Theseus's son and Phaedra's stepson, for preferring Artemis, goddess of chastity. The goddess causes Phaedra to fall in love with him. Hippolytus rejects her advances, and Phaedra hangs herself in despair after denouncing him as her seducer. Theseus banishes Hippolytus, who is killed fighting a bull sent from the sea to punish him. Artemis reveals the truth to Theseus, and father and son are reconciled before Hippolytus's death. As Racine's title change indicates, *Phèdre* shifts the emphasis from the chaste Hippolytus to his stepmother's monstrous passion. If Euripides dramatizes what happens when love is resisted, Racine looks at a love that is irresistible and self-destructive. In one of the stage's greatest female roles, Phèdre is devoured by an uncontrollable passion that overmasters her reason and consumes her with guilt, jealousy, and self-loathing. In Racine's version, the gods, who play an active role in controlling human fate in Euripides' play, are no longer central as the drama shifts from the clash between gods and men to the inner conflict within the human psyche, between reason and the irrational, desire and conscience. Good and evil are not opposed in Racine's drama by representative characters but are shown battling within Phèdre herself.

How does Act 1 establish the play's conflict?

As the play opens, the austere and chaste Hippolytus of Euripides' play becomes, in Racine's handling, a young, guilt-ridden lover who confesses his passion for Aricie, the daughter of his father's enemy, who has been condemned to celibacy. Racine's Hippolyte is, therefore, shown confronting a similar conflict between desire and duty that afflicts Phèdre. The power of the play is derived from the skill Racine displays in offering variations of the same theme—the potentially destructive power of passion to overbalance reason, duty, and responsibility. The most damning example is Phèdre. Unable to resist her shameful passion, Phèdre is tormented to illness and tempted by suicide. Her nurse and confidant Oenone described Phèdre as "dying from a hidden malady" in which "eternal discord reigns within her mind." Phèdre confesses to Oenone that the source of her suicidal anguish is her helpless and hateful passion for her stepson, her "adored enemy":

I have a fitting horror for my crime;

Phèdre is a character from Greek mythology whose story is retold in the Racine tragedy (1880 painting *Phaedra* by Alexandre Cabanel).

292

I hate this passion and I loathe my life
Dying, I could have kept my name unstained,
And my dark passion from the light of day....

Phèdre reveals herself as both wracked by guilt and heroic in her resistance to what she knows to be immoral yet overpowering. She refuses to mitigate or justify her passion and is her own defendant and prosecutioner. However, news arrives that Thésée has died, leaving open the possibility that Phèdre might overcome the illicitness of her passion and her desire as Oenone asserts that it is now no longer shameful for her mistress to love Hippolyte. It is the first in a series of temptations that Phèdre cannot resist.

How do Acts 2 and 3 complicate the conflict?

The second act opens with a third confession: of Aricie's love for Hippolyte. Yet another character is struggling to control passion. Significantly for Phèdre, Aricie will become a rival for Hippolyte's love, thereby adding jealousy to the mix of lust and guilt that torments Phèdre. In the act's impressive fifth scene, Phèdre finally confronts Hippolyte. In a brilliant psychological study of tentative probing and disguised wooing, Phèdre expresses her love for the son by recalling her love of the father. Describing Thésée's arrival in her native Crete when he mastered the labyrinth and slayed the Minotaur, Phèdre states:

He had your eyes, your bearing, and your speech.
His face flushed with your noble modesty....
Why could you not, too young, alas, have fared
Forth with the ship that brought him to our shores?
You would have slain the monstrous Cretan bull
Despite the windings of his endless lair....
I, only I, would have revealed to you
The subtle windings of the labyrinth.
What care I would have lavished on your head!
A thread would not have reassured my fears.
Affronting danger side by side with you,
I would myself have wished to lead the way,
And Phèdre, with you in the labyrinth,
Would have returned with you or met her doom.

To this Hippolyte sensibly asked if Phèdre has forgotten that Thésée is his father and her husband. He is embarrassed and disgusted by what Phèdre's words imply. Her response conveys her failed struggle to master her shameful passion, and Phèdre begs Hippolyte to punish her with his sword in language that is simultaneously masochistic, sexual, and coaxing:

Take vengeance. Punish me for loving you.
Come, prove yourself your father's worthy son,
And of a vicious monster rid the world.
I, Thésée's widow, dare to love his son!

This frightful monster must not now escape.
Here is my heart. Here must your blow strike home.
Impatient to atone for its offence,
I feel it strain to meet your mighty arm.
Strike. Or if it's unworthy of your blows,
Or such a death too mild for my deserts,
Or if you deem my blood too vile to stain
Your hand, lend me, if not your arm, your sword.
Give me it!

Rescued by Oenone before she can take her own life, Phèdre in the third act is alternately humiliated by Hippolyte's rejection and sustained by hope that he will relent. Thésée's return, the reversal that sets in motion the play's climax, presents Phèdre with the choice of revealing or concealing her love for Hippolyte. Yet again she is tempted to do the wrong thing, and the frightened Phèdre accedes to Oenone's plan to deceive Thésée by accusing Hippolyte of attempting to dishonor his stepmother.

How is the conflict resolved in Act 4?

In Act 4, Thésée confronts his son with Oenone's charges, refuses to believe his claim of innocence based on Hippolyte's avowed love for Aricie, and banishes him, invoking the vengeance of Neptune upon his son. Phèdre, on the brink of confessing all to Thésée and saving Hippolyte, is stunned into silence and murderous jealousy by the revelation of Hippolyte's love for Aricie. The news of Hippolyte's death, from an encounter with the sea monster Neptune has sent in response to Thésée's appeal, reaches the palace. Phèdre, having taken poison, dies onstage, in a singular violation of neoclassical conventions, after the play's ultimate confession of her guilt to Thésée. Every attempt Phèdre has made to overcome her passion has failed, leaving only death to resolve her conflict. Racine comments in the play's preface that Phèdre "is neither entirely guilty nor altogether innocent. She is involved by her destiny, and by the anger of the gods, in an unlawful passion at which she is the very first to be horrified. She prefers to let herself die rather than declare it to anyone. And, when she is forced to disclose it, she speaks with such embarrassment that it is clear that her crime is a punishment of the gods rather than an urge flowing from her own will." Racine's mitigation of Phèdre as tragic victim is curiously not a consolation that she seizes on herself. Racine's cosmology more closely resembles the fatalistic worldview of the Jansenists than the Greeks in which sin is the rule, not the exception. What makes *Phèdre* so powerful and so modern is its refusal to locate the source of its conflicts outside the range of human nature itself. If Molière offered in compensation for destroyed illusions a sustaining moderation and common sense, Racine indicts these as well, as hopeless against human desires. Phèdre's losing battle to control and master her passion is both heroic in her resistance and inevitable in Racine's dark vision of human limitations.

SEVENTEENTH–CENTURY THEATER CONTINUED

How did theatrical practices change in the seventeenth century?

The stage innovations of Restoration Comedy, the Spanish *comedia nueva,* and French neoclassical drama all grew out of and reflected important changes in theatrical practices that have defined the Western theater ever since.

An increasing realism in acting styles and stage effects was a direct result of taking drama indoors to smaller, purpose-built theaters. After moving outside in the Middle Ages through the Renaissance, plays had been performed in improvised, makeshift indoor spaces in courts and halls, such as the Inns of Court in Elizabethan London. During the Renaissance, the first modern, enclosed theaters were constructed in Italy, initially replicating ancient theaters with a viewing area surrounding a skene-like structure representing a city street. At the beginning of the seventeenth century, theater design began to resemble the conventions that remain today's standard: a raised stage separated from the audience by a proscenium arch, revealing increasingly elaborate and lifelike stage design. Scenery as we know it today derives from the discovery of the rules of perspective in the Italian Renaissance that were adapted for theatrical performance. The stage is raised to eye level of the so-called "duke or king's seat," with its perfect view of the scenery of painted backdrops giving the illusion of depth. Perspective scenery was first introduced to the English court theater of James I in the beginning of the seventeenth century by Inigo Jones (1573–1652), England's first major scene designer. Realistic stage illusion would be further enhanced by sets that could replicate a drawing room or other realistically detailed interior space, perfect for productions of Restoration and Neoclassical comedies of manners.

Moving the theater indoors required artificial lighting, and the evolution of stage lighting would be provided first by candles mounted on chandeliers over the stage and the auditorium, then by oil lamps, introduced in the 1780s, also mounted on chandeliers. Gas lighting was introduced at the Chestnut Theatre in Philadelphia in 1816 and at London's Drury Lane and Covent Garden theaters a year later. Mounting positions included footlights across the border of the stage and in wing lights between each pair of scenic wings. Developed in the 1820s, limelight (a term now synonymous with the theater) offered a new type of arti-

English architect Inigo Jones was also important for his stage design work, which he often did for playwright Ben Jonson.

ficial illumination as a gas flame was used to ignite a cylinder of quicklime (calcium oxide). Reflectors and lenses could direct its incandescence. London's Savoy Theatre, the home of D'Oyly Carte company's productions of Gilbert and Sullivan operettas, introduced the first electric lighting system in 1881. By the end of the century, most theaters had switched from gas to the safer electric lights. In 1903, the Kliegl Brothers installed their electric lighting system of multiple dimmers in the Metropolitan Opera House in New York City. In the 1920s, an incandescent spotlight was introduced. All these innovations could be used to enhance the illusion of onstage reality, suited for the developing naturalism and psychological realism of modern drama. The term coined by Samuel Taylor Coleridge in 1817, the "willing suspension of disbelief," could be assisted onstage, as the so-called conceptual fourth wall, a term used by Molière to mean separating a performance from the audience, is removed to create modern realistic theater.

What was the state of drama before drama's third great flowering in the modern period?

Despite the considerable innovation and vitality of European drama from the late sixteenth through the seventeenth centuries, what theater followed in the eighteenth and nineteenth centuries is more derivative than groundbreaking. Important plays were written and performed, such as John Gay's *Beggar's Opera* (1728), Carlo Goldoni's *The Servant of Two Masters* (1745), Oliver Goldsmith's *She Stoops to Conquer* (1773), Richard Sheridan's *School for Scandal* (1777), Friedrich Schiller's *The Robbers* (1782), Beaumarchais's *The Marriage of Figaro* (1784), and Nikolai Gogol's *The Inspector General* (1836), but drama's preeminence as a literary form for presenting the crucial ideas and concerns of its time had clearly passed to poetry and the emerging novel.

In the Romantic period (between the 1770s and 1830s), poetry best expressed the cultural moment and its core concerns with, in Wordsworth's definition of a new, vital poetry, the "spontaneous overflow of powerful emotions." None of the major English Romantics—Blake, Wordsworth, Coleridge, Byron, Shelley, and Keats—turned to the stage to express themselves and their age's concerns. The highest literary aspirations were in poetry—in lyrics, epics, or verse tragedies (not meant for the stage)—not in the commercial theater.

The new, upstart literary form, the novel, emerging in England and France in the eighteenth century, would become the unrivaled popular form to reflect everyday life and the recognizable experiences of readers. Henry Fielding, for example, would abandon his successful career as a dramatist in 1737, after legislation restricted the number of legitimate theaters in London, and turn to the novel, which he declared was "the comic epic in prose." The novel's evolving, unique, flexible, dual focus—outward to encompass the widest-possible social range and inward to explore private consciousness and emotions—exposed the limitations of drama to do the same. In the hands of great English practitioners, such as Jane Austen, Charles Dickens, William Thackeray, Charlotte and Emily Brontë, Anthony Trollope, and George Eliot, the novel would shed its reputation as a debased popular literary form, incapable of the seriousness of poetry and tragedy, to become the age's source for a critique of human nature and human experience. Meanwhile, drama declined to serve as a conventional vehicle for entertainment alone for it was spectacle and sentiment in the preferred melodramas that dominated the stage.

Surprisingly, as a moribund European theater in the late nineteenth century served up either revivals of accepted classics or light and forgettable new works, the cultural moment shifted once again to produce a third great flowering of Western drama.

What are the chief characteristics of modern drama?

It can be argued that the exact moment when modern drama began, when drama reasserted its preeminence as the literary form to communicate an age's most crucial and vexing questions, was December 4, 1879, with the publication of Henrik Ibsen's *A Doll's House*, or perhaps it was at the explosive climax of the first performance in Copenhagen on December 21, 1879, when Nora Helmer slammed the door behind her as she shockingly leaves her comfortable home, respectable marriage, husband, and children for an uncertain future of self-discovery. Nora's shattering exit ushered in a new dramatic era, legitimizing the exploration of serious social and psychological concerns for the modern theater. As Ibsen's biographer Michael Meyer has observed, "No play had ever before contributed so momentously to the social debate, or been so widely and furiously discussed among people who were not normally interested in theatrical or even artistic matter." A contemporary reviewer of the play declared, "When Nora slammed the door shut on her marriage, walls shook in a thousand homes."

Ibsen (1828–1906) set in motion a transformation of drama as distinctive in the history of the theater as the one that occurred in fifth century B.C.E. Athens or Elizabethan London. Like the great Athenian dramatists and Shakespeare, Ibsen fundamentally redefined drama and set a standard that later playwrights have had to absorb or challenge. The stage that he inherited had largely ceased to function as a serious medium for the deepest consideration of human themes and values. After Ibsen, drama was restored as an important truth-telling vehicle for a comprehensive criticism of life. *A Doll's House* anatomized onstage for the first time the social, psychological, emotional, and moral truths beneath the placid surface of a conventional, respectable marriage while creating a new, psychologically complex modern heroine who still manages to shock and unsettle audiences more than a century later.

READING MODERN DRAMA–
IBSEN'S *A DOLL'S HOUSE*

How does an understanding of Ibsen's life and temperament help to explain his drama?

The momentum that propelled Ibsen's daring artistic and social revolt was sustained principally by his outsider status as an exile both at home and abroad. His last deathbed word was "Tvertimod!" ("On the contrary!"), a fitting epitaph and description of his artistic and intellectual mindset. Born in Skien, Norway, a logging town southwest of Oslo, Ibsen endured a lonely and impoverished childhood, particularly after the bankruptcy of his businessman father when Ibsen was eight. At fifteen, he was sent to Grimstad as an apothecary's apprentice, where he lived for six years in an attic room on meager pay, sustained by reading romantic poetry, sagas, and folk ballads. He later recalled feeling "on a war footing with the little community where I felt I was being suppressed by my situation and by circumstances in general." His first play was *Cataline*, a historical drama featuring a revolutionary hero who reflects Ibsen's own alienation. "*Cataline* was written," the playwright later recalled, "in a little provincial town, where it was impossible for me to give expression to all that fermented in me except by mad, riotous pranks, which brought down upon me the ill will of all the respectable citizens who could not enter into that world which I was wrestling with alone."

Largely self-educated, Ibsen failed the university entrance examination to pursue medical training and instead pursued a career in the theater. In 1851, he began a thirteen-year stage apprenticeship in Bergen and Oslo, doing everything from sweeping the stage to directing, stage managing, and writing mostly verse dramas based on Norwegian legends and historical subjects. The experience gave him a solid knowledge of the stage conventions of the day, particularly of the so-called "well-made play" of the popular French playwright Augustin Eugène Scribe and his many imitators, with its emphasis on a complicated, artificial plot based on secrets, suspense, and surprises. Ibsen would transform the conventions of the "well-made play" into the modern problem play, exploring controversial social and human questions that had never before been dramatized. Although his stage experience in Norway was marked chiefly by failure, Ibsen's apprenticeship was a crucial testing ground for perfecting his craft and providing him

What dramas by Ibsen preceded *A Doll's House*?

In 1864, Ibsen began a self-imposed exile from Norway that would last for twenty-seven years. He traveled first to Italy, where he was joined by his wife Susannah, whom he had married in 1858, and his son. The family divided its time between Italy and Germany. The experience was liberating for Ibsen; he felt that he had "escaped from darkness into light," releasing the productive energy with which he composed the succession of plays that brought him worldwide fame. His first important works, *Brand* (1866) and *Peer Gynt* (1867), were poetic dramas, very much in the Romantic mode of the individual's conflict with experience and the gap between heroic assertion and accomplishment, between sobering reality and blind idealism. *Pillars of Society* (1877) shows him experimenting with ways of introducing these central themes into a play reflecting modern life, the first in a series of realistic dramas that redefined the conventions and subjects of the modern theater.

with the skills to mount the assault on theatrical conventions and moral complacency in his mature work.

How did *A Doll's House* originate?

The first inklings of his next play, *A Doll's House,* are glimpsed in Ibsen's journal ideas headed "Notes for a Modern Tragedy":

> There are two kinds of moral laws, two kinds of conscience, one for men and one, quite different, for women. They don't understand each other; but in practical life, woman is judged by masculine law, as though she weren't a woman but a man.

> The wife in the play ends by having no idea what is right and what is wrong; natural feelings on the one hand and belief in authority on the other lead her to utter distraction....

> Moral conflict. Weighed down and confused by her trust in authority, she loses faith in her own morality, and in her fitness to bring up her children. Bitterness. A mother in modern society, like certain insects, retires and dies once she has done her duty by propagating the race. Love of life, of home, of husband and children and family. Now and then, as women do, she shrugs off her thoughts. Suddenly anguish and fear return. Everything must be borne alone. The catastrophe approaches, mercilessly, inevitably. Despair, conflict, and defeat.

How is *A Doll's House* structured?

To tell his modern tragedy based on gender relations, Ibsen takes his audience on an unprecedented, intimate tour of a contemporary, respectable marriage. Set during the Christmas holidays, *A Doll's House* begins with Nora Helmer completing the finishing touches on the family's celebrations. Her husband, Torvald, has recently been named a bank manager, promising an end to the family's former straightened financial circumstances, and Nora is determined to celebrate the holiday with her husband and three children in style. Despite Torvald's disapproval of her indulgences, he relents, giving her the money she desires, softened by Nora's childish play-acting that gratifies his sense of what is expected of his "lark" and "squirrel." Beneath the surface of this apparently charming domestic scene is a

A Doll's House is a very modern work in its feminist sensibilities. The heroine, Nora, is shown as a much more moral character than her shallow husband, Torvald (title page from the original manuscript).

potentially damning and destructive secret. Seven years before, Nora had saved the life of her critically ill husband by secretly borrowing the money needed for a rest cure in Italy. Knowing that Torvald would be too proud to borrow money himself, Nora forged her dying father's name on the loan she received from Krogstad, a banking associate of Torvald.

What is the crisis in *A Doll's House,* and what does it reveal?

The crisis comes when Nora's old school friend Christina Linde arrives in need of a job. At Nora's urging, Torvald aids her friend by giving her Krogstad's position at the bank. Learning that he is to be dismissed, Krogstad threatens to expose Nora's forgery unless she can persuade Torvald to reinstate him. Nora fails to convince Torvald to relent, and, after receiving his dismissal notice, Krogstad sends Torvald a letter disclosing the details of the forgery. The incriminating letter remains in the Helmers' mailbox like a ticking time bomb as Nora tries to distract Torvald from reading it and Christina attempts to convince Krogstad to withdraw his accusation. Torvald eventually reads the letter following the couple's return from a Christmas ball and explodes in recriminations against his wife, calling her a liar and a criminal, unfit to be his wife and his children's mother. "Now you've wrecked all my happiness—ruined my whole future," Torvald insists. "Oh, it's awful to think of. I'm in a cheap little grafter's hands; he can do anything he wants with me, ask me for anything, play with me like a puppet—and I can't breathe a word. I'll be swept down miserably into the depths on account of a featherbrained woman." Torvald's reaction reveals that his formerly expressed high moral rectitude is hypocritical and self-serving. He shows himself worried more about appearances than true morality, caring principally about *his* reputation than his wife. However, when Krogstad's second letter arrives in which he announces his intention of pursuing the matter no further, Torvald joyfully informs Nora that he is "saved" and that Nora should forget all that he has said, assuming that the normal relationship with his "frightened little songbird" can be resumed. Nora, however, shocks Torvald with her reaction.

How is the play's conflict resolved?

Nora, profoundly disillusioned by Torvald's response to Krogstad's letter, which is bereft of the sympathy and heroic self-sacrifice she had hoped would come, orders him to sit down for a serious talk, the first in their married life, in which she reviews their relationship. "I've been your doll-wife here, just as at home I was Papa's doll-child," Nora explains. "And in turn the children have been my dolls. I thought it was fun when you played with me, just as they thought it fun when I played with them. That's been our marriage, Torvald." Nora has acted out the nineteenth-century ideal of the submissive, unthinking, dutiful daughter and wife, and it has taken Torvald's reaction to shatter the illusion and to force an illumination. "When the big fright was over," Nora explains, "—and it wasn't from any threat against me, only for what might damage you—when all the danger was past, for you it was just as if nothing had happened. I was exactly the same, your little lark, your doll, that you'd have to handle with double care now that I'd turned out so brittle and frail. Torvald—in that instant it dawned on me that I've been living here with a stranger...." Nora tells Torvald that she no longer loves him because he is not the man she thought he was, that he was incapable of heroic action on her behalf. When Torvald insists that "no man would sacrifice his honor for love," Nora replies, "Millions of women have done just that."

Nora finally resists the claims Torvald mounts in response, that she must honor her duties as a wife and mother, stating that "I don't believe in that anymore. I believe that, before all else, I'm a human being, no less than you—or anyway, I ought to try to become one. I know the majority thinks you're right, Torvald, and plenty of books agree with you, too. But I can't go on believing what the majority says, or what's written in books. I have to think over these things myself and try to understand them." The finality of Nora's decision to forgo her assigned role as wife and mother for the authenticity of selfhood is marked by the sound of the door slamming and her exit into the wider world, leaving Torvald to survey the wreckage of their marriage.

What is the impact of the play on its audience and its legacy?

Ibsen leaves his audience and readers to consider sobering truths: that married women are the decorative playthings and servants of their husbands, who require their submissiveness, that a man's authority in the home should not go unchallenged, and that the prime duty of anyone is to arrive at an authentic human identity, not to accept the role determined by social conventions. That Nora would be willing to sacrifice everything, even her children, to become her own person proved to be, and remains, the controversial shock of *A Doll's House,* provoking continued debate over Nora's motivations and justifications. The first edition of 8,000 copies of the play quickly sold out, and the play was so heatedly debated in Scandanavia in 1879 that, as critic Frances Lord observes, "Many a social invitation in Stockholm during that winter bore the words, 'You are requested not to mention Ibsen's *Doll's House!*'" Ibsen was obliged to supply an alternative ending for the first German production when the famous leading lady Hedwig Niemann-Raabe refused to perform the role of Nora, stating that "I would never leave *my children!*" Ibsen provided what he would call a "barbaric outrage," an ending in which Nora's departure is halted at the doorway of her children's bedroom. The play served as a catalyst for an ongoing debate over feminism and women's rights. In 1898 Ibsen was honored by the Norwegian Society for Women's Rights and toasted as the "creator of Nora." Always the contrarian, Ibsen rejected the notion that *A Doll's House* champions the cause of women's rights:

> I have been more of a poet and less of a social philosopher than people generally tend to suppose. I thank you for your toast, but must disclaim the honor of having consciously worked for women's rights. I am not even quite sure what women's rights really are. To me it has been a question of human rights. And if you read my books carefully you will realize that. Of course it is incidentally desirable to solve the problem of women; but that has not been my whole object. My task has been the portrayal of human beings.

Despite Ibsen's disclaimer that *A Doll's House* should be appreciated as more than a piece of gender propaganda, that it deals with universal truths of human identity, it is nevertheless the case that his drama is one of the milestones of the sexual revolution, sounding themes and advancing the cause of women's autonomy and liberation that echoes Mary Wollstonecraft's *A Vindication of the Rights of Woman* and anticipates subsequent works as Virginia Woolf's *A Room of One's Own* and Betty Friedan's *The Feminine Mystique*. The impact of Nora's slamming the door of her doll's house is still being felt more than a century later.

Why is Ibsen considered the founding figure of modern drama?

In central ways, Ibsen stands behind the restoration of drama as a vital literary genre for a consideration of the most im-

Norwegian playwright Henrik Ibsen has been called "the father of realism."

portant human questions. Largely moribund as a serious art form through much of the nineteenth century, drama was little more than light entertainment or pleasing diversion and idealization in the melodramas and spectacles that dominated the stage that Ibsen inherited and transformed.

Ibsen's remarkable series of plays include *Ghosts* (1881), *The Wild Duck* (1884), *An Enemy of the People* (1886), *Rosmersholm* (1886), *The Lady from the Sea* (1888), and *Hedda Gabler* (1890). In them Ibsen replaced an idealistic vision with a realistic method in which the spectator is made to feel, as he explains, "as if he were actually sitting, listening, and looking at events happening in real life." His plays reworked the staid and artificial conventions of the stage to focus on ordinary individuals whose dramas were based on the details and circumstances of recognizable middle-class life in contemporary society. Ibsen would help to initiate a third golden age of the drama, rivaling the dominance of drama in Attic Greece in the fifth century B.C.E. and during the Elizabethan period. After Ibsen, life's most important questions would be dramatized by the playwrights whom he influenced: August Strindberg, George Bernard Shaw, Eugene O'Neill, Arthur Miller, Tennessee Williams, and others who contributed to the tradition of contemporary drama.

READING MODERN DRAMA— CHEKHOV'S *THE CHERRY ORCHARD*

How did Anton Chekhov continue the revolution in the modern drama?

If Ibsen established a dominant trait of modern drama with its heightened social and psychological realism that peeked into ordinary lives, his cofounder of modern drama is unquestionably Anton Chekhov. If Ibsen liberated drama's subject matter and restored the play as a serious criticism of life, then Chekhov supplied the theater with a radical new method and dramatic form that altered all the available conventions of production, which had needed a new theory of acting and a radical reconceptualization. No less a literary titan than Leo Tolstoy, who often disparaged Chekhov's plays in which "nothing happened," regarded him as his chief artistic rival. Chekhov, Tolstoy declared, "is an incomparable artist" who "created new forms of writing, completely new, in my opinion, to the entire world, the likes of which I have encountered nowhere." Of his drama, Tolstoy predicted that "in the future, perhaps a hundred years hence, people will be amazed at what they find in Chekhov about the inner workings of the human soul." Chekhov himself, with characteristic modesty, diminished his achievement, except as an innovator. "Everything I have written," he remarked, "will be forgotten in five or ten years; but the paths I have cut out will be safe and sound—my only service lies in this."

No other dramatist in as few major works has asserted a comparable influence on the development of theater than has Chekhov. As expressed in *The Seagull, The Cherry Orchard, The Three Sisters,* and *Uncle Vanya*, Chekhov's art features an essential humane truthfulness based on the compelling drama of the unexceptional. "A play should be written," he argued, "in which people arrive, go away, have dinner, talk about the weather, and play cards. Life must be exactly as it is, and people as they are—not on stilts…. Let everything on the stage be just as complicated, and at the same time just as simple as it is in life." Chekhov pioneered a new conception of drama, reflecting not the extraordinary but the commonplace and unexceptional. Traditional dramatic conflict between characters is replaced by inner conflict within characters. Meaning is generated beyond stage action by counterpoint and juxtaposition of ideas and images, a dramatic method perfectly suited to the rich interplay of text, subtle stagecraft, and the psychological penetration pioneered by Konstantin Stanislavky and the Moscow Art Theater, which first produced Chekhov's works.

How does an understanding of Chekhov's biography provide a context for understanding his drama?

Remarkably, Chekhov fundamentally shaped two literary genres: modern drama and the modern short story, and he is commonly viewed as a fiction writer who turned to drama only in his final years. It is far more accurate to consider him a lifelong dramatist who resorted to fiction by necessity to earn a living while the contemporary Russian theater caught up with his dramatic vision.

Chekhov was born in 1860 in Taganrog on the Black Sea. His father was a former serf who rose to become a grocer but whose artistic interests as a choirmaster, violinist, and occasional painter took precedence over more practical considerations. Chekhov's interest in the theater was sparked by trips to the Taganrog Theatre and in-home reenactments of such plays as Gogol's *The Inspector General*. When Chekhov was sixteen, his father became bankrupt and relocated his family to a Moscow slum to avoid his creditors. Chekhov remained behind to finish his education at the local gymnasium, supporting himself by tutoring younger students. When he was nineteen, Chekhov joined his family in Moscow and assumed their financial support while enrolled in the medical program at Moscow University. He paid for his education and his family's upkeep by writing comic sketches and short stories for humorous magazines. When he became a doctor in 1884, he continued writing stories and one-act satirical farces based on many of them while juggling a medical career ("my lawful spouse") and his writing ("my mistress").

By 1898, when Chekhov achieved his first great success with the Moscow Art Theater's landmark production of *The Seagull*, the tuberculosis that Chekhov had contracted during his student days had advanced beyond a cure. Chekhov settled in Yalta after suffering a pulmonary hemorrhage and did not see his plays staged by the Moscow Art Theater until their Crimean tour in 1900. At a rehearsal, however, he had met the actress Olga Knipper, who played Arkadina in *The Seagull*, and they were married in May 1901. Chekhov would draw on personal experiences, particularly his dispossession from Taganrog because of his father's bankruptcy to write his masterpiece, *The Cherry Orchard*.

What is *The Cherry Orchard*: comedy or tragedy?

The Cherry Orchard was conceived and composed during the final stage of the illness that would take his life in 1904, yet Chekhov was adamant that what turned out to be his final work should be a comedy. Following the success of *Three Sisters* in 1901, Chekhov wrote to his wife, "I keep dreaming of writing a comic play, in which all hell will break loose. I don't know whether anything will come of it." He began work on the play in 1902 and completed it in September 1903. "It has turned out not a drama," Chekhov asserted, "but a comedy, in places even a farce." Konstantin Stanislavsky, who would produce and direct the play for the Moscow Art Theater, disagreed: "It isn't a comedy or a farce, as you claim—it's a tragedy." The dispute between playwright and director over *The Cherry Orchard*'s tone and intention that began with its first production has persisted in performances ever since. *The Cherry Orchard* is a play of such intriguing complexity and multiple (and at times contradictory) modes and methods that it can support either interpretation, while it ultimately is neither one nor the other—neither simply comedy nor tragedy—but something new altogether. In its challenge to the established dramatic genres, *The Cherry Orchard* helped establish the tragicomic as the dominant modern dramatic mode, while its linkage of surface realism and the symbolic anticipated the techniques of the great literary modernists of the twentieth century, such as James Joyce and T. S. Eliot.

How is *The Cherry Orchard* structured?

The Cherry Orchard begins with an arrival: widow Lyubov Andreevna Ranevskaya returns to her heavily mortgaged Russian estate from Paris, where she has gone to forget the drowning death of her son five years before. Like *Three Sisters*, in which the usual

This photo is of a 1903 Moscow Art Theater production of Ibsen's *The Cherry Orchard,* one year before the author's death. The play presciently reflects upon the socio-economic changes in Russia that would later come to a head with the 1917 revolution.

dramatic action is excluded, waiting establishes the central dramatic tension, as Samuel Beckett would later exploit in *Waiting for Godot.* Dominating the action is the suspended question what will become of the estate, with its renowned cherry orchard, which must be sold unless the family recovers its fortune. Chekhov gathers a large cast together to react collectively to the threat to the family while revealing its causes. They include Madame Ranevskaya's indolent brother Leonid Andreyevitch Gaev, her daughter Anya and adopted daughter Varya, her son's former tutor Trofimov, fellow landowner Pischchik, the bookkeeper Yephikhov, and a former serf, now successful businessman, Lopakhin. Included as well is a full complement of servants—Charlotta, the governess, Yasha, the valet, Dunyasha, the maid, and Fiers, the ancient footman. Act 1 of the play, subtitled "A Comedy in Four Acts," appropriately is set in the nursery, where the family can evade the present crisis by summoning up and recalling the past. As the Russian critic A. R. Kugel has observed, "All the inhabitants of *The Cherry Orchard* are children and their behavior is childish." To avoid the estate being auctioned, Lopakhin offers the practical solution that the cherry orchard should be cut down and the land divided into building lots for summer holiday makers. This suggestion, which would pay off the family's debts and secure their future, is greeted with shock and incredulity. "If there's anything of interest in the entire district," Lyubov asserts, "even outstanding, it's none other than our cherry orchard." For Gaev, reference to the orchard in the *Encyclopedia* puts an end to such a suggestion. Both brother and sister reveal themselves as incapable of decisive action or adult responsibility. Lyubov is a generous but impractical sentimentalist; Gaev is more focused on his mental games of billiards, his fruit candies, and hosting a jubilee celebration for an old bookcase. His ideas to rescue the situation—Anya's marriage to a rich man, Varya's marriage to Lopakhin, a gift from their rich great-aunt—are, in his words, "several remedies, very many, and that really means I've none at all." The often ridiculous, self-deluded behavior of all sets the play's mixed tonality in which the absurd collides with the portentous.

How does the play's conflict develop in Act 1?

The threat to the cherry orchard begins to accumulate symbolic significance, expressing the demise of an era in which the Russian landed gentry and their entire leisured way of life are about to be destroyed by the practicalities of a new materialistic order. Characteristically, Chekhov balances the accounts on both sides of the equation: Lyubov and Gaev cherish the past and appreciate the beauty of the cherry orchard but are incapable of maintaining it; Lopakhin is so consumed by the practical that the orchard and house are nothing more than commodities. Lyubov and Gaev exist in the past; Lopakhin for the future, and the present is squandered in the often inconsequential and absurd behavior of all.

What happens in Act 2?

Act 2 shifts the scene outside near the orchard at sunset as each of the characters reacts to the impending sale, which begins to push them to a deeper understanding of themselves and their circumstances. Each member of the household is allowed a sympathetic moment. By revealing their suffering, loneliness, and isolation, Chekhov complicates and deepens his presentation of characters who are far too foolish to be taken as wholly tragic but far too sensitive and recognizable in their suffering to be only laughed at. The breakup of the estate begins, putting into perspective the characters' past, their natures, and a new set of future challenges. For Fiers, the coming auction means that the old order is passing. In the *ancien régime* he says, "The peasants stood by the masters, the masters stood by the peasants, but now everything is all smashed up, you can't tell about anything." This tone of melancholy and nostalgic appraisal is countered by the young people, Anya and Trofimov, whose idealism and commitment to a new future redeemed by work and selfless dedication cause Anya to ask, "What have you done to me, Petya, why don't I love the cherry orchard any longer the way I used to?"

The cherry orchard (and its eventual destruction) in Chekhov's play serves as a symbol of how the old Russia and its gentry are coming to an end.

What happens in Act 3?

The party scene of Act 3—the ball following the auction—has been described by Chekhov scholar Laurence Senelick as "the supreme example of Chekhov's intermingling of subliminal symbol and surface reality." As desultory conversation takes place in the drawing room against the forced gaiety of the dancing in the background, the characters await word about the result of the auction. The underlying tension surfaces in Madame Ranevskaya's argument with Trifimov about the value of her estate and her announcement of her intention to return to Paris and the lover who fleeced and deserted her. The tone of impending doom is interrupted by the comic elements of Charlotte's ventriloquism and magic tricks and by Trofimov's tripping and falling down the stairs after delivering his moral judgments. The fateful news about the auction is delivered at the end of a farcical sequence in which Varya, squabbling with Yephikhov, strikes out at him with a pool cue only to hit the entering Lopakhin, who manages to announce that he has purchased the cherry orchard.

How does the play conclude in Act 4?

Symbolically, Act 4 returns to the nursery setting but reverses its arrivals with departures. The dispossession and dispersal of the family are now complete as they all depart for an uncertain future as an entire way of life is falling under the axe that can be heard outside. We are left suspended in uncertainty. As critic John Gassner observes, "Chekhov maintained a sensitive equilibrium between regret for the loss of old values and jubilation over the dawn of a new day. And it is the quality of detachment that also enabled him to equalize pathos and humor, and to render a probing account of the contradictions of human character."

Only Fiers remains as the curtain comes down:

[*The stage is empty. The sound of keys being turned in the locks is heard, and then the noise of the carriages going away. It is quiet. Then the sound of an axe against the trees is heard in the silence sadly and by itself. Steps are heard. Fiers comes in from the door on the right. He is dressed as usual, in a short jacket and white waistcoat; slippers on his feet. He is ill. He goes to the door and tries the handle.*]

FIERS: It's locked. They've gone away. [Sits on a sofa] They've forgotten about me…. Never mind, I'll sit here…. And Leonid Andreyevitch will have gone in a light overcoat instead of putting on his fur coat…. [Sighs anxiously] I didn't see…. Oh, these young people! [Mumbles something that cannot be understood] Life's gone on as if I'd never lived. [Lying down] I'll lie down…. You've no strength left in you, nothing left at all…. Oh, you … bungler! [He lies immobile.]

[*The distant sound is heard, as if from the sky, of a breaking string, dying away sadly. Silence follows it, and only the sound is heard, some ways away in the orchard, of the axe falling on the trees.*]

Curtain.

The conclusion here, despite a shared sonic effect, is contrary to that of Ibsen's *A Doll's House*. This is not the explosion of Nora's liberation and its blast to conventional orthodoxy. Rather, it is a slow and steady expiration with the death of Fiers and the ceasing of his heartbeat echoed by the relentless sound of the axe falling on the trees. To the bang of Ibsen, Chekhov offers the whimper of a dying fall, frustrated wills and desires, a serious comedy of human errors and loss.

Modern drama gravitates between the poles of bang and whimper, between exploding the past certainties in decisive action and turning the focus from action to inaction and paralysis. Chekhov is the master dramatist of inaction who pioneered its stage representation by replacing the long-functioning Aristotelian premises with a radically new method. He replaced the reliance on a main plot and main characters with multiple plotlines collective protagonists, and the fusion of all into a unified thematic whole. Chekhov's art, as expressed in *The Cherry Orchard* and his other works, features an unidealized truthfulness, shorn of consoling delusions or empty distractions. Stripped of the usual dramatic action, Chekhov's plays locate their interest in the gradual revelation of character and circumstance "in all the grayness of their everyday life."

MODERN DRAMA

What are the chief characteristics of modern drama?

Ibsen and Chekhov supplied modern drama with a purpose (to provoke and pose the most important human questions), a subject (ordinary, often unexceptional modern life), and a method (nuanced and gradual revelations, often from the most commonplace action). They helped to usher in an unprecedented century of major dramatic achievement by successors such as August Strindberg, Gerhart Hauptmann, Maxim Gorky, George Bernard Shaw, John Millington Synge, Sean O'Casey, Eugene O'Neill, Tennessee Williams, Arthur Miller, John Osborne, and many more.

A primary source of modern drama's energy and innovation stems from locating the profound, existential issues of its age in the turmoil of everyday life. Modern drama seized on the novel's concern for average, ordinary experience and found a way to make it compelling. In the process, drama attacked and scrambled core categories and distinctions in place since Aristotle. Is *A Doll's House* a tragedy or a comedy? Is it mainly detailing the destruction of a marriage, asserting Nora's liberation and fulfillment in independence (not in love or in reconciliation), or both? Is Willy Loman, the protagonist in Arthur Miller's *The Death of a Salesman*, a tragic hero? As his surname makes clear, he possesses neither the stature nor greatness of the Aristotelian heroic ideal. Both plays show the modern dramatist detonating theatrical norms. Both Ibsen and Miller create their drama out of the mundane life of characters who had never served as protagonists before: a lying, grasping, petty housewife and a used-up traveling salesman whose delusions and despair are disguised by "a smile and a shoeshine." In a modern age in which uncertainty is the dominant cultural condition, in which plot itself is exposed as a consoling artifice, is writing pure tragedy or comedy even possible? Do the melodramatic simplifications of hero and villain, or even protagonist and antagonist, apply when all characters seem unalterably mixed? In modern drama, it's the blurring of those distinctions into tragicomedy, neither the one nor the other, that seems far more plausible.

What besides its realism is a central characteristic of modern drama?

If social and psychological realism is a dominant feature of modern drama, another is its antirealism, its imaginative breaking of the conventions that insist on a deceptive surface realism or even a stable, cause-and-effect sequence of action. With drama's restrictions to the exterior of character and actions, modern playwrights sought alternate methods to show inner states of consciousness and alternative modes of perceiving reality. Modern movements of symbolism, expressionism, and surrealism are represented by modern playwrights including Alfred Jarry, August Strindberg (*The Ghost Sonata, The Father, The Dream Play*), William Butler Yeats, Luigi Pirandello, Jean Cocteau, Eugène Ionesco, and Jean Genet.

Perhaps the best illustrations of the antirealism of modern drama are the works of Bertolt Brecht and Samuel Beckett. For Brecht, stage realism was too focused on the particular, in which the audience is lulled into identification rather than provoked into criticism or action. His conception of "epic theater," expressed in such plays as *The Threepenny Opera, Mother Courage and Her Children, The Good Person of Szechwan*, and *The Caucasian Chalk Circle*, sought to change the fundamental relationship between the audience and the performance. By disrupting lifelike presentation, by highlighting the performance as performance, Brecht sought to "make strange" stage action, employing distancing effects that called attention to the theatricality of the experience to encourage an audience's critical attitude. Beckett, in *Waiting for Godot*, detonated the operating principles of drama that we expect to find in a play: a coherent sequence of action, motives, and conflicts leading to a resolution. He substituted the core dramatic element of suspense—waiting—and forces the audience to experience the same anticipation and uncertainty of his two tramps pointlessly awaiting the arrival of Godot, who never appears.

READING A MODERN DRAMA–
BRECHT'S *MOTHER COURAGE*

What is the significance of *Mother Courage*?

Described by Tennessee Williams as the greatest drama of the twentieth century, Bertolt Brecht's *Mother Courage and Her Children* (1941) is both one of the most powerful antiwar dramas ever written and one of the masterworks of the playwright's conception of "epic theater," which was Brecht's innovative and influential contribution to modern drama.

What is the background for Brecht's *Mother Courage*?

Written on the eve of World War II in Scandinavia, where Brecht was living in exile from Nazi Germany and first performed in Switzerland in 1941, *Mother Courage and Her Children* debuted in Germany in 1949 under Brecht's direction amidst the ruins of Berlin, a horrifyingly appropriate setting reflecting the consequences of ignoring Brecht's jeremiad on the all-consuming destructiveness of war. *Mother Courage* has become one of Brecht's most performed and admired plays, a classic of modern theater as well as a justification of and a challenge to Brecht's notions of drama. Set during the devastating seventeenth-century Thirty Years' War, the play chronicles the en-

German playwright Bertolt Brecht was a primary advocate of epic theater, which concerned itself with political and other modern issues.

counters of a canteen woman, Anna Fierling, nicknamed Mother Courage, as she tries to make her living selling her wares from her cart to the soldiers. As critic Victor Wittner wrote about the play's wartime premier, "With all its cynicism, *Mutter Courage* is a compelling portrait, often with subtle humor, often with diabolical undercurrents of meaning, often with a certain fatalism, but also often with pure human simplicity and tenderness. And what moves us even more than that is the parallel with today's events, the actual recognition that one war is like another, one misery yields nothing to another in gruesomeness." *Mother Courage* has gone on to reflect and respond to other wars and other atrocities, revealing powerful truths about the human condition.

How should you understand the play's central figure?

At the play's center is one of drama's great paradoxical protagonists. Mother Courage defines the modern conception of the antihero as both an ultimate survivor of the worst humans can devise—a pathetic victim of war who loses her three children to it—and a collaborator in her own and her family's destruction. As critic Richard Brustein has argued, "Like Falstaff (her Shakespearean prototype), she is an escaped character who baffles the author's original intentions. Salty, shrewd, hardbitten, and skeptical, Courage is a full-blooded personification of the anti-heroic view of life. At the end, childless and desolate, Courage straps herself to her battered wagon and continues to follow the soldiers, having learned nothing except that man's capacity for suffering is limitless. But this knowledge is the tragic perception; and Brecht, for all his ideologizing, has recreated a tragic universe in which the cruelty of men, the venality of society, and the indifference of the gods seem immutable conditions of life." The brilliance of the play stems from the complex and ambiguous Mother Courage, who both embodies Brecht's polemical lesson of the consequences of war and a dehumanizing materialism and evades reductive ideological and moral categories.

How does an understanding of Brecht's biography and background provide a helpful context?

Mother Courage is no less complex or paradoxical than her creator. Brecht was born in 1898 in the Bavarian city of Augsburg into a respectable, middle-class family. His father, the business director of a paper factory, was a Catholic; his mother, a Protestant. An indifferent and at times rebellious student, Brecht excelled at writing and published his first poems and reviews as a teenager in local newspapers. To evade the draft during World War I, Brecht studied medicine at the University of Munich but was called up in 1918 to serve as a medical orderly in an Augsburg military hospital. There he witnessed firsthand the terrible cost of war, which reinforced a lifelong pacifism. Following Germany's defeat, Brecht responded to the postwar social chaos, including the turbulent formation of the Weimar Republic and the brutal suppression of the 1918–1919 revolution, with his initial dramatic works and a commitment to socialism and the German Communist Party. His first play, *Baal*, written in 1918, concerns a poet who murders his best friend in a fit of jealousy. Composed of twenty-two loosely connected scenes, the play shows the combined influence of Büchner's *Woyzeck* and the expressionists. His second play, *Trommeln in der Nacht* (*Drums in the Night*), a bitterly nihilistic drama about a war veteran who learns that his fiancée was seduced by a war profiteer, was performed to acclaim in Munich in 1922. Praised for his stark and challenging assessment of postwar reality and innovative dramatic techniques, Brecht moved to Berlin in 1924, where he served as a play reader for the great German director Max Reinhardt while continuing his theatrical experimentation in such plays as *In the Jungle of the Cities* and *A Man's a Man*. He achieved his greatest popular success in 1928 with the musical *The Threepenny Opera*, an adaptation of John Gay's comedy, written in collaboration with composer Kurt Weill. A direct assault on the audience's expectations and complacency, *The Threepenny Opera* innovatively combines social and moral instruction with entertainment, employing the methods that Brecht would later codify in his conception of the *"episches Theatre."*

What is Brecht's concept of "Epic Theater"?

Initially conceived in articles and notebooks during the 1920s and worked out in several essays in the early 1930s, Brecht's formulation of a new theory of drama is a crucial contribution to modern drama. "No other twentieth-century writer," drama historian Marvin Carlson has argued, "has influenced the theatre both as a dramatist and theorist

311

as profoundly as Bertolt Brecht." Rejecting the assumptions of naturalism that had dominated the European theater after Ibsen, Brecht opposed the realistic "theater of illusion" that encouraged an audience's emotional involvement and complacency through verisimilitude by a different kind of drama designed to stimulate thought and action. Traditional Aristotelean or Dramatic Theater, in Brecht's view, was restrictive and falsifying. Brecht's alternative was a dramatic structure derived from the epic: an episodic narrative form in which each episode is significant not only for what it contributes to the whole but also in itself. The epic further differs from drama in that it deals with past events rather than with the imaginary "present" of the drama, which unfolds before us as if it were happening for the first time. In his epic theater, Brecht wants the audience to see the action as something that has happened and is now being re-enacted on a stage.

The deliberate distancing of the audience from the onstage experience is encapsulated in the key Brechtian term *verfremdung*, "to make strange," or the so-called alienation principle. Contrary to the theater of verisimilitude that draws the audience into the illusion of life enacted onstage, Brecht endorsed techniques of dramatic structure, staging, and acting to maintain the audience's critical distance and judgment to "make strange" habitual ways of seeing experience and thereby opening up new possibilities and perceptions.

How does *Mother Courage* embody Brecht's concepts of "Epic Theater"?

Mother Courage and Her Children brilliantly illustrates both Brecht's dramatic method and its achievement. Composed of twelve scenes set in numerous locations in Sweden, Poland, and Germany between 1624 and 1636, the play dramatizes the central ironic contradiction between Mother Courage's struggles to provide for and protect her children and to maintain her business that insures their loss. Each scene is introduced by a summary of setting and situation, including outcomes that undermine dramatic suspense in favor of the audience's critique of characters and action. As the play opens, Mother Courage and her wagon—the two constants in the succession of scenes—appear onstage being drawn by her two sons, Eilif and Swiss Cheese. Kattrin, her mute, traumatized daughter, rides in the wagon with her mother. Encountering Swedish recruiting soldiers, Anna tells how she got her nickname by intrepidly driving her cart through the bombardment of Riga to sell fifty loaves of moldy bread and sings the first of several songs that ironically comment on the play's themes:

Set during the seventeenth century's Thirty Years' War, *Mother Courage and Her Children* comments on the rise of Nazism in Germany and the hopelessness of a life of war about which nothing, not even the title character, is immune.

Captains, how can you make them face it—
Marching to death without a brew?
Courage has rum with which to lace it
And boil their souls and bodies through.
Their musket primed, their stomach hollow—
Captains, your men don't look so well.
So feed them up and let them follow
While you command them into hell.
The new year's come. The watchmen shout.
The thaw sets in. The dead remain.
Whatever life has not died out
It staggers to its feet again.

Mother Courage's clear-eyed awareness of the horrors and stupidity of war, sounded in the song, is also evident as she distracts efforts to recruit Eilif by fortune-telling, in which the recruiting officers and all her children draw the black cross of death. However, while she is busy haggling with the sergeant over the sale of a belt, Eilif is led away to join the army. The scene closes as the sergeant sings in parting to Mother Courage and her remaining two children: "Like the war to nourish you? / Have to feed it something too."

How does *Mother Courage* develop its central themes?

Two years later while still following the Swedish army on their Polish campaign, the reduced family is briefly reunited as Eilif has achieved acclaim for having slaughtered peasants and stolen their oxen. Three years later, Swiss Cheese has become paymaster of the Second Protestant Regiment, which is being overrun by Catholic forces. Mother Courage remains convinced of the superiority of the Protestant side, observing, "To go by what the big shots say, they're waging war for almighty God and in the name of everything that's good and lovely. But look closer, they ain't so silly, they're waging it for what they can get. Else little folk like me wouldn't be in it all." The cost for the "little folk" is made clear when Mother Courage attempts to ransom her captured son. Willing to part with her wagon for two hundred guilders, she reserves some of the money to live on, and the offered sum proves insufficient to save Swiss Cheese, who is executed. Mother Courage, therefore, loses a son a second time when her commercial practicality comes in conflict with her love and duty to her children. In one of the most intense moments of the play, the scene closes as Mother Courage is shown the dead body of her son but must show no recognition to save herself. "Know him?" the sergeant asks. "What, never seen him before he had that meal here? Pick him up. Chuck him in the pit. He's got nobody knows him."

What are the climactic moments in *Mother Courage*?

In Scene 5, two years have passed and the war has widened, taking Mother Courage and her wagon to Italy and Bavaria, where she resists an appeal to convert the officer's shirts she is planning to sell into bandages for dying peasants unable to pay. By showing

Mother Courage carrying on business as usual amid the carnage of the war, Brecht seeks to offset some of the sympathy the audience may feel for her as a war victim. War and capitalism are conjoined, each an aspect of the other, with greed and exploitation warping Mother Courage into a "hyena of the battlefield." This is made especially clear as peace momentarily breaks out in Scene 8, and Mother Courage's first response is to lament the armistice's impact on her trade ("Peace'll wring my neck"). In her absence, the condemned Eilif is led onto the stage to be executed for continuing to kill and rob peasants during peacetime, the same actions that formerly brought him commendation. The scene closes with Mother Courage announcing that the war has resumed, and she encourages it and her trade in song:

> From Ulm to Metz, from Metz to Munich
> Courage will see the war gets fed.
> The war will show a well-filled tunic
> Given its daily shot of lead.
> But lead alone can hardly nourish
> It must have soldiers to subsist.
> It's you it needs to make it flourish.
> The war's still hungry. So enlist!

Now down to her final child, Mother Courage in Scene 11 is outside the Protestant village of Halle. Unprotected when Mother Courage goes for supplies to sell, Kattrin is captured along with several peasants who fear that the Catholic forces will strike the village without warning. In what has been called by critic Eric Bentley "possibly the most powerful scene, emotionally, in twentieth century drama," Kattrin climbs onto a roof and sounds the alarm with a drum before she is shot. In the play's final scene, Mother Courage sings a lullaby to her dead daughter, trying to convince herself that her child is only sleeping. Eventually realizing the truth but still unaware that Eilif has been killed, Mother Courage, paying the peasants to bury Kattrin, follows the army, hitching herself to her wagon and closing the play with a final song:

> With all its luck and all its danger
> The war is dragging on a bit
> Another hundred years or longer
> The common man won't benefit.
> Filthy his food, no soap to shave him
> The regiment steals half his pay.
> But still a miracle may save him:
> Tomorrow is another day!
> The new year's come. The watchmen shout.
> The thaw sets in. The dead remain.
> Wherever life has not died out
> It staggers to its feet again.

How does *Mother Courage* embody Brecht's dramatic method and its justification?

Strategically, with its antirealistic staging, its choral songs, soliloquies, and narrative structure that proceeds by repetition, contrast, and juxtaposition of scenes and images, *Mother Courage* reaches a level of mythic resonance that universalizes the human condition. Brecht's comments and revisions of the play make clear that he was concerned that audiences would overly sympathize with Mother Courage, that her losses, suffering, and indomitable spirit would obscure the play's thesis that war benefits no one, least of all the "little folk," and that the pursuit of profit dehumanizes and destroys as inexorably as combat. Ultimately, Brecht's efforts to overrule empathy in favor of criticism, reducing the vital complexity of the despicable *and* admirable Mother Courage down to a political and moral assertion, failed. In a sense, audiences have continued to perceive an even greater play than the one Brecht intended by responding to its ambiguous protagonist who is heroic in her endurance and suffering but condemned by her foolish pursuit of profiteering that has cost her so much. Brecht's stage innovations make clear both how the theater can dramatize the most profound and complex human and social questions yet can never fully dispense with the power of felt experience to communicate, modify, and expand the message.

By the end of the play, Mother Courage has not changed her ways even after losing all her children. She continues to leech her income off the soldiers who fight an ongoing war, selling them food and other goods.

315

What dramatic characteristics does Beckett share with Brecht?

If Brecht's antirealism serves his interest in reinforcing drama's capacity to provoke and challenge intellectually and emotionally, Beckett provides a similar assault on realism's certainty and the Aristotelian rules that had governed drama from its beginning. Reacting to a modern human condition shaped by the experiences of two world wars, the Holocaust, and imminent nuclear annihilation, logic, cause and effect, and contingency all seemed now quaintly inoperative with existential absurdity the most reasonable response. Other postwar dramatists, such as Camus and Sartre, diagnosed a contemporary absurdist response in plays that made perfect sense. Beckett would pioneer a dramatic method to reflect fully the absurdity of modern life.

READING A MODERN DRAMA— BECKETT'S *WAITING FOR GODOT*

What is the significance of *Waiting for Godot*?

Two tramps in bowler hats, a desolate country road, a single bare tree: these iconic images of a radically new modern drama confronted the audience at the Théâtre de Babylone in Paris on January 5, 1953, at the premiere of *En attendant Godot* (*Waiting for Godot*). Written during the winter of 1948–1949, the play would take Samuel Beckett four years to get it produced. It is easy to see why. As the play's first director, Roger Blin, commented, "Imagine a play that contains no action, but characters that have nothing to say to each other." The main characters—Vladimir and Estragon, nicknamed Didi and Gogo—are awaiting the arrival of Godot, but we never learn why, nor who he is, because he never arrives. The tramps frequently say, "Let's go," but they never move. We never learn where the road leads nor see the tramps taking it. The play gratifies no expectations and resolves nothing. Instead, it detonates the accepted operating principles of drama that we expect to find in a play: a coherent sequence of actions, motives, and conflicts leading to a resolution. It substitutes instead the core dramatic element of suspense—waiting—and forces the audience to experience the same anticipation and uncertainty of Vladimir and Estragon while raising fundamental issues about the nature and purpose of existence itself, our own elemental version of waiting. If modern drama originates in the nineteenth century with Ibsen and Chekhov, both Brecht and Beckett extend the implications of their innovations into a radical new kind of theatrical experience and method. The theatrical and existential vision of *Waiting for Godot* makes it *the* watershed twentieth-century drama—as explosive, groundbreaking, and influential a work as T. S. Eliot's *The Waste Land* is for modern poetry and James Joyce's *Ulysses* is for modern fiction. From its initial baffling premiere, *Waiting for Godot* would be seen by more than a million people in the next five years. Eventually, it would become the most frequently produced modern drama worldwide, entering the collective consciousness with a "Beckettlike landscape" and the illusive Godot established as images of modern futility and angst.

How does an understanding of Beckett's life and background contribute to an understanding of *Waiting for Godot*?

Like his fellow countryman and mentor James Joyce, Beckett oriented himself in exile from his native Ireland, but unlike Joyce, who managed to remain relatively safe on the fringes of a modern world spinning out of control, Beckett was very much plunged into the maelstrom. He was born in Foxrock, a respectable suburb of Dublin, to Protestant Anglo-Irish parents. His education at Portora Royal School (where Oscar Wilde had been a student) and at Trinity College, Dublin, where he received his degree in French and Italian, pointed him toward a distinguished academic career. In 1928 Beckett won an exchange lectureship at l'Ecole normale supérieure in Paris, where he met Joyce and assisted him in his labors on *Finnegans Wake*. Beckett returned to Trinity as a lecturer in French but found teaching "grim." He would state that "I could not bear the absurdity of teaching others what I did not know myself." In 1932, he left Ireland for good, except for short visits to his family. When World War II broke out, Beckett ended a visit home and returned to Paris, later stating, "I preferred France in war to Ireland in peace." During the war, Beckett joined the French resistance in Paris. When his group was infiltrated by a double agent and betrayed to the Gestapo, he was forced to escape to unoccupied France in 1942, where he worked as a farm laborer until the war's end.

In 1946 Beckett struggled to restart his interrupted and stalled literary career, which had produced a critical study of Proust, a collection of short stories (*More Pricks Than Kicks*), a volume of poems (*Echo's Bones*), and two novels (*Murphy* and *Watt*). The turning point came during a visit to his mother in Foxrock. He would later transfer the epiphany that gave him a new subject and method to the more dramatic setting of the pier in Dún Laoghaire on a stormy night in *Krapp's Last Tape*.

> Spiritually a year of profound gloom and indigence until that memorable night in March, at the end of the jetty, in the howling wind, never to be forgotten, when suddenly I saw the whole thing. The vision at last…. What I suddenly saw then was this … that the dark I have always struggled to keep under is in reality my most….

Krapp's revelation breaks off, but Beckett himself completed his sentence, saying "that the dark I have always struggled to keep under" was "my most precious ally." As Beckett biographer James

One of the last giants of modern theater, Irish playwright and Nobel Prize winner Samuel Beckett would produce increasingly minimalist works as he turned his focus to his own inner consciousness and the absurdity of existence.

317

Knowlson summarizes, Beckett's insight meant that he would "draw henceforward on his own inner world for his subjects; outside reality would be refracted through the filter of his own imagination; inner desires and needs would be allowed a much greater freedom of expression; rational contradictions would be allowed in; and the imagination would be allowed to create alternative worlds to those of conventional reality." Beckett would thereby find the way to bypass the specific to deal directly with the universal. His fiction and plays would not be social or psychological but ontological. To mine those inner recesses, Beckett would reverse the centrifugal direction of most writers to contain and comprehend the world for the centripetal, of reduction down to essentials.

What is the characteristic Beckett style and method?

Beckett, who had assisted Joyce in the endlessly proliferating *Finnegans Wake*, would overturn the encyclopedic method of his mentor. "I realized that Joyce had gone as far as one could in the direction of knowing more, in control of one's material," Beckett would observe. "He was always adding to it; you only have to look at his proofs to see that. I realized that my own way was in impoverishment, in lack of knowledge and in taking away, in subtracting rather than in adding." This realization required a means of presentation that Beckett found in minimalism and composition in French, which he found "easier to write without style." Restricted to a voice and its consciousness, Beckett would eliminate the conventional narrative requirements of specificity of time and place, elaborate background for characters, and a complex sequence of causes and effects to form his plots. In Beckett's work the atmosphere of futility and stagnation around which Chekhov devised several of his plays and stories would become pervasive and inescapable. The world is drained of meaning; human relationships are reduced to tensions between hope and despair in which consciousness itself is problematic. Beckett's protagonists, who lack the possibility of significant action, are paralyzed or forced to repeat an unchanging condition. Beckett compresses his language and situations down to the level of elemental forces without the possibility of escape from the predicament of the basic absurdity of existence.

How did *Waiting for Godot* originate?

Returning to Paris after the war, Beckett began what he called "the siege in the room": his most sustained and prolific period of writing that produced in five years the plays *Eleutheria, Waiting for Godot*, and *Endgame*, the novel trilogy *Molloy, Malone Dies*, and *The Unnamable*, and short stories published under the title *Stories and Texts for Nothing*. Beckett has stated that *Waiting for Godot* began "as a relaxation, to get away from the awful prose I was writing at the time." It gave dramatic form to the intense interior explorations of his fiction. The play's setting is nonspecific but symbolically suggestive of the modern wasteland as the play's protagonists, Vladimir and Estragon, engage in chatter derived equally from metaphysics and the music hall while they await the arrival of Godot, who never comes. What Godot represents (Beckett remarked, "If I knew, I would have said so in the play" and "If by Godot I had meant God, I would have said God, not Godot") is far less important than the defining condition of fruitless and pointless waiting that the play dramatizes. Beckett explores onstage the implications of a world in which nothing happens, in which a desired revelation and meaningful resolution are endlessly deferred. At art's core is a fundamental ordering of the world, but Beckett's art is based on the world's ultimate incomprehensibility. "I think anyone nowadays," Beckett has remarked, "who pays the slightest attention to his own experience finds it the experience of a nonknower, a noncaner." By powerfully staging radical uncertainty and the absurdity of futile waiting, *Godot* epitomizes the operating assumptions of the Theater of the Absurd.

How is *Waiting for Godot* structured?

The most repeated critique of *Waiting for Godot* is Irish critic Vivian Mercier's succinct summary: "Nothing happens, twice." The play, subtitled "a tragi-comedy in two acts," does not, in the words of Martin Esslin, "tell a story; it explores a static situation" that is encapsulated by the words of Estragon: "Nothing happens, nobody comes, nobody goes, it's awful."

What "happens" in Act 1?

In Act 1, Vladimir and Estragon (who refer to each other by the pet names "Didi" and "Gogo") await the anticipated arrival of Godot, to whom they have made "a kind of prayer," a "vague supplication" for something unspecified that Godot has agreed to consider. However, it is by no means certain whether this is the right place or day for the meeting. To pass the time, they consider hanging themselves ("It'd give us an erection"), but the only available tree seems too frail to hold them, and they cannot agree who should go first. Another pair arrives—Lucky, with a rope around his neck, loaded down with a bag, picnic basket, stool, and great coat, being whipped on by the domineering Pozzo, who claims to be a landowner taking Lucky to a fair to sell him. They halt for Pozzo to eat, and he asks Gogo and Didi if they would like to be entertained by Lucky's "thinking," which turns out to be a long, nonsensical monologue. After Pozzo and Lucky depart, a boy enters, addresses Vladimir as Mr. Albert, and delivers the message that Mr. Godot will not be coming this evening but will surely come tomorrow. After the boy exits, Vladimir and Estragon also decide to leave but make no move to do so.

What "happens" in Act 2?

Act 2 takes place apparently the next day at the same time and place, although the tree now has four or five leaves. Again, Vladimir and Estragon begin their vigil,

In *Waiting for Godot* two characters, Vladimir and Estragon, wait fruitlessly for the arrival of a man with whom they have made an unspecified request for assistance.

passing the time by exchanging questions, contradictions, insults, and hats, as well as pretending to be Pozzo and Lucky, until the originals arrive. However, Pozzo is now blind and bumps into Lucky, knocking them both down. After debating whether they should help them get up, Didi and Gogo also find themselves on the ground, unable to rise, with Vladimir announcing, "We've arrived … we are men." Eventually, they regain their footing, supporting Pozzo between them. Pozzo has no recollection of their previous encounter, and when asked what they do if they fall where there is no one to help them, says, "We wait till we can get up. Then we go on." When Didi asks if Lucky can "think" again for them before they leave, Pozzo reveals that Lucky is now "dumb"—"he can't even groan." Vladimir wonders about their transformation since yesterday, but Pozzo insists time is a meaningless concept: "Have you not done tormenting me with your accursed time! It's abominable! When! When! One day, is that not enough for you, one day he went dumb, one day I went blind, one day we'll go deaf, one day we were born, one day we shall die, the same day, the same second, is that not enough for you? They give birth astride of a grave, the light gleams an instant, then it's night once more."

After Pozzo and Lucky exit (with the sound of their falling again offstage), the boy arrives to announce that Godot will not be coming this evening but will be there without fail tomorrow. Although he appears to be the same boy as yesterday, he denies this and runs off when a frustrated Vladimir lunges at him. Estragon proposes going far away, but Vladimir reminds him that they must wait for Godot to come tomorrow. They return to the idea of hanging themselves, but when they try to use Estragon's belt cord, it breaks, and Estragon's pants fall down. They decide to bring a stronger rope the next day and say, "We'll hang ourselves tomorrow. (*Pause.*) Unless Godot comes." The play concludes:

Vladimir: Well? Shall we go?
Estragon: Yes, let's go.
They do not move.
Curtain.

How does Beckett generate meaning in *Waiting for Godot*?

Beckett in *Waiting for Godot* creates meaning through image, repetition, and counterpoint. In their bowler hats and pratfalls, Vladimir and Estragon are versions of Charlie Chaplin's tramp, tragic clowns poised between despair and hope. Act 2 repeats the sequence of action of Act 1 but deepens the absurdity as well as the significance of their waiting for Godot. Unlike Pozzo and Lucky, whose relationship parodies the master-slave dynamic and a sadomasochistic conception of existence in which death is the only outcome of birth, Vladimir and Estragon complement one another and live in hope for Godot's arrival and the revelation and resolution it implies ("Tonight perhaps we shall sleep in his place, in the warmth, our bellies full, on the straw. It is worth waiting for that, is it not?"). The hope that Godot might come, that purpose is possible even in the face of almost certain disappointment, is their sustaining illusion and the play's ultimate comic affirmation. As Vladimir explains, "What are we doing here, *that* is the question. And we

> ## What is the legacy of *Waiting for Godot* and Beckett's drama?
>
> Beckett, in what has been called the Theater of the Absurd by critic Martin Esslin, embodies the futility and purposelessness of modern life with plays that radically disrupt everything upon which drama had depended: stable characters engaged in a meaningful series of actions, leading to a decisive climax and resolution. Beckett and Brecht pioneered modern drama's antirealism that was taken up by such dramatists as Edward Albee, Peter Weiss, Harold Pinter, Dario Fo, Amiri Baraka, Tom Stoppard, Caryl Churchill, Tony Kushner, and others.

are blessed in this, that we happen to know the answer. Yes, in this immense confusion one thing alone is clear. We are waiting for Godot to come.... We have kept our appointment and that's an end to that. We are not saints, but we have kept our appointment. How many people can boast as much?" To which Estragon replies: "Billions." By the comic calculus of *Waiting for Godot*, continuing to believe in the absence of the possibility of belief is true heroism and the closest we get to human fulfillment. Beckett's play makes clear that the illusions that prevent us from confronting the core truth of human existence must be stripped away, whether in the storm scene of Act 3 of *King Lear* when bare, unaccommodated man is revealed or here on a "country road. A tree. Evening."

What are the challenges in understanding modern drama?

In its embodying both realism and its opposite, in breaking and reconstituting theatrical conventions, modern drama presents clear challenges in reading and understanding. As is the case with much modern art, its novelty shocks and often forces readers and viewers to discover its operating assumptions and standards of evaluation. Picasso's cubist distortions are not failed realism but something else entirely. Picasso's art does not conform to the methods and standards of realism and needs to be judged by what it does do, not what it does not. Similarly, modern drama need not operate under any of the established rules and conventions. A better approach is to accept the rules under which each play operates. A valid critique of a tragedy is not "I only like comedies and this play fails to make me laugh." You would be judging the tragedy by the wrong standard. It's better to evaluate a play based on what it's trying to do and see whether it is successful in meeting those challenges. You may still not like it or prefer other dramatic forms, but at least you have tried to see the play for what it is and not for what it isn't.

Ultimately, effective drama provokes a response in its audience (or reader), which may not be pleasurable. Whatever response Shakespeare's momentous *King Lear* provokes, pleasure seems an inadequate or inappropriate outcome. Great drama does far more than just entertain: it challenges and provokes; it shocks us with both the surprising and the familiar. Modern dramatists like Ibsen, Chekov, Shaw, Beckett, and others wanted to start a dialogue with the audience—posing the most interesting questions,   321 not answers—and to get their audience to feel and to think. The supreme test for any work of literature can be distilled into this essential question: Does the work tell us something about human nature and human experience? How it does so, though critical to its strategy, is ultimately less important than if it does.

CONTEMPORARY DRAMA

What is the status of contemporary drama?

Premature predictions of the death of drama were no doubt offered in Attic Greece and Elizabethan England. The history of drama is the history of imminent collapse and extinction, as well as persistence in various shapes and forms. Recall how out of the collapse of the Roman Empire and its stage tradition drama re-emerged, gratifying the same religious and moral imperatives that produced it in the first place. English drama returned after an eighteen-year ban, and a modern renaissance followed one of its most fallow periods in the nineteenth century. These instances remind us of drama's tenacity. Despite a sense of decline, it seems as though every age gets the drama it deserves.

There is no question, however, that the vitality of live drama today seems to be in serious danger, if not in critical condition. Drama, the great democratic and inclusive literary form, has become more an exclusive entertainment for the well-heeled few. Ticket prices on Broadway and the West End have turned live theater into a special occasion; the commercial theater leans heavily on spectacle rather than drama featuring existential, cultural, and political challenges. The economics of contemporary theater work against risky productions. Subsidized national theater has picked up the slack as have regional companies who can afford to take chances on new dramatic voices.

If live theater's purpose to provoke and engage is under threat, it can certainly be argued that no previous age is as saturated in drama as ours. Whether in films or on television, drama has become our preeminent literary entertainment. Far more people see literary works today than read them. With the rise of cable television and its relaxed censorship compared to broadcast television, a so-called new "Golden Age" of televised drama has emerged with such productions as *The Sopranos, The Wire, Breaking Bad, Mad Men,* and *Game of Thrones,* providing examples of popular dramas that extend boundaries and capture the cultural moment in challenging ways. Playwrights today no doubt feel the lure of also being screenwriters to reach a wider popular audience.

But what about contemporary theater?

Despite the economic and competitive barriers of the commercial theater, contemporary drama, to paraphrase William Faulkner's Nobel Prize speech, somehow not only endures but prevails. Consider this list of winners of the Pulitzer Prize for drama since 2000:

Year: 2000
Play: *Dinner with Friends*
Playwright: Donald Margulies (1954–)
Subject: The breakup of a marriage of a middle-aged couple in Connecticut with scenes from their lives and another couple
First Performed: Premiered at the 1998 Humana Festival in Louisville, KY, before opening off-Broadway in 1999

Year: 2001
Play: *Proof*
Playwright: David Auburn (1969–)
Subject: A daughter's struggle to cope with her father's mathematical genius and mental illness and her own
First Performed: Developed at George Street Playhouse in New Brunswick, NJ, before premiering off-Broadway in 2000 and transferring to Broadway

Year: 2002
Play: *Topdog/Underdog*
Playwright: Suzan-Lori Parks (1963–)
Subject: Chronicles the lives of two African American brothers and the existential traps of being African American and male in the United States
First Performed: Premiered off-Broadway in 2001 at The Public Theater

Year: 2003
Play: *Anna in the Tropics*
Playwright: Nilo Cruz (1960–)
Subject: Set in 1929, chronicles the lives of Cuban American cigar factory workers and the story of *Anna Karenina* that is read to them
First Performed: Premiered in Coral Gables, FL

Year: 2004
Play: *I Am My Own Wife*
Playwright: Doug Wright (1962–)
Subject: Examines the life of German antiquarian Charlotte von Mahlsdorf, who survived the Nazi and communist regimes in East Berlin as a transgender woman
First Performed: Premiered off-Broadway in 2003 at Playwrights Horizons, opening on Broadway the next year

Year: 2005
Play: *Doubt*
Playwright: John Patrick Shanley (1950–)
Subject: Set in a fictional Catholic school in the Bronx, the play pits the questioning parish priest against a rigidly conservative nun over the issue of sexual abuse
First Performed: Originally staged off-Broadway at the Manhattan Theatre Club before transferring to Broadway

Year: 2006   No award

Year: 2007
Play: *Rabbit Hole*

Playwright: David Lindsay-Abaire (1969–)
Subject: Explores how a family survives loss and addiction
First Performed: First presented at Pacific Playwrights Festival of the South Coast Repertory, Costa Mesa, CA, which commissioned it

Year: 2008
Play: *August: Osage County*
Playwright: Tracy Letts (1965–)
Subject: Scenes from a family reunion over several weeks in August at a home outside Pawhuska, Oklahoma
First Performed: Premiered at the Steppenwolf Theatre in Chicago, before transferring to Broadway

Year: 2009
Play: *Ruined*
Playwright: Lynn Nottage (1964–)
Subject: Dramatizes the plight of women in civil war-torn Democratic Republic of Congo
First Performed: Comissioned by the Goodman Theatre in Chicago where it premiered before opening off-Broadway at the Manhattan Theatre Club

Year: 2010
Play: *Next to Normal*
Playwright: Tom Kitt (1974–) and Brian Yorkey (1970–)
Subject: Rock musical dealing with a mother who struggles with bipolar disorder, exploring issues of grief, suicide, drug abuse, modern psychiatry, and the dark side of surburban life
First Performed: Off-Broadway and a year run at the Arena Stage in Crystal City, VA, before opening on Broadway in 2009

Year: 2011
Play: *Clybourne Park*
Playwright: Bruce Norris (1960–)
Subject: A prequel and sequel to Lorraine Hansberry's *A Raisin in the Sun* (1959), depicting an African American family in Chicago
First Performed: Premiered off-Broadway at Playwrights Horizons in New York, opening in London and performed in several regional theaters before opening on Broadway in 2012

Year: 2012
Play: *Water by the Spoonful*
Playwright: Quiara Alegría Hudes (1977–)
Subject: A search for meaning by a returning Iraq War veteran, set in a sandwich shop in Philadelphia
First Performed: Commissioned by Hartford Stage, where it was first performed in 2011 before premiering off-Broadway at the Second Stage Theatre

Year: 2013
Play: *Disgraced*
Playwright: Ayad Akhtar (1970–)
Subject: A dinner party exploring racial and ethnic prejudices and the challenge for Muslim Americans in post-9/11 America

First Performed: Premiered at the American Theater Company, Chicago, before off-Broadway and off-West End productions, opening on Broadway in 2014

Year: 2014
Play: *The Flick*
Playwright: Annie Baker (1981–)
Subject: Set in a run-down movie theater in Worcester, Massachusetts, and dramatizes the interactions of three underpaid movie ushers
First Performed: Debuted off-Broadway at Playwrights Horizons

Year: 2015
Play: *Between Riverside and Crazy*
Playwright: Stephen Adly Guiris (1965–)
Subject: Concerns a retired New York City policeman in his Upper West Side rent-controlled apartment
First Performed: Opened off-Broadway at the Atlantic Theater Company's Linda Gross Theater

Year: 2016
Play: *Hamilton*
Playwright: Lin-Manuel Miranda (1980–)
Subject: A musical about the life and times of Alexander Hamilton
First Performed: Debuted off-Broadway at The Public Theater before transferring to Broadway

Year: 2017
Play: *Sweat*
Playwright: Lynn Nottage (1964–)
Subject: Set in a bar in Reading, Pennsylvania, intertwines the relationship among a parole officer and two ex-convicts and three childhood woman friends working in the same factory
First Performed: First performed at the Oregon Shakespeare Festival before performances at the Arena Stage in Washington, D.C. Opened off-Broadway at The Public Theater and transferring to Broadway

What is striking in this list is the diversity of subjects and viewpoints, as well as the different routes that productions now take to find their audiences. Of the seventeen playwrights, the two oldest are in their sixties; the two youngest are in their thirties, with fifty the average age of the winners. Although men predominate (72 percent), there is an impressive ethnic diversity: Suzan-Lori Parks is the first African American woman winner; Lynn Nottage became the second and the first woman ever to win the Pulitzer for Drama twice, Nilo Cruz is the first Latino to win; Quiara Alegría Hudes became the second (and the first Latina); Lin-Manuel Miranda became the third. Aynd Akhtar, a Pakistan American, is the first playwright of South Asian ancestry to win. The playwrights' diverse viewpoints are evident in the range of subject matter: plays tackle big cultural topics, such as the Catholic clergy sexual abuse scandal (*Doubt*), the civil war in the Congo (*Ruined*), the consequences of the Iraq War (*Water by the Spoonful*), the collapse of the American Dream (*Sweat*), and the fate of Muslim Americans after 9/11 (*Disgraced*). They also dramatize smaller, private stories: a dissolving marriage (*Dinner with Friends*) and family struggles (*Rabbit Hole, Next to Normal, August: Osage County, Be-*

tween Riverside and Crazy). These plays consider grand historical subjects (*Hamilton*) as well as unfamiliar people and places: German antiquarian and transgender survivor of the Nazis and communists, Charlotte von Mohlsdorf (*I Am My Own Wife*), Tampa, Florida, in 1929 (*Anna in the Tropics*), Pawhuska, Oklahoma (*August: Osage County*), Worcester, Massachusetts (*The Flick*), and Reading, Pennsylvania (*Sweat*). American identity is defined through the multiple lenses of race, gender, class, and ethnicity in *Topdog/Underdog, Clybourne Park, Disgraced*, and *Between Riverside and Crazy*. None of the plays premiered on Broadway; all came through vital and supportive regional theaters that commissioned several of the works or from the off-Broadway theatrical scene.

These plays demonstrate a clear lineage with the development of modern drama from Ibsen's re-establishing the relevance and urgency of the problem play to Chekhov pushing it to reflect unexceptional, everyday life. While realism defines many of the plays, others (*Next to Normal, Hamilton, Anna in the Tropics, The Flick*) push well beyond its boundaries to echo the experimental antirealism of Brecht and Beckett.

Take a closer look at both the realism and antirealism of contemporary drama in an analysis of two plays, August Wilson's *Fences* and Tony Kushner's *Angels in America*.

READING CONTEMPORARY DRAMA– WILSON'S *FENCES*

Why is *Fences* significant?

One of the most ambitious projects ever undertaken by an American dramatist is August Wilson's ten-play "Pittsburgh Cycle," *Fences*. Each play is set in a different decade of the twentieth century to chronicle black experience in America. "I'm taking each decade," Wilson (1945–2005) said about his work in progress, "and looking at one of the most important questions that blacks confronted in that decade and writing a play about it. Put them all together, and you have a history." Beginning with *Ma Rainey's Black Bottom* in 1984, the cycle was completed with *Radio Golf*, which opened only a few months before Wilson's death from liver cancer in 2005. It has been described by critic Lawrence Bommer as "the most complete cultural chronicle since Balzac wrote his vast *Human Comedy*, an artistic whole that has grown even greater than its prize-winning parts." In a playwriting career of a little more than twenty years, August Wilson dominated the American stage as few other dramatists have ever done. Since 1984, no American playwright had more productions on Broadway than Wilson. Two of them, *Fences* (1987) and *The Piano Lesson* (1990), won both Pulitzer Prizes and Tony Awards for best drama. He received seven New York Drama Critics' Circle Awards for best play. Since the award was inaugurated in 1936, only Tennessee Williams, who won it four times, had ever won it more than twice. His plays' critical acclaim and wide popularity are also unique and significant. "His audience appeal," critic John

Lahr has observed, "almost single-handedly broke down the wall for other black artists, many of whom would not otherwise be working in the mainstream." As a dramatist, Wilson set out to change the ways "white America looks at blacks, and the way blacks look at themselves." Toni Morrison has called her efforts of bearing witness to previous generations' racial experiences "re-membering," that is, revivifying and embodying what has been lost in the past as too painful to recall. Wilson's plays function in a similar way. "What I want to do," he told an interviewer in 1987, "is place the culture of black America onstage, to demonstrate that it has the ability to offer sustenance, so that when you leave your parents' house, you are not in the world alone." *Fences* epitomizes Wilson's efforts to dramatize the reality of black experience in America while probing its depths and complexity.

How does Wilson's background inform his plays?

The search for self-definition and a sustaining racial heritage that dominates Wilson's plays are reflected in his background. Born Frederick August Kittel in 1945, Wilson grew up in Pittsburgh's black ghetto known as the Hill. His white father abandoned the family when Wilson was a child. His mother, Daisy Wilson Kittel, worked as a cleaning woman to support her six children; they lived in a two-room apartment above a grocery store. Wilson would later take his mother's maiden name to honor her and his African American heritage. When Wilson was twelve, his mother remarried, and the family moved to the predominantly white, working-class suburb of Hazelwood, where they were the target of racial abuse. At fourteen, Wilson was the only black student at Central Catholic High School. He subsequently transferred to a vocational school and then to a public high school, where he was falsely accused of plagiarism. Disgusted by the injustice and the racism he experienced, Wilson dropped out of school at age fifteen, spending his time at a public library where he educated himself, reading all he could of writers such as Richard Wright, Ralph Ellison, and Langston Hughes.

In 1965, Wilson moved out of his mother's home to a rooming house and began to associate with a group of local, young, black intellectuals and writers. Wilson heard Malcolm X speak for the first time and discovered the blues in the records of Bessie Smith. Both would have an important impact on his development. Wilson has called the black pride and

Malcolm X and the Nation of Islam were powerful influences on playwright August Wilson.

327

power message of Malcolm X and the Nation of Islam "the kiln in which I was fired," while he has described the blues, with its complexity and distinctness as an African American folk expression, as the wellspring of his art. In 1968, Wilson cofounded with Rob Penny the Black Horizons theater in the Hill. In operation until 1978, the theater served as a forum for his initial plays and exposure to the works of other black dramatists, such as Amiri Baraka, Ed Bullins, and Lonnie Elder. Wilson's evolving dramatic aesthetic would differ from that of other black dramatists of the period by avoiding an overt political and didactic take on the African American experience. Although also dealing with confrontations with whites as critic Mark William Rocha has explained, "in Wilson's plays the confrontation occurs off-stage so that the emphasis is placed not so much on the confrontation itself, but on how the black community invests itself in that face-to-face encounter." Moreover, contrary to the often racially exclusionary aesthetic of members of the Black Arts Movement, Wilson embraced a cross-cultural diversity of influences. "When I sat down to write," Wilson recalled about his first experience as a playwright, "I realized I was sitting in the same chair as Eugene O'Neill, Tennessee Williams, Arthur Miller, Henrik Ibsen, Amiri Baraka, and Ed Bullins."

What were Wilson's early experiences as a dramatist?

Wilson's career as a dramatist began in 1978, when he took a job writing dramatic skits for the Science Museum in Minnesota. He founded the Playwrights Center and discovered his dramatic voice recalling situations and characters from his hometown. Among his early plays, *Jitney* is a realistic drama set in a Pittsburgh gypsy taxi stand. *Fullerton Street*, a play set in the 1940s on the night of a famous Joe Louis prizefight, followed. In 1981, Wilson began submitting his plays to the National Playwrights Conference of the Eugene O'Neill Center in Connecticut. Four were rejected, but a fifth, *Ma Rainey's Black Bottom*, was accepted for a staged reading. This began Wilson's long association with Lloyd Richards, who directed the play at the Yale Repertory Theatre before it came to Broadway in 1984. This would set the model for most of Wilson's subsequent dramas, directed by Richards and premiering first at Yale before going on to Broadway. Set in a Chicago recording studio in 1927, *Ma Rainey's Black Bottom* focuses on blues singer Gertrude "Ma" Rainey and four male members of her backup band and the racial exploitation and frustration they experience. Reviewer Frank Rich declared Wilson "a major find for the American theater" who "sends the entire history of black America crashing down upon our head" through the play's "searing inside account of what white racism does to its victims."

How does *Fences* reflect Wilson's intentions?

Wilson has acknowledged that he never set out to write a play cycle by decades. After completing *Ma Rainey*, he realized, "I've written three plays in three different decades, so why don't I just continue to do that?" The scheme "gave me an agenda, a focus, something to hone in on, so that I never had to worry about what the next play would be about. I could always pick a decade and work on that." For his next play, Wilson chose the 1950s and set *Fences* in his hometown. Wilson has described the play as "the odd one, more conventional in structure with its large character." As he recalled its genesis, "I kept hearing *Ma Rainey* described as oddly constructed and I thought, 'I can write one of those plays where you have a big character and everything revolves around him.'" In *Fences* that character is fifty-three-year-old garbage collector Troy Maxson, the patriarch of a large, extended family living in a tenement in Pittsburgh in 1957. Gradually, through the play's nine scenes, Troy's complex personality, experiences, and relationships are revealed. As the play opens, Troy and his friend Jim Bono sit on the front porch of his home discussing Troy's challenge to his employer and the union over being denied the same opportunities as whites. Troy's strength of character in insisting on fairness and justice to provide for his family is balanced by Bono's accusation that Troy has been unfaithful to his wife, Rose, by seeing a woman named Alberta. When Lyons, Troy's son by a previous marriage, arrives to borrow money from his father, Troy urges him to get a job, to which Lyons replies, "I don't wanna hear all that about how I live.... If you wanted to change me, you should have been there when I was growing up." Troy's conflict with Lyons is repeated in his relationship with his younger son, Cory. Annoyed that his high school-aged son is neglecting his job at a supermarket to play football in the hopes of winning a college scholarship, Troy has informed the football coach that he has forbidden Cory to play any longer. The reasons behind Troy's actions eventually are revealed. His own father was selfish, insensitive, and angry at the world. His mother ran off when he was eight. Beaten by his father, Troy left home, resorting to crime to survive. After accidentally killing a man in a robbery, Troy was sent to prison, where he learned to play baseball. After his release, he became a star in the Negro League but was too old to take advantage of the integration of the Major Leagues. He is still resentful that he was denied the opportunity for success because of his race. Rather than compensating vicariously by his son's success, Troy worries that Cory will repeat his experience. When Cory is given the chance to play football in college on a scholarship, Troy sees not the social change that could help his son but his own denial. Racism makes Troy into both a victim and a victimizer in which the pain and resentment he has experienced become the principal legacy that he passes on to his family.

How does *Fences* develop in Act 2?

In the second act, the consequences of Troy's actions escalate. Confessing to Rose that he has been seeing another woman who is going to have his baby, Troy explains his betrayal: Alberta lets him forget his family responsibilities. In baseball terms, Troy says:

> I done locked myself into a pattern trying to take care of you all that I forgot about myself.... Rose, I done tried all my life to live decent ... to live a clean ... hard ... useful life. I tried to be a good husband to you. In every way I knew how. Maybe I come into the world backwards. I don't know. But ... you born with two strikes on you before you come to the plate. You got to guard it closely ... always looking for the curve-ball on the inside corner. You can't afford to let none get past you. You can't afford a call strike. If you going down ... you going

down swinging. Everything lined up against you. What you gonna do. I fooled them, Rose. I bunted. When I found you and Cory and a halfway decent job … I was safe. Couldn't nothing touch me. I wasn't gonna strike out no more.… Then when I saw that gal … she firmed up my backbone. And I got to thinking that if I tried … I just might be able to steal second. Do you understand after eighteen years I wanted to steal second.

The baseball analogy appears as well in the metaphor of the fence that Rose has asked Troy to complete around their property. For Rose, the fence represents protection and security for her family; for Troy, fences have restrained him all his life, and as a power hitter, his goal has always been to clear the fences. The climax for metaphor and man comes after Alberta has died in childbirth and Troy brings the infant, Raynell, home to be raised by Rose. She agrees, extending compassion to the innocent baby, but tells her husband, "I'll take care of your baby for you … this child got a mother. But you a womanless man."

What is the climax of *Fences*?

Troy's control over the people in his life is slipping away, culminating in his climactic confrontation with Cory, who stands up to his father: "You ain't never done anything but hold me back. Afraid I was gonna be better than you. All you ever did was try and make me scared of you." Troy advances to strike his son, but Cory defends himself with his father's baseball bat. Taunted by his father to "put me out," Cory swings and misses twice before Troy retrieves his bat and orders Cory out of his house. As his son departs, Troy exults: "I can't taste nothing. Hellujah! I can't taste nothing no more." Assuming his batting stance, he taunts Death to get a fastball by him: "Come on! It's between you and me now! Come on! Anytime you want! Come on! I be ready for you … but I ain't gonna be easy."

How does *Fences* conclude?

The final scene is set in 1965 on the morning of Troy's funeral. Rose is devoted to the seven-year-old Raynell and to involvement in her church. Lyons is serving time for cashing other people's checks. Cory arrives as a Marine corporal, determined not to attend his father's funeral. Rose, however, comes to Troy's defense:

Your daddy wanted you to be everything he wasn't … and at the same time he tried to make you into everything he was. I don't know if he was right or wrong … but I do know he meant to do more good than he meant to do harm. He wasn't always right. Sometimes when he touched he bruised. And sometimes when he took me in his arms he cut.

Rose's muted elegy for her flawed husband serves to reconcile Cory sufficiently that he relents. The play closes, emphasizing the fences that divide and protect. "At the end of *Fences* every person," Wilson has stated, "with the exception of Raynell, is institutionalized. Rose is in church. Lyons is in a penitentiary. Gabriel's in a mental hospital, and Cory's in the Marines. The only free person is the girl, Troy's daughter, the hope for the future."

August Wilson would go on documenting the past and suggesting a basis for the future in a remarkable series of plays, including *Joe Turner's Come and Gone* (1988), *The Piano Lesson* (1990), *Two Trains Running* (1992), *Seven Guitars* (1996), *and King Hedley II* (2001). All, in a sense, deal with the central issue of *Fences* as Wilson explained it: "I was trying to get at why Troy made the choices he made, how they have influenced his values and how he attempts to pass those along to his son. Each generation gives the succeeding generation what they think they need. One question in the play is 'Are the tools we are given sufficient to compete in a world that is different from the one our parents knew?' I think they are—it's just that we have to do different things with the tools. That's all Troy has to give. Troy's flaw is that he does not recognize that the world was changing."

READING CONTEMPORARY DRAMA– KUSHNER'S *ANGELS IN AMERICA*

What is important about *Angels in America*?

Without doubt, the most important drama to appear in the last decade of the twentieth century is *Angels in America* by Tony Kushner (1956–), a play that fundamentally challenged the conventional wisdom that had dominated contemporary theater. Kushner's play demonstrated that popularity and critical acclaim are not mutually exclusive, that the marginalized could claim the mainstream stage in a drama conceived on the grandest scale. If contemporary drama often seems shrunken down to isolated, private consciousness into what one reviewer has called "an era of apolitical American isolationist theatre," Kushner suggests a panoramic, engaged alternative. As reviewer Frank Rich asserted, *Angels in America* is "a searching and radical rethinking of the whole esthetic of American political drama in which far-flung hallucinations, explicit sexual encounters and camp humor are given as much weight as erudite ideological argument." Oversized and risky, mixing reality and fantasy, the current and the cosmological, hilarity and wrenching pain, *Angels in America* is an encyclopedia of dramatic and intellectual possibilities, a reflection of the messy contradictions of American democracy itself. Its aspirations stem from a Whitmanesque ambition to contain multitudes. Kushner has acknowledged the risk he took: "When I started to

Tony Kushner won the Pulitzer Prize for Drama, a Tony Award for Best Play, and the Drama Desk Award for Outstanding Play for his *Angels in America*.

331

write these plays, I wanted to attempt something of ambition and size even if that meant I might be accused of straying too close to ambition's ugly twin, pretentiousness. Given the bloody opulence of this country's great and terrible history, given its newness and its grand improbability, its artists are bound to be tempted towards large gestures and big embraces.… Melville, my favorite American writer, strikes inflated, even hysterical, chords on occasion. It's the sound of the Individual ballooning, overreaching. We are all children of 'Song of Myself.'" The young, relatively unknown playwright's attempt to elbow his way into the grand American literary tradition while treating homosexuality, the AIDS crisis, and the avowed cherished ideals of difference and diversity in the widest possible context of history, politics, metaphysics, and mysticism helped to make *Angels in America*, in the words of scholar John M. Clum, "a turning point in the history of gay drama, the history of American drama, and of American literary culture." Critic John Lahr has argued, "Not since [Tennessee] Williams has a playwright announced his poetic vision with such authority on the Broadway stage. Kushner is the heir apparent to Williams' romantic theatrical heritage: he, too, has tricks in his pocket and things up his sleeve, and he gives the audience 'truth in the pleasant disguise of illusion.' And, also like Williams, Kushner has forged an original, impressionistic theatrical vocabulary to show us the heart of a new age."

How does Kushner's background inform *Angels in America*?

Kushner was born in New York City in 1956. His parents, both classically trained musicians, moved their family to Lake Charles, Louisiana, when Kushner was an infant. He attributes his interest in opera and literature to his father and his passion for theater to his mother, who acted in local productions. "That's the major reason I went into the theater," Kushner reported. "I saw some of her performances when I was four or five years old and they were so powerful. I had vivid dreams afterwards." He also recollects from childhood "fairly clear memories of being gay since I was six. I knew that I felt slightly different than most of the boys I was growing up with. By the time I was eleven, there was no doubt. But I was completely in the closet." Kushner would not "come out" until his twenties. After graduating from high school, Kushner returned to New York City to attend Columbia University, where he graduated in 1978 with a concentration in medieval studies. He then worked as a switchboard operator at the United Nations Plaza Hotel in New York City for six years before deciding to pursue a career in the theater. Kushner enrolled at New York University, where he studied with Bertolt Brecht specialist Carl Weber and earned an M.F.A. in directing in 1984. It was the year that Ronald Reagan was reelected as president, the growing AIDS epidemic made headlines, and Kushner dealt with a number of personal setbacks. He recalled, "The desolate political sphere mirrored in an exact and ugly way an equally desolate personal sphere." He would choose to set *Angels in America* around this time.

In 1985 Kushner left New York to become assistant director at the St. Louis Repertory Theatre for one season and saw an eclectic group of his initial plays first performed. His early works include an opera, *La Fin de la Baleine: An Opera for the Apocalypse*

(1983), some children's plays, including *Yes, Yes, No, No* (1985), an adaptation of Goethe's drama *Stella* (1987), *The Illusion* (1988), adapted from Corneille, and one-act and full-length original plays, including *The Heavenly Theatre* (1986), *In Great Eliza's Golden Time* (1986), and *Hydriotaphia, or The Death of Dr. Browne* (1987). Kushner's first professional production was *A Bright Room Called Day* (1985), concerning a group of friends in Germany during the early years of Hitler's rise to power. Their story is juxtaposed with commentary from a narrator who draws parallels between Hitler's regime and current politics. When it opened in New York, it was called "an ambitious, disturbing mess of a play" that Frank Rich dismissed as "fatuous" and "an early front-runner for the most infuriating play of 1991." Oskar Eustis, the artistic director of the Eureka Theater Company in San Francisco, where the earliest version of *A Bright Room Called Day* was staged, was, however, impressed by Kushner's talent enough to commission him to write a play about the impact of AIDS on the gay community in San Francisco. This would become *Angels in America,* which grew into a seven-hour, two-part drama, developed in a workshop production at Los Angeles's Mark Taper Forum in 1990 before the first part, *Millennium Approaches,* premiered in San Francisco in 1991. Part two, *Perestroika,* premiered at the Mark Taper Forum in 1992. The first production of both parts occurred in Los Angeles before transferring to Broadway in 1993. By then Kushner had received international acclaim, and *Angels in America* was being called "The Great American Play."

What theory of drama does Kushner pursue in *Angels in America*?

The intentions and methods behind *Angels in America* reflect Kushner's influences and aims as a dramatist. An overtly socially engaged dramatist, Kushner has asserted that all drama is political and that he "cannot be a playwright without having some temptation to let the audiences know what I think when I read the newspaper in the morning. What I find is that the things that make you the most uncomfortable are the best things to write about." Unlike other American dramatists such as Clifford Odets and Arthur Miller, however, Kushner has not followed a predominant realistic method. Citing dramatists such as Ibsen and Shaw as influences for the drama of ideas that interests him, Kushner also is an admirer of the lyricism and overt sexual themes of Tennessee Williams. "The first time I read *Streetcar*," Kushner has asserted, "I was annihilated." Kushner's greatest influence, however, is Brecht:

> To me, Brecht is central. Playwrights who aspire to a theater of political analysis and engagement and who envision the theater as a platform for social debate—can see in the life and work of Brecht what the marriage of art and politics has to offer. I don't think anybody interested in writing progressive, politically committed theater can possibly avoid dealing with him. His theoretical writings are incredibly important, not just for the theater, but for film and all the arts. Everyone seems to dip into him. His notion of the relationship between the means of production, art and the audience is fundamental. *Mother Courage* is my favorite play. I think he's one of the great poets of the Twentieth Century.

Angels in America is a complex story with a mix of storylines and characters, some of whom are even ghosts and angels.

In Brecht, Kushner found the conjunction of "radical, dignified left politics and theatrical practice" that he would emulate, particularly in *Angels in America*, which conforms in its social themes and anti-illusionist method to Brecht's concept of epic theater.

How is *Angels in America* organized?

Kushner has said that with *Angels in America*, he set out to write a play on "AIDS, Mormons, and Roy Cohn." Linking these three disparate subjects—the disease that was destroying and isolating gays in America, the religious group committed to godliness but also intolerant toward gays, and the notorious conservative power broker who, though he persecuted gays, was himself a closet homosexual, only outed when he contracted AIDS and died in 1986—Kushner attempts to chronicle a particularly crucial moment of the testing of American values in a "Gay Fantasia on National Themes," featuring thirty characters played by eight actors. Set in New York City in 1985, the play explores its era when, in the words of Yeats, "things fall apart" through the linked narrative of two couples and the collapse of their relationships. Joe Porter Pitt, who is married to Harper ("an agoraphobic with a mild Valium addiction"), is a conservative Mormon and friend of power lawyer Roy Cohn. Joe and Harper's marriage is dissolving because of Joe's growing awareness that he is gay. The other couple is Louis Ironson and Prior Walter, whose relationship is threatened by Prior's worsening health from AIDS as Louis finds it impossible to remain with his partner. Their stories intersect and are thematically joined in split scenes and plot developments, such as Louis becoming Joe's lover; Belize, a former drag queen and lover of Prior's, serving as Roy Cohn's nurse; and Joe's mother, Hannah, who comes to the aid of Prior. The play also orchestrates its themes and connects its multiple plots and characters with the techniques of magic realism (as when Harper and Prior participate in a mutual dream sequence) as well as staging characters' fantasies and suffusing the narrative with ghosts, such as the spirit of Ethel Rosenberg who haunts Roy Cohn, and the supernatural, in which an Angel appears to Prior at the conclusion of *Millennium Approaches*.

Kushner has stated that the play is "about people being trapped in systems that they didn't participate in creating. The point being we're now in a new world in so many ways, we have to reinvent ourselves.... The characters need to create their own myths to empower themselves." To achieve this new empowering myth, the characters first must contend with forces that test their values and identities as the American democratic ideals of diversity and inclusion are being tested both by "Reaganomics" and the AIDS epidemic. Joe struggles to reconcile his Mormon faith and conservative Republicanism with his actual sexual preference, while Harper copes with the collapse of their marriage by drug-assisted fantasies of global destruction and flight. The liberal Louis, racked with guilt over his betrayal of Prior, calls Joe and himself "children of the new morning, criminal minds. Selfish and greedy and loveless and blind. Reagan's children." Perhaps the most staggering response to the trap of circumstances comes from Roy Cohn when he refuses his doctor's diagnosis of AIDS and the definitions that society forces on him:

ROY: AIDS. Your problem, Henry, is that you are hung up on words, on labels, that you believe they mean what they seem to mean. AIDS. Homosexual. Gay. Lesbian. You think these are names that tell you who someone sleeps with, but they don't tell you that.

HENRY: No?

ROY: No. Like all labels they tell you one thing and one thing only: where does an individual so identified fit in the food chain, in the pecking order? Not ideology, or sexual taste, but something much simpler: clout. Not who I fuck or who fucks me, but who will pick up the phone when I call, who owes me favors. This is what a label refers to. Now to someone who does not understand this, homosexual is what I am because I have sex with men. But really this is wrong. Homosexuals are not men who sleep with other men. Homosexuals are men who in fifteen years of trying cannot get a pissant antidiscrimination bill through City Council. Homosexuals are men who know nobody and who nobody knows. Who have zero clout. Does this sound like me, Henry?... I have sex with men. But unlike nearly every other man of whom this is true, I bring the guy I'm screwing to the White House and President Reagan smiles at us and shakes his hand. Because *what* I am is defined entirely by *who* I am. Roy Cohn is not a homosexual. Roy Cohn is a heterosexual man, Henry, who fucks around with guys.

335

HENRY: OK, Roy.

ROY: And what is my diagnosis, Henry?

HENRY: You have AIDS, Roy.

ROY: No, Henry, no. AIDS is what homosexuals have. I have liver cancer.

By the end of *Millennium Approaches*, the characters face a reckoning as they attempt to adjust to a changing reality. An Angel appears near the end ("*very* Steven Spielberg," Prior exclaims) to hail Prior as the new prophet of deliverance from the changes and struggles that have terrified the characters and altered their world.

What about Part 2 of *Angels in America?*

Kushner has asserted that Part 2 of *Angels in America, Perestroika*, "proceeds forward from the wreckage made by the Angel's traumatic entry" and "is about the characters' learning how to change. The problems the characters face are finally among the hardest problems—how we let go of the past, how to change and lose with grace, how to keep going in the face of overwhelming suffering." Opposing the otherworldly perfection of the Angel, a metaphor for ideals that have lost touch with reality, *Perestroika* celebrates messy, imperfect, and contradictory humanity. Belize reluctantly but compassionately nurses the dying Cohn, despite his taunts. Louis repents for his abandonment of Prior and seeks the means to make amends. Cohn's decline and death are

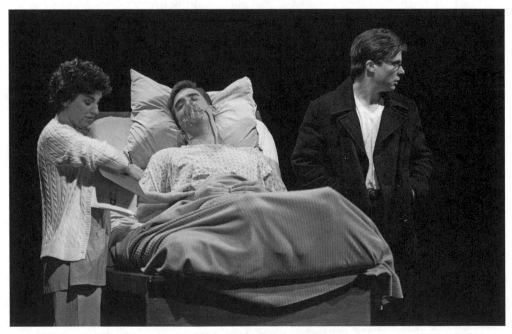

Kushner uses poignant subjects such as AIDS as forces that insert themselves into his characters' lives to test their values and identities.

matched by Prior's hard-fought coping with his disease and rejecting the role of the prophet of humanity's death. Wrestling with the Angel and storming heaven, Prior asserts to the assembled "Celestial Apparatchik/Bureaucrat-Angels" humanity's imperative: "We can't just stop. We're not rocks—progress, migration, motion is … modernity. It's *animate*, it's what living things do. We desire. Even if all we desire is stillness, it's still desire *for*." Prior's affirmation of life and change, despite all their pain and anguish, is matched by Harper's concluding vision of the souls of the dead rising to close the hole in the ozone protecting the earth: "Nothing's lost forever. In this world, there is a kind of painful progress. Longing for what we've left behind and dreaming ahead."

How does *Angels in America* conclude?

In the play's epilogue, set five years later, a new family and a new reflection of American democratic values have been constituted as Prior, Hannah, Belize, and Louis assemble before the angel statue of Central Park's Bethesda fountain. Affirming a common humanity transcending race and sexual preference, the play closes with Prior's direct address to the audience:

> This disease will be the end of many of us, but not nearly all, and the dead will be commemorated and will struggle on with the living, and we are not going away. We won't die secret deaths anymore. The world only spins forward. We will be citizens. The time has come. Bye now. You are fabulous creatures, each and every one. And I bless you: *More Life*. The Great Work Begins.

A triumph in its moral and intellectual challenges and its avoidance of the easy, sentimental assignment of villainy and victimization, *Angels in America* is also a liberating theater experience, pointing the way for drama to reclaim a primary role as interpreter of the historical moment and the human condition.

HOW TO READ LITERARY NONFICTION

What is literary nonfiction?

In this section, we will look at types of nonfiction that aspire to more than providing information or analysis alone. As discussed in the first chapter, most nonfiction falls under the class of "everyday reading"—a newspaper article, a recipe in a cookbook, a textbook. These are designed to deliver clear and concise key communication: Who won? What ingredients are needed? What formula or key dates apply? The writer uses a transparent style (not to obscure the message) and eliminates ambiguity (an undesired uncertainty of meaning or intention resulting from imprecision in the use of diction or syntax). Most nonfiction is practical and utilitarian: a vehicle to deliver information whose purpose and interest are fulfilled when the delivery is accomplished. We rarely go back to these nonfiction sources except to refresh our memory, and we rarely settle in to reread a nonfiction work for pleasure.

Rereading for pleasure is precisely what characterizes the kinds of nonfiction we will treat here. In its ambition and its style, certain kinds of nonfiction attempt more than just the basic transfer of information. Literary nonfiction, in its use of language, ideas, and in its expressive nature, meets Ezra Pound's definition of literature: "News that stays news." The essay, the memoir, and what has come to be called creative nonfiction, can all be categorized as literary nonfiction: often provocative and challenging forms of creative self-expression that possess their own rules for reading and understanding them. If literature—poetry, fiction, and drama—reaches truth through imaginative invention, literary nonfiction, still relying on creativity, finds its way to truth tethered to what is known rather than what can be imagined.

What are some early examples of literary nonfiction?

The best early examples of this kind of literary nonfiction are the nonfiction prose texts that are still read not just for the information they provide but also for their greater insights into the writers and their culture, as well as for their literary style. An example is Herodotus's *Histories*, written in the fifth century B.C.E., a long account of the Greco-Persian Wars. His history (the Greek word "historia" means "inquiry") is both the earliest surviving historical account as well as the first example of "creative nonfiction." Herodotus set out to "prevent the traces of human events from being erased by time, and to preserve the fame of the important and remarkable achievements produced by both Greeks and non-Greeks." He freely speculates and imagines what his historical figures might have said "as they seem true to me." Mixing the verifiable and the imagined, Herodotus was criticized as "The Father of Lies," particularly in comparison with fellow fifth-century B.C.E. historian Thucydides, whose rigorous, evidence-based histories were deemed more acceptable. Herodotus, however, would later be praised as one of the most modern of the ancient Greeks for recognizing that all well-told history is a version of creative storytelling, a matter of selection and idealization, that incorporates both myth and fact in its truth-telling.

Herodotus's successor, Greek writer Plutarch (46–120), displays a similar handling of myth and fact in his best-known work *Parallel Lives*, a series of biographies of famous Greeks and Romans, arranged in pairs to display common moral virtues and vices. The importance of the work includes both the insights provided about so many ancient historical figures as well as the lessons drawn in the arrangement. Like Herodotus, Plutarch shows that nonfiction depends on selection and can be driven by a larger purpose to find moral lessons in past lives. Plutarch's *Moralia* ("Customs and Mores") is an eclectic collection of reflections and transcribed speeches with such titles as "On Fraternal Affection," "On the Fortune or the Virtue of Alexander the Great," and "On Peace of Mind." The *Moralia* serves as a volume of proto-essay models that would influence Montaigne in his formulation of the unique nature of the essay form that he pioneered in the sixteenth century.

How did the essay originate?

The modern essay is named by and conceived by Michel de Montaigne (1533–1592). It may seem surprising to suggest a point of origin for such a ubiquitous and familiar form of writing. However, the first sustained writing you ever did, from the "what I did on my summer vacation" to a book report, derived from the essay pioneered by Montaigne: a personal reflection on a specific topic. We might try our hand at writing a poem, a play, a short story, or a novel, but the essay is the go-to writing task from papers in school to quarterly reports and planning documents. Whenever you have felt the need or desire to go beyond straightforward reporting in a letter, email, or text message—"It's snowing" or "meet you at 8"—you enter the territory of the essay. As soon as you aspire to render vividly and expressively in writing the nature and meaning of your experience and what it makes you think and feel, you are following the path laid out by Montaigne more than four centuries ago.

It is ironic that a literary form that plays so much a part in our writing life is a late invention. Only the novel and the short story postdate the essay's development. It was not until the late sixteenth century that the essay was named and recognized as a distinct, independent, and respectable literary form. Drama and lyric and epic poetry precede it by more than a millennium. In interesting ways, the invention of the essay, or literary nonfiction, is directly connected with the creation of fiction as a form of self-expression and an analysis of our world. The essay, novel, and short story all needed some cultural and consciousness shifts to be possible.

What explains the origin of the essay?

As a form of literary expression, the essay is directly connected with the relatively new, radical notion that the individual's perspective on the world mattered. The missing ingredient that made the essay into an available form of self-expression and communication is the Renaissance's emphasis on subjective experience in its discovery of the importance of the "I." It was during the Renaissance when the profound notion took hold that the individual, not some received authority, could make sense of the world, that the subjective experience of individuals merited consideration in literary expression, that the "I" had important things to tell "Us." In classical literature, except in the lyric, the individual who created the epic or drama is subsumed in the work itself, whose subject is derived from the culture's myths, legends, and history, not an individual's experiences. Homer only emerges as an individualized voice indirectly: what he thinks and feels about his characters or events is largely beside the point of the dominant stance of objectivity. Even as late as Shakespeare, objectivity still reigned supreme. It is simply not possible to learn anything certain about the author through his plays (though many have tried to do so). For most of literary history, the writer was largely anonymous, a craftsman producing an object that communicated significance and meaning.

French philosopher Michel de Montaigne is credited with popularizing the essay as a literary form.

We can begin to see the shift from objectivity to subjectivity by comparing Medieval and Renaissance painting. In Medieval art, figures are depicted on the same spatial plane; there is little attempt to render figures in three dimensions—height, width, and depth—only in two: height and width. With Renaissance paintings, the two-dimensional surface also shows depth. Renaissance art is distinguished by this discovery of linear perspective, that is, the illusion of the third dimension of depth on a two-dimensional surface. It works because the painting depends on an "I" view in which all that we see is oriented from that perspective.

It is this discovery of perspective that helped to define the Renaissance but not just in the visual arts. Consider what the discovery of perspective means philosophically: the

341

"I" now matters; that is, how we see the world depends on where we are viewing it, by our vantage point and perspective. Perspective in art is just one example of the widespread discovery in the Renaissance that called attention to and considered the importance of subjective, individual evaluation and assessment. The essay would become the prose equivalent of perspectivism in art. It would express the sense of the world from a distinctive, individual, and subjective, rather than objective, viewpoint.

What were Montaigne's contributions to the creation of the essay?

Prior to Montaigne, throughout the classical period and later, there had been long and short prose reflections on various subjects, by Herodotus, Plato, Plutarch, Cicero, Seneca, Horace, Augustine, and Machiavelli, but Montaigne's originality and distinctiveness fully reflected the Renaissance view and set the pattern for the essay form as it is known today.

Born in 1533, Montaigne had the advantage of being the son of a well-to-do merchant father who was inspired by the philosophy of the Renaissance to raise his son on its principles of humanistic learning and its faith in the potential of the individual to know and understand the world. Montaigne would be educated by some of the leading humanist scholars of the day, and, after a career in the law and as a magistrate and legislator, he had the wealth to retire at age thirty-eight to his chateau to devote himself to reading and writing. Montaigne began asking "What do I know?" and tried to answer that question first by compiling a collection of quotations from his extensive reading of classical and Renaissance sources with his own commentary. As he continued to write, his comments began to overwhelm the quotations, and Montaigne began to develop a new literary style: loose, anecdotal, almost free association in a series of meditations on multiple topics with titles such as "Of Age," "Of Drunkenness," "Of Vanity," "Of Constancy," and "Of Fear." He called his efforts *Essais,* meaning "attempts," or explorations, and as he stated throughout his collection of 102 meditations: "I am myself the subject of my book," reflecting his constantly shifting, subjective view of the world. In 1580, volumes one and two of *Essais* were published. In 1586, a third volume appeared with a revision and expansion of the first two volumes. Montaigne would spend his last years further revising and expanding his collection before his death in 1592.

In a sense, Montaigne combined in his new essay form metaphysics (what can we know and how do we know it), sociology (how do human beings live), and psychology (how do human beings think and feel). No subject was off-limits, including his own often contradictory and fallible personality and temperament. Rather than the formal eloquence of previous writers, Montaigne's style is easygoing and informal, marked by a witty, self-deprecating tone, along with a series of amusing and ingenious anecdotes, examples, and quotations. The one constant connecting the diverse subject matter is his own subjective awareness. In Montaigne's *Essais,* the "I" comes to the center of the stage as he examines his own nature, what he considered the *only* subject on which one can speak with any degree of certainty.

Given Montaigne's fascination with himself, you would expect that he would flatter himself about his privileged and central position in the universe as well as his special power of understanding it, but the opposite is the case. Montaigne continually insists on how average and mediocre his view is and how fallible, unreliable, untrustworthy, and limited he and his fellow human beings can be. There is little preaching or pontificating in the *Essais* but more a sense of the ongoing struggle of an intelligent, all-too-human speaker trying to make sense of a chaotic world. Think of humorist Dave Barry as a contemporary descendant of Montaigne!

What are some examples of Montaigne's voice and intention in the *Essais?*

- So, Reader, I am myself the subject of my book; it is not reasonable to expect you to' waste your leisure on a matter so frivolous and empty.
- 'Tis a book consubstantial with the author, of a peculiar design, a member of my life, and whose business is not designed for others, as that of all other books is.
- Authors communicate themselves to the world by some special and extrinsic mark; I am the first to do so by my general being, as Michel de Montaigne, not as a grammarian or a poet or a lawyer. If the world finds fault with me for speaking too much of myself, I find fault with the world for not even thinking of itself.
- I speak my mind freely on all things, even on those which perhaps exceed my capacity and which I by no means hold to be within my jurisdiction. And so the opinion I give of them is to declare the measure of my sight, not the measure of things.

These four famous quotations from Montaigne perfectly capture the nature of his work and the confidential, confessional tone and voice in *Essais*. In the first, Montaigne makes clear that he is the real subject of his book. Rather than an egotist claiming importance for this subject, Montaigne expresses the opposite, humbly marveling that the reader would be the least bit interested in such a frivolous and mediocre subject. In the second, he makes the connection between "I" and his subject even more explicit. His book is not really "for" others; it's for himself, for self-understanding. The suggestion here is that his essays should be understood more as explorations than sermons, more about questions than answers. The third clarifies the difference between Montaigne and other writers. Montaigne declares that he is the first writer to appear before his readers not defined by a role or a profession— neither as a grammarian, poet, nor lawyer—but as just an individual, as Michel de Montaigne. This makes for a radically new kind of authenticity and hon-

Humorist and essayist Dave Barry may be considered a modern-day version of Montaigne, a man who portrayed himself as an everyday person trying to make sense of the world.

esty in his essays. The fourth makes clear that Montaigne is neither the expert nor the authority nor the final word on any of his subjects. Instead, he will declare "the measure of my sight," that is, how he sees the world and understands it.

ANALYSIS OF MONTAIGNE'S "OF SMELLS"

What is "Of Smells" about?

Despite evidence to the contrary, most believe that the best smell is an absence of smell. Yet Montaigne is drawn to certain smells as he is repelled by others. Physicians, Montaigne suggests, should promote the benefits of odors because he has noticed how smells "cause an alteration in me." An example of beneficial fragrances is incense in churches that "rouse up and purify the senses, the better to fit us for contemplation."

Likewise, cooks can captivate with their aromas as was the case when the cook to the king of Tunis visited Naples and produced smells that filled nearby streets and persisted for a long time.

Montaigne concludes by saying that his first concern in choosing lodgings when traveling is to avoid bad smells, and in this regard, both Venice and Paris "lessen the kindness I have for them" by their offensive smells.

How does "Of Smells" work as an essay?

Such a bald summary of Montaigne's argument in "Of Smells" misses the essence of the writer as well as the appeal of the essay form he pioneered. Consider first its subjects: smells of all kinds, offensive as well as pleasant. It is often said that the first thing one would notice time-traveling back to another era like Montaigne's would be its smells: an expected, overpowering, and omnipresent sensation. But who before Montaigne, other than noting pleasure or offense, considered smells in all their dimensions and in their effects? Montaigne announces here that no topic is out of bounds for his consideration, and his essays will tackle topics from the profound to the mundane.

The essay in its first paragraph establishes Montaigne's credentials as a learned authority, with references to Plutarch and quotations from Plautus and Martial. Yet Montaigne's scholarship plays against the essay's subject matter, orchestrating several classical voices to weigh in on such a low and presumably indecorous topic. Montaigne's scholarship here is handled not ponderously or pompously but playfully. It supports the essay's opening surprising paradox: we mostly value smells by their absence ("She smells sweetest, who smells not at all"). In fact, Montaigne points out, those who smell the strongest, even if perfumed, have the most to hide: "To smell, though well, is to stink," Montaigne declares. With both these initial observations that the absence of smells is the accepted standard of excellence and that excessive smells, even if inoffensive, call attention to its opposite are both witty and clever. They prepare us for the essay's central procedure: to surprise us with reflections that are both fresh and inventive, supported by a tone that is conversational rather than lecturing, informal even in its formality of quotations and citations.

How does "Of Smells" proceed?

The essay shifts attention from basic dichotomies of good and foul smells to consider the multiplicity and gradations of smells. To draw his distinctions, Montaigne freely offers himself as the prime example: "I am nevertheless a great lover of good smells, and as much abominate the ill ones, which also I scent at a greater distance, I think, than other men." The "I" here recurs three times in a single sentence. The effect is to establish a more informal conversational and confessional relationship with the reader, drawing examples and generalities from the author's own experiences, treated not as definitive but typical. "Physicians might, I believe," Montaigne suggests, "extract greater utility from odours than they do, for I have often observed that they cause an alteration in me and work upon my spirits according to their several virtues...."

Anticipating the concept of aromatherapy, Montaigne considers the various purposes smells serve. For support, he offers the example of incense in churches "to cheer us, and to rouse and purify the senses, the better to fit us for contemplation." A second example are cooks who have "so rare a way of seasoning exotic odours," such as a renowned chef to the royal court of Charles the Emperor, whose dishes filled the room and nearby streets with "an aromatic vapour which did not presently vanish." Here, not

classical scholarship but reliable observation (use of incense in church services) and documented testimony of Muley-Hassan support the generalizations. His examples move from the profound (worship) to the mundane (cooking smells) that serve the same purpose: smells alter our moods and reception of the spirit and the flesh. Montaigne displays here both a range of ideas and experiences that move at the speed of association, barely controlled by his paragraph units. The effect is to take the reader inside Montaigne's mental processes, almost like a Joycean stream of consciousness.

How does "Of Smells" conclude?

The essay more accurately trails off, rather than concludes, with another example from the author's experience: how his enjoyment

Montaigne notes how churches use incense in services to put us in a better state of mind for contemplation.

345

of Venice and Paris are directly related to avoidance of the "thick and stinking air" of "those beautiful cities." Montaigne simply ends his observations, violating the principle that an author should offer some concluding summation, tying together the various claims into a central thesis or clear takeaway. None of this is done in "Of Smells." Montaigne ends without assessment. Instead, the essay concludes having posed some interesting exceptions to the conventional rule that the best smells are no smells. Montaigne offers examples of how smell can do more than offend. It can elevate and intensify experience, both adding to our contemplation and pleasure and decisively ruining it. Smell, therefore, is shown as no trivial power or unseemly subject. The essay succeeds in forcing the reader to look at something in a new way, much like the church smells that he mentions "to cheer us, and to rouse and purify the senses, the better to fit us for contemplation." There is no better description of what an essay should attempt to accomplish.

German philosopher Friedrich Nietzche considered Montaigne to be an author who highlighted the joy of being alive.

What have others said about Montaigne?

It is not often that we can date with any approach to accuracy the arrival of a new class of literature into the world. But it was the month of March 1571 that the essay was invented.

—Edmund Gosse

This great French writer deserves to be regarded as a classic, not only in the land of his birth, but in all countries and in all literatures.… He was, without being aware of it, the leader of a new school in letters and morals. His book was different from all others which were at that date in the world. It diverted the ancient currents of thought into new channels. It told its readers, with unexampled frankness, what its writer's opinion was about men and things, and threw what must have been a strange kind of new light on many matters but darkly understood. Above all, the essayist uncased himself, and made his intellectual and physical organism public property. He took the world into his confidence on all subjects. His essays were a sort of literary anatomy, where we get a diagnosis of the writer's mind, made by himself at different levels and under a large variety of operating influences.

—William Hazlitt

That such a man wrote has truly augmented the joy of living on this Earth.

—Friedrich Nietzsche

Montaigne is the frankest and honestest of all writers. His French freedom runs into grossness; but he has anticipated all censure by the bounty of his own confessions.... He parades it: he makes the most of it: nobody can think or say worse of him than he does. He pretends to most of the vices; and, if there be any virtue in him, he says, it got in by stealth. There is no man, in his opinion, who has not deserved hanging five or six times; and he pretends no exception in his own behalf.

—Ralph Waldo Emerson

It is life that emerges more and more clearly as these essays reach not their end, but their suspension in full career. It is life that becomes more and more absorbing as death draws near, one's self, one's soul, every fact of existence: that one wears silk stockings summer and winter; puts water in one's wine; has one's hair cut after dinner; must have glass to drink from; has never worn spectacles; has a loud voice; carries a switch in one's hand; bites one's tongue; fidgets with one's feet; is apt to scratch one's ears; likes meat to be high; rubs one's teeth with a napkin (thank God, they are good!); must have curtains to one's bed; and, what is rather curious, began by liking radishes, then disliked them, and now likes them again. No fact is too little to let it slip through one's fingers, and besides the interest of facts themselves there is the strange power we have of changing facts by the force of the imagination.

—Virginia Woolf

What is Montaigne's legacy?

In the seventeenth century, the French philosopher Pascal would complain about Montaigne's "foolish project of painting himself," but the world has basically gotten Montaigne's point. Montaigne has been recognized as one of the great literary originators who stands clearly behind so many subsequent essayists. In 1597, Montaigne's term *Essais* entered English when Francis Bacon applied it to his own *Essays* (1597–1625). The form would be imitated and modified: in Blaise Pascal's own *Pensées* (*Thoughts*) (1670), in the works of eighteenth-century writers Jonathan Swift, Voltaire, Rousseau, Joseph Addison, Richard Steele, and Samuel Johnson; in the nineteenth century by Samuel Taylor Coleridge, William Hazlitt, Charles Lamb, and Thomas de Quincy; in America by Ralph Waldo Emerson, Henry David Thoreau, and Mark Twain; and during the twentieth and twenty-first centuries by Virginia Woolf, George Orwell, James Baldwin, Joan Didion, Ralph Ellison, Maxine Hong Kingston, Barbara Kingsolver, David Sedaris, and many more.

As the essay has evolved, it has retained Montaigne's pioneering conception of a prose work that makes no claim to an exhaustive or technical examination of a subject;

rather, essays seek to record thoughts and ruminations on diverse topics for a general audience. Influenced by Montaigne's example, subsequent writers have multiplied the essay into several types: informal, formal, narrative, descriptive, expository (explaining something), and argumentative. These categories can overlap but help to establish the essay's range and utility.

ESSAYS

How should you read an essay?

With Montaigne's example in mind, he offers some excellent initial ideas on how to read an essay:

No subject is off-limits—An essay may tell a story, but it doesn't have to, or, like a poem, it may only recount a feeling or a thought. It need not be more than a glimpse. It can trade in questions rather than answers. Approach each essay on its own terms, and see what you learn.

Not just assertions—Essays persuade by their ability to offer vivid and convincing examples and evidence. What sets most essays apart from other forms of nonfiction is how effectively the essay makes its ideas and feelings tangible. Pay attention to the interaction between the abstract and the specific.

The "I" is central—The essay offers access to a particular point of view, a specific perspective. Unlocking an essay's meaning and significance is often a matter of understanding that point of view.

Tone matters—Montaigne generally features an informal, conversational tone. In reading other essays, let the tone establish your criteria for assessment. Some essays read less like an intimate conversation between writer and reader and more like a well-scripted speech (or sermon). Both kinds of essays are valid, and one need not be more significant than the other.

Read it like a short story—The essay's short form, to be read in a single sitting, should remind you of the intentions and procedures of the short story: achieving a unity of effect through a principle of exclusion. As in a short story, assume that everything is there for a purpose. Ask yourself how and why this detail, sentence, and paragraph contribute to the essay's outcome and overall meaning.

Nonfiction contract—You can read an essay like a short story, but an essay is not a short story. Instead, essays abide by a contract with the reader to stick to the actual, and speculation and invention in an essay needs to be identified as such. A short story writer is not constrained by fact; an essayist needs to be. There are many examples of essay writers violating this contract, for example investigative journalists making up sources or a writer falsely claiming to tell a true story, with career-ending consequences. In reading an essay, trust the writer who honors the nonfiction contract unreservedly.

348

Questions, not answers—Many great essays, like great works of literature, are concerned less about solving a problem or providing answers and more about formulating interesting questions to provoke continuing reflections and debate, not to close them off. Remember what *essais* means in French: an attempt or an exploration in which the journey of discovery matters more than any definitive conclusion.

Violate rules—Montaigne shows that the essayist can violate every rule of subject matter or procedure, provided inquiry and communication are enhanced. The test for any essay is: Does it make you think? Does it tell you something you didn't know before? Does it make the familiar surprising or the surprising familiar?

What other approach should you take in reading an essay?

Essays, or indeed any literary nonfiction, need to be read in the same way as you read literature: actively and closely. Here are some suggestions:

Pre-reading—Before plunging into an essay, get your bearings by attending to any biographical or publication information provided. Who is the author? What is his or her background and expertise? Where the essay was first published can tell you what to expect: was this an op-ed piece, an essay in a scholarly journal, or a periodical for a more general reader? By answering these questions, you can anticipate issues like tone, formality, and standards of persuasiveness in the essay. Look at the essay before you start to read it: what does the title tell you about the subject and the approach? Skim the first paragraph to see if you learn more about the topic and vantage point. Look at the opening sentences for each paragraph to determine what the essay is about and its organization. Look at the conclusion to see if the thesis (the central point the essay wants to show) has been clarified.

Read the essay actively—Read, and reread, the essay as if you are having a conversation with the writer. What is the chain of thought or organizational principle here: deductive (generalization to particular) or inductive (particular to the general). Find the thesis statement that drives the essay. It's the essay's central point: what it wants to show or prove. Usually, writers state the thesis early to focus the reader's attention on the claims in support of the thesis that follows. Sometimes, the thesis is the "a-ha!" moment of revelation at the end: here's what to make of what I have just shown you. Sometimes, the essay forces the reader to formulate the thesis with no direct help by the author. Identifying the thesis, whether stated directly or indirectly, is often the key to understanding the essay and judging its effectiveness.

Ask questions—Continually ask "why this and not that" questions. An essay, like any work of literature, is all about choices and selection. Ask why this word and not some other, why this detail and not some other, why this reaction and not some other. It may seem that your questions are one-sided because you won't get any direct response, but these questions tend to take you deeply into not just the "what" of the essay but also the "how." You may not need to know how an engine works to take advantage of a car ride, but looking "under the hood" of an essay repays the effort in understanding.

Summarize—One of the best tests of your understanding of an essay is to force yourself to write a brief summary of it, what finally stands out in what the essay says and how the essay says it? Finally, write down your takeaway from this essay: How has it made you feel? What has it said that you either didn't know before or never quite viewed what you do know in the same way? Ultimately, the test of an essay, like any work of literature, is what it tells the reader about human nature and human experience.

AUTOBIOGRAPHY AND MEMOIR

What is the relationship between the essay and autobiography?

Although Montaigne would pioneer the first-person, subjective approach, which subsequent essayists would imitate, there are earlier versions of autobiographical writing in literary history. St. Augustine's *Confessions*, written between 397 and 400, is generally considered the first autobiography in Western literature. He chronicles his first forty years, recording his sinful early years and eventual conversion to Christianity, providing one of the earliest detailed accounts of a life and times that would influence many similar works during the Middle Ages. Another is *The Confessio* of St. Patrick (fifth century), containing almost all the known information about him that exists. *The Confessio* follows Augustine's pattern of conversion to faith and spiritual rebirth. The most important early secular autobiography is that of Benvenuto Cellini (1500–1571), Florentine goldsmith, sculptor, and painter. It was begun in 1558 when Cellini was fifty-eight and offers a detailed account of his career as well as his loves and enemies, ending abruptly three years before his death. In it, Cellini offers advice to all who might follow him in writing an account of their lives: "No matter what sort he is, everyone who has to his credit what are or really seem great achievements, if he cares for truth and goodness, ought to write the story of his own life in his own hand; but no one should venture on such a splendid undertaking before he is over forty." Cellini's criteria of a life in full, or at least from a mature perspective to enhance distance and understanding, has been followed in countless subsequent autobiographies, including Jean-Jacques Rousseau's *Confessions* (1789), *The Autobiography of Benjamin Franklin* (1791), *The History of My Life* (1822) by Casanova, *The Story of My Life* (1903) by Helen Keller, *Mein Kampf* (1925) by Adolf Hitler, *The Story of My Experiments with Truth* (1927) by Mahatma Gandhi, *Long Walk to Freedom* (1994) by Nelson Mandela, and *Dreams from My Father* (1995) by Barack Obama.

What are the key differences between the essay and autobiography?

Compared to the discursive glimpse of the essay, the autobiography echoes the novel's amplitude and inclusion. Like the novelist, the autobiographer constructs a narrative of a life, selecting the salient events and experiences, which from the writer's vantage point explain how the writer developed and became the person he or she is. Great autobiographies must adhere to the factual record, but selection is everything. A bald episodic chronology may set a biographical record straight, but to reach literary status, the autobiographical writer needs to do much more. Great autobiographies bring episodes to life with vivid details and insights that help the reader gain not just the facts but also their importance and significance.

To see how a novelist does it, examine classic fictional autobiographies: Charles Dickens's *David Copperfield* (1851), Tolstoy's *Childhood, Boyhood,* and *Youth* (1852–1856), D. H. Lawrence's *Sons and Lovers* (1913), James Joyce's *A Portrait of the Artist as a Young Man* (1916), Marcel Proust's *In Search of Lost Time* (1927), Ralph Ellison's *Invisible Man* (1952), Sylvia Plath's *The Bell Jar* (1963), J. M. Coetzee's *Boyhood: Scenes from Provincial Life* (1997), and many more. In all, a life in full (or over a significant portion) is treated in a succession of incidents and revelations in the development of the speaker. Unlike the novelist, the writer of an autobiography cannot invent or contrive a more satisfactory sequence of events or outcomes. Instead of invention, the autobiographical writer relies on memory. An autobiography is anchored by the facts of the author's life, but memory often fails and tricks us. Autobiographies are different from biographies in which the historical record and corroboration provide more reliability, if less intimacy and authenticity.

What are the key differences between autobiography and memoir?

Closer in scope and method to the essay is the memoir. If the essay resembles the short story and the autobiography is similar to the novel, then the memoir is somewhere in between— like the novella, without the amplitude of the novel but more extended than the short story. A memoir need not detail a life in full but can deal with just significant portions of that life. Examples include Julius Caesar's account of his nine-year campaign in the Gallic Wars in *Commentaries* (58–49 B.C.E.) or the *Personal Memoirs of Ulysses S. Grant* (1885), focused on his military career during the Mexican–American War and the Civil War, or presidential accounts, such as Richard Nixon's *Six Crises* (1962) or Jimmy Carter's *Keeping Faith: Memoirs of a President* (1982). Robert Graves treats his World War I experiences in *Goodbye to All That* (1929). Vladimir Nabokov's *Speak, Memory* (1951) re-creates his life until his emigration to America in 1940. Frank McCourt's *Angela's Ashes* (1996) and Mary Karr's *The Liars' Club* (1995) chronicle their tragic-comic childhoods in Limerick, Ireland, and east Texas, respectively. Memoirs often are produced by the famous but need not be. Frank McCourt was an unpublished New York City high school teacher before winning the Pulitzer Prize for *Angela's Ashes*.

Freed from the autobiography's encompassing summation and chronology of an entire life (or its most significant part), the memoir narrows its focus to a specific aspect of a life. It can be less formal, more tentative, more an inquiry or exploration and, therefore, more like Montaigne's *Essais* than an autobiography. Gore Vidal in his own memoir, *Palimpsest* (1995), described the difference as follows: "A memoir is how one remembers one's own life, while an autobiography is history, requiring research, dates, facts double-checked." In other words, the memoir tries to do more than just record a person's history; it wants to re-create that history. Think of the difference between a narrative summary of a résumé and a much closer, more introspective, more imaginative reconstruction of a section of that résumé. Characteristically, autobiography tells and the memoir shows. The memoirist often borrows from the resources of fiction, in its evocative use of detail and in a more expressive style, to achieve a more literary quality, to be interesting and significant not just in what it records but how it does so.

What has contributed to the popularity of the memoir?

William Zinsser in *Inventing the Truth: The Art and Craft of Memoir* (1998) has called the end of the last century "the age of memoir." Ben Yagoda in his book *Memoir: A History* (2009) identifies the period 1990–2010 as the boom years, when "total sales in the categories of Personal Memoir, Childhood Memoirs, and Parental Memoirs increased more than 400 percent between 2004 and 2008." There is no sign of let-up, and it's hard to say whether boom has finally shifted to bust with overproduction, or whether memoirs remain the ideal vehicle for Andy Warhol's celebrated prediction that "in the future, everyone will be world famous for fifteen minutes." Is the memoir the literary expression of our "selfie" culture? Or will pictures and social media posts eliminate the hard work needed to examine a life?

If the memoir's future is unclear, it is still interesting to speculate on why it has achieved such popularity and pervasiveness in our culture. One argument might be that the memoir has filled a gap left by modern literature. Modernism's retreat from reality to subjective consciousness, from public to private concerns, and postmodernism's assertion that there is nothing "real" and that all truth is problematic, have left readers scrambling for the verifiable, in which "a true story," or an account based on an actual life, is reassuring. There are readers today who have foregone the literary for the solidity and consolation of nonfiction. History, biography, autobiography, memoir, and the essay make sense of the world in ways modern fiction and poetry have failed to deliver for many readers. Modern literature is just too much effort for some to work out the connection between the imagined and a relevant truthfulness. Nonfiction secures its truths at the outset in promising to deliver facts or, at least, the actual.

Another argument is that the memoir is simply a rediscovery of Socrates's maxim that "the unexamined life is not worth living." Self, according to Montaigne, is not just the best subject but is the only subject we can discuss with confidence. Fledgling writers are forever being advised to "write about what you know"—and who or what do you know any better than yourself? Memories are ready-made narratives, already fleshed out with whatever vivid details can be recalled. It is not surprising that when looking for a writing subject, a personal story is the first that comes to mind. It does not require invention; plot and character are already formed. The "theme" of a life or a part of a life might be difficult to decipher, but significance is assured: is any story more consequential than yours? The trick with the self-centered memoir is to make what is naturally interesting to you—your life and times—interesting to someone else. A diary makes riveting reading to its author; for a reader, not so much. It's like all those photos of restaurant dishes posted on social media; they're not really nourishing for the viewer. Memoirs and essays make the risky and presumptuous assertion that one person's life can represent all, that what interests and fascinates the writer will also interest and fascinate the reader. The memoir's continued popularity will largely depend on the degree to which it aspires to the universal relevance of literature.

How should you read a memoir?

Here are some suggestions on what to look for in reading and evaluating a memoir:

- Does it have an interesting story to tell? Memoirs of the famous have an advantage over others because we generally want to read about people we are familiar with or want to know more about. Readers bring to a memoir of a former president or celebrity a built-in motivation to follow their accounts. The memoirs of the famous have thereby cleared the first hurdle in any memoir: motivate the reader to read on. However, fame does not guarantee literary success or valuable insights. Sometimes, setting the record straight by a celebrity memoirist means burnishing an image and defensively evading unpleasantness. Perhaps the best example of this is *RN: The Memoirs of Richard Nixon* (1978), a maddening series of evasions, lacking either authenticity or introspection: a memoir as press release. We have reached the moment when classic rock legends—Keith Richards, Neil Young, Pete Townshend, Brian Wilson, Bruce Springsteen, and many more—have all issued autobiographies or memoirs. Sex, drugs, and rock 'n' roll—what could be more interesting? However, writing about a great song's hook or a chronicle of life on the road does not necessarily ensure a great memoir.

Ultimately, the test for a successful memoir is not just potential reader interest but also whether there is a story, or rather, a plot at all. As discussed earlier, a story is a chronological sequence of episodes, while a plot depends on causality: how episodes are related, how they lead to something greater in terms of outcome and significance. Plot, rather than story, is the key ingredient for a great memoir. A lasting memoir needs to be more than just a chronological account. It needs to make sense of that chronology in an interesting or surprising way. It needs to move from telling the story of a life to revealing its plot.

This is particularly true for memoirs written by the less than famous, by private rather than public figures. Lacking the name recognition or the built-in appeal of the famous, many of these memoirs claim attention through stories that rely heavily on sensation, on personal tragedies, dysfunctional families, addiction, and sexual abuse, so much so that they have been categorized Misery Lit or Victim Lit—leading a famous bookstore chain to group these in a "Painful Lives" section. Tolstoy's famous opening line to *Anna Karenina* is: "All happy families are alike; each unhappy family is unhappy in its own way." Misery Lit threatens Tolstoy's maxim with unhappy sameness. A great memoir needs more than dreadful and sensational circumstances. It needs to convert all into a plot or a journey that takes us to unexpected places and shows how and why we got there.

- Does it justify your time and attention? For a memoir to reach beyond the shocking to the significant, it needs to do more than titillate. Lasting memoirs tell us things we don't know, expose us to perspectives, settings, and situations that are new to us, or re-introduce the familiar in unexpected and surprising ways. It is often said that there are only two subjects for literature: love and death. *How* we deal with them makes all the difference whether in a poem, drama, fiction, or memoir. The best question to ask of any memoir after evaluating its story or plot is how it performs on your interest scale, with "Ho-hum" or "So what" at one end and "Wow" and "I never knew that" on the other.

- Does it tell its story in an interesting way? To become a memoir of lasting value, one that invites rereading after the revelations are exposed, it needs to be well written. Otherwise, memoirs risk falling back into the category of everyday reading for information transfer. Even the most fascinating life can revert to the commonplace, can fail to come to life at all, under the weight of deadening and leaden prose. For a memoir to merit consideration as literature, it needs to be written artfully beginning with its principle of selection. In telling a story based on a life, potentially every aspect of that life is relevant, but clearly, not every aspect is *equally* relevant. Imagine answering the question "How was your day?" around the family dinner table. Think about all that you would edit out as uninteresting or unessential. You would instead focus on just the key incidents and details that collectively answer the question about your day. In other words, you find in the myriad details of a day the blueprint for a plot, excluding all other details as irrelevant or beside the point. Memoirists must do the same for a life or a significant portion of one. Great memoirs, like great stories, first must determine why to tell this story in the first place, what is the point or significance that the story will reveal, then eliminate every scene, detail, and encounter that does not drive the story forward and is not connected to the central theme the story is trying to reveal. Evaluate a memoir in the same way you would a short story or novel: does it achieve momentum, driving your reading forward, whether by suspense or surprise, to complete its journey to a predetermined destination. The principle of exclusion applies not just to the blueprint or thematic pattern of the memoir as a whole but also to all its particulars: are the details well-chosen, do they contribute in putting the reader vividly into its scene and in showing rather than telling meaning and significance? Are individual scenes well paced to underline tension and emotion? Does the telling, as opposed to the showing, register as more than generic or clichéd? At the most basic level of diction and syntax, is the writing appropriate, concise, original, and evocative?

- Does the memoir mean more? A memoir may be therapeutic for its writer, but it isn't justified as therapy alone. Every recalled memory may be relevant to the therapist but not to the reader. To have lasting value, to reach the level of the literary, the memoir needs to go beyond the specific to reveal the universal. Self-expression is not enough. A memoir needs to matter to the reader. It needs to entertain, certainly, but more than that, it must find a way to connect one life to all lives. In this regard, a memoir is no different than other works of literature, with the same challenge of converting the data of an individual's experience into truths about all our lives. The memoir that can achieve this is valuable indeed.

ANALYSIS OF LANGSTON HUGHES'S "SALVATION"

What is notable about "Salvation"?

Langston Hughes (1902–1967), poet, playwright, fiction writer, and critic, was a central figure in the cultural explosion of the Harlem Renaissance in the 1920s and '30s and became a powerful influence and mentor for such African American writers as Richard Wright and Ralph Ellison. "Salvation" is the second chapter of Hughes's autobiography, *The Big Sea* (1940) and can serve as a concise and compelling example of the medley of the essay, memoir, and autobiography. Read the short essay online using the guidelines above.

The striking difference between Montaigne's discursive and free-form essays is Hughes's more tightly controlled dramatic narrative structure. "Salvation" reads more like a taut first-person short story than an expository essay. We know that this is not an invented "I" since the author is clearly named in the story, but the strategies of the short story are in play here: a narrative with a clear beginning (the "big revival at my Auntie Reed's church"), middle (Langston's call to be saved), and ending (the consequences of Langston's lie). The conflict between the believers and Langston's confusion over what salvation actually is drives the narrative, and the consequences of his actions and understanding produce the narrative's conclusion. Moreover, the skill of the storyteller is demonstrated by the careful use of dialogue and descriptive detail that visualize the scene. Like a skilled film director, Hughes shifts the perspective from tight close-ups: "A great many old people came

Poet, playwright, and novelist Langston Hughes was also a gifted essayist.

355

and knelt around us and prayed, old women with jet-black faces and braided hair, old men with work-gnarled hands" to long shots: "Suddenly the room broke in a sea of shouting. Waves of rejoicing swept the place." Hughes also shifts perspective from what young Langston is seeing and what the older Langston now understands.

How does "Salvation" conclude?

This culminates in the essay's powerful final paragraph which, along with the first two sentences—"I was saved from sin when I was going on thirteen. But not really saved."—frames the entire piece:

> That night, for the first time in my life but one for I was a big boy, twelve years old—I cried. I cried, in bed alone, and couldn't stop. I buried my head under the quilts, but my aunt heard me. She woke up and told my uncle I was crying because the Holy Ghost had come into my life, and because I had seen Jesus. But I was really crying because I couldn't bear to tell her that I had lied, that I had deceived everybody in the church, that I hadn't seen Jesus, and that now I didn't believe there was a Jesus anymore, since he didn't come to help me.

The power of this conclusion, as in the rest of "Salvation," comes from Hughes's willingness to pose the most interesting questions rather than rush to provide some easy answers. This links Hughes to Montaigne as does the narrative turning on a paradox: the boy thinks salvation is literal, that he must actually "see" Jesus; the elders understand it as figurative. What the young Langston experiences as a result is even more shattering: the power of the lie to deceive, console, and finally to ostracize the nonbeliever. The reader is left contemplating multiple issues here: What exactly is salvation? How does the lie here operate? Salvation has been replaced by a sin, but can the case be made that the boy is actually "saved" from the hypocrisy of the congregation who similarly fail to "see" Jesus? How do you reconcile and comprehend the difference between the child's literalness and an adult's figurativeness? How does language itself mislead and confuse? These questions, and several more, reverberate from Hughes's taut narrative essay.

ANALYSIS OF MAXINE HONG KINGSTON'S *THE WOMAN WARRIOR*

What is notable about *The Woman Warrior*?

Maxine Hong Kingston's work (1976) is one of the singular achievements of modern American literature. The first work by an Asian American writer to gain widespread popularity and critical acclaim, it revolutionized accepted literary forms, creating a new genre that has been called "the creative memoir" and spawning an ongoing, important exploration of the American experience from personal, ethnic, cultural, and gender perspectives. Subtitled "Memoirs of a Girlhood Among Ghosts," *The Woman Warrior* presents the coming-of-age and coming-to-terms saga of an Asian American woman's attempt to achieve an authentic identity as well as liberation from the cultural and gender restrictions imposed by the intimidating and threatening spectres of both Caucasian American life and her often mystifying and stultifying Chinese heritage. The work has been described as the first postmodern autobiography in which chronological, objective narrative is abandoned in favor of fragmented, subjective moments of illumination, mixing fact and fiction that blurs the distinction between biography and legend, reality and fantasy, truth and myth.

What has been the impact of *The Woman Warrior*?

A work of remarkable originality and popular appeal, *The Woman Warrior* has become one of the most assigned texts on college campuses, appearing on syllabi in course offerings in English, ethnic studies, women's studies, American studies, Asian studies, Asian American studies, anthropology, sociology, history, and psychology. Clearly, the relevance and resonance of *The Woman Warrior* has exceeded the reach of the standard memoir of growth and development from a particular ethnic, cultural, historical, or regional perspective. As scholar Sau-Ling Wong has observed, "It is safe to say that many readers who otherwise do not concern themselves with Asian American literature have read [*The Woman Warrior*]." Through the remarkable poetic and vibrant quality of her prose, her daring, experimental mixture of fictional and nonfictional elements, and her balancing of rival cultural imperatives in pursuit of synthesis, Kingston has moved in *The Woman Warrior* from the particular to the universal, chronicling an Asian American woman's personal story that is also a profound exploration of gender, cultural, and human identity.

What is the biographical background to *The Woman Warrior*?

Born Maxine Ting Ting Hong in Stockton, California, in 1940, the writer was the first of six American-born children of Chinese immigrants Chew Ling Yan and Tom Hong. Her father was trained in China as a scholar and teacher and immigrated to the United States in 1925. Working as a laborer, he was eventually able to save enough to invest in a laundry in New York's Chinatown. Maxine's mother (Brave Orchid in *The Woman Warrior*) remained in China and was separated from her husband for fifteen years. During the interim, she trained in medicine and midwifery and worked as a physician, a remarkable accomplishment for a Chinese woman of the time. She joined her husband

Chinese American author Maxine Hong Kingston draws upon her family background and cultural experiences in her fiction and nonfiction writings.

in the United States in 1939 in Stockton, California, where Tom Hong had become the manager of an illegal gambling house owned by a wealthy Chinese immigrant. Maxine was named for an often lucky blonde gambler. During World War II, the Hongs started a laundry in Stockton where Kingston and her siblings were put to work as soon as they were old enough to help. The laundry became an informal Chinese community center where Kingston heard the "talk-stories" she would later draw on in her writing and characterized as "a tradition that goes back to prewriting time in China, where people verbally pass on history and mythology and genealogy and how-to stories and bedtime stories and legends.... [At the laundry] I would hear talk-story from everyone who came in. So I inherited this amazing amount of information, culture, history, mythology, and poetry." Speaking only Chinese until she started school, Kingston failed kindergarten in part because she refused to speak. Gaining fluency and an increased mastery of expression in English, Kingston eventually excelled as a student, publishing her first essay, "I Am an American," in *American Girl* in 1955 when she was still in high school. She attended the University of California at Berkeley on a scholarship, graduating in 1962 with a degree in English. The same year, she married Earll Kingston, an actor and fellow Berkeley graduate. Earning a teaching certificate, Kingston taught English and mathematics in a California high school for five years. Disillusioned with the 1960s drug culture and the ineffectiveness of the protest movement against the Vietnam War, the couple, with their young son, left California in 1967 en route to Japan. Stopping off in Hawaii, they would remain there for the next seventeen years. Kingston taught English, language arts, and English as a second language at several high schools and business and technical colleges. For more than two years, she worked on the manuscript that would become *The Woman Warrior*.

How is *The Woman Warrior* organized?

Kingston originally intended the work to be combined with the stories that eventually made up *China Men* (1980) as "one big book" exploring identity formation and cultural conflict faced by Chinese Americans, which was based on her own experiences and her relationships with her parents and other relatives. Avoiding the restrictions of "standard autobiography," which she identified as dealing with "exterior things" or "big historical events that you publicly participate in," Kingston concentrated instead on what she called "real stories," narratives mixing facts and the imagination, dramatizing "the rich, personal inner life." Her publisher insisted that the project be divided into two volumes and categorized as nonfiction. *The Woman Warrior* was published in 1976 to universal acclaim, winning the National Book Critics Circle Award, and established Kingston as a major writing talent. The book was described by reviewer William McPherson as "a strange, sometimes savagely terrifying and, in a literal sense, wonderful story of growing up caught between two highly sophisticated and utterly alien cultures, both vivid, often menacing and equally mysterious." *The Woman Warrior* explores the forces of heritage, family, and personal experience that impact the lives of women and must be confronted before any genuine autonomy and liberation can be achieved. "Chinese-Americans," Kingston writes, "when you try to understand what things in you are Chinese, how do you separate what is peculiar to childhood, to poverty, insanities, one family, your mother who marked your growing with stories, from what is Chinese? What is Chinese tradition and what is the movies?" *The Woman Warrior* attempts to answer these questions, dealing in imaginative terms with the status of Asian women in America and the various burdens and responsibilities faced by all women.

Divided into five sections, each centered on a talk-story, *The Woman Warrior* provocatively begins with a family secret and a warning: "You must not tell anyone," my mother said, "what I am about to tell you. In China your father had a sister who killed herself. She jumped into the family well. We say that your father has all brothers because it is as if she had never been born."

As told to the narrator by her mother, Brave Orchid, as a "story to grow up on," the fate of "No Name Woman," who bears a child two years after her husband's departure for America, is intended as a sobering lesson about the dangers of unsanctioned sexuality and the consequences of transgressing the traditional gender roles—subservience to male authority and repression of personal desires—that a Chinese woman is expected to obey. For her sexual indiscretion, the narrator's aunt provokes the community's wrath as the villagers kill the family's livestock and destroy their possessions. A pariah who has caused family shame and misery, No Name Woman gives birth unattended in a pigsty, kills herself and her newborn, and is sentenced by her own family to the anonymity of a nonperson in which even her name is obliterated. This striking story establishes the costs and consequences of challenging the established, patriachal values of Chinese tradition, while the narrator's breaking the taboo of silence and imaginatively restoring aspects of her aunt's history and identity establish central themes of *The Woman Warrior*, including the repression faced by Chinese women and the harsh retribution suffered by transgressors as well as the redemptive power of the imagination to restore the life of the voiceless and forgotten.

How does Kingston build on the first section, "No Name Woman"?

The second section, "White Tigers," recasts the legendary story of Fa Mu Lan, a woman warrior who takes her father's place in bat-

Kingston reworks the old Chinese tale of the warrior heroine Fa Mu Lan (or Hua Mulan, shown here in an eighteenth-century painting) into *The Woman Warrior* as a model of the nonsubmissive woman.

tle and avenges her family's wrongs that are carved onto her back, as an alternative Chinese myth—in contrast to the submissive, subservient female myth revealed by the fate of No Name Woman. For the narrator, the thrilling adventures of a fantasized woman warrior invite a sustaining identification. Refusing to be the passive victim of racist and sexist acts like Fa Mu Lan, the narrator sees her writing as a different kind of fighting, declaring:

> The swordswoman and I are not so dissimilar. May my people understand the resemblance soon so I can return to them. What we have in common are the words at our backs. The idiom for *revenge* are "report a crime" and "report to five families." The reporting is the vengeance—not the beheading, not the gutting, but the words. And I have so many words—"chink" words and "gook" words too—that they do not fit on my skin.

The middle chapter, "Shaman," presents a biographical sketch of the narrator's mother, Brave Orchid, as the story of a modern woman warrior. Like Fa Mu Lan, who went "away ordinary and came back miraculous, like the ancient magicians who came down from the mountains," Brave Orchid earns a medical degree, bravely exorcises the malevolent "Sitting Ghost" that threatens her school, and establishes a respectable career as a physician in China before joining her husband in America. In contrast, "At the Western Palace" presents the fate of Brave Orchid's sister, Moon Orchid, a victim of sexual manipulation and submissiveness that leads to madness. Moon Orchid has been left in Hong Kong by her husband, who has come to America and bigamously married a young, assimilated Chinese American woman. Brought to America by her sister to reclaim her rights as her husband's first wife, Moon Orchid's passivity, timidity, and subservience to established Chinese values prohibit her from reaching a positive settlement with her husband, and the radically different values she finds in America leads to her gradual loss of sanity and self-identity and eventual confinement to a mental asylum.

How does *The Woman Warrior* conclude?

The silence and madness of No Name Woman and Moon Orchid, therefore, stand in sharp contrast to the liberating possibilities of Fa Mu Lan and Brave Orchid. The conflict among competing gender and cultural assumptions are applied in the book's concluding section, "A Song for a Barbarian Reed Pipe," to the narrator's development through several events in her childhood and adolescence. The cost of silence is the dominating theme of this portion of *The Woman Warrior* as the narrator recalls "the worst thing [she] had yet done to another person," cruelly trying to force a silent classmate to speak, a metaphor of the narrator's own inner trauma of inarticulateness suspended between the opposing ghosts in her life—her Chinese heritage and American life. "Once upon a time," the narrator recalls, "the world was so thick with ghosts, I could hardly breathe; I could hardly walk, limping my way around the White Ghosts and their cars." The narrator's haunting is a result both of her parents' refusal to acknowledge the reality of their American life and their imposition of the shadowy world of their Chinese past and childhood on their offspring. Regarded by the older generation of Chinese immigrants as not completely Chinese, the narrator also finds herself insufficiently American at school, alienated both from her ancestral past

and her Amerian present. She is also female, judged inferior and a burden by Chinese standards, and an outsider by the dominating American patriarchy. The disjunction makes the
narrator a double victim of sexual stereotypes and racist stigmatism that threatens to destroy one's identity if one is unable to resolve these contradictions. As the narrator achieves
the power to confront her mother for imposing silence on her and to speak out against the
various gender and racial forces that threaten her, she finds a new model in the second-cen-
tury Chinese woman poet, Ts'ai Yen, to displace the swordswoman Fa Mu Lan. A prisoner
of the barbarians for twelve years, Ts'ai Yen is able to recover her voice as she listens to the
music of barbarian flutes and is inspired to write poetry that distills her experiences into
an enduring voice that challenges her repression and achieves valuable communication:

> Ts'ai Yen sang about China and her family there. Her words seemed to be Chinese,
> but the barbarians understood their sadness and anger. Sometimes they thought
> they could catch barbarian phrases about forever wandering. Her children did not
> laugh, but eventually sang along when she left her tent to sit by the winter camp-
> fires, ringed by barbarians.

Ts'ai Yen is the final version of the woman warrior who, like the narrator, lives among
people of a different race and offers the narrator as a word warrior a model for using self-
expression as a means of reclaiming self-identity, liberation, and autonomy. By setting
Ts'ai Yen's story—along with those of No Name Woman, Fa Mu Lan, Brave Orchid, and
Moon Orchid—in the context of her own experiences, the narrator ultimately achieves
the means to exorcise her own ghosts, to find her own voice, and to achieve self-definition out of the various forces of gender and culture that silence, repress, and destroy.

What is the significance of *The Woman Warrior* as cultural record and as memoir?

The Woman Warrior functions both as a crucial record of Chinese American experience
and a dramatization of the process by which a woman, of any ethnicity, is forced to fashion an identity out of gender and cultural imperatives. It blurs the distinctions between
fiction and nonfiction, essay and autobiography. Drawing freely on her own experiences,
Kingston imagines and fictionalizes others' stories, whether from the past or in myths
and legends, to serve as counterpoints and comparisons, always under the pressure of
the narrator's speculative analysis.

Consider, for example, the conclusion of "No Name Woman":

"Don't tell anyone you had an aunt. Your father does not want to hear her name.
She has never been born." I have believed that sex was unspeakable and words
so strong and fathers so frail that "aunt" would do my father mysterious harm.
I have thought that my family, having settled among immigrants who had also
been their neighbors in the ancestral land, needed to clean their name, and a
wrong word would incite the kinspeople even here. But there is more to this silence: they want me to participate in her punishment. And I have.

In the twenty years since I heard this story, I have not asked for details nor said
my aunt's name; I do not know it. People who can comfort the dead can also

chase after them to hurt them further—a reverse ancestor worship. The real punishment was not the raid swiftly inflicted by the villagers, but the family's deliberately forgetting her. Her betrayal so maddened them, they saw to it that she would suffer forever, even after death. Always hungry, always needing, she would have to beg food from other ghosts, snatch and steal it from those whose living descendants give them gifts. She would have to fight the ghosts massed at crossroads for the buns a few thoughtful citizens leave to decoy her away from village and home so that the ancestral spirits could feast unharassed. At peace, they could act like gods, not ghosts, their descent lines providing them with paper suits and dresses, spirit money, paper houses, paper automobiles, chicken, meat, and rice into eternity essences delivered up in smoke and flames, steam and incense rising from each rice bowl. In an attempt to make the Chinese care for people outside the family, Chairman Mao encourages us now to give our paper replicas to the spirits of outstanding soldiers and workers, no matter whose ancestors they may be. My aunt remains forever hungry. Goods are not distributed evenly among the dead.

My aunt haunts me—her ghost drawn to me because now, after fifty years of neglect, I alone devote pages of paper to her, though not origamied into houses and clothes. I do not think she always means me well. I am telling on her, and she was a spite suicide, drowning herself in the drinking water. The Chinese are always very frightened of the drowned one, whose weeping ghost, wet hair hanging and skin bloated, waits silently by the water to pull down a substitute.

In language as chilling as it is lyrical, Kingston orchestrates something strikingly new: an analytical essay illuminated with the skills and techniques of the fiction writer, in which reflection and the imagination converge in a potent new form of literary expression.

CREATIVE NONFICTION

What is creative nonfiction?

For some time now, various types of literary nonfiction have been designated by the term "creative nonfiction." The label is problematic because it is based on a false distinction, implying that all nonfiction isn't "creative." Anyone who has ever written any kind of nonfiction—a newspaper account, a report, instructions—knows that to do it well, creativity (originality, ingenuity, resourcefulness) is essential. The creativity in creative nonfiction, however, has a narrower application. Creative nonfiction is based on the actual instead of the imagined or invented. It is, therefore, nonfiction as opposed to drama, poetry, or fiction but draws upon the techniques of the literary artists to instill factually accurate prose with a compelling, vivid, and dramatic style. The guru of creative nonfiction, Lee Gutkind, a longtime practitioner and instructor, in the journal *Creative Nonfiction* that he edits, defines the genre succinctly: "True stories, well told."

Creative nonfiction is currently publishing's hottest commodity, and undergraduate and graduate creative writing programs now offer it as a specialty. Creative nonfiction, in all its various guises as journalism, essay, memoir, meditation, and profile, dominates publications such as the *New Yorker, The Atlantic*, and *Vanity Fair* but can also now be found in such hard-news outlets as *The New York Times* and *The Wall Street Journal*. As au courant as creative nonfiction may appear, the form derives from the traditional literary nonfiction sources: the essay, autobiography, and memoir.

Lee Gutkind is the founder of the magazine *Creative Nonfiction* and is considered the guru of the genre.

What are the chief characteristics of Creative Nonfiction?

The chief attributes of Creative Nonfiction are these:

1. *The presence of "I"*—Traditional journalism, expository prose, analysis, even argumentation insists upon detached objectivity, a third-person omniscient approach, in which the author disappears, or, as Flaubert asserted, "The artist must be in his work like God is in creation, invisible and all-powerful; one must sense him everywhere but never see him." This hard-news conception of nonfiction adheres to the Joe Friday edict: "Just the facts." Just who, what, when, and where. It's the reader's job to interpret and draw conclusions (why). Any attempt to intrude upon the factual record with opinions or biases are out of bounds or are reserved for the columnist, not the reporter. Creative nonfiction breaks with this objective approach by freely admitting a first-person presence and an undisguised subjectivity. The factual, therefore, is processed through an "I" perspective that becomes part of the story or the analysis.

The more recent antecedent for the restoration of the personal in nonfiction and the evolving techniques of Creative Nonfiction is Truman Capote's *In Cold Blood* (1966), which he labeled a "nonfiction novel," and Norman Mailer's *The Armies of the Night* (1968) with its subtitle "The Novel as History; History as the Novel." The so-called New Journalism emerged in the 1960s and 1970s with works by Joan Didion, Jimmy Breslin, Pete Hamill, Hunter S. Thompson, Gay Talese, and especially Tom Wolfe, whose 1973 book *New Journalism* serves as both a manifesto and a collection of notable ex-

363

amples. In New Journalism, facts are distilled through the now-visible and often intrusive presence of the shaping reporter, whose biases, interpretations, opinions, and ruminations break down the journalistic equivalent of drama's "fourth wall," the invisible, imagined wall separating actors from the audience.

To be fair, Tom Wolfe admitted that he never liked the term New Journalism, that "any movement, group, party, program, philosophy or theory that goes under a name with 'New' in it is just begging for trouble." New Journalism begs the question: what exactly is new about the journalism here? The presence of a first-person, speculative, and inventive perspective is as old as Herodotus. One of the earliest-surviving journalistic accounts is Daniel Defoe's *A Journal of the Plague Year* (1722), which purports to be a factual, eyewitness account of one man's experiences during the Great Plague of London in 1665. Its author, Defoe, who was only five years old in 1665, converts a great deal of research into his fictionalized narrative. Initially read as nonfiction, Defoe's account has subsequently been classified as a novel, although modern scholars have defended his accuracy and reliability compared to actual eyewitness accounts, with one scholar declaring that his invented detail is "small and inessential." By any standard, however, Defoe meets (and even exceeds with his fictionalized narrative) the core concept of New Journalism and Creative Nonfiction. Other examples are Mark Twain's travel books, such as *The Innocent Abroad* (1869), *Roughing It* (1872), *A Tramp Abroad* (1880), and *Following the Equator* (1897). Twain's reporting might not be as "gonzo" as Hunter S. Thompson's, but his persona, whether real or imagined, dominates the discussion, providing the lens through which the world is seen. This is no less true of famously caustic early mid-twentieth-century reporter H. L. Mencken, who rarely conceals from the reader where he stands, and in Ernest Hemingway's nonfiction, such as *Death in the Afternoon* (1932), *Green Hills of Africa* (1935), *The Spanish Earth* (1938), and his actual memoir *A Moveable Feast* (1964). In all these examples, the guiding perspective of the author is unmistakable.

If New Journalism and the flood of Creative Nonfiction that followed did not initiate the deployment of first-person subjectivity in fact-based writing, they certainly embraced it with a verve and energy that challenged accepted nonfiction standards. In the process, they disputed the accepted notion that objectivity is even possible, honestly admitting that so-called facts-only journalism is as compromised by subjectivity as any personal approach.

Truman Capote based his novel *In Cold Blood* on the true story of a family who was murdered in Kansas, thus pioneering what he called the "nonfiction novel."

2. *The techniques of literature*—Traditional journalism and expository nonfiction aspires to a straightforward factual account rendered in a style that values clarity and conciseness above all. Its prose seeks a transparency to avoid distorting or distracting from its subject. A style that calls attention to itself as consciously literary (ingenious turns of phrase, clever wordplay, poetic elements calling attention to the sound and rhythm of the words) rarely makes it past the copy editor. This is from the copy style sheet for *The Kansas City Star* that Ernest Hemingway mastered during his tenure writing police and emergency room items in 1917 and 1918: "Use short sentences. Use short first paragraphs. Use vigorous English. Be positive, not negative.... Never use old slang.... Eliminate every superfluous word.... Avoid the use of adjectives." The *Star's* rules that predict Hemingway's future terse, to-the-bone fictional style was the journalistic norm, predicated on delivering the facts as precisely as possible.

With the New Journalists and Creative Nonfiction, literary techniques borrowed from drama, fiction, and poetry become part of nonfiction's message and manner. Structurally, just-the-facts-driven prose, organized by importance, is characteristically replaced by writing in scenes as the basic unit of dramatic construction. Core narrative components like setting, action, dialogue, point of view, suspense, and surprise all become key elements of Creative Nonfiction. Linear chronology can be altered with flashbacks and flash-forwards. Nuanced characters are constructed from details of action, dialogue, and description and are shown from multiple vantage points. At the level of diction and syntax, poetic devices—metaphor, symbolism, personification, imagery, assonance, alliteration, irony, and allusion—are exploited. The result is nonfiction that calls attention to itself as constructed and written, no longer a transparent lens but a delivery system for expressive communication.

Tom Wolfe famously defended New Journalism's assimilation of the literary expression in a 1972 *Esquire* article called "Why They Aren't Writing the Great American Novel Anymore." In it, Wolfe identified techniques that he and the other New Journalists had co-opted from fiction, including scene-by-scene construction, full record of dialogue, and the "manifold incidental details to round out character." The result, Wolfe declares, "is a form that is not merely like a *novel*. It consumes devices that happen to have originated with the novel and mixes them with every other device known to prose. And all the while, quite beyond matters of technique, it enjoys an advantage so obvious, so built-in, one almost forgets what power it has: the simple fact that the reader knows *all this actually happened*. The disclaimers have been erased. The screen is gone. The writer is one step closer to the absolute involvement of the reader that Henry James and James Joyce dreamed of but never achieved."

Creative nonfiction then makes full use of literary devices to enhance expression but without literary fiction's need to reach truth and reality through imaginary means. A "willing suspension of disbelief" (Coleridge's phrase about believing the unbelievable in literature) is unnecessary because of the nonfiction writer's pledge to abide by the actual.

3. *The nonfiction contract*—Keeping Creative Nonfiction honest is the abiding contract with the reader that what is being presented actually happened—or, at least, when facts shift to surmise and supposition, they are clearly identified as such. As innovative as Creative Nonfiction can be in exploiting techniques of imaginative literature, it is still held to an exacting adherence to the actual. Scenes can be manipulated by viewpoint, close-ups on telling details, or through a filter of irony and sarcasm, but they cannot be made up and passed off as actual. A character can be developed, but he cannot be invented. Literary and journalistic careers have been destroyed after revelations of fabrication in factual accounts. The most famous example is the addiction memoir of James Frey, *A Million Little Pieces* (2003), that was selected for Oprah's Book Club and ascended to the top of the nonfiction bestseller list. Evidence of falsification was first denied, justified, and later apologized for by Frey, who eventually admitted that he had made himself "tougher and more daring and more aggressive than in reality I was, or I am" and that "I wanted the stories in the book to ebb and flow, to have dramatic arcs, to have the tension that all great stories require." What Frey failed to realize is that great stories may require these things, but Creative Nonfiction requires accuracy and reliability above all.

Writers of Creative Nonfiction can employ imaginative invention provided it is identified as such. A great example of this is Maxine Hong Kingston's "No Name Woman" from her collection *The Woman Warrior.* Her essay begins, "'You must not tell anyone,' my mother said, 'what I am about to tell you. In China your father had a sister who killed herself. She jumped into the family well.'" Piecing together the details from her mother, Kingston tries to imagine the how and the why of her aunt's death. She conjures a dramatic and believable story, despite having never known her aunt or, at the time, ever having been to China. Her account is harrowing and vivid though the reader never loses sight that it is imagined and speculative, not based on actual evidence. In "No-Name Woman," Kingston is as creative as Creative Nonfiction writers can be: constructing a "true story, well told," but adhering to the nonfiction contract that no matter what might have happened or might have been said, do not mislead the reader by presenting it as actuality.

It is Creative Nonfiction's commitment to the actual, despite its subjectivity and creativity, that is one of the genre's greatest strengths. Readers have long preferred stories based on the actual. It is one of the reasons that Daniel Defoe, in inventing the English novel, passed off both *Robinson Crusoe* and *Moll Flanders* as the real-life accounts of actual individuals. It is also why films make a point of saying that what is shown is "based on a true story." Creative writing is based on the imagination, reaching its truth through a version of lying; Creative Nonfiction must protect its veracity. As Annie Dillard writes in a defense of the form she is best known for, the personal essay: "The essay can do everything a poem can do, and everything a short story can do—everything but fake it. The elements in any nonfiction should be true not only artistically—the connections must hold at base and must be veracious, for that is the convention and the covenant between the nonfiction writer and his reader." Dillard goes on to challenge the notion that veracity is a drawback for either the writer or the reader: "The real world arguably exerts a greater fascination on people than any fictional one; many people, at least, spend their whole lives there, apparently by choice. The essayist does what we do with our lives; the essayist thinks about actual things. He can make sense of them analytically or artistically. In either case he renders the real world coherent and meaningful, even if only bits of it, and even if that coherence and meaning reside only inside small texts."

How have others described Creative Nonfiction?

Creative nonfiction ... is fact-based writing that remains compelling, undiminished by the passage of time, that has at heart an interest in enduring human values: foremost a fidelity to accuracy, to truthfulness.

—Carolyn Forché and Philip Gerard

[Creative nonfiction] denotes a broad category of prose works such as personal essays and memoirs, profiles, nature and travel writing, narrative essays, observational or descriptive essays, general-interest technical writing, argumentative or idea-based essays, general-interest criticism, literary journalism, and so on. The term's constituent words suggest a conceptual axis on which these sorts of prose works lie. As nonfiction, the works are connected to actual states of affairs in the world, are "true" to some reliable extent. If, for example, a certain event is alleged to have occurred, it must really have occurred; if a proposition is asserted, the reader expects some proof of (or argument for) its accuracy. At the same time, the adjective creative signifies that some goal(s) other than sheer truthfulness motivates the writer and informs her work. This creative goal, broadly stated, may be to interest readers, or to instruct them, or to entertain them, to move or persuade, to edify, to redeem, to amuse, to get readers to look more closely at or think more deeply about something that's worth their attention ... or some combination(s) of these.

—David Foster Wallace

What Is Creative About Nonfiction? It takes a whole semester to try to answer that, but here are a few points: The creativity lies in what you choose to write about, how you go about doing it, the arrangement through which you present things, the skill and the touch with which you describe people and succeed in developing them as characters, the rhythms of your prose, the integrity of the composition, the anatomy of the piece (does it get up and walk around on its own?), the extent to which you see and tell the story that exists in your material, and so forth. Creative nonfiction is not making something up but making the most of what you have.

—John McPhee   367

"Creative nonfiction" seems slightly bogus. It's like patting yourself on the back and saying, "My nonfiction is creative." Let the reader be the judge of that.... There is [also] a bit of self-congratulations in "literary nonfiction." One reason I prefer it is because it embeds the work in a tradition and a lineage. Instead of implying this is something new, it says this type of writing has been around for a long, long time. In English literature, there is the great tradition of the English essay, with Samuel Johnson, Hazlitt and Lamb, Robert Louis Stevenson and de Quincey, Matthew Arnold, McCauley, Carlisle, Beerbohm, and on into the twentieth century, with Virginia Woolf and George Orwell. By saying you write literary nonfiction, you're saying that you're part of that grand parade.... Creative nonfiction is somewhat distortedly being characterized as nonfiction that reads like fiction. Why can't nonfiction be nonfiction? Why does it have to tart itself up and be something else? I make no apologies for the essay form, for the memoir form, or for any kind of literary nonfiction. These are genres that have been around for a long time, and we don't have to apologize for them, or act like they're new fads when they're not.

—Philip Lopate

Poetry seems to have priced itself out of a job; sadly, it often handles few materials of significance and addresses a tiny audience. Literary fiction is scarcely published; it's getting to be like conceptual art—all the unknown writer can do is tell people about his work, and all they can say is, "good idea." The short story is to some extent going the way of poetry, willfully limiting its subject matter to such narrow surfaces that it cannot address the things that most engage our hearts and minds. So the narrative essay may become the genre of choice for writers devoted to significant literature.

—Annie Dillard

And yet in the early 1960s a curious new notion, just hot enough to inflame the ego, had begun to intrude into the tiny confines of the feature statusphere. It was in the nature of a discovery. This discovery, modest at first, humble, in fact, deferential, you might say, was that it just might be possible to write journalism that

Having written fiction, poetry, a memoir, and nonfiction, Annie Dillard has predicted that the narrative essay might become the genre of choice for authors.

would … read like a novel. *Like* a novel, if you get the picture. This was the sincerest form of homage to The Novel and to those greats, the novelists, of course. Not even the journalists who pioneered in this direction doubted for a moment that the novelist was the reigning literary artist, now and forever. All they were asking for was the privilege of dressing up like him … until the day when they themselves would work up their nerve and go into the shack and try it for real … They were dreamers, all right, but one thing they never dreamed of. They never dreamed of the approaching irony. They never guessed for a minute that the work they would do over the next ten years, as journalists, would wipe out the novel as literature's main event.

—Tom Wolfe

What should you look for when reading Creative Nonfiction?

By combining two previously exclusive evaluative standards—literary creativity and nonfictional truth-telling—Creative Nonfiction invites the application of both in reading and assessing it.

Creative Nonfiction as nonfiction—The essence of all nonfiction is practical: Does it provide a description of someone or something, an analysis of a complex process, event, or object, an argument identifying a problem and offering a solution that a reader finds useful and valuable? Does it extend your knowledge of the world or yourself in helpful ways? Does it tell you something you didn't know or re-introduce you to the familiar in a new and surprising way? How it does so is also a crucial consideration in any evaluation: Does it have a compelling focus or thesis that is developed fully and convincingly? Are generalizations and assertions backed up with evidence and examples that persuade? If it is an analysis, is it easy to follow? Does it prioritize its information in a helpful way, often marked by clear steps and stages? If it is an argument, does it convincingly present both the problem it is addressing and the solution offered? Is it logical in its approach? What about the voice or tone? How is credibility established, trustworthiness, reliability? All of these issues matter in evaluating Creative Nonfiction. To raise them, you should read and reread a text to understand what it says but also how it says it. In this regard, the techniques of active reading we have recommended for literature apply here as well: annotating, asking questions, summarizing. One of the best techniques in close reading of a nonfiction text is to do a reverse outline, that is, turning the work back into an outline that identifies:

- Topic. What is it about: what issue is the work addressing, the problem addressed, the solution offered?

- Thesis. What is its main point? The thesis is usually announced early in an essay in the first or second introductory paragraph. Look as well at the conclusion, where a thesis restatement is often offered.

- Main claims. What are the main assertions in support of that thesis? These can usually be identified in the first sentence of each body paragraph, its topic sentence, that is, its general idea that will be supported by the evidence that makes up the paragraph.

- Key evidence. What evidence is being offered to prove each claim?

- Conclusion. What is the writer asking the reader to do or think now that we have completed the essay?

Constructing a reverse outline with these elements will guide your ability to evaluate the strengths and weaknesses of the work and will enhance your understanding of what is being said and how.

Creative nonfiction as literature—The creative part of Creative Nonfiction is the way in which the presentation takes advantage of the same literary tools we have discussed in our consideration of poetry, fiction, and drama. If the work is constructed as a narrative in a succession of scenes, how does the presentation and arrangement impact meaning? How is tension, conflict, narrative arc (the work's forward momentum driving the reader to the conclusion), and dramatic unity (exposition, rising action, climax, denouement, and resolution) achieved? In formulating answers, the five key questions we have introduced in discussing all literary works—significance of the title, why start here, what is the conflict, how is it resolved, and why end here—are helpful. What characters emerge? Round or flat? How are they developed? By telling or showing? By what characters do or say (or don't say or don't do)? What point of view is employed? First-person or third-person? Is the perspective reliable? How does the point of view intrude and affect interpretation of what is shown? Is the work narrative or lyrical, that is, more focused on a thought or feeling, a meditation instead of a story of events with a clear beginning, middle, and ending? How and why does it employ poetic devices, such as simile, metaphor, imagery, symbolism, personification, irony, and allusion? Does the writing style call attention to sound qualities like alliteration, assonance, and rhythmic effects? What do they contribute to the work, whether in enhancing reading pleasure or shaping meaning?

Combining the two—In any final assessment of Creative Nonfiction, the dual components of creativity and fact-finding truth need to come together, supporting one another in a satisfying whole. The Horacian platitude that "the aim of the poet is to teach and delight" applies no less to the writer of Creative Nonfiction. Another way of expressing Horace's literary duality is to say that Creative Nonfiction, like all literary work, strives for permanent, pleasing truths. Does the work achieve a continual relevance? To adapt Ben Jonson's praise of Shakespeare: Is it "not of an age, but for all time"? There is nothing wrong with a work bound by its age, providing an intimate historical view, but to reach the permanence of literature, it needs to do more. Pleasing, as used here, does not necessarily mean "entertaining." Creative nonfiction, like other literary works, can unsettle and disturb rather than entertain. It's hard, for example, to call *King Lear* entertaining, but its terrifying profundity can still be pleasing in the sense of satisfying deep intellectual and emotional needs. Without needing to reach the magnitude of *King Lear*, Creative Nonfiction, if it deserves classification as literature, needs to satisfy with the truths it provides. They may be great truths about love and death, of great heroism in the world, or smaller truths about ordinary life and unexceptional individuals, a close look at what might be deemed unimportant or ignored. But if it goes small in this regard, it still needs to get big by magnifying the unexamined or unexplored and discovering importance and relevance that surprises and endures in its relevance. The challenge for the Creative Nonfiction writer is to convert its facts into truths. It is the same challenge for any work of literature in which the specific and the concrete matter of literature in a particularized scene, setting, and situation is transformed into the universal. In *A Portrait of the Artist as a Young Man*, James Joyce has his character, the undergraduate, Stephen Dedalus, describe the role of the literary artist like that of the priest at Mass, converting the humblest bread and wine into spiritual essence, becoming "a priest of the eternal imagination, transmuting the daily bread of existence into the radiant body of everliving life." It's a grandiloquent assertion and the precocious and impossibly pretentious Stephen, as readers discover in *Ulysses*, has a lot to learn, but behind the hyperbole there is a core truth that applies particularly to Creative Nonfiction. It is, and must be, about the actual, quotidian world, and it takes the efforts and skills of a master writer to reach beyond to permanent truth.

CRITICAL APPROACHES TO LITERATURE

What is literary criticism, and why is it important?

The evaluation and interpretation of literature is nearly as old as literature itself. The English word "criticism" derives from the Greek word *krites*, meaning "to judge," and the judgment about literature—in literary aims and methods in a collective understanding of more than two millennia that has formed a critical tradition—is fundamental to our ability to understand it at all. As M. A. R. Habib writes in *Literary Criticism from Plato to the Present*:

> If we had no tradition of critical interpretation, if we were left with the "texts" themselves, we would be completely bewildered. We would not know how to classify a given writer as Romantic, classical, or modern. We would not know that a given poem was epic or lyric, mock-heroic, or even that it was a poem. We would be largely unaware of which tradition a given writer was working in and how she was trying to subvert it in certain ways. We would not be able to arrive at any comparative assessment of writers in terms of literary merit. We would not even be able to interpret the meanings of individual lines or words in any appropriate context. It has been the long tradition of literary interpretation—refined and evolved over many centuries—which has addressed these questions.

It is literary criticism that has, like the work of the natural scientists, provided us with a taxonomy of literature, identifying the major literary genres—poetry, drama, fiction, and nonfiction—as well as subgenres (for poetry: lyric, narrative, dramatic; for drama: tragedy, comedy, and tragicomedy, etc.). Literary criticism has supplied us with both an understanding of literature's nature and an analysis of literary practice that provides a common basis of evaluative comparison, as well as theoretical understanding of how literature functions from the perspective of the text, the writer, and the reader. Without the collective consensus of literary criticism, we would be without a standard of evaluation as well as the means of understanding a literary text beyond the rudimentary. Literary criticism has given us the keys to translating literature into a common vocabulary that makes communication possible.

What is the difference between literary theory and critical approaches?

Literary criticism can be usefully subdivided into two complementary subgroups: literary theory and critical approaches. While these terms can be used interchangeably and as synonyms, for our discussion, literary theory designates consideration of the nature of literature and the function and purpose of its three component parts (author, text, and reader), while critical approaches are the application of theory to an interpretation of literary works. In other words, literary theory examines what literature can mean; critical approaches, applying various methods based in theory, interpret what an individual literary work may mean.

All readers, whether they are aware of it or not, base their encounter with any literary text on some kind of literary theory. We all understand what a work of literature should be and do, based on past experience that establishes our critical standard. It's how we know we are reading literature in the first place: a work conforms to (or fails to meet) our ideal of what literature is in its form, content, and meaning. Experience and expectations also inform a reader's criticism of a literary work. For example, we know that mysteries should feature a secret that is only gradually revealed; that's the theory of the genre. How well an individual mystery conforms to this principle becomes at least one of the critical questions you might ask, applying theory to practice.

In looking at the tradition of literary theory and critical approaches, you realize just how many ways of understanding literature's methods and purposes exist as well as how many different critical approaches are available to assist your interpretation. An awareness of both literary theory and critical approaches helps to explain just how contentious interpreting literature can be and why distinguished and expert literary critics so often disagree on both the merits of individual works and the significance of literature as a whole. It is worth noting that the term "theory" comes from a Greek theatrical term, *theoria*, meaning a view or perspective of the Greek stage. Even though many theorists regard their views as singular and essential, for the reader, however, it is wise to keep in mind that a theory is only one of many views to be judged on how well it helps you see the stage. The same is true of critical approaches to literature, which can best be regarded as lenses to assist a reader's view of the text. Each lens may call attention to different aspects of the literary work, and no particular critical approach should necessarily exclude others. The question always should be: how does a literary theory or a critical approach help the reader to see more that the literary work expresses?

What are the questions that literary theory has tried to answer?

Literary theory seeks to answer the essential questions about the nature of literature and its value and function. Some key questions that literary theorists have considered for the last two and a half millennia are:

- *Where does literature originate?* What is the source of literature's appeal and points of origin?

- *What is the relationship of literature to truth?* Is literature a trustworthy reflection of the world or a potentially dangerous distraction and distortion of truth? Is literature a form of truth-telling or appealing lies, substituting fancy for truth?

- *What purpose does literature serve?* Is literature good or bad? Moral and beneficial or immoral and dangerous? If it pleases: why does it? If it teaches: what does it teach and how?

- *Does literature serve a useful social function?* What purpose beyond individual enrichment does literature serve?

- *What role does the author play in the creation of literature?* Is literature inspired? The work of genius? Or is it a craft, perfected through skill and expertise?

- *What is the relationship in literature between form and content?* Do form and content exist independent of each other, or are they inextricably linked?

- *How can literature be classified and its subgenres understood and compared?* How are poetry, drama, and fiction similar and different?

- *What is the basis for judging a work of literature?* What standard of excellence can be applied to literature? What makes a particular work of literature good or bad?

- *What is the relationship between the author, the historical moment, and the work of literature?* Are works of literature reflections of the era in which they were written, or do they transcend the specific culture or conditions of their creation? Is an author's biography and culture relevant or irrelevant in considering a work or literature?

- *Who determines the literary canon?* Why are some works of literature valued, and what assumptions govern literary works that are regarded as classics? What are the standards that admit a work of literature to the canon?

- *What is literary criticism, and how should it operate?* What is the purpose and function of the literary critic and criticism in general in treating literature?

What are the landmark works and authors of literary theory?

Literary theory that examines the nature and purpose of literature is as old as some of our oldest surviving texts and deals with the key questions surrounding author, work, and audience.

CLASSICAL PERIOD

What is Plato's *Republic*?

In Book X of Plato's *Republic* (c. 373 B.C.E.), a Socratic dialogue on the nature of justice and the ideal society, Plato provides the earliest extant theory of literature as well as its first criticism. According to Plato, truth resides in the ideal, not in the imitation of the nature offered by poets, which is already a pale reflection of the ideal, making poetry an imitation of an imitation and an unreliable source of truth. "What poets do," Plato argues, "is hold the mirror up to nature: They copy the appearances of men, animals, and objects in the physical world." Appearances, in Plato's view, both deceive and distract from truth. Moreover, unlike our reason, fanciful poetry tends toward the illogical and irrational, with the composition of poetry closer to madness, from the poet being carried away irrationally by divine inspiration. A talented artist could transform a morally bad subject and encourage others to do bad deeds through poetry's power to appeal to the irrational part of man's soul. Accordingly, Plato bans poets from his ideal Republic and allows only works of art, such as hymns to the gods or praise of the state, which are morally uplifting and help citizens live a good life.

While Plato's *Republic* is primarily noted for its discourse about what makes the best society, the work also contains the first known example of literary criticism and theories of literature.

At the conclusion of Book X, Plato sets poets a challenge that will become the bedrock upon which all subsequent literary criticism will take shape. Plato will allow poets back into his Republic if they can prove that poetry serves a useful purpose and enhances our knowledge of truth rather than deceives it. Nearly all subsequent critical theory takes up Plato's challenge to assert literature's capacity to reflect human nature and human experience truthfully and to assess its benefits.

What important work did Plato's pupil produce?

In *Poetics* (c. 330 B.C.E.), Plato's pupil, Aristotle, treats poetry (in verse and drama) for the first time as a distinct facet of knowledge, like physics, ethics, and rhetoric, and as a separate discipline with its own rules, procedures, and purposes. The *Poetics*, therefore, becomes the first handbook describing how literature operates. Unlike Plato's concern for what art does or ought to do, Aristotle looks at what literature is, classifying its various forms—epic, tragedy, comedy, lyric, music, and dance—before arriving at literature's unifying principle: "Art is an imitation of nature." For Plato, imitation of the actual is a deceptive corruption of the source of truth in the ideal; for Aristotle, the real is the source of truth, and imitation is central to how all humans learn. We take delight in recognizing a skilled imitation. For Aristotle, artistic imitation is not simply a copy of the real but a completion of it, not necessarily life as it is but how it might be. Art is nature perfected with the randomness and chaos replaced by patterns of causality and meaning. Artistic imitation differs, according to Aristotle, by its medium, its objects, and its manner. The *Poetics* describe how poetry and drama differ in this regard and how they originated.

The *Poetics* is the foundation document in the development of the philosophy of aesthetics upon which critical theory and approaches to literature are derived. Aristotle's chief contribution to this debate is his insistence that art is independent from ethical considerations and should be judged by its own aesthetic standards alone. The discovery of these standards will become critical theory's central preoccupation.

What work by Horace offers advice on writing poetry?

Horace (65–8 B.C.E.), one of the greatest poets of Rome's Augustan Age, produced *Ars Poetica* around 20 B.C.E. This verse epistle offers advice to the sons of his patron, the Piso family, on how to write great poetry. It has proven to be one of the great fountainheads of critical theory, like Aristotle's *Poetics*, providing key concepts and terms that have established aesthetic standards in judging literature. Of central importance, particularly for neoclassical literary theory, is Horace's articulation of the rules of decorum that poets should obey: not to mix unlike things, such as comedy and tragedy, and that each genre should have its own distinctive style and possess a unity of action, character, and mood. Horace famously defined the proper goal of poetry to please and teach (*dulce et utile*):

> The Old, if Moral's wanting, damn the Play;
> And Sentiment disgusts the Young and Gay.
> He who instruction and delight can blend,
> Please with his fancy, with his moral mend.

The true poet, Horace argues, combines genius and craft. Like an athlete, he needs both innate ability and rigorous training to achieve the unity and perfection that looks easy and natural.

So much of *Ars Poetica* has entered our critical language from Horace's admonition not to begin a work at the beginning (*ab ovo*, "from the egg") but *in media res* ("in the middle of things") to his urging against employing a *deus ex machina* ("god from the machine") to resolve a convoluted plot by the onstage arrival of a god to untangle it to his caution against *purpureus pannus* ("purple prose"), or flowery language.

What work is credited with starting the dialogue on what literature achieves and how it does so?

The author of the Roman-era Greek work *On the Sublime* (c. first century C.E.) is unknown, though the work is often attributed to Longinus. Written in epistolary form, it is a treatise on aesthetics and a work of literary criticism that identifies good and bad writing as well as the principles of achieving sublimity in writing. Previous studies of writing, notably Aristotle's *Rhetoric*, focused on the ways to persuade an audience; Longinus, who defines the sublime as "a consummate excellence and distinction of language," insists that "the effect of genius is not to persuade the audience but rather to transport them out of themselves." He adds that "what inspires wonder casts a spell upon us and is always superior to what is merely convincing and pleasing."

According to *On the Sublime*, sublimity is not produced by inflated, hyperbolic language or melodramatic contrivance. It is "a certain distinction and excellence in composition," which raises style above the ordinary to elevate the reader to a striking comprehension. The treatise identifies five principal sources of the sublime: 1) grandeur of thought, 2) capacity for strong emotion, 3) appropriate use of figures of speech, 4) nobility of diction, and 5) dignity of composition that fully integrates the first four. For Longinus, the sublime requires both genius and craft, both the capacity for conceiving great thoughts and feeling great passion and the ability to harness both in effective language. To demonstrate, the treatise analyzes passages from Homer, Sappho, and others who unite form and content to produce the sublime. One of his most important exemplars of sublime writing is Plato himself, critic of poetic inspiration as irrational and counterproductive. Longinus shows how much of Plato's genius stems from his own transport into the realm of the sublime.

On the Sublime would help initiate a critical discussion of exactly what literature achieves and how it does so. The topic would be taken up by John Baillie in *An Essay on the Sublime* (1747), by Edmund Burke in *A Philosophical Inquiry into the Origin of Our Ideas of the Sublime and the Beautiful* (1757), by Immanuel Kant in *The Critique of Judgment* (1790), and by the ideas and practices that defined Romanticism.

MEDIEVAL PERIOD

What advances in literary criticism were made in medieval Europe?

During the medieval period, no comparable works of literary criticism rivaling those by Plato, Aristotle, Horace, or Longinus were produced. Instead, several writers either directly or indirectly addressed issues related to the importance (or lack of importance) of imaginative literature and the nature of beauty.

Who was St. Augustine?

St. Augustine of Hippo (354–430) was the author of *Confessions* (400), which be-

St. Augustine was a philosopher and theologian who served as bishop of Hippo Regius (now Annaba, Algeria). He is also the author of the first autobiography, *Confessions*.

came the first modern autobiography, challenging the classical standard of objectivity with subjectivity derived from the experiences of the individual. This would have an enormous impact on the future conception of literature and its procedures. In the *Confessions*, Augustine, however, expresses his regret over his own "foolish" immersion in classical literature. Augustine sympathizes with Plato's argument for banishing poets on moral grounds and offers his own reason for art's falsity: art cannot be otherwise, since beauty and truth have nothing to do with the physical world. In Augustine's view, which became central to later medieval thinkers as Professor Habib summarizes, "The world is thus divested of any *literal* significance: its meaning resides in another realm, a transcendent goal. No object in the world can have any significance, importance, or meaning except in reference to God. Only God is to be loved for his own sake, and all other things are to be loved in reference to God."

According to Augustine, the world as experienced by a Christian is transformed from things to a series of signs revealing God. Learning to read these signs demanded study and practice demonstrated in the medieval practice of exegesis of scriptural texts, a forerunner of literary criticism's close reading and semiotics.

Who were Dante Alighieri and Giovanni Boccaccio?

Dante Alighieri (c. 1265–1321) and Giovanni Boccaccio (1311–1375) were two late medieval writers whose works stand out as heralds of what was to come in the Renaissance. Dante's *De vulgari eloquentia* ("On Eloquence in the Vernacular"; c. 1304–1307) argues for consideration of the Italian language over Latin as a literary language in the earliest work of literary criticism dealing with a vernacular language. Dante provides a theory of the evolution of language, mapping the ones that he knows, and describes his search for the "illustrious vernacular" among the fourteen varieties he claims to have identified in Italy to use in poetry. The second book of his essay examines literary gen-

Why is the *Summa theologica* important?

The greatest philosopher of the late medieval period, St. Thomas Aquinas (1224–1274) wrote proofs of the existence of God and offered an influential aesthetic doctrine on the intellectual conception of beauty in his *Summa theologica*. Aquinas argues that beauty requires three components: integrity (*integritas*) or wholeness, harmony or consonance (*consonantia*), and radiance (*claritas*). For an exercise in "applied Aquinas," see chapter five James Joyce's *A Portrait of the Artist as a Young Man,* in which Stephen Dedalus explains Aquinas's aesthetics to a classmate. The significance of Aquinas's aesthetic doctrine is the shift—ever so slightly from Augustine's conception of spiritual beauty and earthy imperfection derived from Plato—to an Aristotelian orientation toward actuality that will pave the way for the Renaissance.

res best suited to the vernacular. Dante's work is an important challenge to the supremacy of Latin as the literary language and the capacity of the everyday, common language as a literary medium.

Boccaccio likewise was a proponent of Italian vernacular literature with his best-known contribution, the *Decameron* (1358), his story collection. His most important work of literary criticism, however, was in Latin, *Geneaologia Deorum Gentilium* ("Genealogy of the Gentile Gods"; 1350–1362), a fifteen-volume encyclopedia of classical mythology. The last two books consist of a comprehensive defense of poetry. Boccaccio rejects the charge that reading poetry is an "unprofitable" activity, arguing that it "moves the minds of a few men from on high to a yearning for the eternal." Echoing both Horace and Longinus, Boccaccio asserts poetry's power to teach and delight, with literature sharing with theology an interest beyond the literal in embodying divine mysteries and spiritual meaning. Boccaccio's case in favor of poetry includes for one of the first times fiction as well, "a legitimate work of another art than oratory."

RENAISSANCE PERIOD

What key work of literary criticism was published during the Renaissance?

It can be argued that the crucial work of literary criticism during the Renaissance is Aristotle's *Poetics*, the Greek text that was made available in 1508 with a Latin translation in 1536. Prior to this, the *Poetics* had only been known through an Arabic commentary. Along with the circulation of numerous editions of Horace's *Ars Poetica*, the *Poetics* help shift literary criticism in the Renaissance from purpose to procedures, from the medieval Platonic focus on the ideal to the Aristotelian reliance on the actual, which bolstered an evolving Renaissance humanism.

Why was Giambattista Giraldi's *Discourse on the Composition of Romances* significant?

One of the most important Renaissance works of literary criticism, *Discourse on the Composition of Romances* (1554) by the Italian dramatist, poet, and critic Giraldi (1504–1573), was very much influenced by Aristotle's formalism in the *Poetics*. As Aristotle had both supported the excellence of tragedy and examined its methods, Giraldi makes a case for the new literary genre, the romance, a lengthy, narrative poem combining elements of classical epic and the medieval prose romance, the most notable example of which was Ariosto's *Orlando Furioso* (1516). Giraldi breaks with Aristotle's precept that an epic should imitate a single action, justifying the romance's many episodes and characters. By advocating on behalf of a literary form that did not derive from either the Greeks or Romans, written "laudably from our own language," Giraldi offers one of the first salvos in an ongoing critical battle between the "ancients" and the "moderns." In essence, Giraldi suggests that authors need not be bound by the precepts of their predecessors, that literary values are historically based and not eternal, that they evolve to reflect different tastes and standards.

Which work is considered the most important to be written in English during the Renaissance?

An Apology for Poetry (1595) by the Elizabethan poet, courtier, soldier, and scholar Sir Philip Sidney (1554–1586) is the most important contribution to literary theory written in English during the Renaissance and a seminal synthesis of Renaissance literary criticism. In it, Sidney mounts a two-pronged defense arguing the merits of poetry and refuting the main arguments against poetry as unprofitable, full of lies, and leading to sin. Drawing on a wide range of sources, Sidney asserts that poetry is the "first light-giver to ignorance." Since a prerequisite of knowledge is pleasure in learning, poetry has made all knowledge—scientific, moral, philosophical, and political—accessible by expressing them pleasurably. Moreover, poetry, unlike other arts and sciences, is not constrained to a particular aspect of nature but ranges freely by the boundless poet's wit, producing that which is superior to nature. "Nature never set forth the earth in so rich a tapestry," Sidney asserts, "as diverse poets have done.... Her world is brazen, the poets only deliver gold." Rather than profane falsifiers, Sidney insists, poets are linked closely to the divine as seers and prophets, whose imitations transcend and improve upon the natural world. Agreeing with Horace that the end of poetry is to teach and delight, Sidney affirms poetry's utility in inspiring readers to scorn the vices of its villains and imitate the nobility and virtues of its heroes.

To the argument that poetry is an unprofitable waste of time, Sidney insists poetry is the most fruitful of all knowledge, more effective than either philosophy or history in its teaching, because it teaches pleasurably. To the charge that poetry is a form of lies, Sidney argues that poetry never claims to be the truth and it shows not what is but what should or should not be. It is not poetry that leads to sin but its abuse. Why not, Sidney asks, condemn the Bible as well for the heresy and sins that have been committed in its name? Sidney concludes with a curse on all poetry deniers: "Thus much Curse I must send you in the behalfe of all Poets, that while you live, you live in love, and never get favour, for lacking skill of a Sonet, and when you die, your memorie die from the earth for want of an Epitaphe."

An English courtier, soldier, and poet, Sir Philip Sidney was the author of one of the most important books on literary theory of the Renaissance period.

NEOCLASSICAL PERIOD

What is neoclassicism?

Neoclassicism refers to the movement in literature and art during the seventeenth and eighteenth centuries calling for a return to the classical models, prescribed decorum, and values of the ancient Greeks and Romans. Neoclassicists extended the rediscovery of classical art during the Renaissance into a literary theory and critical standards that first took root in France and spread throughout Europe, notably in England.

Which work justified the playwright's right to violate Aristotelian principles of drama?

French playwright Pierre Corneille (1606–1684) produced the treatise *Three Discourses on Dramatic Poetry* (1660) to answer attacks on his play *Le Cid* (1637), which critics had charged violated the classical unities of action, time, and place. While rejecting a slavish adherence to Aristotelian principles in practice, Corneille nevertheless affirms his intention to "make ancient rules agree with modern pleasures." By doing so, Corneille articulated core principles of neoclassical literary theory.

Who explained the core ideas of French neoclassicism?

French poet and critic Nicholas Boileau (1636–1711) enumerates the core precepts of French neoclassicism in *The Art of Poetry* (1674), which would prove influential throughout Europe. Written in poetic form that echoed Horace's *Ars Poetica*, Boileau's text reaffirms poetry's central purpose to instruct and delight and reinforces the primacy of reason in the poetic endeavor, admonishing the poet to "love reason then; and let what'er you write / Borrow from her its beauty, force, and light." In Boileau's view, reason demands both resistance to religious censorship and an advocacy of control over poetic material exemplified in the classical rules of decorum.

What important contribution to the debate did John Dryden provide?

In *Essay of Dramatic Poesy* (1668), poet and playwright John Dryden (1673–1700), whom Samuel Johnson called "the father of English criticism," provides an extensive, formal treatment of literary genres, including epic, tragedy, comedy, and satire as well as contributing to the debate of the ancients versus the moderns—that is, the conflict between classical literary archetypes and modern violations of them, most notably in the works of Shakespeare. Written in a series of debates among four speakers crossing the Thames in a boat discussing the issues of the day, Dryden stages an overview of the main critical issues that mattered to the neoclassicists. All four support the notions that art is a form of imitation that should teach and delight and that requires writers to abide, if flexi-

John Dryden, who was England's first poet laureate, has been called the father of English criticism.

bly, to the classical rules of decorum. They differ on the relationship to the ancients whether they should imitate them closely or surpass them in alternative literary archetypes. They examine in detail the classical unities, defined by Aristotle and Horace and codified by French neoclassicists, such as Corneille, Racine, and Boileau, as well as the similarities and differences between the French and English theater. The speaker, Neander ("new man"), who becomes a mouthpiece for Dryden himself, asserts that English drama is superior because the rules and examples of the ancients are honored and observed but only as the laws of nature dictate.

What did Alexander Pope say criticism should accomplish for readers?

An Essay on Criticism (1711), the verse epistle by Alexander Pope (1688–1744), captures memorably in epigrammatic couplets core neoclassical principles. Pope calls for a "return to nature" in art that should celebrate the universal in human experience with "wit," which he defines as "nature to advantage dress'd, / What oft was thought, but ne'er so well expressed." Much of the poem focuses on the proper role of the critic, who, Pope admonishes, should write out of a love of poetry and not out of envy or spite. Criticism, Pope argues, should serve as "the Muse's handmaid prov'd / To dress her charms, and make her more belov'd." That is, criticism should help readers appreciate poetic genius and should judge works of literature on their own merits, freed from biases and narrow-minded attitudes. Pope offers a prescription for criticism that remains relevant today when the ingenuity of the critic is raised above the genius of the artist and works of art are made to fit the theory, rather than the theory to support the art, with sufficient judgment, humility, and generosity:

> But where's the man, who counsel can bestow,
> Still pleas'd to teach, and yet not proud to know?
> Unbias'd, or by favour or by spite;
> Not dully prepossess'd, nor blindly right;
> Though learn'd, well-bred; and though well-bred, sincere;
> Modestly bold, and humanly severe?
> Who to a friend his faults can freely show,
> And gladly praise the merit of a foe?
> Blest with a taste exact, yet unconfin'd;
> A knowledge both of books and human kind;
> Gen'rous converse; a soul exempt from pride;
> And love to praise, with reason on his side?
> Such once were critics; such a happy few....

ROMANTIC PERIOD

What happened during the Romantic period of criticism?

A fundamental challenge to the conception of literature and the nature of the artist that had ruled discussions of literature from the times of the Greeks and Romans would begin to emerge around the middle of the eighteenth century in reaction to the Enlightenment's primacy of reason, supported by the neoclassical standards of order, control, and harmony.

What was Edmund Burke's most famous work?

Philosophical Inquiry into the Origin of Our Ideas of the Sublime and Beautiful (1757) by Irish statesman and political theorist Edmund Burke (1729–1797) is an attack on the revolutionary energies that would help to fuel Romanticism and his conservative argument in support of tradition and authority. Burke's earlier treatise would, ironically, bolster many of the central ideas behind Romanticism, particularly in the growing shift from an ontological, objective definition of literature to a more subjective, epistemological understanding—in other words, Burke's essay expresses a shift in critical interest from artistic form to how literature pleases and is perceived, from beauty as an inherent component of an artistic object to beauty as an emotional and intellectual response to an object. Burke agrees with John Locke that the basis of all human knowledge is sense perception, and he shows how the imagination and judgment convert the raw data of sense impressions into more complex responses, including aesthetic judgments. For Burke, whatever excites ideas of pain, danger, and terror is a source of the sublime, the "strongest emotions which the mind is capable of feeling." The sublime differs from the beautiful in its evoking more than simple pleasure, stimulated by the wild, untamed, dark, and rugged. It would be this shift of emphasis from beauty as order to the sublime as overwhelming and awful, in its original sense of "full of awe" that would define the shift from neoclassical to Romantic art.

How did Immanuel Kant's view of aesthetic judgment affect the Romantic period?

It is impossible to treat the aesthetic theories of Immanuel Kant (1724–1804) in brief except by touching on its key concepts. As with Burke, beauty for Kant is connected to the subjective perception of an object, not inherently in an object. The work of art, Kant argues in *Critique of Judgment* (1790), is free from any moral or political responsibility, existing simply to give pleasure. It is from Kant that the concept of "art for art's sake"—of art as autonomous, having no purpose beyond itself—is derived. For Kant, aesthetic judg-

German philosopher Immanuel Kant believed in art for art's sake and that beauty is in the eye of the beholder. These principles would be influential in Romantic and later critical theory.

ment must be "disinterested," with no concern over art's utility or moral capacity. As Kant asserts, "beautiful objects have no meaning" beyond their capacity to provoke pleasure. The supreme agent in aesthetic judgment, according to Kant, is the imagination, the role of which would serve as the key for Romantic theory and literary practice. In aesthetic judgment, the imagination is not as constrained by rules of association or understanding but can act in "free lawfulness," becoming productive, rather than reproductive, and spontaneous, combining images in new and surprising ways. This notion of aesthetic perception as dynamic and creative would point the way to the radical reconceptualization of literary theory by the Romantics.

Who built on Kant's theories in his books on aesthetics and literature?

Poet, dramatist, and literary theorist Friedrich Schiller (1759–1805) derived from Kant the core notion of aesthetics as a form of liberation in his *Letters on the Aesthetic Education of Man* (1795) and *On Naïve and Sentimental Poetry* (1795–1796). The modern world, according to Schiller, is a tyranny of the material in which "utility is the great idol of the time, for which all powers slave and all talents should pay homage." The solution for Schiller is to pursue beauty instead, "through which one proceeds to freedom." For Schiller, modern society has extended human knowledge but at a cost of wholeness and harmony: "Eternally chained to only a single fragment of the Whole, man only develops himself as a fragment." The solution, according to Schiller, lies in the synthesizing power of the poet to recreate the world based on eternal ideals with art superior to politics or ethics in serving moral and spiritual ends.

What did William Wordsworth's *Preface to Lyrical Ballads* help clarify?

The publication of *Lyrical Ballads*, a collaboration of William Wordsworth (1770–1850) and Samuel Taylor Coleridge (1772–1834) in 1798, is widely regarded as one of the great literary events announcing a new conception of poetry and the ways and means of the poet. Wordsworth added his *Preface* to the second edition of the collection (1800) to clarify the poets' intentions and justify their break with poetic tradition. Prior to the Romantics, literature had been held as the product of a skilled craftsman, objectively reflecting nature but improving upon it in its subject matter and rules of decorum. The Romantics shifted the emphasis to the subjective expressiveness of the poet as the touchstone for art. Literary critic M. H. Abrams memorably captures this shift in the title of his critical study of Romanticism, *The Mirror and the Lamp*. Mimesis, or the reflection of nature, defined literature until the Romantics changed the paradigm to a lamp, an illumination or projection rather than a reflection, whose source is the poet's own consciousness.

This distinction is clearly evident in the *Preface* in Wordsworth's definition of poetry as the "spontaneous overflow of powerful emotions," a radical reconceptualization of poetry as a subjective, expressive art form, as an externalization of the poet's inner state of emotions, perceptions, and memories in response to feelings and ideas that are evoked in a contemplation of nature. Following from Wordsworth's premise of a new kind of poetry, the *Preface* calls for a radically altered set of methods and rules of decorum that had applied since Aristotle's *Poetics*. For Aristotle, tragic drama was "an imitation of an action" that led to the feelings of fear and pity; for Wordsworth, this process is reversed: poetry starts with the feelings of the poet to embodying them in scene and action. According to Wordsworth, poetry could evoke the strongest feelings, not from grand and noble subjects but from common, ordinary experiences and the humblest characters. The hierarchy of literary forms supported by Aristotle that privileged the epic and tragedy is similarly overthrown by Wordsworth's elevation of the lyric. To depict ordinary life, Wordsworth calls for a new poetic diction, replacing the inflated and artificial language of past poetry with "the real language of men": simple, direct, and natural.

Wordsworth's *Preface* and the poems that make up *Lyrical Ballads* announced a revolution that would have a profound impact on the literature that would follow and the critical theory that helped to explain it.

What was Samuel Taylor Coleridge's contribution to critical theory?

Samuel Taylor Coleridge (1772–1834) contributed to critical theory with his two-volume *Biographia Literaria: Biographical Sketches of My Literary Life and Opinions* (1817). Less an autobiography than a meditation and critical treatise, the *Biographia*, which has been called "the greatest book of criticism in English," is Coleridge's defense of his own and Wordsworth's poetic practices and the key conceptions that define Romanticism, linking the English Romantics with German philosophers, such as Immanuel Kant, Johann Gottlieb Fichte, and Friedrich Wilhelm Joseph von Schelling. One of Coleridge's key distinctions is between the natural philosopher who begins with nature and moves inductively to the general and ideal (the Aristotelian) and the transcendental philosopher who begins with the ideal and finds deductively its embodiment in the real (the Platonist). For Coleridge, these two different starting points both must arrive at a shared destination resolving the dichotomies of subject and object, real and ideal, mind and nature. The key agent for doing so, in Coleridge's view, is the imagination, which has the perceptive power to discover the deepest truths. Coleridge further distinguishes between the "primary imagination," in which one is passively inspired, and the "secondary imagination," the true source of poetry, which actively "dissolves, dissipates, diffuses, in order to

One of the founders of the Romantic Movement, Samuel Taylor Coleridge, believed that poetry involved the creation of something completely unique in which every part is essential to the whole.

recreate." Finally, Coleridge articulates an organic theory of poetry in which it is not imitation but creation of a near-living entity, in which each part is essential to the whole and nothing is unnecessary or missing. For Coleridge, a poem's form is determined by its content, and its form is essential to that content. Coleridge's demonstration of the organic wholeness of a poem is one of his singular contributions to literary theory. As critic David Daiches argues, "It was Coleridge who finally, for the first time, resolved the age-old problem of the relation between the form and content of poetry." It is mainly from Coleridge that modern, formalistic literary criticism is derived.

How did Percy Bysshe Shelley defend poetry against the rising tide of scientific rationalism?

Percy Bysshe Shelley's *A Defense of Poetry* (1821, published 1840) serves as a lyrical and impassioned synthesis of Romantic critical theory. Written in response to a satirical essay by Thomas Love Peacock, "The Four Ages of Poetry" (1820), which argued that scientific progress was making poetry obsolete, Shelley's *Defense* argues for the moral and social imperatives of poetry. In it, Shelley exalts the synthesizing power of the imagination, which he calls "the great instrument of moral good" over reason as the source of key truths. Completely reversing Plato's key precept, Shelley asserts that reason is to the imagination as the shadow is to the substance. "Poetry," Shelley declares, "redeems from decay the visitations of the divinity in man." The poet, Shelley argues, is like an Aeolian harp, producing music when the wind of inspiration blows over its strings. Although this inspiration is both unpredictable and short-lived, it makes the poet into a prophet of "the eternal, the infinite, and the one": "Poetry turns all things to loveliness; it exalts the beauty of that which is most beautiful, and it adds beauty to that which is most deformed; it marries exultation and horror, grief and pleasure, eternity and change; it subdues to union under its light yoke all irreconcilable things. It transmutes all that it touches, and every form moving within the radiance of its presence is changed by wondrous sympathy to an incarnation of the spirit which it breathes: its secret alchemy turns to potable gold the poisonous waters which flow from death through life; it strips the veil of familiarity from the world, and lays bare the naked and sleeping beauty, which is the spirit of its forms." Poets, Shelley declares, invent language, all art, laws, and religion, and the *Defense* concludes by famously declaring that "poets are the unacknowledged legislators of the world."

MODERNISM

What is Modernism?

Modern critical theory is shaped by a rejection of Romantic subjectivism, by a return to formalism, and by crucial nineteenth- and twentieth-century ideas (by Darwin, Marx, Nietzsche, Freud, Einstein, and others) that radically redefined human nature and the human experience and would have a major impact on how literature would be understood and interpreted.

What work by Matthew Arnold ushered in Modernism?

In "The Function of Criticism at the Present Time" (1864), the preface to the 1853 edition of *Poems*, Matthew Arnold (1822–1888) heralded the arrival of the modern and modernism by declaring, "The calm, the cheerfulness, the disinterested objectivity have disappeared: the dialogue of the mind have commenced." In "The Function of Criticism at the Present Time," Arnold asserts the crucial importance of criticism to make sense of the complexity of the modern age and its assault on traditional authority and understanding. Defining criticism as "a disinterested endeavor to learn and propagate the best that is known and thought in the world," Arnold argues that the analytical function of criticism prepares the way for creation, generating new

English cultural critic Matthew Arnold helped usher in the era of modern literary criticism with his "The Function of Criticism at the Present Time."

and fresh ideas that literature synthesizes and applies. Arnold identifies two epochs in the "life cycle" of a culture: an epoch of expansion, in which new ideas abound (such as Periclean Athens and Elizabethan England), and an epoch of concentration, in which ideas are consolidated and hardened and which Arnold regards as the contemporary period in which the critic is crucial to facilitate a new set of ideas that will initiate a new epoch of expansion and new opportunities for the literary artist. In Arnold's view, therefore, the poet and critic are interdependent: the critic is essential to assess cultural values of an age and the poet to harness the critic's intellectual energy and convert it into great art. Arnold's conception of the interplay between criticism and creativity would be important in raising the value of the critic and criticism in the functioning of literature, while shifting the debate from the subjective, expressive nature of literary expression promoted by the Romantics, to a new analytic formalism of New Criticism and modern critical approaches.

How did T. S. Eliot's "Tradition and the Individual Talent" help define literary modernism?

Prufrock and Other Observations (1917), the first collection by T. S. Eliot (1888–1965), is one of the singular events in literary history, comparable to the publication of *Lyrical Ballads* in announcing a new direction for poetry. Like Wordsworth's *Preface*, Eliot's critical essays serve to justify his methods and to provide core critical principles that would define literary modernism. "Tradition and the Individual Talent" (1919) is one of Eliot's crucial texts in which he argues that poetry should be essentially "impersonal," independent, and distinct from the personality of the poet. Eliot rejects the subjective expressive conception of literary art of the Romantics and advocates on behalf of a renewed sense of artistic objectivity. "Poetry is not a turning loose of emotion," Eliot argues, "but an escape from emotion; it is not the expression of personality, but an escape from personality." The poet, in Eliot's view, is "a medium and not a personality," a passive "receptacle" of images, ideas, and feelings, who combines them into new "art emotion," discovering what he will define in his essay "Hamlet and His Problem" (1920) as the "objective correlative," "a set of objects, a situation, a chain of events which shall be the formula of that particular emotion." Eliot's conception is an attempt to find an alternative to the self-projecting emotionality, vagueness, and excesses of the Romantics. Eliot further attempts to establish a foundation for literary influence and canon formation in his conception of "tradition." Rejecting the Romantic emphasis on individual genius, spontaneity, and originality as the source of poetry, Eliot insisted that poetic creation is dependent on "the historical sense," forming an order or "tradition" that is continually being transformed by new work. "The past," Eliot asserts, "should be altered by the present as much as the present is directed by the past." Poetry, in Eliot's view, only achieves its full value when it is understood in the context of all the poetry that has come before. Eliot's historical and objective conceptions of poetic practice will help to define modern poetics and critical understanding.

Which essays by W. K. Wimsatt challenged Romantic and Neoclassical literary theory?

American academic, literary theorist, and critic W. K. Wimsatt (1907–1975) is best known for the essays "The Intentional Fallacy" (1947) and "The Affective Fallacy" (1949),

Who provided the theoretical foundations of New Criticism?

Cambridge and Harvard academic and literary critic I. A. Richards (1893–1979) would be instrumental in providing the theoretical foundations of New Criticism in *Principles of Literary Criticism* (1924) and *Practical Criticism* (1929). New Criticism is the formalist movement in literary theory that emphasized the self-contained, autonomous nature of literature to be approached by close reading and analysis of a work's form. Arguing that literary criticism is too often impressionistic and imprecise, Richards sought a better means for responding to poetry in a close reading that analyzes the way poetry creates meaning and reader responses. In classroom experiments, he asked students to examine poems in which authorial and contextual information was removed before asking for interpretation. By forcing students to focus just on the text, Richards shifted critical emphasis from authorial intent and context to the formal aspects of a text. "It is never what a poem says that matters," Richards insists, "but what it is."

cowritten with Monroe Beardsley (1915–1985), that take direct aim both at the Romantic notion that a poem is the expression of the poet and the neoclassical assertion that a poem's worth is measured by the effect it has on the reader. Both essays are foundational in establishing the formalistic critical approach of New Criticism. In "The Intentional Fallacy," the authors reject critical analysis that attempts to uncover the author's intent derived from biographical details; in "The Affective Fallacy," they deny the pragmatic approach to literature, as asserted by Horace and others, in poetry's capacity to teach and delight. In both cases, according to Wimsatt and Beardsley, external standards, based on psychological causes or effects not inherent to the poem, are arbitrarily applied. Rather than guessing at what a poem might have intended or relying on imprecise reader response, the critic, Wimsatt asserts, should instead focus on the inner workings of the poem itself. This internal, as opposed to external, source of meaning and significance ought to be the basis for critical interpretation and assessment. Both essays share the New Critics' desire to establish an objective measure for literary criticism based on the inherent qualities of the poem's language and structure, freed from reference to external criteria of history, biography, or reader response.

Who is considered to be the most influential New Critic?

American literary critic and professor Cleanth Brooks (1906–1994) is perhaps the most influential advocate of New Criticism that dominated the teaching of poetry in the mid-twentieth century. In his book *The Well Wrought Urn: Studies in the Structure of Poetry* (1947), Brooks demonstrates his central critical tenet that literary study should be "concerned primarily with the work itself." He pursues the logical extension of this premise in "The Heresy of Paraphrase" by arguing that extracting a "paraphrasable core" of meaning in a poem is not possible, that meaning in a poem is inextricably linked to its structure and texture. A poem, Brooks argues, is a "pattern of resolved stresses," in which details, images, and ideas exert their own unique pressures. It is the critic's job not to reduce a poem to extract meaning but to reveal the poem's multiple tensions and underlying structure.

Who was the most prominent advocate of Archetypal and Mythic Criticism?

Canadian literary theorist Northrop Frye (1912–1991) is the most influential theorist of Archetypal and Mythic Criticism, which displaced New Criticism as the most important critical theory of the 1940s to 1960s, before the arrival of structuralism and deconstruction (which will be discussed in the Critical Approaches section

Literary critic and theorist Northrop Frye was key in advancing the Archetypal and Mythic schools of criticism.

of this chapter). Frye in *Anatomy of Criticism* (1957) postulated for the first time "a unified commentary on the theory of criticism," attempting "a synoptic view of the scope, theory, principles, and techniques of literary criticism." For Frye, literary archetypes "play an essential role in refashioning the material universe into an alternative verbal universe that is humanly intelligible and viable, because it is adapted to essential needs and concerns." For example, archetypes of Spring, Summer, Autumn, and Winter give rise to the literary forms of comedy, tragedy, irony, and romance, with each expressing shared symbolic elements. Frye shares with New Criticism a conviction of the autonomy and integrity of the "literary verbal structure." Expanding New Criticism's concern with the autonomous form of a literary work, Frye attempts to demonstrate how each poem makes up a network of references to an archetype, which he defines as "a symbol which connects one poem with another." Codifying the ways in which literary meaning repeats central mythical patterns, Frye demonstrates how, in its archetypal context, each work becomes a "microcosm of all literature."

POSTMODERNISM

What is postmodern critical theory?

Postmodern critical theory supports multiple critical approaches, such as Semiotics, Structuralism, Post-Structuralism, and Deconstruction. What unites them all under a general banner of postmodernism is a radical skepticism at the core of the most basic precepts of literary analysis from the formalist doctrine of New Criticism to the genre assumptions upon which Northrop Frye bases archetypal criticism. Postmodern critical theory problematizes virtually every component of literature from text, to author, to reader, as well as language itself, which is seen as a self-referential system, not as an unambiguous tool for representing reality. Friedrich Nietzsche's statement, "There are no facts. Only interpretations," could serve as the credo of postmodernism, elevating critical interpretation into an art form of its own, with the critic, not the author, as the ultimate source for literature's meaning.

Which literary theorist played a central role in connecting the ideas of postmodernist theory?

In many ways French literary theorist Roland Barthes (1915–1980) connects multiple postmodernist critical approaches. His many works, including *Writing Degree Zero* (1953), *Criticism and Truth* (1966), *S/Z* (1970), and *Mythologies* (1975), influenced the emerging discourse in semiotics, structuralism, and post-structuralist deconstruction. Perhaps no single work by Barthes has had such currency as his essay "The Death of the Author" (1967), in which he extends the intentional fallacy argument of New Criticism in devastating fashion that destablilizes critical interpretation itself. For Barthes, not only is the author's intent an invalid critical distinction, but he denies that any author is at the center or origin of a text, which he calls a "tissue of signs, endless imitation, infinitely postponed." The author is called a "scriptor," who merely combines pre-existing texts in new ways and "who is born simultaneously with the text." Every work is "eternally written here and now," with each rereading because its origin rests exclusively in "language itself" and its impressions on the reader. It's the reader who "authors" any text, and Barthes dismisses as deluded literary critics who claim to be able to interpret meaning for the reader.

CRITICAL APPROACHES TO LITERATURE

How did different critical approaches develop?

Literary theory is concerned with the nature of literature as a whole, while critical approaches apply theory to an interpretation of literary genres and individual literary works. We have treated literary theory historically. But what about critical approaches to literature? How have they developed and changed? For most of literary history, a single set of theories, derived from the philosophical idealism of Plato, the mimetic philosophy of Aristotle, and the moral philosophy of Horace and others instructed the ways literature should be understood, judged, read, and taught. Accepting Aristotle's classification of literature as a productive art and Horace's core notion that literature should please and teach, literary criticism up until the modern period mainly assisted in forming the canon of literary works that included those that best achieved Horace's dual purpose. From the Renaissance, these were largely works of literature that stood the test of time, the works of classical writers. The questions of literature's utility and social function, first raised by Plato, would continue to direct literary discourse, prompting the suppression of dramatic theater through much of its history and other censorship as literature was judged to have failed in its moral mission.

As the age of print took hold in the seventeenth and eighteenth centuries, the first professional literary critics, periodical reviewers, came to prominence, whose reviews evaluating new publications helped establish literary taste and standards, though their work was a source of frequent complaints by writers such as John Dryden, Alexander Pope, Samuel Johnson, and others who decried reviewers' lack of both taste and standards.

Literary criticism in academia, up until the twentieth century, reflected a consensus of the books that every educated man (women were, of course, mainly excluded here) should read and the aims and purpose of literature. From the medieval period down through the twentieth century, colleges and universities offered not courses of study but key books to read and master. These were mainly classical works that had stood the test of time. Literary scholars mainly curated literary history: establishing the key texts, tracking influences, identifying literary periods, and clarifying, much in the manner of the medieval monastic tradition of exegesis of sacred texts, allusions, etymology, and historical contexts of accepted, important texts. Literary scholars, first mainly of classical literature and eventually in the twentieth century of modern languages, did the work of *philology* (from the Greek "love of language"), the study of the historical development of languages and literary texts. It is from this scholarly tradition that certain critical approaches to literature, such as formalism and historic criticism, would emerge in the twentieth century.

BIOGRAPHICAL CRITICISM

What is one of the earliest critical approaches to literature?

In addition to approaching literature from a historical perspective, treating it in the context of an author's life is one of the earliest critical approaches that goes back to the classical period. It used existing knowledge of an author's life as a way of explaining a work, or, in the absence of direct evidence, scoured the text for clues to construct a biographical profile. Homer was one of the earliest candidates for this treatment, which has persisted, with the notoriously elusive Shakespeare, an inescapable quarry for Biographical Criticism. Samuel Johnson's (1709–1784) *Lives of the Most Eminent English Poets* (1779–1781), a compendium of short biographies and critical appraisals of fifty-two mostly eighteenth-century English poets, is one of the most important examples of a Biographical Critical approach. Johnson himself would serve as the subject for the first modern literary biography, James Boswell's *Life of Samuel Johnson* (1791). Biographical Critical approaches would be considerably enhanced with the shift in literary theory during the Romantic period from literature as objective reflection to literature as expressive projection by the author. Works were inescapably seen as versions of autobiography that changed the critical approach from the text to the author. Perhaps the most outspoken advocate of Biographical Criticism is French critic Charles Augustin Sainte-Beuve (1804–1869), who has been called the inventor of modern literary criticism and who argued that a work of literature could be entirely explained in terms of a biographical approach. Literary formalism, or New Criticism, would emerge to counter Sainte-Beuve and the Biographical Critical approach, but it persists in various modern critical approaches, such as Psychological Criticism and Historical Criticism, in scholarly production of writers' letters and biographies, even in the biographical blurb that publishers feel obligated to include on book jackets.

Author, critic, editor, and lexicographer Samuel Johnson penned an important early work of Biographical Criticism, *Lives of the Most Eminent English Poets.*

393

What critical questions does Biographical Criticism ask?

A Biographical Critical approach focuses on the connections between the work and the author's life and personal experiences. The theory supporting the approach is that since the work of literature is the creation of a specific author, knowledge about the author's biography as well as statements about the work by the author provide a helpful context in appreciating and understanding it. Some key questions raised by a Biographical Critical approach include:

- *How are details of the author's life relevant to an understanding of the work?* How does biography and historical context help to explain the work?
- *How are the author's views, values, and beliefs relevant to an understanding of the work?* What light does the author's stated opinions and intentions, evident from letters, interviews, etc., shed on understanding the work?
- *Are there correspondences between the concerns and issues of the work and what we know about the author's personal experiences and beliefs?* Is a work's meaning related to the author's background? Do specific elements of the work resemble events experienced by the author?
- *Do any of the characters in the work correspond to real people?* Can the work be read as a form of autobiography? If so, what light does the work shed on its author?

What are leading examples of Biographical Criticism?

The best representatives of effective Biographical Critical approaches are found in the many exemplary literary biographies that integrate details about an author's life with critical readings of their works. Some standouts are:

Author	Book	Significance
Edel, Leon	*Henry James* (1953–1972)	A five-volume, magisterial literary biography
Ellmann, Richard	*James Joyce* (1959)	One of the models of the form with always sensible critical analysis informed by the biography
Frank, Joseph	*Dostoevsky*	Frank's monumental biography is a model for literary biography and the most comprehensive and definitive account of Dostoevky's life and times
Greenblatt, Stephen	*Will in the World: How Shakespeare Became Shakespeare* (2004)	One of the best on the Bard in a crowded field, combining narrative excellence and outstanding scholarship
Holmes, Richard	*Shelley* (1974)	Demonstrates how the literary biographer can revise our sense of this Romantic poet
Johnson, Edgar	*Charles Dickens: His Tragedy and Triumph* (1962)	A classic. Look for the two-volume edition that includes the author's superb critical analysis of the novels
Lee, Hermione	*Virginia Woolf* (1996)	Has been described as a "majestic" biography that "rediscovers Virginia Woolf afresh"

Author	Book	Significance
Rampersad, Arnold	*The Life of Langston Hughes* (1986, 2002)	A definitive two-volume biography by one of the foremost African American scholars
Reynolds, Barbara	*Dante: The Poet, the Political Thinker, the Man* (2006)	A fascinating re-assessment of Dante's life and career with intriguing speculation
Tomalin, Claire	*Jane Austen* (1997)	Considered definitive, this biography "radiates intelligence, wit, and insight"
Wilson, A. N.	*Tolstoy* (1989)	Written with novelistic skill and critical intelligence

What led to the development of multiple, competing critical views of literature?

In many ways, the proliferation of critical approaches to literature begins during the opening decades of the twentieth century in reaction to Romantic literary theory and Biographical Critical approaches. This is directly attributed to the assault on traditional beliefs in the destabilizing ideas of Darwin, Marx, Nietzsche, Freud, Einstein, and others and the breakdown of the centuries-old consensus view of what constitutes the literary canon, as well as the aims and purposes of literature. Romantic literary theory challenged the established objective, mimetic theory of literature offering different conceptions of the source of literature, its value and purpose, and the role of the author in society as outsider and critic rather than an advocate of the shared values of a culture and community. "Make it new," the rallying cry of Modernism, signaled a direct assault on traditional literary values and stimulated alternate critical approaches to understand and appreciate a new kind of literature. To understand this new literature that originated and reflected a radically different worldview, critical approaches emerged that both sought more precision in treating literature and ways of incorporating unfolding ideas in psychology, sociology, politics, and gender roles.

FORMALISM AND NEW CRITICISM

What is Formalism?

Formalism is a critical approach focused on the formal elements of a literary text, such as structure, tone, images, setting, symbols, and diction and excludes extrinsic considerations of the author's intent, historical context, and the work's purpose. Formalism in various types would dominate the way in which literature was studied and taught through much of the twentieth century, persisting as a core method in literature courses and as a foundational element in later critical approaches such as structuralism and deconstruction.

What is the origin of Formalist Criticism?

Literary formalism can trace its origin to several nineteenth-century literary theories. One is a reaction to author-centered, subjective expressive theory of literature promulgated by the Romantics that shifted focus from the author and the emotional effect of a text to the classical norm of objectivism. Another is Aestheticism and the Aesthetic Movement, the intellectual and art movement during the second half of the nineteenth century that emphasized aesthetic values over the moral and social justification for art and argued "Art for Art's sake," and the autonomous integrity of a literary work that severed the connection between art and morality. A third influence is the late nineteenth-century French Symbolist Movement that located the source of key truths and powerful emotions in particular images or objects with symbolic meanings. Literary theorist Jean Moréas, in his "Symbolist Manifesto" (1886), decried "plain meaning, declamations, false sentimentality, and matter-of-fact descriptions" in literature and advocated for a method to "clothe the ideal in a perceptible form." The French Symbolists would in turn influence the European Imagist Movement during the first two decades of the twentieth century, which sought to replace the "emotional slither" of Romanticism with concrete images that generated meaning and feeling, what T. S. Eliot would call the "objective correlative." These literary theories encouraged a new critical approach of formalism.

What is New Criticism?

The Formalist Critical approach called New Criticism emerged from a loose collection of American academics and literary critics in the 1920s and 1930s, becoming the dominant critical approach for more than thirty years. It was named for the book *The New Criticism* (1941) by scholar, poet, and critic John Crowe Ransom (1888–1974). Its criticism was "new" in the sense of its break from past critical approaches that focused on extrinsic issues of the author's biography, historical context, or moral, social, and political impact rather than intrinsic elements of literary form. Cleanth Brooks (1906–

What is Russian Formalism?

The earliest was a loose collection of Russian and Soviet literary critics from the 1910s to the 1930s, including such scholars as Viktor Shklovsky, Vladimir Propp, Boris Eichenbaum, and Roman Jacobson. They shared a pursuit of a "scientific" method for studying literature with an emphasis on the functional role of literary devices and an exclusion of traditional Historical and Psychological Critical approaches. For the Russian Formalists, the features that distinguish literature from other human activities constitute the proper object of critical inquiry, which attempted to identify the various mechanical "devices," such as imagery, rhythm, and meter, of literature to show how a work operated.

Important critical works in this area include Victor Erlich's *Russian Formalism: History—Doctrine* (1981); Vladimir Propp's *The Morphology of the Folktale* (1928), and Viktor Shklovsky's *Theory of Prose* (1925).

1994) in a 1951 essay called "The Formalist Critics" laid out a set of assumptions that help define New Criticism:

- That literary criticism is a description and an evaluation of its object.
- That the primary concern of criticism is with the problem of unity—the kind of whole that the literary work forms or fails to form and the relation of the various parts to each other in building up this whole....
- That in a successful work, form and content cannot be separated.
- That form is meaning.
- That literature is ultimately metaphorical and symbolic.

New Criticism got its name from a book title by John Crowe Ransom, who is considered the founding voice of this school of criticism.

- That the general and the universal are not seized upon by abstraction but got at through the concrete and the particular.

Brooks summarizes the operating principles of New Criticism in the primacy and automony of the literary work, in which its medium is its message, requiring close reading to explore the interconnections, ambiguities, and multiple tensions. For the New Critic (see W. K. Wimsatt's "Intentional Fallacy" and "Affective Fallacy" above), neither the author's intention nor the reader's emotional response to a text is relevant. What matters is what the text actually says and does. Important critical works in this area include:

- *The Well Wrought Urn: Studies in the Structure of Poetry* (1947) by Cleanth Brooks
- *Understanding Poetry* (1938) by Cleanth Brooks and Robert Penn Warren
- *Understanding Fiction* (1943) by Cleanth Brooks and Robert Penn Warren
- *The New Criticism* (1941) by John Crowe Ransom
- *The Verbal Icon: Studies in the Meaning of Poetry* (1954) by W. K. Wimsatt

What is Neo-Aristotelian Criticism (Chicago School)?

The Neo-Aristotelians were formalist literary critics associated with the University of Chicago in the 1930s through the 1960s who broke with New Criticism over questions of the proper focus for formalist studies of literature. The New Critics looked at texts from the micro-perspective of language and diction; the Neo-Aristotleans were interested in the macro-perspective of form and genre as derived by Aristotle's *Poetics* and *Rhetoric*. Like Aristotle, the Neo-Aristotelians attempted to identify the rules governing literary structure and what distinguished one genre from another. Agreeing with the New Critics that criticism should move away from a primarily historical toward an aesthetic approach, the Neo-Aristotelians advocated on behalf of a systematic theory of literature informed by the history of literary theory as well as close readings and explication of texts. Important works include:

- *The Rhetoric of Fiction* (1951) by Wayne C. Booth
- *Critics and Criticism: Ancient and Modern* (1952) by Ronald Salmon
- *The Language of Criticism and the Structure of Poetry* (1952) by Ronald Salmon
- *Tragedy and the Theory of Drama* (1961) by Elder Olson

What questions do Formalist Critics ask?

- *How do the components of the literary work—diction, imagery, rhyme, and rhythm, for example—interact to form the work's structure and pattern of meaning?* How do the parts of the work unite to form a literary whole?
- *How does the form of the work create the content of the work?* How does form reflect function in creating meaning and significance in the work? How is meaning created in the text? How do the various elements of work reinforce its meaning?
- *What tensions and contradictions are evident in the work, and how are they resolved?* How do the various elements of the work contribute to the unity of the work? Do elements of the work resist or contradict resolution into an organic whole?
- *What figures of speech (metaphor, simile, etc.) and recurring patterns (repeated or related words, images, etc.) reveal or reflect the work's meaning?* Do these elements rise to the level of the symbolic?
- *How do ambiguity, irony, and paradox work in the text?* How do these elements contribute to the meaning of the work?
- *What is the tone or mood of the work?* How are tone and mood created?
- *How does the sequence of action described form a plot that explains causality?* How are the events related? How does one lead to another, and how does plot relate to character?

PSYCHOLOGICAL AND PSYCHOANALYTICAL CRITICISM

What is the origin of Psychological Criticism?

Aristotle in the *Poetics* placed character just below plot in importance in tragedy, and his analysis of the nature of character needed in drama is the first instance we have of what could be called a psychological approach to literature, that is, the relationship between literature and human character types. Through much of the literary history that followed, through the medieval period and the Renaissance, human psychology was fundamentally regarded as fixed and stable, expressed in terms of clear moral categories (virtue and vice) or by the four fundamental personality types or humours (sanguine, choleric, melancholic, and phlegmatic). It would not be until John Locke (1632–1704), the English Enlightenment philosopher, provided a theory of human understanding derived from experience that a dynamic and developmental concept of human psychology began to emerge. By the eighteenth century, various evolving literary forms—biography, autobiography, and the novel—reflected the Lockian view of the experiential nature of personality that would culminate in a modern theory of psychology, identity, and consciousness as articulated by Sigmund Freud, Carl Jung, and others. The psychological or psychoanalytic approach to literature applies these theories to an understanding and interpretation of literary works.

What is Freudian Criticism?

Without question, the first Freudian critic of literature was Sigmund Freud (1856–1939) himself, who relied on literature for examples and confirmation of his theory of human nature and development. "Everywhere I go," Freud declared, "I find a poet has been there before me." He would, for example, name his most controversial theory of childhood sexual desire the Oedipus complex after the Greek myth dramatized by Sophocles. It is not surprising, therefore, that literature would later serve as case histories for an application of Freud's psychoanalytical theories that transformed our understanding of human nature and experience. Freud's core concept of the role of the unconscious in shaping behavior and desires as well as the three parts of the human personality (id, ego, and superego) would lead literary critics to look for an underlying dynamic of Freud's teachings in literary works not on their surface but in the unconscious motives of both characters and authors. If, as Freud declared, "Dreams are the royal road to the unconscious," then imaginative literature could be regarded as the symbolic wish fulfilment of the unconscious desires of its author and its characters in the text as embodiment of repression, childhood sexual memory, and neuroses. The Freudian Psychological Critical approach would elevate the importance of biographical information about an author as well as encourage a close reading of a text, not as in New Criticism for the relationship between form and content but for underlying symbolic patterns revealing psychological truths operating in the text.

The founder of psychoanalysis, Sigmund Freud, also had his influence on the interpretation of literature.

What are Jungian and Myth or Archetypal Criticism?

For Carl Jung (1875–1961), the notion of the unconscious led not to Freud's theory of repressed childhood sexual desire but to the conception of a universal or collective unconscious that is expressed in shared patterns of human experiences, or archetypes. Like Freud, Jung saw the human psyche as a battlefield of conflicting forces, both personal and collective. These forces are expressed in archetypes, forms of beliefs, actions, and symbols in which the unconscious becomes conscious to us. In Jung's view, there are two kinds of archetypes: those of the collective unconscious in the form of recurring patterns to be found in any culture and those of the personal unconscious, dispositions that each individual needs to recognize and accommodate to function as a mature member of society. Both are uncovered by Jungian analysis.

Jung's psychological theories stand behind the school of archetypal or myth criticism of Northrop Frye (see his *Approaches to Criticism* above) and others that emerged in the 1940s and 1950s. Archetypal literary critics attempted to classify literary texts based on recurring myths and archetypes, such as the hero's quest and a seasonal understanding of literary genre—Summer: Romance (birth of the hero), Autumn: Tragedy (death or defeat of the hero), Winter: Satire (absence of the hero), Spring: Comedy (rebirth of the hero). Archetypal literary critics focus on the universal patterns connecting the surface and particularized details of a literary text and an understanding of these patterns (archetypes) in both its form and content.

What is Lacanian Criticism?

French psychoanalytical theorist Jacques Lacan (1901–1981) provides yet a third construct of the unconscious—neither Freud's realm of suppressed desire nor Jung's source of shared patterns of human experiences—but as sophisticated as consciousness itself and "structured like a language." Lacan, who described his work as "returning to the meaning of Freud," refashions Freudian theory in light of current theories of semiotics and poststructuralist linguistics. Lacan replaces Freud's psychic construct of id, ego, and superego with an Imaginary stage (the undifferentiated union with the mother in which self and other are united), the Mirror stage (recognition of identity and the difference of self and other), and the Symbolic stage (in which language is acquired with the separation between subject and object). It is language or culture rather than nature, in Lacan's view, that codifies identity and gender differences as well as marking the barriers between desires and fulfilment. For the literary critic, Lacan's psychoanalytic theory has provided a methodology beyond sexual desire and myth for explaining how consciousness of a separate self operates and under what symbolic constraints of language. Lacan's critical method redirects psychological interest back to the formal elements of the texts without the necessity of framing critical responses in relation to the author's biography or mythical patterns of meaning.

Important critical works include:

• *A Theory of Poetry* (1973) by Harold Bloom

- *Archetypal Patterns in Poetry* (1934) by Maud Bodkin

- *Psychoanalysis and the Future of Theory* (1994) by Malcolm Bowie

- *Psychoanlytic Literary Criticism* (2014) edited by Maud Ellman

- *Ancient Myth in Modern Poetry* (1971) by Lillian Feder

- *Reading Lacan* (1985) by Jane Gallop

- *A Jungian Approach to Literature* (1984) by Bettina L. Knapp

- *Jacques Lacan: Psychoanalysis and the Subject of Literature* (2001) by Jean-Michel Rabate

- *Lacan and Literature* (1996) by Ben Stoltzfus

- *Jungian Literary Criticism* (1993) by Richard Sugg

What questions does Psychological Criticism ask?

- *What unconscious motives are operating in the main characters?* What repressed wounds, fears, unresolved conflicts, or guilty desires are evident? How do they impact behavior?

- *Can a character's adult behavior be traced to early experience and family relations?* What do these behavior patterns and family dynamics reveal and signify?

- *How do the plot, characters, and images reflect psychoanalytic concepts, such as a fear or fascination with death and sexuality, as central expressions of psychological identity?* How does the Freudian psychic construct of id, ego, and superego operate in the text?

- *How does the work reflect the writer's experiences and psychology?* How do the writer's biographical details illuminate the work?

- *How do details in the work, such as images and setting, function symbolically in the story clarifying conscious and unconscious motive and behavior?* As in a dream, to what extent is every element potentially meaningful?

- *How does the work resemble other stories? How do the characters reflect character types?* What archetypal pattern of experience is being expressed in the plot and characters?

- *What common human concerns are expressed?* Does the work deal with issues such as death or rebirth? A journey of initiation or discovery?

- *What trials or obstacles does the protagonist face?* What is implied by these obstacles and the rewards for surmounting them?

- *What archetypal images or settings appear?* For example, water, rising or setting sun, a garden, or wasteland.

- *How can the central character be understood in the context of the Lacanian stages of Imaginary, Mirror, and Symbolic?* How is the protagonist's identity expressed by language patterns that define subject–object relationships?

- *How are concepts like the father and law represented?* What conflicts emerge in the protagonist's conception of both?

- *How do various details in the text coalesce into a psychological understanding of the ways in which the unconscious functions?* How do the details and language establish patterns of association and tensions to understand motive and behavior?

MARXIST CRITICAL APPROACH

What is the basis of Marxist Criticism?

If literature is a productive subject for the psychological approach, examining the inner mental and emotional responses of its characters, it is also, particularly in the outward range of the novel, reflective of how society operates. Long before sociology existed as an academic discipline, literature discussed the functioning of class and the implications of cultural change produced by urbanization and technology. Interest in these themes has been guided by the social theories of Karl Marx (1818–1883) in his series of groundbreaking books—*The Communist Manifesto* (1848), *Preface to the Contribution to the Critique of Political Economy* (1859), and *Das Kapital* (*Capital*, 1867). Marx radically re-examined the underlying tenets of capitalism to suggest that the individual is prey to massive forces of class and economic imperatives that he cannot hope to control. In Marx's view, these forces obliterate the old pieties about human agency—the individual's ability to control his own destiny. For Marx, the base (or structure) of society is the economic means and modes of production upon which rest the social, political, and intellectual superstructure. All art, Marx asserted, reflects and expresses these economic forces. The Marxist Critical approach applies Marx's social theories to literary interpretation.

What are the main concerns of the Marxist Critical approach?

Marxist literary criticism focuses on the ways in which a text represents social issues of class conflict and economic imperatives, not just in story or characters but also in literary forms and the author's assumptions about society and politics. For the Marxist Critic, a work of literature is treated as a product of history and should

Marxist Criticism is grounded in the social theories of political theorist and economist Karl Marx, who examined the individual as a victim of class distinctions and economic systems.

402

be analyzed by looking at the social and economic conditions in which it was constructed as well as the social and political ideas expressed. As Marx asserts, "It is not consciousness of men that determines their being, but on the contrary their social being, that determines their consciousness." Accordingly, the focus of the Marxist Critical approach is how are social issues addressed in the work, what underlying social assumptions dictate both form and content. Marxist literary critics take a historical approach rather than the aesthetic approach of the literary formalist, carefully locating the work in its historical and cultural context. Marxist Critics generally assert that no literary work can be understood in isolation from the social, cultural, and historical conditions in which it was produced and that even the aesthetic categories by which a text is measured are determined by the same conditions. Moreover, Marxist Critics are also concerned with what a work does *not* say or cannot say, based on the author's or the work's underlying ideology. Finally, Marxist Critics are divided over the issue of whether their function is to describe a work's ideology or to advocate for change. As Marx asserted, "The philosophers have only *interpreted* the world in various ways; the point is to *change* it." Single-minded Marxist criticism that ignores everything but socioeconomic forces has been labeled *vulgar* Marxism, and an application of Marxist perspectives that works in concert with other critical approaches makes the most sense for the general reader. Important Marxist Criticism books include:

- *Marxism and Literary Criticism* (1976) by Terry Eagleton
- *Marxist Literary Theory: A Reader* (1996) by Terry Eagleton
- *The Philosophical Discourse of Modernity* (1990) by Jürgen Habermas
- *Marxism and Form* (1971) by Fredric Jameson
- "The Ideology of Modernism" (1956) by Georg Lukács
- *Marxism and Literature* (1977) by Raymond Williams

What questions does Marxist Criticism ask?

- *What role does class play in the work?* What is the author's analysis of class relations?
- *In what ways does the work support certain socioeconomic values and what ways does it challenge or resist them?* How are social and economic issues represented in the work?
- *What class assumptions are evident in the work?* How are characters' identities, motives, and values shaped by class affiliation?
- *What happens when characters of various classes interact?* How does class difference define the conflict in the work?
- *What forms of oppression are evident in the work?* How do characters respond to social and economic forces and overcome them or are overcome by them?
- *What solution is being offered to the problems encountered in the work?* Does the work simply diagnose socioeconomic issues, or are their solutions provided?

403

STRUCTURALISM

What is Structuralism?

Structuralism, a critical approach that would gain popularity in 1960s, extended the Formalists' focus on the formal and linguistic elements of a text to the structures that order our thinking rather than the internal architecture of a literary work. The theoretical basis for structuralism is derived from the linguistic studies of Swiss linguist and semiotician Ferdinand de Saussure (1857–1913) and the French anthropologist Claude Lévi-Strauss (1908–2009) as adapted to literary studies by French critics Michel Foucault (1926–1984) and Roland Barthes (1915–1980). Saussure, regarded as the founder of modern linguistics, regarded signifiers (words and symbols) as arbitrary and distinct from the signified (objects in the real world) to which they referred. Language, as understood by Saussure, worked by a system of "differences," and he was interested in identifying the underlying structures that made meaning possible, that is, the rules and functions of languages and their interrelations rather than language particulars. For the structuralist literary critic, Saussure's focus on the structure common to language as a whole signaled the shift of inquiry to shared systems of meaning, such as genres and myths common to multiple cultures and historical periods, rather than their individual expressions in particular poems or stories as favored by New Criticism. Structuralists regard a text as part of a network of conventions, such as the rules governing a language system, that pattern the work in its entirety. These conventions can be cultural (from history, politics, religion, etc.) and/or literary, in the form of the norms of textual genre, as well as similarity and difference with other works. Only by carefully relating an individual work to its cultural and literary context does the structuralist reveal the structural rules of the work that makes meaning and understanding possible. With the risk of oversimplifying a complex and often dense approach, structuralism attempts to identify and understand fundamental structures of a text by relating it to larger systems that communicate meaning. The structuralist resembles the grammarian who is less interested in the content of the sentences examined but in how certain words function within the sentence. For the structuralist, everything is part of a sign system that can be "read" and understood based on core structures of meaning. A literary text, for the structuralist, is just one of many sign systems, no different in operating principles from a

Structuralism draws its inspiration from linguist and semiotician Ferdinand de Saussure.

film, television program, or commercial. With the Structuralist Critical approach, the critic, not the author, is supreme.

Important Structuralist works include:

- "Structuralist Activity" in *Collected Essays* (1972) by Roland Barthes
- *Structuralist Poetics* (1975) by Jonathan Culler
- *Death and the Labyrinth* (1963) by Michel Foucault
- "Truth and Power" (1977) by Michel Foucault
- *After the New Criticism* (1980) by Frank Lentricchia
- *Structural Anthropology* (1976) by Claude Lévi-Strauss
- *Course in General Linguistics* (1916) by Ferdinand de Saussure
- *Structuralism: An Introduction* (1973) by Robert Scholes

What questions does Structuralist Criticism ask?

- *How does the work's form relate to established literary genres?* What are the conventions of the literary genre to which the work belongs? How are those conventions observed or violated?
- *How do elements in the work refer to the culture from which the text was created?* How do patterns in the text (in its narrative operation, its images and details) relate to similar systems in other texts or in culture?
- *How can the work be read as a series of signs specifying meaning?* What pattern of significance is evident?
- *How do the elements of the work's action suggest a meaningful pattern?* What narrative rules are observed?
- *How are differences in the text (characters, images, events) expressed, and what do they signify?* If language works by binary opposites (day/night, good/bad, for example), what differences are established in the text and for what purposes?
- *What assumptions and rules govern the interpretation of the text?* What cultural assumptions do individual judgments on the work suggest? How are those judgments derived?
- *What pattern of meaning can be identified from the various images and motifs in the work?* How are completing patterns of meaning related and resolved?

POST–STRUCTURALISM AND DECONSTRUCTION

What is Post-Structuralism?

Post-Structuralist Criticism extends the structuralist's core belief that we can understand things only in terms of other things to encompass the notion that any final, conclusive meaning is an impossibility. Meaning exists in an interconnected web of ideas leading to other ideas, and, therefore, for the post-structuralist, a literary text has no fixed or final meaning outside of the network of meaning to which it is connected. For the post-structuralists, the systems and meaning patterns deciphered by the structuralists are ingenious but fictional constructs that can neither be trusted nor provide any conclusive truths because that very notion is a delusion. Instead, the post-structuralists radically doubt that both the world and literary texts are ever really knowable and that any system of understanding is inherently unstable and shifting. Post-structuralism is similar to Heisenberg's uncertainty principle in physics; the literary text, like the velocity and position of an object, cannot be measured with certainty. For the post-structuralist, literary critic interpretation reveals more about our biases and assumptions rather than anything certain about a text, with all interpretation to an extent equally valid and invalid. Literary criticism is thereby reduced to a dizzying exercise of what post-structuralist guru Jacques Derrida called "full free play of meaning": interpretation unmoored from any reliable connection to truth. At its best, post-structuralist criticism can be ingenious and liberating, suggesting new ways of understanding a literary text; at its worst, it can be maddeningly relativistic and self-serving with the literary critic the reigning connoisseur of interpretative chaos.

What is Deconstruction?

The most pervasive and controversial of the various Post-Structuralist Critical approaches (others include Reader-Response Theory and Gender Theory, treated below) is deconstruction. Its main tenets were revealed by French philosopher and semiotician Jacques Derrida (1930–2004) in a famous lecture, "Structure, Sign and Play in the Discourse of the Human Sciences" (1966). In it, Derrida disputed both the core assumption of Western philosophy that stable, central truths are possible, and the structuralist's basic notion that fundamental patterns of meaning underlie language and discourse. For Derrida and the deconstructionists, the relationship between signifier and signified in language is untrustworthy, resulting in a breakdown of certainty. As Derrida asserts, "There is no getting outside text" to any fixed, stable meaning. Instead, literary texts, like any ideology or communication, are to be deconstructed to reveal their inherent contradictions and infinite associational possibilities. For the deconstructionist, the traditional notion of an author as creative

French philosopher Jacques Derrida developed Deconstruction criticism, which asserts that texts can only be constructed to reveal their contradictions, not stable truths.

originator is replaced by the creative power of language or the text and the ingenuity of the critic to unpack and translate it in new and provocative ways. Like the New Critic, Deconstruction depends on close reading, but the formalists' confidence in literature's coherence and unity is suspect, and literature itself as the privileged source of literary criticism is undermined. The focus of deconstruction's interest in a text are the fissures and cracks in its seeming unity or coherence. The text is self-referential only and does not refer outside itself to the author's intentions or the outside world.

In practice, deconstruction, which literary critic Richard Ellmann has called "the systematic undoing of understanding," focuses on the contradictions and internal oppositions upon which meaning in a literary text rests, demonstrating how such meaning is endlessly complex and unstable. For the deconstructionist, a literary text has multiple and contradictory interpretations that are never fully resolved. As J. Hillis Miller observes, "Deconstruction is not a dismantling of the structure of a text, but a demonstration that it has already dismantled itself. Its apparently solid ground is no rock, but thin air."

Important Deconstructionist works include:

- *Deconstruction & Criticism* (1979) by Harold Bloom, Paul de Man, Jacques Derrida, Geoffrey Hartman, and J. Hillis Miller
- *On Deconstruction: Theory and Criticism after Structuralism* (1982) by Jonathan Culler
- "Structure, Sign and Play in the Discourses of the Human Sciences" (1966) and *Of Grammatology* (1967) by Jacques Derrida
- *Literary Theory: An Introduction*, Chapter 4 (1983) by Terry Eagleton
- *Against Deconstruction* (1989) by John Ellis
- *After the New Criticism* (1980) by Frank Lentricchia
- *Theory Now and Then* (1991) by J. Hillis Miller

What questions does deconstruction criticism ask?

- *What assumptions does the work reveal?* How might those assumptions bias the interpretation of the meanings the text suggests?
- *What is the logic or argument that is evident in the text, and what are its flaws?* How can the work as a whole be broken down to its constituent parts, and how are these parts unified?
- *What ambiguities or paradoxes are evident in the text?* What can you learn from what the text fails to resolve?
- *What tensions are evident in the text?* What contradictions are revealed between what the author intends and what the text actually says? How does the work undermine or contradict generally accepted truths?
- *How does the work use different kinds of words (nouns, verbs, adverbs, etc.), and what do they reveal about the text's assumptions?* The language of a work functions as a hypothesis about the world it depicts. What are these hypotheses?

- *How does the language in the text show multiple meanings in words?* How does this contribute to the instability of text?

- *What key binary oppositions (masculine/feminine, reason/emotion, or for example) are evident?* Which terms in these oppositions is being given preference, and how does such privileging impose an interpretative template on the work being examined?

- *What meanings can be detected beyond its explicit or common meaning?* Are there alternative explanations that are ignored by many readers? Are there unconventional ideas and possibilities that may have been overlooked?

- *How can your reading of a text become a creative, not a passive, act?* Your reaction, ideas, even your misreading can be as meaningful as the author's presumed intention.

- *What happens if we shift the point of view in a work to another character?* How would the story change? What is not told in the text, and why not?

HISTORICAL CRITICISM AND NEW HISTORICISM

What is the Historical approach to literary criticism?

Until the advent of formalistic and New Critical methods in the opening decades of the twentieth century, the dominant academic literary approach was some form of Historical Criticism. Literary scholars established the historical and biographical context for literary works, debated the canon, and annotated texts to clarify language and allusion in their historical contexts. They saw their interpretative role as elucidating literary works in their original context. The formalists shifted interest to the intrinsic functioning of literary text itself, relegating biographical and historical issues to the extrinsic and unnecessary for the primacy of aesthetic values. For the formalists and New Critics, literature's appeal is universal, not historical, and dependent on the reader's attention to the details of the work rather than requiring scholarly expertise on an author's biography or the work's historical background. While such an approach restored the predominance of the literary work in critical study, close readings of texts unanchored by historical insights can lead to misunderstanding and anachronistic interpretations. Even granting the New Critics' suspicion of an author's intentions and the free play of the deconstructionists, foregoing all historical contexts in a literary work is like playing tennis without a net (which was Robert Frost's response when asked why he did not write free verse). Literary works are always re-interpreted based on contemporary values, but should literary judgments not consider the values that informed the work's creation? In watching a performance of Shakespeare, you can appreciate and enjoy the play without the annotations of a scholarly print version, but don't you understand more if you know the accepted meaning of the language when it was written and the specific historical or cultural allusions it refers to? Don't you understand more about Dickens's methods by understanding how his works were first published? That, at least, is the assumption of the historical approach that attempts to explore the connections between the work and historical period in which it was created.

What is New Historicism?

A renewed justification of the Historical Critical approach began in the 1980s, in part influenced by Structuralist and Post-Structuralist Critical theories and in part as a reaction to them. The term "New Historicism" was coined by American Shakespearean scholar Stephen Greenblatt (1943–) in his introduction to an essay collection, *The Power of Forms in the English Renaissance* (1982), in which he asserts the "mutual permeability of the literary and the historical." Greenblatt has later asserted that "my deep, ongoing interest is in the relation between literature and history, the process through which certain remarkable works of art are at once embedded in a highly specific life-world and seem to pull free of that life-world." Like the structuralists who are interested in the ideological structures underlying a text and the deconstructionists who focus on the cracks in the presumed unity and coherence of a text, the New Historicist looks at the ways in which a literary work subscribes to and subverts its historical circumstances. Its central precept, according to scholar Louis Montrose, is its belief in "the textuality of history and the historicity of texts." Attacked by critics as "neither new

nor historical"—as misapplying the historical method and as antithetical to aesthetic values, of turning history into literature and literature into history—New Historicism has nevertheless become, in the words of scholar Jonathan Date, "the most influential strand of criticism over the last 25 years, with its view that literary creations are cultural formations shaped by the circulation of social energy."

In practice, the New Historicist focuses on the social, political, cultural, and historical assumptions that a text reveals to demonstrate the ways in which the literary work responds to the historical moment as well as how history helps explain the text. New Historicist scholars research the documentary record of the period to explicate details in the work and clarify the meaning of a work as its original readers would have understood it. They connect the work to others written at the time and earlier to

Harvard University professor and Shakespearean scholar Stephen Greenblatt is one of the founders of New Historicism, a term he coined.

trace similarities, differences, and influences. New Historicism would move the debate over literary works back to the context from which they were created, influencing multiple critical approaches, including Marxist, feminist, gender, and cultural criticism.

Important critical works in New Historicism include:

- *New Historicism and Cultural Materialism* (1998) by John Brannigan
- *New Literary Histories* (1997) by Claire Colebrook
- *The Power of Forms in the English Renaissance* (1982) by Stephen Greenblatt
- *The Purpose of Playing* (1996) by Louis Montrose
- *The New Historicism in Literary Study* (1989) by D. G. Myers
- *The New Historicism* (1989) edited by Harold Aram Veeser

What questions does Historical Criticism ask?

- *How does the work reflect the time in which it was written?* How accurately does it reflect and distort its era? Consider issues of race, religion, politics, gender, philosophy, etc.
- *How does the literary background and production of the literary work influence the text?* What literary, social, economic, and historical influences helped shape the form and content of the work?
- *What similarities and differences are evident in comparing the work with others written at the same time?* Do the works share key assumptions or differ in their presentations of core values?
- *How would the characters and events of the work have been viewed by the author's contemporaries?* What cultural assumptions and values at the time help to explain the work's reception?
- *Does the work support or contradict prevailing values of the time in which it was written?* What elements oppose or maintain core assumptions of the age in which it was written?
- *How are actual historical events or historical figures depicted in the work?* How do the depictions vary from the historical record?

What is Reader-Response Criticism?

Reader-Response Criticism, like formalism and New Criticism, originated in reaction to historical and biographical approaches. The formalists would emphasize the text, not the context, while Reader-Response critics emphasize the role of the reader in the literary process. One of the earliest Reader-Response proponents was Barnard College professor Louise Rosenblatt, who asserted in an influential book, *Literature as Exploration* (1936), that a literary work's meaning resided not within the text but in the reader's transaction with it. Rosenblatt's so-called "transactional theory," a core premise of the Reader-Response Critical approach, is that each "transaction" with a text is unique, in which the reader continually relies on beliefs and background knowledge in the reading act. This requires readers to pay close attention to every detail of the text and their own responses to it. Rosenblatt's work emphasizes that the role of the reader in the interpretative process ought not be omitted important and that readers are not passive receivers of a text's meaning and impact.

Rosenblatt's transactional theory of Reader-Response would be elaborated and codified into critical strategies and renewed support by German scholars at the University of Constance in the 1970s, including Wolfgang Iser and Hans Robert Jauss; in France in Roland Barthes' provocative 1967 essay, "The Death of the Author"; and in America by academics such as Stanley Fish and Wayne Booth. The Reader-Response Critical approach regards the literary text as closer to a musical score or a performative art that depends on the reader to give it life and expression in an interpretive collaboration between the creator and the audience. Isher asserts that there is a fundamental tension between the "implied reader," which is assumed and created by the work itself, and the "actual reader," who brings to the work unique experiences and assumptions, and that interpretation stems from the collision of both. As Fish argues, "Interpretation is not the art of construing but of constructing. Interpreters do not decode poems; they make them."

In practice, reader-response critics argue over the extent a literary work is a stable, objective artifice that directs and sets limits to the reader's response and to what extent the subjective power of the reader predominates, in which a text means whatever a reader says it does. At the subjective extreme is Barthes' contention that ultimately it is the reader who "authors" the text and what is of interest is not the text but the reaction to it. To set limits to the sense that anything goes and every reader response is equally valid, critics have posited the notion of "interpretative communities," groups of readers with shared backgrounds and assumptions (such as scholars or professional reviewers) who have reached a consensus view on how a literary work functions and what meanings predominate. These communities reach not a definitive "right" reading but offer judgment on which readings are better and worse. Readers then can refer their own responses to these communities for comparison to inform interpretative judgment. The constraint on response, therefore, is not bounded by the text but by the different strategies, assumptions, and approaches of the various interpretative communities.

Important works in Reader-Response Criticism include:
- *Subjective Criticism* (1978) by David Bleich
- *The Rhetoric of Fiction* (1961) by Wayne Booth
- *Is There a Text in This Class?* (1980) by Stanley Fish
- *The Return of the Reader* (1987) by Elizabeth Freund
- *The Implied Reader* (1972) and *The Act of Reading* (1976) by Wolfgang Iser
- *Literary History as a Challenge to Literary Theory* (1969) by Hans Robert Jauss
- *Literature as Exploration* (1938) and *The Reader, The Text, The Poem: The Transactional Theory of the Literary Work* (1978) by Louise Rosenblatt
- *Reader-Response Criticism* (1980) by Jane Thompkins

What questions does Reader-Response Criticism ask?

- *What was the reader's reaction to the work?* How did the work agree or clash with your understanding of the world? With your understanding of right and wrong?

- *How does meaning in the work depend on an interaction between the text and the reader?* What limits to the reader's responses are evident, and how do they contrast with other responses?

- *How does the text guide, constrain, and control the reader's response?* What "implied reader" is evident in the text? And how does the actual reading experience share or differ with the implied reader?

- *How do readers reach conclusions about the meaning of the work?* What details in the text elicit the strongest reactions and why?

- *What reader responses are better than others?* Are certain responses more valid than others? And why?

- *What consensus is there in the body of criticism of how a work should be read and understood?* What assumptions explain different critical reactions?

GENDER STUDIES

What are gender studies?

Gender studies, which focus on the ways in which gender is reflected and functions in literary works, is an extension of feminist literary criticism. Initially concerned with a reappraisal of gender assumptions by male writers, a reexamination of woman authors in the canon, and a rediscovery of neglected and forgotten woman writers, gender studies have expanded attention to the ways in which texts are traditionally read from heterosexual perspectives, excluding or invalidating gay or lesbian viewpoints or literary achievements. The result of feminist, gay, and lesbian critical approaches has been a provocative revisionist rereading of the literary canon as well as an expanding of the canon to admit formerly ignored or marginalized voices. The core of the gender studies critical debate concerns both equality and difference: that is, how can oppressed and disregarded literary voices claim equal importance with a dominant masculine, heterosexual canon and how can distinctive difference in gender and sexuality be recognized and examined.

What is Feminist Criticism?

The Feminist Critical approach applies to literature insights derived from feminist theory and cultural studies that include such works as Christine de Pisan's *The Book of the City of Ladies* (1405), Mary Wollstonecraft's *A Vindication of the Rights of Woman* (1794), Virginia Woolf's "A Room of One's Own" (1929), Simone de Beauvoir's *The Second Sex* (1949), Betty Friedan's *The Feminine Mystique* (1963), Kate Millett's *Sexual*

Politics (1969), Germaine Greer's *The Female Eunuch* (1970), and other influential feminist works. Feminist literary criticism would emerge out of the so-called "second wave" of feminism in the 1960s and '70s that advocated on behalf of women's rights and explored women's identity and the representation of women in media and culture. American academic Elaine Showalter, a founding figure of feminist literary criticism, called for "gynocriticism," which she characterized as an "ideological, righteous, angry, and admonitory search for the sins and errors of the past," focused on the study of works by woman authors (both included and excluded from the canon) and the depiction of woman and gender issues by male-authored canonical texts.

In practice, Feminist Criticism is less a method of literary interpretation, such as New Criticism, than a perspective focused on gender issues that can be combined with a variety of critical approaches, including Reader-Response Criticism, Psychological Criticism, New Historicism, and deconstruction. The Feminist Critical approach has both enlarged the canon to include overlooked and neglected woman writers while stimulating new readings of classic texts from the perspective of patriarchal assumptions in determining how women have been characterized in literary texts. Feminist literary critics such as Judith Butler, Hélène Cixous, and others are also in the forefront of the reassessment of gender itself as a human construct in which the systematic repression of women is encoded in the male-dominated discourse of the Western intellectual tradition.

Important Feminist Criticism works include:

- *Gender Trouble: Feminism and the Subversion of Identity* (1990) by Judith Butler
- *The Madwoman in the Attic: The Woman Writer and the Nineteenth-Century Literary Imagination* (1979) by Sandra Gilbert and Susan Gubar
- *Literary Women* (1976) by Ellen Moers
- *Sexual/Textual Politics: Feminist Literary Theory* (1985; 2nd ed. 2002) by Toril Moi
- *A Literature of Their Own* (1977) and "Toward a Feminist Poetics" (1979) by Elaine Showalter
- *The Female Imagination* (1975) by Patricia Meyer Spacks

What questions does Feminist Criticism ask?

- *How are women portrayed in the work?* What defines the relationship of men and women in the work, and what assumptions about gender are evident?
- *How does the work define masculinity and femininity?* Are these views conventional or challenging to established norms?
- *Does the work challenge or affirm traditional views of women?* How might the work have been different from the perspective of one of the woman characters? By changing the sex of each, how would the work be different?
- *What elements of patriarchal society are evident?* How does the perspective and characters embody or disrupt patriarchal assumptions?

413

- *Does the work's reception and reputation in literary history reveal gender assumptions?* Are the values regarding masculinity and femininity in the period when the work was written evident and are they factors in the work's reception and reputation?

How does Gay and Lesbian Criticism approach literature?

Gay and lesbian literary criticism trace their development to the evolving examination of gender, first promoted by feminist literary criticism, around issues of sexuality, power, and marginalized groups and voices in the literary canon. If Feminist Critics attacked the prevailing patriarchy, gay and lesbian literary critics consider heterosexual cultural dominance and its impact on gay and lesbian writers and in the literary canon. Like Feminist Criticism, Gay and Lesbian Critical approaches depend not on a particular method of interpretation but on a perspective and sensitivity to the ways in which sexual identity have been portrayed, promoted, and denied. The result has been, similar to feminist literary criticism, an enlargement in the literary canon to include the perspective of marginalized authors and a provocative, revisionist interpretation of classical texts viewed from a lens of sexual ideology.

The central distinction between heterosexuality and homosexuality has been deconstructed in Queer Theory, a set of critical assumptions that emerged in the 1990s and that called into question the concept of sexual identity itself. For queer theorists, sexuality is a fluid cultural construct, to be viewed historically rather than biologically or psychologically, that calls into question the cultural binaries of "normal" and "deviant." Queer Theory rejects the idea of a fixed sexual identity or innate or essential gender norms and is interested in the multiple and contradictory ways sexuality is expressed whether by supposedly "straight," "gay," "lesbian," "bisexual," or "transgender" writers or characters. Queer theorists exploit the resources of formalism, structuralism, Reader-Response Criticism, and deconstruction to examine how sexuality and gender is encoded in a literary work and subverts assumptions.

Important critical works include:

- *Bodies that Matter* (1990) and *Undoing Gender* (2004) by Judith Butler
- *The Laugh of the Medusa* (1975) by Hélène Cixous
- *Homographesis: Essays in Gay Literary and Cultural Theory* (1993) by Lee Edelman
- "Toward a Definition of the Lesbian Literary Imagination" (1988) by Marilyn R. Farwell
- *History of Sexuality* (1976) by Michel Foucault
- *Thinking Queerly* (2010) by David Fryer
- *Lesbian and Gay Writing: An Anthology of Critical Essays* (1990) edited by Mark Lilly
- *The Novel and the Police* (1988) and *Jane Austen, or The Secret of Style* (2003) by D. A. Miller

- *Between Men* (1985) and *Epistemology of the Closet* (1994) by Eve Kosofsky Sedgwick
- *The Trouble with Normal* (1999) by Michael Warner
- *Gender Theory, Queer Theory* (2004) by Riki Wilchins

What questions do Gay, Lesbian, and Queer Criticism ask?

- *How are traditional reflections of masculinity and femininity, heterosexuality and homosexuality evident in the text?* How are these values presented by works written by gay, lesbian, and queer writers? By apparently heterosexual writers?

- *What evidence in the text suggests challenges to or questioning of sexual roles and sexual identity?* How does the text illustrate problems of sexuality and sexual identity? Is there a challenge to the understanding of the usual categories of homosexual and heterosexual?

- *How does the work portray the operations (socially, politically, psychologically) of heterosexism?* Is the work, either consciously or unconsciously, homophobic? Does it critique or accept heterosexist values?

- *How do openly lesbian, gay, or queer works differ in term of content, form, and ideology from work by assumed heterosexual writers?* What does the work reveal about theme and characterization that appears unique and distinctive, and how does it contribute to an understanding of a distinctive gay, lesbian, and queer poetics or literary canon?

- *How might the works of heterosexual writers be reread from a gay, lesbian, or queer perspective?* How does our understanding of a classic text change when heterosexual assumptions are challenged?

CULTURAL STUDIES AND POST-COLONIAL CRITICISM

What are Cultural Studies and Post-Colonial Criticism?

Less a methodology than a re-examination of the traditional subjects of literary scholarship, Cultural Studies is an interdisciplinary perspective with theory and methods from sociology, anthropology, politics, economics, ethnic and gender studies, historical, Marxist, feminist, and post-structuralist literary criticism. Cultural critics look at the shaping dynamics and historical foundations of cultures while shifting the understanding of culture from the more traditional, privileged, elitist conception of "high culture" to an inclusive multiculturalism that recognizes a diversity of overlapping and competing cultures, created by people from a variety of social, economic, and ethnic backgrounds. In examining literary works, Cultural Studies is interested in the ways in which literature is produced, distributed, and consumed in a society and in the intersections between so-called "highbrow" and "lowbrow" literary achievements. That is, why are some literary forms given serious consideration while others are relegated to less important consideration as popular entertainment? Cultural critics attempt to broaden the understanding of what texts can be read and interpreted, beyond the usual suspects in the literary canon (the Shakespeares, Miltons, Dantes), to historically neglected and ignored sources from gay, lesbian, and ethnic minorities. Believing that all texts are artistic expressions of a culture, they might choose to examine not books, poems, or plays but movies and television shows, advertisements, graffiti, and comic books. These and virtually all verbal and visual expressions can be interpreted by the cultural critics, employing the same rigorous analysis to a bumper sticker as the New Critic devotes to a sonnet.

A popular branch of Cultural Studies is Postcolonial Criticism, which looks at the cultural impact on former European and American colonies around the world to explore the fate of indigenous cultures under colonial rule as well as the blending of cultures in the colonial experience and the emerging cultures following independence. Like cultural critics generally, Post-Colonial Critics celebrate neglected writers, broaden the literary canon, and challenge narrow cultural assumptions that do not consider the hybrid nature of culture.

Important critical works in this area include:

- *The Field of Cultural Production* (1993) by Pierre Bourdieu
- *The Cultural Studies Reader* (2007) edited by Simon During
- *The Order of Things: An Archeology of the Human Sciences* (1970) by Michel Foucault
- *The Interpretation of Cultures* (1973) by Clifford Geertz
- *The Uses of Literacy* (1957) by Richard Hoggart
- *Orientalism* (1978) by Edward Said
- *Cultural Studies* (1994) by Ziauddin Sardar
- *Culture and Society* (1966) by Raymond Williams

What questions do Cultural Studies and Post-Colonial Criticism ask?

- *What does the work convey about social attitudes and social relations?* What is the impact of sex, class, ethnicity, power, and privilege on the work? What do they convey about cultural values?

- *How are the events, ideas, and attitudes in the work influenced by economic, political, and social conditions?* What is the cultural context underpinning the work?

- *What does the text reveal about the interaction of race, religion, class, gender, and sexual orientation in cultural identity?* How is cultural difference expressed?

- *What does the work reveal about colonial oppression and attitudes?* What is the dominant culture, and how are characters and events judged against that culture?

- *What conflicts are evident between indigenous and colonial cultures?* How are these conflicts resolved?

- *What constitutes post-colonial values?* How is the impact of colonialism expressed in the work in indigenous culture? On emerging cultural expressions?

- *What does the text reveal about the challenges of post-colonial identity?* How is the conflict between personal and cultural identity expressed?

ETHNIC STUDIES AND CRITICAL RACE THEORY

How do Ethnic Studies and Critical Race Theory approach literature?

With clear parallels to postcolonial criticism in its focus on alternative voices, Ethnic Studies treats the literature of ethnic groups that have been marginalized or subordinated to a dominant culture. The first such group to claim attention for a distinctive literary tradition and aesthetic were African Americans during the period of the Harlem Renaissance of the 1920s and the Black Arts or Black Aesthetic Movement of the 1960s. Critical interest in Native American, Asian American, Hispanic, and Chicano American literatures would follow. All would express similar core beliefs of equality—urging inclusion of neglected sources and authors on established aesthetic grounds—and of difference by exploring the ways in which ethnic identity produced alternative aesthetic forms and values. New histories of American literature began to appear that challenged previous established views of the canon and its reflections of race.

Critical Race Theory (CRT) is a theoretical movement that originated within American law schools and social science departments in the 1970s by scholars such as Derrick Bell, Alan Freeman, and Richard Delgado that attempted to trace the impact of race and racism across dominant cultural modes of expression. Originally conceived to examine how African American victims of systematic racism are affected by cultural perceptions of race, CRT has been subsequently applied to Asian American, Latino, and Native American racial experience. Applied to literature, CRT focuses on the sociocultural forces that shape how we perceive and respond to race and the connection between race, class, and gender in both the construction of literary works and the response to them.

Important critical works in this area include:

- "Who's Afraid of Critical Race Theory" (1995) by Derrick A. Bell

- *Critical Race Theory: The Key Writings that Formed the Movement* (1995) edited by Kimberlé Crenshaw and others

- *Critical Race Theory: An Introduction* (2012) by Richard Delgado and Jean Stefancic

- *The Signifying Monkey: A Theory of African American Literary Criticism* (2014) by Henry Louis Gates

- *Asian American Literary Studies* (2005) edited by Guiyou Huang

- *Native American Literature: An Introduction* (2004) by Suzanne Eversten Lundquist

- *Seeing a Color-Blind Future* (1998) by Patricia Williams

What questions do Ethnic Studies and Critical Race Theory ask?

- *How are race and racial issues depicted in the work?* How are racial attitudes and assumptions reflected in the characters and situations?

- *What values are expressed and methods employed that can be explained by ethnicity?* Are the values of the dominant culture celebrated or subverted in the work?

- *What calls to combat racism are evident in the text?* What solutions are offered for contending with racism in the work?

- *How are differing views of race depicted in the work?* What is the relationship between ethnic identity, class, gender, and sexual orientation in the text?

- *How does the work change our understanding of literary history and the accepted canon?* Does the work's focus on race and ethnic identity force a reconsideration of other works in the canon?

- *How are the various social, political, and economic advantages of white privilege expressed in the work?* What are the obvious or subtle differences in the access to power, social status, educational opportunities, and experiences of prejudice expressed or ignored in the work?

- *What evidence is there of "microaggressions"—instances of minute or unconscious instances of prejudice in the work?* Does prejudice emerge beyond blatant and obvious ways?

CHOOSING AN APPROACH

Which critical approach should you choose?

Having surveyed and sampled the many critical approaches discussed here, you may be asking: Which critical approach should I choose? A better question would be: Which critical *approaches* should I choose? Critical approaches are not mutually exclusive but rather different lenses that magnify and focus attention on specific features of a literary text from a distinctive vantage point. Just as one approach may illuminate an important aspect of a literary work, it can also obscure or discount other equally important features. Scholarly proponents of a critical approach are often fierce advocates for the advantages and efficacy of their approach; they need to be consistent in their application of their approach to demonstrate it convincingly, but readers are under no such requirement to forsake one critical approach for another or not to take into account several different critical approaches in interpreting a literary work. A historical and New Critical approach need not be incompatable. Neither would psychological, Marxist, or feminist perspectives working in tandem. Henry James famously observed that "the house of fiction has … not one window, but a million … every one of which has been pierced, or is still pierceable, in its vast front, by the need of the individual vision and by the pressure of the individual will." This is no less true for the house of literary criticism: perhaps not a million windows (though it can seem like it) but enough for multiple views to accommodate "the need of the individual vision."

What standard should you apply in assessing the usefulness of a critical approach?

Since no single critical approach is inherently better than another and each helps the reader to focus on different features of the literary work, what standard should you use in employing different critical approaches? The most sensible is for a preference of approaches that open up, rather than shut down, interpretation. A work of literature is great not because it answers one or more important questions but because it raises countless important questions. This should be no less true for the critical approaches serving a literary work. For literature, one critical approach does not fit all; some works are more amenable to one perspective over another, but great works of literature encourage multiple perspectives. An approach that reduces a work of literature to one thing alone is not as useful as one that reminds the reader how deep and rich a literary work truly is. A first principle, therefore, in assessing any critical approach is does it illuminate the literary work in important ways? Does it shed new light on a familiar text or offer an essential re-assessment?

Ultimately, critical approaches need to serve a literary work, not the other way around. They are not a substitute for that work, and literature ought not be the excuse for a theory or an approach. Literature is not ideology, and critical approaches that reduce a literary work to a single truth, that fit an expansive imaginative expression into a narrow and rigid viewpoint, are less useful than approaches that embrace a work's multiplicity and are fair to literature's many questions and methods. The best critical approaches are descriptive rather than prescriptive, helping readers to see the work afresh, but most importantly, they help to really see it, not just some abstract generalization about it. The great Victorian novelist George Eliot defined literature as "aesthetic teaching," that is, embodied or dramatized lessons in human nature and human experience. Critical approaches that neglect the aesthetic issues on behalf of the perceived lessons do a disservice to literature. Hamlet's caution to Horatio, "There are more things in heaven and earth, Horatio / Than are dreamt of in your philosophy," applies no less to literature, whose capacity to tell us things we don't know far exceeds any attempt to make it fit a single philosophy or critical approach.

Glossary of Essential Literary Terms

Affective Fallacy—Critical concept introduced by W. K. Wimsatt and M. C. Beardsley in *The Verbal Icon* (1954) suggesting "a confusion between the poem and its results (what it is and what it does)." The affective fallacy represents the attempt of New Critics to shift the focus of criticism to the work itself, not on the author's intentions or the reader's response. See also *Intentional Fallacy, Pathetic Fallacy*.

Allegory—Derived from the Greek *allergia* ("speaking otherwise"), an allegory is a consistent, extended metaphorical correspondence between literal details (objects, characters, settings, events, and actions) and abstract, figurative concepts (innocence, death, virtue, and villainy). See also *Symbol*.

Alliteration—A literary sound device in poetry and prose in which initial consonant sounds of words in close proximity are repeated to create emphasis and enhance musicality and retention. See also *Assonance, Consonance, Rhyme*.

Allusion—A direct or indirect reference to previous literary, historical legendary, or cultural figures, events, or languages to widen or enhance a context for the work. See also *Symbol*.

Ambiguity—The uncertainty and multiplicity of meaning in a literary work. Intentional ambiguity encourages readers to actively and imaginatively engage with a work to determine its significance.

Antagonist—From the Greek *antagonistes* ("opponent" or "rival"), the character(s) or force(s), external or internal, that opposes the protagonist's action, will, or desire, producing conflict in a literary work. See *Conflict, Protagonist*.

Archetype—An image, detail, plot pattern, or character type that appears frequently in literature, myths, fairytales, and folklore and which suggests a universal, recurring, and collective human understanding or response. Swiss psychologist Carl Jung argued that archetypes come from the "collective unconscious" of mankind: experiences such as death, birth, love, survival, etc. shared by a race or culture. See also *Allegory, Hero/Heroine, Symbol*.

Assonance—A literary technique in poetry and prose created by the repetition of identical or similar vowel sounds in words, usually close together and achieving a musical effect of euphony (from the Greek "sweetness of sound").

Atmosphere—The feeling conveyed to a reader through descriptions of setting and objects that enhances the reader's emotional engagement with the work, contributing to suspense, and foreshadowing the action. See also *Setting*.

Bildungsroman—From the German "novel of education," the bildungsroman focuses on the growth and development of its main character from youth and innocence to experience and adulthood. A subcategory of the bildungsroman is the künstlerroman (German for "artist novel") about the growth and development of an artist.

Blank Verse—Verse line of ten unrhymed syllables (pentameter) with alternating unstressed and stressed meter (iambic): da-DUM da-DUM, da-DUM, da-DUM, da-DUM. Introduced into English by the Earl of Surrey in the sixteenth century in his translation of the *Aeneid* (1557), blank verse would become the most widely used of English verse forms and is the one closest to rhythms of everyday English speech.

Catastrophe—From the Greek meaning "an overturning or sudden end." As a literary term, a catastrophe refers to the final, decisive event in a tragedy that produces the downfall or death of the protagonist. Also referred to as the dénouement, the catastrophe follows the climax. See also *Climax, Dénouement*

Catharsis—From the Greek word meaning "cleansing" or "purgation," catharsis is the term used by Aristotle in his *Poetics* to explain the impact of a tragedy on an audience: "through pity and fear effecting the proper catharsis of these emotions." Aristotle suggests that the power of tragedy comes from expressing powerful emotions that serve a therapeutic purpose for an audience, vicariously summoning up and experiencing emotions otherwise suppressed.

Characters—Characters are the human or nonhuman personalities depicted, acted upon, or acting in a poem, story, or drama. Characters have been categorized as "flat," with static, singular traits and "round": multidimensional, changeable, and dynamic. Characters have been further classified morally as "hero," "villain," "protagonist," and "antagonist." See also *Characterization*.

Characterization—Characterization describes the methods of presenting characters in description, in speech, in what other characters say about them, and in what the characters say, think, or feel themselves. The illusion created by the writer in which believable and identifiable characters are involved in the action is one of the core strengths of literature. See also *Antagonist, Protagonist*.

Climax—From the Greek term "ladder," a climax is the culmination of a conflict, the decisive turning point in drama, and the moment of greatest plot intensity and tension. In graphic terms, the climax is the apex of the triangle, the peak moment in the conflict, dividing the rising action of a developing conflict and the falling action of the consequences of the climax. See also *Conflict, Dénouement, Falling Action, Rising Action*.

Conceit—See *Metaphor.*

Conflict—The struggle that ensues from the opposition in a plot between and within characters. A conflict may be external (between a character and a force of nature or between a protagonist and an antagonist) or internal (psychological, or moral conflict between conflicting desires). See also *Catastrophe, Climax, Falling Action, Rising Action.*

Connotation—From the Latin *connotare* or "to mark in addition," connotation refers to the associations and emotional implications that words suggest. As opposed to a word's denotation, or its literal, dictionary definition, connotation is a word's implicit meaning. See also *Denotation, Diction.*

Consonance—Literary device in prose and poetry in which the same or similar consonant sounds are repeated. Akin to alliteration that depends on similar sounds at the start of words, whether consonants or vowels, consonance occurs in the repetition of consonant sounds at the beginning or end of words. See also *Alliteration, Assonance.*

Crisis—See *Climax, Conflict.*

Denotation—The literal or dictionary definition of a word, as opposed to a word's connotation (a word's implied association). A word's denotation, like connotation, may shift and change over time, and in order to appreciate precisely what a literary work means, readers must understand and fully consider the denotation and connotation of the words chosen. See also *Connotation, Diction.*

Dénouement—From the French for "untying," in dramatic terms dénouement refers to the untangling or resolution of the complications produced by conflict, following the climax, in which the various loose ends of the plot are resolved into the conclusion. The dénouement serves as the final resolution or clarification in a literary work. See also *Catastrophe, Climax, Conflict, Falling Action.*

Description—Language used to create a vivid and concrete picture of a character, object, or setting of a literary work, which helps readers to form mental images about the things described. See also *Imagery.*

Dialogue—Conversation between two or more characters in a narrative, story, or play. In drama, dialogue is the principle vehicle for expression. In nondramatic works dialogue is usually set off in quotation marks. Dialogue is an important means of advancing the plot and in characterization, calling attention not only to what is said but how. See also *Character, Characterization.*

Diction—The kinds of words, phrases, and figurative language that a writer selects. As sound is to the musician and color is to the painter, diction is the fundamental medium of literature that depends on both the denotation (literal dictionary definition) and the connotation (implied association) of words. See also *Connotation, Denotation.*

Dramatic Irony—See *Irony.*

Dramatic Monologue—See *Monologue.*

Epic—A type of poetic literature in which a narrative is recounted rather than enacted (as in the dramatic narrative form). A long narrative form, the epic was originally performed orally and improvised by the epic poet, the most famous of which is Homer in his *Iliad* and *Odyssey*. The term "Epic" has come to mean all-encompassing, serious, and definitive, applied to diverse, ambitious narratives. See also *Lyric, Narrative*.

Epiphany—The liturgical commemoration of the manifestation of Jesus' divinity to the Magi adapted and secularized as a literary term by James Joyce, who defined an epiphany as "a sudden spiritual manifestation, whether in the vulgarity of speech or of gesture or in a memorable phase of the mind itself." The epiphany became a key technique of the modern short story in which all the details of the story work toward a revelation of meaning and significance by a character or the reader.

Episodic Narrative—Narrative method organized by episodes that follow each other in a straightforward chronological order; each episode is not a cause or necessarily an effect of another. The most famous narratives employing an episodic structure are picaresque stories in which the protagonist sets out on a journey or adventure. See also *Plot, Story*.

Exposition—The background information supplied by a narrator or individual characters that explains an event, setting, the nature of a character, or the context for a situation in a story or drama. Skillful handling of exposition presents essential details naturally and seamlessly integrated into the action. See also *Description*.

Fable—See *Myth*.

Falling Action—In drama, the action following the climax in which the peak tension provided by the conflict is lessened or the consequence of action taken leads to the catastrophe or resolution. In Aristotle's conception of tragic action, the hero must fall from a position of high rank and power, and the falling action of a tragedy traces that descent. See also *Catastrophe, Climax, Dénouement, Resolution*.

Figurative Language—The use of words beyond their literal meaning to enhance meaning and impact. The most common figurative language includes metaphors, similes, hyperbole, and personification. See a definition of each.

First-Person Narration—Point of view provided by an outside observer or someone directly or indirectly involved in a narrative. So-called *I* narration has the advantage of immediacy but is limited to what the narrator can report so that reliability becomes an issue in first-person narration: whether or not the narrator can be trusted to report events honestly and objectively. See also *Point of View*

Flashback—A cinematic term adapted to literature describing a scene or episode that took place in the past and interrupts a linear, chronological narrative. A device that provides background details and explanations for a current situation or character's behavior, flashbacks are ways to show rather than tell important past details. So-called "Flash Forwards" show the future results of present action. See also *Exposition*.

Flat Characters—Designation of character types popularized by E. M. Forster in *Aspects of the Novel* (1927), contrasting rounded characters (contradictory, dynamic, and changeable) with flat characters who are static, functional, and stock. Some flat characters serve only a functional role that is only necessary for the advancement of the plot. See also *Character, Characterization, Round Characters.*

Foreshadowing—Anticipations in information, details, or action preparing for and suggesting future events or outcomes. Providing structural and thematic unity, foreshadowing also enhances suspense and anticipation in suggesting developments to come. See also *Suspense.*

Free, Indirect Discourse—See *Third-Person Narration.*

Free Verse—Poetry written in no regular meter or line length, depending instead on natural speech rhythms and other syntactical and image patterns to determine unity and cadence. Pioneered in the poetry of Walt Whitman and in France as *vers libre,* free verse became a standard practice in modern poetry.

Genres—Term used in literary criticism to designate types or categories of literary works, historically beginning with epic, lyric, and tragedy, and subsequently organized in conventional groupings, such as poetry, drama, fiction, and non-fiction, with multiple subgenres for each. Modern literary criticism frequently rejects conventional genre designation (and the rules that apply to each) as arbitrary and reductive.

Hamartia—From the Greek meaning "to miss the mark" or "to err," hamartia is a term used to explain the tragic hero's change of fortune and fall. Often translated as "tragic flaw"—the weakness or inadequacy of the protagonist—it might be better understood as a "tragic capacity," that is, the defining aspect of the tragic hero that leads to a downfall. Hamartia is crucial to a tragedy's catharsis, arousing pity and fear based on the mixture of the good and bad qualities of the protagonist.

Hero/Heroine—See *Protagonist*

Hyperbole—From the Greek meaning "overcasting," hyperbole is a figure of speech in which emphasis is gained by exaggeration. Common examples include "old as the hills," "weighs a ton," and "dying of shame."

Image —Language in a poem or prose that represent ideas, objects, actions, and feelings in sensory terms. An image may be literal (a specific detail to suggest a mental picture) or figurative (using metaphor and simile to make the abstract vivid and concrete). Based on placement, prominence, and emphasis, an image may take on the significance of a symbol. See also *Figurative Language, Imagism, Symbol.*

Imagery—See *Image*

Imagism—An early twentieth-century English poetic movement that rejected traditional poetic diction, meter, and abstraction for a reliance on concrete, concise, image-focused poetry to express meaning. Imagism declined as a coherent movement by the 1920s, but its tenets became an important legacy for modernist poetry and prose. See also *Image.*

In medias res—Latin for "in the middle of things," describing the narrative technique of plunging the reader directly into the action at an engaging point without exposition.

425

The opposite of *in medias res* is an opening that is *ab ovo* ("from the egg"), that is, from the beginning.

Intentional Fallacy—Term used by proponents of New Criticism to attempt to shift the focus in criticism away from the author's intent or the reader's response onto the text itself. See also *Affective Fallacy, Pathetic Fallacy*.

Interior Monologue—Literary technique originating in the late nineteenth century and popularized by twentieth-century modernist novelists to render a character's consciousness directly in all its fragmented, associational logic, mixing observations, feelings, and memories. The technique can be handled as direct interior monologue (without author presence) or as indirect (with the author guiding, selecting, and framing a character's thoughts). See also *Point of View, Stream of Consciousness*.

Irony—From the Greek meaning "dissimulation," the term was first used by Plato to indicate a means of deception. Verbal irony is a figure of speech in which what is meant is expressed in words with an opposite meaning. Situational irony refers to behavior that is incongruous from what is expected. In dramatic irony, the audience or reader knows more about a situation than the characters do. See also *Figurative Language*.

Juxtaposition—The technique of arranging details, settings, or situations in proximity for the purpose of establishing comparison or contrast. In music, the combination of two or more independent melodies creating a single harmony is called counterpoint. Similar outcomes are possible in literature through juxtaposition, linking different elements to form a more complex whole.

Künstleroman—See *Bildungsroman*.

Legends—See *Myth*.

Leitmotif—See *Motif*.

Lyric Poem—Originally defined by the ancient Greeks as the expression of a single singer accompanied by a lyre, lyric poetry came to describe poetry that emphasizes subjectivity and emotional expression, together with a pronounced musical or melodic structure. It is mostly contrasted with narrative poetry that tells a story.

Magic Realism—Literary technique combining real world verisimilitude with fantasy elements. Magic realism became the distinguishing characteristic of the Latin American literary boom of the 1960s and 1970s and has since become an accepted technique of postmodern fiction in which core concepts of realism are undermined. See also *Metafiction*.

Melodrama—From the Greek, meaning "sound drama," melodrama originally referred to plays with musical accompaniment to enhance their emotional impact and later came to describe drama that emphasized spectacle, action, sensationalism, and extravagant emotional appeals with clear moral types and poetic justice in which virtue is rewarded and villainy punished. Victorian novelists joined melodramatic elements to secrets and surprise to create the genre of the Sensation Novel.

Metafiction—A narrative technique in which the illusion of realism is disrupted by openly calling attention to the imaginary and constructed nature of a work. The term was coined by writer William Gass in 1970 and is associated with modernist and post-modern literature.

Metaphor, Simile, Conceit—From the Greek meaning "carrying from one place to another," metaphor is a figure of speech that makes an implicit or implied comparison between two things that are otherwise unrelated. Unlike a direct comparison, similes announce resemblance with the use of "like" or "as." A conceit, associated with the Metaphysical Poets, is an unlikely comparison between two very dissimilar things. See also *Figurative Language.*

Metaphysical Poetry—Type of poetry associated with seventeenth-century English poets who challenged the conventions of Elizabethan lyricism with psychological analysis of emotions. Metaphysical poets used striking, unexpected, and original metaphors or conceits drawn from diverse sources, including contemporary science. The metaphysical poets would be reclaimed in the twentieth century as models for modernism. See also *Metaphor, Simile, Conceit.*

Meter—From the Greek, meaning "measure" and referring to the pattern of stressed and unstressed syllables in verse. The rhythmic unit within a poetic line is called a foot. The standard English verse lines are monometer (one foot), diameter (two feet), trimeter (three feet), tetrameter (four feet), pentameter (five feet), hexameter (six feet), and heptameter (seven feet). Meter functions in establishing distinct rhythm in poetry and prose, which can be arranged for various musical effects and emphasis.

Modernism—A literary movement describing innovative and experimental literature produced from the 1880s to the 1940s. Defined by a break from traditional ways of writing, modernist authors found new literary subjects in the myriad details of ordinary life and subjective consciousness, aligned with new literary methods such as interior monologue and fragmentation. See also *Postmodernism.*

Mood—See *Atmosphere* and *Tone.*

Motif—A recurring element—an image, word, or action—that contributes to an understanding of the dominant idea or theme of a literary work. Allied to symbols, motifs underscore and reinforce key ideas, providing conceptual and associational bridges among diverse narrative elements. The term *leitmotif*—a recurring musical phrase associated with a particular person, place, or idea—has also been applied to literature. See also *Atmosphere, Image, Theme.*

Motivation—The forces, whether of personality or circumstances, that compel a character to act in a particular way. See also *Character, Plot.*

Myth—From the Greek *mythos,* meaning "word" or "tale," derived from *myo,* meaning "to teach" or "initiate into mysteries," myths are a culture's anonymous stories rooted in folk beliefs and oral tradition, and they serve to explain or interpret natural events or express core communal values. Myths differ from legends by being less historically based with more supernatural elements and are distinguished from fables by being less morally didactic and not originating from an individual. See also *Narrative, Story*.

Narration—See *Point of View*.

Narrative—An account, in prose or verse, of a sequence of actions, real or imagined, recounted by a narrator or storyteller. Drama enacts stories: narrative, whether an essay, poem, or fiction, describes stories. See also *Plot, Point of View*.

Naturalism—A form of extreme realism originating in the late nineteenth and early twentieth centuries in which writers extended the goal of literary realism of verisimilitude and plausibility and embraced the objective methods of a scientist observing phenomena. Realism recognizes the capacity of individual's free will to make choices; naturalism accepts the predominance of external determinist forces that control human behavior. See also *Realism*.

Neoclassical Literature—Literary movement of the late seventeenth century through the eighteenth century that advocated standards of literary forms derived from the classical literature of ancient Greece and Rome (hence *neo* or "new" classical). Characteristics included an emphasis on reason, order, and harmony and an adherence to decorum, as outlined by Aristotle and Horace, that prescribed consistency and proper diction and action appropriate to the subject matter.

Novella—A narrative genre that falls in length between a short story and a short novel, while sharing characteristics of both forms. A novella may introduce more characters and incidents than in a short story but fewer subplots and expansion than a novel.

Omniscient Narration—A third-person narrative point of view in which the narrator, possessing a freedom of movement in time and space, is capable of revealing what the characters are thinking or feeling and is not restricted to a particular viewpoint. However, just because an omniscient narrator can see all does not mean the narrator will tell all; the omniscient narrator is free to choose how and when to comment directly or reveal details, thoughts, and feelings of characters. See also *Point of View, Third-Person Narration*.

Pathetic Fallacy—A term that refers to the ascribing of human feelings or sympathetic correspondences to nature or inanimate objects. The pathetic fallacy is a kind of personification referring to the attribution of human emotions to the nonhuman. See also *Personification*.

Persona—From the Latin for "mask," personae were the masks worn by actors in Greek drama depicting the characters they portrayed (the *dramatis personae*). As a literary term, persona refers to the character created by the author to serve as the first-person narrator. In poetry, a persona is used in dramatic monologues. See also *First Person Narration, Point of View*.

Personification—Figurative language that endows human characteristics to nonhuman objects. Personification serves to animate the inanimate, adding vividness by finding resemblances between human traits and the nonhuman to create novel and original perspectives. See also *Figurative Language, Pathetic Fallacy.*

Picaresque—From the Spanish word *picaresco* meaning "relating to a picaro," Spanish for rogue or vagabond. The picaresque is an early narrative genre that originated in sixteenth-century Spain, depicting the adventures of a lower-class hero that combined a realistic style, comedy, and satire in an episodic narrative. See also *Episodic Narrative.*

Plot—The arrangement of narrative elements in a literary work—details, action, episodes—into a significant, unified whole. Modernist authors rejected traditional concepts of plot as a sequence of extraordinary actions for open-ended and undramatic arrangements of ordinary events, while postmodern writers would evoke traditional plots ironically. See also *Episodic Narrative, Narrative, Point of View.*

Point of View—The vantage point from which a story is narrated or the angle of vision in a non-narrative work, such as a lyric poem. The decisions made by writers about point of view are crucial in constructing narratives and are essential to determining significance in a literary work. See also *First-Person Narration, Interior Monologue, Stream of Consciousness, Third-Person Narration.*

Postmodernism—As a literary movement, postmodernism may refer to the second half of the twentieth century and after, following literary modernism, or more broadly as a rejection of core concepts such as the primacy of reason and the scientific method that characterize the modern world since the Enlightenment of the seventeenth century. Characteristics of postmodern literature are a pervasive ironic approach, playfulness, black humor, and a rejection of conventional ways of understanding and categorizing literature. See also *Modernism.*

Protagonist—From the Greek for "first combatant or competitor," protagonist was the first actor in early Greek drama and subsequently the chief character in a literary work to engage the audience/reader's interest and sympathy. Sometimes referred to as the hero or heroine, or the central character, the fate of the protagonist and his/her growth and development provide the focus for literary works, which can include multiple protagonists. See also *Antagonist, Character and Characterization, Conflict.*

Realism—A literary technique that emphasizes the faithful representation of the actual and denotes both a subject matter (interest in ordinary life), as well as a style of verisimilitude and plausibility. Realism became a dominant literary mode in nineteenth-century fiction and drama. See also *Naturalism, Romance.*

Resolution—The outcome of the climax in a plot. See also *Climax, Dénouement, Falling Action.*

Rhyme—The repetition of accented vowel sounds and all succeeding consonant sounds typically at the end of two or more lines of verse. Rhyme provides a means to enhance rhythm and musicality in a poem and is one of the major attributes differentiating poetry from prose. See also *Alliteration, Assonance, Consonance.*

Rhythm—See *Meter*

Rising Action—The escalating tension and complications in a plot stemming from the conflict that leads to the climax. Rising action is instigated by some kind of catalyst (arrival of a stranger, departure on a journey, for example) that disrupts the routine, provoking decisions or actions taken that lead to the climax. See also *Conflict, Climax, Falling Action, Suspense.*

Romance—A narrative genre designating medieval tales (in verse or prose) of chivalry and love, often marvel-filled adventures such as quests, sometimes with supernatural elements. The evolving novel form replaced romance's emphasis on the extraordinary, generic settings, and character types with an emphasis on the average, ordinary experiences of recognizable characters. Romance narrative elements persisted in the Gothic romances of the eighteenth and nineteenth centuries and appear in diverse contemporary fiction.

Romanticism—A cultural and literary movement of the eighteenth- and nineteenth-centuries that harkened back to the faith and belief that characterized the medieval romance. Romanticism elevated feeling and the imagination, the sustaining power of uncontrolled nature, and the imperatives of the individual, and offered a dynamic, experiential encounter between the world and the artist's subjective consciousness. See also *Neoclassicism.*

Round Characters—A designation of characterization, round characters are multidimensional or dynamic and are shown developing and changing based on their experiences. See also *Characters, Characterization, Flat Characters.*

Setting—The background against which the action of a narrative takes place. A setting can be the geographical place where the story is enacted, the time in which it takes place, and the environment (such as urban or country, upper or lower class) that impacts the action. Setting may work as simply a backdrop of little importance to the plot or easily substituted with another setting, or it can be integral to the action, theme, and character development of a story. See also *Atmosphere.*

Simile—See *Metaphor.*

Stock Character—See *Flat Characters.*

Story—See *Plot.*

Stream of Consciousness—A term that describes the subjective life and flow of thought that comprise the inner workings of human consciousness. One method used by writers is the interior monologue: the direct or indirect rendering of a character's associative thought that mixes memory and observation. See also *Interior Monologue.*

Style—The characteristic manner of expression in prose or poetry used by a writer, based on a writer's choice of words (diction) and arrangement of those words in sentences (syntax), as well as the use of figures or speech employed in a particular or distinctive way. Great writers create a seamless connection between ideas and the methods of expression. See also *Tone.*

Subplot—A secondary or subordinate plot to the main plot. In tragedy, a subplot may supply comic relief, and in narratives a subplot can enhance suspense, cutting between it and the main plot while providing a thematic comparison or contrast with the main plot to add tension, complexity, and depth to a story. See also *Plot*.

Suspense—Literary device designed to create anticipation in the audience or reader by the desire to know what happens next. Suspense enhances engagement in the work, and, when handled with skill, provides an irresistible forward pressure on the narrative, carrying audience and reader to the climax and resolution. See also *Plot*.

Symbol—From the Greek meaning "throwing together," a symbol is an image in a literary text that stands for something beyond its original meaning or function. Literary symbols may be universal or public—such as the color red symbolizing passion or spring suggesting rebirth and renewal—or private, determined in the context of the work. See also *Allegory, Figurative Language, Image*.

Syntax—From the Greek meaning "together arrangement," syntax is the arrangement of words into sentences, one of the three basic choices writers have, along with diction and the arrangement of sentences into larger units, such as paragraphs, to express meaning. See also *Diction*.

Theme—The central or important underlying meaning of a literary work, thematic unity binds the various elements of a narrative. A theme can be expressed in the action and events of the story, in characters' experiences, and in the characters' and the narrator's attitudes. See also *Atmosphere, Tone*.

Third-Person Narration—The use of the grammatical third person in narration, using a third-person pronoun. Third-person narration can be omniscient (unrestricted to a particular character or place, able to reveal internal as well as external character details); objective (concentrating on the externals of characters); limited (restricting the view to a particular character), or free indirect discourse (combining third-person narration with first-person by slipping in and out of the consciousness of a character and narrating as if in the character's voice). See also *First-Person Narration, Omniscient Narration, Point of View*.

Tone—The attitude expressed either directly or indirectly on the subject of a literary work. The tone reflects the writer's attitude toward a work's subject and is established through diction, syntax, and multiple elements like imagery, symbolism, and figurative language. See also *Atmosphere, Diction, Figurative Language, Image, Symbols, Theme*.

Villain—See *Antagonist*.

Recommended Essential Works of Literature

POETRY

ANCIENT WORLD

Bible	*Psalms* and *The Song of Solomon*
Catullus	*Poems*
Hesiod	*Works and Days*
Homer	*The Iliad* and *The Odyssey*
Horace	*Satires, Odes, Ars poetica*
Ovid	*Metamorphoses, The Art of Love*
Pindar	*Odes*
Sappho	*Lyrics*
Virgil	*The Aeneid, The Georgics*

OLD ENGLISH

	Beowulf
Caedmon	*Caedmon's Hymn*
	The Battle of Maldon
	The Seafarer
	The Wanderer
	Dream of the Rood

CHINESE T'ANG ERA (SEVENTH CENTURY)

Li Po	Alone and Drinking Under the Mountain, Drinking Alone, Autumn River Song, A Vindication
Tu Fu	Advent of Spring, Full Moon, Day's End, Lone Wild Goose, Morning Rain

MIDDLE AGES

	Sir Gawain and the Green Knight, Pearl
	The Nibelungenlied
	The Song of Roland

Chaucer, Geoffrey	*The Canterbury Tales, Troilus and Criseyde*
Chrétien de Troyes	*Arthurian Romances*
Dante	*The Divine Comedy*
Dunbar, William	To a Lady, To the City of London, Sweet Rose of Virtue, Lament for the Makers
Eschenbach, Wolfram von	*Parzival*
Gower, John	*Confessio Amantis*
Guillaume de Lorris	*Roman de la Rose*
Khayyam, Omar	*The Rubaiyat*
Langland, William	*Piers Plowman*
Marie de France	*Lais*
Villon, Françoise	The Ballad of the Proverbs, Ballade, Ballade to Our Lady

1400s–1700

Basho, Matshuo	A Bee, A Snowy Morning, Autumn Moonlight, Don't Imitate Me, A Monk Sips Morning Tea
Bradstreet, Anne	Here Follows Some Verses upon the Burning of Our House, To My Dear and Loving Husband
Donne, John	*Songs and Sonnets*
Dryden, John	*Absalom and Achitophel*
Herbert, George	Easter Wings, Affliction, Peace, The Pulley
Herrick, Robert	To the Virgins, to Make Much of Time, Upon Julia's Clothes
Jonson, Ben	On My First Son, To Celia, To Penshurst
Marlowe, Christopher	The Passionate Shepard to His Love
Marvell, Andrew	To His Coy Mistress, Eyes and Tears, Bermudas, A Dialogue Between the Soul and Body
Milton, John	On His Blindness, *Lycidas, Paradise Lost*
Petrarch, Francesco	*Il Canzoniere*
Raleigh, Sir Walter	The Nymph's Reply to the Shepherd, The Lie
Ronsard, Pierre de	To His Young Mistress, To the Moon
Shakespeare, William	*Sonnets*
Sidney, Sir Philip	*Astrophel and Stella*
Spencer, Edmund	*The Fairie Queene, Amoretti and Epithalamion*
Taylor, Edward	Preparatory Meditations, Upon a Spider Catching a Fly, The Preface, Ebb and Flow
Wyatt, Sir Thomas	They Flee from Me, Is It Possible, Farewell, Love, I Find No Peace

1701–1900

Arnold, Matthew	Dover Beach, Growing Old, Immortality
Baudelaire, Charles	*Les Fleurs du mal*
Blake, William	*Songs of Innocence and of Experience*
Browning, Elizabeth Barrett	The Deserted Garden, How Do I Love Thee?, My Heart and I
Browning, Robert	My Last Duchess
Burns, Robert	Song—A Red, Red Rose, To a Mouse
Byron	*Childe Harold's Poilgrimage, Don Juan,* She Walks in Beauty
Carroll, Lewis	Jabberwocky, The Hunting of the Snark, The Walrus and the Carpenter, A Valentine

Coleridge, Samuel Taylor	The Rime of the Ancient Mariner, Kubla Khan, Frost at Midnight, Dejection: An Ode
Dickinson, Emily	*Poems*
Emerson, Ralph Waldo	Each and All, Give All to Love
Goethe, Johann Wolfgang	A Legacy, Autumn Feelings, Prometheus, April, At Midnight Hour
Goldsmith, Oliver	*The Deserted Village*
Gray, Thomas	Elegy Written in a Country Churchyard
Hardy, Thomas	Hap, The Darkling Thrush, Neutral Tones
Heine, Heinrich	Death, A Palm-Tree, Death and His Brother Sleep
Henley, William Ernest	Invictus, A Love by the Sea, O Gather Me the Rose
Hopkins, Gerard Manley	The Windhover, Spring and Fall, God's Grandeur
Hugo, Victor	More Strong Than Time, A Sunset, The Genesis of the Butterfly, Luna
Johnson, Samuel	London, *The Vanity of Human Wishes*
Keats, John	*Odes,* When I Have Fears that I May Cease to Be
Mallarmé, Stephen	L'apres-Midi d'un Faune, Sea Breeze, Album Leaf, Anxiety
Poe, Edgar Allan	The City in the Sea, To Helen, The Raven, Annabel Lee
Pope, Alexander	*The Rape of the Lock, An Essay on Man, An Essay on Criticism, The Dunciad*
Rimbaud, Arthur	*Poems*
Rossetti, Christina	Goblin Market, The Poor Ghost
Rossetti, Dante Gabriel	The Blessed Damozel
Shelley, Percy Bysshe	Ozymandias, Ode to the West Wind, Adonais
Swift, John	Verses on the Death of Dr. Swift, A Description of a City Shower, A Description of the Morning
Tennyson, Alfred	In Memoriam A.H.H., Ulysses
Valery, Paul	*Poems*
Verlaine, Paul	*Poems*
Wheatley, Phillis	A Hymn to Evening, On Being Brought to America
Whitman, Walt	*Song of Myself,* When Lilacs Last in the Dooryard Bloom'd
Wordsworth, William	Lines Composed a Few Miles Above Tintern Abbey, I Wandered Lonely as a Cloud, *The Prelude*
Yeats, W. B.	The Lake Isle of Innisfree, The Song of Wandering Aengus

1901–2017

Ammons, A. R.	The City Limits, Poetics, Gravelly Run, Autonomy
Ashbery, John	Self-Portrait in a Convex Mirror, Daffy Duck in Hollywood, My Philosophy of Life, My Erotic Double, And Ut Pictura Poesis Is Her Name
Auden, W. H.	Musée des Beaux Arts, September 1, 1939, In Memory of W.B. Yeats
Berryman, John	*Dream Songs*
Bishop, Elizabeth	One Art, I Am in Need of Music, The Fish, A Miracle for Breakfast, In the Waiting Room, Sestina
Boland, Evan	And Soul, The Pomegranate, Outside History, Domestic Violence
Brooks, Gwendolyn	We Real Cool, The Mother, To Be in Love, The Crazy Woman
Collins, Billy	Forgetfulness, Introduction to Poetry, Litany

Crane, Hart	*The Bridge*
Cummings, E. E.	I Carry Your Heart with Me, In Just-, Buffalo Bill's
Eliot, T. S.	The Love Song of J. Alfred Prufrock, *The Waste Land, Four Quartets*
Frost, Robert	The Road Not Taken, Stopping by Woods on a Snowy Evening, Birches, Mending Wall, Birches
Ginsberg, Allan	Howl, America
Hayden, Robert	Those Winter Sundays, Middle Passage
Heaney, Seamus	Digging, Blackberry Picking, Death of a Naturalist, Mid-Term Break, Bogland, Two Lorries, Clearances, Requiem for the Croppies
Hecht, Anthony	More Light! More Light!, The End of the Weekend, A Letter
Housman, A.E.	*A Shropshire Lad*, To an Athlete Dying Young
Hughes, Langston	Dream Deferred, Life Is Fine, The Weary Blues
Hughes, Ted	The Thought-Fox, Pike, View of a Pig, Hawk Roosting, Relic, *Crow*
Jarrell, Randall	The Death of the Ball Turret Gunner
Jeffers, Robinson	Hurt Hawks, Vulture, Be Angry at the Sun, Shine, Perishing Republic
Kavanagh, Patrick	*The Great Hunger*
Komunyakaa, Yusef	Facing It, My Father's Love Letters, Prisoners
Larkin, Philip	Church Going, Aubade, Faith Healing, Ambulances
Levertov, Denise	What Were They Like?, Talking to Grief, The Secret, Tenebrae
Lowell, Robert	*Life Studies,* For the Union Dead
Meredith, William	Rhode Island, The Illiterate, Parents, Accidents of Birth
Merrill, James	Home Fires, Voices from the Other World, The Broken Home
Merwin, W. S.	Losing a Language, For a Coming Extinction, It Is March
Moore, Marianne	Poetry, The Mind Is an Enchanting Thing, The Fish
Neruda, Pablo	If You Forget Me, Walking Around
O'Hara, Frank	The Day Lady Died, Why I Am Not a Painter
Olds, Sharon	Young Mothers, The Unborn, The Victims, The End
Oliver, May	A Dream of Trees, Wild Geese, When Death Comes, Morning Poem
Owens, Wilfred	Dulce et Decorum Est, Anthem for Doomed Youth
Plath, Sylvia	Daddy, Lady Lazarus, Ariel
Pound, Ezra	A Girl, *Hugh Selwyn Mauberley, The Cantos*
Rich, Adrienne	Diving into the Wreck, Aunt Jennifer's Tigers, A Valediction Forbidding Mourning, For the Dead, Planetarium
Rilke, Rainer Maria	*Duino Elegies*
Robinson, Edwin Arlington	Miniver Cheevy, Richard Cory, Mr. Flood's Party
Roethke, Theodore	My Papa's Waltz, I Knew a Woman, In a Dark Time, Elegy for Jane, Journey into the Interior
Rosenberg, Isaac	Break of Day in the Trenches
Sandburg, Carl	Chicago, Fog
Sexton, Anne	Wanting to Die, 45 Mercy Street, After Auschwitz, Anna Who Was Mad
Shapiro, Karl	The Alphabet, California Winter, The Conscientious Objector, A Garden in Chicago
Snodgrass, W. D.	Lasting, Heart's Needle, April Inventory
Stafford, William	A Ritual to Read to Each Other, How to Regain Your Soul, Trav-

	eling through the Dark, Just Thinking
Stevens, Wallace	Sunday Morning, Anecdote of the Jar, Emperor of Ice-Cream, Thirteen Ways of Looking at a Blackbird, The Idea of Order in Key West
Thomas, Dylan	Do Not Go Gentle into that Good Night, Deaths and Entrances, Fern Hill
Wilbur, Richard	Love Calls Us to the Things of the World, Boy at the Window, Parable
Williams, William Carlos	*Patterson,* The Red Wheelbarrow, Spring and All
Wright, Charles	After Reading Tu Fu, Last Supper, A Short History of the Shadow, Homage to Paul Cezanne
Wright, James	Autumn Begins in Martins Ferry, Ohio, The Alarm, Between Wars, The Blessing
Yeats, W. B.	Easter 1916, The Second Coming, Sailing to Byzantium

SHORT STORIES

Alexie, Sherman	The Lone Ranger and Tonto Fistfight in Heaven
Anderson, Sherwood	Death in the Woods, I Want to Know Why, The Other Woman
Asimov, Isaac	I Robot, Nightfall
Atwood, Margaret	Happy Endings
Babel, Isaac	My First Goose
Baldwin, James	Sonny's Blues
Bambara, Toni Cade	The Lesson
Barth, John	Lost in the Funhouse
Barthelme, Donald	The Indian Uprising, The School, Views of My Father Weeping
Beattie, Ann	Shifting
Bellow, Saul	Seize the Day
Bierce, Ambrose	An Occurrence at Owl Creek
Bloom, Amy	Silver Water
Borges, Jorge Luis	Pierre Menard, Author of Quixote, The Library of Babel, The Aleph, The Circular Ruins, The End of the Duel
Boyle, T. C.	Greasy Lake, After the Plague
Caputo, Philip	In the Forest of the Laughing Elephant
Carver, Raymond	Cathedral, A Small, Good Thing, Will You Please Be Quiet, Please? Why Don't You Dance?
Cather, Willa	Paul's Case
Cheever, John	The Swimmer, Goodbye, My Brother, The Enormous Radio, The Country Husband
Chekhov, Anton	The Lady with the Dog, The Looking Glass, The Bet
Chopin, Kate	Désirée's Baby, The Story of an Hour, A Pair of Silk Stockings
Cisneros, Sandra	The House on Mango Street
Colette	The Other Woman
Connell, Richard	The Most Dangerous Game
Conrad, Joseph	The Secret Sharer
Coover, Robert	The Babysitter
Cortazar, Julio	Blow-Up, The Night Face-Up

Crane, Stephen	The Open Boat, The Blue Hotel
Cunningham, Michael	White Angel
Danticat, Edwidge	Night Women
Díaz, Junot	How to Date a Brown Girl (Black Girl, White Girl, or Halfie), The Sun, the Moon, the Stars
Dickens, Charles	The Signalman
Dostoyevsky, Fyodor	White Nights
Doyle, Arthur Conan	A Scandal in Bohemia
Erdrich, Louise	The Red Convertible
Faulkner, William	The Bear, Barn Burning, A Rose for Emily, That Evening Sun
Fitzgerald, F. Scott	Babylon Revisited, The Diamond as Big as the Ritz
Flaubert, Gustave	A Simple Heart
Gaitskill, Mary	A Romantic Weekend
Garcia Marquez, Gabriel	The Very Old Man with Enormous Wings
Gilb, D'Agoberto	Shout
Gish, Jen	In the American Society, Who's Irish?
Glaspell, Susan	A Jury of Her Peers
Gogol, Nikolai	The Overcoat, The Nose
Ha Jin	The Russian Prisoner
Hale, Edward Everett	The Man without a Country
Harte, Bret	The Luck of Roaring Camp, The Outcasts of Poker Flat
Hawthorne, Nathaniel	Young Goodman Brown, The Minister's Black Veil, The Birthmark
Hemingway, Ernest	Indian Camp, Big Two-Hearted River, The Killers, Hills Like White Elephants, The Snows of Kilimanjaro, The Short Happy Life of Francis Macomber
Henry, O.	The Gift of the Magi, The Last Leaf
Irving, Washington	Rip Van Winkle, The Legend of Sleepy Hallow
Jackson, Shirley	The Lottery
James, Henry	The Beast in the Jungle, The Real Thing
Jewett, Sarah Orne	A White Heron
Johnson, Denis	Emergency
Joyce, James	Araby, The Dead
Kafka, Franz	A Hunger Artist, In the Penal Colony
Kincaid, Jamaica	Girl
King, Stephen	The Body
Kipling, Rudyard	The Man Who Would Be King, Rikki Tikki Tavi
Lahiri, Jhumpa	Interpreter of Maladies, The Third and Final Continent, A Temporary Matter
Lardner, Ring	Haircut
Lawrence, D. H.	Odour of Chrysanthemums, The Rocking Horse Winner
Le Guin, Ursula	The Once Who Walk Away from Omelas
Lessing, Doris	Our Friend Judith, To Room Nineteen
Lethem, Jonathan	The Happy Man
Li, Yiyun	A Thousand Years of Good Prayers
London, Jack	To Build a Fire
Lu Xun	Regret for the Dead, Diary of a Mad Man

Malamud, Bernard	The Magic Barrel, The Jewbird
Mann, Thomas	Tonio Kroger
Mansfield, Katherine	The Garden Party, The Fly
Mason, Bobbie Ann	Shiloh
Maupassant, Guy de	Boule de Suif, The Necklace
McCullers, Carson	The Ballad of the Sad Café
Melville, Herman	Bartleby the Scrivener
Moore, Lorrie	Dance in America, How to Become a Writer, You're Ugly, Too
Mukherjee, Bharati	The Management of Grief
Munro, Alice	How I Met My Husband, Meneseteung, Boys and Girls, The Turkey Season, Love of a Good Woman
Murakami, Haruki	The Second Bakery Attack, The Seventh Man
Nabokov, Vladimir	Signs and Symbols
O'Brien, Tim	The Things They Carried
O'Connor, Flannery	A Good Man Is Hard to Find, Good Country People, The Displaced Person
O'Connor, Frank	Guests of the Nation
Oates, Joyce Carol	Where Are You Going, Where Have You Been?, How I Contemplated the World from the Detroit House of Corrections and Began My Life Over Again
Olsen, Tillie	I Stand Here Ironing
Ozick, Cynthia	The Shawl
Packer, ZZ	Drinking Coffee Elsewhere, Brownies
Paley, Grace	A Conversation with My Father
Perkins, Charlotte Gilman	The Yellow Wallpaper
Poe, Edgar Allan	The Tell-Tale Heart, The Cask of Amontillado, The Fall of the House of Usher
Porter, Katherine Ann	Flowering Judas, Pale Horse, Pale Rider, The Jilting of Granny Wetherall
Proulx, Annie	Brokeback Mountain, The Blood Bay
Pushkin, Alexander	The Queen of Spades
Pynchon, Thomas	Entropy
Roth, Philip	Goodbye, Columbus
Salinger, J. D.	A Perfect Day for Bananafish, For Esmé—With Love and Squalor
Sanders, George	Pastoralia, Sea Oak
Saroyan, William	The Daring Young Man on the Flying Trapeze
Schwartz, Delmore	In Dreams Begin Responsibilities
Scott, Walter	The Two Drovers
Silko, Leslie Marmon	Storyteller, Yellow Woman
Simpson, Mona	Lawns
Singer, Isaac Bashevis	The Spinoza of Market Street, Gimpel the Fool
Stafford, Jean	In the Zoo
Stein, Gertrude	Melanctha
Steinbeck, John	The Chrysanthemums
Stockton, Frank R.	The Lady, or the Tiger?
Stone, Robert	Helping
Strout, Elizabeth	Olive Kitteridge

Tan, Amy	Half and Half, Rules of the Game
Thomas, Dylan	A Child's Christmas in Wales
Thurber, James	The Secret Life of Walter Mitty
Tolstoy, Leo	The Death of Ivan Ilyich, Three Questions, How Much Land Does a Man Need
Trevor, William	The Ballroom of Romance
Turgenev, Ivan	First Love, Bezhin Meadow, Torrents of Spring
Twain, Mark	The Celebrated Jumping Frog of Calaveras County, The Man That Corrupted Hadleyburg
Updike, John	A & P, Pigeon Feathers
Vonnegut, Kurt	Harrison Bergeron
Walker, Alice	Everyday Use
Welty, Eudora	A Worn Path, Why I Live at the P.O.
Wharton, Edith	Roman Fever
Williams, William Carlos	The Use of Force
Wolff, Tobias	Bullet in the Brain, Hunters in the Snow, The Rich Brother
Woolf, Virginia	Kew Gardens, A Haunted House
Wright, Richard	The Man Who Was Almost a Man, The Man Who Lived Underground
Yamamoto, Hisaye	Seventeen Syllables, Wilshire Bus

NOVELS (IN CHRONOLOGICAL ORDER)

Murasaki Shikibu	*The Tale of Genji* (Eleventh Century)
Rojas, Fernando de	*La Celestina* (1499)
Cervantes, Miguel de	*Don Quixote* (1605, 1615)
La Fayette, Madame de	*The Princess of Cleves* (1678)
Defoe, Daniel	*Robinson Crusoe* (1719), *Moll Flanders* (1722)
Prévost, Abbé	*Manon Lescaut* (1731)
Richardson, Samuel	*Pamela* (1740), *Clarissa* (1747–48)
Fielding, Henry	*Joseph Andrews* (1742), *Tom Jones* (1749)
Voltaire	*Candide* (1759)
Sterne, Laurence	*Tristram Shandy* (1760–67)
Rousseau, Jean-Jacques	*Julie; or, The New Eloise* (1761)
Goldsmith, Oliver	*The Vicar of Wakefield* (1766)
Goethe, Johann Wolfgang von	*The Sorrows of Young Werther* (1774)
Burney, Fanny	*Evelina* (1778)
Laclos, Pierre Choderlos de	*Les Liaisons dangereuses* (1782)
Cao Xueqin	*Dream of the Red Chamber* (1791)
Marquis de Sade	*Justine* (1791)
Radcliffe, Ann	*The Mysteries of Udolpho* (1794)
Chateaubriand, François-René	*René* (1802)
Austen, Jane	*Pride and Prejudice* (1813), *Emma* (1816), *Persuasion* (1818)
Scott, Walter	*Waverley* (1814), *The Heart of Midlothian* (1818)
Constant, Benjamin	*Adolphe* (1816)
Shelley, Mary	*Frankenstein* (1818)
Cooper, James Fennimore	*The Last of the Mohicans* (1826)

Manzoni, Alessandro	*The Betrothed* (1827)
Stendhal	*The Red and the Black* (1830), *The Charterhouse of Parma* (1839)
Balzac, Honoré de	*Eugénie Grandet* (1833), *Le Père Goriot* (1835), *Illusions perdues* (1843)
Dickens, Charles	*The Pickwick Papers* (1836–37), *David Copperfield* (1849–50), *Bleak House* (1852–53), *Little Dorrit* (1857–59), *Great Expectations* (1861)
Lermontov, Mikhail	*A Hero of Our Time* (1840)
Gogol, Nikolai	*Dead Souls* (1842)
Dumas, Alexandre	*The Three Musketeers* (1844)
Brontë, Charlotte	*Jane Eyre* (1847), *Villette* (1853)
Brontë, Emily	*Wuthering Heights* (1847)
Thackeray, William Makepeace	*Vanity Fair* (1847–48)
Hawthorne, Nathaniel	*The Scarlet Letter* (1850)
Melville, Herman	*Moby-Dick* (1851)
Stowe, Harriet Beecher	*Uncle Tom's Cabin* (1852)
Trollope, Anthony	*Barchester Towers* (1857), *The Last Chronicle of Barset* (1866–67)
Flaubert, Gustave	*Madame Bovary* (1857), *Sentimental Education* (1869)
Goncharov, Ivan	*Oblomov* (1859)
Meredith, George	*The Ordeal of Richard Feverel* (1859)
Collins, Wilkie	*The Woman in White* (1860), *The Moonstone* (1868)
Turgenev, Ivan	*Fathers and Sons* (1862)
Hugo, Victor	*Les Misérables* (1862)
Gaskell, Elizabeth	*Wives and Daughters* (1864–66)
Dostoyevsky, Fyodor	*Crime and Punishment* (1866), *The Idiot* (1869), *The Brothers Karamazov* (1880)
Zola, Émile	*Thérèse Raquin* (1867), *Germinal* (1885), *L'Assommoir* (1877)
Tolstoy, Leo	*War and Peace* (1869), *Anna Karenina* (1877)
James, Henry	*The Portrait of a Lady* (1881), *The Ambassadors* (1902), *The Wings of the Dove* (1902), *The Golden Bowl* (1904)
Stevenson, Robert Louis	*Treasure Island* (1883), *The Strange Case of Dr. Jekyll and Mr. Hyde* (1886)
Twain, Mark	*Adventures of Huckleberry Finn* (1884)
Huysmans, Joris Karl	*Against the Grain* (1884)
Perez Galdós, Benito	*Fortunata and Jacinto* (1886–67)
Hardy, Thomas	*The Mayor of Casterbridge* (1886), *Tess of the D'Urbervilles* (1891), *Jude the Obscure* (1895)
Hamsun, Knut	*Hunger* (1890)
Gissing, George	*New Grub Street* (1891)
Fontane, Theodor	*Effi Briest* (1894)
Crane, Stephen	*The Red Badge of Courage* (1895)
Stoker, Bram	*Dracula* (1897)
Chopin, Kate	*The Awakening* (1897)
Machado de Assis, Joaquim Maria	*Dom Casmurro* (1899)
Norris, Frank	*McTeague* (1899)

Conrad, Joseph	*Lord Jim* (1900), *Nostromo* (1904), *The Secret Agent* (1907)
Dreiser, Theodore	*Sister Carrie* (1900), *An American Tragedy* (1925)
Mann, Thomas	*Buddenbrooks* (1901), *The Magic Mountain* (1924), *Doctor Faustus* (1947)
Doyle, Arthur Conan	*The Hound of the Baskervilles* (1901)
Kipling, Rudyard	*Kim* (1901)
Wharton, Edith	*House of Mirth* (1905), *The Age of Innocence* (1920)
Lawrence, D. H.	*Sons and Lovers* (1913), *The Rainbow* (1915), *Women in Love* (1920)
Proust, Marcel	*In Search of Lost Time* (1913–27)
Soseki, Natsume	*Kokoro* (1914)
Ford, Ford Maddox	*The Good Soldier* (1915)
Bely, Andrey	*Petersburg* (1916, 1922)
Joyce, James	*A Portrait of the Artist as a Young Man* (1916), *Ulysses* (1922), *Finnegans Wake* (1939)
Cather, Willa	*My Antonia* (1918)
Undset, Sigrid	*Kristin Lavransdatter* (1920–22)
Hasek, Jaroslav	*The Good Soldier Svejk* (1921–23)
Svevo, Italo	*The Confessions of Zeno* (1923)
Forster, E. M.	*A Passage to India* (1924)
Woolf, Virginia	*Mrs. Dalloway* (1925), *To the Lighthouse* (1927)
Fitzgerald, F. Scott	*The Great Gatsby* (1925), *Tender Is the Night* (1934)
Kafka, Franz	*The Trial* (1925)
Hemingway, Ernest	*The Sun Also Rises* (1926), *A Farewell to Arms* (1929), *For Whom the Bell Tolls* (1940), *The Old Man and the Sea* (1958)
Gide, André	*The Counterfeiters* (1926)
Hesse, Hermann	*Steppenwolf* (1927)
Sholokhov, Mikhail	*Quiet Flows the Don* (1928–40)
Döblin, Alfred	*Berlin Alexanderplatz* (1929)
Tanizaki, Jun'ichiro	*Some Prefer Nettles* (1929)
Faulkner, William	*The Sound and the Fury* (1929), *As I Lay Dying* (1930), *Light in August* (1932), *Absalom, Absalom!* (1936)
Dos Passos, John	*U.S.A.* (1930–38)
Musil, Robert	*The Man without Qualities* (1930–33)
Agnon, S. Y.	*The Bridal Canopy* (1931)
Broch, Hermann	*The Sleepwalkers* (1932), *The Death of Virgil* (1945)
Celine, Louis-Ferdinand	*Journey to the End of Night* (1932)
Roth, Joseph	*The Radetzky March* (1932)
Malraux, André	*Man's Fate* (1933)
West, Nathanael	*Miss Lonelyhearts* (1933)
Miller, Henry	*Tropic of Cancer* (1934)
Roth, Henry	*Call It Sleep* (1934)
Anand, Mulk Raj	*Untouchable* (1935)
Mitchell, Margaret	*Gone with the Wind* (1936)
Barnes, Djuna	*Nightwood* (1936)
Lao She	*Camel Xiangzi* (1936)
Gombrowicz, Witold	*Ferdydurke* (1937)

Kawabata Yasunari	*Snow Country* (1937, 1948)
Hurston, Zora Neale	*Their Eyes Were Watching God* (1937)
Bowen, Elizabeth	*The Death of the Heart* (1938)
Sartre, Jean-Paul	*Nausea* (1938)
O'Brien, Flann	*At Swim-Two-Birds* (1939)
Steinbeck, John	*The Grapes of Wrath* (1939)
Wright, Richard	*Native Son* (1940)
Camus, Albert	*The Stranger* (1940)
Cela, Camilo José	*The Family of Pascual Duarte* (1942)
Genet, Jean	*Our Lady of the Flowers* (1942)
Andric, Ivo	*The Bridge on the Drina* (1945)
Waugh, Evelyn	*Brideshead Revisited* (1945)
Asturias, Miguel Angel	*Mr. President* (1946)
Warren, Robert Penn	*All the King's Men* (1946)
Welty, Eudora	*Delta Wedding* (1948)
Ba Jin	*Cold Nights* (1947)
Lowry, Malcolm	*Under the Volcano* (1947)
Greene, Graham	*The Heart of the Matter* (1948)
Mailer, Norman	*The Naked and the Dead* (1948)
Paton, Alan	*Cry, the Beloved Country* (1948)
Bowles, Paul	*The Sheltering Sky* (1949)
Salinger, J. D.	*The Catcher in the Rye* (1951)
Beckett, Samuel	*Molloy, Malone Dies, The Unnamable* (1951–53)
Ellison, Ralph	*Invisible Man* (1952)
Amis, Kingsley	*Lucky Jim* (1954)
Nabokov, Vladimir	*Lolita* (1955), *Pale Fire* (1962), *Ada* (1969)
Gaddis, William	*The Recognitions* (1955)
Kazantzakis, Nikos	*The Last Temptation of Christ* (1955)
Mahfouz, Naguib	*The Cairo Trilogy* (1956–57)
Kerouac, Jack	*On the Road* (1957)
Pasternak, Boris	*Doctor Zhivago* (1957)
Robbe-Grillet, Alain	*Jealousy* (1957)
White, Patrick	*Voss* (1957)
Durrell, Lawrence	*The Alexandria Quartet* (1957–60)
Lampedusa, Giuseppe Tomasi di	*The Leopard* (1958)
Achebe, Chinua	*Things Fall Apart* (1958)
Grass, Günter	*The Tin Drum* (1959)
Lee, Harper	*To Kill a Mockingbird* (1960)
Updike, John	*Rabbit Run* (1960)
Heller, Joseph	*Catch-22* (1961)
Fuentes, Carlos	*The Death of Artemio Cruz* (1962), *Terra Nostra* (1975)
Lessing, Doris	*The Golden Notebook* (1962)
Abé, Kobo	*Woman in the Dunes* (1962)
Singer, Isaac Bashevis	*The Slave* (1962)
Solzhenitsyn, Aleksandr	*One Day in the Life of Ivan Denisovich* (1962)
Cortazar, Julio	*Hopscotch* (1963)
Bellow, Saul	*Herzog* (1964)
Ibuse Masuji	*Black Rain* (1965)

Pynchon, Thomas	*The Crying of Lot 49* (1965), *Gravity's Rainbow* (1973)
Soyinka, Wole	*The Interpreters* (1965)
Amado, Jorge	*Dona Flora and Her Two Husbands* (1966)
Rhys, Jean	*Wide Sargasso Sea* (1966)
Bulgakov, Mikhail	*The Master and Margarita* (1966–67)
García Márquez, Gabriel	*One Hundred Years of Solitude* (1967), *Love in the Time of Cholera* (1985)
Thiong'o, Ngugi wa	*A Grain of Wheat* (1969)
Roth, Philip	*Portnoy's Complaint* (1969), *American Pastoral* (1997)
Davies, Robertson	*The Deptford Trilogy* (1970–75)
Calvino, Italo	*Invisible Cities* (1972)
Boll, Heinrich	*The Lost Honor of Katharina Blum* (1974)
Gordimer, Nadine	*The Conservationist* (1974)
Naipaul, V.S.	*A Bend in the River* (1979)
Rushdie, Salmon	*Midnight's Children* (1981)
Allende, Isabel	*The House of the Spirits* (1982)
Hulme, Keri	*The Bone People* (1983)
Kundera, Milan	*The Unbearable Lightness of Being* (1984)
Erdrich, Louise	*Love Medicine* (1984)
Munif, 'Abd al-Rahman	*Cities of Salt* (1985)
Atwood, Margaret	*The Handmaid's Tale* (1985), *The Blind Assassin* (2000)
Morrison, Toni	*Beloved* (1987)
Murakami, Haruki	*Norwegian Wood* (1987), *1Q84* (2009)
Doyle, Roddy	*The Barrytown Trilogy* (1987–91)
Ford, Richard	*Independence Day* (1995)
Wallace, David Foster	*Infinite Jest* (1996)
DeLillo, Don	*Underworld* (1997)
Coetzee, J. M.	*Disgrace* (1999)
Chabon, Michael	*The Amazing Adventures of Kavalier & Clay* (2000)
Pamuk, Orhan	*My Name Is Red* (2000), *Snow* (2002)
Smith, Zadie	*White Teeth* (2004), *NW* (2012)
McEwan, Ian	*Atonement* (2001)
Franzen, Jonathan	*The Corrections* (2001)
Russo, Richard	*Empire Falls* (2001)
Sebald, W. G.	*Austerlitz* (2001)
Eugenides, Jeffrey	*Middlesex* (2002)
Hazzard, Shirley	*The Great Fire* (2003)
Jones, Edward P.	*The Known World* (2003)
Lahiri, Jhumpa	*The Namesake* (2003)
Bolaño, Roberto	*2666* (2004)
Clarke, Susanna	*Jonathan Strange & Mr. Norrell* (2004)
Hollinghurst, Alan	*The Line of Beauty* (2004)
Mitchell, David	*Cloud Atlas* (2004)
Robinson, Marilynne	*Gilead* (2004)
Adichie, Chimamanda Ngozi	*Half of a Yellow Sun* (2006), *Americanah* (2013)
McCarthy, Cormac	*The Road* (2006)
Díaz, Junot	*The Brief Wondrous Life of Oscar Wao* (2007)
Johnson, Denis	*Tree of Smoke* (2007)

Mantel, Hilary	*Wolf Hall* (2009)	
Egan, Jennifer	*A Visit from the Goon Squad* (2010)	
Ferrante, Elena	*My Brilliant Friend* (2011)	
Harbach, Chad	*The Art of Fielding* (2011)	
Fountain, Ben	*Billy Lynn's Long Halftime Walk* (2012)	
Tartt, Donna	*The Goldfinch* (2013)	
Doerr, Anthony	*All the Light We Cannot See* (2014)	
McGuire, Ian	*The North Water* (2016)	
Whitehead, Colson	*Underground Railroad* (2016)	

HISTORICAL FICTION

Author	Title	Subject
Auchincloss, Louis	*The Cat and the King* (1981)	Seventeenth and eighteenth centuries
Auel, Jean	*The Clan of the Cave Bear* (1980)	Prehistory
Banks, Russell	*Cloudsplitter* (1998)	Nineteenth century
Barker, Pat	*Regeneration* (1992), *The Eye in the Door* (1994), *The Ghost Road* (1996)	Twentieth century
Barth, John	*The Sot-Weed Factor* (1966)	Colonial America
Bell, Madison Smartt	*All Souls' Rising* (1995)	Seventeenth and eighteenth centuries
Bell, Madison Smartt	*Devil's Dream* (2009)	American Civil War
Berger, Thomas	*Little Big Man* (1964)	Nineteenth century American West
Boyden, Joseph	*Three Day Road* (2005)	Twentieth century
Brooks, Geraldine	*Year of Wonders* (2001)	Seventeenth and eighteenth centuries
Brooks, Geraldine	*March* (2005)	American Civil War
Brooks, Geraldine	*People of the Book* (2008)	Twentieth century
Buck, Pearl S.	*The Good Earth* (1931)	Chinese village life before World War I
Butler, Margaret	*The Lion of England* (1973), *The Lion of Justice* (1975), *The Lion of Christ* (1977)	Middle Ages
Carey, Peter	*True History of the Kelly Gang* (2001)	Australia
Chabon, Michael	*The Amazing Adventures of Kavalier & Clay* (2000)	Twentieth century
Chevalier, Tracy	*At the Edge of the Orchard* (2016)	Nineteenth century
Clarke, Susanna	*Jonathan Strange & Mr Norrell* (2004)	Napoleonic Wars

Clavell, James	*Shogun* (1975)	Japan
Cowell, Stephanie	*Nicholas Cooke, The Physician of London* (1995)	Seventeenth and eighteenth centuries
Crane, Stephen	*The Red Badge of Courage* (1895)	American Civil War
Dickens, Charles	*A Tale of Two Cities* (1859)	Seventeenth and eighteenth centuries
Doctorow, E. L.	*Ragtime* (1976)	Twentieth century
Doctorow, E. L.	*The March* (2005)	American Civil War
Doerr, Anthony	*All the Light We Cannot See* (2015)	Twentieth century
Druon, Maurice	*The Poisoned Crown* (1957), *The Strangled Queen* (1957), *Royal Succession* (1958)	Middle Ages
Drury, Allen	*A God Against the Gods* (1976), *Return to Thebes* (1977)	Ancient Egypt
Dumas, Alexandre	*The Three Musketeers* (1844)	Seventeenth and eighteenth centuries
Eco, Umberto	*The Name of the Rose* (1983)	Middle Ages
Edmonds, Walter D.	*Drums Along the Mohawk* (1936)	American Revolution
Egan, Jennifer	*Manhattan Beach* (2017)	Twentieth century
Eliot, George	*Romola* (1863)	Renaissance
Falconer, Colin	*When We Were Gods* (2000)	Ancient Rome
Fast, Howard	*April Morning* (1961)	American Revolution
Faulks, Sebastian	*Birdsong* (1996)	Twentieth century
Flanagan, Thomas	*The Year of the French* (1979)	Seventeenth and eighteenth centuries
	The Tennants of Time (1988)	Nineteenth century
	The End of the Hunt (1994)	Twentieth century
Fleming, Thomas	*Liberty Tavern* (1976)	American Revolution
Follett, Ken	*The Pillars of the Earth* (1989), *World Without End* (2007), *A Column of Fire* (2017)	Middle Ages
Foote, Shelby	*Shiloh* (1980)	American Civil War
Fowles, John	*The French Lieutenant's Woman* (1969)	Nineteenth century
Frazier, Charles	*Cold Mountain* (1997)	American Civil War
Garrett, George	*Death of the Fox* (1971), *The Succession* (1983), *Entered from the Sun* (1990)	Tudor and Elizabethan England
George, Margaret	*The Autobiography of Henry VIII* (1986)	Tudor and Elizabethan England
George, Margaret	*Memoirs of Cleopatra* (1997)	Ancient Rome
Ghosh, Amitav	*Sea of Poppies* (2008), *River of Smoke* (2013)	Nineteenth century
Golding, William	*The Inheritors* (1962)	Prehistory
Graves, Robert	*I Claudius* (1934), *Claudius the God* (1935)	Ancient Rome

Guthrie, A. B.	*The Way West* (1949), *The Big Sky* (1958)	Nineteenth-century American West
Hill, Lawrence	*Book of Negroes* (2012)	Seventeenth and eighteenth centuries
Hugo, Victor	*Les Miserables* (1862)	Nineteenth-century France
Iggulden, Conn	*Emperor: The Gates of Rome* (2002)	Ancient Rome
Jiles, Paulette	*Enemy Women* (2002)	American Civil War
Jones, Edwin P.	*The Known World* (2003)	Nineteenth century
Kantor, MacKinlay	*Long Remember* (1934), *Andersonville* (1955)	American Civil War
Kidd, Sue Monk	*The Invention of Wings* (2014)	Nineteenth century
Mantel, Hilary	*Wolf Hall* (2009), *Bring Up the Bodies* (2012)	Tudor and Elizabethan England
Martin, Valerie	*Property* (2003)	Nineteenth century
McBride, James	*The Good Lord Bird* (2013)	Nineteenth century
McCann, Maria	*As Meat Loves Salt* (2001), *The Wilding* (2010)	Seventeenth and eighteenth centuries
McCullough, Colleen	*Caesar* (1997), *The October Horse* (2002)	Ancient Rome
McDermott, Alice	*The Ninth Hour* (2017)	Twentieth century
McEwan, Ian	*Atonement* (2001)	Twentieth century
McMurtry, Larry	*Lonesome Dove* (1985)	Nineteenth-Century American West
Miles, Rosalind	*I, Elizabeth* (1994)	Tudor and Elizabethan England
Min, Anchee	*The Last Empress* (2007)	China
Mitchell, David	*The Thousand Autumns of Jacob de Zoet* (2010)	Seventeenth and eighteenth centuries
Mitchell, Margaret	*Gone with the Wind* (1936)	Antebellum and Civil War South
Morrison, Toni	*Beloved* (1987)	Nineteenth century
Nordhoff, Charles & James Hall	*The Bounty Trilogy*	Pacific
O'Brian, Patrick	*The Aubrey/Maturin Series*	Napoleonic Wars
O'Connor, Joseph	*Redemption Falls* (2008)	Nineteenth century
Oldenbourg, Zoe	*The World Is Not Enough* (1948), *The Cornerstone* (1955), *Destiny of Fire* (1961), *Cities of the Flesh* (1961), *Cities of Flesh* (1971)	Middle Ages
Pasternak, Boris	*Doctor Zhivago* (1958)	Twentieth century
Penman, Sharon Kay	*The Sunne in Splendour* (19872), *Here Be Dragons* (1987), *Falls the Shadows* (1988), *When Christ and His Saints Slept* (1995)	Middle Ages
Pressfield, Stephen	*Gates of Fire* (1998), *Tides of War* (2000)	Ancient Greece
Proulx, Annie	*Barkskins* (2016)	Seventeenth and eighteenth centuries

Renault, Mary	*The Last of the Wine* (1956), *The King Must Die* (1958), *The Mask of Apollo* (1966), *Fire from Heaven* (1969), *The Persian Boy* (1972), *The Praise Singer* (1978), *Funeral Games* (1981)	Ancient Greece
Roberts, Kenneth	*Northwest Passage* (1937)	Colonial America
	Arundel (1930), *Rabble in Arms* (1933), *Oliver Wiswell* (1940)	American Revolution
Saunders, George	*Lincoln in the Bardo* (2017)	American Civil War
Schmidt, Sarah	*See What I Have Done* (2017)	Nineteenth century
Scott, Paul	*The Raj Quartet*	India
Scott, Walter	*Waverley* (1814)	Seventeenth and eighteenth centuries
See, Lisa	*Secret Fan* (2005)	Nineteenth century
Shaara, Jeff	*The Killer Angels* (1974)	American Civil War
Sienkiewicz, Henryk	*Quo Vadis* (1964)	Ancient Rome
Sontag, Susan	*The Volcano Lover* (1992)	Napoleonic Wars
Stone, Irving	*The Agony and the Ecstasy* (1961)	Renaissance
Styron, William	*The Confessions of Nat Turner* (1967)	Nineteenth century
Sundaresan, Indu	*The Twentieth Wife* (2002)	India
Tan, Amy	*The Valley of Amazement* (2014)	China
Tey, Josephine	*The Daughter of Time* (1952)	Middle Ages
Toibin, Colm	*The Master* (2004)	Twentieth century
Tolstoy, Leo	*War and Peace* (1872)	Napoleonic Wars
Tremaine, Rose	*Restoration* (1990), *Merivel: A Man of His Time* (2013)	Seventeenth and eighteenth centuries
Vidal, Gore	*Julian* (1958)	Ancient Rome
Wallace, Lew	*Ben-Hur* (1880)	Ancient Rome
Waters, Sarah	*The Night Watch* (2011)	Twentieth century
Waters, Sarah	*Fingersmith* (2002)	Nineteenth century
Whitehead, Colson	*The Underground Railroad* (2016)	Nineteenth century
Wilder, Thornton	*Ides of March* (1948)	Ancient Rome
Yourcenar, Marguerite	*Hadrian's Memoirs* (1954)	Ancient Rome

LITERARY NONFICTION (ESSAYS, AUTO–BIOGRAPHIES, MEMOIRS, NARRATIVE NONFICTION, CREATIVE NONFICTION)

Abbey, Edward
Desert Solitaire (1968)

Angelou, Maya
I Know Why the Caged Bird Sings (1969)

Augustine
Confessions (397–400 C.E.)

Baker, Russell
Growing Up (1982)

Baldwin, James
Notes of a Native Son (1955), *The Fire Next Time* (1963)

Berendt, John
Midnight in the Garden of Good and Evil (1994)

Berry, Wendell
Recollected Essays (1981)

Boo, Katherine
Behind the Beautiful Forevers (2012)

Brittain, Vera
Testament of Youth (1933)

Capote, Truman
In Cold Blood (1966)

Diderot, Denis
Rameau's Nephew (1761–74)

Didion, Joan
Slouching Towards Bethlehem (1968), *The Year of Magical Thinking* (2005)

Dillard, Annie
Pilgrim at Tinker Creek (1974), *An American Childhood* (1987)

Dinesen, Isak
Out of Africa (1937)

Douglass, Frederick
Narrative of the Life of Frederick Douglass (1845)

Eggers, Dave
What Is the What (2006)

Ellison, Ralph
Shadow and Act (1964)

Emerson, Ralph Waldo
Essays

Ephron, Nora
Crazy Salad (1975)

Frank, Anne
The Diary of a Young Girl (1947)

Franklin, Benjamin
The Autobiography of Benjamin Franklin (1791)

Grant, Ulysses S.
Personal Memoirs of Ulysses S. Grant (1885)

Graves, Robert
Good-Bye to All That (1929)

Haley, Alex
The Autobiography of Malcolm X (1965)

Hamill, Pete
A Drinking Life (1994)

Heat-Moon, William Least
Blue Highways (1982)

Hemingway, Ernest
A Moveable Feast (1964)

Herr, Michael
Dispatches (1977)

Herriot, James
All Creatures Great and Small (1972)

Hersey, John
Hiroshima (1946)

Hoagland, Edward
Edward Hoagland Reader (1979)

Howard, Maureen
Facts of Life (1978)

Hughes, Langston
The Big Sea (1940)

Karr, Mary
The Liars' Club (1995)

Kazin, Alfred
A Walker in the City (1951)

Keller, Helen
The Story of My Life (1903)

Kingston, Maxine Hong
The Woman Warrior (1976)

Kotlowitz, Alex
There Are No Children Here (1991)

Krakauer, Jon
Into Thin Air (1996)

Kruif, Paul de
Microbe Hunters (1926)

Lawrence, T. E.
The Seven Pillars of Wisdom (1926)

Mailer, Norman
The Armies of the Night (1968), *Of a Fire on the Moon* (1970), *The Executioner's Song* (1979)

Markham, Beryl
West with the Night (1942)

McBride, James
The Color of Water (1995)

McCourt, Frank
Angela's Ashes (1996)

McPhee, John
Coming into the Country (1977)

Montaigne, Michel de
Essays (1580)

Morris, Willie
North Toward Home (1967)

Nabokov, Vladimir
Speak, Memory (1951)

Nafisi, Azar
Reading Lolita in Tehran (2003)

Orwell, George
Down and Out in Paris and London (1933), *Homage to Catalonia* (1938)

Plutarch
Parallel Lives (1517)

Rousseau, Jean-Jacques
Confessions (1782)

Sacks, Oliver
The Man Who Mistook His Wife for a Hat (1985)

Sassoon, Siegfried
Memoirs of a Fox-Hunting Man (1928)

Sedaris, David
Me Talk Pretty One Day (2000)

Sontag, Susan
Against Interpretation (1966)

Spiegelman, Art
Maus (1986)

Stein, Gertrude
The Autobiography of Alice B. Toklas (1933)

Strachey, Lytton
Eminent Victorians (1918)

Styron, William
Darkness Visible (1990)

Suetonius
The Lives of the Twelve Caesars (121 C.E.)

Thomas, Lewis
The Lives of a Cell (1974)

Thompson, Hunter S.
Fear and Loathing in Las Vegas (1971)

Thoreau, Henry David
Walden (1854)

Twain, Mark
The Innocents Abroad (1869), *Roughing It* (1872), *Life on the Mississippi* (1883), *The Autobiography of Mark Twain* (1924)

Updike, John
Self-Consciousness (1989)

Vidal, Gore
United States: Essays 1952–1992 (1993)

Vowell, Sarah
The Wordy Shipmates (2008)

Wallace, David Foster
A Supposedly Fun Thing I'll Never Do Again (1997), *Consider the Lobster* (2005)

Walls, Jeannette
The Glass Castle (2005)

Welty, Eudora
One Writer's Beginnings (1984)

White, E. B.
Essays (1977)

Wiesel, Elie
Night (1956)

Williams, William Carlos
In the American Grain (1925)

Wolfe, Tom
The Electric Kool-Aid Acid Test (1968), *The Right Stuff* (1979)

Wolff, Tobias
This Boy's Life (1989)

Woolf, Virginia
A Room of One's Own (1929)

Wright, Richard
Black Boy (1945)

Further Reading

Abbott, H. Porter. *The Cambridge Introduction to Narrative.* New York: Cambridge University Press, 2008.

Abrams, M. H. *A Glossary of Literary Terms.* 7th ed. New York: Harcourt Brace Jovanovich, 1999.

———. *The Mirror and the Lamp: Romantic Theory and the Critical Tradition.* Oxford: Oxford University Press, 1953.

———. *Natural Supernaturalism: Tradition and Revolution in Romantic Literature.* New York: W. W. Norton, 1971.

Adams, Hazard, ed. *Critical Theory since Plato.* Revised ed. New York: Harcourt Brace Jovanovich, 1992.

Adler, Mortimer J., and Charles Van Doren. *How to Read a Book.* Rev. and updated ed. New York: Simon & Schuster, 1972.

Allen, Walter. *The Short Story in English.* Oxford: Clarendon Press, 1981.

Aquinas, Thomas. *Summa Theologica.* (Project Gutenberg, 2006). http://www.gutenberg.org/cache/epub/17611/pg17611.txt.

Aristotle. *The Poetics.* (Project Gutenberg, 2008). https://www.gutenberg.org/files/1974/1974-h/1974-h.htm.

Armstrong, Nancy. *Desire and Domestic Fiction: A Political History of the Novel.* New York: Oxford University Press, 1987.

———. *How Novels Think: The Limits of Individualism from 1719–1900.* New York: Columbia University Press, 2005.

Arnold, Matthew. *Selections from the Prose Works of Matthew Arnold.* (Project Gutenberg, 2008). http://www.gutenberg.org/cache/epub/12628/pg12628.txt.

Arp, Thomas R. , et al. *Perrine's Sound and Sense: An Introduction to Poetry.* 12th ed., Boston: Thomson/Wadsworth, 2008.

Attridge, Derek. *Poetic Rhythm, an Introduction.* New York: Cambridge University Press, 1995.

Auerbach, Erich. *Mimesis: The Representation of Reality in Western Literature*. New York: Doubleday, 1957.

Augustine. *Confessions*. (Project Gutenberg, 2002). http://www.gutenberg.org/cache/epub/3296/pg3296.txt.

Baker, David. *Meter in English: A Critical Engagement*. Fayetteville: University of Arkansas Press, 1996.

Barth, John. "The Literature of Exhaustion" in *The Friday Book: Essays and Other Non-fiction*. New York: Putnam, 1984.

Barthes, Roland. "The Death of the Author" in *Image, Music, Text*. New York: Hill & Wang, 1978.

Bates, H. E. *The Modern Short Story: A Critical Survey*. Boston: Writer, 1972.

Bates, W. J., ed. *Criticism: The Major Texts*. Enlarged ed. New York: Harcourt Brace Jovanovich, 1970.

Bayley, John. *The Short Story: Henry James to Elizabeth Bowen*. New York: St. Martin's Press, 1988.

Bell, Madison Smartt. *Narrative Design: A Writer's Guide to Structure*. New York: W. W. Norton, 1997.

Bentley, Phyllis. *Some Observations on the Art of Narrative*. New York: Macmillan, 1947.

Bevington, David. *How to Read a Shakespeare Play*. Malden, MA: Blackwell Pub, 2006.

Bieber, Margaret. *The History of Greek and Roman Theatr*. 2nd ed. Princeton: Princeton University Press, 1961.

Bloom, Harold. *How to Read and Why*. New York: Scribner, 2000.

———. *Shakespeare: The Invention of the Human*. New York: Riverhead Books, 1998.

———. *The Western Canon: The Books and School of the Ages*. New York: Harcourt Brace, 1994.

Boccaccio, Giovanni. "Literary Criticism" in *Critical Theory since Plato*. Ed. Hazard Adams. Revised ed. New York: Harcourt Brace Jovanovich, 1992.

Boileau, Nicolas. *The Art of Poetry*. Charlottesville: University of Virginia Library, 2000.

Booth, Wayne C. *The Rhetoric of Fiction*. 2nd ed. Chicago: University of Chicago Press, 1983.

Bradford, Richard. *Poetry: The Ultimate Guide*. Basingstoke, Hampshire: Palgrave Macmillan, 2010.

Brantlinger, Patrick, and William B. Thesing. *A Companion to the Victorian Novel*. Oxford: Blackwell, 2002.

Brockett, Oscar G., and Franklin J. Hildy. *History of the Theatre*. 10th ed. Boston: Pearson Education, 2008

Brooks, Cleanth. *The Well-Wrought Urn: Studies in the Structure of Poetry*. New York: Harcourt Brace, 1947.

Brooks, Cleanth, and Robert Heilman, eds. *Understanding Drama: Twelve Plays.* New York: H. Holt, 1948.

Brooks, Cleanth, and Robert Penn Warren, eds. *Understanding Fiction.* 3rd ed. Englewood Cliffs, NJ: Prentice-Hall, 1979.

———. *Understanding Poetry.* 4th ed. New York: Holt, Rinehart & Winston, 1976.

Brooks, Peter. *Reading for Plot: Design and Intention in Narrative.* New York: Knopf, 1984.

———. *The Empty Space.* New York: Avon Books, 1969.

Brown, John Russell. *The Oxford Illustrated History of Theatre.* New York: Oxford University Press, 2001.

Brustein, Robert. *The Theatre of Revolt: An Approach to Modern Drama.* Boston: Little, Brown, 1964.

Burke, Edmund. *A Philosophical Enquiry into the Origin of Our Ideas of the Sublime and Beautiful.* Ed. James T. Boulton. South Bend, IN: University of Notre Dame Press, 1958.

Butcher, S. H. *Aristotle's Theory of Poetry and Fine Arts.* London: Macmillan, 1902.

Cellini, Benvenuto. *The Autobiography of Benevenuto Cellini.* Rev. ed. New York: Penguin Books, 1998.

Chase, Richard. *The American Novel and Its Tradition.* New York: Doubleday, 1957.

Chatman, Seymour. *Story and Discourse: Narrative Structure in Fiction and Film.* Ithaca, NY: Cornell University Press, 1978.

Chatman, Seymour, and Samuel R. Levin, eds. *Essays in the Language of Literature.* Boston: Houghton Mifflin, 1967.

Chiardi, John, and Miller Williams. *How Does a Poem Mean?* 2nd ed. Boston: Houghton Mifflin, 1975.

Cobley, Paul. *Narrative: The New Critical Idiom.* London: Routledge, 2001.

Coleridge, Samuel Taylor. *Biographia Literaria.* Ed. James Engell and W. Jackson Bate. Princeton, NJ: Princeton University Press, 1983.

Conway, Jill Ker. *When Memory Speaks: Reflections on Autobiography.* New York: Knopf, 1998.

Corbett, Edward P. J., and Robert J. Connors. *Style and Statement.* New York: Oxford University Press, 1998.

Corn, Alfred. *The Poem's Heartbeat: A Manual of Prosody.* Port Townsend, WA: Copper Canyon Press, 2008.

Corneille, Pierre. *Three Discourses on Dramatic Poetry.* In *The Continental Model: Selected French Critical Essays of the Seventeenth Century.* Ed. Scott Elledge and Donald S. Schier. Ithaca, NY: Cornell University Press, 1970.

Crane, R. S., ed. *Critics and Criticism.* Chicago: University of Chicago Press, 1952.

Culler, Jonathan. *Literary Theory: A Very Short Introduction.* 2nd ed. Oxford: Oxford University Press, 2011.

———. *Structuralist Poetics: Structuralism, Linguistics, and the Study of Literature.* Ithaca, NY: Cornell University Press, 1975.

Current-Garcia, Eugen, and Walton R. Patrick, eds. *What Is the Short Story?* Rev. ed. Glenview, IL: Scott, Foresman, 1974.

Currie, Gregory. "Does Great Literature Make Us Better?" *New York Times* (1 June 2013). https://opinionator.blogs.nytimes.com/2013/06/01/does-great-literature-make-us-better/.

Daiches, David. *Critical Approaches to Literature.* New York: W. W. Norton, 1956.

Damrosch, David. *How to Read World Literature.* Chichester, UK: Wiley-Blackwell, 2009.0

Dante Alighieri. "On Eloquence in the Vernacular." Trans. by Steven Botterill. http://alighieri.letteraturaoperaomnia.org/translate_english/alighieri_dante_de_vulgari_eloquentia.html.

David, Deidre. *The Cambridge Companion to the Victorian Novel.* 2nd ed. Cambridge: Cambridge University Press, 2012.

Davie, David. *Purity of Diction in English Verse.* New York: Schocken Books, 1967.

Day, Geoffrey. *From Fiction to the Novel.* London: Routledge & Kegan Paul, 1987.

Dillard, Annie. *Living by Fiction.* New York: Perennial Library, 1989.

Dryden, John. *Literary Criticism of John Dryden.* Ed. Arthur C. Kirsch. Lincoln: University of Nebraska Press, 1967.

Eagleton, Terry. *The English Novel: An Introduction.* Malden, MA: Blackwell, 2005.

———. *How to Read Literature.* New Haven, CT: Yale University Press, 2013.

———. *Literary Theory: An Introduction.* 3rd ed. Minneapolis: University of Minnesota Press, 2008.

Eliot, T. S. *Selected Prose.* Ed. Frank Kermode. New York: Harcourt, Brace Jovanovich, 1975.

Else, Gerald F. *Plato and Aristotle on Poetry.* Chapel Hill: University of North Carolina Press, 1986.

Engell, James. *The Creative Imagination: Enlightenment to Romanticism.* Cambridge: Harvard University Press, 1981.

———. *Forming the Critical Mind: Dryden to Coleridge.* Cambridge: Harvard University Press, 1989.

Esslin, Martin. *The Theatre of the Absurd.* Rev. Updated ed. Garden City, NY: Anchor Books, 1969.

Fenton, James. *An Introduction to English Poetry.* New York: Farrar, Straus & Giroux, 2002.

Forché, Carolyn, and Philip Gerard, eds. *Writing Creative Nonfiction*. Cincinnati: Story Press, 2001.

Forster, E. M. *Aspects of the Novel*. (1927). New York: Harcourt, Brace & World, 1954.

Foster, Thomas C. *How to Read Literature Like a Professor*. Rev. ed. New York: Harper, 2017.

———. *How to Read Novels Like a Professor*. New York: Harper, 2008.

Frow, John. *Genre*. 2nd ed. London: Routledge, 2015.

Frye, Northrup. *Anatomy of Criticism: Four Essays*. Princeton, NJ: Princeton University Press, 1957.

Fussell, Paul. *Poetic Meter and Poetic Form*. Rev. ed. New York: Random House, 1979.

Garrett, Peter. *The Victorian Multiplot Novel: Studies in Dialogical Form*. New Haven, CT: Yale University Press, 1980.

Gassner, John, ed. *Medieval and Tudor Drama*. New York: Bantam Books, 1963.

Gibson, Andrew. *Towards a Postmodern Theory of Narrative*. Edinburgh, Scotland: Edinburgh University Press, 1996.

Gilman, Richard. *The Making of Modern Drama*. New York: Farrar, Straus & Giroux, 1974.

Giraldi, Giovanni Battista. *On Romances*. Ed. Henry L. Snuggs. Lexington: University of Kentucky Press, 1968.

Gornick, Vivian. *The Situation and the Story: The Art of the Personal Essay*. New York: Farrar, Straus & Giroux, 2001.

Greenblatt, Stephen. *The Power of Forms in the English Renaissance*. Norman, OK: Pilgrim Books, 1982.

Griffin, Connie E. *To Tell the Truth: Practice and Craft in Narrative Nonfiction*. New York: Pearson/Longman, 2009.

Gross, Harvey, and Robert McDowell. *Sound and Form in Modern Poetry*. 2nd ed. Ann Arbor: University of Michigan Press, 1996.

Guerin, Wilfrid L., et al. *A Handbook of Critical Approaches to Literature*. 4th ed. Oxford: Oxford University Press, 1999.

Gutkind, Lee. *The Art of Creative Nonfiction*. New York: Wiley, 1997.

———. *In Fact: The Best of Creative Nonfiction*. New York: W. W. Norton, 2005.

———. *You Can't Make This Stuff Up: The Complete Guide to Writing Creative Nonfiction*. Boston: Da Capo Press, 2012.

Habib, Rafey. *History of Literary Criticism: From Plato to the Present*. Malden, MA: Blackwell, 2005.

Hampl, Patricia. *I Could Tell You Stories: Sojourns in the Land of Memory*. New York: W. W. Norton, 1999.

Hanson, Claire. *Short Stories and Short Fiction, 1880–1980*. New York: St. Martin's Press, 1985.

Hart, Jack. *Story Craft: The Complete Guide to Writing Narrative Nonfiction*. Chicago: University of Chicago Press, 2011.

Head, Dominic. *The Modernist Short Story*. Cambridge: Cambridge University Press, 1992.

Herodotus. *The Histories*. Ed. Walter Blanco and Jennifer Tolbert Roberts. New York: W. W. Norton, 1992.

Hirsch, Edward. *How to Read a Poem: And Fall in Love with Poetry*. New York: Harcourt, 1999.

Hoffman, M. J., & P. D. Murphy, eds. *Essentials of the Theory of Fiction*. 3rd ed. Durham: Duke University Press, 2005.

Hollander, John. *Rhyme's Reason: A Guide to English Verse*. 3rd ed. New Haven, CT: Yale University Press, 2001.

Horace. *Ars poetica*. (Project Gutenberg, 2003). http://www.gutenberg.org/cache/epub/9175/pg9175.txt.

Hunter, J. Paul. *Before Novels: The Cultural Contexts of Eighteenth-Century English Fiction*. New York: W. W. Norton, 1990.

Jacobus, Lee A. *The Bedford Introduction to Drama*. 6th ed. Boston: Bedford/St. Martin's, 2009.

James, Henry. *The Art of Fiction: And Other Essays*. (1884). New York: Oxford University Press, 1948.

Jones, John. *On Aristotle and Greek Tragedy*. New York: Oxford University Press, 1962.

Kahler, Erich. *The Inward Turn of Narrative*. Princeton, NJ: Princeton University Press, 2017.

Kant, Immanuel. *The Critique of Judgment*. Ed. Paul Guyer. Cambridge: Cambridge University Press, 2000.

Kaplan, Charles, and William Anderson, eds. *Criticism: The Major Statements*. 3rd ed. New York: St. Martin's Press, 1991.

Karr, Mary. *The Art of Memoir*. New York: Harper, 2015.

Kennedy, George A. *The Cambridge History of Literary Criticism*. Cambridge: Cambridge University Press, 1989.

Kermode, Frank. *The Sense of an Ending; Studies in the Theory of Fiction*. New ed. New York: Oxford University Press, 2000.

King, Stephen. *On Writing: A Memoir of the Craft*. New York: Scribner, 2000.

Kingston, Maxine Hong. *The Woman Warrior: Memoirs of a Girlhood among Ghosts*. New York: Vintage Books, 1977.

Kinzie, Mary. *A Poet's Guide to Poetry*. Chicago: University of Chicago Press, 1999.

Klinkenborg, Verlyn. "Some Thoughts on the Pleasures of Being a Re-Reader." *New York Times*. (29 May 2009). http://www.nytimes.com/2009/05/30/opinion/30sat4.html.

Krutch, Joseph Wood. *Modernism in Modern Drama: A Definition and a Critical Estimate*. Ithaca, NY: Cornell University Press, 1953.

Lawall, Sarah, ed. *Norton Anthology of World Literature*. 2nd ed. New York: W. W. Norton, 2002.

Leitch, Vincent B., ed. *Norton Anthology of Theory and Criticism*. 2nd ed. New York: W. W. Norton, 2010.

Lennard, John. *The Poetry Handbook: A Guide to Reading Poetry for Pleasure and Practical Criticism*. New York: Oxford University Press, 1996.

Lentricchia, Frank. *After the New Criticism*. Chicago: University of Chicago Press, 1980.

Levine, George. *How to Read the Victorian Novel*. Malden, MA: Blackwell, 2008.

Lodge, David. *The Art of Fiction*. New York: Viking, 1993.

———. *Consciousness and the Novel: Connected Essays*. Cambridge. MA: Harvard University Press, 2002.

Loftis, John, ed. *Restoration Drama: Modern Essays in Criticism*. New York: Oxford University Press, 1966.

Lohafer, Susan. *Coming to Terms with the Short Story*. Baton Rouge: Louisiana State University Press, 1983.

Longinus. *On the Sublime*. (Project Gutenberg, 2006). https://www.gutenberg.org/files/17957/17957-h/17957-h.htm.

Lopate, Philip, ed. *The Art of the Personal Essay: An Anthology from the Classical Era to the Present*. New York: Anchor Books, 1994.

———. *To Show and To Tell: The Craft of Literary Nonfiction*. New York: Free Press, 2013.

Lounsberry, Barbara. *The Art of Fact: Contemporary Artists of Nonfiction*. New York: Greenwood Press, 1990.

Lubbock, Percy. *The Craft of Fiction*. (1921). New York: Scribner, 1955.

MacKay, Marina. *The Cambridge Introduction to the Novel*. Cambridge: Cambridge University Press, 2011.

May, Charles, ed. *Story Theories*. Athens: Ohio University Press, 1976.

McKeon, Michael. *Theory of the Novel: A Historical Approach*. Baltimore: Johns Hopkins University Press, 2000.

Miller, Brenda, and Suzanne Paola. *Tell It Slant: Creating, Refining, and Publishing Creative Nonfiction*. 2nd ed. New York: McGraw-Hill, 2012.

Montaigne, Michel de. *The Complete Essays of Montaigne*. Stanford, CA: Stanford University Press, 1976.

Moore, Dinty. *The Truth of the Matter: Art and Craft in Creative Nonfiction.* New York: Pearson/Longman, 2007.

Moretti, Franco. *Atlas of the European Novel, 1800–1900.* London: Verso, 1998.

Mullan, John. *How Novels Work.* Oxford: Oxford University Press, 2006.

Nabokov, Vladimir. *Lectures on Literature.* New York: Harcourt Brace Jovanovich, 1980.

O'Connor, Flannery. "Writing Short Stories" in *Mystery and Manners: Occasional Prose.* New York: Farrar, Straus & Giroux, 1969.

O'Connor, Frank. *The Lonely Voice: A Study of the Short Story.* Cleveland: World Pub., 1963.

O'Faolain, Sean. *The Short Story.* New York: Devin-Adair, 1951.

Oliver, Mary. *A Poetry Handbook.* San Diego: Harcourt Brace, 1994.

Ortolani, Benito. *The Japanese Theatre: From Shamanistic Ritual to Contemporary Pluralism.* Revised ed. Princeton, NJ: Princeton University Press, 1995.

Paul, Annie Murphy. "Reading Literature Makes Us Smarter and Nicer." *Time.com.* (3 June 2013). http://ideas.time.com/2013/06/03/why-we-should-read-literature/.

Perl, Sondra, and Mimi Schwartz. *Writing It True: The Art and Craft of Creative Nonfiction.* 2nd ed. Boston: Wadsworth/Cengage Learning, 2014.

Pinsky, Robert. *The Sounds of Poetry: A Brief Guide.* New York: Farrar, Straus & Giroux, 1998.

Plato. *The Republic.* Trans. by Richard W. Sterling and William C. Scott. New York: W. W. Norton, 1985.

Plutarch. *Works of Plutarch.* Boston: MobileReference.com, 2010.

Pollack, Ellen. *Creative Nonfiction; A Guide to Form, Content, and Style.* Boston: Wadsworth/Cengage Learning, 2010.

Prose, Francine. *Reading Like a Writer: A Guide for People Who Love Books and Those Who Want to Write Them.* New York: HarperCollins, 2006.

Rehm, Rush. *Understanding Greek Tragic Theatre.* 2nd ed. London: Routledge, 2017.

Richards, I. A. *Practical Criticism: A Study of Literary Judgment.* New York: Harcourt, Brace & World, 1956.

———. *Principles of Literary Criticism.* New York: Harcourt, Brace, 1952.

Roorbach, Bill. *Writing Life Stories: How to Make Memories into Memoirs.* Cincinnati: Story Press, 1998.

Root, Robert L., and Michael Steinberg. *The Fourth Genre: Contemporary Writers of/on Creative Nonfiction.* 6th ed. Boston: Pearson, 2012.

Rosenthal, M. L. *Poetry and the Common Life.* New York: Oxford University Press, 1974.

Ryan, Michael. *Literary Theory: A Practical Introduction.* Malden, MA: Blackwell, 1999.

Schiller, Freidrich. *Aesthetical and Philosophical Essays.* (Project Gutenberg, 2012). https://www.gutenberg.org/files/6798/6798-h/6798-h.htm.

Scholes, Robert. *The Fabulators.* New York: Oxford University Press, 1967

———. *Structuralism in Literature: An Introduction.* New Haven: Yale University Press, 1974.

Scholes, Robert, et al., eds. *Elements of Literature: Essay, Fiction, Poetry, Drama, Film.* 3rd ed. New York: Oxford University Press, 2004.

Scholes, Robert, James Phelan, and Robert Kellogg. *The Nature of Narrative.* Revised ed. New York: Oxford University Press, 2006.

Shaw, Harry E.. *The Forms of Historical Fiction: Sir Walter Scott and His Successors.* Ithaca: Cornell University Press, 1983.

Shelley, Percy Bysshe. *A Defence of Poetry and Other Essays.* (Project Gutenberg, 2013). https://www.gutenberg.org/files/5428/5428-h/5428-h.htm.

Showalter, Elaine. *The New Feminist Criticism: Essays on Women, Literature, and Theory.* New York: Pantheon Books, 1985.

Showerman, Grant. *Horace and His Influence.* New York: Cooper Square, 1963.

Smiley, Jane. *Thirteen Ways of Looking at the Novel.* New York: Knopf, 2005.

Spacks, Patricia. *On Rereading.* Cambridge: Harvard University Press, 2011.

Steele, Timothy. *Missing Measures: Modern Poetry and the Revolt Against Meter.* Fayetteville: University of Arkansas Press, 1990.

Steiner, George. *The Death of Tragedy.* New York: Knopf, 1961.

Strand, Mark, and Eavan Boland. *The Making of a Poem: A Norton Anthology of Poetic Forms.* New York: W. W. Norton, 2000.

Styan, J. L. *Modern Drama in Theory and Practice.* Cambridge: Cambridge University Press, 1981.

Sidney, Philip. *Apology for Poetry.* (Project Gutenberg, 1999). https://www.gutenberg.org/files/1962/1962-h/1962-h.htm.

Sutherland, John. *How to Read a Novel.* New York: St. Martin's Press, 2006.

Thompkins, Jane P., ed. *Reader-Response Criticism: From Formalist to Post-Structuralism.* Baltimore: Johns Hopkins University Press, 1980.

Trilling, Lionel. "Manners, Morals, and the Novel" in *The Liberal Imagination: Essays in Literature and Society.* Uniform Edition. *The Works of Lionel Trilling.* New York: Harcourt Brace Jovanovich, 1979.

Trotter, David. "The Modernist Novel" in *The Cambridge Companion to Modernism.* Ed. Michael H. Levenson. Cambridge: Cambridge University Press, 1999.

Turnell, Martin. *The Classical Moment: Studies in Corneille, Molière, and Racine.* New York: New Directions, 1948.

Van Ghent, Dorothy. *The English Novel: Form and Function.* 2nd ed. New York: Harper & Row, 1967.

Vendler, Helen. *Poems, Poets, Poetry: An Introduction and an Anthology.* 2nd ed. Boston: Bedford/St. Martin's, 2002.

Watt, Ian. *The Rise of the Novel: Studies in Defoe, Richardson, and Fielding.* Berkeley: University of California Press, 1957.

Waugh, Patricia. *Metafiction: The Theory and Practice of Self-Conscious Fiction.* London: Methuen, 1984.

Weber, Ronald. *The Literature of Fact: Literary Nonfiction in American Writing.* Athens: Ohio University Press, 1980.

Webster, Roger. *Studying Literary Theory: An Introduction.* 2nd ed. London: Arnold, 1996.

Weiss, Shira. *The Art of Poetry: How to Read a Poem.* New York: Oxford University Press, 2001.

Wellek, René, and Austin Warren. *Theory of Literature.* Rev. ed. New York: Harvest Books, 1964.

Wiles, David, and Christine Dymkowski. *The Cambridge Companion to Theatre History.* Cambridge: Cambridge University Press, 2013.

Wimsatt, W. K. *The Verbal Icon: Studies in the Meaning of Poetry.* Lexington: University of Kentucky Press, 1982. Includes "The Intentional Fallacy" and "The Pathetic Fallacy," co-written with Monroe Beardsley.

Wimsatt, W. K., and Cleanth Brooks. *Literary Criticism: A Short History.* New York: Knopf, 1957.

Wolfe, Tom. *The New Journalism.* Ed. E. W. Johnson. New York: Harper & Row, 1973.

———. "Why They Aren't Writing the Great American Novel Anymore." *Esquire* (December 1972).

Wood, James. *How Fiction Works.* New York: Farrar, Straus & Giroux, 2008.

Wordsworth, William, and Samuel Taylor Coleridge. *Lyrical Ballads: 1798.* Ed. W. J. B. Owen. 2nd ed. Oxford: Oxford University Press, 1969.

Yagoda, Ben. *Memoir: A History.* New York: Riverhead Books, 2009.

Yates, Frances A. *Theatre of the World.* Chicago: University of Chicago Press, 1969.

Zinsser, William, ed. *Inventing the Truth: The Art and Craft of Memoir.* 2nd ed. Boston: Houghton Mifflin, 1995.

———. *On Writing Well: The Classic Guide to Writing Nonfiction.* 7th ed. New York: HarperCollins, 2006.

Zunshine, Lisa. *Why We Read Fiction: A Theory of Mind and the Novel.* Columbus: Ohio State University Press, 2006.

Index

Note: (ill.) indicates photos and illustrations.

Rattigan, Terence, 249
Ray, Gordon, 191
reader, role in literature, 11
Reader-Response Criticism, 410–12
Reagan, Ronald, 332
realism, 200–201, 309
The Red Badge of Courage (Crane), 216
red herring, 235
Reed, Ishmael, 155
Reinhardt, Max, 311
Renaissance period, 380–81
Republic (Plato), 375–76, 376 (ill.)
rereading, 25–27
Reynolds, Barbara, 395
Rich, Adrienne, 44
Rich, Frank, 333
Richards, I. A., 389
Richards, Keith, 353
Richards, Lloyd, 328
Richardson, Samuel, 167–68, 172 (ill.), 172–73, 179
"Rip Van Winkle" (Irving), 131
Robinson Crusoe (Defoe), 161, 162
Roman drama, 260–64
Roman Empire, fall of, 262–64, 263 (ill.)
romance, 152–54, 200
The Romance of King Arthur, 153 (ill.)
Romantic period, 296, 383–87
Rosenblatt, Louise, 410–11
Roth, Philip, 149, 157, 158 (ill.)
Les Rougon-Macquart (Zola), 214
round characters, 107–8
Rousseau, Jean-Jacques, 347, 350
Rowley, William, 279
Rowson, Susanna, 199
Ruined (Nottage), 324, 325
Rushdie, Salman, 5, 6
Russell, George, 210
Russian Formalism, 396
Russian literature, 132

S

Sackville, Thomas, 266
Said, Edward, 416
Sainte-Beuve, Charles Augustin, 393
Salander, Lisbeth (character), 235
Salinger, J. D., 138, 148
Salmon, Ronald, 398
"Salvation" (Hughes), 355–56
Sandburg, Carl, 44
Sardar, Ziauddin, 416
Saunders, George, 149
Saussure, Ferdinand de, 404, 404 (ill.), 405
Sayers, Dorothy, 234
saying, 107

scapegoat, 257
The Scarlet Letter (Hawthorne), 200
Schelling, Friedrich Wilhelm Joseph von, 386
Schiller, Friedrich, 296, 385
Scholes, Robert, 405
science fiction
    definition, 238
    fantasy novels vs., 241
    Frankenstein (Shelley), 239–40
    hard vs. soft, 238
    origin of, 239
    reading, 242
    as speculative fiction, 238
    subgenres, 240–41
Scott, Walter, 131, 178, 200, 231, 231 (ill.)
Scribe, Augustin Eugène, 298
Sedaris, David, 347
Sedgwick, Eve Kosofsky, 415
Selkirk, Alexander, 163
Seneca the Younger, 262, 262 (ill.)
Senelick, Laurence, 306
serial novel, 188 (ill.), 188–91
Serling, Rod, 241
setting, 128–29
Seymour, Robert, 185–86, 186 (ill.)
Shakespeare, William, 267 (ill.). *See also* Elizabethan era
    best way to understand and appreciate drama of, 268–70
    biographical criticism, 393, 394
    comparisons, 60–66
    defines poetry, 42
    drama in a play, 278
    fantasy, 241
    Hamlet, 25, 102 (ill.), 237
    history's greatest dramatist, 266–68
    imagery, 67
    as inventor of humanity, 15
    metaphors, 61–63
    A Midsummer Night's Dream, 270–78
    similes, 61–63
    soliloquy, 245
    Sonnet 18, 16, 60–64
    Sonnet 73, 67
Shanley, John Patrick, 323
Shaw, George Bernard, 238, 250, 279, 302, 308, 333
Shelley, Mary, 239, 239 (ill.)
Shelley, Percy Bysshe, 43, 239, 387, 394
Shelley (Holmes), 394
Shepard, Sam, 250
Shepherd, Scott, 3 (ill.)
Sheridan, Richard, 296
Shields, Carol, 149
Shklovsky, Viktor, 396

short story
    American emergence of, 90–91
    assumptions about, 92
    authors' understanding of, 94 (ill.), 94–100, 98 (ill.)
    beginning of, 103–4
    best way to read, 101
    character creation, 106–7
    character in, 101–2
    characters vs. plot, 106
    Chekhov, Anton, 135–37
    climax, 105–6
    definition, 91–92
    developments outside U.S., 149
    drama vs., 93
    earliest, 89–90
    ending, 105
    essay vs., 348
    first-person narration, 115
    French, 132–34
    "The Gift of the Magi" (Henry), 109–13
    Hemingway, Ernest, 146–48
    images, 119–20
    importance of plot in reading, 103
    Joyce, James, 138–47
    meaning, 113, 118
    middle, 104–5
    nineteenth-century, 130–47
    novel vs., 93–94, 151
    origin as literary genre, 90
    plot, 101–3
    poetry vs., 92–93
    point of view, 113–14, 117
    post-modernist period, 148–49
    questions to ask to best understand characters, 109
    revelations and concealment, 104
    Russian, 132
    setting, 118–19, 121–22
    significance, 118
    "The Story of an Hour" (Chopin), 122–30
    symbols, 120–22
    third-person narration, 115–17
    twentieth-century, 147–49
    types of characters in, 107–8
    understanding and significance of, 101
Showalter, Elaine, 413
showing, 107
Shute, Nevil, 240
Sidney, Sir Philip, 381, 381 (ill.)
significance, 118
Silko, Leslie Marmon, 149
similes, 61–63
Simmons, John, 273 (ill.)
Sister Carrie (Dreiser), 216
skene, 252

473